Applied and Computational
Mathematics for Digital Environments

Applied and Computational Mathematics for Digital Environments

Editor

Liliya Demidova

MDPI • Basel • Beijing • Wuhan • Barcelona • Belgrade • Manchester • Tokyo • Cluj • Tianjin

Editor
Liliya Demidova
MIREA—Russian
Technological University
Moscow
Russia

Editorial Office
MDPI
St. Alban-Anlage 66
4052 Basel, Switzerland

This is a reprint of articles from the Special Issue published online in the open access journal *Mathematics* (ISSN 2227-7390) (available at: https://www.mdpi.com/si/mathematics/Appl_Comput_Math_Digit_Environ).

For citation purposes, cite each article independently as indicated on the article page online and as indicated below:

LastName, A.A.; LastName, B.B.; LastName, C.C. Article Title. *Journal Name* **Year**, *Volume Number*, Page Range.

ISBN 978-3-0365-7266-6 (Hbk)
ISBN 978-3-0365-7267-3 (PDF)

© 2023 by the authors. Articles in this book are Open Access and distributed under the Creative Commons Attribution (CC BY) license, which allows users to download, copy and build upon published articles, as long as the author and publisher are properly credited, which ensures maximum dissemination and a wider impact of our publications.

The book as a whole is distributed by MDPI under the terms and conditions of the Creative Commons license CC BY-NC-ND.

Contents

About the Editor . . . . **vii**

Preface to "Applied and Computational Mathematics for Digital Environments" . . . . **ix**

Liliya A. Demidova
Applied and Computational Mathematics for Digital Environments
Reprinted from: *Mathematics* **2023**, *11*, 1629, doi:10.3390/math11071629 . . . . **1**

Evgeny Nikulchev, Dmitry Ilin and Alexander Gusev
Technology Stack Selection Model for Software Design of Digital Platforms
Reprinted from: *Mathematics* **2021**, *9*, 308, doi:10.3390/math9040308 . . . . **7**

Ilya E. Tarasov
A Mathematical Method for Determining the Parameters of Functional Dependencies Using Multiscale Probability Distribution Functions
Reprinted from: *Mathematics* **2021**, *9*, 1085, doi:10.3390/math9101085 . . . . **19**

Anton Aleshkin
The Influence of Transport Link Density on Conductivity If Junctions and/or Links Are Blocked
Reprinted from: *Mathematics* **2021**, *9*, 1278, doi:10.3390/math9111278 . . . . **33**

Natanael Karjanto and Husty Serviana Husain
Not Another Computer Algebra System: Highlighting *wxMaxima* in Calculus
Reprinted from: *Mathematics* **2021**, *9*, 1317, doi:10.3390/math9121317 . . . . **51**

Bogdan Aman and Gabriel Ciobanu
Knowledge Dynamics and Behavioural Equivalences in Multi-Agent Systems
Reprinted from: *Mathematics* **2021**, *9*, 2869, doi:10.3390/math9222869 . . . . **71**

Dmitry Zhukov, Julia Perova and Vladimir Kalinin
Description of the Distribution Law and Non-Linear Dynamics of Growth of Comments Number in News and Blogs Based on the Fokker-Planck Equation
Reprinted from: *Mathematics* **2022**, *10*, 989, doi:10.3390/math10060989 . . . . **97**

Juan-Jose Cardenas-Cornejo, Mario-Alberto Ibarra-Manzano, Daniel-Alberto Razo-Medina and Dora-Luz Almanza-Ojeda
Complex Color Space Segmentation to Classify Objects in Urban Environments
Reprinted from: *Mathematics* **2022**, *10*, 3752, doi:10.3390/math10203752 . . . . **121**

Vladimir Krutikov, Svetlana Gutova, Elena Tovbis, Lev Kazakovtsev and Eugene Semenkin
Relaxation Subgradient Algorithms with Machine Learning Procedures
Reprinted from: *Mathematics* **2022**, *10*, 3959, doi:10.3390/math10213959 . . . . **139**

Askhat Diveev and Elizaveta Shmalko
Machine Learning Feedback Control Approach Based on Symbolic Regression for Robotic Systems
Reprinted from: *Mathematics* **2022**, *10*, 4100, doi:10.3390/math10214100 . . . . **173**

Aleksei Vakhnin, Evgenii Sopov and Eugene Semenkin
On Improving Adaptive Problem Decomposition Using Differential Evolution for Large-Scale Optimization Problems
Reprinted from: *Mathematics* **2022**, *10*, 4297, doi:10.3390/math10224297 . . . . **205**

Liliya A. Demidova
A Novel Approach to Decision-Making on Diagnosing Oncological Diseases Using Machine Learning Classifiers Based on Datasets Combining Known and/or New Generated Features of a Different Nature
Reprinted from: *Mathematics* **2023**, *11*, 792, doi:10.3390/math11040792 . . . . **233**

About the Editor

Liliya Demidova

Liliya Demidova is Professor at the MIREA—Russian Technological University (Moscow, Russia). She is the author of seven books and over two hundred papers that have been published in reputable journals in both Russian and English. Her research interests include fuzzy logic, machine learning, data mining, decision support, time series forecasting, and image processing.

Preface to "Applied and Computational Mathematics for Digital Environments"

Currently, digitalization and digital transformation are actively expanding into various areas of human activity, and researchers are identifying urgent problems and offering new solutions for digital environments in industry, economics, business, medicine, ecology, education, etc.

Undeniably, when we seek to solve problems that challenge the global community, the advanced principles and technologies of applied and computational mathematics must be involved. The application of such principles and technologies will ensure the study and modeling of various phenomena in the real world using intelligent software, hardware platforms, and corresponding modules.

The present book contains the 11 papers that were accepted for publication among the 12 manuscripts that were submitted to the Special Issue "Applied and Computational Mathematics for Digital Environments" of the MDPI "*Mathematics*" journal. The 11 papers, which appear in the present book in the series that they have been published in, Volumes 9 (2021), 10 (2022), and 11 (2023) of the journal, cover a wide range of topics connected to the principles and technologies of applied and computational mathematics, which can be applied to solve various practical problems in digital environments.

The topics of interest include, among others, scientific research, applied tasks, and problems in the following areas:

- The construction of mathematical and information models of intelligent computer systems for monitoring and controlling the parameters of digital environments;
- The development of intelligent optimization algorithms that search for optimal parameter values of mathematical and information models in digital environments;
- Software and mathematical technologies in the implementation of intelligent monitoring and computer control of the parameters of digital environments;
- The development and application of mathematical and information models, machine learning methods, and artificial intelligence for the analysis and processing of big data in digital environments.

I hope that this book will be useful to those who are interested in the real-world applications of applied and computational mathematics for digital environments in terms of solving actual, practical problems in all spheres of human life and activity.

As the Guest Editor of the Special Issue "Applied and Computational Mathematics for Digital Environments" of the MDPI "*Mathematics*" journal, I am grateful to the contributing authors, the reviewers of this paper for their valuable comments, which greatly improved the quality of the submitted papers, and the administrative staff of MDPI publications for the support toward completing this project. Furthermore, special thanks are due to the Managing Editor of the Special Issue, Dr. Syna Mu, for his excellent collaboration, valuable assistance, and support.

Liliya Demidova
Editor

Editorial

Applied and Computational Mathematics for Digital Environments

Liliya A. Demidova

Institute of Information Technologies, Federal State Budget Educational Institution of Higher Education, MIREA–Russian Technological University, 78, Vernadsky Avenue, 119454 Moscow, Russia; liliya.demidova@rambler.ru

1. Introduction

Currently, digitalization and digital transformation are actively expanding into various areas of human activity, and researchers are identifying urgent problems and offering new solutions regarding digital environments in industry [1,2], economics [3,4], medicine [5,6], ecology [7,8], education [9,10], etc.

The advanced principles and technologies of applied and computational mathematics should be used to address challenges faced by the global community. The application of such principles and technologies enables the study and modeling of various phenomena of the real world using intelligent software and hardware platforms and corresponding modules.

In this regard, topics of interest in this Special Issue, "Applied and Computational Mathematics for Digital Environments", include but are not limited to scientific research, applied tasks and problems in the following areas:

- Construction of mathematical and information models of intelligent computer systems for monitoring and controlling the parameters of digital environments;
- Development of intelligent optimization algorithms that search for optimal parameters values of mathematical and information models in digital environments;
- Software and mathematical technologies in the implementation of intelligent monitoring and computer control of the parameters of digital environments;
- Development and application of mathematical and information models, machine learning methods, and artificial intelligence for the analysis and processing of big data in digital environments.

2. Statistics of the Special Issue

A total of 12 papers were submitted to this Special Issue, of which 11 were published (91.67%) [11–21] and only 1 was rejected (8.33%), indicating the very high quality of the original submissions.

These 11 papers were accepted for publication in this Special Issue after a careful, comprehensive and iterative peer-review process based on criteria related to their high quality and novelty.

The geographical distribution of the authors of the submitted papers is presented in Figure 1, and the published papers are represented by 26 authors from 5 different countries.

We also note that three papers were written by one author each, three papers were written by teams of two authors, three papers were written by teams of three authors, one paper was written by a team of four authors, and one paper was written by a team of five authors.

At the same time, many papers were written as collaborations between authors from different countries, cities and scientific organizations.

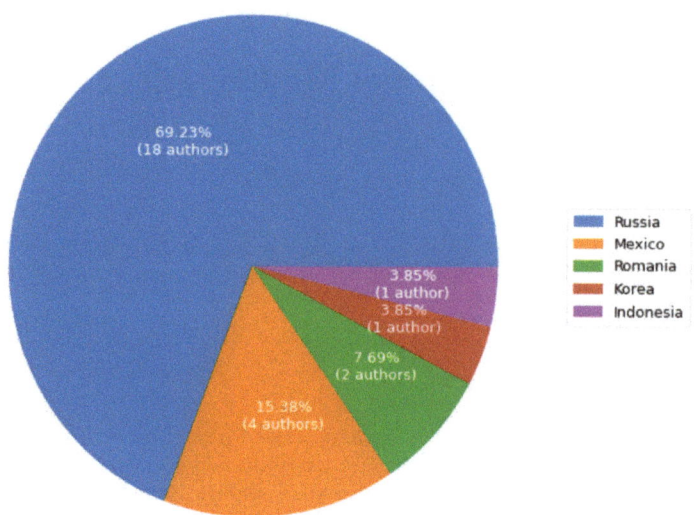

Figure 1. The geographical distribution of the authors of the papers.

3. Authors of the Special Issue

The authors of this Special Issue and their affiliations are shown in Table 1.

Table 1. Affiliations and bibliometric indicators for authors.

Author	Affiliation	References
Evgeny Nikulchev	Department of Intelligent Information Security Systems, MIREA—Russian Technological University, 119454 Moscow, Russia	[11]
Dmitry Ilin	Department of Intelligent Information Security Systems, MIREA—Russian Technological University, 119454 Moscow, Russia	[11]
Alexander Gusev	Data Center, Russian Academy of Education, Moscow 119121, Russia; Kuban State Technological University, 350072 Krasnodar, Russia	[11]
Ilya E. Tarasov	Institute of Informational Technologies, RTU MIREA, Vernadsky pr. 78, 119454 Moscow, Russia	[12]
Anton Aleshkin	Department of Systems Management and Modelling, MIREA—Russian Technological University, 78 Vernadsky Prospect, 119454 Moscow, Russia	[13]
Natanael Karjanto	Department of Mathematics, University College, Natural Science Campus, Sungkyunkwan University, Suwon 16419, Korea	[14]
Husty Serviana Husain	Department of Mathematics Education, Faculty of Mathematics and Natural Science Education, Indonesia University of Education, Bandung 40154, Indonesia	[14]
Bogdan Aman	Institute of Computer Science, Romanian Academy, 700505 Iași, Romania; Faculty of Computer Science, Alexandru Ioan Cuza University, 700506 Iași, Romania	[15]
Gabriel Ciobanu	Faculty of Computer Science, Alexandru Ioan Cuza University, 700506 Iași, Romania	[15]
Dmitry Zhukov	Institute of Cybersecurity and Digital Technologies, MIREA—Russian Technological University, 78 Vernadsky Avenue, 119454 Moscow, Russia	[16]

Table 1. *Cont.*

Author	Affiliation	References
Julia Perova	Institute of Radio Electronics and Computer Science, MIREA—Russian Technological University, 78 Vernadsky Avenue, 119454 Moscow, Russia	[16]
Vladimir Kalinin	Institute of Cybersecurity and Digital Technologies, MIREA—Russian Technological University, 78 Vernadsky Avenue, 119454 Moscow, Russia	[16]
Juan-Jose Cardenas-Cornejo	Electronics Engineering Department, DICIS, University of Guanajuato, Carr. Salamanca-Valle de Santiago KM. 3.5 + 1.8 Km., Salamanca 36885, Mexico	[17]
Mario-Alberto Ibarra-Manzano	Electronics Engineering Department, DICIS, University of Guanajuato, Carr. Salamanca-Valle de Santiago KM. 3.5 + 1.8 Km., Salamanca 36885, Mexico	[17]
Daniel-Alberto Razo-Medina	Electronics Engineering Department, DICIS, University of Guanajuato, Carr. Salamanca-Valle de Santiago KM. 3.5 + 1.8 Km., Salamanca 36885, Mexico	[17]
Dora-Luz Almanza-Ojeda	Electronics Engineering Department, DICIS, University of Guanajuato, Carr. Salamanca-Valle de Santiago KM. 3.5 + 1.8 Km., Salamanca 36885, Mexico	[17]
Vladimir Krutikov	Department of Applied Mathematics, Kemerovo State University, Krasnaya Street 6, 650043 Kemerovo, Russia	[18]
Svetlana Gutova	Department of Applied Mathematics, Kemerovo State University, Krasnaya Street 6, 650043 Kemerovo, Russia	[18]
Elena Tovbis	Institute of Informatics and Telecommunications, Reshetnev Siberian State University of Science and Technology, Prosp. Krasnoyarskiy Rabochiy 31, 660031 Krasnoyarsk, Russia	[18]
Lev Kazakovtsev	Institute of Informatics and Telecommunications, Reshetnev Siberian State University of Science and Technology, Prosp. Krasnoyarskiy Rabochiy 31, 660031 Krasnoyarsk, Russia	[18]
Eugene Semenkin	Institute of Informatics and Telecommunications, Reshetnev Siberian State University of Science and Technology, Prosp. Krasnoyarskiy Rabochiy 31, 660031 Krasnoyarsk, Russia	[18,20]
Askhat Diveev	Federal Research Center "Computer Science and Control", the Russian Academy of Sciences, 119333 Moscow, Russia	[19]
Elizaveta Shmalko	Federal Research Center "Computer Science and Control", the Russian Academy of Sciences, 119333 Moscow, Russia	[19]
Aleksei Vakhnin	Department of System Analysis and Operations Research, Reshetnev Siberian State University of Science and Technology, 660037 Krasnoyarsk, Russia	[20]
Evgenii Sopov	Department of System Analysis and Operations Research, Reshetnev Siberian State University of Science and Technology, 660037 Krasnoyarsk, Russia	[20]
Liliya A. Demidova	Institute of Information Technologies, Federal State Budget Educational Institution of Higher Education, MIREA—Russian Technological University, 78, Vernadsky Avenue, 119454 Moscow, Russia	[21]

4. Overview of the Contributions to the Special Issue

Nikulchev et al. [11] evaluated the efficiency of integrating information technology solutions into digital platforms by developing a mathematical model and methodology based on the use of fuzzy logic.

Tarasov [12] studied the application of an approximation method of experimental data using functional dependencies. The author introduced an independent parameter "scale of the error probability distribution function" that considers the architecture and practical approaches to its implementation.

Aleshkin [13] proposed an approach to modeling and managing traffic flows based on percolation theory. The author studied the properties of transport networks and proposes algorithms for building planar random networks and calculating their percolation thresholds.

The study by Karjanto et al. [14] is dedicated to a computer algebra system (CAS) wxMaxima for calculus teaching and learning at a tertiary level. The authors study the strengths and limitations of the software under consideration.

Aman et al. [15] address the behavior of multi-agent systems. The authors consider how knowledge is handled and exchanged between agents, and study the evolution of the system that is caused by these exchanges.

Zhukov et al. [16] consider distributions of news items via the number of comments, including both comments at the first level and comments under these. The authors state that under certain assumptions the law for the stationary probability distribution can be derived from the Fokker–Planck differential equation.

Cardenas-Cornejo et al. [17] propose a new chromatic segmentation approach for detecting and classifying objects in urban environments. This approach yields centroids of patches on the color image, which are subsequently classified using a convolutional neural network (CNN) with a high accuracy score.

The study by Krutikov et al. [18] is dedicated to a new relaxation subgradient minimization method (RSMM). The computational experiments conducted by the authors confirmed the effectiveness of the proposed algorithm, showing that it outperforms currently known methods.

Diveev et al. [19] propose a universal numerical approach to solving the problem of optimal control with feedback using machine learning methods based on symbolic regression. First, authors introduce and discuss such notions as machine learning control, stability, optimality and feasibility of machine-made control systems. Then, they provide a substantiation for the machine learning feedback control approach based on symbolic regression and evolutionary algorithms.

Vakhnin et al. [20] address large-scale global black-box optimization (LSGO). The authors propose a self-adaptive approach that combines ideas from state-of-the-art algorithms and implements Coordination of Self-adaptive Cooperative Co-evolution algorithms with Local Search (COSACC-LS1).

Demidova [21] proposes an approach for diagnosing oncological diseases based on blood protein markers, new features generated using non-linear dimensionality reduction algorithm UMAP, formulas for various entropies and fractal dimensions. The author used resulting datasets with various combinations of features to develop multiclass kNN and SVM classifiers.

The published papers cover a wide range of tasks and problems in various fields of human activity and offer solutions by applying modern tools to analyze and process data in digital environments.

5. Acknowledgments to the Authors and Reviewers

As Guest Editor of the Special Issue, "Applied and Computational Mathematics for Digital Environments", I am grateful to all contributing authors. I also express my gratitude to all the reviewers for their painstaking work and valuable comments that helped to improve the quality of the submitted papers.

6. Conclusions

The purpose of this Special Issue was to attract high-quality new papers in the field of applied and computational mathematics for digital environments, offering original solutions to various problems that are relevant and in demand in various fields of human activity.

I hope that these selected research papers are recognized as important and meaningful by the international scientific community and can form the basis for further research in the field of applied and computational mathematics for digital environments, solving complex problems in various disciplines and application areas.

Institutional Review Board Statement: Not applicable.

Informed Consent Statement: Not applicable.

Data Availability Statement: Not applicable.

Conflicts of Interest: The author declares no conflict of interest.

References

1. Fonseca, L. Industry 4.0 and the digital society: Concepts, dimensions and envisioned benefits. *Proc. Int. Conf. Bus. Excell.* **2018**, *12*, 386–397. [CrossRef]
2. Schnell, P.; Haag, P.; Jünger, H.C. Implementation of Digital Technologies in Construction Companies: Establishing a Holistic Process which Addresses Current Barriers. *Businesses* **2023**, *3*, 1–18. [CrossRef]
3. Zhu, H.; Wang, C. Digital economy leads the high-quality development of industries: Theory, mechanism, and path. *Financ. Econ. Theory Pract.* **2020**, *41*, 2–10.
4. Yang, S.; Jia, J. Digital Economy, Technological Innovation, and Environmental Quality Improvement. *Sustainability* **2022**, *14*, 15289. [CrossRef]
5. Sun, M.; Xie, L.; Liu, Y.; Li, K.; Jiang, B.; Lu, Y.; Yang, Y.; Yu, H.; Song, Y.; Bai, C.; et al. The metaverse in current digital medicine. *Clin. eHealth* **2022**, *5*, 52–57. [CrossRef]
6. Syamimi Masrani, A.; Nik Husain, N.R. Digital environment: An evolutionary component in environmental health. *J. Public Health Res.* **2022**, *11*, 1–6. [CrossRef]
7. Truong, T.C. The Impact of Digital Transformation on Environmental Sustainability. *Adv. Multimed.* **2022**, *2022*, 6324325. [CrossRef]
8. Marton, A. Steps toward a Digital Ecology Ecological Principles for the Study of Digital Ecosystems. *J. Inf. Technol.* **2022**, *37*, 250–265. [CrossRef]
9. Lodge, J.; Kennedy, G.; Lockyer, L. Digital learning environments, the science of learning and the relationship between the teacher and the learner. In *Learning Under the Lens: Applying Findings from the Science of Learning to the Classroom*; Carroll, A., Cunnington, R., Nugent, A., Eds.; Routledge: Abingdon, UK, 2020.
10. Andrianova, E.G.; Demidova, L.A.; Sovetov, P.N. Pedagogical design of a digital teaching assistant in massive professional training for the digital economy. *Russ. Technol. J.* **2022**, *10*, 7–23. [CrossRef]
11. Nikulchev, E.; Ilin, D.; Gusev, A. Technology Stack Selection Model for Software Design of Digital Platforms. *Mathematics* **2021**, *9*, 308. [CrossRef]
12. Tarasov, I.E. A Mathematical Method for Determining the Parameters of Functional Dependencies Using Multiscale Probability Distribution Functions. *Mathematics* **2021**, *9*, 1085. [CrossRef]
13. Aleshkin, A. The Influence of Transport Link Density on Conductivity If Junctions and/or Links Are Blocked. *Mathematics* **2021**, *9*, 1278. [CrossRef]
14. Karjanto, N.; Husain, H.S. Not Another Computer Algebra System: Highlighting *wxMaxima* in Calculus. *Mathematics* **2021**, *9*, 1317. [CrossRef]
15. Aman, B.; Ciobanu, G. Knowledge Dynamics and Behavioural Equivalences in Multi-Agent Systems. *Mathematics* **2021**, *9*, 2869. [CrossRef]
16. Zhukov, D.; Perova, J.; Kalinin, V. Description of the Distribution Law and Non-Linear Dynamics of Growth of Comments Number in News and Blogs Based on the Fokker-Planck Equation. *Mathematics* **2022**, *10*, 989. [CrossRef]
17. Cardenas-Cornejo, J.-J.; Ibarra-Manzano, M.-A.; Razo-Medina, D.-A.; Almanza-Ojeda, D.-L. Complex Color Space Segmentation to Classify Objects in Urban Environments. *Mathematics* **2022**, *10*, 3752. [CrossRef]
18. Krutikov, V.; Gutova, S.; Tovbis, E.; Kazakovtsev, L.; Semenkin, E. Relaxation Subgradient Algorithms with Machine Learning Procedures. *Mathematics* **2022**, *10*, 3959. [CrossRef]
19. Diveev, A.; Shmalko, E. Machine Learning Feedback Control Approach Based on Symbolic Regression for Robotic Systems. *Mathematics* **2022**, *10*, 4100. [CrossRef]
20. Vakhnin, A.; Sopov, E.; Semenkin, E. On Improving Adaptive Problem Decomposition Using Differential Evolution for Large-Scale Optimization Problems. *Mathematics* **2022**, *10*, 4297. [CrossRef]
21. Demidova, L.A. A Novel Approach to Decision-Making on Diagnosing Oncological Diseases Using Machine Learning Classifiers Based on Datasets Combining Known and/or New Generated Features of a Different Nature. *Mathematics* **2023**, *11*, 792. [CrossRef]

Disclaimer/Publisher's Note: The statements, opinions and data contained in all publications are solely those of the individual author(s) and contributor(s) and not of MDPI and/or the editor(s). MDPI and/or the editor(s) disclaim responsibility for any injury to people or property resulting from any ideas, methods, instructions or products referred to in the content.

Article

Technology Stack Selection Model for Software Design of Digital Platforms

Evgeny Nikulchev [1,*], Dmitry Ilin [1] and Alexander Gusev [2,3]

1. Department of Intelligent Information Security Systems, MIREA—Russian Technological University, Moscow 119454, Russia; ilin_dyu@mirea.ru
2. Data Center, Russian Academy of Education, Moscow 119121, Russia; alexander.gusev@rusacademedu.ru
3. Kuban State Technological University, Krasnodar 350072, Russia
* Correspondence: nikulchev@mail.ru

Citation: Nikulchev, E.; Ilin, D.; Gusev, A. Technology Stack Selection Model for Software Design of Digital Platforms. *Mathematics* **2021**, *9*, 308. https://doi.org/10.3390/math9040308

Academic Editor: Hsien-Chung Wu

Received: 17 December 2020
Accepted: 30 January 2021
Published: 4 February 2021

Publisher's Note: MDPI stays neutral with regard to jurisdictional claims in published maps and institutional affiliations.

Copyright: © 2021 by the authors. Licensee MDPI, Basel, Switzerland. This article is an open access article distributed under the terms and conditions of the Creative Commons Attribution (CC BY) license (https://creativecommons.org/licenses/by/4.0/).

Abstract: The article is dedicated to the development of a mathematical model and methodology for evaluating the effectiveness of integrating information technology solutions into digital platforms using virtual simulation infrastructures. The task of selecting a stack of technologies is formulated as the task of selecting elements from sets of possible solutions. This allows us to develop a mathematically unified approach to evaluating the effectiveness of different solutions, such as choosing programming languages, choosing Database Management System (DBMS), choosing operating systems and data technologies, and choosing the frameworks used. Introduced technology compatibility operation and decomposition of the evaluation of the efficiency of the technology stack at the stages of the life cycle of the digital platform development allowed us to reduce the computational complexity of the formation of the technology stack. A methodology based on performance assessments for experimental research in a virtual software-configurable simulation environment has been proposed. The developed solution allows the evaluation of the performance of the digital platform before its final implementation, while reducing the cost of conducting an experiment to assess the characteristics of the digital platform. It is proposed to compare the characteristics of digital platform efficiency based on the use of fuzzy logic, providing the software developer with an intuitive tool to support decision-making on the inclusion of the solution in the technology stack.

Keywords: mathematical model for evaluating the effectiveness of integrating information technology; digital platforms; virtual simulation infrastructures; experimental virtual environment

1. Introduction

The proliferation of web applications, driven by their platform and hardware independence, ubiquity of use, interfaces, data transfer protocols, and programmable capabilities, has defined the development of the IT sector—the creation of digital platforms. Using a platform allows the collection and sharing of information between a huge number of users, combining results into big data. Information technologies, which are used in the development of digital platforms, are commonly called technology stacks. An important feature of IT solutions integrated into the stack is their replaceability, meaning one of the technologies can be replaced with an alternative, either newly created or a new version of the existing one. There are many techniques for individual software design phases [1,2] for specific technologies and software systems such as digital platforms.

The system performance depends on the efficiency of each of the components of the technology stack [3] and on the effectiveness of their interaction [4]. At the same time, there can be more than one ready-made technology solution for one task, both commercial and free of charge. In practice, the choice is based on load tests or expert assessments. The approaches summarize the experience of using specific components or the technology stack, but are not based on formal assessments and cannot be used to compare efficiency. Formal methods are focused on solving identification and optimization tasks that are of greater dimensionality. The proposed methods do not consider the specifics of the operation of the digital platform and its infrastructure.

The quality of the technology selection can only be judged after the entire stack of technologies has been formed, a digital platform has been developed, and characteristics are calculated. In practice, there are situations where large digital systems stop working when they start at high load. For example, the logging framework accessed the database where the main data was stored, which resulted in a significant increase in the latency of access to the data. It is typical that when the system is commissioned, it turns out that some of its write/reading functions are slower than expected, the method of storing data was incorrectly selected, and so on. In high load systems with integrated modules used, it is difficult or impossible to assess theoretically their effectiveness. In these conditions, a model and an approach are proposed, which consist of identifying a subset of technologies of the required technology stack and choosing based on an assessment of quality characteristics in conditions that simulate a real environment, e.g., parameters of network loading, parameters of virtual machines, data transfer rate, and so on.

The paper also proposes use of fuzzy logic. For example, when choosing technological solutions based on minimizing the consumption of a resource, the key indicator is not the specific number of bytes or microseconds spent on the execution of an algorithm that changes slightly from experiment to experiment, but a qualitative estimate of whether resource consumption is "high", "medium", or "low" in accordance with the developer's goals and perceptions. The introduction of such quality categories makes it possible to significantly simplify the evaluation of the technological solution, breaking all the many available technological solutions into a small number of classes relative to the consumption of the resource, corresponding to the quality categories.

The article consists of six sections. Section 2 provides an overview of related works, Section 3 proposes a basic model, Section 4 describes the virtual environment used for experimental research, and Section 5 describes the example of decision-making for specific experimental studies. Section 6 provides key results and conclusions.

2. Related Works

The basics of evaluating information technology solutions are considered within the algorithmic efficiency theory. However, in the development of digital platforms, each solution can include a large number of algorithms. Evaluating the effectiveness of each individual algorithm will require laborious research. In addition, the solutions under consideration may contain closed source code.

There are many approaches to the task of selecting effective software components [5–7], methods for solving the problem of optimization, and formal models for the decision-making support [8,9]. However, the tasks under consideration are of great dimensionality and the existing solutions do not take into account the specifics of the operation of the digital platform and its infrastructure. Various methods of Database Management System (DBMS) benchmarking are well known for SQL, NoSQL, and hybrid solutions, but these methods do not address the DBMS in the context of the technology stack.

Development practices (load testing, benchmarking, expert review etc.) generalize experience in specific solutions or technology stacks and are actively applied in digital platform development practices. A significant drawback of these practices is the lack of consideration of the specifics of the operation of the digital platform and its infrastructure.

The need for experimental evaluation of the technology solutions before integration into the digital platform can be due to various reasons. For example, the software developer may need to test the hypothesis about the pros or cons of the solution under consideration [10]. The need for cross-platform functioning [11] also can be the reason for experimental evaluation to ensure the resulting digital platform components can run in various environments (browsers, mobile devices, operating systems etc.).

Distributed software development teams have a practice of using virtual development environments [12]. This technology uses virtualization and virtual machine configuration management [13] to apply the right settings and install the required components. It automates the process of synchronizing, setting up, and starting the developer's work environment. Configuration management systems facilitate simultaneous distributed work on multiple components of the software being developed [14] and automate the process of installing and customizing all the necessary components of the development environment [15]. Upgrading and modifying the virtual environment also becomes simplified [16] because configuration files can be easily distributed among developers.

To test the compatibility of technology solutions, services are used to bootstrap a virtual machine with the chosen operating system, software, and browser of a given version. Microsoft has a number of virtual machines for Internet Explorer and Edge browsers that do not require the purchase of a Windows license. However, since there are many other browsers, there are tools with a large set of options. For example, BrowserStack provides the ability to run virtual machines with a predetermined configuration on a remote server. It also provides means to run automated test scenarios, such as regression testing, during development.

A well-established approach to experimental software evaluation is software testing [17]. In papers [18,19], a number of approaches to testing are considered, which differ in their types: functional, non-functional, compatibility, reliability, recoverability, performance, maintainability, security, and others. As noted in [20], there are noticeable differences in views on the problems of software testing in industry and in science. At the stage of software maintenance, automation tools are actively used [21,22]. Testing the software is commonly included into the overall sequence of operations required to verify that the software meets the requirements. In addition, experiments are being carried out to assess the quality of the system [23,24] for the end users.

3. Technology Stack Selection Model

The concept and corresponding model for choosing a technology stack have been developed and can be described as follows. It is necessary to construct a p-dimensional vector of the technology stack to build the digital platform:

$$\Xi = \{\xi_1, \xi_2, \ldots, \xi_p\}, \xi_i \in \hat{S}_i, (i = \overline{1, p}),$$

where ξ_i—information technology solution for the technology stack (communication protocols, type of DBMS, frameworks used, Operating system (OS) version, etc.); $\hat{S}_i$—the set of possible alternatives for each information technology solution type. Let each set with specific selected technology options denote Ξ_q.

For the given operating conditions (that is, when the digital platform is used after its complete implementation, during the workload on software and hardware of a computing system), each set of the technology stack can be associated with a vector of efficiency characteristics, such as memory consumption, processing time of a given number of records, processing queue size, failure frequency, maximum number of users, average CPU load, client data transfer time, etc.:

$$\forall \Xi_q \to \vartheta_q = [\varphi_{q,1}, \ldots, \varphi_{q,n}]^T \in \mathbb{R}^n.$$

The stack Ξ_o will be effective if

$$\exists \Xi_o, \forall \Xi_l, l \neq o : \max_{\Omega}(\vartheta_l, \vartheta_o) = \vartheta_o.$$

Here, Ω is the configuration and operating conditions of the digital platform after its implementation; max—operation of comparison of vectors characterizing qualities. In this paper, the operation max is proposed to be implemented using fuzzy logic.

In this case, the choice is a problem with computational complexity determined by a complete enumeration of all elements of the sets $\hat{S}_i(i = \overline{1,p})$ in p places of the technology stack, i.e., it is necessary to enumerate all the options.

$$O = n_1 \cdot n_2 \cdot \ldots \cdot n_p,$$

where n_i is cardinality of $\hat{S}_i(i = \overline{1,p})$.

The complexity of the problem lies in the necessity of complete enumeration of possible solutions, and in the fact that efficiency can be determined only by forming the entire technology stack and assessing its performance after implementation. It is proposed to solve the problem of evaluating the effectiveness by its approximation on the basis of experimental virtual environments simulating the given operating conditions, decomposing the general problem in accordance with the stages of the life cycle of the development of digital platforms. To achieve this goal, the concept of a configuration is introduced at t stages of the life cycle for a given configuration and operating conditions Ω: $\omega^i(i = \overline{1,t}) \subset \Omega$. At each stage ω^i, each information technology solution of the technology stack is selected so that the values of the efficiency characteristics are greater or equal in a given set of alternatives.

In addition, technologies depend on the selection of previous information technology solutions included into the technology stack. For example, the programming languages chosen at the first stage limit the sets of libraries, the choice of the type of data storage limits the choice of DBMS, and the choice of the OS also introduces restrictions.

Let an operation of compatibility of solutions be introduced such that

$$\xi_k \rhd\lhd \xi_g, \text{ if } \Xi = (\xi_1, \ldots, \xi_k, \ldots, \xi_g, \ldots, \xi_p) \to \vartheta,$$
wherein ϑ has no zero elements,

In other words, compatible solutions are those that do not give zero efficiency values; that is, they are able to function when used together.

At each m-th stage of the life cycle, the problem of choosing an information technology solution for the formation of a technology stack is solved, i.e., a subset of the required Ξ_o is formed. The procedure for choosing an information technology solution is as follows. For each valid and compatible set $\Sigma_m = \{s_1^m, \ldots, s_\eta^m\}, \eta < p$.

Let $s_1^m \in \hat{S}_1$, then
$s_2^m \in \tilde{S}_2 \subseteq \hat{S}_2, \forall \tilde{s}_2 \in \tilde{S}_2 : \tilde{s}_2 \rhd\lhd s_1^m;$
$s_3^m \in \tilde{S}_3 \subseteq \hat{S}_3, \forall \tilde{s}_3 \in \tilde{S}_3 : \tilde{s}_3 \rhd\lhd s_2^m;$
$\ldots$
$s_\eta^m \in \tilde{S}_\eta \subseteq \hat{S}_\eta, \forall \tilde{s}_\eta \in \tilde{S}_\eta : \tilde{s}_\eta \rhd\lhd s_{\eta-1}^m;$

For the efficiency vector given at the m-th stage out of M^i characteristics $\forall \Sigma_m \to \Phi_m \in \mathbb{R}^{M^m}$:

$$\exists \Sigma_o, \forall \Sigma_l, l \neq o : \max_{\omega^m}(\Phi_l, \Sigma_o) = \Sigma_o, \text{ for } \omega_i \text{ obtaining a solution set for the technology stack } \Sigma_o \subset \Xi_o.$$

When choosing solutions with the introduced operation of compatibility of information technology solutions, the number of options for enumeration is reduced, so the complexity estimate will be

$$\tilde{O} = n_1 \cdot n_2(1 - \Delta_1) \cdot n_3(1 - \Delta_2) \cdot \ldots \cdot n_p(1 - \Delta_{p-1}),$$

where n_i is the set cardinality $\hat{S}_i(i = \overline{1,p}); \Delta_i(i = \overline{1, p-1}, \Delta_1 \leq \Delta_2 \leq .. \leq \Delta_{p-1})$ is the coefficient characterizing the decrease in cardinality $\hat{S}_i$ down to $\tilde{S}_i$, considering solution compatibility.

The original problem of evaluating a technology stack is divided into stages. Thus, the technology stack is evaluated at each stage instead of a single evaluation after the digital platform is launched. If the completely assembled digital platform does not meet the requirements (in terms of speed, resources used, the ability to provide desired Quality-of-service (QoS) to users, etc.), it will be necessary to identify which of the technology solutions used affect efficiency (which is a very time-consuming task), and it will be necessary to reimplement or to replace these technology solutions. When using the proposed approach, assessments of the effectiveness of various alternative options are obtained at the stage of selecting technological solutions. These assessments make it possible to select effective and appropriate technological solutions before the time the platform is put into operation.

Thus, the approach allows the reduction of the number of options required to be evaluated for forming a technology stack and makes it possible to evaluate information technology solutions at the stages of the digital platforms' development life cycle. The introduced decomposition of the selection problem allows us to reduce the dimension of the original problem and reduce the number of options under consideration, the effectiveness of which can only be assessed by conducting experiments including each of the information technology solutions into the digital platform.

The approach has limitations that must be considered when using it. The initial selection of the information technology solutions is carried out with the involvement of expert assessments, and therefore the list of options may not be complete. If initial expert assessments have led to an ineffective set of solutions, then the choice of subsequent solutions for implementation in the technology stack will be limited by the need to ensure compatibility with existing ineffective solutions. Thus, a systematic error in expert assessments can hypothetically lead to a decrease in the efficiency of the digital platform.

4. Experimental Virtual Environment

When setting up an experiment, it is important to minimize the influence of the observer on the object. To isolate the evaluated information technology solution from the influence of the observer, it is necessary to form an independent infrastructure [25]. It can be prepared both in hardware, using physical computing devices (computers, servers, routers, etc.), and software, using virtual machines. The second option should be considered preferable, since the implementation of the infrastructure using software means more rational use of resources and portability. In addition, the use of virtual machines provides infrastructure reusability.

It should be noted that infrastructure provisioned with virtual machines has several disadvantages—it requires a large amount of disk space, it is difficult to monitor the current state of virtual machines, and the changes you make need to be documented separately.

To mitigate the shortcomings, one can use the "infrastructure as code" approach. The approach is implemented using systems such as:

- Systems for creating and configuring a virtual development environment (for example, the Vagrant system);
- Systems for automating the deployment and management of applications in environments with containerization support (for example, Docker);
- Configuration management systems (for example, Ansible, Puppet).

Studies show that containerization systems are less suitable for setting up computational experiments. They provide less isolation of computational resources, which can affect results.

To obtain experimental evaluations of the integration of information technology solutions into digital platforms, a virtual simulation bench has been developed, as shown in Figure 1.

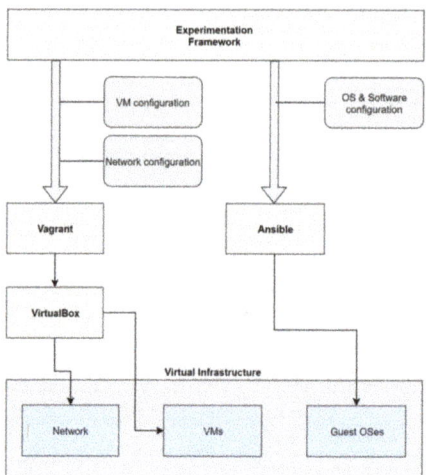

Figure 1. Scheme of the virtual bench for obtaining experimental evaluations of the integration of information technology solutions.

Figure 1 contains a general scheme of the experimental bench. Configuration files in YAML and Ruby languages are used as initial data. Based on the configuration files, virtual machines are launched with the specified parameters and network connection settings. Then the reference image of the operating system is loaded and launched. After launch, the necessary software is installed on the guest operating systems using the configuration management system (Ansible). The detailed description of the experiment, the source code of the virtual environment, the settings of the swarm intelligence algorithm, and other parameters are presented in the paper [25].

The proposed approach based on a virtual environment allows the obtaining of reliable estimates of the effectiveness of information technology solutions. If the requirements and operating conditions are changed (for example, the computing infrastructure is changed, servers were replaced, the amount of data received, and the number of users were changed), then the reliability of the estimates could be arguable. In this case, the estimates of the effectiveness of information technology solutions need to be recalculated. However, the methodology makes it possible to recalculate the value of the estimates using the experimental virtual environment, even if the requirements and operating conditions are subject to change.

Incorrect decomposition of the technology stack into subsets also can significantly affect the reliability of the estimates obtained. That is, the technology stack can be decomposed so that interrelated and interacting information technology solutions are selected at different stages, while the experimental evaluation of the effectiveness of these solutions occurs independently of each other, which excludes the possibility of testing and evaluating their mutual influence. In this case, the reliability of efficiency estimates can be lower than expected; however, this limitation is general for all decomposition problems. Decomposition of a single problem into many elementary problems increases the speed and reduces computational costs of solving them, but it excludes the possibility of assessing their mutual influence. Therefore, the depth of decomposition of the problem into subsets is determined by the researcher depending on the available time and computational resources for solving problems of assessing the effectiveness of information technology solutions.

5. Examples

Let there be given n functional requirements q_i ($i = \overline{1, n}$) for the digital platform, as well as t different configurations ω^k ($k = \overline{1, t}$) of the infrastructure, reflecting the set of conditions for the functioning of the platform. The platform developer defines M

solutions of the technology stack to choose from. Each of the M solutions implement at least one of the functional requirements q_i. The subsets of alternative information technology solutions from M capable of implementing the functional requirement q_i can be denoted as m_i $(i = \overline{1,n})$. The subsets of information technology solutions, where for each functional requirement q_i there is at least one component from M, are defined as technology stacks s^j $(j = \overline{1,p})$. S is the set of all possible stacks. To assess the quality of integration of information technology solutions, f quality indicators $r_\xi^{k,j}$, $(\xi = \overline{1,f})$: $R^{k,j} = [r_1^{k,j}, \ldots, r_\xi^{k,j}, \ldots, r_f^{k,j}]^T$, $(k = \overline{1,t}, j = \overline{1,p})$ are introduced [26]. These quality indicators belong to $\mathbb{R}^f$ space. Thus,

$$\forall \omega^k : s^j \to R^{k,j} \in \mathbb{R}^f,$$

where $R^{k,j}$ is a vector consisting of the values of the experimentally calculated quality indicators for the infrastructure configuration ω^k and the evaluated stack s^j.

The following methodology for the integral quality assessment of the technology stack is proposed:

1. Mathematical formalization of the problem of choosing the appropriate technology stack in accordance with the above definitions.
2. Formation of fuzzy inference rules based on the goals and priorities of the digital platform developer.
3. Study of the fuzzy inference system for the completeness of coverage of the range of input values by the rules, the absence of redundant rules, and the elimination of the ambiguous choice situation by setting the weights of the rules.
4. The choice of the method of normalizing the values of quality indicators $r_\xi^{k,j}$ for transmission to the input of the fuzzy inference system.
5. Organization of experiments in a virtual simulation environment to obtain normalized quality values $r_\xi^{k,j}$ for transferring to the input of the fuzzy inference system and obtaining an integral quality indicator of the evaluated stack s^j for infrastructure configuration ω^k.
6. To organize a directed search of the s^* technology stack for configuration ω^k, it is proposed to use the swarm intelligence algorithm [27].

Let us consider the application of the methodology on the example of choosing Node.js modules for developing a digital platform DigitalPsyTools [28], designed to provide information support for population and longitudinal psychological research in Russia.

The following functional requirements are imposed on the modules used for data transmission and processing in the digital platform:

- q_1—sequentially check all elements of the array for compliance with the condition and return an array consisting of elements for which the check gave the value "True" (given alternatives: Lodash, Underscore);
- q_2—apply the specified function to all elements of the array, returning a new array consisting of the transformed elements (given alternatives: Lodash, Underscore, native JavaScript);
- q_3—return the first element of the array (given alternatives: Lodash, Underscore);
- q_4—build full path to file or directory based on specified array of path elements (given alternatives: native path module);
- q_5—find and replace a substring in the given string (given alternatives: native JavaScript);
- q_6—zip the transferred file array and return the generated Zip archive (given alternatives: Adm-zip, jszip, zipit);
- q_7—calculate the MD5 hash sum for the specified dataset (given alternatives: Hasha, md5, Ts-md5);
- q_8—read data from file (given alternatives: Fs-extra, native fs module);
- q_9—read the contents of a directory by returning an array of filenames and subdirectories inside the directory (given alternatives: Fs-extra);

- q_{10}—recursively read the contents of a directory and return an array of filenames and subdirectories inside the directory (given alternatives: Recursive-readdir).

Thus, $n = 10, p = 216$.

The quality of functioning is evaluated using $f = 3$ quality indicators: $r_1^{k,j}$—physical time spent on the experiment, ns; $r_2^{k,j}$—microprocessor time spent on executing user code during the experiment, μs; $r_3^{k,j}$—increase in the size of memory pages allocated to the experiment process (including heap, code segment, and stack), bytes. During the experiment, the quality indicators were normalized relative to their maximum values in the experiment, taking values on the interval [0; 1].

The use of these quality indicators is explained by the need to choose a technology stack for which resource consumption in terms of increasing the size of memory pages, processor, and physical time of program execution are minimal, which will ensure the best user experience on various desktop and mobile devices.

The Fuzzy Logic Toolbox for MATLAB engineering software package is used for fuzzy inference. It allows us to make the process of creating and configuring fuzzy inference systems interactive. The developer visually configures the number of fuzzy sets, the type of the membership function, the method of fuzzification of the initial quantitative data for the transition to a qualitative representation, and the defuzzification method to obtain a quantitative value at the output of the system. In the given example, the following standard fuzzy inference parameters are set: *and method: min*; *or method: max*; *implication: min*; *aggregation: max*; *defuzzification: centroid*.

Two different fuzzy inference systems of the Mamdani type were developed to obtain integral quality indicators of the evaluated technology stack $\Psi(\omega^k, s^j)$. Both systems are described in Appendix A.

The first fuzzy inference system led to the following technology stack for the implementation of functional requirements:

- q_1 is implemented by the "Underscore" component;
- q_2 and q_5 are implemented by the JavaScript language tools;
- q_3—by the "Lodash" component;
- q_4—by the "Path" component;
- q_6—by the "Adm-zip" component;
- q_7—by the "Hasha" component;
- q_8—by the "Fs" component;
- q_9—by the "Fs-extra" component;
- q_{10}—by the "Recursive-readdir" component.

The integral quality indicator value for the technology stack is 0.8123.

The second fuzzy inference system led to the following technology stack for the implementation of functional requirements of the given digital platform:

- q_1 is implemented by the "Underscore" component;
- q_2 and q_5 are implemented by the JavaScript language tools;
- q_3—by the "Lodash" component;
- q_4—by the "Path" component;
- q_6—by the "Adm-zip" component;
- q_7—by the "Ts-md5" component;
- q_8—by the "Fs-extra" component;
- q_9—by the "Fs-extra" component;
- q_{10}—by the "Recursive-readdir" component.

The integral quality indicator value for the technology stack is 0.8647.

6. Conclusions

A methodology for the selection of information technology solutions for a technology stack of digital platforms based on fuzzy logic has been developed. The methodology was tested on the choice of a technology stack for the component of data processing and transmission in the digital platform of population psychological research. The obtained results were confirmed experimentally, as the implementation of the selected technologies provided the required level of quality and efficiency in the collection and transmission of data in population studies. In this paper, studies of two alternative methods of fuzzy inference are carried out, demonstrating the use of fuzzy logic for the developed methodology.

The contribution of the paper to the developer community lays in demonstration of the importance of conducting experimental research and obtaining numerical estimates of technology solution efficiency during the process of digital platform development. It is shown that the software system will satisfy the specified requirements if the choice of the technology stack is reasonable. The limitation of the approach is the need to allocate additional computing resources and specialists for experimental research and analysis of the results obtained. However, these costs are justified for digital platforms that process big data or work with a large number of users, since the methodology helps to avoid many of the errors that are commonly detected at the launch stage.

The proposed methodology can be applied in various models of the digital platforms' life cycle. Since correct experiments are time consuming, it is quite possible that the approach is difficult to apply in agile development methodologies with short sprints. The methodology is suited better to the incremental and agile methodologies with a longer sprint or iteration duration as it gives the advantage during the search of the effective information technology solutions based on the previously selected technology stack.

The proposed methodology can be used when choosing technological solutions for the technology stack of modern digital platforms and similar software systems with integrated architecture.

Author Contributions: Conceptualization, E.N.; methodology, E.N., A.G., and D.I.; software, D.I.; validation, A.G.; formal analysis, E.N. and A.G.; investigation, D.I.; resources, D.I.; writing—original draft preparation, E.N., D.I.; writing—review and editing, A.G.; visualization, A.G.; supervision, E.N.; project administration, E.N. All authors have read and agreed to the published version of the manuscript.

Funding: This research was funded by the Ministry of Science and Higher Education of the Russian Federation.

Institutional Review Board Statement: Not applicable.

Informed Consent Statement: Not applicable.

Data Availability Statement: Not applicable.

Conflicts of Interest: The authors declare no conflict of interest.

Appendix A

Two different fuzzy inference systems of the Mamdani type (hereinafter FIS) were developed, as shown in Figure A1, to obtain integral quality indicators $\Psi(\omega^k, s^j)$ of the evaluated technology stack. These systems take as input the three quality indicators described above, with $r_1{}^{k,j}$ being denoted as **t**, $r_2{}^{k,j}$ being denoted as **cpu**, and $r_3{}^{k,j}$ being denoted as **ram**. The integral quality indicator $\Psi(\omega^k, s^j)$ is denoted as **quality**.

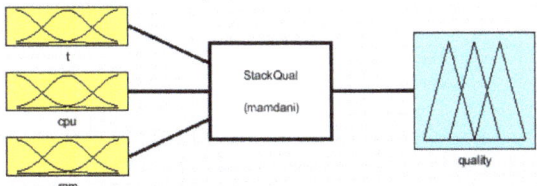

Figure A1. Structure of fuzzy inference system.

In both fuzzy inference systems, the numerical values of the indicators **t**, **cpu**, **ram** are associated with fuzzy sets "low"—low resource consumption, "med"—average resource consumption, "high"—high resource consumption, for which triangular membership functions are defined with coordinates vertices [−0.4 0 0.4], [0.1 0.5 0.9], [0.6 1 1.4] for "low", "med", "high", respectively.

The integral quality indicator named **quality** is associated with fuzzy sets "low"—low quality, "med"—medium quality, "high"—high quality in accordance with defined membership functions, as shown in Figure A2.

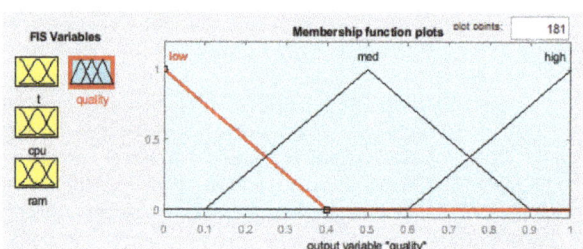

Figure A2. Membership functions of fuzzy sets for the integral quality indicator.

When determining the value of the integral quality indicator in FIS, the following rules are used (the weight of the rule is indicated in brackets):

1. If (**t** is low) and (**cpu** is low) then (**quality** is high) (0.5);
2. If (**t** is low) and (**cpu** is med) then (**quality** is high) (0.5);
3. If (**t** is low) and (**cpu** is high) then (**quality** is med) (0.5);
4. If (**t** is med) and (**cpu** is low) then (**quality** is high) (0.5);
5. If (**t** is med) and (**cpu** is med) then (**quality** is med) (0.5);
6. If (**t** is med) and (**cpu** is high) then (**quality** is med) (0.5);
7. If (**t** is high) and (**cpu** is low) then (**quality** is med) (0.5);
8. If (**t** is high) and (**cpu** is med) then (**quality** is med) (0.5);
9. If (**t** is high) and (**cpu** is high) then (**quality** is med) (0.5);
10. If (**ram** is med) then (**quality** is med) (1);
11. If (**ram** is high) then (**quality** is low) (1).

For verification, an alternative output is considered, using more rules. When determining the value of the integral quality indicator in FIS$_A$, the following rules are used (the weight of the rule is indicated in brackets):

1. If (**t** is low) and (**cpu** is low) and (**ram** is low) then (**quality** is high) (1);
2. If (**t** is low) and (**cpu** is low) and (**ram** is med) then (**quality** is high) (1);
3. If (**t** is low) and (**cpu** is low) and (**ram** is high) then (**quality** is med) (1);
4. If (**t** is low) and (**cpu** is med) and (**ram** is low) then (**quality** is high) (1);
5. If (**t** is low) and (**cpu** is med) and (**ram** is med) then (**quality** is med) (1);
6. If (**t** is low) and (**cpu** is med) and (**ram** is high) then (**quality** is low) (1);
7. If (**t** is low) and (**cpu** is high) and (**ram** is low) then (**quality** is med) (1);
8. If (**t** is low) and (**cpu** is high) and (**ram** is med) then (**quality** is low) (1);
9. If (**t** is low) and (**cpu** is high) and (**ram** is high) then (**quality** is low) (1);
10. If (**t** is med) and (**cpu** is low) and (**ram** is low) then (**quality** is high) (1);
11. If (**t** is med) and (**cpu** is low) and (**ram** is med) then (**quality** is med) (1);
12. If (**t** is med) and (**cpu** is low) and (**ram** is high) then (**quality** is low) (1);
13. If (**t** is med) and (**cpu** is med) and (**ram** is low) then (**quality** is med) (1);
14. If (**t** is med) and (**cpu** is med) and (**ram** is med) then (**quality** is med) (1);
15. If (**t** is med) and (**cpu** is med) and (**ram** is high) then (**quality** is low) (1);
16. If (**t** is med) and (**cpu** is high) and (**ram** is low) then (**quality** is med) (1);
17. If (**t** is med) and (**cpu** is high) and (**ram** is med) then (**quality** is med) (1);
18. If (**t** is med) and (**cpu** is high) and (**ram** is high) then (**quality** is low) (1);

19. If (**t** is high) and (**cpu** is low) and (**ram** is low) then (**quality** is med) (1);
20. If (**t** is high) and (**cpu** is low) and (**ram** is med) then (**quality** is low) (1);
21. If (**t** is high) and (**cpu** is low) and (**ram** is high) then (**quality** is low) (1);
22. If (**t** is high) and (**cpu** is med) and (**ram** is low) then (**quality** is med) (1);
23. If (**t** is high) and (**cpu** is med) and (**ram** is med) then (**quality** is med) (1);
24. If (**t** is high) and (**cpu** is med) and (**ram** is high) then (**quality** is low) (1);
25. If (**t** is high) and (**cpu** is high) and (**ram** is low) then (**quality** is med) (1);
26. If (**t** is high) and (**cpu** is high) and (**ram** is med) then (**quality** is low) (1);
27. If (**t** is high) and (**cpu** is high) and (**ram** is high) then (**quality** is low) (1).

FIS and FIS$_A$ decision surfaces are shown in Figure A3.

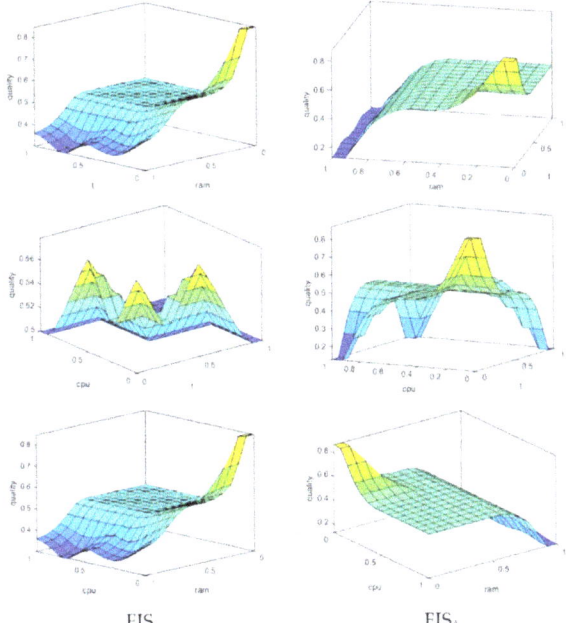

Figure A3. Decision surfaces for fuzzy inference systems, FIS and FIS$_A$.

Consideration of decision surfaces for pairs of indicators for FIS and FIS$_A$ indicates the applicability of both fuzzy inference systems for the choice of information technology solutions. However, due to a more compact rule base and the use of weight priorities, FIS is distinguished by a higher steepness of the surface in terms of **t**, **cpu** and by the presence of local maximum, which is compensated by the superior weight of the selection rules in terms of the **ram** indicator (Rules 10 and 11) to eliminate the ambiguity of the choice in terms of **t**, **cpu**.

References

1. Ramirez, A.; Romero, J.R.; Ventura, S. Interactive multi-objective evolutionary optimization of software architectures. *Inf. Sci.* **2018**, *463*, 92–109. [CrossRef]
2. Yang, Y.; Yang, B.; Wang, S.; Jin, T.; Li, S. An enhanced multi-objective grey wolf optimizer for service composition in cloud manufacturing. *Appl. Soft Comput.* **2020**, *87*, 106003. [CrossRef]
3. Gholamshahi, S.; Hasheminejad, S.M.H. Software component identification and selection: A research review. *Softw. Pract. Exp.* **2019**, *49*, 40–69. [CrossRef]
4. Beran, P.P.; Vinek, E.; Schikuta, E. A cloud-based framework for QoS-aware service selection optimization. In Proceedings of the 13th International Conference on Information Integration and Web-based Applications and Services, Ho Chi Minh City, Vietnam, 5–7 December 2011; pp. 284–287.

5. Ramírez, A.; Parejo, J.A.; Romero, J.R.; Segura, S.; Ruiz-Cortés, A. Evolutionary composition of QoS-aware web services: A many-objective perspective. *Expert Syst. Appl.* **2017**, *72*, 357–370. [CrossRef]
6. Vinek, E.; Beran, P.P.; Schikuta, E. A dynamic multi-objective optimization framework for selecting distributed deployments in a heterogeneous environment. *Procedia Comput. Sci.* **2011**, *4*, 166–175. [CrossRef]
7. Kudzh, S.A.; Tsvetkov, V.Y.; Rogov, I.E. Life cycle support software components. *Russ. Technol. J.* **2020**, *8*, 19–33. [CrossRef]
8. Ezenwoke, A.; Daramola, O.; Adigun, M. QoS-based ranking and selection of SaaS applications using heterogeneous similarity metrics. *J. Cloud Comput.* **2018**, *7*, 15. [CrossRef]
9. Belov, V.; Tatarintsev, A.; Nikulchev, E. Choosing a Data Storage Format in the Apache Hadoop System Based on Experimental Evaluation Using Apache Spark. *Symmetry* **2021**, *13*, 195. [CrossRef]
10. Beyer, D.; Lemberger, T. Software verification: Testing vs. model checking. In *Haifa Verification Conference*; Springer: Cham, Switzerland, 2017; pp. 99–114.
11. Yigitbas, E.; Anjorin, A.; Jovanovikj, I.; Kern, T.; Sauer, S.; Engels, G. Usability evaluation of model-driven cross-device web user interfaces. In *International Conference on Human-Centred Software Engineering*; Springer: Cham, Switzerland, 2018; pp. 231–247.
12. Caballer, M.; Blanquer, I.; Moltó, G.; De Alfonso, C. Dynamic management of virtual infrastructures. *J. Grid Comput.* **2015**, *13*, 53–70. [CrossRef]
13. Giannakopoulos, I.; Konstantinou, I.; Tsoumakos, D.; Koziris, N. Cloud application deployment with transient failure recovery. *J. Cloud Comput.* **2018**, *7*, 1–20. [CrossRef]
14. Xuan, N.P.N.; Lim, S.; Jung, S. Centralized management solution for vagrant in development environment. In Proceedings of the 11th International Conference on Ubiquitous Information Management and Communication, Beppu, Japan, 5–7 January 2017. [CrossRef]
15. Peacock, M. *Creating Development Environments with Vagrant*; Packt Publishing Ltd.: Birmingham, UK, 2015.
16. Iuhasz, G.; Pop, D.; Dragan, I. Architecture of a scalable platform for monitoring multiple big data frameworks. *Scalable Comput.* **2016**, *17*, 313–321. [CrossRef]
17. Garousi, V.; Giray, G.; Tüzün, E.; Catal, C.; Felderer, M. Aligning software engineering education with industrial needs: A meta-analysis. *J. Syst. Softw.* **2019**, *156*, 65–83. [CrossRef]
18. Lemos, O.A.L.; Silveira, F.F.; Ferrari, F.C.; Garcia, A. The impact of Software Testing education on code reliability: An empirical assessment. *J. Syst. Softw.* **2018**, *137*, 497–511. [CrossRef]
19. Nachiyappan, S.; Justus, S. Cloud testing tools and its challenges: A comparative study. *Procedia Comput. Sci.* **2015**, *50*, 482–489. [CrossRef]
20. Garousi, V.; Felderer, M. Worlds apart: Industrial and academic focus areas in software testing. *IEEE Softw.* **2017**, *34*, 38–45.
21. Couto, L.D.; Tran-Jørgensen, P.W.V.; Nilsson, R.S.; Larsen, P.G. Enabling continuous integration in a formal methods setting. *Int. J. Softw. Tools Technol. Transf.* **2020**, *2*, 667–683. [CrossRef]
22. Mäntylä, M.V.; Adams, B.; Khomh, F.; Engström, E.; Petersen, K. On rapid releases and software testing: A case study and a semi-systematic literature review. *Empir. Softw. Eng.* **2015**, *20*, 1384–1425. [CrossRef]
23. Lindgren, E.; Münch, J. Raising the odds of success: The current state of experimentation in product development. *Inf. Softw. Technol.* **2016**, *77*, 80–91. [CrossRef]
24. Dingsøyr, T.; Lassenius, C. Emerging themes in agile software development: Introduction to the special section on continuous value delivery. *Inf. Softw. Technol.* **2016**, *77*, 56–60. [CrossRef]
25. Gusev, A.; Nikulchev, E.; Ilin, D. The Dataset of the Experimental Evaluation of Software Components for Application Design Selection Directed by the Artificial Bee Colony Algorithm. *Data* **2020**, *5*, 59. [CrossRef]
26. Brondolin, R.; Ferroni, M.; Santambrogio, M. Performance-aware load shedding for monitoring events in container based environments. *ACM Sigbed Rev.* **2019**, *16*, 27–32. [CrossRef]
27. Gusev, A.; Ilin, D.; Kolyasnikov, P.; Nikulchev, E. Effective selection of software components based on experimental evaluations of quality of operation. *Eng. Lett.* **2020**, *28*, 420–427.
28. Nikulchev, E.; Ilin, D.; Silaeva, A.; Kolyasnikov, P.; Belov, V.; Runtov, A.; Pushkin, P.; Laptev, N.; Alexeenko, A.; Magomedov, S.; et al. Digital Psychological Platform for Mass Web-Surveys. *Data* **2020**, *5*, 95. [CrossRef]

Article

A Mathematical Method for Determining the Parameters of Functional Dependencies Using Multiscale Probability Distribution Functions

Ilya E. Tarasov

Institute of Informational Technologies, RTU MIREA, Vernadsky pr. 78, 119454 Moscow, Russia; tarasov_i@mirea.ru

Abstract: This article discusses the application of the method of approximation of experimental data by functional dependencies, which uses a probabilistic assessment of the deviation of the assumed dependence from experimental data. The application of this method involves the introduction of an independent parameter "scale of the error probability distribution function" and allows one to synthesize the deviation functions, forming spaces with a nonlinear metric, based on the existing assumptions about the sources of errors and noise. The existing method of regression analysis can be obtained from the considered method as a special case. The article examines examples of analysis of experimental data and shows the high resistance of the method to the appearance of single outliers in the sample under study. Since the introduction of an independent parameter increases the number of computations, for the practical application of the method in measuring and information systems, the architecture of a specialized computing device of the "system on a chip" class and practical approaches to its implementation based on programmable logic integrated circuits are considered.

Keywords: statistics; multiscale analysis; data analysis; system on chip

Citation: Tarasov, I.E. A Mathematical Method for Determining the Parameters of Functional Dependencies Using Multiscale Probability Distribution Functions. *Mathematics* **2021**, *9*, 1085. https://doi.org/10.3390/math9101085

Academic Editor: Liliya Demidova

Received: 27 March 2021
Accepted: 7 May 2021
Published: 12 May 2021

Publisher's Note: MDPI stays neutral with regard to jurisdictional claims in published maps and institutional affiliations.

Copyright: © 2021 by the author. Licensee MDPI, Basel, Switzerland. This article is an open access article distributed under the terms and conditions of the Creative Commons Attribution (CC BY) license (https://creativecommons.org/licenses/by/4.0/).

1. Introduction

Currently, data to be analyzed are subject to the action of many factors, which is due to both the increasing complexity of objects and systems that are the sources of such data, and the increasing requirements for the quality of analysis of complex multi-parameter systems. An additional factor is the effect of interference, including outliers, which complicates the analysis in an automated mode, forcing researchers to perform additional operations to identify data that incorrectly describe the process under study and to eliminate them from the analyzed samples.

On the other hand, advances in computing technology and increased computing performance make it attractive to use digital computing systems to implement advanced data analysis techniques that could benefit from such increased performance. Therefore, the search for new methods of data analysis can improve the quality of information, measuring and analytical systems, if modern high-performance computing systems can be used for their implementation.

The presented method is an original study inspired by the positive results and experience of using multiscale analysis for processing experimental results in applied physics. Practical results include the application of the method in a number of precision measuring devices, for example, a series of dielectric loss tangent meters (Tangent-M3, RU.C.34.010A reg. No. 52972, MEP-6IS, reg. No. 44621-10). The noted disadvantage of the method, as will be shown below, is the large number of computations for its implementation; therefore, during the research process, it had limited application. At present, the development of computer technology, especially FPGA, makes it possible to revise the practical aspects of the presented method and re-iterate it taking into account the new possibilities of computer technology.

An approach based on the synthesis of hypotheses with subsequent verification of their quality can be significantly more effective compared to analytical approaches based on the use of predetermined statistical parameters. The Anscombe quartet [1] is a well-known example illustrating the ambiguous nature of regression analysis. It represents four sets of data (pairs of points) with the same statistical characteristics, but visually significantly different.

The literature notes that all sets of points have the same function, determined based on a regression analysis:

$$y(x) = 0.5x + 3, \tag{1}$$

Thus, the application of the least squares method does not allow one to distinguish datasets either by the characteristics of the regression dependence, by the correlation coefficient or by the main statistical characteristics of the datasets, which also coincide. In general, the role of the Anscombe quartet is to demonstrate the imperfection of regression analysis when applied to data that are the result of various processes that cannot be taken into account in the formulation of the regression analysis problem. The modern reference to the Anscombe quartet is usually made in the context of the importance of data visualization [2,3]. In this article, the Anscombe quartet will be used as a widespread example to illustrate the analysis results.

2. Theoretical Description of the Method of Approximating the Parameters of Functional Dependencies Using Multiscale Probability Distribution Functions

The analysis method considered below, first described in [4], consists of using the Bayes' theorem for data analysis, in which a free parameter "scale of the probability density function" is introduced, and the posterior probabilities are calculated for different values of this parameter. This approach is intended to partially compensate for the well-known drawback of Bayes' theorem in the form of insufficient substantiation of the choice of the a priori error distribution law.

The essence of the approach considered here is to accept a probabilistic hypothesis of the form "the quantity has a real value equal to X_i." Then, the probability that the observed (measured) value will have a value x is determined by the probability density function of the error distribution, where the argument is the deviation value $X_i - x$. In accordance with Bayes' theorem, the posterior probability that a series of measurements $x_1, x_2, \ldots x_n$ appeared in the process of measuring a quantity with a real value Xi is determined by the formula:

$$f_A(x, \sigma) = \frac{1}{N} \sum_{i=1}^{n} P(x_i | x_{real}, \sigma), \tag{2}$$

There is a known maximum likelihood method, which is based on a similar formula, but estimates the product of probability density functions, not the sum:

$$L(x, \sigma) = \prod_{i=1}^{n} P(x - x_i, \sigma), \tag{3}$$

There is a significant difference between the method of maximum likelihood and the considered method of statistical analysis. There is an obvious difference in the mathematical formulation, which consists of the summation of the probabilities in the considered method and in their multiplication in the maximum likelihood method. From the point of view of probability theory, the multiplication of the probability of independent events corresponds to the probability of their simultaneous occurrence. In relation to the measurement process, this means that all measured values objectively reflect the state of the measured object. The presence of disturbances, partial inconsistency between the object and the measuring system, interference in the measuring channel, etc. calls into question the correctness of such an assumption. At the same time, the addition of probabilities corresponds to a situation where some (but not necessarily all) measured values can be used to assess the state of an object. In this case, there is an implicit filtering of misses (although in reality they all participate in determining the probability), since the analysis technique provides for the determination of such a value of the measured quantity x, at which the appearance of all quantities in the analyzed sample can be explained taking into account any possible interference in the measuring system.

At the same time, the appearance of a single slip for the maximum likelihood method will lead to the appearance of a sample element with a large deviation from the considered variant of the approximating dependence, for which the probability density function will be close to zero.

The provisions of the considered method can be applied to modify the regression analysis. It is known that regression analysis uses the method of least squares, which minimizes the sum of squares of deviations of experimental points from the corresponding values obtained from the analytical dependence:

$$P(\beta) = \sum_{i=1}^{N}(f(x_i,\beta) - y_i)^2, \qquad (4)$$

where β is the vector of dependence parameters.

Let us introduce the function $\rho(x_1, x_2) = (x_1 - x_2)^2$ for the least squares method. In this case, Equation (4) can be represented as:

$$P(\beta) = \sum_{i=1}^{N} \rho(f(x_i,\beta), y_i), \qquad (5)$$

Since the function $\rho(x_1, x_2)$ is a function of the distance between the points x_1, x_2 in some space R(x, ρ), the least squares method can be considered as a method that minimizes the sum of distances in the space R from the approximating dependence to the experimental points. Moreover, for the LSM the function R is quadratic.

An idea of using a distance function other than quadratic is known. For example, the least absolute deviation method is based on the linear distance. Alternatives to the least squares method are known, such as quantile regression, least trimmed squares and others, and this shows that the disadvantages of the least squares method are significant and practical applications require alternative methods of analysis.

In Equation (5), the distance function can be replaced. It is easy to imagine that with an arbitrary choice of distance functions, the results of the analysis will be radically different, but no particular case will be preferable. The choice and justification of the distance function in this work is proposed to be made on the basis of the known or assumed distribution law of the measurement error. Taking into account the mentioned analysis method based on Bayes' theorem, it is proposed to carry out statistical analysis for a series of functions with different values of σ. For this, a relationship should be established between the distance function and the probability function. One can introduce the operator $g : L(x) \to \rho(x)$, which maps the probability of a dependence with these parameters to the distance from the approximating dependence to the next experimental point in the space R.

If the distance function $\rho\,(\Delta x) \in [0; \infty)$, and the probability density function P (Δx) [0; P$_{max}$] and, obviously, the zero distance in the space R correspond to the maximum probability, then $g(x)$ can be taken as:

$$g : P_{max} - P(x) \qquad (6)$$

When using such a mapping, the minimum (zero) distance corresponds to the maximum probability density. This is the easiest way to convert the maximum probability to the minimum distance and should be reviewed and improved upon in the future. Consequently, the condition for the maximum of the probability function defined by Equation (2) can also be written as an adequate condition for minimizing the total distance in some space R between the assumed dependence and the points of the original sample.

From the point of view of the assessment method by the probability criterion, Equation (5) can be written as:

$$P(\beta) = \sum_{i=1}^{N} p(f(x_i,\beta) - y_i, \sigma) \qquad (7)$$

When using this criterion, it is necessary to determine the set of parameters β, upon substitution of which in Equation (5) the function P(β) reaches its maximum value.

From the above, it follows that for a set of experimental readings, a space is constructed with a function of the distance between points determined by the characteristics of the measuring channel (including the digital part). For this space, the fulfillment of the triangle axiom is not obvious (moreover, it can be shown that this axiom does not hold in the case of a Gaussian distribution of the error); thus, in the general case, one cannot speak of its metric. For such spaces, where the triangle axiom does not hold (however, the rest of the axioms characteristic of metric spaces hold), the terms "symmetric" or "pseudo metrics" are used. Due to this replacement, it is incorrect to designate the resulting function as "regression dependence," since this implies a search for a minimum of deviations using the least squares method. In this case, it is more correct to use the more general term "approximating dependence."

If we consider the widely used Gaussian function and construct a distance function based on it, it will look compared to the quadratic distance function, as shown in Figure 1.

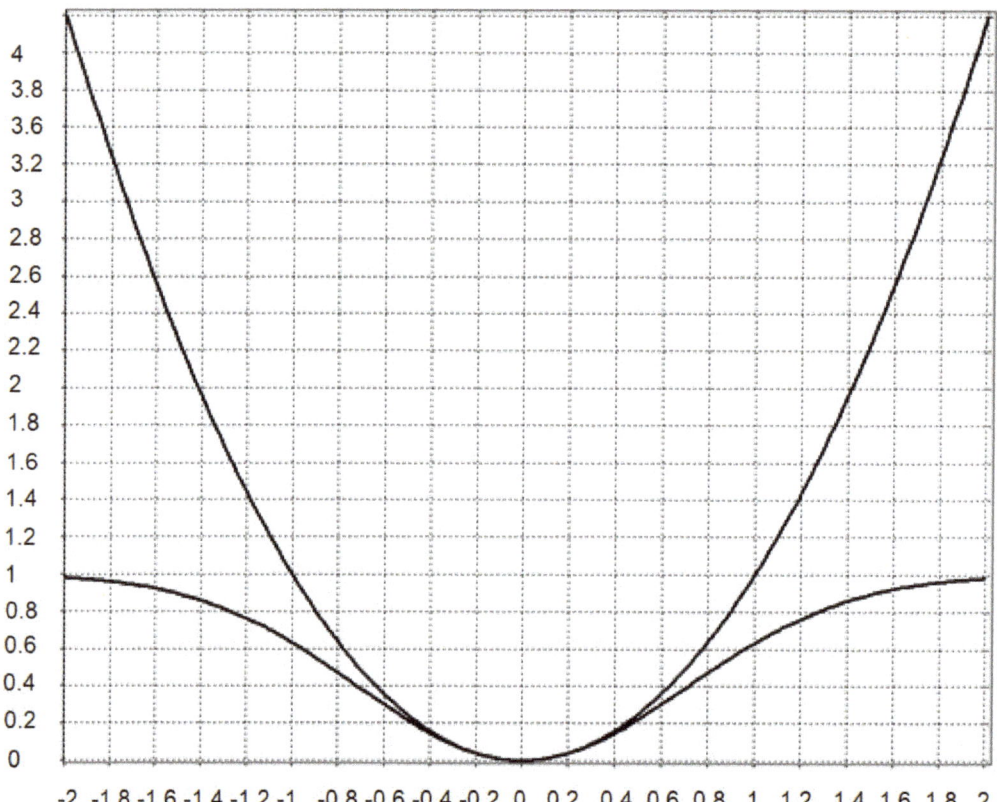

Figure 1. Comparative representation of the quadratic distance function and the distance function constructed under the assumption that the error has a Gaussian probability distribution.

Thus, in the considered approach, the procedure for analyzing the parameters of the regression dependence is replaced by the procedure for synthesizing a possible vector of parameters and estimating its probability in accordance with a modified Bayesian estimate, in which the independent parameter "scale of the probability density function" is introduced. Based on this function, a space is formed in which the sum of the distances from the hypothetical dependence to the available points of the analyzed sample is minimized.

An obvious objection to the proposed approach is the sharply increasing volume of computational operations. Indeed, in addition to the synthesis of hypotheses about the possible values of the parameters of the approximating dependence, it is also required to change the parameter "scale of the probability distribution function," which forms the corresponding distance function. Thus, for n parameters of the dependence to be analyzed, there is $n + 1$ parameter, which in this work is proposed to be obtained not analytically, but by methods of computational mathematics.

The development of computer technology and the emergence of new architectures, including a great deal of attention to parallel computing, makes it attractive to use numerical methods of analysis if the use of high-performance computing systems allows new possibilities to be obtained. For example, in [5], the author considered the practical issues of building a high-performance computing system with parallel computing nodes based on an FPGA. The current state of the architecture of high-performance computing devices demonstrates the widespread use of parallel operating nodes and systems [6–9].

As an example, consider the process of analyzing the parameters of a linear relationship. Among the possible options for representing a linear function, it seems advisable to choose the option with the direction vector angle and the distance to the origin of coordinates (θ, p). This form of representation, in particular, allows one to find vertical and horizontal lines, and also provides a more uniform distribution of hypotheses when the angle of the direction vector changes linearly.

The straight line equation is represented by the formula:

$$R = X \cos\theta + Y \sin\theta - p \tag{8}$$

In this representation of straight line, R is a distance between point with $(X; Y)$ coordinates and a line described by (θ, p). This is very useful for the described method, because Equation (8) may be easily converted to a distance in any other space, including quadratic, Gaussian etc.

If we introduce the criterion of the quality of an approximation in the form of a function that takes the maximum value when the distance between the pixel and the generated line representation is zero, then the search for a set of parameters for a straight line can be performed by maximizing Equation (7):

$$S(\theta, p) = \sum_{X,Y} f(X \cos\theta + Y \sin\theta - p) \tag{9}$$

In a more general form, Equation (9) can be represented as:

$$S(\vec{a}) = \sum_{X,Y} f(X, Y, \vec{a}) \tag{10}$$

where $\vec{a}$ is the vector of the line parameters.

As follows from Equations (8)–(10), an important role is played by the choice of the function f, which is used to determine the quality criterion of the approximation. It can be pointed out that similar approaches were previously used in problems of approximating functions from experimental data. For example, the Hough transformation [10] assumes, instead of analyzing image pixels, the synthesis of hypotheses about the presence of a line with certain parameters and counting the number of image pixels belonging to each of these lines. Similarly, "voting for hypotheses" is implemented, which is mathematically similar to performing a probabilistic estimate.

For the Hough transform, the function S can be represented as:

$$f = \begin{cases} 0 \text{ with } |X \cos\theta + Y \sin\theta - p| > 1 \\ 1 \text{ with } |X \cos\theta + Y \sin\theta - p| \leq 1 \end{cases} \tag{11}$$

From Equation (11) it can be seen that Equation (10) can be reduced to the Hough transformation by passing to the limit if the approximation quality function is presented as a delta function (according to the principle of the presence or absence of a pixel). The possibility of using nearby pixels for analysis appears when using functions that make sense of the probability of deviation of pixels in an image from an idealized line representation with specified parameters. This property seems to be significant in the analysis of high-resolution images, where graphic objects, visually perceived as straight lines, have deviations from the idealized straight line when they are presented in a discrete form using a video matrix subject to interference.

It can be noted that a number of publications devoted to the Hough transformation provide for the transformation of the original image with blurring on the basis of the corresponding convolution kernels [11,12]. The proposed approach is mathematically close to this effect, though it is not the original image that is blurred, but rather the analyzing function. In this case, the function used for such blurring is based on the known form of the error distribution law, which can be qualitatively obtained from the analysis of the subject area and its characteristic processes. Additionally, the introduction of an independent parameter "distribution function scale" allows a number of analysis procedures to be performed with a comparison of the results.

3. Illustration of the Characteristics of the Method Using the Example of the Anscombe Quartet

The data presented in the Anscombe quartet were analyzed using the method described in this paper. The purpose of this analysis was to identify the ability of the method to distinguish between datasets based on the quantitative characteristics obtained. We used the representation of a straight line in Equation (8), with several options for the values of the scale σ. A probabilistic representation of the result was used, since it involves finding the maximum probability (and not the minimum distance in a nonlinear distance space), which provides a better visual representation of the results. The analysis results are shown in Figure 2, where the left side of the figure visualizes the value of the probability function depending on the parameters (θ, p), and the right side shows the corresponding datasets of the Anscombe quartet with superimposed straight lines corresponding to the maximum of the probability function.

The plotting algorithm is quite simple. For each pair of values, the probability density function is calculated according to Equation (7) and is represented as a color in the hot palette. The horizontal axis represents the θ value, and the vertical axis represents the p value.

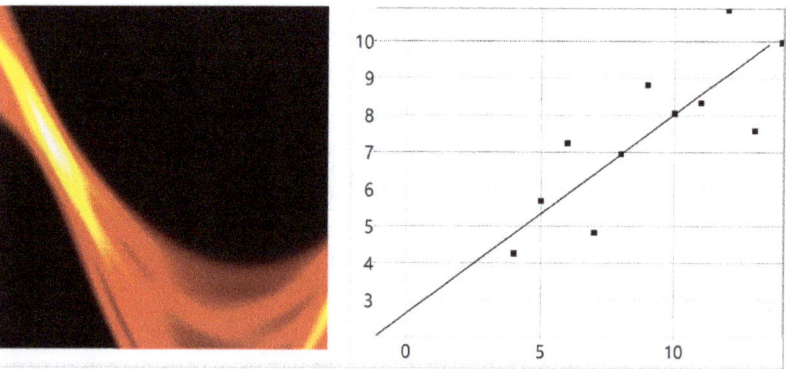

Figure 2. *Cont.*

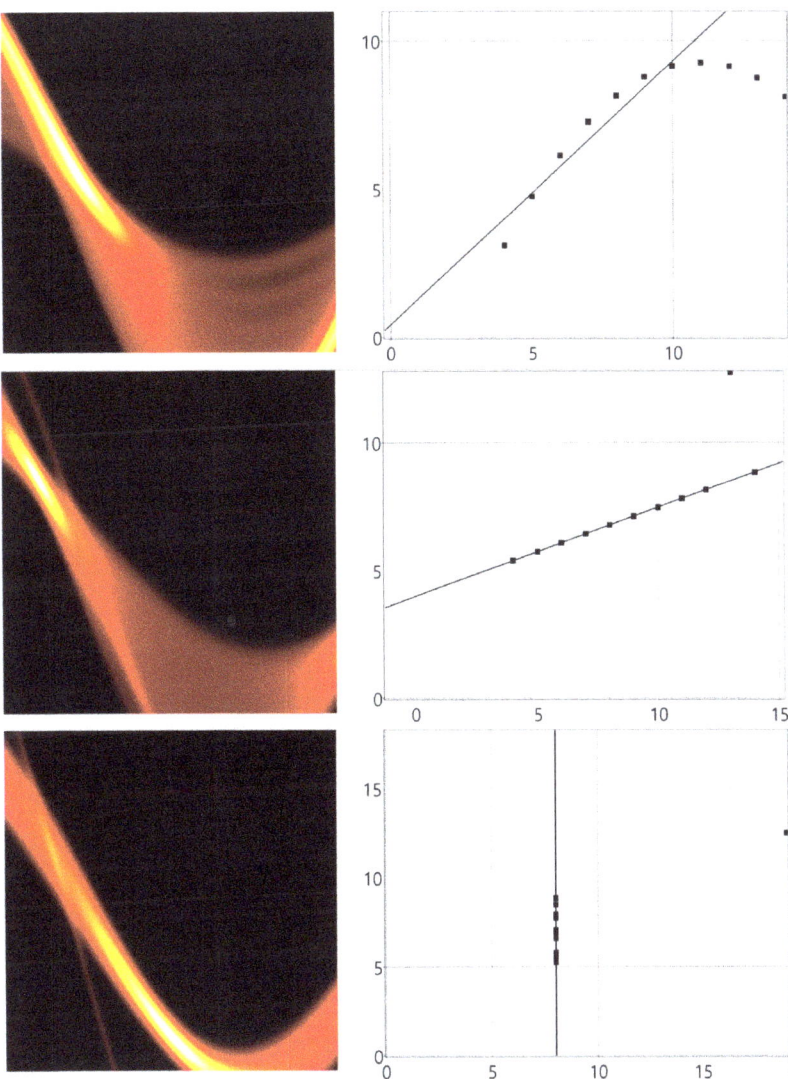

Figure 2. Results of the analysis of the data presented in the Anscombe quartet ($\sigma = 1$).

The data in Figure 2 clearly show the cardinal difference of the proposed method, which provided the identification of the assumed straight lines, which can be determined by taking into account the presence of specially introduced outliers in cases 3, 4. For case 2, the initial data are a parabola; therefore, the search for the parameters of the straight line is obviously inappropriate.

It can be noted that as the parameter "distribution scale" increases, the results of the analysis tend to the results obtained for the regression dependence. This is illustrated in Figure 3, where the analysis was carried out with $\sigma = 10$.

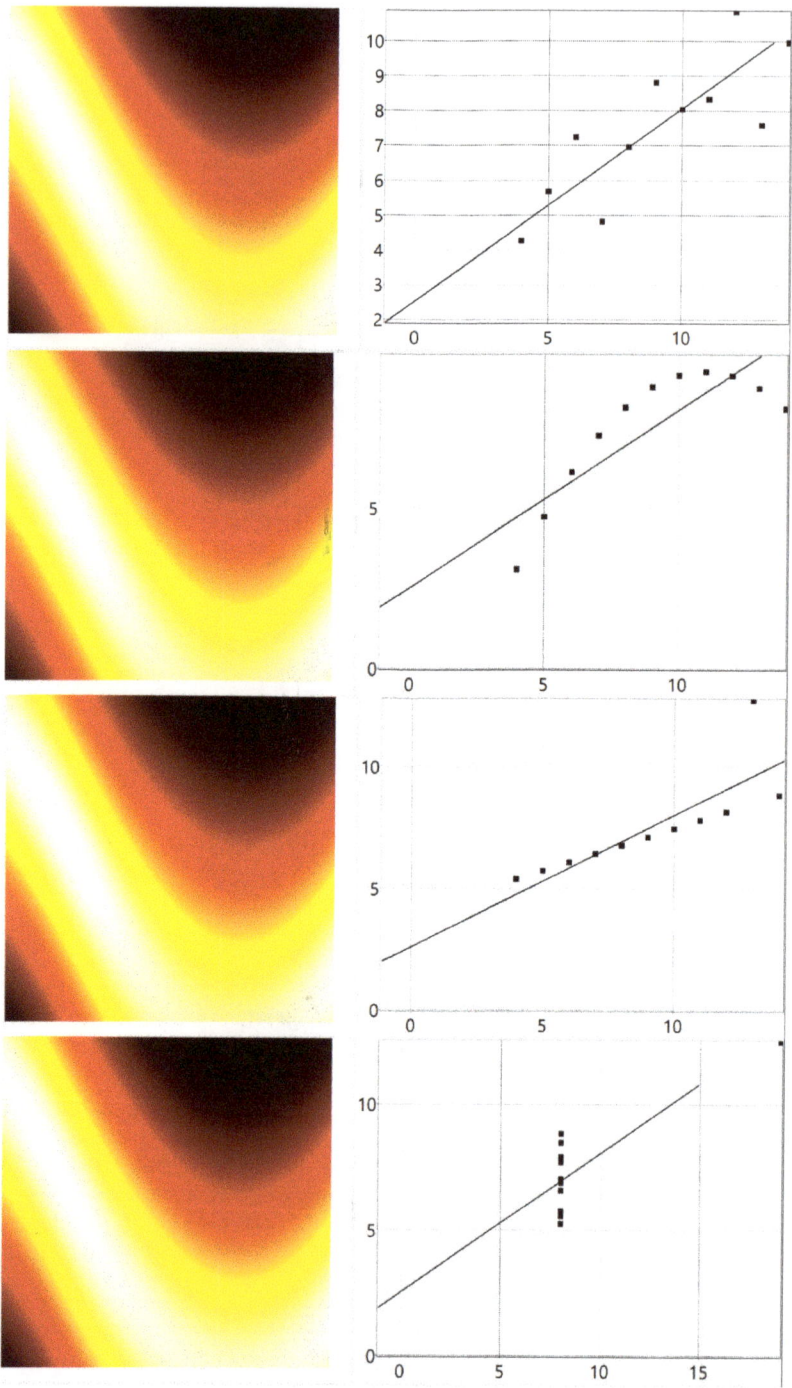

Figure 3. Results of the analysis of the data presented in the Anscombe quartet, with an increase in the scale of the probability distribution function ($\sigma = 10$).

Thus, the method considered in the article can be reduced to the well-known method of regression analysis by the passage to the limit ($\sigma \to \infty$). At the same time, the analysis with other values of σ, including in the range determined based on the analysis of the experimental distribution of the error in the initial data, is able to give results that adequately reflect the dependences in the analyzed data, being stable to the single outliers in the sample.

4. Examples of Using the Method for Analyzing Samples of Various Types

The positive effect of sample analysis using the developed method is manifested primarily for situations where the data generally correspond to the assumed analytical law describing the relationship between them. In this section of the article, the results of the analysis of a number of synthetic and experimentally obtained samples are considered.

Figures 4 and 5 show the results of the analysis of a sample containing two sets of points belonging to different straight lines with the same slope, but with a different constant coefficient.

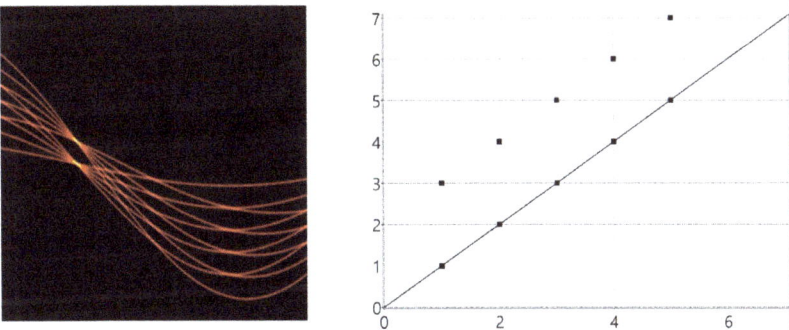

Figure 4. Analysis results of the data sample, $\sigma = 0.1$.

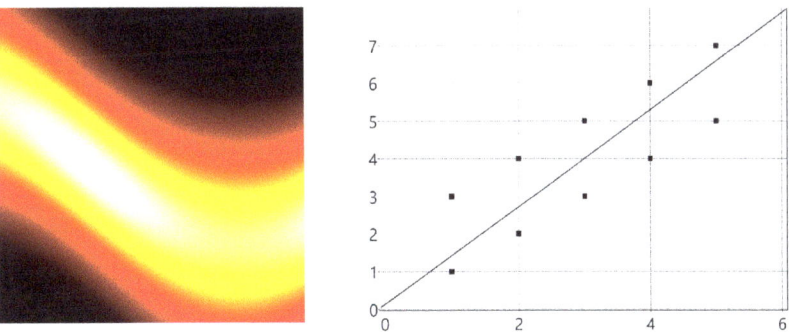

Figure 5. Analysis results of the data sample, $\sigma = 5$.

In Figure 4 it can be seen that the assumed straight lines corresponding to the analytically specified functions $y = x$ and $y = x + 2$ are reflected in the graph of the function P as two bright points corresponding to the local maxima of the probability function for these hypotheses. At the same time, an increase in the scale of σ to a value of 5, exceeding the distance between the straight lines, led to the obtaining of the "averaged line." This allows us to talk about the possibility of managing the results of the analysis by choosing such a scale of the probability density function that most adequately reflects the processes occurring in the system under study and measuring devices.

Figure 6 shows the results of an experimental study of the transient process in a test RC circuit connected to a source of rectangular voltage pulses. The sample is the voltage readings across the capacitor measured with a digital oscilloscope. In Figure 6, artifacts can be seen in the form of digital noise caused by interference in the measurement path. The presence of horizontal sections and fragments where the investigated function decreases will not allow investigating the characteristics of the RC chain using only local analysis, since the time constant calculated for such fragments will tend to infinity or go beyond the domain of the logarithmic function.

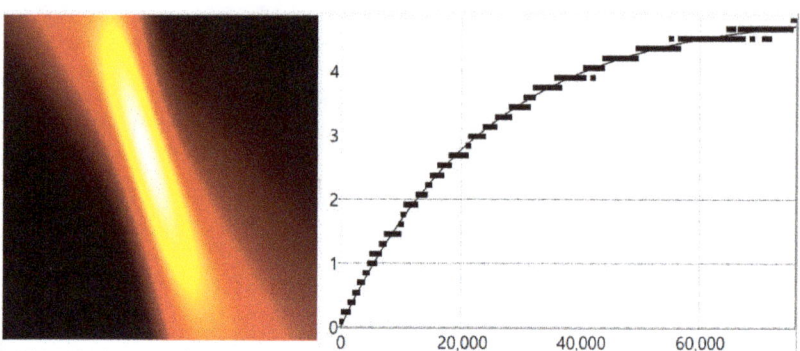

Figure 6. Results of the analysis of a sample of data describing the transient process in the RC chain.

At the same time, an expression can be chosen in the form of an approximating function:

$$V(t) = V_0(1 - exp(-t/\tau)), \tag{12}$$

where V_0 is the amplitude voltage value and τ is the time constant of the RC chain.

In Figure 6, it can be seen that the discovered function passes through the main experimental points, making it possible to quantitatively determine the parameters of the dependences approximating the experimental data.

Interestingly, in Figure 6 there are artifacts originating from the measuring equipment. The measurement mode with low voltage resolution was deliberately chosen so that the experimental data contained horizontal segments that cannot be adequately described by an exponential function. At the same time, the considered method makes it possible to find the analytical parameters of the exponential function that adequately describes the experimental data and is robust to artifacts.

5. Implementation of the Method in Measuring and Information Systems

As mentioned above, the considered method is demanding on the performance of the computing device for its implementation. The synthesis of n parameters of the approximating dependence, performed in the range of their possible values, supplemented by a change in the "scale" parameter, in the direct calculation of the probabilities of hypotheses has a computational complexity of $O(n + 1)$. This significantly distinguishes the considered analysis method from averaging and even digital filtering. Therefore, for the practical application of the method, it is necessary to consider the issues of its implementation in measuring and information systems.

At present, for high-performance computing, along with general-purpose processors (CPUs), graphic processors (GPUs) [13–15] and programmable logic integrated circuits with FPGA architecture [16–20] are also widely used.

Taking into account the fact that the calculations of individual probabilities of individual hypotheses about the parameters of the approximating function are independent processes, parallel computing architectures can be effectively used for this method. Therefore, GPUs and FPGAs appear to be promising hardware platforms, since they provide a large number of computational nodes, the capabilities of which are sufficient to calculate the probability of hypotheses about the parameters of the approximating dependence.

At the same time, the use of a GPU for this task is fraught with certain difficulties. For example, when using a GPU with a program based on the CUDA SDK, the measured data preparation time in the CPU was 0.2–0.3 s, and the calculation time was 27 ms (for 100 CUDA cores and 1000 iterations in each core) with a tabular presentation error probability density function. Computing the Gaussian function in the GPU increases the computation time to 61 ms. Thus, up to 90% of the analysis time is spent on data transfer operations between the CPU and GPU. Therefore, one should also consider computational architectures that process data as it is received.

A specialized computing device of the "system on a chip" (SNC) class, combining data reception and processing, will eliminate the operations of sending data and probability functions, replacing them with storing (or generating) probability functions in the SNC and processing the incoming values in real time (or in combination with their storage in the buffer memory). Prototyping of such a device is now widely performed using FPGAs. The feasibility of implementing a specialized VLSI is determined by technical and economic factors; however, the high cost of preparing VLSI production determines the widespread use of FPGAs in systems manufactured in small quantities.

When considering the architecture and implementation of a specialized computing device, it is necessary to be guided by the following considerations. Since GPUs are effective in the tasks of building three-dimensional graphics and are structurally similar to them, most likely, it will not be possible to exceed their technical and economic characteristics when implementing similar architectures or repeating existing ones. Therefore, for a dedicated FPGA-based device, the following must be done:

1. Reduce the functionality of the computational units compared to the CUDA cores used in a GPU.
2. Provide storage or generation of probability density functions in a computing device, thereby eliminating the need to transfer them from a control device (for example, a PC).

A variant of the structural diagram of a specialized computing device for determining the parameters of the approximating dependence is shown in Figure 7.

Additional advantages of the proposed approach from the point of view of specialized computing systems can be indicated. For example, in Figure 7, the analyzed data and the error probability distribution function can be generalized for a number of computing units. However, it is more important that there are no requirements for constant transmission of input data and results, since for the operation of such a computing system, it is sufficient to load the analyzed sample and the table representing the error probability distribution function. This significantly reduces the load on the peripheral devices of such a computer.

Prototyping of the computing device was carried out on the basis of an FPGA with APSOC Xilinx Zynq-7020 architecture. The obtained characteristics of the module for calculating the probability are shown in Table 1. The module has an internal table for storing the values of the probability density function and an external interface for entering individual values of the sample under study in integer format. The clock frequency of the module was 150 MHz for the XC7Z20 FPGA.

From the data in the table, it can be seen that when describing a highly specialized module in the hardware description language (HDL), a compact implementation of a computational node can be obtained. Thus, for the considered FPGA ZC7020, related to the initial-middle level, it is possible to estimate the number of parallel working nodes in 80–90 (which is limited by the number of memory blocks). For other FPGAs, the number of channels will be correspondingly higher.

Table 2 shows estimates of the comparative performance characteristics of some FPGAs, assuming that the number of placed modules is determined by the number of memory blocks, and the practically achievable clock frequency is 150 MHz for the Zynq-7000 and 200 MHz for the more productive UltraScale+ and Versal FPGAs.

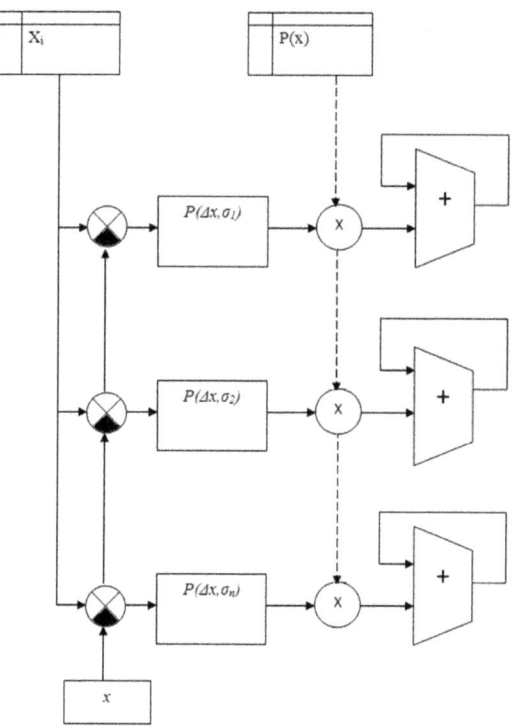

Figure 7. Block diagram of a specialized computing device for determining the parameters of the approximating dependence.

Table 1. Using the resources of FPGA XC7Z7020 when implementing one module for calculating the probability of a hypothesis.

Resource	Utilization	Available	Utilization %
LUT	214	53,200	0.40
FF	158	106,400	0.15
BRAM	1.50	140	1.07
DSP	2	220	0.91

Table 2. Comparative characteristics of FPGA performance when calculating the probability of hypotheses.

FPGA	Number of Channels	Performance, 10^9 Samples/Sec
Zynq-7000 XC7Z20	90	13.5
Kintex UltraScale+ XCKU3P	240	48
Kintex UltraScale+ XCKU19P	1000	200
Zynq MPSOC ZU2CG	100	15
Zynq MPSOC ZU19EG	600	120
Versal VM1102	100	20
Versal VM2902	1300	260

As can be seen from Table 2, FPGA performance ranges from approximately 10 to 250 billion samples per second. Sample processing means calculating the probability that a given sample belongs to one of the sets of approximating dependencies and adding this probability to the accumulator. In this case, the digital interfaces of the FPGA provide direct transfer of the analyzed data to the computing device, and the probability density functions are specified in the considered implementation by tables.

6. Conclusions

The method presented in the article is proposed for processing data exposed to unpredictable impulse noise. The noted disadvantage of the method is the large number of computations required for its implementation, which can be compensated for by using a high-performance element base, such as FPGA. Several issues outlined in the article require additional research and development. For example, the construction of the distance function is of great theoretical interest, and this publication presents it only briefly. Similar to other methods of multiscale analysis, the study and classification of distance functions and their properties opens up great opportunities for research.

An important practical issue is the improvement of algorithms for finding the extrema of the distance or probability function. The examples shown use brute force to construct an entire surface that illustrates the behavior of the probability function. The amount of computation can be significantly reduced using known or new algorithms for finding the extremum of a function. In this area, it is possible to create software implementations of the method, frameworks and libraries, as well as hardware accelerators for high-performance data analysis.

Funding: This research received no external funding.

Institutional Review Board Statement: Not applicable.

Informed Consent Statement: Not applicable.

Data Availability Statement: Not applicable.

Conflicts of Interest: The author declares no conflict of interest.

References

1. Anscombe, F.J. Graphs in Statistical Analysis. *Am. Stat.* **1973**, *27*, 17–21.
2. Li, Q. Overview of data visualization. In *Embodying Data*; Springer: Singapore, 2020. [CrossRef]
3. Embarak, O. The importance of data visualization in business intelligence. In *Data Analysis and Visualization Using Python*; Apress: Berkeley, CA, USA, 2018. [CrossRef]
4. Tarasov, I.E. Estimation of measurements data with use of probability distribution functions with variable scale Zavodskaya Laboratoriya. *Diagn. Mater.* **2004**, *70*, 55–61.
5. Tarasov, I.E.; Potekhin, D.S. Real-time kernel function synthesis for software defined radio and phase-frequency measuring digital systems. *Russ. Technol. J.* **2018**, *6*, 41–54. (In Russian) [CrossRef]
6. Jouppi, N.P.; Young, C.; Patil, N.; Patterson, D.; Agrawal, G.; Bajwa, R.; Bates, S.; Bhatia, S.; Boden, N.; Borchers, A.; et al. In-Datacenter Performance Analysis of a Tensor Processing Unit. In Proceedings of the 44th International Symposium on Computer Architecture (ISCA), Toronto, ON, Canada, 26 June 2017.
7. Hennessy, J.L.; Patterson, D.A. *Computer Architecture*, 6th ed.; A Quantitative Approach (The Morgan Kaufmann Series in Computer Architecture and Design); Morgan Kaufmann: Burlington, MA, USA, 2017; 936p.
8. Olofsson A 2016 Epiphany-V: A 1024 Processor 64-Bit RISC System-on-Chip. Available online: https://www.parallella.org/wp-content/uploads/2016/10/e5_1024core_soc.pdf (accessed on 2 February 2021).
9. Japan's Own Processor "PEZY-SC2" and Equipped with Supercomputers "Gyoko" Details. Available online: https://pc.watch.impress.co.jp/docs/news/1091458.html (accessed on 2 February 2021).
10. Hough, P.V.C. Method and Means for Recognizing Complex Patterns. U.S. Patent 3,069,654, 18 December 1962.
11. Hassanein, A.S.; Mohammad, S.; Sameer, M.; Ragab, M.E. A Survey on Hough Transform, Theory, Techniques and Applications. *arXiv* **2015**, arXiv:1502.02160.
12. Barbosa, W.O.; Vieira, A. On the Improvement of Multiple Circles Detection from Images using Hough Transform. *TEMA* **2019**, *20*, 331–342. [CrossRef]
13. Perepelkin, E.E.; Sadovnikov, B.I.; Inozemtseva, N.T. *Computing on Graphics Processing Units (GPU) in Problems of Mathematical and Theoretical Physics*, 3rd ed.; Lenand: Moscow, Russia, 2019; 240p, ISBN 978-5-9710-6490-9.

14. Boreskov, A.V.; Kharlamov, A.A. *Basics of Working with CUDA Technology*; DMK Press: Moscow, Russia, 2019; 232p, ISBN 978-5-9760-715-2.
15. Sanders, J.; Kendroth, E. *CUDA Technology in Examples: An Introduction to GPU Programming: Translate from English*; Slinkina, A.A., Boreskov, A.V., Eds.; DMK Press: Moscow, Russia, 2018; 232p, ISBN 978-5-97060-581-3.
16. Tarasov, I.E. FPGA Xilinx. In *VHDL and Verilog Hardware Description Languages, CAD, Design Techniques*; Hotline-Telecom: Moscow, Russia, 2019; p. 538. ISBN 978-5-9912-0802-4.
17. Available online: www.xilinx.com (accessed on 2 February 2021).
18. Available online: https://www.xilinx.com/products/silicon-devices/fpga/kintex-ultrascale.html (accessed on 2 February 2021).
19. Available online: https://www.xilinx.com/products/silicon-devices/soc.html (accessed on 2 February 2021).
20. Available online: https://www.xilinx.com/products/silicon-devices/acap/versal.html (accessed on 2 February 2021).

Article

The Influence of Transport Link Density on Conductivity If Junctions and/or Links Are Blocked

Anton Aleshkin

Department of Systems Management and Modelling, MIREA—Russian Technological University, 78 Vernadsky Prospect, 119454 Moscow, Russia; Antony@testor.ru; Tel.: +7-916-306-9879

Abstract: This paper examines some approaches to modeling and managing traffic flows in modern megapolises and proposes using the methods and approaches of the percolation theory. The author sets the task of determining the properties of the transport network (percolation threshold) when designing such networks, based on the calculation of network parameters (average number of connections per crossroads, road network density). Particular attention is paid to the planarity and nonplanarity of the road transport network. Algorithms for building a planar random network (for modeling purposes) and calculating the percolation thresholds in the resulting network model are proposed. The article analyzes the resulting percolation thresholds for road networks with different relationship densities per crossroad and analyzes the effect of network density on the percolation threshold for these structures. This dependence is specified mathematically, which allows predicting the qualitative characteristics of road network structures (percolation thresholds) in their design. The conclusion shows how the change in the planar characteristics of the road network (with adding interchanges to it) can improve its quality characteristics, i.e., its overall capacity.

Keywords: increasing traffic capacity; percolation threshold; transport link density; transport network; density of transport links

Citation: Aleshkin, A. The Influence of Transport Link Density on Conductivity If Junctions and/or Links Are Blocked. *Mathematics* **2021**, *9*, 1278. https://doi.org/10.3390/math9111278

Academic Editor: Liliya Demidova

Received: 14 May 2021
Accepted: 30 May 2021
Published: 2 June 2021

Publisher's Note: MDPI stays neutral with regard to jurisdictional claims in published maps and institutional affiliations.

Copyright: © 2021 by the author. Licensee MDPI, Basel, Switzerland. This article is an open access article distributed under the terms and conditions of the Creative Commons Attribution (CC BY) license (https://creativecommons.org/licenses/by/4.0/).

1. Introduction

Controlling and balancing flows in transport networks is one of the main problems of modern conurbations. Urbanization and the development of the motor transport industry have led to the emergence of huge vehicle flows moving within our current limited traffic infrastructures, and this has led to an increase in delays and, consequently, a loss of time and money, as well as increased emissions of harmful substances into the atmosphere.

All this entails the requirement for traffic flow control and balancing models and methods to be developed. In general, it is necessary to look at the topology of a transport network in order to solve the dynamic task of traffic redistribution. The problem in so doing, however, is that the number of vehicles in the network is constantly increasing and, as a result, current management models become outdated and inefficient. It is, therefore, necessary to search for new management tools or to modernize the physical base (road width and length, number of lanes etc.) of the current transport network. Let us consider some of the current approaches to traffic management in transport systems which fall into two categories: local and systematic management.

Local management is carried out on the basis of statistically estimated vehicle characteristics. The result is provided with the estimate of transport flow efficiency per any single road junction regardless of any neighboring ones. Systematic management provides transport flow optimization in the sphere including many junctions and, as a rule, operates considering the macro-characteristics of the flow. Any change in management operations on any single junction inevitably leads to a change in neighboring transport flow characteristics. Conflict between local and systematic management methods is common. Thus, if a network simultaneously uses both management methods, these should be implemented at different times. Local management time is selected with the aim of limiting the influence of transport flow on neighboring junctions.

Without dwelling in detail on transport flow analysis and the development of management models throughout history (which include models proposed by Grinschields, Richards, Grindberg, El Hozaini, Underwood, Drake, and Pipes: optimal speed, "Smart" driver, leader follow, cellular automata models, etc.) and the different methods of classification, this paper instead presents some more recent models.

For example, in [1], a network flow model based on a conservation hyperbolic system with discontinuous flow was investigated. This investigation showed that the model could be quickly developed because additional procedures were not required for solution management. The model developed enables us to automatically select the solution where a flow is maximized in each direction (user's optimum), i.e., there is no need to calculate maximum flow, which could be transferred through any junction (global optimum), as the model is developed according to standard approaches.

In [2], the authors developed a short-term traffic forecasting method. During this investigation, an efficiency comparison of specific algorithms was undertaken using the Volterra prediction model, RBFNN (radial basis function neural network). According to such a comparison, the Volterra model was selected where traffic data were normalized to simplify the programming of algorithms.

In [3], the authors developed an algorithm to calculate the exact average speed of flow movement using mobile detector data for measuring movement speed. The algorithm developed indicates average speed on a given road section, ignoring repetitive messages, and a travel time filter is used to compensate such time selection exceeding the road speed limit. Furthermore, this method comprises errors, such as errors caused by connection failure, dubbing recording, and other factors.

In [4], the authors performed an investigation on the calibration and testing of a macroscopic traffic flow model. Their model was investigated and compared to 10 different algorithms in total (regarding its ability to converge to this solution) for different datasets. Optimization algorithms using particle swarm (PSO) seemed to be the most effective in terms of both convergence rate and solution compilation.

In [5], the authors used a Gaussian regression model (GPR), optimized using particle swarm algorithm (PSO), to predict undefined, nonlinear, and complex traffic in a road tunnel.

Other studies [6,7] described models of stochastic flow dynamics in traffic networks with nondeterministic characteristics of statistical parameter distribution, describing the dependence of the probability of blocking individual nodes from traffic characteristics over time. The developed mathematical models describe the rules of intersection maintenance (time of switching traffic lights), considering the material balance of the number of cars in the system and the connection of their flows between neighboring intersections. The authors of [6,7] showed that the use of percolation theory techniques and the results of the stochastic model of traffic flows allows simulating the operation of the transport network at the level of not only individual nodes, but also the whole structure. The proposed model allows using a real map of the transport network to create its dynamic model, as well as simulate its work and the occurrence of traffic jams.

In [8], the authors studied traffic flow instability in experimental and empirical investigations. To calculate traffic instability, the authors considered the competition between stochastic violations, which can tend to destabilize traffic flow, and how drivers adapt to changing speeds, which can, in contrast, tend to stabilize traffic flow.

In [9], the authors developed a modified algorithm for optimizing the transportation route according to street traffic flow. This study was based on a modified ant algorithm (ant colony optimization algorithm), being one of the most effective polynomial searching solutions for dealing with problems regarding route optimization.

In [10], a structural analysis of public transport routes was performed concerning tariffs and operating mode. To provide more adequate and logical results, the advanced route calculation algorithm was proposed for different structures.

In [11], the authors developed a transport network algorithm in the form of a prefractal graph based on their theory. The search for solutions to multi-objective problems using an indication of the optimal path was carried out by algorithms which searched for optimal solutions on several criteria if the presence of such criteria was proven or based on a solution with specific deviations from the optimal solution. In this paper, the largest maximal chains extraction algorithm (MCEA algorithm) was used with the arbitrary graph.

In [12], the professional system and regulator using the fuzzy logic module was studied for traffic control systems at intersections.

In [13], the authors developed a traffic control method based on a traffic efficiency index they compiled, comprising factors such as traffic and road capacities.

In [14], the authors studied loaded traffic management issues using a prediction model for any specific intersection and within the transport area. Using a solution based on a predictive management algorithm model, the residual queue is distributed, due to a transport demand which exceeds the capacity of the crossing, along all incoming transport links. Simultaneously, in the case of long-term implementation of the intersection, a big queue accumulation in oversaturation mode is observed. In this case, a network-wide delay can be prevented by decreasing transport demand at intersection entrances only.

Another author [15] studied the possibility to use the main network traffic diagram for prediction of traffic functioning conditions in cities. The traffic model studied by the author was based on the use of standard Pipes model for indication of dependencies between speed and density for traffic performance calculation. The model analysis showed that it is necessary to limit a high level of vehicle accumulation and use the correspondent management strategies when controlling traffic on roads in cities.

In [16], the authors studied the nature of traffic interval distribution depending on the distance from the previous signaled crossing. According to the investigation results, the authors made a conclusion that normalized Erlang distribution is the most suitable practice for description of intervals inside traffic groups.

In [17], the principles of using telecommunications technologies based on the protocols of interaction of the type "car-to-car" were examined to organize an efficient infrastructure in terms of ensuring traffic transport. The information used for this method included the parameters of movement, the location, and the parameters of the state of the car's systems. After processing and analyzing this information, it is possible to form recommendations and management effects. These recommendations are used by the driver or an automated driving system. The article described a model that allows realizing the interaction of cars, which can determine the optimal use of the car's resources, as well as the aggressive driving style of the vehicle.

A brief review on the development of recently created models shows that, despite their variety, no investigations studied the general features of transport network structure, indicating its conductivity. No works banded the dynamic characteristics and structural features (topology) of transport systems.

Accordingly, this paper aimed to study the effect of the density of transport network connections on their conductivity when blocking nodes and/or links, analyzing the dependence of such an influence and finding generalized patterns for predicting the properties of the road network (the possibility of determining the percolation threshold based on the calculated density of the road network). This should take into account different types of network structures (planar and nonplanar networks) and various tasks to be solved (node tasks and link tasks).

2. Statement of the Problem

The significant density index of vehicles per area unit of all current roads leads to an inevitable congestion of vehicles at one or other elements of the traffic system (e.g., intersections and roads), i.e., delays (jams). Most traffic investigations, analyses, and subsequent developments of management models focus on local-level solutions, not considering the transport network.

The traffic systems of modern conurbations have very wide, complex, and branching structures (see Figure 1 for example), which may be represented as a graph (junctions—road intersections and edges—roads). When modeling traffic, it is necessary to consider the dynamic of traffic mass change (daily variation of flows) and the fact that all elements of the transport graph (junctions and edges) have different characteristics (traffic capacity).

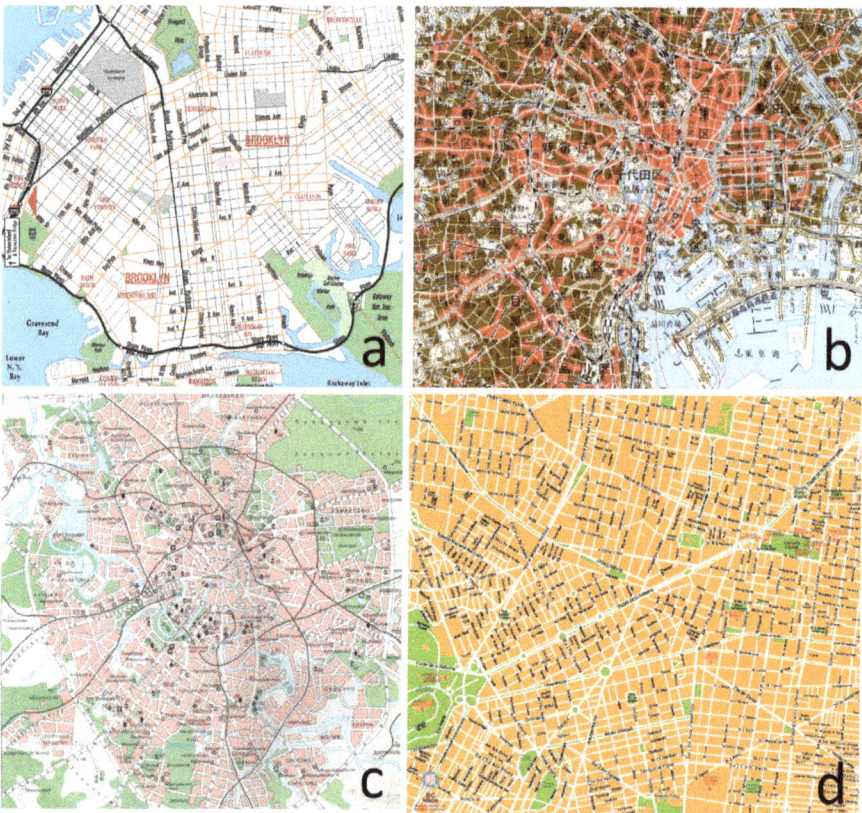

Figure 1. Traffic maps of several world conurbations (**a**—New York, **b**—Tokyo, **c**—Moscow, **d**—Mexico).

If we trace the path of the detailed traffic graph model generated with a detailed description of its attributes (number of lanes, route length, number of directions at intersections, etc.), requiring such a model for the local management of traffic would be extremely complicated and difficult to implement for practical purposes.

It is arguably more convenient to create a traffic percolation model to make the structure more efficient, regardless of which specific elements could be blocked due to the formation of traffic delays. In this case, functioning and reliability mean that at least one freeway is possible which comprises unblocked graph elements between any two arbitrary network junctions.

3. Percolation Theory Methods for the Network Transport Structures

Percolation theory (graph-based probability theory) studies solutions to problems relating to junction and link tasks [18–21] for networks with various regular and accidental structures. When solving the link problem, the link share must be separated by at least two isolated parts (or, conversely, the fraction of conductive nodes (crossroads) when conductivity occurs). When solving junction problems, the fraction of blocked junctions is indicated where the network is broken up into isolated clusters within which links can be kept (or, conversely, the fraction of conductive junctions, when conductivity occurs). Percolation threshold is the fraction of nonblocked junctions (junction task) or unbroken nodes (crossroads) (nodes task), where conductivity occurs between two randomly selected network junctions. For the same structure of percolation threshold values, junction, and nodes (crossroads), tasks have different meanings. Note that, in the case of junction blocking, all links are blocked, and, in the case of node (crossroad) blocking, only one link is blocked between neighboring junctions.

Use of the term "blocked junction fractions" or "blocked road fractions" is equivalent to the occurrence probability that a randomly selected junction (or nodes) will be blocked. Therefore, we may accept that the percolation limit value indicates the probability of passage through the whole network if any of its junctions (or links) are blocked or (removed), i.e., given the average probability of a single junction (or nodes) being blocked.

Achieving the percolation threshold in a network corresponds to a cluster where links exist among random junctions. An endless or contracting conducting cluster is formed. Note that this approach claims to be universal and can be applied not only to the topology of road networks, but also to other topologies [22].

For finite structures, conductivity may appear at different fractions of conducting junctions (or links, see Figure 2). However, if network size L tends toward endlessness, then the sphere of transfer becomes compact (see Figure 2, curve I for small-sized structure or curve II for an endless network).

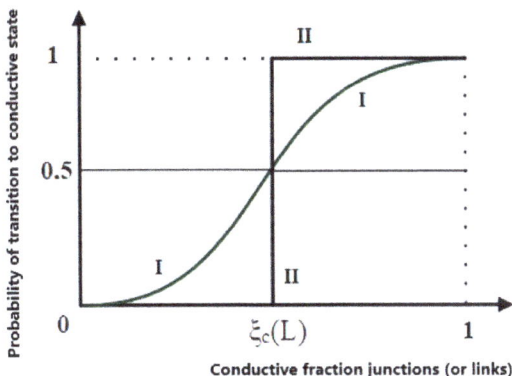

Figure 2. The probability of percolation occurrence depending on the value of the fraction of conductive junctions (or links).

For finite-sized structures, the percolation threshold structure $\xi_c(L)$ may be determined from the fixed value of network transition probability in relation to the conducting state. In Figure 2, this probability is chosen to be equal to 0.5 (50%). However, we could also take a value of 0.95 or 0.99, for example (then, the percolation threshold would correspond to the given criteria of network reliability working); in other words, it is possible to determine what fraction of blocked junctions and/or links influences the decrease in the necessary level of performance.

Based on specified work reliability values (the probability of transition or being in conductive state), we can find the fraction of unblocked junctions (or road).

The fraction of blocked junctions (or links) where network conductivity disappears (which can be calculated as follows: one minus conductive junctions (or links)) causes the blocking of the network as a whole, and this value can be associated with the macro-characteristics of traffic in the current transport system. In the simplest case, we can give the following estimate: the accepted level of intensity of traffic without delays (presented as q_{max}) for European cities is 600–900 vehicles and in the USA up to 1300 vehicles per hour per lane; in Russian cities, this index is 300–700 vehicles per hour per lane. Therefore, knowing the total city road stretch and number of lanes, as well as daily vehicle dynamics, we can use such data to calculate the average traffic intensity at any moment (presented as $q(t)$). Then, the average probability ($P(t)$) of a network element blocking at any moment in time t may be indicated as follows:

$$P(t) = \begin{cases} \frac{q(t)}{q_{max}}, & q(t) \leq q_{max} \\ 1, & q(t) > q_{max} \end{cases}.$$

Furthermore, using such a probability estimate of network element blocking, we can find, at a given time t, the state of the reliability and efficiency of the network as a whole, as well as analyze daily dynamics of changes to the network and, consequently, if necessary, change the structure (for example, link density) of the transport system as appropriate (the way in which the traffic functioning reliability is associated with density of its links, for example, as discussed later in the article).

For exact estimates of average blocking probability, different macroscopic mathematical models of traffic flows can be used (drawing on the models proposed by Grinschilds, Richards, Grindberg, El Khozaini, Underwood, Drake, and Pipes: the optimum speed, "Smart" driver, leader follow, cellular automata models, etc.).

The main problem when investigating percolation features of network structures which have accidental structures is that there are currently no established analytical methods and, as such, it is only possible to study such networks by using computer-aided simulation. First of all, it is necessary to build a topological graph, which is itself a rather difficult task for studying the percolation properties of planar network structures which have accidental structures.

The application of some methods of percolation theory to traffic flow modeling was described in [23]. In this paper, traffic dynamics were seen as a critical phenomenon, in which there was a transition between isolated local and global flows on the roads with the formation of clusters of congested sections of the transport network in local structures and their unification into a global cluster. Local flows are connected by narrow links, and narrow links can occur in different places of the transport network at different times of the day. The authors of [23] described such processes as the percolation of traffic between local clusters. The authors tried to describe how local traffic flows interact and merge into a global stream across the city network.

When modeling a transport structure, it is difficult to assess the entire dynamics of traffic organization throughout the network as a whole and to link it to local traffic characteristics. To solve this problem, the authors [23] used the percolation theory. They collected and analyzed the speeds of more than 1000 roads with record 5 min segments measured on roads in Beijing's central district. The data covered a period of 2 weeks in 2013, with the road network encompassing intersections (nodes) and sections of the road between two intersections. For each road, the speed $V_{ij}(t)$ changed throughout the day in accordance with real time. For each road e_{ij}, authors set the 95th percentile of its maximum speed at each day and defined the model parameter $r_{ij}(t)$ as the ratio between the current speed and the limited maximum speed measured for that day. At some given threshold q, all e_{ij} roads could be divided into two categories: functional at $r_{ij} > q$ and dysfunctional at $r_{ij} < q$. With this assumption, the authors found it possible to build a functional network of traffic for a given value q from the dynamics of road traffic in the network.

At $q = 0$, nothing happens with the traffic in the network, whereas, at $q = 1$, it becomes completely fragmented. The hierarchical organization of road traffic at different scales appears only in the road groups where r_{ij} above q. These clusters are functional modules consisting of connected roads at speeds above q. For example, at $q = 0.69$, there is a speed that the entire transport network cannot maintain. When the value of q is reduced to 0.19, small clusters merge together and form a global cluster, in which the functional network (with less flow speed) extends to almost the entire road network.

The merit of the authors' method for modeling and analyzing traffic is that, by having data on traffic flows in the real network, it is possible to determine the critical value of q_c below which the transport network loses functionality (percolation threshold). In [23], q_c was set to approximately 0.4.

The drawback of the study is that the results are private and only available for a certain part of Beijing's transport network. In this regard, they cannot be generalized to a transport network with an arbitrary structure. In addition, another drawback is the significant laboriousness of the method of analysis and modeling of transport networks proposed by the authors of this work.

A more technological and versatile modeling method may be to use common network characteristics, such as the impact of network density on traffic recycling. In this case, if it turns out that the density of the network, regardless of its real structure, is a universal characteristic, allowing the user to link structural and dynamic (traffic) characteristics, it at least reduces the laboriousness of analysis and modeling of the health of the transport network, thus becoming more universal.

4. Methods and Algorithms for Calculating the Percolation Properties of Random Network Structures: Modeling the Dependence of the Percolation Thresholds of Random Networks on Their Link Density

The main problem when investigating percolation features of network structures which have accidental structures is that there are currently no established analytical methods and, as such, it is only possible to study such networks by using computer-aided simulation.

When studying and modeling percolation processes in transport networks, it is necessary to consider that they have two components: planar and nonplanar (taking into account multi-level interchanges).

First of all, it is necessary to build a topological graph, which is itself a rather difficult task for studying the percolation properties of planar network structures which have accidental structures.

4.1. Algorithm of Planar Networks with Accidental Structures

In order to build a planar network with an accidental number of links for each junction (network density), we may use the following algorithm [24]:

(1) Plot the total number of junctions N and quantity of links E.
(2) Generate a list S consisting of junctions N with accidental coordinates (x, y).
(3) Select the junction n_0 with the smallest coordinate along x; if there are any junctions, then select the point with the maximal y coordinate. Point this junction as n_0 {n_{0x}; n_{0y}}. The first index shows us the number of junctions, and the second one shows the coordinates of the junction.
(4) Sort junctions on the list S by the increase of the distance L value from the junction n_0 as follows:
$$L = \sqrt{(n_{0x} - n_{ix})^2 + (n_{0y} - n_{iy})^2},$$
where n_0 is the selected first junction, i is the junction index, n_{ix} is the x-coordinate of junction i, and n_{iy} is the y-coordinate of junction i. After such a step, we have a sorted junction list: n_0 {n_{0x}; n_{0y}}, n_1, n_2 ...
(5) Join the first three junctions n_0, n_1, n_2 from the list S to the first triangle, adding edges. Moving clockwise from the edge between the first and second junctions in the list, add the triangle edges to the cyclical list H.
(6) Sequentially process all junctions from the list S.
   a. Take the first raw junction n_i.

b. In the H list, take the last edge V, which joins n_a {n_{ax}; n_{ay}} and n_b {n_{bx}; n_{by}} with n_i {n_{ix}; n_{iy}} to form a left turn. The following condition is satisfied:

$$(n_{ix} - n_{ax}) * (n_{by} - n_{ay}) - (n_{iy} - n_{ay}) * (n_{bx} - n_{ax}) > 0.$$

c. Among all the edges H, find the first edge V_L which does not satisfy the left turn condition (appearing before and to the left of edge V).
d. Among the edges H, find the first edge V_R which does not satisfy the left turn condition (being behind and to the right if edge V).
e. Sequentially process all edges from the list H between V_L and V_R. Each of these edges forms a new triangle with junction n_i by adding new edges among them.
f. Remove all edges between V_L and V_R from the list H.
g. From the first triangle added, take the edge between n_i and the edge point, absent from the following processed triangle, and add it to the list H.
h. From the first added triangle, take the edge between n_i and the edge point, absent from the previous processed triangle, and add it to the list H.

(7) Remove the edges from the current graph, until their quantity is no longer equal to E. Edges should be selected randomly but only removed if there is a way to do so without them being between the junctions of such an edge.

Sorting Joints Clockwise

(1) Find the center of the polygon for whole junction as follows:

$$\overline{R} = \frac{\sum_i \overline{r}_i}{i},$$

where i is the index of edges connected to the junction, $\overline{r}_i$ is the i-edge vector with (x, y) coordinates, and $\overline{R}$ is the calculated center of the polygon for the whole junction.

(2) Shift all apexes so that the center is at the beginning of the coordinate.
(3) Take a zero value (for example, radius OA vector = (0, 1) see Figure 3).

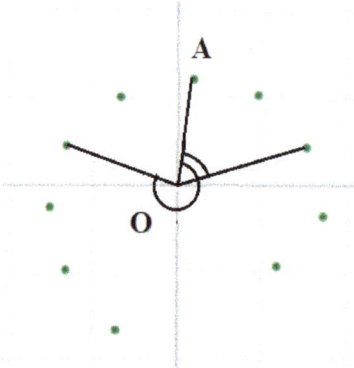

Figure 3. Selection of points while sorting.

(4) Find corners among the vectors from the center to each apex and OA (corners should be over the range of 0–360).
(5) Sort corners from smaller to larger ones.

Using this algorithm, we can build different accidental planar networks; an example is presented in Figure 4.

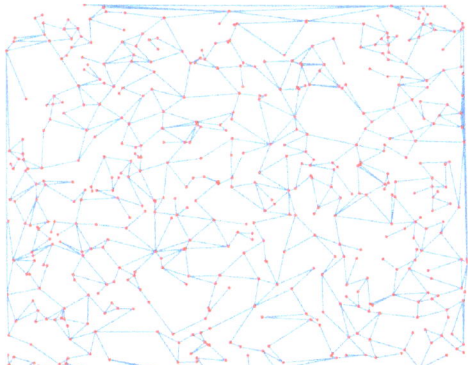

Figure 4. Example of an accidental planar network consisting of 500 junctions with an average number of links equal to 2.9.

4.2. Network Percolation Threshold Calculation Algorithm

The network percolation threshold algorithm used consists of the following steps [24]:

(1) Randomly select two network junctions A and B, considering limits, with at least one intermediate junction between them.
(2) Set the blocking probability value of the single junction (in the junction task) or link (for the link task) and randomly block the junction (or link) fraction which is equal to this probability.
(3) Check for the presence of at least one "free" way in the network (a route which is included in the junction or link list) from junction A to junction B. If no "free" way is present (i.e., number of "free" ways is equal to 0), record 0. Otherwise, record 1.
(4) Increase the blocking probability value of a single junction (for the junction task) or link (for the link task) on any value. Then, randomly block the fraction of network junctions (or links), equal to the specified probability value. Next, indicate the specific network junctions being excluded.
(5) Repeat step 3, until all network junctions have been processed.
(6) Return to step 2 and execute steps 3–5 Q times (for example, several hundred times). Repeat all steps (if the whole network is blocked) on all experiments. Indicate the number of embeddings, where at least one "free" way was indicated (designate as ξ). For example, at step h = 18 in 8, 12, 19, 56, 58, 76, 80, and 89 experiments with at least one "free" way, then $\xi(5) = 8$ (8 is the total number of "free" ways). Find the value $\bar{p}(h) = \xi(h)/Q$, h—step number per step. Calculate the average cluster size of excluded junctions, the quantity of such clusters, etc. (on all N experiments per step). The average size of the cluster may be indicated as the ratio of all value sums obtained for this clustering step (on all Q experiments) to total number of experiments Q. For illustrative purposes, we can consider the following example: assume that, at step h = 6 in the first experiment, four clusters were obtained, each having a size of 15 junctions, whereas three clusters were obtained in the second experiment, two clusters were obtained in the third, etc. Then, the average number of clusters having a size 10 of blocked junctions would be equal to $(4 + 3 + 2 + \ldots + 5)/100$.
(7) Then, return to step 1 and repeat the implementation of steps 2–6, W times. For each W test, we can calculate the value $\bar{p_w}(h) = \xi(h)/Q$. Index w indicates which W-test to study.
(8) After completing the simulation, for each of the h steps, we can calculate the value
$$\bar{p}(h) = \sum_{w=1}^{W=100} \bar{p_w}(h)/W,$$
i.e., the average value of the probability ratio for passage through the network as a whole through unblocked junctions (or links for the task of link blocking) at each of the steps (considering different possible route configurations).

Calculating using this algorithm enables us to obtain a database for the dependency of the average ratio value of the probability of passage through the network $\bar{p}(h)$ as a whole on the fraction of blocked junctions (or links for link blocking tasks), at different average numbers of links, per junction (network density).

4.3. Calculating the Dependency of the Percolation Threshold Dependency on the Network Density (Average Number of Links per Crossroad)

The results of computational modeling and calculation of percolation threshold values for planar networks with an accidental number of links per junction for junction and link blocking tasks are presented in Table 1. Note that column 3 named "density" represents the average number of links per single junction, and the values of reverse link densities are specified in brackets. Column 4 named "threshold" represents the value of the percolation threshold (fraction of conductive junctions or links where network conductivity appears as a whole). The natural log values of percolation thresholds are specified in brackets.

Table 1. Values of percolation thresholds for planar networks with an accidental structure.

No.	Task Type	Density	Threshold
1.		5.99 (0.167)	0.500 (−0.693)
2.		5.40 (0.185)	0.533 (−0.629)
3.		4.80 (0.208)	0.570 (−0.562)
4.		4.50 (0.222)	0.593 (−0.523)
5.		4.20 (0.238)	0.618 (−0.481)
6.	Junction blocking task	3.90 (0.256)	0.650 (−0.431)
7.	[19–21]	3.60 (0.278)	0.683 (−0.381)
8.		3.42 (0.292)	0.708 (−0.345)
9.		3.18 (0.314)	0.750 (−0.288)
10.		2.94 (0.340)	0.793 (−0.232)
11.		2.70 (0.370)	0.852 (−0.160)
12.		2.46 (0.407)	0.925 (−0.078)
13.		5.99 (0.167)	0.395 (−0.929)
14.		5.69 (0.176)	0.405 (−0.904)
15.		5.39 (0.186)	0.435 (−0.832)
16.		5.09 (0.196)	0.445 (−0.810)
17.		4.49 (0.223)	0.480 (−0.734)
18.		4.19 (0.239)	0.510 (−0.673)
19.		3.89 (0.257)	0.550 (−0.598)
20.	Link blocking task	3.59 (0.279)	0.570 (−0.562)
21.		3.29 (0.304)	0.625 (−0.470)
22.		2.99 (0.334)	0.685 (−0.378)
23.		2.87 (0.348)	0.715 (−0.335)
24.		2.70 (0.370)	0.770 (−0.261)
25.		2.58 (0.388)	0.805 (−0.217)
26.		2.39 (0.418)	0.900 (−0.105)

Table 1 includes percolation threshold values as a fraction of conductive junctions (or links), where network conductivity appears. The fraction of blocked junctions (or links), where network conductivity disappears may be found as one minus the fraction of conductive junctions (or links).

Note that the percolation threshold values of planar networks with different densities for junction blocking tasks were calculated by the present authors in earlier works [25–30], where networks consisting of 100,000 junctions were used to carry out computational simulations. In order to undertake numerical experiments while solving network tasks, a network with 5000 junctions was used, requiring significant computational steps to successfully solve the tasks.

A 0.5 value of probability that the network transition is in a conducting state (see Figure 2) was selected as the percolation threshold of percolation network structures.

However, note once again that we may take, for example, another value of transition probability of 0.95 or 0.99 (the percolation threshold would be set by the reliability criteria), i.e., we may calculate the fraction at which the total number of blocked junctions and/or links leads to the network losing the required level of efficiency.

It is important to note that the average number of links per single junction (network density) for a planar graph cannot exceed a value of 6. This is due to the Euler theorem [31], according to which, for a plane graph, the following equation should be fulfilled: $V - E + F = 2$, where V is the number of vertices in the graph, E is the number of edges, and F is the number of areas the graph separates in the plane.

In Figure 5, the dependencies of percolation threshold values of planar networks on the average number of network links per single junction (in junction blocking tasks [24] and in link blocking tasks) are presented.

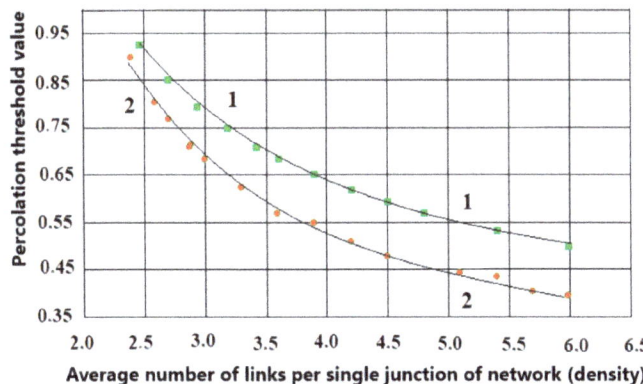

Figure 5. Dependency of values percolation threshold values of planar accidental networks on network density (curve 1—junction task, curve 2—link task).

To calculate the influence of the network's structure density on the value of its percolation limits, it is necessary to analyze the data, shown in Table 1 and in Figure 5, and to calculate a functional dependency which may describe the influence of the network density on the value of its percolation limit. This enables us to calculate the link density of actual transport networks, to estimate the value of their percolation limit and, consequently, draw conclusions on the reliability of their structure, i.e., at which fraction of blocked junctions and/or links the network as a whole loses the required level of efficiency.

The results obtained can be used in the process of transport network construction or renovation in order to increase traffic potential and working capacity.

In [32–34] based on the topological structure of binding clusters proposed by Schklovskiy and de Zhen ("skeleton and dead ends"), the function of conditional flow probability (percolation) in grid $Y(\xi, L)$ was obtained as follows:

$$Y(\xi, L) = \frac{1}{1 + e^{-S(\xi, L)}}, \quad (1)$$

where $S(\xi, L) = \sum_i a_i (\xi^i - \xi_c^i(L))$ is the polynomial of degree i, a_i represents its coefficients, ξ is the fraction of blocked junctions, and $\xi_c(L)$ is the fraction of blocked junctions, corresponding to the percolation threshold value which depends on the size of the network L. The polynomial $S(\xi, L)$ of degree i may depend on the topological features of the network structure (network density, space symmetry, dimensionality etc.), which may be set during phenomenology with coefficients a_i.

The main problem when describing percolation using Equation (1) is indicating the polynomial degree i and its coefficients. The shred use of Equation (1) and Hodge algebraic geometry methods [35], as well as Kadanoff–Wilson renormalization theory [36,37] with groups (see, e.g., [18]), enables us (in all cases) to calculate theoretical values of the percolation threshold for any regular structures [32–34]. In Hodge theory, algebraic varieties are studied (varieties, consisting of subsets, any of which comprise a set of solutions to any polynomial equations). Geometrical representations of algebraic varieties are called Hodge cycles. Linear combinations of such geometrical figures are called algebraic cycles [38].

The core of this approach is that we may depart from using Hodge methods and Kadanoff–Wilson renormalization groups to calculate the dependency of polynomial $S(\xi, L)$ of degree i, from conditional probability $Y(\xi, L)$ of the flow in the grid, as well as to calculate the influence of topological factors on such a dependency. Using Equation (1), we can derive the following:

$$ln Y(\xi, L) = -ln\left\{1 + e^{-S(\xi, L)}\right\},$$

where $S(\xi, L) = \sum_i a_i\{\xi^i - \xi_c^i(L)\}$ is the polynomial of degree i, a_i designates its coefficients, ξ is the current value of the blocked junction fraction, and $\xi_c(L)$ is the fraction of blocked junctions, which corresponds to the percolation threshold value (this depends on the size of network L). Considering that a value near to the percolation threshold is $\xi \approx \xi_c(L)$, then the polynomial value $S(\xi, L)$ is small and $e^{-S(\xi, L)}$ may be expanded in series, restricted by two elements. After some manipulation, we can derive the following:

$$ln Y(\xi, L) \approx 1 - S(\xi, L) = 1 - \sum_i a_i\{\xi^i - \xi_c^i(L)\}. \qquad (2)$$

The righthand side of Equation (2) may be the function (or composed function) of certain variables, each of which is associated with any specific absolute concept of the network. For example, one of the variables may be the average number x of links (network density).

The described approach enables us to analyze the data specified in Table 1 and in Figure 5. It also enables us to present the dependency for the base logarithm of the percolation threshold $lnP(x)$ on topological characteristics, for example, network density reciprocity $(1/x)$, calculated as one divided by the average number of links per single network junction (see Figure 6). As may be inferred from Figure 6, the dependencies identified have a linear form and may be approximated by linear equations.

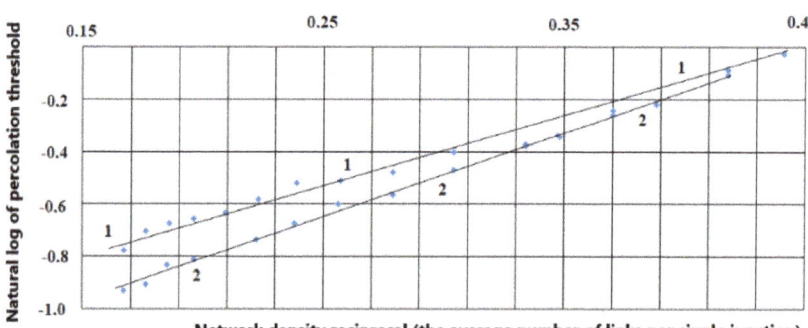

Figure 6. Dependency of natural log percolation threshold value ($lnP(x)$) on accidental planar structures from the reciprocal of density ($1/x$).

For planar structures in nodes tasks, the dependency of a percolation threshold log $lnP(x)$ on the reciprocal of the network density ($1/x$) may be described using the following equation:

$$lnP_{node,\ unreg}(x) = \frac{2.52}{x} - 1.08, \qquad (3)$$

with a correlation number coefficient value and linear dependency equation equal to 0.99 (see righthand line 1 in Figure 6). In the links task, this equation becomes

$$lnP_{bond,\ unreg}(x) = \frac{3.19}{x} - 1.44, \qquad (4)$$

with a correlation number coefficient value and linear dependency equation equal to 0.99 (see the righthand line 2 in Figure 6).

The focus here is a comparison of percolation features for accidental and regular planar networks. For example, the transport networks for New York or Mexico (see Figure 1) have a structure resembling a square lattice, while the transport networks of many other cities have structures which more closely resemble the structure shown in Figure 4. This leads us to question how the thresholds for such network blocking can differ at the same link density.

In Table 2, the percolation threshold values of some regular networks are shown (see Figure 7), and the cited literature is specified (where the source was not specified, the percolation threshold values were indicated in the numerical modeling results).

Table 2. Percolation threshold values for planar networks with regular structures.

No.	Task Type	Density	Threshold
1.		2.7 (0.37)–f in Figure 5.	0.74 (−0.30)
2.		3 (0.33)–d in Figure 5 [17].	0.70 (−0.36)
3.		3.40 (0.29)–g in Figure 5.	0.64 (−0.45)
4.	Node blocking task	4 (0.25)–a in Figure 5 [17].	0.59 (−0.53)
5.		4.5 (0.22)–e in Figure 5.	0.56 (−0.58)
6.		6 (0.17)–b in Figure 5.	0.50 (−0.69)
7.		6 (0.17)–c in Figure 5 [17].	0.50 (−0.69)
8.		2.7 (0.37)–f in Figure 5.	0.69 (−0.37)
9.		3 (0.33)–d in Figure 5 [17].	0.65 (−0.43)
10.	Bond blocking tasks	3.40 (0.29)–g in Figure 5.	0.52 (−0.65)
11.		4 (0.25)–a in Figure 5 [17].	0.50 (−0.69)
12.		6 (0.17)–b in Figure 5.	0.36 (−1.02)
13.		6 (0.17)–c in Figure 5 [17].	0.35 (−1.05)

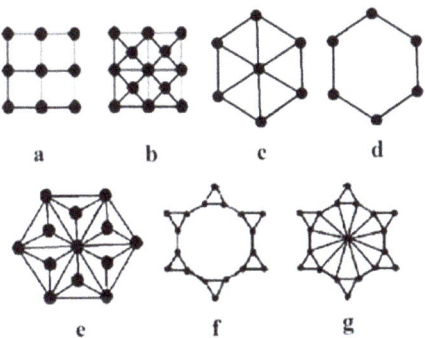

Figure 7. Geometrical representation of some regular network structures (a–g).

Figure 8 shows that dependencies of natural logs for percolation threshold values of regular networks from the reverse density of links are also described accurately using linear equations. For the nodes task, this equation becomes

$$lnP_{node,\ reg}(x) = \frac{1.98}{x} - 1.02, \qquad (5)$$

with the value of the numeric correlation coefficient and linear dependence equation equal to 0.99 (see righthand line 1 in Figure 8). In the links task, this equation becomes

$$lnP_{bond,\,reg}(x) = \frac{3.29}{x} - 1.56, \qquad (6)$$

with the numeric correlation value and linear equations equal to 0.97 (see righthand line 2 in Figure 8).

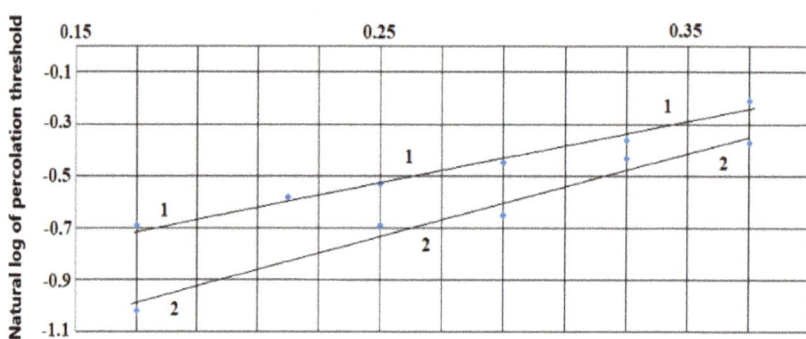

Figure 8. Dependency of natural log percolation threshold value ($lnP(x)$) on planar accidental structures from the reciprocal of density ($1/x$).

Analysis of the results shows that the conductivity of any planar networks at identical densities of its bonds is larger than in the task of bond blocking compared with the task of node blocking. The percolation threshold (fraction of conductive nodes or bonds or where conductivity occurs) in the bond task is less than in the node task.

5. Discussion

Table 3 presents data on the density of transport bonds in any world cities, generated according to its graph analysis, as well as the value of blocking thresholds calculated using Equations (3) and (4). The values of network blocking values are specified in brackets, calculated from the analysis of real transport systems using numerical simulation. The blocking value is calculated using the following equation: one minus the percolation threshold calculated in Equation (3) or Equation (4). The values found in the analysis of the network graph are specified in brackets.

Table 4 presents data on the density of transport bonds in any world cities, calculated from graph analyses, as well as from the value of blocking thresholds calculated using Equations (5) and (6). The values of network blocking values are specified in brackets, calculated in the analysis of real transport systems using numerical simulation. The blocking value is calculated according to the following equation: one minus the percolation threshold calculated using Equation (5) or Equation (6).

Table 3. Densities of transport bonds in any world cities and values of their blocking thresholds identified using models of accidental networks.

No.	City	Density	Blocking Threshold in Node Tasks according to Equation (3)	Blocking Threshold in Link Tasks according to Equation (4)
1.	New York	2.85	0.18 (0.19)	0.27 (0.21)
2.	Istanbul	2.91	0.19 (0.19)	0.29 (0.21)
3.	Madrid	2.77	0.16 (0.18)	0.25 (0.21)
4.	Beijing	2.70	0.14 (0.17)	0.23 (0.27)
5.	Paris	2.63	0.11 (0.16)	0.20 (0.19)
6.	Moscow	2.51	0.08 (0.13)	0.16 (0.17)
7.	London	2.39	0.03 (0.11)	0.10 (0.14)

Table 4. Densities of transport bonds in any world cities and the values of their blocking thresholds calculated using models of regular networks.

No.	City	Density	Blocking Threshold in Node Tasks according to Equation (5)	Blocking Threshold in Link Tasks according to Equation (6)
1.	New York	2.85	0.28 (0.19)	0.33 (0.21)
2.	Istanbul	2.91	0.29 (0.19)	0.35 (0.21)
3.	Madrid	2.77	0.26 (0.18)	0.31 (0.21)
4.	Beijing	2.70	0.25 (0.17)	0.29 (0.27)
5.	Paris	2.63	0.23 (0.16)	0.27 (0.19)
6.	Moscow	2.51	0.21 (0.13)	0.22 (0.17)
7.	London	2.39	0.17 (0.11)	0.17 (0.14)

A comparison of the data presented in Tables 3 and 4 (which consider inaccuracies in reporting of traffic density and numerical simulation) enables us to draw two conclusions:

1. The transport networks of many cities in the world have structures which are close to an accidental structure and not regular planar networks.
2. An increase in network density leads to an increase in the blocking threshold of the network.

Today, rather often, overpasses and multilevel transport interchanges are constructed to increase traffic capacity. From a topological perspective, this changes its planarity. Earlier, in [25], the percolation features of nonplanar accidental networks were studied, and the following equation was found to calculate the conductivity threshold in node tasks:

$$\ln P_{node,\ unreg}^{st}(x) = \frac{4.39}{x} - 2.41, \qquad (7)$$

where $P_{node,\ unreg}^{st}(x)$ is the percolation threshold value, and x is the network density.

Taking the example of a network density equal to 2.65 (the mean density according to data from Tables 3 and 4), for the percolation limit value of an accidental nonplanar network, we obtain 0.47. Thus, loss of conductivity for such structures occurs when the fraction of blocked nodes is greater than 0.53. Therefore, creating many nonplanar interchanges and overpasses in the transport network may significantly increase traffic capacity, but this is nevertheless associated with significant expenses due to the major construction work involved.

Let us consider the change in network topology due to the construction of multilevel interchanges and overpasses and their influence on the loss of efficiency in terms of bond blocking. Earlier, in [25], the percolation features of nonplanar accidental networks were studied, and the following equation was found for the conductivity limit in bond tasks:

$$\ln P_{bond,\ unreg}^{st}(x) = -\frac{6.58}{x} - 0.20, \qquad (8)$$

where $P_{bond,\ unreg}^{st}(x)$ is the percolation threshold value, and x is the network density.

Taking a network density value equal to 2.65 as an example, we obtain 0.07 for the percolation limit value of the accidental nonplanar network. Thus, the loss of conductivity for such structures occurs when the fraction of blocked bonds is greater than 0.93. Accordingly, the creation of a large quantity of planar interchanges and overpasses in the transport network and in the event of bond blocking can also significantly increase its traffic capacity.

However, as mentioned earlier, this is due to the significant cost of capital construction of complex interchanges. When choosing specific urban planning solutions, it is necessary to consider that the percolation threshold of the transport network can be increased not only due to nonplanar overpasses, but also due to changes in density. In other words, you can add a small number of plank connections to the network graph instead of building tiered interchanges (if the cost of building them is higher).

6. Avenues for Future Research

In further investigations, the author plans to study the following issues:

1. Table 3 includes data on the density of transport bonds in cities around the world and specific threshold values of blocking based on the analysis thereof, calculated using Equations (3) and (4). Note that the network blocking values were specified during an analysis of real transport systems using numerical simulation. The author further plans to study more city graphs, from which statistics can be gathered to study the correlation of blocking threshold values, calculated using Equations (3) and (4) and reported in the result of real traffic analysis. This will enable the development of an accurate percolation model.
2. To estimate the reliability and efficiency of traffic, as well as the changes in traffic density throughout the day, it is necessary to indicate the average blocking probability of a network element at any given moment. Hence, different macroscopic traffic models will be studied in order to create an effective and accurate model of the influence of traffic characteristics and topology on the average probability of its elements blocking (drawing on the models proposed by Grinschields, Richards, Grindberg, El Hozaini, Underwood, Drake, and Pipes: the optimal speed, "Smart" driver, leader follow, cellular automata models, etc.). This will enable us to choose these characteristics as the core of the model and, consequently, to provide the required result after its modernization. Moreover, it will be useful to develop new models, for example, based on the description of stochastic systems including the possibility of self-organization and presence of memory of previous states.
3. Further research may also include a wider range of studies by various authors about road traffic management using intelligent vehicles equipped with a variety of sensors and communications [39–44] to integrate new approaches and data streams into the proposed traffic percolation model.

7. Conclusions

Percolation theory methods may be used to investigate the operational reliability and ground transport network fault tolerance where any transport structure may be represented as a planar or almost planar graph with some nonlinear bonds (in real transport networks, this is associated with the presence of overpasses and multilevel interchanges).

In percolation theory, we may consider the solution to problems relating to the indication of blocked nodes and bond fractions for networks with different structures. In order to solve bond tasks, the fraction of nodes and bonds, which must be broken up to separate such a network into at least two isolated areas (or, conversely, the fraction of +–+ conductive bonds when conductivity occurs), is indicated. In the node task, the fraction of blocked nodes where network decomposition occurs to create isolated areas (or, vice versa, the fraction of conductive nodes when conductivity occurs) is indicated. The percolation threshold is the fraction of nonblocked nodes (for the node task) or unbroken bonds (for the bond task), where conductivity occurs between two randomly selected network nodes. For the same structure of percolation threshold values, node and bond tasks have different meanings. The value of the percolation threshold depends on the average number of bonds per single node of the network (density) and is the criterion of work reliability, i.e., it indicates at which fraction of blocked nodes and/or bonds the network loses the required level of efficiency as a whole.

The dependence of the blocking (percolation) threshold value on the network bond density can be mathematically expressed. This enables us to use the traffic map and indicates the average number of bonds per single node to then calculate the threshold value of when it blocks, which can be used when engineering and modernizing the road infrastructure. If such a blocking threshold is increased, we may calculate the necessary number of additional links.

Real transport networks have a topology which is closer to accidental networks than to regular ones. Given equal network density, an accidental planar network (if loss of efficiency is possible) is slightly inferior to regular structures.

Thus, if we know the total city road stretch and number of lanes, as well as daily vehicle dynamics, we may calculate the average traffic intensity on the basis of such data. Then, we can calculate the average probability that a network element will block at any given moment. This enables us to estimate the reliability and efficiency of the network, to analyze daily dynamics, and—if possible—to change the traffic structure accordingly.

Increasing transport bond density may increase the reliability and traffic capacity of the network. Moreover, in order to increase traffic capacity, we can choose to build overpasses and multilevel interchanges. From a topological perspective, this changes its planarity. In the case of the same link density with planar networks, random nonplanar networks have higher blocking threshold values. Creating a small number of nonplanar junctions and overpasses may significantly increase the traffic capacity of the network.

The results of this study can be methodically used as follows: the graph of the real transport network can be applied to investigate their percolation properties using previously described models and techniques. If we want to increase bandwidth and reliability (increase the percolation threshold), then various changes to the network graph may be proposed (either additional connections or tiered interchanges). Next, numerical simulations or calculations can be carried out using the percolation threshold equations obtained in the study for modified graphs (various proposed solutions). Then, the estimated option with the largest percolation threshold and minimal capital cost can be chosen in the implementation of city planning solutions. This solution will claim optimal reliability at minimal cost.

Funding: This research received no external funding.

Institutional Review Board Statement: Not applicable.

Informed Consent Statement: Not applicable.

Conflicts of Interest: The author declares no conflict of interest.

References

1. Briani, M.; Cristiani, E. An easy-to-use algorithm for simulating traffic flow on networks: Theoretical study. *Netw. Heterog. Media* **2014**, *9*, 519–552. [CrossRef]
2. Hui, M.; Bai, L.; Li, Y.; Wu, Q. Highway traffic flow nonlinear character analysis and prediction. *Math. Probl. Eng.* **2015**, 20–27. [CrossRef]
3. Ahn, G.-H.; Ki, Y.-K.; Kim, E.-J. Real-time estimation of travel speed using urban traffic information system and filtering algorithm. *IET Intell. Transp. Syst.* **2014**, *8*, 145–154. [CrossRef]
4. Poole, A.; Kotsialos, A. Swarm intelligence algorithms for macroscopic traffic flow model validation with automatic assignment of fundamental diagrams. *Appl. Soft Comput.* **2016**, *38*, 134–150. [CrossRef]
5. Guo, J.; Chen, F.; Xu, C. Traffic flow forecasting for road tunnel using PSO-GPR algorithm with combined kernel function. *Math. Probl. Eng.* **2017**, 125–135. [CrossRef]
6. Lesko, S.A.; Alyoshkin, A.S.; Barkov, A.A. Mathematical and software development of modeling and management of transport flows based on percolation stochastic model. *CEUR Workshop Proc.* **2017**, *2064*, 454–469.
7. Lesko, S.A.; Alyoshkin, A.S.; Titov, V.V. Models and algorithms of optimization of routes in the transport network of the city. *CEUR Workshop Proc.* **2017**, *2064*, 438–453.
8. Jiang, R.; Jin, C.; Zhang, H. Experimental and empirical investigations of traffic flow instability. *Transp. Res. Procedia* **2017**, *23*, 157–173. [CrossRef]
9. Danchuk, V.; Bakulich, O.; Svatko, V. An Improvement in ant algorithm method for optimizing a transport route with regard to traffic flow. *Procedia Eng.* **2017**, 425–434. [CrossRef]
10. Pun-Cheng, L.S.; Chan, A.W. Optimal route computation for circular public transport routes with differential fare structure. *Travel Behav. Soc.* **2015**, *3*, 71–77. [CrossRef]
11. Baranovskata, T.P.; Pavlov, D.A. Simulation of large-scale traffic networks using multiobjective optimization methods and considering structural dynamics. *Political Netw. Electron. Sci. J. Kuban State Agrar. Univ.* **2016**, *120*, 1686–1705.
12. Pavlenko, P.F. Use of expert system and control module based on fuzzy logic in traffic adaptive management. *Inst. Autom. Inf. Technol. NAN KR* **2014**, *2*, 92–97.
13. Trubicin, V.A.; Golub, D.I. Traffic management based on traffic and road capacity ratio. *Bull. North-Cauc. Fed. Univ.* **2013**, *2*, 89–92.
14. Vlasov, A.A.; Chushkina, Z.A. Saturated Traffic Control Regional Architecture and Construction. *Reg. Archit. Eng.* **2014**, *4*, 152–156.
15. Ziryanov, V.V. Peculiarities of main traffic diagram use on network level. *Energy Resour. Sav. Ind. Transp.* **2013**, *21*, 71–74.

16. Filippova, D.M.; Chernyago, A.B.; Slobodchikova, N.A. Traffic flow distribution organizing coordinated traffic management. *Bull. Irkutsk State Univ.* **2013**, *9*, 172–176.
17. Kaligin, N.N.; Uvaysov, S.U.; Uvaysova, A.S.; Uvaysova, S.S. Infrastructural review of the distributed telecommunication system of road traffic and its protocols. *Russ. Technol. J.* **2019**, *7*, 87–95. (In Russian) [CrossRef]
18. Grimmet, G. *Percolation*, 2nd ed.; Springer: Berlin, Germany, 1999.
19. Sahimi, M. *Applications of Percolation Theory*; Tailor & Francis: London, UK, 1992.
20. Stauffer, D.; Aharony, A. *Introduction to Percolation Theory*; Tailor & Francis: London, UK, 1992.
21. Feder, J. *Fractals*; Plenum Pressl: New York, NY, USA; London, UK, 1998.
22. Lesko, S.A.; Alyoshkin, A.S.; Filatov, V.V. Stochastic and Percolating Models of Blocking Computer Networks Dynamics during Distribution of Epidemics of Evolutionary Computer Viruses. *Russ. Technol. J.* **2019**, *7*, 7–27. [CrossRef]
23. Li, D.; Fu, B.; Wang, Y.; Lu, G.; Yehiel Berezin, H.; Stanley, E.; Havlin, S. Percolation transition in dynamical traffic network with evolving critical bottlenecks. *Proc. Natl. Acad. Sci. USA* **2015**, *112*, 669–672. [CrossRef]
24. Zhukov, D.O.; Andrianova, E.G.; Lesko, S.A. The Influence of a Network's Spatial Symmetry, Topological Dimension, and Density on its Percolation Threshold. *Symmetry* **2019**, *11*, 920. [CrossRef]
25. Zhukov, D.; Khvatova, T.; Lesko, S.; Zaltsman, A. Managing social networks: Applying the Percolation theory methodology to understand individuals' attitudes and moods. *Technol. Forecast. Soc. Chang.* **2017**, *123*, 234–245. [CrossRef]
26. Zhukov, D.O.; Khvatova, T.Y.; Lesko, S.A.; Zaltsman, A.D. The influence of connection density on clusterization and percolation threshold during information distribution in social networks. *Inform. Appl.* **2018**, *12*, 90–97. [CrossRef]
27. Khvatova, T.Y.; Zaltsman, A.D.; Zhukov, D.O. Information processes in social networks: Percolation and stochastic dynamics. *CEUR Workshop Proc.* **2017**, *2064*, 277–288.
28. Lesko, S.; Aleshkin, A.; Zhukov, D. Reliability Analysis of the Air Transportation Network when Blocking Nodes and/or Connections Based on the Methods of Percolation Theory. *IOP Conf. Ser. Mater. Sci. Eng.* **2020**, *714*, 012016. [CrossRef]
29. Zhukov, D.O.; Zaltcman, A.G.; Khvatova, T.Y. Forecasting Changes in States in Social Networks and Sentiment Security Using the Principles of Percolation Theory and Stochastic Dynamics. In Proceedings of the 2019 IEEE International Conference Quality Management, Transport and Information Security, Information Technologies IT and QM and IS 2019, Sochy, Russia, 23–27 September 2019; pp. 149–153. [CrossRef]
30. Lesko, S.A.; Zhukov, D.O. Percolation models of information dissemination in social networks. In Proceedings of the 2015 IEEE International Conference on Smart City/SocialCom/SustainCom (SmartCity), Chengdu, China, 19–21 December 2015; pp. 213–216. [CrossRef]
31. Trudeau, R.J. *Introduction to Graph Theory*; Corrected, Enlarged Republication, Edition; Dover Pub.: New York, NY, USA, 1993; p. 64.
32. Gallyamov, S.R. A passing threshold of a simple cubic lattice in the site problem of Bethe lattice model. *Vestn. Udmurt. Univ. Mat. Mekhanika Komp'yuternye Nauki* **2008**, *3*, 109–115. (In Russian) [CrossRef]
33. Gallyamov, S.R.; Mel'chukov, S.A. On one method of calculating percolation thresholds for square and diamond lattices in the percolation problem of knots. *Vestn. Udmurt. Univ. Mat. Mekhanika Komp'yuternye Nauki* **2009**, *4*, 33–44. (In Russian) [CrossRef]
34. Gallyamov, S.R.; Mel'chukov, S.A. Hodge's idea in percolation percolation threshold estimation by the unit cell. *Vestn. Udmurt. Univ. Mat. Mekhanika Komp'yuternye Nauki* **2011**, 60–79. (In Russian) [CrossRef]
35. Hodge, W.V.D. *The Theory and Applications of Harmonic Integrals*; Cambridge Mathematical Library: Cambridge, UK, 1952.
36. Kadanoff, L.P.; Jotze, W.; Hamblen, D.; Hecht, R.; Lewis, E.A.S.; Palciauskas, V.V.; Rayl, M.; Swift, J.; Aspres, D.; Kane, J. Static Phenomena Near Critical Points: Theory and Experiment. *Rev. Mod. Phys.* **1967**, *39*, 395–431. [CrossRef]
37. Wilson, K.G. Renormalization group and critical phenomena. *Phys. Rev. B* **1971**, *4*, 3174–3183. [CrossRef]
38. Krasnov, V.A. Algebraic cycles on a real algebraic GM-manifold and their applications. *Russ. Acad. Sci. Izv. Math.* **1994**, *43*, 141–160. [CrossRef]
39. Romeo, F.; Campolo, C.; Molinaro, A.; Berthet, A.O. DENM repetitions to enhance reliability of the autonomous mode in NR V2X sidelink. In Proceedings of the 2020 IEEE 91st Vehicular Technology Conference (VTC2020-Spring), Antwerp, Begium, 25–28 May 2020; pp. 1–5. [CrossRef]
40. Qi, W.; Landfeldt, B.; Song, Q.; Guo, L.; Jamalipour, A. Traffic differentiated clustering routing in DSRC and C-V2X hybrid vehicular networks. *IEEE Trans. Veh. Technol.* **2020**, *69*, 7723–7734. [CrossRef]
41. Zadobrischi, E.; Dimian, M. Vehicular Communications Utility in Road Safety Applications: A Step toward Self-Aware Intelligent Traffic Systems. *Symmetry* **2021**, *13*, 438. [CrossRef]
42. Ahmed, S.H.; Bouk, S.H.; Yaqub, M.A.; Kim, D.; Song, H.; Lloret, J. CODIE: COntrolled Data and Interest Evaluation in vehicular named data networks. *IEEE Trans. Veh. Technol.* **2016**, *65*, 3954–3963. [CrossRef]
43. Carli, R.; Dotoli, M.; Epicoco, N. Monitoring Traffic Congestion in Urban Areas through Probe Vehicles: A Case Study Analysis. *Internet Technol. Lett.* **2017**, *1*, e5. [CrossRef]
44. Wang, S.; Zhang, X.; Cao, J.; He, L.; Stenneth, L.; Yu, P.S.; Li, Z.; Huang, Z. Computing urban traffic congestions by incorporating sparse GPS probe data and social media data. *ACM Trans. Inf. Syst.* **2017**, *35*, 30. [CrossRef]

Article

Not Another Computer Algebra System: Highlighting *wxMaxima* in Calculus

Natanael Karjanto [1,*] and Husty Serviana Husain [2]

[1] Department of Mathematics, University College, Natural Science Campus, Sungkyunkwan University Suwon 16419, Korea
[2] Department of Mathematics Education, Faculty of Mathematics and Natural Science Education, Indonesia University of Education, Bandung 40154, Indonesia; serviana@upi.edu
* Correspondence: natanael@skku.edu

Abstract: This article introduces and explains a computer algebra system (CAS) *wxMaxima* for Calculus teaching and learning at the tertiary level. The didactic reasoning behind this approach is the need to implement an element of technology into classrooms to enhance students' understanding of Calculus concepts. For many mathematics educators who have been using CAS, this material is of great interest, particularly for secondary teachers and university instructors who plan to introduce an alternative CAS into their classrooms. By highlighting both the strengths and limitations of the software, we hope that it will stimulate further debate not only among mathematics educators and software users but also also among symbolic computation and software developers.

Keywords: computer algebra system; *wxMaxima*; Calculus; symbolic computation

Citation: Karjanto, N.; Husain, H.S. Not Another Computer Algebra System: Highlighting *wxMaxima* in Calculus. *Mathematics* **2021**, *9*, 1317. https://doi.org/10.3390/math9121317

Academic Editor: Liliya Demidova

Received: 13 May 2021
Accepted: 3 June 2021
Published: 8 June 2021

Publisher's Note: MDPI stays neutral with regard to jurisdictional claims in published maps and institutional affiliations.

Copyright: © 2021 by the authors. Licensee MDPI, Basel, Switzerland. This article is an open access article distributed under the terms and conditions of the Creative Commons Attribution (CC BY) license (https://creativecommons.org/licenses/by/4.0/).

1. Introduction

A computer algebra system (CAS) is a program that can solve mathematical problems by rearranging formulas and finding a formula that solves the problem, as opposed to just outputting the numerical value of the result. *Maxima* is a full-featured open-source CAS: the software can serve as a calculator, provide analytical expressions, and perform symbolic manipulations. Furthermore, it offers a range of numerical analysis methods for equations or systems of equations that otherwise cannot be solved analytically. It can sketch graphical objects with excellent quality.

What is *wxMaxima*, then? *wxMaxima* is a document-based graphical user interface (GUI) for the CAS *Maxima*. It allows us for using all of *Maxima*'s functions. Additionally, it provides convenient wizards for accessing the most commonly used features, including inline plots and simple animations. Similar to *Maxima*, *wxMaxima* is free of charge, and it is released and distributed under the terms of the GNU General Public License (GPL). This allows for everyone to modify and distribute it, as long as its license remains unmodified. In this article, we use the term "*wxMaxima*" more often, but the terms "*Maxima*" and "*wxMaxima*" can be used interchangeably.

Maxima is different from other well-known so-called *3M* mathematical software (*Maple*, *Matlab*, *Mathematica*), as they are commercial and one needs to purchase a license before using them. Other open-source mathematics software include *Axiom*, *Reduce*, *SageMath*, *Octave* and *Scilab* (both are for numerical computation), *R* (for statistical computing), and *GeoGebra* (for interactive geometry and algebra), where the latter is quite well-known globally among mathematics educators.

Apart from being free and easy to install, *Maxima* is also updated continuously. Currently, *Maxima* can run natively without emulation on the following operating systems: *Windows*, *Mac OS X*, *Linux*, *Berkeley Software Distribution* (*FreeBSD*), *Solaris*, and *Android*. An executable file can be downloaded from *Maxima*'s website [1]. In particular, the installation file for *Windows* operating system is available for download at an open-source software community resource *SourceForge* [2]. One can simply double-click the executable file and follow the instruction accordingly. After the installation is completed, the software is ready to be launched. The whole process takes less than three minutes in total, depending on the Internet connection speed.

This software is introduced because it is free and under the GPL. As a comparison, the total combined cost for purchasing *3M* software is almost USD 5500 for an educational license (see Table 1). Although the expenditure for personal and student licenses are much lower than those for commercial and professional licenses, for colleagues and practitioners in many developing countries, the price is still considered to be costly. Having this in mind, we promote an open-source software that benefits many people who have limited resources, particularly in less affluent countries.

For teaching and learning mathematics, *Maxima* is fairly accessible by many people. Although *SageMath* is popular among university professors for teaching Calculus and Linear Algebra thanks to its user-friendly cloud, the server is rather slow, particularly if one attempts to access it from a developing country with modest Internet connectivity. *SageMath* can be downloaded and installed locally, but it is a huge file. Thus, it is another hindrance for many colleagues in developing countries.

Table 1. Software packages and the individuals or institutions through which they were first developed, the year they were launched, and estimated cost in USD.

Software	Creator	Launched	Cost (USD)
Axiom	Richard Jenks	1977	Free
Magma	University of Sydney	1990	USD 1140
Maple	University of Waterloo	1980	USD 2390
Mathematica	Wolfram Research	1986	USD 2495
Maxima	Bill Schelter et al.	1976	Free
Matlab	MathWorks	1989	USD 3150
SageMath	William A. Stein	2005	Free

In what follows, we cover a literature study on *Maxima* for teaching and learning. A study from Malaysia suggests that students who are exposed to *Maxima* while learning Calculus had a significantly better academic performance as compared with the group that followed a traditional teaching method, and showed a better motivation and more confidence towards the subject [3]. Another example comes from Spain, where García et al. proposed to replace *Derive* using *Maxima* [4]. Díaz et al. analyzed the role of *Maxima* in learning Linear Algebra in the context of learning on the basis of competencies [5]. Fedriani and Moyano proposed using *Maxima* in teaching mathematics for business degrees and A-level students [6]. The authors also presented a report of the main strengths and weaknesses of this software when used in the classroom. Additionally, the CAS *wxMaxima* is used for training future mathematics teachers in Ukraine [7].

Advanced mathematics can also be explored using *Maxima*, as demonstrated by Dehl [8]. A new possibility for interactive teaching in engineering module using *Maxima* was discussed by Žáková [9]. There also exist free Calculus electronic textbooks incorporating *wxMaxima* developed by Zachary Hannan from Solano Community College, Fairfield, California [10]. These books could certainly be adopted into Calculus classrooms. Currently, Hannan is working on PreCalculus, Multivariable Calculus (MVC), Linear Algebra, and Differential Equations textbooks that utilize the software. Thus, we hope to see more *Maxima*-based mathematics textbooks, and this is good news for mathematics educators who are interested in embedding technology and CAS into their classrooms.

Beyond mathematics, some authors used *Maxima* successfully in Classical Mechanics [11] and Chemistry [12]. In particular, for an efficient path in understanding *Maxima*, the latter provides a thorough introduction to exploiting *Maxima* with the focus on utilizing the *wxMaxima* interface. Woollett provided a series of tutorial notes on *Maxima*. Designed for new users, particularly *Windows* customers, the notes include some nuts-and-bolts suggestions for working with the CAS [13]. Puentedura designed a *Maxima* tutorial workflow for enhancing and transforming the learning process in science and mathematics. He identified that the CAS has at least three essential roles: as a number-crunching calculator, as a tool for paper-and-pencil symbolic mathematical derivation, and as a typesetter [14].

The list of literature reviews presented above is by no means exhaustive. While the literature offers abundant materials on where *wxMaxima* can outstandingly perform, what it can and cannot do is not entirely clear when it comes to teaching Calculus using the software. This article fills the gap in human–computer interaction, both in the technological and pedagogical senses. Furthermore, by highlighting the software's limitations, we hope to stimulate further debate among the symbolic-computation and mathematics-education communities on how to remedy the situation, perhaps by either providing alternative ways in problem-solving or by improving the technological aspects of the CAS itself. From a pedagogical point of view, the students' feedback that was obtained after implementing *wxMaxima* in teaching and learning for multiple semesters could shed light on its accessibility, digital natives' interaction with technology, and uncover a better way of teaching with technology.

In particular, the limitations of *wxMaxima* are examined by revisiting several examples that were considered in the literature. We present some examples of symbolic integration where *wxMaxima* fails to calculate in most of the cases in relation to results from other software. Interestingly, even other CAS that were often regarded as superior to *wxMaxima* have shortcomings as well. Granted, the field of symbolic integration itself, let alone the area of symbolic computation, particularly with different CAS, is a wide range. Both the cited literature and presented examples are by no means exhaustive lists.

Additionally, although Calculus focuses on the mathematical study of continuous change, the subject in itself contains rich examples of symmetrical objects. For example, even and odd functions are symmetric with respect to the y-axis and origin, respectively. Geometrically, the graph of even and odd functions remains unchanged after reflection about the y-axis and rotation of $180°$ about the origin, respectively. Consequently, the integral of the former with respect to symmetric intervals is twice the integral from zero to the corresponding upper limit, while the integral of the latter vanishes. We assume that either these functions are integrable and the intervals are finite or the integral converges for infinite intervals. Throughout this article, we consider other examples where symmetry occurs in Calculus and illustrate them using *wxMaxima*.

This article is an extended version of our previous work on embedding technology into Calculus teaching and learning [15]. We investigate the following research questions: Where can *wxMaxima* perform exceptionally as a CAS? What is its effectiveness? What are *wxMaxima*'s limitations and weaknesses? This paper is organized as follows. After this introduction, Section 2 discusses *wxMaxima*'s strengths and limitations, which are featured through several examples. Section 3 provides educational benefits when one embeds the software for instructional purposes, in addition to covering some study limitations. Section 4 concludes the study and lays out a future outlook from our discussion.

2. *wxMaxima*'s Strengths and Weaknesses

In this section, we cover both *wxMaxima*'s strengths and weaknesses through examples. Although the considered illustrations are mostly Calculus-related, one may consider examples for other subjects as well, including Linear Algebra, Differential Equations, and Discrete Mathematics.

2.1. *wxMaxima*'s Strengths

When working with Calculus problems, students can verify the result of their manual computations performed by pencil and paper using *wxMaxima*. Since *wxMaxima* is lightweight and fairly straightforward, simple Calculus calculations can be executed within seconds. These include calculating the limit, finding the derivative of a function, and evaluating both definite and indefinite integrals. The syntax is relatively easy to understand by someone who has no or little experience in programming. In what follows, we consider several *wxMaxima* examples that can be useful for Calculus teaching and learning.

Example 1. *Calculating limits, derivatives, and integrals:*

$$\lim_{x \to 0} \frac{\sin(7x)}{x}, \quad \frac{d}{dx}\cos(3x^2), \quad \int \frac{1}{1+x^2}\,dx, \quad \int_0^1 \frac{1}{1+x^2}\,dx.$$

Example 1 provides simple examples of calculating limits, derivatives, and integrals, both definite and indefinite. All functions in this example are even. Table 2 displays the *wxMaxima* command inputs and their corresponding outputs. Our experience as instructors suggests that *wxMaxima* is also handy for obtaining quick and excellent-quality graphical plots, particularly three-dimensional objects that can be hard to sketch manually. In turn, this visualization enhances students' understanding of applying Calculus concepts.

Example 2. *Sketching functions (2D plots):*

$y = f(x) = 2x^3 - 7x^2 - 5x + 4$ [cubic function]
$y = g(x) = e^x$ *and* $L(x) = 1 + x$ [exponential function and its linear approximation].

Example 2 gives examples of generating 2D plots of a single polynomial function and an exponential function together with the corresponding linear approximation. Table 2 shows the *wxMaxima* command inputs, and Figure 1 displays the corresponding outputs. The plot on the left-hand side can be used to verify the theoretical computation of the local extrema, increasing or decreasing test, and concavity test to a cubic function $f(x) = 2x^3 - 7x^2 - 5x + 4$. The plot on the right-hand side shows a linear approximation $L(x)$ of an exponential function $g(x) = e^x$ at $x = 0$. The sketching quality in *wxMaxima* is remarkably excellent, and the task is completed swiftly. *SageMath* is rather slow to produce plots, and *WolframAlpha*'s free version generates poor quality plots.

Table 2. Examples of *wxMaxima* commands and their corresponding outputs covering limit, derivative, integral, and 2D plots.

Input	Output
(%i1) 'limit(sin(7*x)/x,x,0);	$\lim_{x \to 0} \frac{\sin(7x)}{x}$
(%i2) limit(sin(7*x)/x,x,0);	7
(%i3) 'diff(cos(3*x^2),x);	$\frac{d}{dx}\cos(3x^2)$
(%i4) diff(cos(3*x^2),x);	$-6x\sin(3x^2)$
(%i5) 'integrate(1/(1 + x^2),x);	$\int \frac{1}{1+x^2}\,dx$
(%i6) integrate(1/(1 + x^2),x);	$\operatorname{atan}(x)$
(%i7) integrate(1/(1 + x^2),x,0,1);	$\frac{\pi}{4}$
(%i8) plot2d(2*x^3-7*x^2-5*x+4, [x,-2,4.5]);	(Figure 1, left panel)
(%i9) plot2d([exp(x), 1 + x], [x,-3,2]);	(Figure 1, right panel)

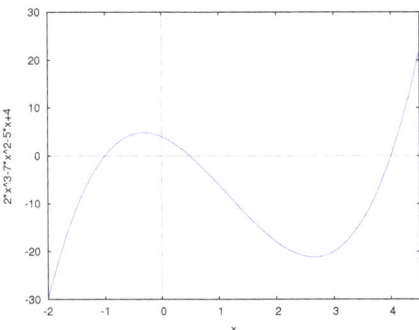 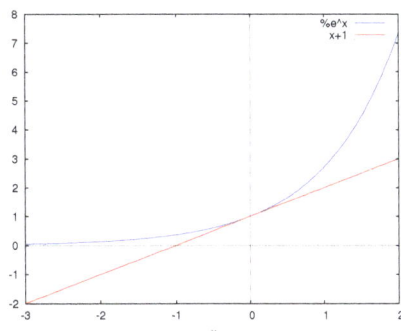

Figure 1. 2D plot outputs of a cubic function $y = f(x) = 2x^3 - 7x^2 - 5x + 4$ (**left**), and the exponential function $y = g(x) = e^x$ and its linear approximation at $(0,1)$, $y = L(x) = 1 + x$ (**right**).

Example 3. *2D and 3D parametric plots:*

$$r(t) = 1 - \sin t, \qquad 0 \leq t \leq 2\pi \qquad [\text{cardioid}]$$
$$\boldsymbol{r}(t) = \langle \cos t, \sin t, t \rangle, \qquad 0 \leq t \leq 5\pi \qquad [\text{helix}].$$

Example 3 gives illustrations of parametric plots in both 2D plane and 3D space. The *wxMaxima* input commands and their corresponding outputs are presented in Table 3. A 2D plot of the polar curve cardioid $r(t) = 1 - \sin t$, $0 \leq t \leq 2\pi$, and a 3D plot of helix $\boldsymbol{r}(t) = \langle \cos t, \sin t, t \rangle$, $0 \leq t \leq 5\pi$ are given on the left and right panels of Figure 2, respectively.

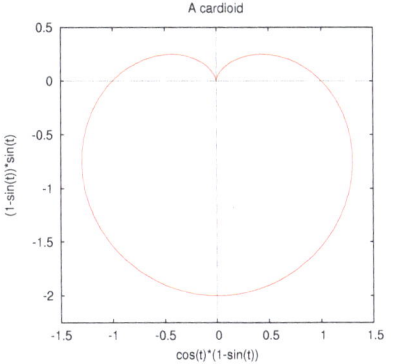 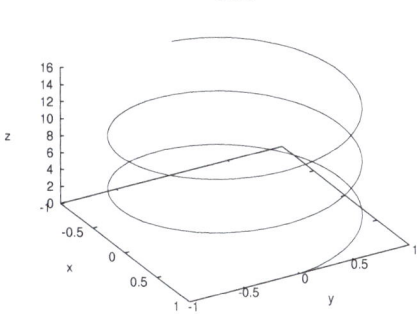

Figure 2. (**left**) The output of 2D parametric plot showing a polar curve cardioid $r(t) = 1 - \sin t$, $0 \leq t \leq 2\pi$. (**right**) An output of a 3D parametric plot displaying a vector-valued function helix $\boldsymbol{r}(t) = \langle \cos t, \sin t, t \rangle$, $0 \leq t \leq 5\pi$. These particular cardioid and helix are symmetric with respect to the *y*- and *z*-axes, respectively.

Two of integral applications are calculating the area enclosed by a polar curve and the arc length of a parametric curve. The commands to calculate the area A enclosed by the cardioid and the length of the helix L and their corresponding results are also given in Table 3. Mathematically, they are performed as follows, where the prime denotes differentiation with respect to t:

$$A = \int_0^{2\pi} \frac{1}{2} r^2 \, dt = \int_0^{2\pi} \frac{1}{2}(1 - \sin t)^2 \, dt = \frac{3\pi}{2}$$

$$L = \int_0^{5\pi} \sqrt{x'(t)^2 + y'(t)^2 + z'(t)^2} \, dt = \int_0^{5\pi} \sqrt{\sin^2 t + \cos^2 t + 1} \, dt = 5\sqrt{2}\pi.$$

Table 3. Examples of *wxMaxima* commands and their corresponding outputs showing 2D and 3D plots of parametric curves cardioid and helix, respectively, and their corresponding arc lengths.

Input	Output
(%i10) r: 1 - sin(t);	$(r)\ 1 - \sin(t)$
(%i11) plot2d([parametric,r*cos(t),r*sin(t)], [t,0,2*%pi],[color,red],[x,-1.5,1.5], [y,-2.25,0.5],same_xy,[title,"A cardioid"]);	(Figure 2, left panel)
(%i12) integrate(1/2*r^2,t,0,2*%pi);	$\dfrac{3\pi}{2}$
(%i13) plot3d([cos(t),sin(t),t],[t,0,5*%pi],[y,-1,1], [grid,100,2],[gnuplot_pm3d,true],[elevation,50], [azimuth,60],[legend,false],[title,"A helix"]);	(Figure 2, right panel)
(%i14) factor(integrate(sqrt(diff(cos(t),t)^2 +diff(sin(t),t)^2+diff(t,t)^2),t,0,5*%pi));	$5\sqrt{2}\pi$

Example 4. *3D surfaces of Möbius band and torus:*

$$s(x,y) = \left\langle \left(3+y\cos\frac{x}{2}\right)\cos x, \left(3+y\cos\frac{x}{2}\right)\sin x, y\sin\frac{x}{2}\right\rangle \qquad \text{[Möbius band]}$$

$$t(\theta,\phi) = \langle (2+\cos\theta)\cos\phi, (2+\cos\theta)\sin\phi, \sin\theta\rangle, \qquad 0 \leq \theta,\phi < 2\pi. \qquad \text{[torus]}$$

The *wxMaxima* input commands and their corresponding outputs are given in Table 4 and Figure 3, respectively. Three-dimensional plots such as this Möbius band and torus can be rotated easily in any direction. Sometimes also called the Möbius strip, the former is a surface with only one side and only one boundary curve, the simplest example of a nonorientable surface. All Möbius bands have a twofold symmetry rotational axis, for which a 180° rotation results in strips indistinguishable from the original. The surface finds abundant applications in physical sciences, including nanostructures [16], metamaterials [17], polymeric materials [18], and photonic crystals [19].

The torus example comes from the problem of calculating the volume of solid revolution. It is obtained from a disk $(x-2)^2 + z^2 \leq 1$ revolved about the z-axis, and thus, it is radially symmetric about the z-axis. The desired viewpoint can be obtained easily by setting the elevation and azimuth angles. This is beneficial in comparison to the *Matlab* plots where figures usually have a high number of pixels and are rather heavy to be rotated. Although the surface of revolution is a fascinating object among geometers and topologists, it also finds ample applications in nanophotonics [20], metamaterials [21], magnetized plasma [22], and polymer chemistry [23].

Table 4. Examples of *wxMaxima* commands and their corresponding outputs showing 3D plots of parametric surfaces Möbius band and torus.

Input	Output
(%i15) plot3d([cos(x)*(3+y*cos(x/2)),sin(x)*(3+y*cos(x/2)), y*sin(x/2)],[x,-%pi,%pi],[y,-1,1],['grid,50,15], [legend,false],[elevation,35],[azimuth,50], [title,"Moebius band"]);	(Figure 3, left panel)
(%i16) plot3d([cos(y)*(2+cos(x)),sin(y)*(2+cos(x)),sin(x)], [x,0,2*%pi],[y,0,2*%pi],[gnuplot_pm3d,true], [grid,50,50],[legend,false],[elevation,30], [azimuth,135],[title,"A torus"]);	(Figure 3, right panel)

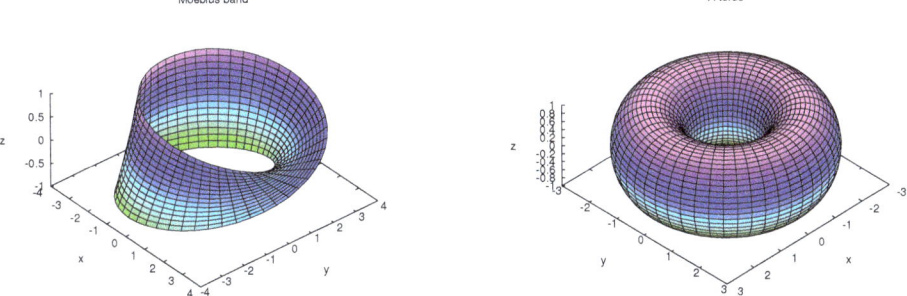

Figure 3. Outputs of (**left**) the 3D surface Möbius band $s(x,y) = (3+y\cos\frac{x}{2})\cos x\,\mathbf{i} + (3+y\cos\frac{x}{2})\sin x\,\mathbf{j} + y\sin\frac{x}{2}\,\mathbf{k}$, and (**right**) the torus $t(\theta,\phi) = (2+\cos\theta)\cos\phi\,\mathbf{i} + (2+\cos\theta)\sin\phi\,\mathbf{j} + \sin\theta\,\mathbf{k}$.

2.2. wxMaxima's Weaknesses

In this subsection, we consider several examples where *wxMaxima* is deficient. When sketching a function with singularities, we can discern an improved plot by including supplementary commands. The CAS *wxMaxima* is not particularly strong when it comes to evaluating integrals, particularly the integral of rational functions. This may come as a surprise since the latter are commonplace and considered to be schematically viable.

Example 5. *A sketch of* $y = f(x) = \dfrac{x^2}{x^2 - 1}$.

In this example, sketching a 2D plot of a function with vertical asymptotes requires an additional instruction. Although the output from "plot2d(x^2/(x^2-1),[x,-4,4]);" input shows that there are two vertical asymptotes at $x = \pm 1$, modifying the input produces a better visibility, cf. [24]:
"plot2d(max(min(x^2/(x^2-1),10),-10),[x,-4,4]);". Figure 4 compares the 2D plots obtained from these two inputs.

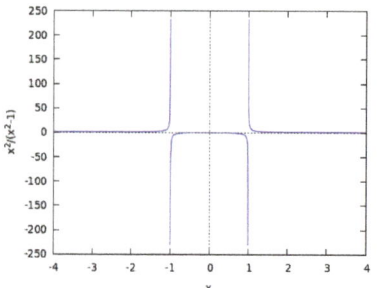 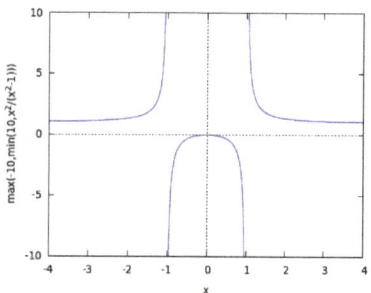

Figure 4. (**left**) A 2D plot of $y = f(x) = \frac{x^2}{x^2-1}$ without any restriction in the vertical scale. (**right**) The same plot as in the left panel but the vertical axis is restricted to $-10 \leq y \leq 10$.

Example 6. *Indefinite and definite integrals involving trigonometric functions:*

$$\int \frac{x \sin x}{1 + \cos^2 x} dx \quad \text{and} \quad \int_0^\pi \frac{x \sin x}{1 + \cos^2 x} dx.$$

Both *wxMaxima* and *Matlab* fail to evaluate both integrals. The indefinite integral above involves a non-elementary function Li$_2(z)$. Special function Li$_s(z)$ is a polylogarithm of order s and argument z. It is also known as the Jonquière's function and is defined by a power series in z; it is also a Dirichlet series in s:

$$\text{Li}_s(z) = \sum_{k=1}^{\infty} \frac{z^k}{k^s}.$$

Both *WolframAlpha* and *Mathematica* can produce a correct answer for the above definite integral: $\pi^2/4$. Although treatment of the indefinite integral is beyond the Calculus course, the definite integral can be evaluated using a simple substitution rule. Appendix A shows how to evaluate it without any help from CAS.

Example 7. *Gärtner's indefinite integral of a rational function [25]:*

$$\int \frac{\sqrt{2} \, dx}{(x-1)^4 + \frac{1}{16}}.$$

When employing the "integrate(sqrt(2)/((x-1)^4+1/16),x);" command, *wxMaxima* could not directly handle this integral. However, using the substitution $y = x - 1$: "changevar(%,x-1-y,y,x);", the integral transforms into

$$\int \frac{16\sqrt{2} \, dy}{16y^4 + 1}.$$

Asking *wxMaxima* to evaluate the integral, "ev(%,integrate);", we obtain

$$2 \log(4y^2 + 2\sqrt{2}y + 1) - 2 \log(4y^2 - 2\sqrt{2}y + 1) + 4 \operatorname{atan}\left(\frac{4y + \sqrt{2}}{\sqrt{2}}\right) + 4 \operatorname{atan}\left(\frac{4y - \sqrt{2}}{\sqrt{2}}\right).$$

Substituting back to the original variable gives us the desired integral, "sfx: %,y=x-1":

$$2 \log(4(x-1)^2 + 2\sqrt{2}(x-1) + 1) - 2 \log(4(x-1)^2 - 2\sqrt{2}(x-1) + 1)$$
$$+ 4 \operatorname{atan}\left(\frac{4(x-1) + \sqrt{2}}{\sqrt{2}}\right) + 4 \operatorname{atan}\left(\frac{4(x-1) - \sqrt{2}}{\sqrt{2}}\right).$$

In attempting to solve indefinite integrals of rational functions, *wxMaxima* essentially still uses the algorithms that were described by Moses [26]. The CAS employs the classical algorithmic tool in symbolic integration known as Hermite reduction. Both Hermite and Ostrogradsky demonstrated decomposing indefinite integral of rational functions as the sum of a function with simple poles and the derivative of another rational function, i.e., for $R \in \mathbb{Q}(x)$

$$\int R(x)\,dx = U(x) + \int A(x)\,dx, \quad U, A \in \mathbb{Q}(x)$$

where A has only simple poles and vanishes at infinity [27–30].

Thus, *wxMaxima* implements the combination of Hermite reduction with either the partial fraction decomposition (Bernoulli–Leibniz algorithm) to compute the rational part of the integrand or with some heuristic methods in computing its transcendental parts for several easier cases. Although other commercial software such as *Axiom* and *3M* might also implement integration using Hermite reduction for the rational part of the integrand, it employs more contemporary and advanced methods to integrate the remaining terms after Hermite reduction is implemented.

Example 8. *Bronstein's definite integral of a rational function* [31]:

$$\int_1^2 \frac{x^4 - 3x^2 + 6}{x^6 - 5x^4 + 5x^2 + 4}\,dx.$$

When we attempt the command "integrate((x^4-3*x^2+6)/(x^6-5*x^4+5*x^2+4), x,1,2);", *wxMaxima* could not compute this integral. However, *Axiom* and *3M* can tackle it. *Axiom*'s output reads:

$$\frac{2\operatorname{atan}(8) + 2\operatorname{atan}(5) + 2\operatorname{atan}(2) + 2\operatorname{atan}\left(\frac{1}{2}\right) - \pi}{2}.$$

Maple's output is given as follows:

$$\arctan\left(\frac{1}{2}\right) - \frac{1}{2}\pi + \arctan(5) + \arctan(8) + \arctan(2).$$

Interestingly, *Mathematica* and *Matlab* give the following outputs, respectively, which were simpler than the ones from the previous two software:

$$\frac{5}{4}\pi - \arctan(2) \quad \text{and} \quad \pi - \arctan(1/3).$$

All of these results correspond to an identical numerical value of approximately 2.819842. The proof is shown in Appendix B.1.

It would also be interesting to observe the corresponding indefinite integral. While *wxMaxima* anticipatedly cannot compute the indefinite integral, *Axiom*, *Maple*, and *Matlab* delivered the same results and agreed with Formula (2.20) in [31]. This reads

$$\int \frac{x^4 - 3x^2 + 6}{x^6 - 5x^4 + 5x^2 + 4}\,dx = \arctan(x) + \arctan(x^3) + \arctan\left(\frac{x^5 - 3x^3 + x}{2}\right) + C.$$

In particular, *Mathematica* is of special interest as the output of the corresponding indefinite integral does not agree with the formula given in [31]. It reads as follows (some terms were rearranged):

$$\int \frac{x^4 - 3x^2 + 6}{x^6 - 5x^4 + 5x^2 + 4}\,dx = \frac{1}{2}\arctan\left[\frac{x(x^2 - 3)}{x^2 - 2}\right] - \frac{1}{2}\arctan\left[\frac{x(x^2 - 3)}{2 - x^2}\right] + C.$$

The definite integral is given as follows:

$$\int_1^2 \frac{x^4 - 3x^2 + 6}{x^6 - 5x^4 + 5x^2 + 4} dx = \lim_{t \to \sqrt{2}^-} \left\{ \frac{1}{2} \arctan\left[\frac{x(x^2-3)}{x^2-2}\right] - \frac{1}{2} \arctan\left[\frac{x(x^2-3)}{2-x^2}\right] \right\} - \arctan(2)$$

$$+ \arctan(1) - \lim_{t \to \sqrt{2}^+} \left\{ \frac{1}{2} \arctan\left[\frac{x(x^2-3)}{x^2-2}\right] - \frac{1}{2} \arctan\left[\frac{x(x^2-3)}{2-x^2}\right] \right\}$$

$$= \left(\frac{\pi}{2} - \arctan(2)\right) + \left(\frac{\pi}{4} + \frac{\pi}{2}\right) = \frac{5}{4}\pi - \arctan(2).$$

The first and second chapters of [31] explain outline algorithms for the integration of rational functions in great detail. All relevant algorithms are given in pseudocodes. With an estimated effort of 500 to 700 lines of code, these algorithms can be implemented in *wxMaxima*.

Example 9. *Adamchik's definite integral of a rational function* [32]:

$$\int_0^4 \frac{x^2 + 2x + 4}{x^4 - 7x^2 + 2x + 17} dx.$$

For an indefinite integral, *wxMaxima* could not compute it. Other software, namely, *Axiom*, *Maple*, and *Matlab*, presented an identical solution but with rather dissimilar expressions:

$$\int \frac{x^2 + 2x + 4}{x^4 - 7x^2 + 2x + 17} dx = \arctan(x - 1) + \arctan\left(\frac{1}{3}x^3 - \frac{1}{2}x^2 - x + \frac{5}{3}\right) + C.$$

On the other hand, the computational result from *Mathematica* produced an antiderivative expression with discontinuities at $x = \pm 2$:

$$\int \frac{x^2 + 2x + 4}{x^4 - 7x^2 + 2x + 17} dx = \frac{1}{2} \arctan\left(\frac{-x-1}{x^2-4}\right) - \frac{1}{2} \arctan\left(\frac{x+1}{x^2-4}\right) + C.$$

For the definite integral, while all numerical results agree, the symbolic outputs yield remarkably distinct expressions. The outputs are given as follows:

$$\int_0^4 \frac{x^2 + 2x + 4}{x^4 - 7x^2 + 2x + 17} dx = \frac{\pi}{4} + \arctan(3) - \arctan\left(\frac{5}{3}\right) + \arctan\left(\frac{41}{3}\right) \qquad \text{[Axiom and Maple]}$$

$$= \frac{5}{4}\pi - \arctan\left(\frac{75}{11}\right) \qquad \text{[Matlab]}$$

$$= \pi - \arctan\left(\frac{1}{4}\right) - \arctan\left(\frac{5}{12}\right) \qquad \text{[Mathematica]}$$

$$= \text{(a tedious and complicated expression)} \qquad \text{[wxMaxima]}$$

$$\approx 2.50182 \qquad \text{[numerical value]}.$$

Although *wxMaxima* computes and produces an output for the definite integral, that expression is exceptionally tedious and complicated. It is also unclear how it was obtained, but possibly by performing a contour integration. Despite that tiresome and intricate expression, its numerical evaluation yields a value that agrees with the one calculated by other software. A high floating-point precision command, e.g., "`fpprec:150`" needs to be imposed to obtain that numerical value. Except for the exact *wxMaxima* output, Appendix B.2 verifies that the above outputs had identical values.

Similar to Example 8, when we want to use *Mathematica*'s antiderivative result to compute the value of the definite integral, we need to split the interval of integration at the point of discontinuity to avoid a wrong result of $-\arctan\left(\frac{1}{4}\right) - \arctan\left(\frac{5}{12}\right)$. The computational summary is given as follows:

$$\int_0^4 \frac{x^2+2x+4}{x^4-7x^2+2x+17}\,dx = \lim_{t\to 2^-}\left\{\frac{1}{2}\arctan\left(\frac{-t-1}{t^2-4}\right) - \frac{1}{2}\arctan\left(\frac{t+1}{t^2-4}\right)\right\} - \arctan\left(\frac{1}{4}\right)$$
$$-\arctan\left(\frac{5}{12}\right) - \lim_{t\to 2^+}\left\{\frac{1}{2}\arctan\left(\frac{-t-1}{t^2-4}\right) - \frac{1}{2}\arctan\left(\frac{t+1}{t^2-4}\right)\right\}$$
$$= \left[\frac{\pi}{2} - \arctan\left(\frac{1}{4}\right)\right] - \left[\arctan\left(\frac{5}{12}\right) - \frac{\pi}{2}\right]$$
$$= \pi - \arctan\left(\frac{1}{4}\right) - \arctan\left(\frac{5}{12}\right).$$

Example 10. *Tobey's indefinite integral of a rational function [33]:*

$$\int \frac{7x^{13}+10x^8+4x^7-7x^6-4x^3-4x^2+3x+3}{x^{14}-2x^8-2x^7-2x^4-4x^3-x^2+2x+1}\,dx.$$

Except for *wxMaxima*, all other CAS can compute this integral. The result can be found on page 502 of [34] using the Rothstein–Trager method. It reads

$$\frac{1}{2}(1+\sqrt{2})\log\left(x^7 - \sqrt{2}\,x^2 - (1+\sqrt{2})x - 1\right) + \frac{1}{2}(1-\sqrt{2})\log\left(x^7 + \sqrt{2}\,x^2 - (1-\sqrt{2})x - 1\right) + C.$$

3. Discussion

3.1. wxMaxima *in Perspective*

There exists a distinct paradigm between the CAS mentioned in the Introduction. While *Matlab* is particularly strong in numerical computation, the real forte of *wxMaxima*, *Maple*, and *Mathematica* is symbolic computation. *Matlab* has also incorporated some symbolic features, and the latter three can also perform numerical computations as well.

When it comes to symbolic functionality, *wxMaxima* still has a long way to go to catch up other commercial software. Together with *Axiom* and *SageMath*, a formula editor is missing in *Maxima*, although *wxMaxima* serves efficiently as its user interface. While *Axiom* does not possess graph-theory symbolic functionality, *wxMaxima* does. Unfortunately, Diophantine equation solvers and quantifier elimination are absent in *wxMaxima*, and *SageMath* acquires these two features via *SymPy* and *qepcad* optional packages, respectively. Table 5 summarizes the significantly developed symbolic functionality in various software systems.

Table 5. A summary of significantly developed symbolic functionality among various software. *Maxima* has a shortfall in quantifier elimination and Diophantine equation solver. The missing formula editor can be overcome by a user interface *wxMaxima*.

Software	Formula Editor	Calculus		Quantifier Elimination	Solvers			
		Integration	Integral Transforms		Inequalities	Diophantine Equations	Differential Equations	Recurrence Relations
Axiom	✗	✓	✓	✓	✓	✓	✓	✓
Magma	✗	✗	✗	✗	✓	✗	✗	✗
Maple	✓	✓	✓	✓	✓	✓	✓	✓
Mathematica	✓	✓	✓	✓	✓	✓	✓	✓
Maxima	✗	✓	✓	✗	✓	✗	✓	✓
Matlab	✓	✓	✓	✓	✓	✗	✓	✗
SageMath	✗	✓	✓	✓	✓	✓	✓	✓

An important feature of *wxMaxima* that trumps other CAS is the admittance of referring to the result of the last evaluated expression with a percentage sign (%). Although we may organize the commands in spatial order, *wxMaxima* stores information in chronological order. Thus, the % always refers to the most recently executed command, and not necessarily to the one that appears directly above the executed command [11]. As already mentioned in the Introduction, since *wxMaxima* is open-source software, it is maintained by an active community of developers, and thus being updated regularly. New releases occur approximately twice annually. For a proprietary software like *3M*, not everyone can inspect, modify, or enhance, but only a team of developers from the company or organization who maintains exclusive control over it can modify the software. Admittedly, the most important reason for utilizing *wxMaxima*, both in teaching and research is the cost, and many authors agreed on this particular notable reason [10–12].

3.2. Educational Benefit

There are many educational benefits of embedding CAS *wxMaxima* into teaching and learning, Calculus in particular, and mathematics in general. The software serves as meaningful assistance not only to students but also to instructors in verifying hand-computed results, obtaining numerical values of tedious expressions, and providing rich-quality graphical plots. Hence, the benefit of algebraic, numerical, and graphical aspects, respectively. The time reduction gained in the labor of manual calculation can be spent for a deeper understanding of key ideas, theoretical concepts, and problem-solving methods.

Some examples discussed in Section 2 support this testimony. By observing the graph of a cubic function, students should establish a connection between the visual plot and the computational result of obtaining intervals where the function is increasing, decreasing, concave up, and concave down. Other features, such as the local maxima and minima, and inflection points should follow naturally. By examining the linear approximation of a function, students should be able to conclude why the approximation works for the variable x near a specified point of interest. At an advanced level, this comprehension is advantageous for linear-stability analysis.

The literature does not lack in supplying educational benefits of using CAS in mathematics lessons. From a coding perspective, the programming language in *wxMaxima* flows more naturally in comparison to that in other software, and hence allows for students to autonomously implement simple algorithms [4]. For current and future calculus teachers, *wxMaxima* could reduce the time spent on course preparation [7]. By allowing students to induce judgments and make mistakes, the adoption of *wxMaxima* stimulates the interactive-learning process through testing, evaluation, decision-making, and error correction [9]. Weigand argued that the wise use of CAS could foster students' ability in problem solving, modeling, proving, and communicating [35]. The CAS can even be blended with an innovative pedagogical approach, such as flipped classrooms [36].

Additional benefits come along as more instructors adopt and implement a CAS, particularly *wxMaxima*, into their teaching and learning. However, *wxMaxima* is not a perfect software, as we elaborated through several examples in Section 2.

3.3. Limitation

This study admits several limitations. First, the extent of course materials in Single-Variable Calculus (SVC) is overwhelmingly profuse while the time is scanty. It covers nine chapters of Stewart's Calculus textbook [37], and they need to be completed in 14 weeks. Embedding technology into teaching and learning contributes an additional burden. In a typical North American university, similar content would be covered in two different courses for two consecutive semesters. Usually called "Calculus 1" and "Calculus 2", they cover Differential and Integral Calculus, respectively. The latter often includes an Introduction to Differential Equations, and Sequence and Series. Hence, teaching Calculus using *wxMaxima* with less material coverage seems to be a promising attempt, as we could pursue in MVC.

Second, despite the superior features of *wxMaxima* and its specialty in symbolic operations, the CAS itself has some weaknesses that could be challenging for beginners to learn, adopt, and adapt, both as instructors and students, where it might be more conspicuous for the latter. The CAS is admittedly far from perfect due to the nature of free and open-source software. Other commercial CAS such as *Mathematica* and *Maple* might be better since the companies that release them possess an army of paid personnel working around the clock to improve the software. Nevertheless, we are not without hope since *wxMaxima* is updated frequently, bugs are fixed, and documentation is improved by a group of volunteer developers who work tirelessly.

4. Conclusions

In this article, we considered several features of *wxMaxima* that could be useful for enhancing the quality of Calculus teaching and learning. Although the CAS itself is far from perfect, focusing on its strengths might benefit both students and instructors when embedding the software into the subject. We included some examples where *wxMaxima* assists well in understanding Calculus concepts better. These include calculating limit, finding a derivative of a function, evaluating definite and indefinite integrals, generating plots for explicit functions, parametric functions, polar curves, and three-dimensional objects. The visualization aspect enhances excellent teaching.

For teachers and instructors who are currently adopting *Maple* or *Mathematica* in their teaching, we are interested in stimulating a discussion on whether it is viable to integrate, or even switch entirely, to *wxMaxima*. This endeavor is not beyond our reach, at least for a sequence of Calculus courses (PreCalculus, SVC, and MVC).

For Linear Algebra, *Matlab* is still the most popular software among both engineers and educators thanks to its many professional contributors, rigorous development, powerful numerical computation, and additional package *Simulink*. *SageMath* is also becoming popular for Linear Algebra teaching and learning since it utilizes existing open-source libraries specifically designed for Linear Algebra, including *LAPack* and *NumPy*. Since *wxMaxima* also possesses many functions for manipulating matrices, we would not be too ambitious to persuade educational practitioners by considering to switch CAS to *wxMaxima* for Linear Algebra teaching and learning. Some Linear Algebra problems are worth testing using *wxMaxima* nonetheless.

Despite the many admirable qualities of *wxMaxima*, our experience in other courses and with different CAS suggests that some students hate when instructors generally attempt to embed any CAS in general into mathematics teaching and learning. For example, after implementing Calculus with *SageMath* in 2012, some students provided feedback suggesting to eliminate *SageMath* from Calculus teaching. For Linear Algebra, a dedicated one-hour problem-solving session using *Matlab* was not favored among the students. Students' feedback on teaching evaluation consistently mentions that the computer laboratory sessions are a waste of time and must be replaced by the traditional problem-solving sessions using pen and paper.

From our experience of embedding *wxMaxima* into Calculus courses, both Single-Variable and Multivariable, very few students gave positive feedback regarding the software. The majority of students' comments voice an atmosphere of negativity and resistance, they tend to push away *wxMaxima*. Even if they seem to embrace the CAS favorably, they might forget it as soon as the semester is over. In subsequent courses, their instructors might not use *wxMaxima* anymore. There are other important programming languages (e.g., *Python*, *C++*, and *Java*) that students could master before they enter the job market.

Author Contributions: Conceptualization, N.K.; methodology, N.K.; software, H.S.H.; validation, N.K. and H.S.H.; formal analysis, N.K.; investigation, N.K.; resources, N.K.; data curation, N.K.; writing—original draft preparation, N.K.; writing—review and editing, N.K.; visualization, N.K.; supervision, N.K.; project administration, N.K.; funding acquisition, N.K. All authors have read and agreed to the published version of the manuscript.

Funding: This research received no external funding.

Institutional Review Board Statement: Not applicable.

Informed Consent Statement: Not applicable.

Data Availability Statement: Not applicable.

Acknowledgments: The authors gratefully acknowledge Boris Gärtner from Munich, Germany for the fruitful discussion on the limitations of *wxMaxima* and for providing references to the relevant literature, particularly [26,31–34].

Conflicts of Interest: The authors declare no conflict of interest.

Dedication

The main author would like to dedicate this article to the memory of his late father Zakaria Karjanto (Khouw Kim Soey, 許金瑞) who not only taught him the alphabet, numbers, and the calendar in his early childhood, but also cultivated the value of hard work, diligence, discipline, perseverance, persistence, and grit. Karjanto Senior was born in Tasikmalaya, West Java, Japanese-occupied Dutch East Indies on 1 January 1944 (Saturday Pahing) and died in Bandung, West Java, Indonesia on 18 April 2021 (Sunday Wage).

Appendix A. Evaluating a Definite Integral without CAS

The definite integral involving trigonometric functions considered in Example 6 can be evaluated without the aid of any CAS. We have the following lemma:

Lemma A1. *For a continuous and rational function* $f(x) \in \mathbb{Q}(x)$

$$\int_0^\pi x f(\sin x)\, dx = \frac{\pi}{2} \int_0^\pi f(\sin x)\, dx.$$

Proof. Let $u = \pi - x$, then $du = -dx$, for $x = 0$, $u = \pi$ and $x = \pi$, $u = 0$. We have

$$\int_0^\pi x f(\sin x)\, dx = \int_\pi^0 (\pi - u) f(\sin(\pi - u))\, (-du) = -\pi \int_\pi^0 f(\sin u)\, du + \int_\pi^0 u f(\sin u)\, du$$

$$= \pi \int_0^\pi f(\sin x)\, dx - \int_0^\pi x f(\sin x)\, dx$$

$$2 \int_0^\pi x f(\sin x)\, dx = \pi \int_0^\pi f(\sin x)\, dx$$

$$\int_0^\pi x f(\sin x)\, dx = \frac{\pi}{2} \int_0^\pi f(\sin x)\, dx.$$

The proof is complete. □

We now have the following proposition.

Proposition A1.
$$\int_0^\pi \frac{x \sin x}{1 + \cos^2 x} dx = \frac{\pi^2}{4}.$$

Proof. There are at least three approaches with subtle differences in tackling this problem. The first method is by taking $f(x) = x/(2 - x^2)$ and applying Lemma A1. We then obtain

$$\int_0^\pi x f(\sin x) dx = \int_0^\pi \frac{x \sin x}{2 - \sin^2 x} dx = \int_0^\pi \frac{x \sin x}{1 + \cos^2 x} dx = \frac{\pi}{2} \int_0^\pi \frac{\sin x}{1 + \cos^2 x} dx$$
$$= -\frac{\pi}{2} \int_0^\pi \frac{d(\cos x)}{1 + \cos^2 x} dx = -\frac{\pi}{2} \tan^{-1}(\cos x)\Big|_0^\pi = -\frac{\pi}{2}\left(\tan^{-1}(-1) - \tan^{-1} 1\right) = \frac{\pi^2}{4}.$$

The second technique is by writing $x = \left(x - \frac{\pi}{2}\right) + \frac{\pi}{2}$ and substituting $u = x - \frac{\pi}{2}$. It becomes

$$\int_0^\pi \frac{x \sin x}{1 + \cos^2 x} dx = \int_{-\frac{\pi}{2}}^{\frac{\pi}{2}} \frac{u \cos u}{1 + \sin^2 u} du + \frac{\pi}{2} \int_0^\pi \frac{\sin x}{1 + \cos^2 x} dx.$$

The first integral of the right-hand side vanishes since the integrand is an odd function. The second integral follows the first method. The third approach is by substituting $u = x - \frac{\pi}{2}$ directly from the beginning. It yields a slightly different expression from the previous two approaches for the second term of the right-hand side:

$$\int_0^\pi \frac{x \sin x}{1 + \cos^2 x} dx = \int_{-\frac{\pi}{2}}^{\frac{\pi}{2}} \frac{u \cos u}{1 + \sin^2 u} du + \frac{\pi}{2} \int_{-\frac{\pi}{2}}^{\frac{\pi}{2}} \frac{\cos u}{1 + \sin^2 u} du.$$

Similar to the second technique, the first integral on the right-hand side is zero. Since the integrand of the second integral on the right-hand side is an even function, it simplifies to twice of the integral from $u = 0$ to $u = \frac{\pi}{2}$. Employing another substitution $y = \sin u$, we obtain the desired result:

$$\int_0^\pi \frac{x \sin x}{1 + \cos^2 x} dx = \pi \int_0^{\frac{\pi}{2}} \frac{d(\sin u)}{1 + \sin^2 u} = \pi \tan^{-1}(\sin u)\Big|_0^{\frac{\pi}{2}} = \pi(\tan^{-1} - 0) = \frac{\pi^2}{4}.$$

The proof is completed. □

Appendix B. CAS Output Comparison

Appendix B.1. Bronstein's Definite Integral of a Rational Function

Before verifying that all outputs in Example 8 have the same value, we need the following identity.

Lemma A2. *For all $x \in \mathbb{R} \setminus \{0\}$*

$$\arctan x + \arctan\left(\frac{1}{x}\right) = \begin{cases} \frac{\pi}{2}, & \text{if } x > 0 \\ -\frac{\pi}{2}, & \text{if } x < 0. \end{cases}$$

Proof. For all $x \in \mathbb{R} \setminus \{0\}$, let

$$f(x) = \arctan x + \arctan\left(\frac{1}{x}\right).$$

Then, f is differentiable for every $x \neq 0$ and

$$f'(x) = \frac{1}{1 + x^2} + \frac{\left(-\frac{1}{x^2}\right)}{1 + \frac{1}{x^2}} = 0.$$

Hence, f is constant on each connected component of all $x \in \mathbb{R} \setminus \{0\}$. Since $f(1) = \frac{\pi}{4} + \frac{\pi}{4} = \frac{\pi}{2}$, we conclude that $f(x) = \frac{\pi}{2}$ for all $x > 0$. And since $f(-1) = -f(1) = -\frac{\pi}{2}$, it follows that $f(x) = -\frac{\pi}{2}$ for all $x < 0$. We have completed the proof. □

Proposition A2. *All outputs in Example 8 are equivalent.*

Proof. To show that all outputs are equivalent, we use the identity $\arctan(2) + \arctan\left(\frac{1}{2}\right) = \frac{\pi}{2}$ from Lemma A2. Hence, for *Mathematica* output, we only need to verify that $\arctan(8) + \arctan(5) = \frac{5}{4}\pi - \arctan(2)$. The left-hand side can be calculated as follows:

$$\arctan(8) + \arctan(5) = \arctan\left(\frac{8+5}{1-8(5)}\right) = \arctan\left(\frac{13}{-39}\right) = \arctan\left(-\frac{1}{3}\right) \bmod \pi.$$

Applying again a similar identity from Lemma A2 for $x = -3 < 0$, $\arctan\left(-\frac{1}{3}\right) = \arctan(3) - \frac{\pi}{2}$, we only need to show that

$$\arctan(3) + \arctan(2) = \frac{5}{4}\pi + \frac{\pi}{2} = \frac{7}{4}\pi.$$

The left-hand side is calculated as previously:

$$\arctan(3) + \arctan(2) = \arctan\left(\frac{3+2}{1-3(2)}\right) = \arctan\left(\frac{5}{-5}\right) = \arctan(-1) \bmod \pi = \frac{7}{4}\pi.$$

For *Matlab* output, we need to show that $\arctan(8) + \arctan(5) = \pi - \arctan\left(\frac{1}{3}\right)$. Using the identity from Lemma A2 that $\arctan(3) + \arctan\left(\frac{1}{3}\right) = \frac{\pi}{2}$, the right-hand side becomes $\frac{\pi}{2} + \arctan(3)$. Combining term arctan 3 with one term on the left-hand side, we obtain either

$$\arctan(5) + \arctan(8) - \arctan(3) = \arctan(5) + \arctan\left(\frac{8-3}{1+8(3)}\right)$$
$$= \arctan(5) + \arctan\left(\frac{1}{5}\right) \bmod \pi = \frac{\pi}{2} \quad \text{or}$$

$$\arctan(8) + \arctan(5) - \arctan(3) = \arctan(8) + \arctan\left(\frac{5-3}{1+5(3)}\right)$$
$$= \arctan(8) + \arctan\left(\frac{1}{8}\right) \bmod \pi = \frac{\pi}{2}.$$

Both identities are correct when we take zero remainder in the congruence relationship. This completes the proof. □

Appendix B.2. Adamchik's Definite Integral of a Rational Function

The results from Adamchik's definite integral of a rational function are verified by the following lemma.

Lemma A3. *All outputs in Example 9 are identical.*

Proof. We show that all exact values are identical. In each case, we take the zero remainder whenever the congruence relationship appears. First, we verify that the *Axiom*/*Maple*'s and *Matlab*'s results are identical, i.e.,

$$\frac{5}{4}\pi - \arctan\left(\frac{75}{11}\right) = \frac{\pi}{4} + \arctan(3) - \arctan\left(\frac{5}{3}\right) + \arctan\left(\frac{41}{3}\right)$$

$$\pi - \arctan\left(\frac{75}{11}\right) = \arctan\left(\frac{2}{9}\right) \bmod \pi + \arctan\left(\frac{41}{3}\right)$$

$$= \arctan\left(\frac{2}{9}\right) + \frac{\pi}{2} - \arctan\left(\frac{3}{41}\right) \quad \text{(by Lemma A2)}$$

$$= \frac{\pi}{2} + \arctan\left(\frac{2/9 - 3/41}{1 + (2/9)(3/41)}\right) \bmod \pi$$

$$\frac{\pi}{2} = \arctan\left(\frac{75}{11}\right) + \arctan\left(\frac{11}{75}\right).$$

Second, we show that the *Matlab*'s and *Mathematica* results are identical, i.e.,

$$\frac{5}{4}\pi - \arctan\left(\frac{75}{11}\right) = \pi - \arctan\left(\frac{1}{4}\right) - \arctan\left(\frac{5}{12}\right).$$

Bringing π to the left-hand side and gathering all inverse tangent terms to the right-hand side, we obtain

$$\frac{\pi}{4} = \arctan\left(\frac{75}{11}\right) - \arctan\left(\frac{1/4 + 5/12}{1 - (1/4)(5/12)}\right) \bmod \pi$$

$$= \arctan\left(\frac{75}{11}\right) - \arctan\left(\frac{32}{48}\right) \bmod \pi = \arctan\left(\frac{75/11 - 32/43}{1 + (75/11)(32/43)}\right) \bmod \pi$$

$$= \arctan 1.$$

Finally, we confirm that the *Axiom*/*Maple*'s and *Mathematica*'s results are identical, i.e.,

$$\pi - \arctan\left(\frac{1}{4}\right) - \arctan\left(\frac{5}{12}\right) = \frac{\pi}{4} + \arctan(3) - \arctan\left(\frac{5}{3}\right) + \arctan\left(\frac{41}{3}\right)$$

$$\frac{3}{4}\pi - \arctan\left(\frac{32}{43}\right) \bmod \pi = \arctan\left(\frac{2}{9}\right) \bmod \pi + \arctan\left(\frac{41}{3}\right)$$

$$\frac{3}{4}\pi = \frac{\pi}{2} - \arctan\left(\frac{43}{32}\right) + \arctan\left(\frac{2}{9}\right) + \arctan\left(\frac{41}{3}\right) \quad \text{(by Lemma A2)}$$

$$\frac{\pi}{4} = \arctan\left(\frac{2}{9}\right) + \arctan\left(\frac{41/3 - 43/32}{1 + (41/3)(43/32)}\right) \bmod \pi$$

$$\frac{\pi}{4} = \arctan\left(\frac{2}{9}\right) + \arctan\left(\frac{7}{11}\right) = \arctan 1.$$

The proof is complete. □

References

1. *Maxima* Website Page. Available online: https://maxima.sourceforge.io/ (accessed on 7 June 2021).
2. *SourceForge* Website Page Hosting *Maxima* Executable File for *Windows*. Available online: http://sourceforge.net/projects/maxima/files/Maxima-Windows/ (accessed on 7 June 2021).
3. Ayub, M.; Fauzi, A.; Ahmad Tarmizi, R.; Abu Bakar, K.; Wong, S.L. Adoption of Wxmaxima software in the classroom: Effect on students' motivation and learning of mathematics. *Malays. J. Math. Sci.* **2014**, *8*, 311–323.
4. García, A.; García, F.; Rodríguez, G.; de la Villa, A. Could it be possible to replace DERIVE with MAXIMA? *Int. J. Technol. Math. Educ.* **2011**, *18*, 137–142.
5. Díaz, A.; García, A.; de la Villa, A. An example of learning based on competences: Use of Maxima in Linear Algebra for Engineers. *Int. J. Technol. Math. Educ.* **2011**, *18*, 177–181.
6. Fedriani, E.M.; Moyano, R. Using Maxima in the Mathematics Classroom. *Int. J. Technol. Math. Educ.* **2011**, *18*, 171–176.
7. Velychko, V. Y.; Stopkin, A.V.; Fedorenko, O.H. Use of computer algebra system Maxima in the process of teaching future mathematics teachers. *Inf. Technol. Learn. Tools* **2019**, *69*, 112–123. [CrossRef]
8. Dehl, M. Exploring Advanced Math with Maxima. *Linux J.* **2009**. Available online: http://www.linuxjournal.com/content/exploring-advanced-math-maxima (accessed on 7 June 2021).
9. Žáková, K. Maxima–An open alternative for engineering education. In Proceedings of the Global Engineering Education Conference (EDUCON), Amman, Jordan, 4–6 April 2011; pp. 1022–1025.
10. Hannan, Z. *wxMaxima for Calculus I. wxMaxima for Calculus II*; Solano Community College: Fairfield, CA, USA, 2015. Available online: https://wxmaximafor.wordpress.com/ (accessed on 7 June 2021).
11. Timberlake, T.K.; Mixon, J.W. *Classical Mechanics with Maxima*; Springer: New York, NY, USA, 2016.
12. Senese, F. *Symbolic Mathematics for Chemists: A Guide for Maxima Users*; John Wiley & Sons: Hoboken, NJ, USA, 2019.
13. Woollett, E.L. *Maxima by Example*; California State University: Long Beach, CA, USA, 2020. Available online: https://web.csulb.edu/~woollett/mbe.html (accessed on 7 June 2021).
14. Puentedura, R.R. *Symbolic Math–A Workflow*; Hippasus: Williamstown, MA, USA, 2020. Available online: http://www.hippasus.com/resources/symmath/index.html (accessed on 7 June 2021).
15. Karjanto, N.; Husain, H.S. Adopting *Maxima* as an open-source Computer Algebra System into mathematics teaching and learning. In *Proceedings of the 13th International Congress on Mathematical Education*; Kaiser, G., Ed.; Springer: Cham, Switzerland, 2017; pp. 733–734.
16. Starostin, E.L.; Van Der Heijden, G.H.M. The shape of a Möbius strip. *Nat. Mater.* **2007**, *6*, 563–567. [CrossRef] [PubMed]
17. Chang, C.W.; Liu, M.; Nam, S.; Zhang, S.; Liu, Y.; Bartal, G.; Zhang, X. Optical Möbius symmetry in metamaterials. *Phys. Rev. Lett.* **2010**, *105*, 235501. [CrossRef] [PubMed]
18. Nie, Z.Z.; Zuo, B.; Wang, M.; Huang, S.; Chen, X.M.; Liu, Z.Y.; Yang, H. Light-driven continuous rotating Möbius strip actuators. *Nat. Commun.* **2021**, *12*, 1–10. [CrossRef] [PubMed]
19. Han, Y.; He, A.L.; Chen, H.J.; Liu, S.Y.; Lin, Z.F. Photonic states on Möbius band. *J. Opt.* **2020**, *22*, 035103. [CrossRef]
20. Ahmadiv, A.; Gerislioglu, B.; Ahuja, R.; Mishra, Y.K. Toroidal metaphotonics and metadevices. *Laser Photonics Rev.* **2020**, *14*, 1900326. [CrossRef]
21. Kaelberer, T.; Fedotov, V.A.; Papasimakis, N.; Tsai, D.P.; Zheludev, N.I. Toroidal dipolar response in a metamaterial. *Science* **2010**, *330*, 1510–1512. [CrossRef] [PubMed]
22. Kliem, B.; Török, T. Torus instability. *Phys. Rev. Lett.* **2006**, *96*, 255002. [CrossRef] [PubMed]
23. Pochan, D.J.; Chen, Z.; Cui, H.; Hales, K.; Qi, K.; Wooley, K.L. Toroidal triblock copolymer assemblies. *Science* **2004**, *306*, 94–97. [CrossRef]
24. Glasner, M.A. *Maxima Guide for Calculus Students*; Pennsylvania State University: University Park, PA, USA, 2004. Available online: http://michel.gosse.free.fr/documentation/fichiers/maxima_sg.pdf (accessed on 7 June 2021).
25. Gärtner, B. *The Computer Algebra Program Maxima–A Tutorial*; Bildungsgüter: München, Germany, 2005. Available online: http://www.bildungsgueter.de/MaximaEN/Contents.htm (accessed on 7 June 2021).
26. Moses, J. Symbolic integration: The Stormy Decade. *Commun. Acm* **1971**, *14*, 548–560. [CrossRef]
27. Subramaniam, T.N.; Malm, D.E. How to integrate rational functions. *Am. Math. Mon.* **1992**, *99*, 762–772. [CrossRef]
28. Bostan, A.; Chen, S.; Chyzak, F.; Li, Z.; Xin, G. Hermite reduction and creative telescoping for hyperexponential functions. In Proceedings of the 38th International Symposium on Symbolic and Algebraic Computation, Boston, MA, USA, 26–29 June 2013; pp. 77–84.
29. Bostan, A.; Chyzak, F.; Lairez, P.; Salvy, B. Generalized Hermite reduction, creative telescoping and definite integration of D-finite functions. In Proceedings of the 2018 ACM International Symposium on Symbolic and Algebraic Computation, New York, NY, USA, 16–19 July 2018; pp. 95–102.
30. Moir, R.H.; Corless, R.M.; Maza, M.M.; Xie, N. Symbolic-numeric integration of rational functions. *Numer. Algorithms* **2020**, *83*, 1295–1320. [CrossRef]
31. Bronstein, M. *Symbolic Integration I: Transcendental Functions*, 2nd ed; Springer: Berlin/Heidelberg, Germany, 2005
32. Adamchik, V.S. *Definite Integration in Mathematica V3.0.*; Preprint; Carnegie Melon University: Pittsburgh, PA, USA, 2008; p. 18. Available online: https://kilthub.cmu.edu/articles/journal_contribution/Definite_Integration_in_Mathematica_V3_0/6604700 (accessed on 7 June 2021). [CrossRef]

33. Tobey, R.G. Algorithms for Antidifferentiation of Rational Functions. Ph.D. Thesis, Harvard University, Boston, MA, USA, 1967.
34. Geddes, K.O.; Czapor, S.R.; Labahn, G. *Algorithms for Computer Algebra*; Kluwer Academic Publishers: Boston, MA, USA; Dordrecht, The Netherlands; London, UK, 1992
35. Weigand, H.G. What is or what might be the benefit of using Computer Algebra Systems in the learning and teaching of Calculus? In *Innovation and Technology Enhancing Mathematics Education*; Faggiano, E., Ferrara, F., Montone, A., Eds.; Springer: Cham, Switzerland, 2017; pp. 161–193.
36. Karjanto, N.; Simon, L. English-medium instruction Calculus in Confucian-Heritage Culture: Flipping the class or overriding the culture? *Stud. Educ. Eval.* **2019**, *63*, 122–135. [CrossRef]
37. Stewart, J. *Calculus: Early Transcendentals for Scientists and Engineers*, Metric Edition; Cengage Learning: Singapore, 2017.

Article

Knowledge Dynamics and Behavioural Equivalences in Multi-Agent Systems

Bogdan Aman [1,2] and Gabriel Ciobanu [2,*]

[1] Institute of Computer Science, Romanian Academy, 700505 Iaşi, Romania; bogdan.aman@iit.academiaromana-is.ro
[2] Faculty of Computer Science, Alexandru Ioan Cuza University, 700506 Iaşi, Romania
* Correspondence: gabriel@info.uaic.ro

Abstract: We define a process calculus to describe multi-agent systems with timeouts for communication and mobility able to handle knowledge. The knowledge of an agent is represented as sets of trees whose nodes carry information; it is used to decide the interactions with other agents. The evolution of the system with exchanges of knowledge between agents is presented by the operational semantics, capturing the concurrent executions by a multiset of actions in a labelled transition system. Several results concerning the relationship between the agents and their knowledge are presented. We introduce and study some specific behavioural equivalences in multi-agent systems, including a knowledge equivalence able to distinguish two systems based on the interaction of the agents with their local knowledge.

Keywords: mobile agents; timeouts; knowledge as set of trees; behavioural equivalences

1. Introduction

Process calculi are used to describe concurrent systems, providing a high-level description of interactions, communications and synchronizations between independent processes or agents. The main features of a process calculus are: (i) interactions between agents/processes are by communication (message-passing), rather than modifying shared variables; (ii) large systems are described in a compositional way by using a small number of primitives and operators; (iii) processes can be manipulated by using equational reasoning and behavioural equivalences. The key primitive distinguishing the process calculi from other models of computation is the parallel composition. The compositionality offered by the parallel composition can help to describe large systems in a modular way, and to better organize their knowledge (for reasoning about them).

In this paper we define an extension of the process calculus TIMO [1] in order to model multi-agent systems and their knowledge. In this framework, the agents can move between locations and exchange information, having explicit timeouts for both migration and communication. Additionally, they have a knowledge of the network used to decide the next interactions with other agents. The knowledge of the agents is inspired by a model of semi-structured data [2] in which it is given by sets of unordered trees containing pairs of labels and values in each node. In our approach, the knowledge is described via sets of trees used to exchange information among agents about migration and communication. Overall, we present a formal way to describe the behaviour of mobile communicating agents and networks of agents in a compositional manner.

A network of mobile agents is a distributed environment composed of locations where several agents act in parallel. Each agent is represented by a process together with its knowledge that is used to decide interactions with other agents. Taking the advantage that there already exists a theory of parallel and concurrent systems, we define a prototyping language for multi-agent systems presented as a process calculus in concurrency theory. Its

semantics is given formally by a labelled transition system; in this way we describe the behaviour of the entire network, and prove some useful properties.

In concurrency, the behavioural equality of two systems is captured by using bisimulations. Bisimulations are important contributions to computer science that appeared as refinements of 'structure-preserving' mappings (morphisms) in mathematics; they can be applied to new fields of study, including multi-agent systems. Bisimilarity is the finest behavioural equivalence; it abstracts from certain details of the systems, focusing only on the studied aspects. The equivalence relations should be compositional such that if two systems are equivalent, then the systems obtained by their compositions with a third system should also be equivalent. This compositional reasoning allows for the development of complex systems in which each component can be replaced by an equivalent one. Furthermore, there exist efficient algorithms for bisimilarity checking and compositionality properties of bisimilarity, algorithms that are usually used to minimize the state-space of systems. These are good reasons why we consider that it is important to define and study some specific behavioural equivalences for multi-agent systems enhanced with a knowledge of the network for deciding the next interactions. To be more realistic, we consider systems of agents with timing constraints on migration and communication. Therefore, a notable advantage of using our framework to model systems of mobile agents is the possibility to naturally express compositionality, mobility, local communication, timeouts, knowledge, and equivalences between systems in a given interval of time (up to a timeout).

The paper is structured as follows: Section 2 presents the syntax and semantics of the new process calculus knowTiMo and provides some results regarding the timing and knowledge aspects of the evolution. In Section 3 we define and study various bisimulations for the multi-agent systems described in knowTiMo . The conclusion, related work and references end the article.

2. The New Process Calculus knowTiMo

In order to model the evolution of multi-agent systems handling knowledge, timed communication and timed migration, we define a process calculus named knowTiMo , where know stands for 'knowledge' and TiMo stands for the family of calculi introduced in [1] and developed in several articles.

In Table 1 we present the syntax of knowTiMo, where:
- $Loc = \{l, l' \ldots\}$ is a set of distributed locations or location variables, $Chan=\{a, b, \ldots\}$ is a set of channels used for communication among agents, $Id= \{id, \ldots\}$ is a set of names used to denote recursive processes, and $\mathcal{N} = \{N, N', \ldots\}$ is a set of networks;
- a unique process definition $id(u_1, \ldots, u_{m_{id}}) \stackrel{def}{=} P_{id}$ is available for all $id \in Id$;
- timeouts of actions are denoted by $t \in \mathbb{N}$; thresholds appearing in tests are denoted by $k \in \mathbb{Z}$; variables are denoted by u; expressions (over values, variables and allowed operations) are denoted by v; fields are denoted by f; path of fields are denoted by p and are used to retrieve/update the value of the fields. Also, if $Q \in Id$ and $Q(u)$ is a process definition, then for $v_1 \neq v_2$ we obtain two different process instances $Q(v_1)$ and $Q(v_2)$.

An agent A is a pair $P \triangleright K$, where A behaves as prescribed by P and K is the knowledge used by process P during its execution. An agent $A = \text{go}^t\, l$ then $P \triangleright K$ is ready to migrate from its current location to the location l by consuming the action $\text{go}^t\, l$ of agent A. In go^t, the timer t indicates the fact that agent A is unavailable for t units of time at the current location; then, once the timer t expires, $\text{go}^t\, l$ then P executes process P at the new location l. Since l can be a location variable, it may be instantiated after communication between agents. The use of location variables allows agents to adapt their behaviours based on the interactions among agents.

An agent $A = a^{\Delta t}!\langle v \rangle$ then P else $Q \triangleright K$ is available for up-to t units of time to communicate on channel a the value v to another agent $A' = a^{\Delta t'}?(u)$ then P' else $Q' \triangleright K'$ available for communication at the same location and awaiting for a value on the same communication channel a. In order to simplify the presentation in this paper, we consider a synchronous calculus; this means that when a communication takes place, the message sent by one process is instantly received by the other process. If the communication happens, then agent A executes process P, while agent A' executes process P' by making use of the received value v. If the timers t and t' of the agents A and A' expire, then they execute processes Q and Q', respectively.

Table 1. Syntax of our Multi-Agent Systems.

Processes	P, Q	::=	$go^t\ l$ then P	(move)
		|	$a^{\Delta t}!\langle v \rangle$ then P else Q	(output)
		|	$a^{\Delta t}?(u)$ then P else Q	(input)
		|	if $test$ then P else Q	(branch)
		|	0	(termination)
		|	$id(v)$	(recursion)
		|	$create(\langle f \mid v; \varnothing \rangle)$ then P	(create)
		|	$update(p/f, v)$ then P	(update)
Knowledge	K	::=	$\varnothing$	(empty)
		|	$\langle f \mid \varepsilon; K \rangle \mid \langle f \mid v; K \rangle$	(tree)
		|	$K\ K$	(set)
Paths	p, p'	::=	$/f \mid p\ p' \mid p[test(p)] \mid p[test(p/f)]$	
Tests	$test(p)$	::=	$true \mid \neg test(p) \mid K(p) > k \mid K(p) = v \mid$	
			...	
	$test$	::=	$test(p) \wedge test(p') \mid \neg test$	
Agents	A, B	::=	$P \triangleright K$	
Set of Agents	$\tilde{A}$	::=	$0 \mid \tilde{A} \parallel A$	
Networks	N	::=	$l[[\tilde{A}]] \mid N \mid N$	

An agent $A =$ if $test$ then P else $Q \triangleright K$ uses its knowledge K to check the truth value of the $test$. If the value is $true$, then agent A executes process P, while if the value is $false$, then agent A executes process Q.

The agent $A = create(\langle f \mid v; \varnothing \rangle)$ then $P \triangleright K$ extends its knowledge K by adding the new piece of knowledge $\langle f \mid v; \varnothing \rangle$ in parallel with K, and then executes process P. The agent $A = update(p/f, v)$ then $P \triangleright K$ updates its knowledge K by adding the value v into the field identified by f reached following path p/f, and then executes process P; if the field f does not exist, then the field is created and the value v is assigned to it. The agent $A = 0 \triangleright K$ has no actions to execute, and its evolution terminates.

The knowledge K of an agent A is used either for storing information needed for communication with other agents or for deciding what process to execute. We define the knowledge as sets of trees in which the nodes carrying the information are of two types: $\langle f \mid \varepsilon; K' \rangle$ and $\langle f \mid v; K' \rangle$. Both types of nodes contain a field f and a knowledge K'; they differ only in the value stored in the field f, which can be either the symbol ε indicating the empty value, or a non-empty value v. An agent $A = P \triangleright K$ can use the information stored in its knowledge K to perform tests. For example, a test $K(p/f) > k$ is $true$ only if, following a path p in knowledge K, the value stored in the field f is greater than k (otherwise, it is evaluated to $false$); a path is used to select a node in knowledge K. Predicates, always embedded in square brackets and attached to fields in a path, are used to analyze either the value of the current node by using $p[test(p)]$ or the values of the inner nodes by using $p[test(p/f)]$. We say that a knowledge K is included in another knowledge K' (denoted $K \subseteq K'$) if for all paths p appearing in K it holds that $K(p) = K'(p)$.

In Table 1 there exist only one possibility to bind variables; namely, the variable u of the process $a^{\Delta t}?(u)$ then P else Q is bound within process P, while it is not bound within process Q. We denote by $fv(P)$ and $fv(N)$ the sets of free variables appearing in process P and network N, respectively. Moreover, we impose that $fv(P_{id}) \subseteq \{u_1, \ldots, u_{m_{id}}\}$, where $id(u_1, \ldots, u_{m_{id}}) \stackrel{def}{=} P_{id}$. We denote by $\{v/u\}P$ the process P having all the free occurrences of the variable u replaced by value v, possibly after using α-conversion to avoid name clashes in process P.

A network is composed of distributed locations, where $l[[\tilde{A}]]$ denotes a location l containing a set $\tilde{A}$ of agents, while $l[[0]]$ denotes a location without any agents. Over the set $\mathcal{N}$ of networks we define the structural equivalence $\equiv$ as the smallest congruence satisfying the equalities:

$$l[[\tilde{A} \parallel 0]] \equiv l[[\tilde{A}]] \, , \, l[[\tilde{A}]] \mid l[[\tilde{B}]] \equiv l[[\tilde{A} \parallel \tilde{B}]] \, ,$$
$$N \equiv N \, , \, N \mid N' \equiv N' \mid N \, , \, (N \mid N') \mid N'' \equiv N \mid (N' \mid N'') \, .$$

The structural congruence $\equiv$ is needed when using the *operational semantics* presented in Tables 2 and 3 for either executing actions or indicating time passing. In Table 2 the relation $N \xrightarrow{\Lambda} N'$ denotes the transformation of a network N into a network N' by executing the actions from the multiset of actions Λ; if the multiset of actions Λ contains only a single action λ, namely $\Lambda = \{\lambda\}$, then we use $N \xrightarrow{\lambda} N'$ instead of $N \xrightarrow{\{\lambda\}} N'$.

The operational semantics of knowTIMO is presented in Table 2.

Table 2. Operational Semantics for our Multi-Agent Systems

(STOP)	$l[[0]] \not\rightarrow$
(COM)	$l[[a^{\Delta t_1}!\langle v\rangle \text{ then } P_1 \text{ else } Q_1 \rhd K_1 \parallel a^{\Delta t_2}?(u) \text{ then } P_2 \text{ else } Q_2 \rhd K_2 \parallel \tilde{A}]] \xrightarrow{a!?@l} l[[P_1 \rhd K_1 \parallel \{v/u\}P_2 \rhd K_2 \parallel \tilde{A}]]$
(PUT0)	$l[[a^{\Delta 0}!\langle v\rangle \text{ then } P \text{ else } Q \rhd K \parallel \tilde{A}]] \xrightarrow{a!^{\Delta 0}@l} l[[Q \rhd K \parallel \tilde{A}]]$
(GET0)	$l[[a^{\Delta 0}?(u) \text{ then } P \text{ else } Q \rhd K \parallel \tilde{A}]] \xrightarrow{a?^{\Delta 0}@l} l[[Q \rhd K \parallel \tilde{A}]]$
(MOVE0)	$l[[\text{go}^0 \, l' \text{ then } P \rhd K \parallel \tilde{A}]] \mid l'[[\tilde{B}]] \xrightarrow{\rhd l'} l[[\tilde{A}]] \mid l'[[P \rhd K \parallel \tilde{B}]]$
(IFT)	$\dfrac{test@K = true}{l[[\text{if } test \text{ then } P \text{ else } Q \rhd K \parallel \tilde{A}]] \xrightarrow{true@l} l[[P \rhd K \parallel \tilde{A}]]}$
(IFF)	$\dfrac{test@K = false}{l[[\text{if } test \text{ then } P \text{ else } Q \rhd K \parallel \tilde{A}]] \xrightarrow{false@l} l[[Q \rhd K \parallel \tilde{A}]]}$
(CREATE)	$l[[\text{create}(\langle f \mid v; \varnothing\rangle) \text{ then } P \rhd K \parallel \tilde{A}]] \xrightarrow{create_f@l} l[[P \rhd K \, \langle f \mid v; \varnothing\rangle \parallel \tilde{A}]]$
(UPDATE)	$\dfrac{\exists p/f = /f' \ldots /f \quad K = \langle f' \mid v'; \ldots \langle f \mid v''; K_1\rangle K_2\rangle K_3 \quad K' = \langle f' \mid v'; \ldots \langle f \mid v; K_1\rangle K_2\rangle K_3}{l[[\text{update}(p/f, v) \text{ then } P \rhd K \parallel \tilde{A}]] \xrightarrow{upd_p@l} l[[P \rhd K' \parallel \tilde{A}]]}$
(EXTEND)	$\dfrac{\exists p = /f' \ldots /f'' \quad \nexists p/f \quad K = \langle f' \mid v'; \ldots \langle f'' \mid v''; K_1\rangle K_2\rangle K_3 \quad K' = \langle f' \mid v'; \ldots \langle f'' \mid v''; \langle f \mid v; \varnothing\rangle K_1\rangle K_2\rangle K_3}{l[[\text{update}(p/f, v) \text{ then } P \rhd K \parallel \tilde{A}]] \xrightarrow{upd_p@l} l[[P \rhd K' \parallel \tilde{A}]]}$
(CALL)	$l[[id(v) \rhd K \parallel \tilde{A}]] \xrightarrow{call@l} l[[\{v/u\}P_{id} \rhd K \parallel \tilde{A}]]$, where $id(u) \stackrel{def}{=} P_{id}$
(PAR)	$\dfrac{N_1 \xrightarrow{\Lambda_1} N'_1 \quad N_2 \xrightarrow{\Lambda_2} N'_2}{N_1 \mid N_2 \xrightarrow{\Lambda_1 \mid \Lambda_2} N'_1 \mid N'_2}$ (EQUIV) $\dfrac{N \equiv N' \quad N' \xrightarrow{\Lambda} N'' \quad N'' \equiv N'''}{N \xrightarrow{\Lambda} N'''}$

In rule (STOP), $l[[0]]$ denotes a network without agents, and thus $\not\rightarrow$ marks the fact that no action is available for execution. Rule (COM) is used if at location l two agents $A_1 = a^{\Delta t_1}!\langle v\rangle$ then P_1 else $Q_1 \rhd K_1$ and $A_2 = a^{\Delta t_2}?(u)$ then P_2 else $Q_2 \rhd K_2$ can communicate successfully over channel a. After communication, both agents remain at the current location l with their knowledge unchanged; agent A_1 executes P_1, while agent A_2 executes $\{v/u\}P_2$. The successful communication over channel a at location l is marked by label $a!?@l$.

Rules (PUT0) and (GET0) are used for an agent $A = a^{\Delta 0} * \text{ then } P \text{ else } Q \triangleright K$ (where $* \in \{!\langle v \rangle, ?(u)\}$) to remove action a when its timer expires. Afterwards, agent A is ready to execute Q. Knowledge K remains unchanged. Since rule (COM) can be applied even if t_1 and t_2 are zero, it follows that when a timer is 0, only one of the rules (COM), (PUT0) and (GET0) is chosen for application in a nondeterministic manner.

Rule (MOVE0) is used when at location l an agent $A = \text{go}^0 \, l' \text{ then } P \triangleright K$ migrates to location l' to execute process P. Rules (IFT) and (IFF) are used when an agent $A = \text{if } test \text{ then } P \text{ else } Q \triangleright K$ should decide what process to execute (P or Q) based on the Boolean value returned by $test@K$; this value is determined by performing the $test$ on the knowledge K of agent A. Notice that in order to perform a $test$, the agent A can only read its knowledge K.

Rule (CREATE) is used when an agent $A = create(\langle f \mid v; \varnothing \rangle) \text{ then } P \triangleright K$ extends its knowledge K with $\langle f \mid v; \varnothing \rangle$; afterwards, the agent A executes process P.

Rule (UPDATE) is used when an agent $A = update(p/f, v) \text{ then } P \triangleright K$ updates to v the value of $K(p/f)$ of the existing field f, while rule (EXTEND) is used when the agent $A = update(p/f, v) \text{ then } P \triangleright K$ expands (at the end of) an existing path p with a field f such that $K(p/f) = v$; afterwards the agent A executes process P.

Rule (CALL) is used when an agent $A = id(v) \triangleright K$ is ready to unfold the process $id(v)$ into $\{v/u\}P_{id}$. Rule (PAR) is used to put together the behaviour of smaller subnetworks. while rule (EQUIV) is used to apply the structures congruence over networks.

In Table 3 are presented the rules for describing time passing, while the knowledge of the involved agents remains unchanged. The relation $N \overset{t}{\leadsto} N'$ indicates the transformation of a network N into a network N' after t units of time.

Table 3. Operational Semantics of knowTiMo : Time Passing.

(DSTOP)	$l[[0]] \overset{t}{\leadsto} l[[0]]$
(DPUT)	$\dfrac{t \geq t' \geq 0}{l[[a^{\Delta t}!\langle v \rangle \text{ then } P \text{ else } Q \triangleright K]] \overset{t'}{\leadsto} l[[a^{\Delta t-t'}!\langle v \rangle \text{ then } P \text{ else } Q \triangleright K]]}$
(DGET)	$\dfrac{t \geq t' \geq 0}{l[[a^{\Delta t}?(u) \text{ then } P \text{ else } Q \triangleright K]] \overset{t'}{\leadsto} l[[a^{\Delta t-t'}?(u) \text{ then } P \text{ else } Q \triangleright K]]}$
(DMOVE)	$\dfrac{t \geq t' \geq 0}{l[[\text{go}^t \, l' \text{ then } P \triangleright K]] \overset{t'}{\leadsto} l[[\text{go}^{t-t'} \, l' \text{ then } P \triangleright K]]}$
(DPAR)	$\dfrac{N_1 \overset{t}{\leadsto} N_1' \quad N_2 \overset{t}{\leadsto} N_2' \quad N_1 \mid N_2 \not\rightarrow}{N_1 \mid N_2 \overset{t}{\leadsto} N_1' \mid N_2'}$
(DEQUIV)	$\dfrac{N \equiv N' \quad N' \overset{t}{\leadsto} N'' \quad N'' \equiv N'''}{N \overset{t}{\leadsto} N'''}$

In rule (STOP), $l[[0]]$ denotes a network without agents; the passing of time does not affect such a network. Rules (DPUT), (DGET) and (DMOVE) are used to decrease the timers of actions, while rules (DPAR) is used to put together the behaviour of composed networks. In rule (DPAR), $N_1 \mid N_2 \not\rightarrow$ denotes a network $N_1 \mid N_2$ that cannot execute any action; this is possible because the use of negative premises in our operational semantics does not lead to inconsistencies.

Given a finite multiset of actions $\Lambda = \{\lambda_1, \ldots, \lambda_k\}$ and a timeout t, a derivation $N \stackrel{\Lambda,t}{\Longrightarrow} N'$ captures a complete computational step of the form:
$$N \stackrel{\lambda_1}{\longrightarrow} N_1 \ldots N_{k-1} \stackrel{\lambda_k}{\longrightarrow} N_k \stackrel{t}{\rightsquigarrow} N'.$$

The fact that a knowTiMo network N is able to perform zero or more actions steps and a time step in order to reach a network N' is denoted by $N \Longrightarrow^* N'$. Notice that the consumed actions and elapsed time are not recorded. By $N \stackrel{\lambda}{\Longrightarrow}^* N'$ we denote the fact that there exist networks N_1 and N_2 such that $N \Longrightarrow^* N_1 \stackrel{\lambda}{\longrightarrow} N_2 \Longrightarrow^* N'$; in this way we emphasize only the consumed action λ out of all consumed actions.

In our setting, at most one time passing rule can be applied for any arbitrary given process. This is the reason why, by inverting a rule, we can describe how the time passes in the subprocesses of a process. This result is useful when reasoning by induction on the structure of processes for which time passes.

Proposition 1. *Assume $N \stackrel{t'}{\rightsquigarrow} N'$. Then exactly one of the following holds:*

- $N = l[[0]]$ and $N' = l[[0]]$;
- $N = l[[a^{\Delta t}!\langle v \rangle \text{ then } P \text{ else } Q \triangleright K]]$ and $N' = l[[a^{\Delta t - t'}!\langle v \rangle \text{ then } P \text{ else } Q \triangleright K]]$, where $t \geq t' \geq 0$;
- $N = l[[a^{\Delta t}?(u) \text{ then } P \text{ else } Q \triangleright K]]$ and $N' = l[[a^{\Delta t - t'}?(u) \text{ then } P \text{ else } Q \triangleright K]]$, where $t \geq t' \geq 0$;
- $N = l[[\text{go}^t \, l' \text{ then } P \triangleright K]]$ and $N' = l[[\text{go}^{t-t'} \, l' \text{ then } P \triangleright K]]$, where $t \geq t' \geq 0$;
- $N = N_1 \mid N_2$ such that $N_1 \mid N_2 \not\rightarrow$, and there exist N_1' and N_2' such that $N' = N_1' \mid N_2'$, $N_1 \stackrel{t'}{\rightsquigarrow} N_1'$ and $N_2 \stackrel{t'}{\rightsquigarrow} N_2'$.

Proof. Straightforward, by observing that the time passing rules in Table 3 can be deterministically inverted; namely, each network of Table 1 performing a time step can use at most one rule of Table 3. □

The following theorem claims that time passing does not introduce nondeterminism in the evolution of a network.

Theorem 1. *The next two statements hold for any three networks N, N' and N'':*

1. *if $N \stackrel{0}{\rightsquigarrow} N'$, then $N = N'$;*
2. *if $N \stackrel{t}{\rightsquigarrow} N'$ and $N \stackrel{t}{\rightsquigarrow} N''$, then $N' = N''$.*

Proof. 1. We proceed by induction on the structure of N.

- Case $N = l[[0]]$. Since $N \stackrel{0}{\rightsquigarrow} N'$, by using Proposition 1, it holds that $N' = l[[0]]$, meaning that $N = N'$ (as desired).
- Case $N = l[[a^{\Delta t}!\langle v \rangle \text{ then } P \text{ else } Q \triangleright K]]$. Since $N \stackrel{0}{\rightsquigarrow} N'$, by using Proposition 1, it holds that $N' = l[[a^{\Delta t - 0}!\langle v \rangle \text{ then } P \text{ else } Q \triangleright K]] = l[[a^{\Delta t}!\langle v \rangle \text{ then } P \text{ else } Q \triangleright K]]$, meaning that $N = N'$ (as desired).
- Case $N = l[[a^{\Delta t}?(u) \text{ then } P \text{ else } Q \triangleright K]]$. Since $N \stackrel{0}{\rightsquigarrow} N'$, by using Proposition 1, it holds that $N' = l[[a^{\Delta t - 0}?(u) \text{ then } P \text{ else } Q \triangleright K]] = l[[a^{\Delta t}?(u) \text{ then } P \text{ else } Q \triangleright K]]$, meaning that $N = N'$ (as desired).
- Case $N = l[[\text{go}^t \, l' \text{ then } P \triangleright K]]$. Since $N \stackrel{0}{\rightsquigarrow} N'$, by using Proposition 1, it holds that $N' = l[[\text{go}^{t-0} \, l' \text{ then } P \triangleright K]] = l[[\text{go}^t \, l' \text{ then } P \triangleright K]]$, meaning that $N = N'$ (as desired).
- Case $N = N_1 \mid N_2$. Since $N \stackrel{0}{\rightsquigarrow} N'$, by using Proposition 1, it holds that there exist N_1' and N_2' such that $N' = N_1' \mid N_2'$, together with $N_1 \stackrel{0}{\rightsquigarrow} N_1'$ and $N_2 \stackrel{0}{\rightsquigarrow} N_2'$. By induction the reductions $N_1 \stackrel{0}{\rightsquigarrow} N_1'$ and $N_2 \stackrel{0}{\rightsquigarrow} N_2'$ imply that $N_1' = N_1$ and

$N_2 = N_2'$, respectively. Thus $N_1' = N_1' \mid N_2' = N_1 \mid N_2$, meaning that $N = N'$ (as desired).

2. We proceed by induction on the structure of N.

- Case $N = l[[\mathbf{0}]]$. Since $N \overset{t}{\leadsto} N'$ and $N \overset{t}{\leadsto} N''$, by using Proposition 1, it holds that $N' = l[[\mathbf{0}]]$ and $N'' = l[[\mathbf{0}]]$, respectively, meaning that $N' = N''$ (as desired).
- Case $N = l[[a^{\Delta t'}!\langle v \rangle$ then P else $Q \triangleright K]]$. Since $N \overset{t}{\leadsto} N'$ and $N \overset{t}{\leadsto} N''$, by using Proposition 1, it holds that $N' = l[[a^{\Delta t'-t}!\langle v \rangle$ then P else $Q \triangleright K]]$ and $N'' = l[[a^{\Delta t'-t}!\langle v \rangle$ then P else $Q \triangleright K]]$, respectively, meaning that $N' = N''$ (as desired).
- Case $N = l[[a^{\Delta t'}?(u)$ then P else $Q \triangleright K]]$. Since $N \overset{t}{\leadsto} N'$ and $N \overset{t}{\leadsto} N''$, by using Proposition 1, it holds that $N' = l[[a^{\Delta t'-t}?(u)$ then P else $Q \triangleright K]]$ and $N'' = l[[a^{\Delta t'-t}?(u)$ then P else $Q \triangleright K]]$, respectively, meaning that $N' = N''$ (as desired).
- Case $N = l[[\text{go}^{t'} \, l'$ then $P \triangleright K]]$. Since $N \overset{t}{\leadsto} N'$ and $N \overset{t}{\leadsto} N''$, by using Proposition 1, it holds that $N' = l[[\text{go}^{t'-t} \, l'$ then $P \triangleright K]]$ and $N'' = l[[\text{go}^{t'-t} \, l'$ then $P \triangleright K]]$, respectively, meaning that $N' = N''$ (as desired).
- Case $N = N_1 \mid N_2$. Since $N \overset{t}{\leadsto} N'$, by using Proposition 1, it holds that there exist N_1' and N_2' such that $N' = N_1' \mid N_2'$, together with $N_1 \overset{t}{\leadsto} N_1'$ and $N_2 \overset{t}{\leadsto} N_2'$. Similarly, since $N \overset{t}{\leadsto} N''$, by using Proposition 1, it holds that there exist N_1'' and N_2'' such that $N'' = N_1'' \mid N_2''$, together with $N_1 \overset{t}{\leadsto} N_1''$ and $N_2 \overset{t}{\leadsto} N_2''$. By induction, $N_1 \overset{t}{\leadsto} N_1'$ and $N_1 \overset{t}{\leadsto} N_1''$ imply that $N_1' = N_1''$, while $N_2 \overset{t}{\leadsto} N_2'$ and $N_2 \overset{t}{\leadsto} N_2''$ imply that $N_2' = N_2''$. Thus, $N_1' = N_1' \mid N_2' = N_1'' \mid N_2''$, meaning that $N = N'$ (as desired). □

The following theorem claims that whenever only the rules of Table 3 can be applied for two time steps of lengths t and t'', then the rules can be applied also for a time step of length $t + t'$.

Theorem 2. *If $N \overset{t}{\leadsto} N'' \overset{t'}{\leadsto} N'$, then $N \overset{t+t'}{\leadsto} N'$.*

Proof. We proceed by induction on the structure of N.

- Case $N = l[[\mathbf{0}]]$. Since $N \overset{t}{\leadsto} N''$ by using Proposition 1, it holds that $N'' = l[[\mathbf{0}]]$. Similarly, since $N'' \overset{t'}{\leadsto} N'$ by using Proposition 1, it holds that $N' = l[[\mathbf{0}]]$. Rule (DSTOP) can be used for network N, namely $N \overset{t+t'}{\leadsto} l[[\mathbf{0}]] = N'$ (as desired).
- Case $N = l[[a^{\Delta t''}!\langle v \rangle$ then P else $Q \triangleright K]]$. Since $N \overset{t}{\leadsto} N''$ by using Proposition 1, it holds that $N'' = l[[a^{\Delta t''-t}!\langle v \rangle$ then P else $Q \triangleright K]]$, where $t'' \geq t \geq 0$. Similarly, since $N'' \overset{t'}{\leadsto} N'$ by using Proposition 1, it holds that $N' = l[[a^{\Delta(t''-t)-t'}!\langle v \rangle$ then P else $Q \triangleright K]]$, where $t'' - t \geq t' \geq 0$. Due to the fact that $0 \leq t+t' \leq t''$, rule (DGET) can be used for network N, namely $N \overset{t+t'}{\leadsto} l[[a^{\Delta t''-(t+t')}!\langle v \rangle$ then P else $Q \triangleright K]] = N'$ (as desired).
- Case $N = l[[a^{\Delta t''}?(u)$ then P else $Q \triangleright K]]$. Since $N \overset{t}{\leadsto} N''$ by using Proposition 1, it holds that $N'' = l[[a^{\Delta t''-t}?(u)$ then P else $Q \triangleright K]]$, with $t'' \geq t \geq 0$. Similarly, since $N'' \overset{t'}{\leadsto} N'$ by using Proposition 1, it holds that $N' = l[[a^{\Delta(t''-t)-t'}?(u)$ then P else $Q \triangleright K]]$, where $t'' - t \geq t' \geq 0$. Due to the fact that $0 \leq t+t' \leq t''$, rule (DPUT) can be used for network N, namely $N \overset{t+t'}{\leadsto} l[[a^{\Delta t''-(t+t')}?(u)$ then P else $Q \triangleright K]] = N'$ (as desired).

- Case $N = l[[\text{go}^{t''} \, l' \text{ then } P \triangleright K]]$. Since $N \xrightarrow{t} N''$ by using Proposition 1, it holds that $N'' = l[[\text{go}^{t''-t} \, l' \text{ then } P \triangleright K]]$, where $t'' \geq t \geq 0$. Similarly, since $N'' \xrightarrow{t'} N'$ by using Proposition 1, it holds that $N' = l[[\text{go}^{(t''-t)-t'} \, l' \text{ then } P \triangleright K]]$, where $t'' - t \geq t' \geq 0$. Due to the fact that $0 \leq t+t' \leq t''$, rule (DMOVE) can be used for network N, namely $N \xrightarrow{t+t'} l[[\text{go}^{t''-(t+t')} \, l' \text{ then } P \triangleright K]] = N'$ (as desired).
- Case $N = N_1 \mid N_2$. Since $N \xrightarrow{t} N''$, by using Proposition 1, it holds that $N_1 \mid N_2 \not\rightarrow$ and there exist N_1'' and N_2'' such that $N'' = N_1'' \mid N_2''$, together with $N_1 \xrightarrow{t} N_1''$ and $N_2 \xrightarrow{t} N_2''$. Similarly, since $N'' \xrightarrow{t'} N'$, by using Proposition 1, it holds that there exist N_1' and N_2' such that $N' = N_1' \mid N_2'$, together with $N_1'' \xrightarrow{t'} N_1'$ and $N_2'' \xrightarrow{t'} N_2'$. By induction, $N_1 \xrightarrow{t} N_1''$ and $N_1'' \xrightarrow{t'} N_1'$ imply that $N_1 \xrightarrow{t+t'} N_1'$, while $N_2 \xrightarrow{t} N_2''$ and $N_2'' \xrightarrow{t'} N_2'$ imply that $N_2' \xrightarrow{t+t'} N_2'$. Since $N_1 \xrightarrow{t+t'} N_1'$, $N_2 \xrightarrow{t+t'} N_2'$ and $N_1 \mid N_2 \not\rightarrow$, rule (DPAR) can be used for network N, namely $N \xrightarrow{t+t'} N_1' \mid N_2' = N'$ (as desired). □

Regarding the knowledge of an agent, we have the following result showing that any given agent can be obtained starting from an agent without any knowledge.

Proposition 2. *If $N'' = l[[P'' \triangleright K'']]$ with $K'' \neq \emptyset$, then there exists $N' = l[[P' \triangleright K']]$ with $K' = \emptyset$ such that $N' \Longrightarrow^* N''$.*

Proof. We proceed by induction on the structure of K''.

- Consider $K'' = \langle f \mid v; \emptyset \rangle$. According to rule (CREATE), this knowledge can be obtain from a process $P' = \text{create}(\langle f \mid v; \emptyset \rangle)$ then P''. This implies that for $N' = l[[P' \triangleright K']]$ with $K' = \emptyset$, it holds that $N' \xrightarrow{\text{create}_f@l} N''$ (as desired).
- Consider $K'' = \langle f \mid v; \emptyset \rangle K$, with $K \neq \emptyset$. By induction, there exists a process P able to create the knowledge K. This implies that for $N = l[[P \triangleright K]]$ with $K \neq \emptyset$, it holds that $N \Longrightarrow^* N''$. According to rule (CREATE), knowledge K'' can be obtain starting from knowledge K by using a process $P' = \text{create}(\langle f \mid v; \emptyset \rangle)$ then P. This implies that for $N' = l[[P' \triangleright K']]$ with $K' = \emptyset$, it holds that $N' \xrightarrow{\text{create}_f@l} N \Longrightarrow^* N''$ (as desired).
- Consider $K'' = \langle f' \mid v'; \ldots \langle f'' \mid v''; \langle f \mid v; \emptyset \rangle K_1 \rangle K_2 \rangle K_3$. By induction, there exists a process P able to create the knowledge $K = \langle f' \mid v'; \ldots \langle f'' \mid v''; K_1 \rangle K_2 \rangle K_3$. This implies that for $N = l[[P \triangleright K]]$ with $K \neq \emptyset$, it holds that $N \Longrightarrow^* N''$. According to rule (EXTEND), knowledge K'' can be obtain starting from knowledge K by using a process $P' = \text{update}(p/f, v)$ then P, where $p = /f' \ldots /f''$. This implies that for $N' = l[[P' \triangleright K']]$ with $K' = \emptyset$, it holds that $N' \xrightarrow{\text{upd}_p@l} N \Longrightarrow^* N''$ (as desired). □

The next result is a consequence of the previous one; it claims that any given network in knowTIMO can be obtained starting from a network containing only agents without knowledge.

Theorem 3. *If $N'' = l_1[[P_{11}'' \triangleright K_{11}'' \mid\mid \ldots \mid\mid P_{1n}'' \triangleright K_{1n}'']] \mid \ldots \mid l_m[[P_{m1}'' \triangleright K_{m1}'' \mid\mid \ldots \mid\mid P_{mn}'' \triangleright K_{mn}'']]$, then there exists $N' = l_1[[P_{11}' \triangleright K_{11}' \mid\mid \ldots \mid\mid P_{1n}' \triangleright K_{1n}']] \mid \ldots \mid l_m[[P_{m1}' \triangleright K_{m1}' \mid\mid \ldots \mid\mid P_{mn}' \triangleright K_{mn}']]$ with $K_{ij}' = \emptyset$ ($1 \leq i \leq m, 1 \leq j \leq n$) such that $N' \Longrightarrow^* N''$.*

The following example illustrates how agents communicate and make use of their knowledge.

Example 1. *To illustrate how multi-agent systems can be described in knowTIMO, we adapt the travel agency example from [3], where all the involved agents have a cyclic behaviour. Consider a travel agency with seven offices (one central and six locals) and five employees (two executives and three travel agents). As the agency is understaffed and all local offices need to be used from time to time, the executives meet with the agents daily at the central office in order to assign them local* offices where they sell travel packages by interacting with potential customers. We consider two customers that are willing to visit the local offices closer to their homes. In what follows we show how each of the involved agents can be described by using the knowTIMO syntax.

Each day, agent A_1 executes the action go^{10} office in order to move after 10 time units from location home$_{A1}$ to the central office. After reaching the central office, in order to find out at which local office will work for the rest of the day, it executes the action $b^{\Delta 5}?$(newloc) to try to communicate with any of the executives in the next 5 time units. The location variable newloc is needed to model a dynamic evolution based on the local office assigned by an available executive. After successfully communicating with an executive, the agent A_1 moves to location office$_i$ after 5 time units in order to communicate with potential customers using channel a_i in order to sell a travel package towards location dest$_{A1}$ at the cost of 100 monetary units. After each working day, the agent returns home by executing the action go^3 home$_{A1}$. The agents A_2 and A_3 behave similarly to A_1, except that they begin and end their days at different locations, work locally at different offices and the travel packages they advertise are different.

Formally, the travel agents are described by the recursive processes $A_X(\text{home}_{AX}) \triangleright K_{AX}$:

$A_X(\text{home}_{AX}) = \text{go}^{10}$ office then $A_X(\text{office})$

$A_X(\text{office}) = b^{\Delta 5}?(\text{newloc})$
          then $(\text{go}^5$ newloc then $A_X(\text{newloc}))$
          else $A_X(\text{office})$

$A_X(\text{office}_i) = update(/\text{work}, \text{office}_i)$
          then $a_i^{\Delta 9}!\langle K_{AX}(/\text{work}/\text{dest}), K_{AX}(/\text{work}/\text{price})\rangle$
          then go^3 home$_{AX}$ then $A_X(\text{home}_{AX})$
          else go^3 home$_{AX}$ then $A_X(\text{home}_{AX})$

$K_{AX} = \langle \text{work} \mid \text{office}; \langle \text{dest} \mid \text{dest}_{AX}\rangle \langle \text{price} \mid 100 \cdot X\rangle\rangle$.

The identifiers AX ($1 \leq X \leq 3$) are uniquely assigned to the three travel agents, and office$_i$ ($1 \leq i \leq 6$) indicate the six local offices.

Given the knowledge K_{AX} defined above, we exemplify how it can be used for some queries:

- $K_{AX}(/\text{work}/\text{price})$ is used to retrieve the price value $100 \cdot X$ by following the path /work/price in K_{AX};
- $K_{AX}(/\text{work}[K_{AX}(/\text{work}/\text{price}) < 200])$ returns the local office in which the agent is trying to sell its travel package whenever the price of the package available by following the path /work/price is below 200 monetary units.

Executives E_1 and E_2 are placed in the central office, being available for communication on channel b for 5 time minutes. In this way, they can assign to the travel agents (in a cyclic manner) the locations office$_1$, office$_3$, office$_5$, and the locations office$_2$, office$_4$, office$_6$, respectively. Formally, the executives are described by $E_X(\text{office}_Y) \triangleright K_{EX}$:

$E_X(\text{office}_Y) = update(/\text{work}, \text{office}_Y)$
          then $b^{\Delta 5}!\langle K_{EX}(/\text{work})\rangle$ then $E_X(\text{office}_{Y+2})$
          else $E_X(\text{office}_Y)$

$K_{EX} = \emptyset$.

The identifiers EX (with $1 \leq X \leq 2$) are uniquely assigned to the two executives, while office$_Y$ (with $Y \in \{X, X+2, X+4\}$) indicate the local offices that each executive EX can assign to travel agents. Defining the index of the local offices in this way ensures that the executives assign the existing local offices in a cyclic way.

The client C_1 initially resides at location home$_{C1}$; being interested in a travel package, client C_1 is willing to visit the local offices closer to his location, namely office$_1$, office$_2$, and office$_3$. For each of these three local offices, the visit has two possible outcomes: if client C_1 interacts with an agent then it will acquire a travel offer, while if the highoffice is closed then client C_1 moves to the next local office from its itinerary. Once its journey through the three local offices ends, client C_1 returns home whenever was unable to collect any travel offer, while goes at the destination for which he has to pay the lowest amount whenever got at least one offer. After the holiday period ends, client C_1 returns home, where can restart the process of searching for a holiday destination. Client C_2 behaves in a similar manner as client C_1 does, except looking for the most expensive travel package while visiting the local offices office$_4$, office$_5$ and office$_6$. Formally, the clients are described by $C_X(\text{home}_{CX}) \triangleright K_{CX}$:

$C_X(\text{home}_{CX}) = \text{go}^{13} \text{ office}_{Z+1}$ then $C_X(\text{office}_{Z+1})$

$C_X(\text{office}_{Z+1}) = a_{Z+1}^{\Delta 4}?(\text{dest}_{CX,1}, \text{cost}_{CX,1})$
$\quad$ then $update(/agency[test_{Z+1}]/dest, dest_{CX,1})$
$\quad$ then $update(/agency[test_{Z+1}]/price, cost_{CX,1})$
$\quad$ then $\text{go}^2 \text{ office}_{Z+2}$ then $C_X(\text{office}_{Z+2})$
$\quad$ else $update(/agency[test_{Z+1}]/dest, \varepsilon)$
$\quad$ then $update(/agency[test_{Z+1}]/price, \varepsilon)$
$\quad$ then $\text{go}^2 \text{ office}_{Z+2}$ then $C_X(\text{office}_{Z+2})$,
$\quad$ where $test_{Z+1} = (K_{CX}(/agency) = \text{office}_{Z+1})$

$C_X(\text{office}_{Z+2}) = a_{Z+2}^{\Delta 4}?(\text{dest}_{CX,2}, \text{cost}_{CX,2})$
$\quad$ then $update(/agency[test_{Z+2}]/dest, dest_{CX,2})$
$\quad$ then $update(/agency[test_{Z+2}]/price, cost_{CX,2})$
$\quad$ then $\text{go}^3 \text{ office}_{Z+3}$ then $C_X(\text{office}_{Z+3})$
$\quad$ else $update(/agency[test_{Z+2}]/dest, \varepsilon)$
$\quad$ then $update(/agency[test_{Z+2}]/price, \varepsilon)$
$\quad$ then $\text{go}^2 \text{ office}_{Z+3}$ then $C_X(\text{office}_{Z+3})$,
$\quad$ where $test_{Z+2} = (K_{CX}(/agency) = \text{office}_{Z+2})$

$C_X(\text{office}_{Z+3}) = a_{Z+3}^{\Delta_4}?(\text{dest}_{CX,3}, \text{cost}_{CX,3})$
$\quad$ then $update(/agency[test_{Z+3}]/dest, dest_{CX,3})$
$\quad$ then $update(/agency[test_{Z+3}]/price, cost_{CX,3})$
$\quad$ then $C_X(\text{next}_{CX})$
$\quad$ else $update(/agency[test_{Z+3}]/dest, \varepsilon)$
$\quad$ then $update(/agency[test_{Z+3}]/price, \varepsilon)$
$\quad$ then $C_X(\text{next}_{CX})$,
$\quad$ where $test_{Z+3} = (K_{CX}(/agency) = \text{office}_{Z+3})$

$C_X(\text{next}_{CX}) = if\ testX$ then $(\text{go}^5 \text{ next}_{CX}$ then $C_X(\text{next}_{CX}))$
$\quad$ else $(\text{go}^5 \text{ home}_{CX}$ then $C_X(\text{home}_{CX}))$

$C_X(\text{dest}_{CX,i}) = \text{go}^5 \text{ dest}_{CX}$ then $C_X(\text{home}_{CX})$

$K_{CX} = \langle agency \mid \text{office}_{Z+1}; \langle dest \mid \varepsilon \rangle \langle price \mid \varepsilon \rangle \rangle$
$\quad \langle agency \mid \text{office}_{Z+2}; \langle dest \mid \varepsilon \rangle \langle price \mid \varepsilon \rangle \rangle$
$\quad \langle agency \mid \text{office}_{Z+3}; \langle dest \mid \varepsilon \rangle \langle price \mid \varepsilon \rangle \rangle$.

The identifiers CX (with $1 \leq X \leq 2$) are uniquely assigned to the two clients, the identifiers $\text{dest}_{CX,i}$ uniquely identify the possible destinations the clients CX can visit, while $Z = 3 * (X-1)$ (with $X \in \{1,2\}$) are used to identify the local offices for each of the clients.
The tests used above are:

$testX = \neg(K_{CX}(/agency/price) = \varepsilon)$,

$\text{next}_{CX} = \begin{cases} K_{CX}(/agency[test_{min}]/dest_{CX,i}) \\ \quad if\ X = 1\ and\ K_{CX}(/agency/price) = \min_{j \in \{1,2,3\}} \text{cost}_{CX,j} \in \mathbb{N}; \\ K_{CX}(/agency[test_{max}]/dest_{CX,i}) \\ \quad if\ X = 2\ and\ K_{CX}(/agency/price) = \max_{j \in \{1,2,3\}} \text{cost}_{CX,j} \in \mathbb{N}; \\ \text{home}_{CX} \quad otherwise. \end{cases}$

The initial state of the system given as the knowTIMO network N is:

$\text{home}_{A1}[[A_1(\text{home}_{A1}) \triangleright K_{A1}]] \mid \text{home}_{A2}[[A_2(\text{home}_{A2}) \triangleright K_{A2}]]$
$\mid \text{home}_{A3}[[A_3(\text{home}_{A3}) \triangleright K_{A3}]] \mid \text{office}[[E_1(\text{office}_1) \triangleright K_{E1} \parallel E_2(\text{office}_2) \triangleright K_{E2}]]$
$\mid \text{home}_{C1}[[C_1(\text{home}_{C1}) \triangleright K_{C1}]] \mid \text{home}_{C2}[[C_2(\text{home}_{C2}) \triangleright K_{C2}]] \mid N'$,

where N' stands for:

$\text{office}_1[[0]] \mid \text{office}_2[[0]] \mid \text{office}_3[[0]] \mid \text{office}_4[[0]] \mid \text{office}_5[[0]] \mid \text{office}_6[[0]]$
$\mid \text{dest}_1[[0]] \mid \text{dest}_2[[0]] \mid \text{dest}_3[[0]]$.

In what follows we show how some of the rules of Tables 2 and 3 are applied such that network N evolves. Since the network N is defined by means of recursive processes, in order to execute their actions we need to use the rules (CALL) and (PAR) for unfolding, namely

$\xrightarrow{\{call,call,call,call,call,call,call\}}$ (CALL), (PAR)

home$_{A1}$[[(go^{10} office then A$_1$(office) $\triangleright$ K$_{A1}$]]
home$_{A2}$[[(go^{10} office then A$_2$(office) $\triangleright$ K$_{A2}$]]
home$_{A3}$[[(go^{10} office then A$_3$(office) $\triangleright$ K$_{A3}$]]
| office[[update(/work, office$_1$)
    then $b^{\Delta 5}!\langle K_{E1}(/work)\rangle$ then E$_1$(office$_3$)
                         else E$_1$(office$_1$)
    $\triangleright$K$_{E1}$
|| update(/work, office$_2$)
    then $b^{\Delta 5}!\langle K_{E2}(/work)\rangle$ then E$_2$(office$_4$)
                         else E$_2$(office$_2$)
    $\triangleright$K$_{E2}$]]
| home$_{C1}$[[go^{13} office$_1$ then C$_1$(office$_1$)]]
| home$_{C2}$[[go^{13} office$_4$ then C$_2$(office$_4$)]]
| N'.

The next step is represented by the two updates performed by the executives; thus, the rules (EXTEND) and (PAR) are applied several times. Since the existing knowledge of the two executives is currently $\oslash$, this means that these updates extend in fact their knowledge.

$\xrightarrow{\{upd,upd\}}$ (EXTEND), (PAR)

home$_{A1}$[[(go^{10} office then A$_1$(office) $\triangleright$ K$_{A1}$]]
home$_{A2}$[[(go^{10} office then A$_2$(office) $\triangleright$ K$_{A2}$]]
home$_{A3}$[[(go^{10} office then A$_3$(office) $\triangleright$ K$_{A3}$]]
| office[[$b^{\Delta 5}!\langle K_{E1}(/work)\rangle$ then E$_1$(office$_3$)
                         else E$_1$(office$_1$)
    $\triangleright\langle work\ |\ office_1; \oslash\rangle$
|| $b^{\Delta 5}!\langle K_{E2}(/work)\rangle$ then E$_2$(office$_4$)
                         else E$_2$(office$_2$)
    $\triangleright\langle work\ |\ office_2; \oslash\rangle$]]
| home$_{C1}$[[go^{13} office$_1$ then C$_1$(office$_1$)]]
| home$_{C2}$[[go^{13} office$_4$ then C$_2$(office$_4$)]]
| N'.

Since the rules of Table 2 are not applicable to the above network, then only time passing can be applied by using the rules of Table 3. The rules (DMOVE), (DGET) and (DPAR) can be applied for $t = 5$, namely the maximum time units that can be performed.

$\xrightarrow{5}$ (DMOVE), (DGET), (DPAR)

home$_{A1}$[[(go^5 office then A$_1$(office) $\triangleright$ K$_{A1}$]]
home$_{A2}$[[(go^5 office then A$_2$(office) $\triangleright$ K$_{A2}$]]
home$_{A3}$[[(go^5 office then A$_3$(office) $\triangleright$ K$_{A3}$]]
| office[[$b^{\Delta 0}!\langle K_{E1}(/work)\rangle$ then E$_1$(office$_3$)
                         else E$_1$(office$_1$)
    $\triangleright\langle work\ |\ office_1; \oslash\rangle$
|| $b^{\Delta 0}!\langle K_{E2}(/work)\rangle$ then E$_2$(office$_4$)
                         else E$_2$(office$_2$)
    $\triangleright\langle work\ |\ office_2; \oslash\rangle$]]
| home$_{C1}$[[go^8 office$_1$ then C$_1$(office$_1$)]]
| home$_{C2}$[[go^8 office$_4$ then C$_2$(office$_4$)]]
| N'.

Since after 5 time units of the evolution there are no agents to communicate with the executives on channel b, then the rules (Put0) and (Par) are applied such that the else branches of the two executives are chosen to be executed next.

$$\xrightarrow{\{b!^{\Delta 0}@\text{office},\ b!^{\Delta 0}@\text{office}\}}$$ (Put0), (Par)

$\text{home}_{A1}[[(\text{go}^5\ \text{office then } A_1(\text{office}) \triangleright K_{A1}]]$
$\text{home}_{A2}[[(\text{go}^5\ \text{office then } A_2(\text{office}) \triangleright K_{A2}]]$
$\text{home}_{A3}[[(\text{go}^5\ \text{office then } A_3(\text{office}) \triangleright K_{A3}]]$
$\mid \text{office}[[\ E_1(\text{office}_1) \triangleright \langle work \mid \text{office}_1; \emptyset \rangle$
$\quad\quad \parallel E_2(\text{office}_2) \triangleright \langle work \mid \text{office}_2; \emptyset \rangle]]$
$\mid \text{home}_{C1}[[\text{go}^8\ \text{office}_1\ \text{then } C_1(\text{office}_1)]]$
$\mid \text{home}_{C2}[[\text{go}^8\ \text{office}_4\ \text{then } C_2(\text{office}_4)]]$
$\mid N'.$

Note that the evolution was deterministic during the first 5 time units. However, since there are two executives and three travel agents into the system, the communication on channel b will take place in a nondeterministic manner, and thus there exists several possible future evolutions of the system.

3. Behavioural Equivalences in knowTiMo

In what follows, we define and study bisimulations for multi-agent systems that consider knowledge dynamics as well as explicit time constraints for communication and migration. Since a bisimilarity is the union of all bisimulations of the same type, in order to demonstrate that two knowTiMo networks N_1 and N_2 are bisimilar it is enough to discover a bisimulation relation containing the pair (N_1, N_2). This standard bisimulation proof method is interesting for the following reasons:

- check-ups are local (only immediate transitions are used);
- No hierarchy exists between the pairs of a bisimulation, and thus we can effectively use bisimilarity to reason about infinite behaviours; this makes it different from inductive techniques, where we can reason about finite behaviour due to the required hierarchy.

3.1. Strong Timed Equivalences

Inspired by the approach taken in [4], we extend the standard notion of strong bisimilarity by allowing also timed transitions to be taken into account.

Definition 1 (Strong timed bisimulation).
Let $\mathcal{R} \subseteq \mathcal{N} \times \mathcal{N}$ be a symmetric binary relation over knowTiMo networks.

1. $\mathcal{R}$ is a strong timed bisimulation if

    - $(N_1, N_2) \in \mathcal{R}$ and $N_1 \xrightarrow{\lambda} N_1'$ implies that there exists $N_2' \in \mathcal{N}$ such that $N_2 \xrightarrow{\lambda} N_2'$ and $(N_1', N_2') \in \mathcal{R}$;
    - $(N_1, N_2) \in \mathcal{R}$ and $N_1 \stackrel{t}{\rightsquigarrow} N_1'$ implies that there exists $N_2' \in \mathcal{N}$ such that $N_2 \stackrel{t}{\rightsquigarrow} N_2'$ and $(N_1', N_2') \in \mathcal{R}$.

2. The strong timed bisimilarity is the union $\sim$ of all strong timed bisimulations $\mathcal{R}$.

Definition 1 treats in a similar manner the timed transitions and the labelled transitions, and so the bisimilarity notion is similar to the bisimilarity notion originally given for labelled transition systems. We can prove that the relation $\sim$ is the largest strong timed bisimulation, and also an equivalence relation.

Proposition 3.
1. Identity, inverse, composition and union of strong timed bisimulations are strong timed bisimulations.
2. $\sim$ is the largest strong timed bisimulation.
3. $\sim$ is an equivalence.

Proof.
1. We treat each relations separately showing that it respects the conditions from Definition 1 for being a strong timed bisimulation.

    (a) The identity relation $Id_\mathcal{R}$ is a strong timed bisimulation.

    i. Assume $(N, N) \in Id_\mathcal{R}$. Consider $N \xrightarrow{\lambda} N'$; then $(N', N') \in Id_\mathcal{R}$.

    ii. Assume $(N, N) \in Id_\mathcal{R}$. Consider $N \xrightarrow{t} N'$; then $(N', N') \in Id_\mathcal{R}$.

    (b) The inverse of a strong timed bisimulation is a strong timed bisimulation.

    i. Assume $(N_1, N_2) \in \mathcal{R}^{-1}$, namely $(N_2, N_1) \in \mathcal{R}$. Consider $N_2 \xrightarrow{\lambda} N_2'$; then for some N_1' we have $N_1 \xrightarrow{\lambda} N_1'$ and $(N_2', N_1') \in \mathcal{R}$, namely $(N_1', N_2') \in \mathcal{R}^{-1}$. By similar reasoning, if $N_1 \xrightarrow{\lambda} N_1'$ then we can find N_2' such that $N_2 \xrightarrow{\lambda} N_2'$ and $(N_1', N_2') \in \mathcal{R}^{-1}$.

    ii. Assume $(N_1, N_2) \in \mathcal{R}^{-1}$, namely $(N_2, N_1) \in \mathcal{R}$. Consider $N_2 \xrightarrow{t} N_2'$; then for some N_1' we have $N_1 \xrightarrow{t} N_1'$ and $(N_2', N_1') \in \mathcal{R}$, namely $(N_1', N_2') \in \mathcal{R}^{-1}$. By similar reasoning, if $N_1 \xrightarrow{t} N_1'$ then we can find N_2' such that $N_2 \xrightarrow{t} N_2'$ and $(N_1', N_2') \in \mathcal{R}^{-1}$.

    (c) The composition of strong timed bisimulations is a strong timed bisimulation.

    i. Assume $(N_1, N_2) \in \mathcal{R}_1 \mathcal{R}_2$. Then for some N we have $(N_1, N) \in \mathcal{R}_1$ and $(N, N_2) \in \mathcal{R}_2$. Consider $N_1 \xrightarrow{\lambda} N_1'$; then for some N', since $(N_1, N) \in \mathcal{R}_1$, we have $N \xrightarrow{\lambda} N'$ and $(N_1', N') \in \mathcal{R}_1$. Also, since $(N, N_2) \in \mathcal{R}_2$ we have for some N_2' that $N_2 \xrightarrow{\lambda} N_2'$ and $(N', N_2') \in \mathcal{R}_2$. Thus, $(N_1', N_2') \in \mathcal{R}_1 \mathcal{R}_2$. By similar reasoning, if $N_2 \xrightarrow{\lambda} N_2'$ then we can find N_1' such that $N_1 \xrightarrow{\lambda} N_1'$ and $(N', N_2') \in \mathcal{R}_2$.

    ii. Assume $(N_1, N_2) \in \mathcal{R}_1 \mathcal{R}_2$. Then for some N we have $(N_1, N) \in \mathcal{R}_1$ and $(N, N_2) \in \mathcal{R}_2$. Consider $N_1 \xrightarrow{t} N_1'$; then for some N', since $(N_1, N) \in \mathcal{R}_1$, we have $N \xrightarrow{t} N'$ and $(N_1', N') \in \mathcal{R}_1$. Also, since $(N, N_2) \in \mathcal{R}_2$ we have for some N_2' that $N_2 \xrightarrow{t} N_2'$ and $(N', N_2') \in \mathcal{R}_2$. Thus, $(N_1', N_2') \in \mathcal{R}_1 \mathcal{R}_2$. By similar reasoning, if $N_2 \xrightarrow{t} N_2'$ then we can find N_1' such that $N_1 \xrightarrow{t} N_1'$ and $(N', N_2') \in \mathcal{R}_2$.

    (d) The union of strong timed bisimulations is a strong timed bisimulation.

    i. Assume $(N_1, N_2) \in \bigcup_{i \in I} \mathcal{R}_i$. Then for some $i \in I$ we have $(N_1, N_2) \in \mathcal{R}_i$. Consider $N_1 \xrightarrow{\lambda} N_1'$; then for some N_2', since $(N_1, N_2) \in \mathcal{R}_i$, we have $N_2 \xrightarrow{\lambda} N_2'$ and $(N_1', N_2') \in \mathcal{R}_i$. Thus, $(N_1', N_2') \in \bigcup_{i \in I} \mathcal{R}_i$. By similar reasoning, if $N_2 \xrightarrow{\lambda} N_2'$ then we can find N_1' such that $N_1 \xrightarrow{\lambda} N_1'$ and $(N_1', N_2') \in \mathcal{R}_i$, namely $(N_1', N_2') \in \bigcup_{i \in I} \mathcal{R}_i$.

    ii. Assume $(N_1, N_2) \in \bigcup_{i \in I} \mathcal{R}_i$. Then for some $i \in I$ we have $(N_1, N_2) \in \mathcal{R}_i$. Consider $N_1 \xrightarrow{t} N_1'$; then for some N_2', since $(N_1, N_2) \in \mathcal{R}_i$, we have $N_2 \xrightarrow{t} N_2'$ and $(N_1', N_2') \in \mathcal{R}_i$. Thus, $(N_1', N_2') \in \bigcup_{i \in I} \mathcal{R}_i$. By similar reasoning, if $N_2 \xrightarrow{t} N_2'$ then we can find N_1' such that $N_1 \xrightarrow{t} N_1'$ and $(N_1', N_2') \in \mathcal{R}_i$, namely $(N_1', N_2') \in \bigcup_{i \in I} \mathcal{R}_i$.

2. By the previous case (the union part), $\sim$ is a strong timed bisimulation and includes any other strong timed bisimulation.
3. Proving that relation $\sim$ is an equivalence requires proving that it satisfies reflexivity, symmetry and transitivity. We consider each of them in the following:

   (a) Reflexivity: For any network N, $N \sim N$ results from the fact that the identity relation is a strong timed bisimulation.

   (b) Symmetry: If $N \sim N'$, then $(N, N') \in \mathcal{R}$ for some strong timed bisimulation $\mathcal{R}$. Hence $(N', N) \in \mathcal{R}^{-1}$, and so $N' \sim N$ because the inverse relation is a strong timed bisimulation.

   (c) Transitivity: If $N \sim N'$ and $N' \sim N''$ then $(N, N') \in \mathcal{R}_1$ and $(N', N'') \in \mathcal{R}_2$ for some strong timed bisimulations $\mathcal{R}_1$ and $\mathcal{R}_2$. Thus, $(N, N'') \in \mathcal{R}_1\mathcal{R}_2$, and so $N \sim N''$ due to the fact that the composition relation is a strong timed bisimulation. □

The next result claims that the strong timed equivalence $\sim$ among processes is preserved even if the local knowledge of the agents is expanded. This is consistent with the fact that the processes affect the same portion of their knowledge. To simplify the presentation, in what follows we assume the notations $|_{i=1}^n N_i = N_1 | \ldots | N_n$ and $||_{i=1}^n A_i = A_1 || \ldots || A_n$.

Proposition 4. *If $K'_{ij} \subseteq K''_{ij}$ for $1 \leq i \leq n, 1 \leq j \leq m$, then*
$$|_{i=1}^n l_i[[||_{j=1}^m P_{ij} \triangleright K'_{ij}]] \sim |_{i=1}^n l_i[[||_{j=1}^m P_{ij} \triangleright K''_{ij}]].$$

Proof. We show that $\mathcal{S}$ is a strong timed bisimulation, where:
$$\mathcal{S} = \{(|_{i=1}^n l_i[[||_{j=1}^m P_{ij} \triangleright K'_{ij}]], |_{i=1}^n l_i[[||_{j=1}^m P_{ij} \triangleright K''_{ij}]]) : K'_{ij} \subseteq K''_{ij}, 1 \leq i \leq n, 1 \leq j \leq m\}.$$
The proof is by induction on the last performed step:

- Let us assume that $|_{i=1}^n l_i[[||_{j=1}^m P_{ij} \triangleright K'_{ij}]] \xrightarrow{\lambda} N'$. Depending on the value of λ, there are several cases:

  – Consider $\lambda = a!?@l_1$. Then there exists $P_{11} = a^{\Delta t_1}!\langle v\rangle$ then P'_{11} else P''_{11} and $P_{12} = a^{\Delta t_2}?(u)$ then P'_{12} else P''_{12} such that $l_1[[P_{11} \triangleright K'_{11} || P_{12} \triangleright K'_{12} ||_{j=3}^m P_{1j} \triangleright K'_{1j}]]$
  $|_{i=2}^n l_i[[||_{j=1}^m P_{ij} \triangleright K'_{ij}]] \xrightarrow{a!?@l_1} l_1[[P'_{11} \triangleright K'_{11} || P'_{12} \triangleright K'_{12} ||_{j=3}^m P_{1j} \triangleright K'_{1j}]]$
  $|_{i=2}^n l_i[[||_{j=1}^m P_{ij} \triangleright K'_{ij}]] = N'$. Then there exists $N'' = [[P'_{11} \triangleright K''_{11} || P'_{12} \triangleright K''_{12}$
  $||_{j=3}^m P_{1j} \triangleright K''_{1j}]] |_{i=2}^n l_i[[||_{j=1}^m P_{ij} \triangleright K''_{ij}]]$ such that $|_{i=1}^n l_i[[||_{j=1}^m P_{ij} \triangleright K''_{ij}]] \xrightarrow{a!?@l_1} N''$.
  Since $K'_{ij} \subseteq K''_{ij}, 1 \leq i \leq n, 1 \leq j \leq m$, clearly $(N', N'') \in \mathcal{S}$.

  – Consider $\lambda = a!^{\Delta 0}@l_1$. Then there exists $P_{11} = a^{\Delta 0}!\langle v\rangle$ then P'_{11} else P''_{11} such that $l_1[[P_{11} \triangleright K'_{11} ||_{j=2}^m P_{1j} \triangleright K'_{1j}]] |_{i=2}^n l_i[[||_{j=1}^m P_{ij} \triangleright K'_{ij}]] \xrightarrow{a!^{\Delta 0}@l_1} l_1[[P'_{11} \triangleright K'_{11}$
  $||_{j=2}^m P_{1j} \triangleright K'_{1j}]] |_{i=2}^n l_i[[||_{j=1}^m P_{ij} \triangleright K'_{ij}]] = N'$. Then there exists $N'' = l_1[[P'_{11} \triangleright K''_{11}$
  $||_{j=2}^m P_{1j} \triangleright K''_{1j}]] |_{i=2}^n l_i[[||_{j=1}^m P_{ij} \triangleright K''_{ij}]]$ such that $|_{i=1}^n l_i[[||_{j=1}^m P_{ij} \triangleright K''_{ij}]]) \xrightarrow{a!^{\Delta 0}@l_1} N''$.
  Since $K'_{ij} \subseteq K''_{ij}, 1 \leq i \leq n, 1 \leq j \leq m$, clearly $(N', N'') \in \mathcal{S}$.

  – Consider $\lambda = a?^{\Delta 0}@l_1$. Then there exists $P_{11} = a^{\Delta 0}?(u)$ then P'_{11} else P''_{11} such that $l_1[[P_{11} \triangleright K'_{11} ||_{j=2}^m P_{1j} \triangleright K'_{1j}]] |_{i=2}^n l_i[[||_{j=1}^m P_{ij} \triangleright K'_{ij}]] \xrightarrow{a?^{\Delta 0}@l_1} l_1[[P'_{11} \triangleright K'_{11}$
  $||_{j=2}^m P_{1j} \triangleright K'_{1j}]] |_{i=2}^n l_i[[||_{j=1}^m P_{ij} \triangleright K'_{ij}]] = N'$. Then there exists $N'' = l_1[[P'_{11} \triangleright K''_{11}$
  $||_{j=2}^m P_{1j} \triangleright K''_{1j}]] |_{i=2}^n l_i[[||_{j=1}^m P_{ij} \triangleright K''_{ij}]]$ such that $|_{i=1}^n l_i[[||_{j=1}^m P_{ij} \triangleright K''_{ij}]]) \xrightarrow{a?^{\Delta 0}@l_1} N''$.
  Since $K'_{ij} \subseteq K''_{ij}, 1 \leq i \leq n, 1 \leq j \leq m$, clearly $(N', N'') \in \mathcal{S}$.

  – Consider $\lambda = l_1 \triangleright l_2$. Then there exists $P_{11} = go^0 \, l_2$ then P'_{11} such that $l_1[[P_{11} \triangleright K'_{11}$
  $||_{j=2}^m P_{1j} \triangleright K'_{1j}]] |_{i=2}^n l_i[[||_{j=1}^m P_{ij} \triangleright K'_{ij}]] \xrightarrow{l_1 \triangleright l_2} l_1[[||_{j=2}^m P_{1j} \triangleright K'_{1j}]] | l_2[[P'_{11} \triangleright K'_{11}$
  $||_{j=1}^m P_{2j} \triangleright K'_{2j}]] |_{i=3}^n l_i[[||_{j=1}^m P_{ij} \triangleright K'_{ij}]] = N'$. Then there exists $N'' = l_1[[||_{j=2}^m P_{1j} \triangleright$
  $K''_{1j}]] | l_2[[P'_{11} \triangleright K''_{11} ||_{j=1}^m P_{2j} \triangleright K''_{2j}]] |_{i=3}^n l_i[[||_{j=1}^m P_{ij} \triangleright K''_{ij}]]$ such that

$|_{i=1}^{n} l_i[[||_{j=1}^{m} P_{ij} \triangleright K''_{ij}]]) \xrightarrow{l_1 \triangleright l_2} N''$. Since $K'_{ij} \subseteq K''_{ij}, 1 \leq i \leq n, 1 \leq j \leq m$, clearly $(N', N'') \in \mathcal{S}$.

- Consider $\lambda = true@l_1$. Then there exists $P_{11} =$ if $test$ then P'_{11} else P''_{11}, where $test@K'_{11} = true$, such that $l_1[[P_{11} \triangleright K'_{11} \ ||_{j=2}^{m} P_{1j} \triangleright K'_{1j}]] \ |_{i=2}^{n} l_i[[||_{j=1}^{m} P_{ij} \triangleright K'_{ij}]]$
$\xrightarrow{true@l_1} l_1[[P'_{11} \triangleright K'_{11} \ ||_{j=2}^{m} P_{1j} \triangleright K'_{1j}]] \ |_{i=2}^{n} l_i[[||_{j=1}^{m} P_{ij} \triangleright K'_{ij}]] = N'$. Then there exists $N'' = l_1[[P'_{11} \triangleright K''_{11} \ ||_{j=2}^{m} P_{1j} \triangleright K''_{1j}]] \ |_{i=2}^{n} l_i[[||_{j=1}^{m} P_{ij} \triangleright K''_{ij}]]$ such that $|_{i=1}^{n} l_i[[||_{j=1}^{m} P_{ij} \triangleright K''_{ij}]]) \xrightarrow{true@l_1} N''$. Since $K'_{ij} \subseteq K''_{ij}, 1 \leq i \leq n, 1 \leq j \leq m$, clearly $(N', N'') \in \mathcal{S}$.

- Consider $\lambda = false@l_1$. Then there exists $P_{11} =$ if $test$ then P'_{11} else P''_{11}, where $test@K'_{11} = false$, such that $l_1[[P_{11} \triangleright K'_{11} \ ||_{j=2}^{m} P_{1j} \triangleright K'_{1j}]] \ |_{i=2}^{n} l_i[[||_{j=1}^{m} P_{ij} \triangleright K'_{ij}]]$
$\xrightarrow{false@l_1} l_1[[P''_{11} \triangleright K'_{11} \ ||_{j=2}^{m} P_{1j} \triangleright K'_{1j}]] \ |_{i=2}^{n} l_i[[||_{j=1}^{m} P_{ij} \triangleright K'_{ij}]] = N'$. Then there exists $N'' = l_1[[P''_{11} \triangleright K''_{11} \ ||_{j=2}^{m} P_{1j} \triangleright K''_{1j}]] \ |_{i=2}^{n} l_i[[||_{j=1}^{m} P_{ij} \triangleright K''_{ij}]]$ such that $|_{i=1}^{n} l_i[[||_{j=1}^{m} P_{ij} \triangleright K''_{ij}]]) \xrightarrow{false@l_1} N''$. Since $K'_{ij} \subseteq K''_{ij}, 1 \leq i \leq n, 1 \leq j \leq m$, clearly $(N', N'') \in \mathcal{S}$.

- Consider $\lambda = create_f@l_1$. Then there exists $P_{11} = create(\langle f \mid v; \varnothing \rangle)$ then P'_{11} such that $l_1[[P_{11} \triangleright K'_{11} \ ||_{j=2}^{m} P_{1j} \triangleright K'_{1j}]] \ |_{i=2}^{n} l_i[[||_{j=1}^{m} P_{ij} \triangleright K'_{ij}]] \xrightarrow{create_f@l_1} l_1[[P'_{11} \triangleright K'_{11} \langle f \mid v; \varnothing \rangle \ ||_{j=2}^{m} P_{1j} \triangleright K'_{1j}]] \ |_{i=2}^{n} l_i[[||_{j=1}^{m} P_{ij} \triangleright K'_{ij}]] = N'$. Then there exists $N'' = l_1[[P'_{11} \triangleright K''_{11} \langle f \mid v; \varnothing \rangle \ ||_{j=2}^{m} P_{1j} \triangleright K''_{1j}]] \ |_{i=2}^{n} l_i[[||_{j=1}^{m} P_{ij} \triangleright K''_{ij}]]$ such that $|_{i=1}^{n} l_i[[||_{j=1}^{m} P_{ij} \triangleright K''_{ij}]]) \xrightarrow{create_f@l_1} N''$. Since $K'_{ij} \subseteq K''_{ij}, 1 \leq i \leq n, 1 \leq j \leq m$, then also $K'_{11} \langle f \mid v; \varnothing \rangle \subseteq K''_{11} \langle f \mid v; \varnothing \rangle$, and clearly $(N', N'') \in \mathcal{S}$.

- Consider $\lambda = upd_p@l_1$. Then there exists $P_{11} = update(p/f, v)$ then P'_{11} such that $l_1[[P_{11} \triangleright K'_{11} \ ||_{j=2}^{m} P_{1j} \triangleright K'_{1j}]] \ |_{i=2}^{n} l_i[[||_{j=1}^{m} P_{ij} \triangleright K'_{ij}]] \xrightarrow{upd_p@l_1} l_1[[P'_{11} \triangleright K^{u'}_{11}$
$||_{j=2}^{m} P_{1j} \triangleright K'_{1j}]] \ |_{i=2}^{n} l_i[[||_{j=1}^{m} P_{ij} \triangleright K'_{ij}]] = N'$. Then there exists $N'' = l_1[[P'_{11} \triangleright K^{u''}_{11}$
$||_{j=2}^{m} P_{1j} \triangleright K''_{1j}]] \ |_{i=2}^{n} l_i[[||_{j=1}^{m} P_{ij} \triangleright K''_{ij}]]$ such that $|_{i=1}^{n} l_i[[||_{j=1}^{m} P_{ij} \triangleright K''_{ij}]]) \xrightarrow{upd_p@l_1} N''$. Since $K'_{ij} \subseteq K''_{ij}, 1 \leq i \leq n, 1 \leq j \leq m$, then also $K^{u'}_{11} \subseteq K^{u''}_{11}$, and clearly $(N', N'') \in \mathcal{S}$.

- Let us assume that $|_{i=1}^{n} l_i[[||_{j=1}^{m} P_{ij} \triangleright K'_{ij}]] \xrightarrow{t} N'$. Then there exists $P'_{ij}, 1 \leq i \leq n$, $1 \leq j \leq m$, such that $|_{i=1}^{n} l_i[[||_{j=1}^{m} P_{ij} \triangleright K'_{ij}]] \xrightarrow{t} |_{i=1}^{n} l_i[[||_{j=1}^{m} P'_{ij} \triangleright K'_{ij}]] = N'$. Then there exists $N'' = |_{i=1}^{n} l_i[[||_{j=1}^{m} P'_{ij} \triangleright K''_{ij}]]$ such that $|_{i=1}^{n} l_i[[||_{j=1}^{m} P_{ij} \triangleright K''_{ij}]] \xrightarrow{t} N''$. Since $K'_{ij} \subseteq K''_{ij}, 1 \leq i \leq n, 1 \leq j \leq m$, clearly $(N', N'') \in \mathcal{S}$.

The symmetric cases follow by similar arguments. □

The following result shows that strong timed bisimulation is preserved even after complete computational steps of two knowTiMO networks.

Proposition 5. *Let N_1, N_2 be two knowTiMO networks. If $N_1 \sim N_2$ and $N_1 \stackrel{\Lambda, t}{\Longrightarrow} N'_1$, then there exists $N'_2 \in \mathcal{N}$ such that $N_2 \stackrel{\Lambda, t}{\Longrightarrow} N'_2$ and $N'_1 \sim N'_2$.*

Proof. Assuming that the finite multiset of actions Λ contains the labels $\{\lambda_1, \ldots, \lambda_k\}$, then the complete computational step $N_1 \stackrel{\Lambda, t}{\Longrightarrow} N'_1$ can be detailed as $N_1 \xrightarrow{\lambda_1} N^1_1 \ldots N^{k-1}_1 \xrightarrow{\lambda_k} N^k_1 \xrightarrow{t} N'_1$. Since $N_1 \xrightarrow{\lambda_1} N^1_1$ and $N_1 \sim N_2$, then according to Definition 1 there exists $N^1_2 \in \mathcal{N}$ such that $N_2 \xrightarrow{\lambda_1} N^1_2$ and $N^1_1 \sim N^1_2$. The same reasoning can be applied for another k steps, meaning that there exist $N^2_2, \ldots, N^k_2, N'_2 \in \mathcal{N}$ such that $N_2 \xrightarrow{\lambda_1} N^1_2 \ldots N^{k-1}_2 \xrightarrow{\lambda_k} N^k_2 \xrightarrow{t} N'_2$ and $N'_1 \sim N'_2$. By the definition of a complete computational step, it holds that $N_2 \xrightarrow{\lambda_1}$

$N_2^1 \ldots N_2^{k-1} \xrightarrow{\lambda_k} N_2^k \xrightarrow{t} N_2'$ can be written as $N_2 \xRightarrow{\Lambda,t} N_2'$. Thus, we obtained that there exists $N_2' \in \mathcal{N}$ such that $N_2 \xRightarrow{\Lambda,t} N_2'$ and $N_1' \sim N_2'$ (as desired). □

The next example illustrates that the relation $\sim$ is able to distinguish between agents with different knowledge if *update* operations are performed.

Example 2. *Consider that client C_2 is at location office$_4$, ready to communicate on channel a_4. To simplify the presentation, we take only a simplified definition of C_2 as follows:*

$C_2'(\text{office}_4) = a_4^{\Delta 4}?(\text{dest}_{C2,1}, \text{cost}_{C2,1})$
    then $update(/\text{agency}[\text{test}_4]/\text{dest}, \text{dest}_{C2,1})$
    else $update(/\text{agency}[\text{test}_4]/\text{dest}, \varepsilon\ )$.

Consider the following three networks in knowTiMo:
$N_1 = \text{office}_4[[C_2'(\text{office}_4) \triangleright K_{C2}]],$
$N_1' = \text{office}_4[[C_2'(\text{office}_4) \triangleright K_{C2}']],$
$N_1'' = \text{office}_4[[C_2'(\text{office}_4) \triangleright K_{C2}'']],$

where the knowledge of the agents is defined as:
$K_{C2} = \langle \text{agency} \mid \text{office}_4; \langle \text{dest} \mid \varepsilon \rangle \langle \text{price} \mid \varepsilon \rangle \rangle,$
$K_{C2}' = \langle \text{agency} \mid \text{office}_5; \langle \text{dest} \mid \varepsilon \rangle \langle \text{price} \mid \varepsilon \rangle \rangle,$
$K_{C2}'' = \emptyset.$

According to Definition 1, it holds that $N_1' \sim N_1''$, while $N_1 \not\sim N_1'$ and $N_1 \not\sim N_1''$. This is due to the fact that while all three networks are able to perform a time step of length 4 and to choose the else branch, only network N_1 is able to perform the update operation. Formally:

$$N_1 \xrightarrow{4} N_2 \xrightarrow{\textit{false}@\text{office}_4} N_3 \xrightarrow{upd/\text{agency}[\text{test}_4]/\text{dest} \ @\text{office}_4} N_4$$

and

$$N_1' \xrightarrow{4} N_2' \xrightarrow{\textit{false}@\text{office}_4} N_3' \not\xrightarrow{upd/\text{agency}[\text{test}_4]/\text{dest} \ @\text{office}_4}$$

$$N_1'' \xrightarrow{4} N_2'' \xrightarrow{\textit{false}@\text{office}_4} N_3'' \not\xrightarrow{upd/\text{agency}[\text{test}_4]/\text{dest} \ @\text{office}_4},$$

where the networks $N_2, N_3, N_4, N_2', N_3', N_2''$ and N_3'' in knowTiMo *are obtained by using the rules of Tables 2 and 3.*

3.2. Strong Bounded Timed Equivalences

We provide some notations used in the rest of the paper:
- A *timed relation* over the set $\mathcal{N}$ of networks is any relation $\mathcal{R} \subseteq \mathcal{N} \times \mathbb{N} \times \mathcal{N}$.
- The *identity timed relation* is
$$\iota \stackrel{df}{=} \{(N, t, N) \mid N \in \mathcal{N}, t \in \mathbb{N}\}.$$
- The *inverse of a timed relation* $\mathcal{R}$ is
$$\mathcal{R}^{-1} \stackrel{df}{=} \{(N_2, t, N_1) \mid (N_1, t, N_2) \in \mathcal{R}\}.$$
- The *composition of timed relations* $\mathcal{R}_1$ and $\mathcal{R}_2$ is
$$\mathcal{R}_1 \mathcal{R}_2 \stackrel{df}{=} \{(N, t, N'') \mid \exists N' \in \mathcal{N} : (N, t, N') \in \mathcal{R}_1 \wedge (N', t, N'') \in \mathcal{R}_2\}.$$
- If $\mathcal{R}$ is a timed relation and $t \in \mathbb{N}$, then
$$\mathcal{R}_t \stackrel{df}{=} \{(N_1, N_2) \mid (N_1, t, N_2) \in \mathcal{R}\}$$
is $\mathcal{R}$'s *t-projection*. We also denote $\mathcal{R}_\infty \stackrel{df}{=} \bigcup_{t \in \mathbb{N}} \mathcal{R}_t$.
- A timed relation $\mathcal{R}$ is a *timed equivalence* if $\mathcal{R}_\infty$ is an equivalence relation, and is an *equivalence up-to time* $t \in \mathbb{N}$ if $\bigcup_{0 \leq t' < t} \mathcal{R}_{t'}$ is an equivalence relation.

The equivalence $\sim$ requires an exact match of transitions of two networks during their entire evolutions. Sometimes this requirement is too strong. In many situations this requirement is relaxed [5], and real-time systems are allowed to behave in an expected way up to a certain amount t of time units. This impels one to define *bounded* timed equivalences up-to a given time t.

Definition 2 (Strong bounded timed bisimulation).
Let $\mathcal{R} \subseteq \mathcal{N} \times \mathbb{N} \times \mathcal{N}$ be a symmetric timed relation on $\mathbb{N}$ and on networks in knowTIMO.
1. $\mathcal{R}$ is a strong bounded timed bisimulation if

    - $(N_1, t, N_2) \in \mathcal{R}$ and $N_1 \xrightarrow{\lambda} N_1'$ implies that there exists $N_2' \in \mathcal{N}$ such that $N_2 \xrightarrow{\lambda} N_2'$ and $(N_1', t, N_2') \in \mathcal{R}$;

    - $(N_1, t, N_2) \in \mathcal{R}$ and $N_1 \xrightarrow{t'} N_1'$ implies that there exists $N_2' \in \mathcal{N}$ such that $N_2 \xrightarrow{t'} N_2'$ and $(N_1', t - t', N_2') \in \mathcal{R}$.

2. The strong bounded timed bisimilarity is the union $\simeq$ of all strong bounded timed bisimulations $\mathcal{R}$.

The following results illustrate some properties of the strong bounded timed bisimulations. In particular, we prove that the equivalence relation $\simeq$ (that is strictly included in relation $\sim$) is the largest strong bounded timed bisimulation.

Proposition 6.
1. Identity, inverse, composition and union of strong bounded timed bisimulations are strong bounded timed bisimulations.
2. $\simeq$ is the largest strong bounded timed bisimulation.
3. $\simeq$ is a timed equivalence.
4. $\simeq \subsetneq \sim$.

Proof.
1. We treat each relations separately showing that it respects the conditions from Definition 2 for being a strong bounded timed bisimulation.

    (a) The identity relation ι is a strong bounded timed bisimulation.
        i. Assume $(N, t, N) \in \iota$. Consider $N \xrightarrow{\lambda} N'$; then $(N', t, N') \in \iota$.
        ii. Assume $(N, t, N) \in \iota$. Consider $N \xrightarrow{t'} N'$; then $(N', t - t', N') \in \iota$.

    (b) The inverse of a strong bounded timed bisimulation is a strong bounded timed bisimulation.
        i. Assume $(N_1, t, N_2) \in \mathcal{R}^{-1}$, namely $(N_2, t, N_1) \in \mathcal{R}$. Consider $N_2 \xrightarrow{\lambda} N_2'$; then for some N_1' we have $N_1 \xrightarrow{\lambda} N_1'$ and $(N_2', t, N_1') \in \mathcal{R}$, namely $(N_1', t, N_2') \in \mathcal{R}^{-1}$. By similar reasoning, if $N_1 \xrightarrow{\lambda} N_1'$ then we can find N_2' such that $N_2 \xrightarrow{\lambda} N_2'$ and $(N_1', t, N_2') \in \mathcal{R}^{-1}$.
        ii. Assume $(N_1, t, N_2) \in \mathcal{R}^{-1}$, namely $(N_2, N_1) \in \mathcal{R}$. Consider $N_2 \xrightarrow{t'} N_2'$; then for some N_1' we have $N_1 \xrightarrow{t'} N_1'$ and $(N_2', t - t', N_1') \in \mathcal{R}$, namely $(N_1', t - t', N_2') \in \mathcal{R}^{-1}$. By similar reasoning, if $N_1 \xrightarrow{t'} N_1'$ then we can find N_2' such that $N_2 \xrightarrow{t'} N_2'$ and $(N_1', t - t', N_2') \in \mathcal{R}^{-1}$.

    (c) The composition of strong bounded timed bisimulations is a strong bounded timed bisimulation.
        i. Assume $(N_1, t, N_2) \in \mathcal{R}_1 \mathcal{R}_2$. Then for some N we have $(N_1, t, N) \in \mathcal{R}_1$ and $(N, t, N_2) \in \mathcal{R}_2$. Consider $N_1 \xrightarrow{\lambda} N_1'$; then for some N', since $(N_1, t, N) \in \mathcal{R}_1$, we have $N \xrightarrow{\lambda} N'$ and $(N_1', t, N') \in \mathcal{R}_1$. Also, since $(N, t, N_2) \in \mathcal{R}_2$ we have for some N_2' that $N_2 \xrightarrow{\lambda} N_2'$ and $(N', t, N_2') \in \mathcal{R}_2$. Thus, $(N_1', t, N_2') \in \mathcal{R}_1 \mathcal{R}_2$. By similar reasoning, if $N_2 \xrightarrow{\lambda} N_2'$ then we can find N_1' such that $N_1 \xrightarrow{\lambda} N_1'$ and $(N', t, N_2') \in \mathcal{R}_2$.

ii. Assume $(N_1, t, N_2) \in \mathcal{R}_1 \mathcal{R}_2$. Then for some N we have $(N_1, t, N) \in \mathcal{R}_1$ and $(N, t, N_2) \in \mathcal{R}_2$. Consider $N_1 \stackrel{t'}{\leadsto} N'_1$; then for some N', since $(N_1, t, N) \in \mathcal{R}_1$, we have $N \stackrel{t'}{\leadsto} N'$ and $(N'_1, t-t', N') \in \mathcal{R}_1$. Also, since $(N, t, N_2) \in \mathcal{R}_2$, for some N'_2 we have $N_2 \stackrel{t'}{\leadsto} N'_2$ and $(N', t-t', N'_2) \in \mathcal{R}_2$. Thus, $(N'_1 t - t', N'_2) \in \mathcal{R}_1 \mathcal{R}_2$. By similar reasoning, if $N_2 \stackrel{t'}{\leadsto} N'_2$ then we can find N'_1 such that $N_1 \stackrel{t'}{\leadsto} N'_1$ and $(N', t-t', N'_2) \in \mathcal{R}_2$.

(d) The union of strong bounded timed bisimulations is a strong bounded timed bisimulation.

i. Assume $(N_1, t, N_2) \in \bigcup_{i \in I} \mathcal{R}_i$. Then for some $i \in I$ we have that $(N_1, t, N_2) \in \mathcal{R}_i$. Consider $N_1 \stackrel{\lambda}{\to} N'_1$; then for some N'_2, since $(N_1, t, N_2) \in \mathcal{R}_i$, we have $N_2 \stackrel{\lambda}{\to} N'_2$ and $(N'_1, t, N'_2) \in \mathcal{R}_i$. Thus, $(N'_1, t, N'_2) \in \bigcup_{i \in I} \mathcal{R}_i$. By similar reasoning, if $N_2 \stackrel{\lambda}{\to} N'_2$ then we can find N'_1 such that $N_1 \stackrel{\lambda}{\to} N'_1$ and $(N'_1, t, N'_2) \in \mathcal{R}_i$, namely $(N'_1, t, N'_2) \in \bigcup_{i \in I} \mathcal{R}_i$.

ii. Assume $(N_1, t, N_2) \in \bigcup_{i \in I} \mathcal{R}_i$. Then for some $i \in I$ we have that $(N_1, t, N_2) \in \mathcal{R}_i$. Consider $N_1 \stackrel{t'}{\leadsto} N'_1$; then for some N'_2, since $(N_1, t, N_2) \in \mathcal{R}_i$, we have $N_2 \stackrel{t'}{\leadsto} N'_2$ and $(N'_1, t-t', N'_2) \in \mathcal{R}_i$. Thus, $(N'_1, t-t', N'_2) \in \bigcup_{i \in I} \mathcal{R}_i$. By similar reasoning, if $N_2 \stackrel{t'}{\leadsto} N'_2$ then we can find N'_1 such that $N_1 \stackrel{t'}{\leadsto} N'_1$ and $(N'_1, t-t', N'_2) \in \mathcal{R}_i$, namely $(N'_1, t-t', N'_2) \in \bigcup_{i \in I} \mathcal{R}_i$.

2. By the previous case (the union part), $\simeq$ is a strong bounded timed bisimulation and includes any other strong bounded timed bisimulation.

3. Proving that relation $\simeq$ is a timed equivalence requires proving that it satisfies reflexivity, symmetry and transitivity. We consider each of them in what follows:

    (a) Reflexivity: For any network N, $N \simeq N$ results from the fact that the identity relation is a strong bounded timed bisimulation.
    (b) Symmetry: If $N \simeq N'$, then $(N, t, N') \in \mathcal{R}$ for some strong bounded timed bisimulation $\mathcal{R}$. Hence $(N', t, N) \in \mathcal{R}^{-1}$, and so $N' \simeq N$ because the inverse relation is a strong bounded timed bisimulation.
    (c) Transitivity: If $N \simeq N'$ and $N' \simeq N''$ then $(N, t, N') \in \mathcal{R}_1$ and $(N', t, N'') \in \mathcal{R}_2$ for some strong bounded timed bisimulations $\mathcal{R}_1$ and $\mathcal{R}_2$. Thus, it holds that $(N, t, N'') \in \mathcal{R}_1 \mathcal{R}_2$, and so $N \simeq N''$ due to the fact that the composition relation is a strong bounded timed bisimulation.

4. We provide Example 3 below that illustrates the strict inclusion. □

The next result claims that strong bounded timed equivalence $\simeq_t$ over processes is preserved even if the local knowledge of the agents is expanded. This is consistent with the fact that the processes affect the same portion of their knowledge.

Proposition 7. *If $K'_{ij} \subseteq K''_{ij}$, for $1 \leq i \leq n$, $1 \leq j \leq m$, then*
$$|_{i=1}^n l_i[[||_{j=1}^m P_{ij} \triangleright K'_{ij}]] \simeq |_{i=1}^n l_i[[||_{j=1}^m P_{ij} \triangleright K''_{ij}]].$$

Proof. We show that $\mathcal{S}$ is a strong bounded timed bisimulation, where:
$$\mathcal{S} = \{(|_{i=1}^n l_i[[||_{j=1}^m P_{ij} \triangleright K'_{ij}]], t, |_{i=1}^n l_i[[||_{j=1}^m P_{ij} \triangleright K''_{ij}]]) : K'_{ij} \subseteq K''_{ij}, 1 \leq i \leq n, 1 \leq j \leq m\}.$$
The proof is by induction on the last performed step:

- Let us assume that $|_{i=1}^n l_i[[||_{j=1}^m P_{ij} \triangleright K'_{ij}]] \stackrel{\lambda}{\to} N'$. Depending on the value of λ, there are several cases:

- Consider $\lambda = a!?@l_1$. Then there exists $P_{11} = a^{\Delta t_1}!\langle v \rangle$ then P'_{11} else P''_{11} and $P_{11} = a^{\Delta t_2}?(u)$ then P'_{12} else P''_{12} such that $l_1[[P_{11} \triangleright K'_{11} \parallel P_{12} \triangleright K'_{12} \parallel\parallel_{j=3}^{m} P_{1j} \triangleright K'_{1j}]]$ $\parallel_{i=2}^{n} l_i[[\parallel_{j=1}^{m} P_{ij} \triangleright K'_{ij}]] \xrightarrow{a!?@l_1} l_1[[P'_{11} \triangleright K'_{11} \parallel P'_{12} \triangleright K'_{12} \parallel\parallel_{j=3}^{m} P_{1j} \triangleright K'_{1j}]]$ $\parallel_{i=2}^{n} l_i[[\parallel_{j=1}^{m} P_{ij} \triangleright K'_{ij}]] = N'$. Then there exists $N'' = [[P'_{11} \triangleright K''_{11} \parallel P'_{12} \triangleright K''_{12}$ $\parallel\parallel_{j=3}^{m} P_{1j} \triangleright K''_{1j}]] \parallel_{i=2}^{n} l_i[[\parallel_{j=1}^{m} P_{ij} \triangleright K''_{ij}]]$ such that $\parallel_{i=1}^{n} l_i[[\parallel_{j=1}^{m} P_{ij} \triangleright K''_{ij}]] \xrightarrow{a!?@l_1} N''$. Since $K'_{ij} \subseteq K''_{ij}, 1 \leq i \leq n, 1 \leq j \leq m$, clearly $(N', t, N'') \in \mathcal{S}$.

- Consider $\lambda = a!^{\Delta 0}@l_1$. Then there exists $P_{11} = a^{\Delta 0}!\langle v \rangle$ then P'_{11} else P''_{11} such that $l_1[[P_{11} \triangleright K'_{11} \parallel\parallel_{j=2}^{m} P_{1j} \triangleright K'_{1j}]] \parallel_{i=2}^{n} l_i[[\parallel_{j=1}^{m} P_{ij} \triangleright K'_{ij}]] \xrightarrow{a!^{\Delta 0}@l_1} l_1[[P'_{11} \triangleright K'_{11}$ $\parallel\parallel_{j=2}^{m} P_{1j} \triangleright K'_{1j}]] \parallel_{i=2}^{n} l_i[[\parallel_{j=1}^{m} P_{ij} \triangleright K'_{ij}]] = N'$. Then there exists $N'' = l_1[[P'_{11} \triangleright K''_{11}$ $\parallel\parallel_{j=2}^{m} P_{1j} \triangleright K''_{1j}]] \parallel_{i=2}^{n} l_i[[\parallel_{j=1}^{m} P_{ij} \triangleright K''_{ij}]]$ such that $\parallel_{i=1}^{n} l_i[[\parallel_{j=1}^{m} P_{ij} \triangleright K''_{ij}]]) \xrightarrow{a!^{\Delta 0}@l_1} N''$. Since $K'_{ij} \subseteq K''_{ij}, 1 \leq i \leq n, 1 \leq j \leq m$, clearly $(N', t, N'') \in \mathcal{S}$.

- Consider $\lambda = a?^{\Delta 0}@l_1$. Then there exists $P_{11} = a^{\Delta 0}?(u)$ then P'_{11} else P''_{11} such that $l_1[[P_{11} \triangleright K'_{11} \parallel\parallel_{j=2}^{m} P_{1j} \triangleright K'_{1j}]] \parallel_{i=2}^{n} l_i[[\parallel_{j=1}^{m} P_{ij} \triangleright K'_{ij}]] \xrightarrow{a?^{\Delta 0}@l_1} l_1[[P'_{11} \triangleright K'_{11}$ $\parallel\parallel_{j=2}^{m} P_{1j} \triangleright K'_{1j}]] \parallel_{i=2}^{n} l_i[[\parallel_{j=1}^{m} P_{ij} \triangleright K'_{ij}]] = N'$. Then there exists $N'' = l_1[[P'_{11} \triangleright K''_{11}$ $\parallel\parallel_{j=2}^{m} P_{1j} \triangleright K''_{1j}]] \parallel_{i=2}^{n} l_i[[\parallel_{j=1}^{m} P_{ij} \triangleright K''_{ij}]]$ such that $\parallel_{i=1}^{n} l_i[[\parallel_{j=1}^{m} P_{ij} \triangleright K''_{ij}]]) \xrightarrow{a?^{\Delta 0}@l_1} N''$. Since $K'_{ij} \subseteq K''_{ij}, 1 \leq i \leq n, 1 \leq j \leq m$, clearly $(N', t, N'') \in \mathcal{S}$.

- Consider $\lambda = l_1 \triangleright l_2$. Then there exists $P_{11} = go^0 \, l_2$ then P'_{11} such that $l_1[[P_{11} \triangleright K'_{11}$ $\parallel\parallel_{j=2}^{m} P_{1j} \triangleright K'_{1j}]] \parallel_{i=2}^{n} l_i[[\parallel_{j=1}^{m} P_{ij} \triangleright K'_{ij}]] \xrightarrow{l_1 \triangleright l_2} l_1[[\parallel_{j=2}^{m} P_{1j} \triangleright K'_{1j}]] \mid l_2[[P'_{11} \triangleright K'_{11}$ $\parallel\parallel_{j=1}^{m} P_{2j} \triangleright K'_{2j}]] \parallel_{i=3}^{n} l_i[[\parallel_{j=1}^{m} P_{ij} \triangleright K'_{ij}]] = N'$. Then there exists $N'' = l_1[[\parallel_{j=2}^{m} P_{1j} \triangleright K''_{1j}]] \mid l_2[[P'_{11} \triangleright K''_{11} \parallel\parallel_{j=1}^{m} P_{2j} \triangleright K''_{2j}]] \parallel_{i=3}^{n} l_i[[\parallel_{j=1}^{m} P_{ij} \triangleright K''_{ij}]]$ such that $\parallel_{i=1}^{n} l_i[[\parallel_{j=1}^{m} P_{ij} \triangleright K''_{ij}]]) \xrightarrow{l_1 \triangleright l_2} N''$. Since $K'_{ij} \subseteq K''_{ij}, 1 \leq i \leq n, 1 \leq j \leq m$, clearly $(N', t, N'') \in \mathcal{S}$.

- Consider $\lambda = true@l_1$. Then there exists $P_{11} = $ if $test$ then P'_{11} else P''_{11}, where $test@K'_{11} = true$, such that $l_1[[P_{11} \triangleright K'_{11} \parallel\parallel_{j=2}^{m} P_{1j} \triangleright K'_{1j}]] \parallel_{i=2}^{n} l_i[[\parallel_{j=1}^{m} P_{ij} \triangleright K'_{ij}]]$ $\xrightarrow{true@l_1} l_1[[P'_{11} \triangleright K'_{11} \parallel\parallel_{j=2}^{m} P_{1j} \triangleright K'_{1j}]] \parallel_{i=2}^{n} l_i[[\parallel_{j=1}^{m} P_{ij} \triangleright K'_{ij}]] = N'$. Then there exists $N'' = l_1[[P'_{11} \triangleright K''_{11} \parallel\parallel_{j=2}^{m} P_{1j} \triangleright K''_{1j}]] \parallel_{i=2}^{n} l_i[[\parallel_{j=1}^{m} P_{ij} \triangleright K''_{ij}]]$ such that $\parallel_{i=1}^{n} l_i[[\parallel_{j=1}^{m} P_{ij} \triangleright K''_{ij}]]) \xrightarrow{true@l_1} N''$. Since $K'_{ij} \subseteq K''_{ij}, 1 \leq i \leq n, 1 \leq j \leq m$, clearly $(N', t, N'') \in \mathcal{S}$.

- Consider $\lambda = false@l_1$. Then there exists $P_{11} = $ if $test$ then P'_{11} else P''_{11}, where $test@K'_{11} = false$, such that $l_1[[P_{11} \triangleright K'_{11} \parallel\parallel_{j=2}^{m} P_{1j} \triangleright K'_{1j}]] \parallel_{i=2}^{n} l_i[[\parallel_{j=1}^{m} P_{ij} \triangleright K'_{ij}]]$ $\xrightarrow{false@l_1} l_1[[P''_{11} \triangleright K'_{11} \parallel\parallel_{j=2}^{m} P_{1j} \triangleright K'_{1j}]] \parallel_{i=2}^{n} l_i[[\parallel_{j=1}^{m} P_{ij} \triangleright K'_{ij}]] = N'$. Then there exists $N'' = l_1[[P''_{11} \triangleright K''_{11} \parallel\parallel_{j=2}^{m} P_{1j} \triangleright K''_{1j}]] \parallel_{i=2}^{n} l_i[[\parallel_{j=1}^{m} P_{ij} \triangleright K''_{ij}]]$ such that $\parallel_{i=1}^{n} l_i[[\parallel_{j=1}^{m} P_{ij} \triangleright K''_{ij}]]) \xrightarrow{false@l_1} N''$. Since $K'_{ij} \subseteq K''_{ij}, 1 \leq i \leq n, 1 \leq j \leq m$, clearly $(N', t, N'') \in \mathcal{S}$.

- Consider $\lambda = create_f@l_1$. Then there exists $P_{11} = create(\langle f \mid v; \varnothing \rangle)$ then P'_{11} such that $l_1[[P_{11} \triangleright K'_{11} \parallel\parallel_{j=2}^{m} P_{1j} \triangleright K'_{1j}]] \parallel_{i=2}^{n} l_i[[\parallel_{j=1}^{m} P_{ij} \triangleright K'_{ij}]] \xrightarrow{create_f@l_1} l_1[[P'_{11} \triangleright K'_{11}$ $\langle f \mid v; \varnothing \rangle \parallel\parallel_{j=2}^{m} P_{1j} \triangleright K'_{1j}]] \parallel_{i=2}^{n} l_i[[\parallel_{j=1}^{m} P_{ij} \triangleright K'_{ij}]] = N'$. Then there exists $N'' = l_1[[P'_{11} \triangleright K''_{11} \, \langle f \mid v; \varnothing \rangle \parallel\parallel_{j=2}^{m} P_{1j} \triangleright K''_{1j}]] \parallel_{i=2}^{n} l_i[[\parallel_{j=1}^{m} P_{ij} \triangleright K''_{ij}]]$ such that $\parallel_{i=1}^{n} l_i[[\parallel_{j=1}^{m} P_{ij} \triangleright K''_{ij}]]) \xrightarrow{create_f@l_1} N''$. Since $K'_{ij} \subseteq K''_{ij}, 1 \leq i \leq n, 1 \leq j \leq m$, then also $K'_{11} \langle f \mid v; \varnothing \rangle \subseteq K''_{11} \langle f \mid v; \varnothing \rangle$, and clearly $(N', t, N'') \in \mathcal{S}$.

- Consider $\lambda = upd_p@l_1$. Then there exists $P_{11} = update(p/f, v)$ then P'_{11} such that $l_1[[P_{11} \triangleright K'_{11} \parallel\parallel_{j=2}^{m} P_{1j} \triangleright K'_{1j}]] \parallel_{i=2}^{n} l_i[[\parallel_{j=1}^{m} P_{ij} \triangleright K'_{ij}]] \xrightarrow{upd_p@l_1} l_1[[P'_{11} \triangleright K^{u'}_{11}$ $\parallel\parallel_{j=2}^{m} P_{1j} \triangleright K'_{1j}]] \parallel_{i=2}^{n} l_i[[\parallel_{j=1}^{m} P_{ij} \triangleright K'_{ij}]] = N'$. Then there exists $N'' = l_1[[P'_{11} \triangleright K^{u''}_{11}$

$||_{j=2}^{m} P_{1j} \triangleright K'_{1j}]] \ |_{i=2}^{n} l_i[[||_{j=1}^{m} P_{ij} \triangleright K'_{ij}]]]$ such that $|_{i=1}^{n} l_i[[||_{j=1}^{m} P_{ij} \triangleright K''_{ij}]]$ $\xrightarrow{upd_p@l_1} N''$. Since $K'_{ij} \subseteq K''_{ij}, 1 \leq i \leq n, 1 \leq j \leq m$, then also $K'^{u}_{11} \subseteq K''^{u}_{11}$, and clearly $(N', t, N'') \in \mathcal{S}$.

- Let us assume that $|_{i=1}^{n} l_i[[||_{j=1}^{m} P_{ij} \triangleright K'_{ij}]] \xrightarrow{t'} N'$. Then there exists $P'_{ij}, 1 \leq i \leq n$, $1 \leq j \leq m$, such that $|_{i=1}^{n} l_i[[||_{j=1}^{m} P_{ij} \triangleright K'_{ij}]] \xrightarrow{t'} |_{i=1}^{n} l_i[[||_{j=1}^{m} P'_{ij} \triangleright K'_{ij}]] = N'$. Then there exists $N'' = |_{i=1}^{n} l_i[[||_{j=1}^{m} P'_{ij} \triangleright K''_{ij}]]$ such that $|_{i=1}^{n} l_i[[||_{j=1}^{m} P_{ij} \triangleright K''_{ij}]] \xrightarrow{t} N''$. Since $K'_{ij} \subseteq K''_{ij}, 1 \leq i \leq n, 1 \leq j \leq m$, clearly $(N', t-t', N'') \in \mathcal{S}$.

The symmetric cases follow by similar arguments. □

The following result shows that strong bounded timed bisimulation is preserved even after complete computational steps of two networks in knowTiMo.

Proposition 8. *Let N_1, N_2 be two knowTiMo networks.*
If $N_1 \simeq_t N_2$ and $N_1 \xrightarrow{\Lambda, t'} N'_1$, then there is $N'_2 \in \mathcal{N}$ such that $N_2 \xrightarrow{\Lambda, t'} N'_2$ and $N'_1 \simeq_{t-t'} N'_2$.

Proof. Assuming that the finite multiset of actions Λ contains the labels $\{\lambda_1, \ldots, \lambda_k\}$, then the complete computational step $N_1 \xrightarrow{\Lambda, t} N'_1$ can be detailed as $N_1 \xrightarrow{\lambda_1} N_1^1 \ldots N_1^{k-1} \xrightarrow{\lambda_k} N_1^k \xrightarrow{t'} N'_1$. Note that $N_1 \simeq_t N_2$ means that $(N_1, t, N_2) \in \simeq$. Since $N_1 \xrightarrow{\lambda_1} N_1^1$ and $(N_1, t, N_2) \in \simeq$, then according to Definition 2 there exists $N_2^1 \in \mathcal{N}$ such that $N_2 \xrightarrow{\lambda_1} N_2^1$ and $(N_1^1, t, N_2^1) \in \simeq$. The same reasoning can be applied for another k steps, meaning that there exist $N_2^2, \ldots, N_2^k, N'_2 \in \mathcal{N}$ such that $N_2 \xrightarrow{\lambda_1} N_2^1 \ldots N_2^{k-1} \xrightarrow{\lambda_k} N_2^k \xrightarrow{t'} N'_2$ and $(N'_1, t-t', N'_2) \in \simeq$, namely $N'_1 \simeq_{t-t'} N'_2$. The definition of a complete computational step implies that $N_2 \xrightarrow{\lambda_1} N_2^1 \ldots N_2^{k-1} \xrightarrow{\lambda_k} N_2^k \xrightarrow{t'} N'_2$ can be written as $N_2 \xrightarrow{\Lambda, t'} N'_2$. Thus, we obtained that there exists $N'_2 \in \mathcal{N}$ such that $N_2 \xrightarrow{\Lambda, t'} N'_2$ and $N'_1 \simeq_{t-t'} N'_2$ (as desired). □

Strong bounded timed bisimulation satisfies the property that if two networks are equivalent up-to a certain deadline t, they are equivalent up-to any deadline t' before t, i.e., $t' \leq t$.

Proposition 9. *If $N \simeq_t N'$ and $t' \leq t$, then $N \simeq_{t'} N'$.*

Proof. Assume $N \simeq_t N'$ and that there exist the networks $N_1, \ldots, N_k \in \mathcal{N}$, the set of actions $\Lambda_1, \ldots, \Lambda_k$ and the timers $t_1, \ldots, t_k \in \mathbb{N}$ such that $N \xrightarrow{\Lambda_1, t_1} N_1 \ldots \xrightarrow{\Lambda_k, t_k} N_k$ and also $t = t_1 + \ldots + t_k$. According to Proposition 8, there exist the networks $N'_1, \ldots, N'_k \in \mathcal{N}$ such that $N' \xrightarrow{\Lambda_1, t_1} N'_1 \ldots \xrightarrow{\Lambda_k, t_k} N'_k$, and also $N_1 \simeq_{t-t_1} N'_1, \ldots, N_k \simeq_0 N'_k$. Since $t' \leq t$, then there exists an $l \leq k$ and a $t'' \in \mathbb{N}$ such that $t_1 + \ldots + t_l + t'' = t'$. By using Theorem 1, it holds that there exists N^1 such that $N \xrightarrow{\Lambda_1, t_1} N_1 \ldots \xrightarrow{\Lambda_l, t_l} N_l \xrightarrow{\Lambda_{l+1}, t''} N^1$. In a similar manner, by using Theorem 1, it holds that there exists N^2 such that $N' \xrightarrow{\Lambda_1, t_1} N'_1 \ldots \xrightarrow{\Lambda_l, t_l} N'_l \xrightarrow{\Lambda_{l+1}, t''} N^2$. Since N^1 and N^2 can perform only time passing steps of length at most $t_{l+1} - t''$, this means that $N^1 \simeq_0 N^2$, However, according to Definition 2, this means that we obtain the desired relation $N \simeq_{t'} N'$ because the networks N and N' can match their behaviour for t' steps. □

The next example illustrates that the relation $\simeq_t$ is able to treat as bisimilar some multi-agent systems that are not bisimilar using the relation $\sim$.

Example 3. Let us consider the networks of Example 2, namely:
$$N_1 = \text{office}_4[[C'_2(\text{office}_4) \triangleright K_{C2}]],$$
$$N'_1 = \text{office}_4[[C'_2(\text{office}_4) \triangleright K'_{C2}]],$$
$$N''_1 = \text{office}_4[[C'_2(\text{office}_4) \triangleright K''_{C2}]],$$
where the knowledge of the agents is defined as:
$$K_{C2} = \langle \text{agency} \mid \text{office}_4; \langle \text{dest} \mid \varepsilon \rangle \langle \text{price} \mid \varepsilon \rangle \rangle,$$
$$K'_{C2} = \langle \text{agency} \mid \text{office}_5; \langle \text{dest} \mid \varepsilon \rangle \langle \text{price} \mid \varepsilon \rangle \rangle,$$
$$K''_{C2} = \emptyset.$$

Even if it holds that $N'_1 \sim N''_1$ while $N_1 \not\sim N'_1$ and $N_1 \not\sim N''_1$, by applying Definition 2, it results that N_1, N'_1 and N''_1 are strong bounded timed bisimilar before the 4th time unit since they have the same evolutions during this deadline, namely $N'_1 \simeq_4 N''_1$, $N_1 \simeq_4 N'_1$ and $N_1 \simeq_4 N''_1$. If $t > 4$, we have that $N'_1 \simeq_t N''_1$, while $N_1 \not\simeq_t N'_1$ and $N_1 \not\simeq_t N''_1$. Thus, both Definitions 1 and 2 return the same relations among N_1, N'_1 and N''_1 for $t > 4$.

This example illustrates also the strict inclusion relation from item 4 of Proposition 6.

3.3. Weak Knowledge Equivalences

Both equivalence relations $\sim$ and $\simeq$ require an exact match of transitions and time steps of two networks in knowTIMO; this makes them too restrictive. We can introduce a weaker version of network equivalence by looking only at the steps that affect the knowledge data, namely the *create* and *update* steps. Thus, we introduce a knowledge equivalence in order to distinguish between networks based on the interaction of the agents with their local knowledge: the networks are equivalent if we observe only *create* and *update* actions along same paths, regardless of the values added to the knowledge.

Definition 3 (Weak knowledge bisimulation). *Let $\mathcal{R} \subseteq \mathcal{N} \times \mathcal{N}$ be a symmetric binary relation over networks in knowTIMO.*

1. *$\mathcal{R}$ is a weak knowledge bisimulation if*

    - *$(N_1, N_2) \in \mathcal{R}$ and $N_1 \xrightarrow{create_f@l} {}^* N'_1$ implies that there exists $N'_2 \in \mathcal{N}$ such that $N_2 \xrightarrow{create_f@l} {}^* N'_2$ and $(N'_1, N'_2) \in \mathcal{R}$;*
    - *$(N_1, N_2) \in \mathcal{R}$ and $N_1 \xrightarrow{upd_p@l} {}^* N'_1$ implies that there exists $N'_2 \in \mathcal{N}$ such that $N_2 \xrightarrow{upd_p@l} {}^* N'_2$ and $(N'_1, N'_2) \in \mathcal{R}$;*

2. *The weak knowledge bisimilarity is the union $\cong$ of all weak knowledge bisimulations $\mathcal{R}$.*

The following results present some properties of the weak knowledge bisimulations. In particular, we prove that the equivalence relation $\cong$ (that is strictly included in relation $\sim$) is the largest weak knowledge bisimulation.

Proposition 10.
1. *Identity, inverse, composition and union of weak knowledge bisimulations are weak knowledge bisimulations.*
2. *$\cong$ is the largest weak knowledge bisimulation.*
3. *$\cong$ is an equivalence.*
4. *$\cong \subsetneq \sim$.*

Proof.
1. We treat each relation separately showing that it respects the conditions from Definition 3 for being a weak knowledge bisimulation.

    (a) The identity relation $Id_\mathcal{R}$ is a weak knowledge bisimulation.

      i. Assume $(N, N) \in Id_\mathcal{R}$. Consider $N \xrightarrow{create_f@l} {}^* N'$; then $(N', N') \in Id_\mathcal{R}$.

ii. Assume $(N, N) \in Id_\mathcal{R}$. Consider $N \xRightarrow{upd_p@l}{}^* N'$; then $(N', N') \in Id_\mathcal{R}$.

(b) The inverse of a weak knowledge bisimulation is a weak knowledge bisimulation.

i. Assume $(N_1, N_2) \in \mathcal{R}^{-1}$, namely $(N_2, N_1) \in \mathcal{R}$. Consider $N_2 \xRightarrow{create_f@l}{}^* N_2'$; then for some N_1' we have $N_1 \xRightarrow{create_f@l}{}^* N_1'$ and $(N_2', N_1') \in \mathcal{R}$, namely $(N_1', N_2') \in \mathcal{R}^{-1}$. By similar reasoning, if $N_1 \xRightarrow{create_f@l}{}^* N_1'$ then we can find N_2' such that $N_2 \xRightarrow{create_f@l}{}^* N_2'$ and $(N_1', N_2') \in \mathcal{R}^{-1}$.

ii. Assume $(N_1, N_2) \in \mathcal{R}^{-1}$, namely $(N_2, N_1) \in \mathcal{R}$. Consider $N_2 \xRightarrow{upd_f@l}{}^* N_2'$; then for some N_1' we have $N_1 \xRightarrow{upd_f@l}{}^* N_1'$ and $(N_2', N_1') \in \mathcal{R}$, namely $(N_1', N_2') \in \mathcal{R}^{-1}$. By similar reasoning, if $N_1 \xRightarrow{upd_f@l}{}^* N_1'$ then we can find N_2' such that $N_2 \xRightarrow{upd_f@l}{}^* N_2'$ and $(N_1', N_2') \in \mathcal{R}^{-1}$.

(c) The composition of weak knowledge bisimulations is a weak knowledge bisimulation.

i. Assume $(N_1, N_2) \in \mathcal{R}_1 \mathcal{R}_2$. Then for some N we have $(N_1, N) \in \mathcal{R}_1$ and $(N, N_2) \in \mathcal{R}_2$. Consider $N_1 \xRightarrow{create_f@l}{}^* N_1'$; then for some N', since $(N_1, N) \in \mathcal{R}_1$, we have $N \xRightarrow{create_f@l}{}^* N'$ and $(N_1', N') \in \mathcal{R}_1$. Also, since $(N, N_2) \in \mathcal{R}_2$ we have for some N_2' that $N_2 \xRightarrow{create_f@l}{}^* N_2'$ and $(N', N_2') \in \mathcal{R}_2$. Thus, $(N_1', N_2') \in \mathcal{R}_1 \mathcal{R}_2$. By similar reasoning, if $N_2 \xRightarrow{create_f@l}{}^* N_2'$ then we can find N_1' such that $N_1 \xRightarrow{create_f@l}{}^* N_1'$ and $(N', N_2') \in \mathcal{R}_2$.

ii. Assume $(N_1, N_2) \in \mathcal{R}_1 \mathcal{R}_2$. Then for some N we have $(N_1, N) \in \mathcal{R}_1$ and $(N, N_2) \in \mathcal{R}_2$. Consider $N_1 \xRightarrow{upd_f@l}{}^* N_1'$; then for some N', since $(N_1, N) \in \mathcal{R}_1$, we have $N \xRightarrow{upd_f@l}{}^* N'$ and $(N_1', N') \in \mathcal{R}_1$. Also, since $(N, N_2) \in \mathcal{R}_2$ we have for some N_2' that $N_2 \xRightarrow{upd_f@l}{}^* N_2'$ and $(N', N_2') \in \mathcal{R}_2$. Thus, $(N_1', N_2') \in \mathcal{R}_1 \mathcal{R}_2$. By similar reasoning, if $N_2 \xRightarrow{upd_f@l}{}^* N_2'$ then we can find N_1' such that $N_1 \xRightarrow{upd_f@l}{}^* N_1'$ and $(N', N_2') \in \mathcal{R}_2$.

(d) The union of weak knowledge bisimulations is a weak knowledge bisimulation.

i. Assume $(N_1, N_2) \in \bigcup_{i \in I} \mathcal{R}_i$. Then for some $i \in I$ we have $(N_1, N_2) \in \mathcal{R}_i$. Consider $N_1 \xRightarrow{create_f@l}{}^* N_1'$; then for some N_2', since $(N_1, N_2) \in \mathcal{R}_i$, we have $N_2 \xRightarrow{create_f@l}{}^* N_2'$ and $(N_1', N_2') \in \mathcal{R}_i$. Thus, $(N_1', N_2') \in \bigcup_{i \in I} \mathcal{R}_i$. By similar reasoning, if $N_2 \xRightarrow{create_f@l}{}^* N_2'$ then we can find N_1' such that $N_1 \xRightarrow{create_f@l}{}^* N_1'$ and $(N_1', N_2') \in \mathcal{R}_i$, namely $(N_1', N_2') \in \bigcup_{i \in I} \mathcal{R}_i$.

ii. Assume $(N_1, N_2) \in \bigcup_{i \in I} \mathcal{R}_i$. Then for some $i \in I$ we have $(N_1, N_2) \in \mathcal{R}_i$. Consider $N_1 \xRightarrow{upd_f@l}{}^* N_1'$; then for some N_2', since $(N_1, N_2) \in \mathcal{R}_i$, we have $N_2 \xRightarrow{upd_f@l}{}^* N_2'$ and $(N_1', N_2') \in \mathcal{R}_i$. Thus, $(N_1', N_2') \in \bigcup_{i \in I} \mathcal{R}_i$. By similar reasoning, if $N_2 \xRightarrow{upd_f@l}{}^* N_2'$ then we can find N_1' such that $N_1 \xRightarrow{upd_f@l}{}^* N_1'$ and $(N_1', N_2') \in \mathcal{R}_i$, namely $(N_1', N_2') \in \bigcup_{i \in I} \mathcal{R}_i$.

2. By the previous case (the union part), $\cong$ is a weak knowledge bisimulation and includes any other weak knowledge bisimulation.

3. Proving that relation $\cong$ is an equivalence requires proving that it satisfies reflexivity, symmetry and transitivity. We consider each of them in what follows:

(a) Reflexivity: For any network N, $N \cong N$ results from the fact that the identity relation is a weak knowledge bisimulation.

(b) Symmetry: If $N \cong N'$, then $(N, N') \in \mathcal{R}$ for some weak knowledge bisimulation $\mathcal{R}$. Hence $(N', N) \in \mathcal{R}^{-1}$, and so $N' \cong N$ because the inverse relation is a weak knowledge bisimulation.

(c) Transitivity: If $N \cong N'$ and $N' \cong N''$ then $(N, N') \in \mathcal{R}_1$ and $(N', N'') \in \mathcal{R}_2$ for some weak knowledge bisimulations $\mathcal{R}_1$ and $\mathcal{R}_2$. Thus, $(N, N'') \in \mathcal{R}_1 \mathcal{R}_2$, and so $N \cong N''$ due to the fact that the composition relation is a weak knowledge bisimulation.

4. We provide Example 4 below illustrating the strict inclusion. □

The next result claims that weak knowledge equivalence $\cong$ among processes is preserved even if the local knowledge of the agents is expanded. This is consistent with the fact that the processes affect the same portion of their knowledge.

Proposition 11. *If $K'_{ij} \subseteq K''_{ij}$, for $1 \leq i \leq n, 1 \leq j \leq m$, then*
$$\|_{i=1}^n l_i[[\|_{j=1}^m P_{ij} \triangleright K'_{ij}]] \cong \|_{i=1}^n l_i[[\|_{j=1}^m P_{ij} \triangleright K''_{ij}]].$$

Proof. We show that $\mathcal{S}$ is a weak knowledge bisimulation, where:
$$\mathcal{S} = \{(\|_{i=1}^n l_i[[\|_{j=1}^m P_{ij} \triangleright K'_{ij}]] \, , \, \|_{i=1}^n l_i[[\|_{j=1}^m P_{ij} \triangleright K''_{ij}]]) \, : \, K'_{ij} \subseteq K''_{ij}, 1 \leq i \leq n, 1 \leq j \leq m\}.$$

The proof is by induction on the last performed step. Let us assume that $\|_{i=1}^n l_i[[\|_{j=1}^m P_{ij} \triangleright K'_{ij}]] \overset{\lambda}{\Longrightarrow}^* N'$. Depending on the value of λ, there are several cases:

- Consider $\lambda = create_f@l_1$. Then there exists P_{11} such that $l_1[[P_{11} \triangleright K'_{11} \|_{j=2}^m P_{1j} \triangleright K'_{1j}]] \|_{i=2}^n l_i[[\|_{j=1}^m P_{ij} \triangleright K'_{ij}]] \overset{create_f@l}{\Longrightarrow}^* l_1[[P'_{11} \triangleright K'_{11} \langle f \mid v; \emptyset \rangle \|_{j=2}^m P'_{1j} \triangleright K'_{1j}]] \|_{i=2}^n l_i[[\|_{j=1}^m P'_{ij} \triangleright K'_{ij}]] = N'$. Then there exists $N'' = l_1[[P'_{11} \triangleright K''_{11} \langle f \mid v; \emptyset \rangle \|_{j=2}^m P'_{1j} \triangleright K''_{1j}]] \|_{i=2}^n l_i[[\|_{j=1}^m P'_{ij} \triangleright K''_{ij}]]$ such that $\|_{i=1}^n l_i[[\|_{j=1}^m P_{ij} \triangleright K''_{ij}]]) \overset{create_f@l}{\Longrightarrow}^* N''$. Since $K'_{ij} \subseteq K''_{ij}$, $1 \leq i \leq n, 1 \leq j \leq m$, then also $K'_{11} \langle f \mid v; \emptyset \rangle \subseteq K''_{11} \langle f \mid v; \emptyset \rangle$, and clearly $(N', N'') \in \mathcal{S}$.

- Consider $\lambda = upd_p@l_1$. Then there exists P_{11} such that $l_1[[P_{11} \triangleright K'_{11} \|_{j=2}^m P_{1j} \triangleright K'_{1j}]] \|_{i=2}^n l_i[[\|_{j=1}^m P_{ij} \triangleright K'_{ij}]] \overset{upd_f@l}{\Longrightarrow} l_1[[P'_{11} \triangleright K'^{u'}_{11} \|_{j=2}^m P'_{1j} \triangleright K'_{1j}]] \|_{i=2}^n l_i[[\|_{j=1}^m P'_{ij} \triangleright K'_{ij}]] = N'$. Then there exists $N'' = l_1[[P'_{11} \triangleright K''^{u''}_{11} \|_{j=2}^m P'_{1j} \triangleright K''_{1j}]] \|_{i=2}^n l_i[[\|_{j=1}^m P'_{ij} \triangleright K''_{ij}]]$ such that $\|_{i=1}^n l_i[[\|_{j=1}^m P_{ij} \triangleright K''_{ij}]]) \overset{upd_f@l}{\Longrightarrow}^* N''$. Since $K'_{ij} \subseteq K''_{ij}$, $1 \leq i \leq n, 1 \leq j \leq m$, then also $K'^{u'}_{11} \subseteq K''^{u''}_{11}$, and clearly $(N', N'') \in \mathcal{S}$.

The symmetric cases follow by similar arguments. □

The following result shows that weak knowledge bisimulation is preserved after complete computational steps of two networks in knowTIMO only if the knowledge is modified at least once during such a step.

Proposition 12. *Let N_1, N_2 be two knowTIMO networks and $\exists create_f@l \in \Lambda$ or $\exists upd_f@l \in \Lambda$. If $N_1 \cong N_2$ and $N_1 \overset{\Lambda,t}{\Longrightarrow} N'_1$, then there exists $N'_2 \in \mathcal{N}$ such that $N_2 \overset{\Lambda,t}{\Longrightarrow}'_2$ and $N'_1 \cong N'_2$.*

Proof. Assuming that the finite multiset of actions Λ contains the labels $\{\lambda_1, \ldots, \lambda_k\}$ that denote modifications to the knowledge, then the complete computational step $N_1 \overset{\Lambda,t}{\Longrightarrow} N'_1$ can be detailed as $N_1 \overset{\lambda_1}{\Longrightarrow}^* N_1^1 \ldots N_1^{k-1} \overset{\lambda_k}{\Longrightarrow}^* N'_1$. Since $N_1 \overset{\lambda_1}{\Longrightarrow}^* N_1^1$ and $N_1 \cong N_2$, then according to Definition 3 there exists $N_2^1 \in \mathcal{N}$ such that $N_2 \overset{\lambda_1}{\Longrightarrow}^* N_2^1$ and $N_1^1 \cong N_2^1$. The same reasoning can be applied for another k times, meaning that there exist $N_2^2, \ldots, N'_2 \in \mathcal{N}$ such that $N_2 \overset{\lambda_1}{\Longrightarrow}^* N_2^1 \ldots N_2^{k-1} \overset{\lambda_k}{\Longrightarrow}^* N'_2$ and $N'_1 \cong N'_2$. By the definition of a complete computational step, it holds that $N_2 \overset{\lambda_1}{\Longrightarrow}^* N_2^1 \ldots N_2^{k-1} \overset{\lambda_k}{\Longrightarrow}^* N'_2$ can be written as $N_2 \overset{\Lambda,t}{\Longrightarrow} N'_2$. Thus, we obtained that there exists $N'_2 \in \mathcal{N}$ such that $N_2 \overset{\Lambda,t}{\Longrightarrow} N'_2$ and $N'_1 \cong N'_2$ (as desired). □

The next example illustrates that the relation $\cong$ is able to treat bisimilar systems that are not bisimilar using the relation $\sim$.

Example 4. *Consider the network N_1 of Example 2, and a network*
$$N_1''' = \text{office}_4[[C_2''(\text{office}_4) \triangleright K_{C2}]],$$
in which the client can perform only an update action:
$$C_2''(\text{office}_4) = \text{update}(/\text{agency}[\text{test}_4]/\text{dest}, \text{dest}_{C2,1}).$$
According to Definition 1, it holds that $N_1 \not\sim N_1'''$. This is due to the fact that the network N_1 can perform a time step of length 4 and choose the else branch, while the network N_1''' can perform only the update operation. Formally:

$$N_1 \xrightarrow{4} N_2 \xrightarrow{\text{false}@\text{office}_4} N_3 \xrightarrow{\text{upd}/\text{agency}[\text{test}_4]/\text{dest}@\text{office}_4} N_4$$

and

$$N_1''' \xrightarrow{\text{upd}/\text{agency}[\text{test}_4]/\text{dest}@\text{office}_4} N_2'''$$

The above reductions can also be written as

$$N_1 \Longrightarrow^* N_3 \xrightarrow{\text{upd}/\text{agency}[\text{test}_4]/\text{dest}@\text{office}_4} N_4,$$

and

$$N_1''' \Longrightarrow^* N_1''' \xrightarrow{\text{upd}/\text{agency}[\text{test}_4]/\text{dest}@\text{office}_4} N_2'''.$$

By applying Definition 3, it results that N_1 and N_1''' are weak knowledge bisimilar because they are able to perform an update on the same path at the same location, i.e., $N_1 \cong N_1'''$.

This example is also an illustration of the strict inclusion relation from item 4 of Proposition 10.

4. Conclusions and Related Work

In multi-agent systems, knowledge is usually treated by using epistemic logics [6]; in particular, the multi-agent epistemic logic [7,8]. These epistemic logics are modal logics describing different types of knowledge, being different not only syntactically, but also in expressiveness and complexity. Essentially, they are based on two concepts: Kripke structures (to model their semantics) and logic formulas (to represent the knowledge of the agents).

The initial version of TIMO presented in [1] leads to some extensions: with access permissions in perTIMO [9], with real-time in rTIMO [10], combining TIMO and the bigraphs [11] to obtain the BigTiMo calculus [12]. However, in all these approaches an implicit knowledge is used inside the processes. In this article we defined knowTIMO to describe multi-agent systems operating according to their accumulated knowledge. Essentially, the agents get an explicit representation of the knowledge about the other agents of a distributed network in order to decide their next interactions. The knowledge is defined as sets of trees whose nodes contain pairs of labels and values; this tree representation is similar to the data representation in Petri nets with structured data [13] and $Xd\pi$ process calculus [14]. The network dynamics involving exchanges of knowledge between agents is presented by the operational semantics of this process calculus; its labelled transition system is able to capture the concurrent execution by using a multiset of actions. We proved that time passing in such a multi-agent system does not introduce any nondeterminism in the evolution of a network, and that the progression of the network is smooth (there are no time gaps). Several results are devoted to the relationship between the evolution of the agents and their knowledge.

According to [15], the notion of bisimulation was independently discovered in computer science [16,17], modal logic [18] and set theory [19,20]. Bisimulation is currently used in several domains: to test the behavioural equality of processes in concurrency [21]; to solve the state-explosion problem in model checking [22]; to index and compress semistructured data in databases [23,24]; to solve Markov decision processes efficiently in stochastic planning [25]; to understand for some languages their expressiveness in description logics [26]; and to study the observational indistinguishability and computational complexity on data graphs in XPath (a language extending modal logic with equality tests for data) [27]. It is worth noting that the notion of bisimulation is related to the modal equivalence in various logics of knowledge and structures presented in [28]. In some of these logics it is proved that certain forms of bisimulation correspond to modal equivalence of knowledge, and this is used to compare the logics expressivity [29,30].

Inspired by the bisimulation notion defined in computer science, in this paper we defined and studied some specific behavioural equivalences involving the network knowledge and timing constraints on communication and migration; the defined behavioural equivalences are preserved during complete computational steps of two multi-agent systems. Strong timed bisimulation takes also into account timed transitions, being able to distinguish between different systems regardless of the evolution time; strong bounded timed bisimulation imposes limits for the evolution time, including the equivalences up to any bound below that deadline. A knowledge equivalence is able to distinguish between systems based on the interaction of the agents with their local knowledge. In the literature, a related but weaker/simpler approach of knowledge bisimulation appeared in [14], where the authors used only barbs (not equivalences), looking only at the *update* steps.

Author Contributions: All authors have read and agreed to the published version of the manuscript. All authors contributed equally to this work.

Funding: This research received no external funding.

Conflicts of Interest: The authors declare that there is no conflict of interest.

References

1. Ciobanu, G.; Koutny, M. Modelling and Verification of Timed Interaction and Migration. In Proceedings of the Fundamental Approaches to Software Engineering, 11th International Conference, FASE 2008, Held as Part of the Joint European Conferences on Theory and Practice of Software, ETAPS 2008, Budapest, Hungary, 29 March–6 April 2008; Lecture Notes in Computer Science. Fiadeiro, J.L., Inverardi, P., Eds.; Springer: Berlin/Heidelberg, Germany, 2008; Volume 4961, pp. 215–229. [CrossRef]
2. Abiteboul, S.; Buneman, P.; Suciu, D. *Data on the Web: From Relations to Semistructured Data and XML*; Morgan Kaufmann: Burlington, MA, USA, 1999.
3. Aman, B.; Ciobanu, G. Verification of distributed systems involving bounded-time migration. *Int. J. Crit.-Comput.-Based Syst.* **2017**, *7*, 279–301. [CrossRef]
4. Ciobanu, G. Behaviour Equivalences in Timed Distributed pi-Calculus. In *Software-Intensive Systems and New Computing Paradigms—Challenges and Visions*; Lecture Notes in Computer Science; Wirsing, M., Banâtre, J., Hölzl, M.M., Rauschmayer, A., Eds.; Springer: Berlin/Heidelberg, Germany, 2008; Volume 5380, pp. 190–208. [CrossRef]
5. Posse, E.; Dingel, J. Theory and Implementation of a Real-Time Extension to the *pi*-Calculus. In Proceedings of the Formal Techniques for Distributed Systems, Joint 12th IFIP WG 6.1 International Conference, FMOODS 2010 and 30th IFIP WG 6.1 International Conference, FORTE 2010, Amsterdam, The Netherlands, 7–9 June 2010; Lecture Notes in Computer Science. Hatcliff, J., Zucca, E., Eds.; Springer: Berlin/Heidelberg, Germany, 2010; Volume 6117, pp. 125–139. [CrossRef]
6. Hintikka, J. *Knowledge and Belief. An Introduction to the Logic of the Two Notions*; Cornell University Press: Ithaca, NY, USA, 1962.
7. Fagin, R.; Halpern, J.Y. Belief, Awareness, and Limited Reasoning. *Artif. Intell.* **1987**, *34*, 39–76. [CrossRef]
8. Modica, S.; Rustichini, A. Awareness and partitional information structures. *Theory Decis.* **1994**, *37*, 107–124. [CrossRef]
9. Ciobanu, G.; Koutny, M. Timed Migration and Interaction with Access Permissions. In Proceedings of the FM 2011: Formal Methods—17th International Symposium on Formal Methods, Limerick, Ireland, 20–24 June 2011; Lecture Notes in Computer Science. Butler, M.J., Schulte, W., Eds.; Springer: Berlin/Heidelberg, Germany, 2011; Volume 6664, pp. 293–307. [CrossRef]
10. Aman, B.; Ciobanu, G. Real-Time Migration Properties of rTiMo Verified in Uppaal. In Proceedings of the Software Engineering and Formal Methods—11th International Conference, SEFM 2013, Madrid, Spain, 25–27 September 2013; Lecture Notes in Computer Science. Hierons, R.M., Merayo, M.G., Bravetti, M., Eds.; Springer: Berlin/Heidelberg, Germany, 2013; Volume 8137, pp. 31–45. [CrossRef]
11. Milner, R. *The Space and Motion of Communicating Agents*; Cambridge University Press: Cambridge, UK, 2009.
12. Xie, W.; Zhu, H.; Zhang, M.; Lu, G.; Fang, Y. Formalization and Verification of Mobile Systems Calculus Using the Rewriting Engine Maude. In Proceedings of the 2018 IEEE 42nd Annual Computer Software and Applications Conference, COMPSAC 2018, Tokyo, Japan, 23–27 July 2018; Reisman, S., Ahamed, S.I., Demartini, C., Conte, T.M., Liu, L., Claycomb, W.R., Nakamura, M., Tovar, E., Cimato, S., Lung, C., et al., Eds.; IEEE Computer Society: New York, NY, USA, 2018; Volume 1, pp. 213–218. [CrossRef]
13. Badouel, É.; Hélouët, L.; Morvan, C. Petri Nets with Structured Data. *Fundam. Inform.* **2016**, *146*, 35–82. [CrossRef]
14. Gardner, P.; Maffeis, S. Modelling dynamic web data. *Theor. Comput. Sci.* **2005**, *342*, 104–131. [CrossRef]
15. Sangiorgi, D. On the origins of bisimulation and coinduction. *ACM Trans. Program. Lang. Syst.* **2009**, *31*, 15:1–15:41. [CrossRef]
16. Ginzburg, A. *Algebraic Theory of Automata*, 1st ed.; Academic Press: Cambridge, MA, USA, 1968.

17. Milner, R. An Algebraic Definition of Simulation between Programs. In Proceedings of the 2nd International Joint Conference on Artificial Intelligence, London, UK, 1–3 September 1971; Cooper, D.C., Ed.; William Kaufmann: Pleasant Hill, CA, USA, 1971; pp. 481–489.
18. van Benthem, J. *Modal Logic and Classical Logic*; Bibliopolis: Asheville, NC, USA, 1985.
19. Forti, M.; Honsell, F. Set theory with free construction principles. *Ann. Della Sc. Norm. Super. Pisa Cl. Sci. 4E SÉRie* **1983**, *10*, 493–522.
20. Hinnion, R. Extensional quotients of structures and applications to the study of the axiom of extensionality. *Bull. Soci'Et'E Mathmatique Belg.* **1981**, *XXXIII*, 173–206.
21. Aman, B.; Ciobanu, G.; Koutny, M. Behavioural Equivalences over Migrating Processes with Timers. In Proceedings of the Formal Techniques for Distributed Systems—Joint 14th IFIP WG 6.1 International Conference, FMOODS 2012 and 32nd IFIP WG 6.1 International Conference, FORTE 2012, Stockholm, Sweden, 13–16 June 2012; Lecture Notes in Computer Science. Giese, H., Rosu, G., Eds.; Springer: Berlin/Heidelberg, Germany, 2012; Volume 7273, pp. 52–66. [CrossRef]
22. Clarke, E.M.; Grumberg, O.; Peled, D.A. *Model Checking*; MIT Press: Cambridge, MA, USA, 2001.
23. Milo, T.; Suciu, D. Index Structures for Path Expressions. In Proceedings of the Database Theory—ICDT '99, 7th International Conference, Jerusalem, Israel, 10–12 January 1999; Lecture Notes in Computer Science. Beeri, C., Buneman, P., Eds.; Springer: Berlin/Heidelberg, Germany, 1999; Volume 1540, pp. 277–295. [CrossRef]
24. Fan, W.; Li, J.; Wang, X.; Wu, Y. Query preserving graph compression. In Proceedings of the ACM SIGMOD International Conference on Management of Data, SIGMOD 2012, Scottsdale, AZ, USA, 20–24 May 2012; Candan, K.S., Chen, Y., Snodgrass, R.T., Gravano, L., Fuxman, A., Eds.; ACM: New York, NY, USA, 2012; pp. 157–168. [CrossRef]
25. Givan, R.; Dean, T.L.; Greig, M. Equivalence notions and model minimization in Markov decision processes. *Artif. Intell.* **2003**, *147*, 163–223. [CrossRef]
26. Kurtonina, N.; de Rijke, M. Expressiveness of Concept Expressions in First-Order Description Logics. *Artif. Intell.* **1999**, *107*, 303–333. [CrossRef]
27. Abriola, S.; Barceló, P.; Figueira, D.; Figueira, S. Bisimulations on Data Graphs. *J. Artif. Intell. Res.* **2018**, *61*, 171–213. [CrossRef]
28. Fagin, R.; Halpern, J.Y.; Moses, Y.; Vardi, M.Y. *Reasoning about Knowledge*; MIT Press: Cambridge, MA, USA, 1995. [CrossRef]
29. van Ditmarsch, H.; French, T.; Velázquez-Quesada, F.R.; Wáng, Y.N. Knowledge, awareness, and bisimulation. In Proceedings of the 14th Conference on Theoretical Aspects of Rationality and Knowledge (TARK 2013), Chennai, India, 7–9 January 2013; Schipper, B.C., Ed.; 2013.
30. Velázquez-Quesada, F.R. Bisimulation characterization and expressivity hierarchy of languages for epistemic awareness models. *J. Log. Comput.* **2018**, *28*, 1805–1832. [CrossRef]

Article

Description of the Distribution Law and Non-Linear Dynamics of Growth of Comments Number in News and Blogs Based on the Fokker-Planck Equation

Dmitry Zhukov [1], Julia Perova [2,*] and Vladimir Kalinin [1]

[1] Institute of Cybersecurity and Digital Technologies, MIREA-Russian Technological University, 78 Vernadsky Avenue, 119454 Moscow, Russia; zhukovdm@yandex.ru (D.Z.); vkalininz@mail.ru (V.K.)

[2] Institute of Radio Electronics and Computer Science, MIREA-Russian Technological University, 78 Vernadsky Avenue, 119454 Moscow, Russia

* Correspondence: jul-np@yandex.ru; Tel.: +7-916-368-05-34

Citation: Zhukov, D.; Perova, J.; Kalinin, V. Description of the Distribution Law and Non-Linear Dynamics of Growth of Comments Number in News and Blogs Based on the Fokker-Planck Equation. *Mathematics* 2022, *10*, 989. https://doi.org/10.3390/math10060989

Academic Editors: Liliya Demidova and Amir Mosavi

Received: 12 January 2022
Accepted: 16 March 2022
Published: 19 March 2022

Publisher's Note: MDPI stays neutral with regard to jurisdictional claims in published maps and institutional affiliations.

Copyright: © 2022 by the authors. Licensee MDPI, Basel, Switzerland. This article is an open access article distributed under the terms and conditions of the Creative Commons Attribution (CC BY) license (https://creativecommons.org/licenses/by/4.0/).

Abstract: The article considers stationary and dynamic distributions of news by the number of comments. The processing of the observed data showed that static distribution of news by the number of comments relating to that news obeys a power law, and the dynamic distribution (the change in number of comments over time) in some cases has an S-shaped character, and in some cases a more complex two-stage character. This depends on the time interval between the appearance of a comment at the first level and a comment attached to that comment. The power law for the stationary probability density of news distribution by the number of comments can be obtained from the solution of the stationary Fokker-Planck equation, if a number of assumptions are made in its derivation. In particular, we assume that the drift coefficient $\mu(x)$ responsible in the Fokker-Planck equation for a purposeful change in the state of system x (x is the current number of comments on that piece of news) linearly depends on the state x, and the diffusion coefficient $D(x)$ responsible for a random change depends quadratically on x. The solution of the unsteady Fokker-Planck differential equation with these assumptions made it possible to obtain an analytical equation for the probability density of transitions between the states of the system per unit of time, which is in good agreement with the observed data, considering the effect of the delay time between the appearance of the first-level comment and the comment on that comment.

Keywords: nonlinear dynamics; processes in social systems; Fokker-Planck equation; power law; monitoring; management

1. Introduction

The description of social network behavior and information resources is one of the most important areas of mathematical sociology. From a practical point of view, the development of models describing user opinion dynamics and preferences contributes to the development of systems for automated monitoring of the public mood and its changes. Compared to traditional methods of studying public opinion, the advantage of such systems is that of automated information processing. Social surveys require the development of questionnaires and sampling, which is complicated by the necessity to cover all strata of society. In addition, respondents tend to provide socially desirable responses.

Another advantage of automated information processing for social networks and comments to newsfeed is that it identifies straightforward comments related to a socially significant topic and to highly-publicized news. Therefore, the development of automated information processing tools provides feedback between society and government bodies, starting from the municipal level and ending at the level of state authorities.

The development of automated tools assumes that their work should be based on algorithms based on approved mathematical models. In addition, it is of the utmost importance not only to monitor and analyze the processes involved in research but also to predict their evolution, which is necessary to ensure sustainable social development.

The dynamics of the changes in opinions and moods of Internet users can be largely attributed to stochastic processes, but with the possibility of targeted impact. On the one hand, the human factor (many people with different opinions, preferences, and behavior patterns) creates random changes (due to the wide variety of behavioral models of users). On the other hand, elements of opinion consistency are introduced into the dynamics of changes. A detailed description of the use of stochastic methods for modeling the dynamics of social processes can be found in [1].

In this regard, we consider models based on the Fokker-Planck equation to be the most promising to develop models of the changes in public mood dynamics, which takes into account both ordered and random changes.

The Fokker-Planck equation is widely used for analyzing and modeling the behavior of time series when describing processes in complex systems [2–5], for example, when analyzing the dynamics of the non-stationary time series of stock and commodity indices. To predict changes, based on the Fokker-Planck equation and sample data, the distribution functions of the series levels are constructed in the form of a sum of polynomials in which the coefficients of drift and diffusion may depend on a specific parameter, which is the level of the series according to various laws and is empirical.

It should be noted that, apart from the Fokker-Planck equation, other approaches are used for modeling based on differential equations, for example, the Liouville equations [5,6], the diffusion equations [4,7] and many others. A detailed review of modeling social processes is presented in [8].

The Fokker-Planck equation is a second-order partial differential equation that not only contains a term responsible for stochastic changes ("diffusion"), but also an element responsible for opinion consistency ("draft"). From the Fokker-Planck equation, it is possible to obtain a probability density function of transitions per unit of time between states of a system. A system can be defined as a blog or newsfeed that users comment on, and its state will be the number of comments that are observed at a given time.

In addition to describing dynamic processes, stationary solutions can be obtained from the Fokker-Planck equation, which can describe the state of a system in a stationary state, when, for example, its evolution has already ended, and changes do not occur. One example of such stationarity may be the final static distribution of newsfeed or blogs by the number of comments on them.

The study of processes occurring in complex systems with the participation of the human factor shows that very often a power law of distribution is performed for the observed characteristics of the parameters of these processes. If we imagine the interconnection of the elements forming a complex system as a diagram, it turns out that the networks that arise in this case—social, communication, Internet link networks, citations, and others—are well described by scale–free models (scale-invariant), in which the degrees of vertices (nodes) are distributed according to the power law $p(x) \sim x - \gamma$ (where γ is the characteristic degree) [9–14]. Scale-free networks are self-similar, i.e., in any part of the network, the distribution of degrees will be the same.

The power model is widely used in the analysis of processes in complex social systems, but at the same time the issue of the theoretical justification of the possibility for its application requires further study. In our opinion, this justification is very crucial. The identification of the nature of the processes from which the power law arises is necessary for a deeper study of behavior and analysis of complex social systems.

In addition, we are not aware of attempts to apply a theoretical description of processes in social networks and network mass media based on the Fokker-Planck equation from the standpoint of formulating and solving boundary value problems based on it.

The purpose of our work is to investigate the possibility of obtaining from the Fokker-Planck equation, often observed in practice in complex social systems, the power law of the distribution of parameters of the processes occurring, and to show that under certain assumptions this equation can be used to describe both static and dynamic characteristics.

2. Research Methods

As described in the lead section, our article is devoted to solving the following issues. First, we collected statistics on the dynamics of changes for the number of comments on the news on the feed portal of the Russian radio station «Echo of Moscow» https://echo.msk.ru/ (accessed on 13 September 2021) (one of the leading Russian commercial radio stations and newsfeeds). Then, we describe the processing of the collected data and the results obtained (in particular, in a stationary state, a power law of the news distribution by the number of observed comments). The observed dynamics of change in the number pf comments (to news feeds and blogs) is described by either two-stage or S-shaped curves. Further, using the stationary Fokker-Planck equation and a number of assumptions about the dependence of coefficients describing a random and purposeful change in the state of the system x (x is the current number of comments on the news) on the magnitude of this current state x, we derive from the Fokker-Planck equation the power law of the distribution of news by the number of comments. Then, based on the Fokker-Planck equation, we construct a dynamic model of changes in the state of the systems under consideration over time. The analysis of the models showed good agreement with the observed characteristics of the processes. This suggests that the models we have developed can be used not only to analyze social processes, but also to predict their evolution, which is very important for managing the stable development of social relations. In conclusion, we discuss the possible application of our models in practice and the creation of algorithms for automated systems for the monitoring of public opinion.

3. A Brief Overview of Existing Studies of the Structure of Complex Social Systems and the Processes Observed

One of the directions in the study of complex networks is the study of their structure, based on the possibility of representing processes at the graph level, using a set of attachments at the level of individual nodes for data aggregation (of the properties of the whole from the properties of the quotient). Aggregation is crucial, since it should, in principle, provide an isomorphism-invariant representation of the graph, i.e., the representation of the graph should be a function of the nodes of the graph, considered as some set.

In [15], the DeepSets aggregation operator based on self-organizing maps (SOM) is considered. Using SOM allows calculation of representations of nodes that include information about their resemblance. Experimental results on real data sets show that the proposed approach provides improved predictive performance compared to the generally accepted summing aggregation and many modern graph neural network architectures in the literature.

Since, with the growth of the network, the search for similarities between nodes in the network is a time-consuming process, to optimize the process of solving problems of predicting connections and detecting communities' researchers in [16] use swarm algorithms. Swarm-based optimization methods used in social network analysis are compared in this article with community analysis and link analysis based on traditionally used approaches.

In [17], the authors consider the mathematical model of mixed membership in user groups, which are formed stochastically. This preliminary solution the authors base on the method of detecting pairwise measurements, which subsequently show the presence or absence of connections between a pair of nodes. When analyzing the approach for probabilistic changes between pairs of objects, it is usually necessary to introduce assumptions, for example, independence, or assumptions of the inconsistency of this connection (mixed membership in stochastically forming groups). The proposed model allows, under certain assumptions, the tracking of dynamic changes in the number of nodes in the forming of groups and their clustering by groups.

In the presented model, from the development of choice and influence on social networks [18], the authors consider a model for which the number of nodes and the network topology (structure of connections) are dynamic. A significant disadvantage of this model is that it explicitly considers the connections between all pairs of nodes. This action leads to quadratic difficulty in calculating the change in the number of participants in various social groups and a significant increase in the calculation time. It is worth noting that real social networks and systems are sparse. This means that most participants do not have paired connections, and the number of their connections is itself random. Introducing the concept of sparsity into the model [18], as well as taking into account the random nature of the number of connections for each node (user) of the network, can significantly increase the speed and efficiency of using this model.

The authors in [19] use a structure analysis technique that dynamically develops, and therefore has a multimodality of, the graph of the social network. Using this approach to real graph structures in practice shows that there is temporary online regularity in people's social interactions. Moreover, correlations are found between the occurrence of friendship between participants and the settings of the interactive social network. Separately, it is worth noting that physical contacts between people can be considered as an interactive dynamically changing network.

In article [20], the authors described methods of structuring and influencing the dissemination of information on mobile social networks. In these networks, a group of users is typically treated as some kind of entity in which individuals can exchange messages. The authors also note that there is a variety of models for analyzing the dissemination of information on mobile social networks, but none of the existing methods considers the concept of information dissemination in the group. Therefore, the authors of the paper used the SIR model, which is used to spread viruses in computer networks, and applied this to the dynamics of the information dissemination process in groups. Simulations using the Monte Carlo method showed that group propagation increases the overall speed of information propagation on the network. In addition, the authors note that the presence of groups with a significant number of participants is most effective in disseminating information than the presence of a huge number of groups but with a small number of participants. This analysis of the impact of the structure on the dissemination of information within it proves that their distribution in the networks of Erdesh-Rennie and Barabashi-Albert does not show any differences. Ref. [20] analyses the stochastic model of opinion dynamics in social networks. This model is based on a multi-agent approach, for which the opinion of each network member is randomly influenced by the actions of others (its neighboring nodes). Examples were given that, since the number of users (nodes) in the network is not infinite, the model as a result asymptotically creates consensus. The consensus value usually corresponds to one of the absorbing states of the Markov system. However, when the number of nodes is large, some metastable transition states are observed in places. The duration of these transient states may be as long as desired in time, and the state data may be characterized using the mean field approximation for the Markov system. Ultimately, the authors propose a model by which opinion control in the social network is possible.

We can consider several statistical studies [21–23] that have widely used the method of studying profiles in social networks. The purpose of these studies is to identify the social mobility of people based on their publications accompanied by geodata. The authors found a large number of such publications, and based on these an approximate map of the user's movements was compiled, the main centers of activity were identified, and the person's place of residence was established. According to the data on the place of residence, the people's names were found. Further, using a database of names distributed by gender, it was possible to determine the gender of more than half of all the accounts studied; according to the surname data, the researchers tried to establish information about the race and age of users, successfully in 38% and 14% of cases, respectively. These studies have shown that it is possible to establish some demographic characteristics, knowing only about the movements of a person or knowing his first and last name.

Using the comparison of time slices, it is possible to determine dynamically changing temporary communities of users of social network structures. The study of these dynamic communities makes it possible to significantly simplify the analysis of the dynamics of a complex system of social interactions as it evolves over time.

Consider [24], which presents the fundamental structures of dynamic social networks based on a high-resolution dataset describing a tightly connected population of 1000 first-year students at a large European university. The authors of this article consider the physically short interactions that they measured using Bluetooth, supplemented with information received from telecommunications networks (information about calls and messages), social networks and the demographic and geolocation data of users.

Human social communities by their nature overlap due to individuals participating in several different groups (in the theory of complex networks, such nodes are called jumpers). During the week, meetings of the subjects of the created compact structure take place, either a meeting of friends outside the university, or of all students (such structures are called cores). In a network of short physical interactions, all participants are present at the same time and are in physical contact.

The location of the core members can also be forecast. The objects that helps to do this are the kernels themselves. By observing the usual routes of the people who make up the core and their behavioral habits, it is possible to predict the geographical location of a person in the next time interval with high accuracy (on average in 93% of cases), such high accuracy proving that human mobility patterns are regular. It is also worth noting that the members of the core have fewer location states than individuals, which leads to lower values of information entropy on average.

The condition that geospatial studies are conducted for a part of the social group, yet the study is limited to certain time frames, shows any complex interaction between time, place and social context. It also supports the hypothesis that often. when people are most unpredictable in the geospatial domain, they exhibit some predictable social behavior. Linking the results of this article with the literature on dynamic community detection, it can be noted that there are many methods in the literature that would allow the detection gatherings in everyday life, but here the authors used a simple comparison of graph components to emphasize the fact that emerging social structures are natural, and these complex methods are not needed to determine their occurrence.

In fact, Ref. [24] provides a quantitative assessment of long-term patterns encoded in the micro dynamics for a huge system of interacting nodes, which are characterized by predictability and a high degree of order.

Let us consider another paper on dynamic models [25]. Recent developments in the field of social networks have shifted the focus from static representations to dynamic ones, requiring new methods of analysis and modeling. Observations in real social systems have revealed two main facts that play a very important role in the evolution of networks and affect the current processes of distribution: the strategies that individuals adopt when choosing between new or old social systems, connections, and the turbulent nature of social activity that sets the pace of these choices. The results are verified using numerical simulation and compared with two observable data sets.

In [26], methods of assessing public opinion and highlighting the mood of users are carried out using a method based on the use of vocabulary and semantics and inherited from the classical approach to the analysis of public sentiment. Neural networks are used for this method. The task of the neural network is to determine important keywords, which are then checked by experts in this subject area. Formally, the program first analyzes articles and determines how often different words are found in them. Next, the program identifies the most commonly used words and expressions, and makes them significant. Then, on their basis, the program builds a lexicon that characterizes the public mood based on the transmitted news articles.

In [27], the authors described the workings of the algorithm for analyzing certain topics from the social network. In addition to collecting information, there are methods for processing and sorting information. In addition, the time elapsed between publications is measured so that it is subsequently possible to restore the order of publications and obtain a time scale based on these data. Following from the above, the result is a graph that can be used to track the growth and decline in popularity of certain topics discussed on social networks. You can also trace what moods are accompanied by what events in society. In addition, it is possible to determine the period of active discussion for certain topics.

Article [28] describes the method of studying political sentiments in society, based on the analysis of the social network. This method is carried out by searching for special words in the text that are previously entered in the program database. The main task of this system is to track by how much different political parties are preferable to citizens, and which are less significant. In addition, which topics are most resonant and most discussed in society are monitored. Additionally, with the help of the program, it is possible to find out how many people in percentage terms support a certain political party.

The subject of [29] is that of microblogs. The authors of this study used the method of keyword analysis. With the help of such analysis and machine learning, they managed to divide the initial sample into six age groups and identify the topics that participants in each age group most often discuss and on which they most often express their thoughts. Teenagers under 18 most often discuss sports; young people aged 18–25 most often talk about entertainment; people aged 25 to 30 mainly discuss family and business, older people (31–36 years old) are most interested in technology, users aged 26–40 begin to worry about their health and speak about this more often, and those over 40 like to discuss politics. Thus, the most frequent topic for discussion was determined for each age group; this does not mean that each member of this group necessarily discusses this topic, but it is more likely that the person discussing this topic belongs to this age group.

The authors of [30–34] proposed a method that evaluates the mass media according to several criteria (topic, evaluation criteria/properties, classes), which combine thematic modeling of context and multi-criteria decision-making. This evaluation system is based on corporate analysis as follows: the conditional distribution of media probabilities by topic, detail and class is calculated after the formation of the thematic model of corporations. Several approaches, including manual labeling, a multi-corporate approach and an automatic approach, are used to obtain coefficients that show the interaction regarding how each topic relates to each evaluation criterion and to each class described in the document. The multi-corporate approach proposed in the study involves assessing the thematic asymmetry of text enclosures to obtain coefficients describing the relationship of each topic to a certain criterion. These factors, in combination with the thematic model, can be used to evaluate each document in the enclosures according to each of the criteria and classes considered. This method was applied to a body of texts consisting of 804,829 news publications from 40 Kazakh sources, published from 1 January 2018 to 31 December 2019 (over a period of 2 years) to classify negative information on socially significant topics. The study produced a BigARTM model (200 topics) and applied this model, including completion of the analytical hierarchical process table (AHP) and all necessary high-level labeling procedures. The experiments carried out confirm the general possibility of evaluating media using the thematic model of text enclosures, since the classification problem achieved an area estimate under the receiver performance curve (ROC AUC) of 0.81, which is comparable to the results obtained for the same task using the BERT model.

The developed system, in which the proposed model was integrated, allows the solution of classic problems, such as simple reports or sentiment analysis. Moreover, it has a number of unique possibilities for use. It provides options such as automatically analyzing a specific topic, event, or object without having to create a keyword-based query. The analysis is based on an arbitrary list of criteria and not limited to sentiment alone. This list includes social significance, popularity, manipulation, propaganda content, attitude to a certain country, attitude to a certain area, analysis of the dynamic behavior of topics, predictive analysis at the thematic level, etc.

In [35–37], the KroMFac technique is proposed, which performs community detection using regularized non-negative matrix factorization (NMF) based on the Kronecker graph model. KroMFac combines network analysis and community discovery methods in a single unified structure. This technique connects four areas of research, namely the detection of communities on graphs, of overlapping communities, of communities in incomplete networks with missing edges, and of complete networks.

It is possible to consider several works, close to the subject of our research, on the description of processes in complex social network structures.

Article [38] considers a model describing the spatial and temporal distribution of information in social networks based on a partial differential equation. In this paper, a non-autonomous diffusion logistic model with Dirichlet boundary conditions was created and investigated, which showed that the diffusion of data is strongly influenced by the diffusion coefficient and internal growth rate (the spread of information or rumors can be considered as a kind of virus that does not have a physical form).

Article [39] proposes a mathematical model of information dissemination and a mechanism of evolution of the state of the information node using the theory of thermodynamic molecular thermo-diffusion motion in combination with the model of epidemic infection. Four different network topologies are used for the time-varying online social network (OSN) information dissemination process (regular network, small worlds network, random network, and non-scale network).

When distributing OSN information, the concept of information entropy is used. The process of information dissemination determines the transition of the system from one stable state to another. The transfer function is set by such information parameters as information energy, information temperature and energy entropy. The considered model is based on the relationship between the state of microscopic network nodes and the rules of macroevolutionary evolution. The authors of the article conduct simulation experiments and empirical comparative experiments in networks with different topological structures. The proposed model is trained and evaluated using experimental data collected from the Chinese network Baidu.

The authors of article [40] propose a model for describing the distribution of messages in social networks. This proposal is based on systems described by means of differential equations that show the propagation of various information in a network graph chain. The authors are convinced that this model allows the taking into account of specific mechanisms for transmitting messages. In this model, the vertices of the graph are people who, when a message is received, form their attitude to it. After this, people decide on further transmission of this message over the network, provided that the corresponding interaction potential of the two persons exceeds a certain threshold level.

The authors developed a mathematical method for calculating the timing of the distribution of messages in the corresponding graph chain, which is reduced to solving a number of Cauchy problems for systems of ordinary nonlinear differential equations. Formally, these systems can be simplified, and some equations can be replaced by the Boussinesque or Corteweg de Frieze equations. The presence of soliton solutions for these equations gives us reason to consider social and communicative solitons as an effective tool for modeling the processes of disseminating messages on social networks and studying various influences on their distribution. If certain assumptions are allowed, this model, considered in [33] has some analogies with the spread of viral epidemics.

In conclusion, it should be noted that almost no one has studied models based on the Fokker-Planck equation to describe processes in complex network social systems.

4. The Analysis of the Observed Statistics of Comments from Users of Newsfeed Resources and Blogs—Statement of the Research Problem

4.1. Data Source Selection and Presentation

Newsfeed and blogs, on which Internet users leave their comments, are one of the most important among network objects, since they can indicate public opinion in real time.

A socially significant topic usually attracts both supporters and opponents, who enter into discussions and leave comments. The more highly-publicized the news or blog, the higher the user activity and the greater the number of commentators (a multi-level structure of comments on comments appears). The analysis of the structure of comments of users of news posts and blogs is one of the most practically significant and relevant scientific tasks, the solution to which ensures sustainable social development.

To study the nature of the observed processes and collect data, we have selected the commercial radio station and newsfeed «Echo of Moscow» https://echo.msk.ru/ (accessed on 13 October 2021). The choice is determined by the following reasons:

1. News portal (The commercial radio station) is among the top 10 news sites in Russia and in July of 2021 took ninth place for attendance and seventh for user activity, also at the end of July 2021 ranking in the top eight of the cited radio stations and occupying first place through hyperlinks in social media at the end of August 2021 and fourth place according to the citation index in the media.
2. The portal has various themes (presents news from the political, sporting, economic and scientific arenas, cultural orientation, etc.).
3. The news portal has been in existence since 1990 and has established itself as a reliable, truthful and publicly available news source, and also publishes blogs of well-known media personalities.
4. There is practically no pre-moderation of comments (pre-moderation applies only to new users or users who have previously violated the rules of the news portal), but there is post-moderation of discussions (the requirements for comments and prohibitions on their placement can be found at the link: https://echo.msk.ru/moderate.html (accessed on 13 October 2021)). Users can express different opinions (which do not have to coincide with the official position) and their comments are deleted only for violating the rules.

At first, we downloaded the news range we were interested in, using a special software application (parser). The portal distributes news by day, and each individual day can be found at the link (https://echo.msk.ru/news, (accessed on 13 October 2021), where day is the day, month is the month, year is the year). Each news item has a number of parameters such as: news text, unique identification number on the portal, title, web page address (URL), metadata (date and time of publication, number of views and comments), texts of user comments (as well as unique identification number of the comment, unique identification number of the user, date and time of comment, comment hierarchy level, relationship by level of commenting to the parent comment) and available information about authors (unique identification number of the user on the webpage, city, occupation, place of work, name or nickname, registration date, the number of recommendations and user profile views, the total number of comments for the observed period, etc.). On average, the number of news items varied from 160 to 190 per day. While collecting the data, we downloaded information about which of the users commented on other users' reaction to news. Based on the data obtained, a database of the newsfeed archive was created.

Figure 1 shows the correspondence of the share of commentators to the number of comments they wrote (the observed density of the distribution of commentators by their number of comments) for the period from 1 January to 31 December 2020. Similar dependencies can be built for any period (day, week, month, quarter, year). The total number of news items published in 2020 was 65,560, of views 196,609,650, and of comments 564,764.

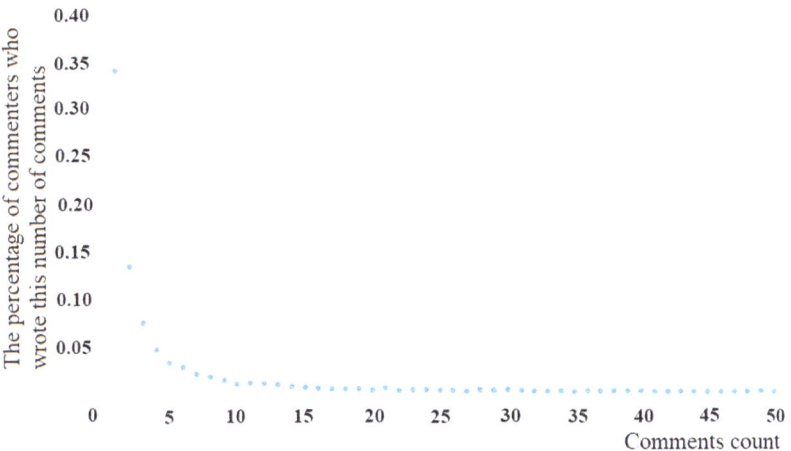

Figure 1. Density of distribution of commentators by their number of comments for the period from 1 January to 31 December 2020.

Note that Figure 1 shows only part of the data. Some users managed to write several hundred comments during the year (the maximum number of comments on one news item was 239), but their share is rather small. So, for clarity of presentation, the right part of the chart has been reduced, because it is uninformative.

4.2. Processing of Observed Data

When analyzing the observed data (see Figure 1), it is crucial to establish the distribution law that the observed distribution density is subject to. Otherwise, se of the data obtained is difficult in terms of predicting the behavior of the process and making recommendations for decision-making.

Considering the process of creating comments by users to be largely random (due to the different probability of occurrence of various news events and the degree of interest in them, etc.), let us consider the three most frequently observed distribution laws:

1. Gaussian distribution: $\rho(x) = e^{-\frac{x^2}{2\sigma^2}} / \sigma\sqrt{2\pi}$
2. Exponential distribution: $\rho(x) = a \cdot e^{-ax}$
3. Power distribution: $\rho(x) = \beta \cdot x^{-\gamma}$

If any of these distributions is fulfilled, then the observed data should be linearized in the appropriate coordinates with an acceptable value of the correlation coefficient (0.95–0.98):

1. For the Gaussian distribution: $ln\{\rho(x)\} = -ln\{\sigma\sqrt{2\pi}\} - \frac{1}{2\cdot\sigma^2} \cdot x^2$
2. For exponential distribution: $ln\{\rho(x)\} = ln\{a\} - ax$
3. For the power distribution: $ln\{\rho(x)\} = ln\{\beta\} - \gamma ln\{x\}$

The linearization of the observed data for various types of distribution is shown in Figures 2–4 ("1"—The area in which the "fluffy tail" is observed.).

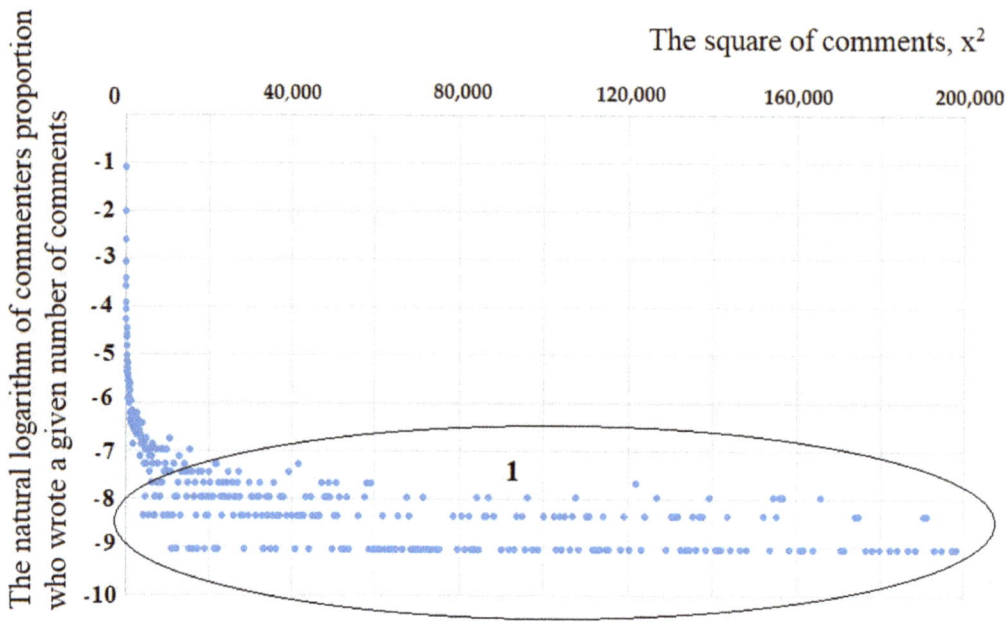

Figure 2. Linearization of the observed data for the Gaussian distribution.

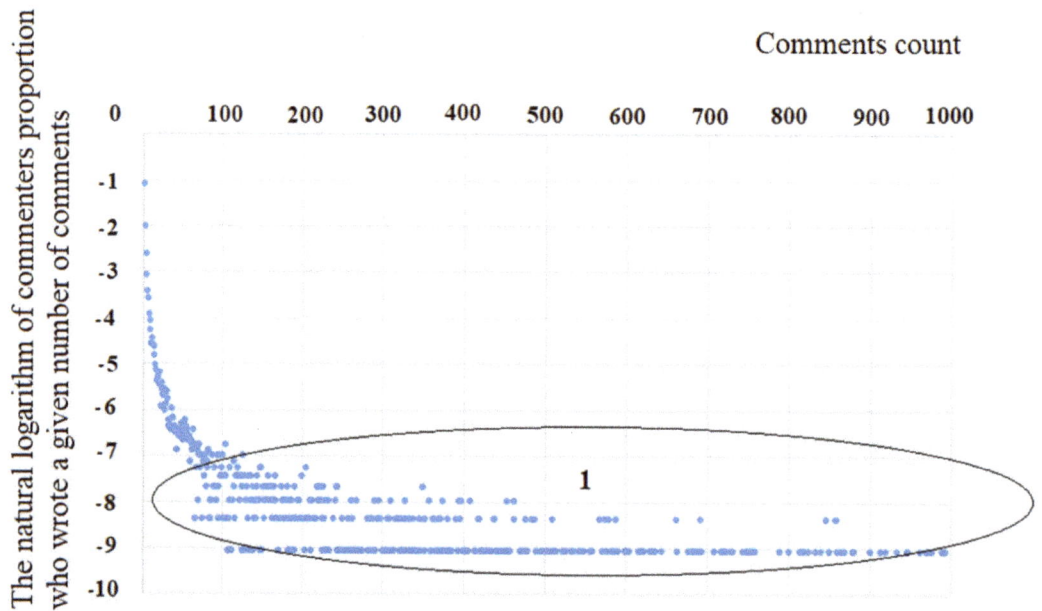

Figure 3. Linearization of observed data for exponential distribution.

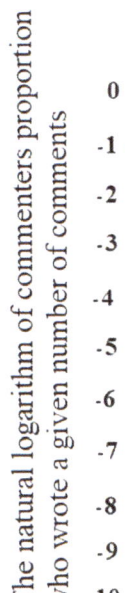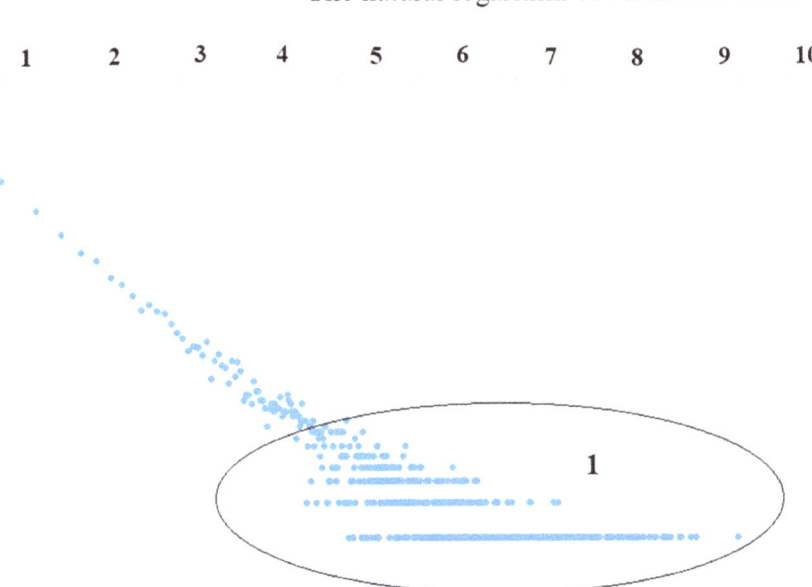

Figure 4. Linearization of the observed data for power distribution.

As can be seen from Figures 2–4, the best linearization is observed for approximating the observed data by the power law of distribution (see Figure 4). However, the areas shown in Figures 2–4 by the oval figure, which we called the "fluffy tail", deserve special discussion. Their appearance is due to the fact that, in addition to the so-called conscientious users, there are chatbots and users who write comments on a professional basis among the commentators. A rule can be introduced according to which unscrupulous users and chatbots can include those commentators who make more than 6–10 comments per day, as well as those who create several comments in a very short time interval (high-frequency commenting).

After appropriate purification, data can be obtained, the linearization of which, for the power law, is shown in Figure 5. There is no acceptable linearization for the exponential distribution and the Gaussian distribution. The straight line in Figure 5 shows that the trend line is well described by the linear approximation $y = -1.49 - 1.23z$, where $y = ln\{\rho(x)\}$, $z = ln\{x\}$, $ln\{\beta\} = -1.47$, and the correlation coefficient is 0.98.

In addition, to confirm the conclusion regarding linear approximation, it is possible to investigate the behavior of the residuals, and test the hypothesis that they are normally distributed with an average value equal to zero and have a homogeneous variance. The calculation of the residuals can be carried out on the basis of the actually observed values of the natural logarithm of the proportion of commentators who gave a given number of comments and the equation we obtained, for a given logarithm of the number of comments. The calculated value of the mathematical expectation for the distribution of residues is 0.25 and the variance is 0.13. The asymmetry is 0.64; the kurtosis is 0.14. Testing the slope hypothesis (two-sample F-test for variances) shows that the variance of the residuals (calculated relative to the trend line) is significantly less than the variance of the deviation of linear regression points from the average value of the observed data ($\Sigma y_i/n = \Sigma ln\{\rho(x_i)\}/n$). This is equal to 2.11 (0.13 << 2.11). Thus, the resulting regression is significant. The asymmetry characterizes the "skewness" of the distribution function, and for symmetric functions (for example, the normal distribution) it is zero (in our case, it is small and close to zero). The kurtosis characterizes the "tail" of the distribution. With large positive values for the kurtosis, the distribution function decreases more slowly with further distance from the average value than with small ones. If the excess value is greater than zero, the distribution density graph will lie above the normal distribution graph and, for less than zero, below the graph (in our case, this is small and very close to zero). Thus, from the data obtained, it can be concluded that the distribution of residuals is very close to normal, which confirms the conclusion that the natural logarithm of the proportion of commentators who wrote these comments linearly depends on the natural logarithm of the number of comments, which confirms the fulfillment of the power law.

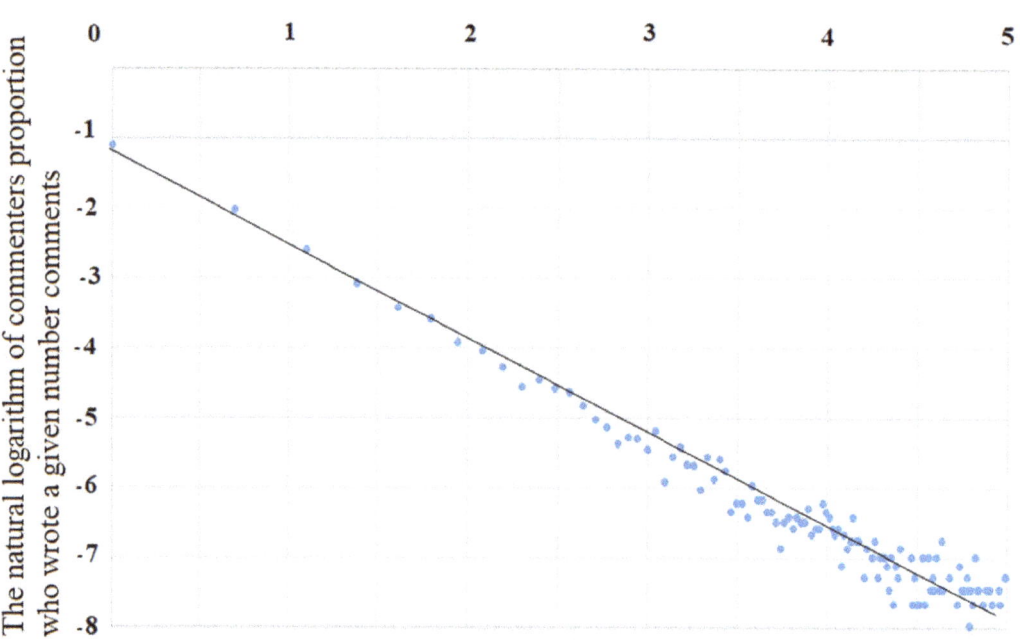

Figure 5. Linearization of the observed data for power distribution after cleaning unscrupulous users.

Thus, it can be assumed with great certainty that the density of the distribution of commentators by their number of comments obeys a power law.

It seems interesting to consider the dynamics of the changes in the number of comments on news of great public interest (during viewing, such types of newsfeed or blogs gain hundreds of comments) over time.

As an illustrative example, the news that appeared on the Echo of Moscow portal (https://echo.msk.ru/news/2626290-echo.html, accessed on 21 November 2021) can be chosen. On 21 November 2021: "The Public Council under the Ministry of Defense made a proposal to rename the Prague metro station in honor of Marshal Konev." The total number of comments was 221. Figure 6 shows the dynamics of changes in the number of comments on this news item over time. The number of comments at the first level (comments one news itself) was 107, at the second level (comments of the comments at the first level) 26, at the third 24, and at the fourth and more, the average time for second-level comments to appear is about 130 min.

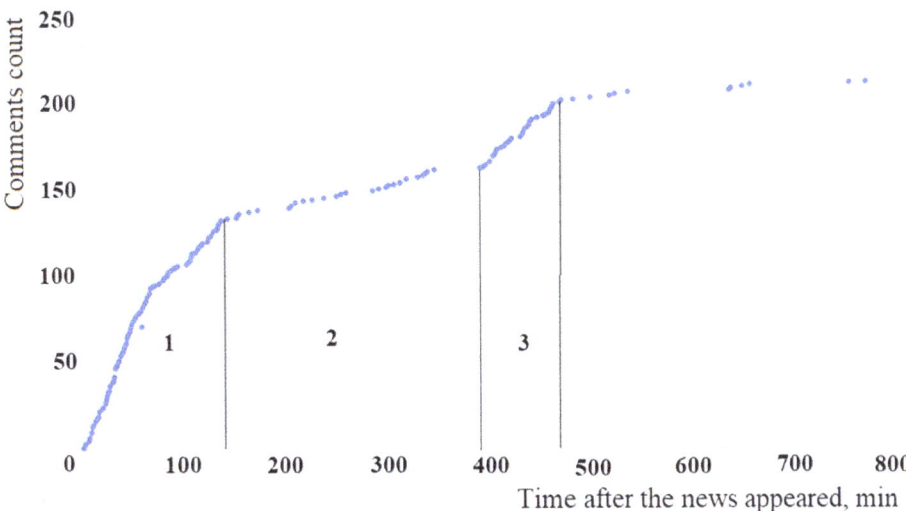

Figure 6. The observed dynamics of change over time, the number of comments on a news item of public interest that appeared on the portal https://echo.msk.ru/news/2626290-echo.html on 16 April 2020.

As another illustrative example, the news that appeared on the Echo of Moscow portal (https://echo.msk.ru/news/2740844-echo.html, accessed on 21 November 2021) on 12 November 2020 can be chosen: "Lavrov said that the Russian Federation has reason to believe that Navalny was poisoned on a plane or in Germany." The total number of comments was 220. The dynamics of the change in the number of comments on this news item over time is shown in Figure 7.

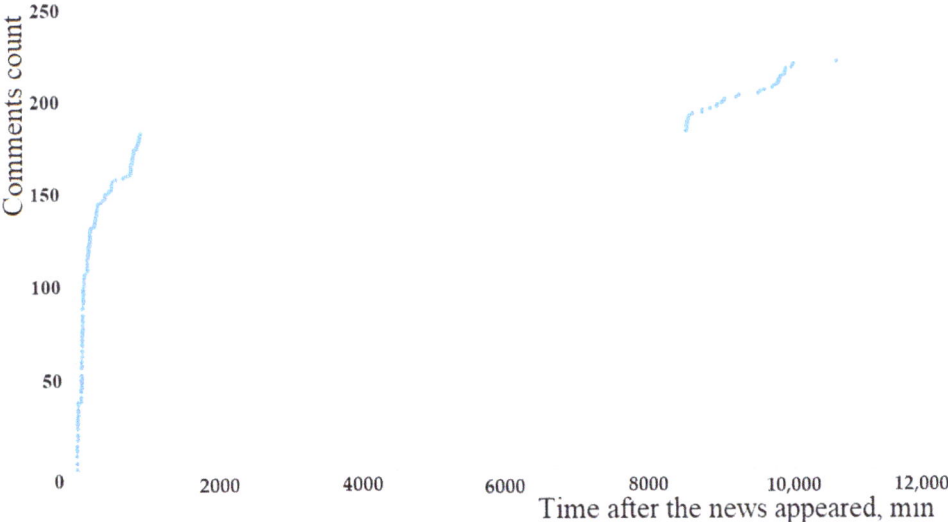

Figure 7. The observed dynamics of change over time, the number of comments on a news item of public interest that appeared on the portal https://echo.msk.ru/news/2740844-echo.html on 12 November 2020.

After removing the time gaps, the dynamics take the form shown in Figure 8.

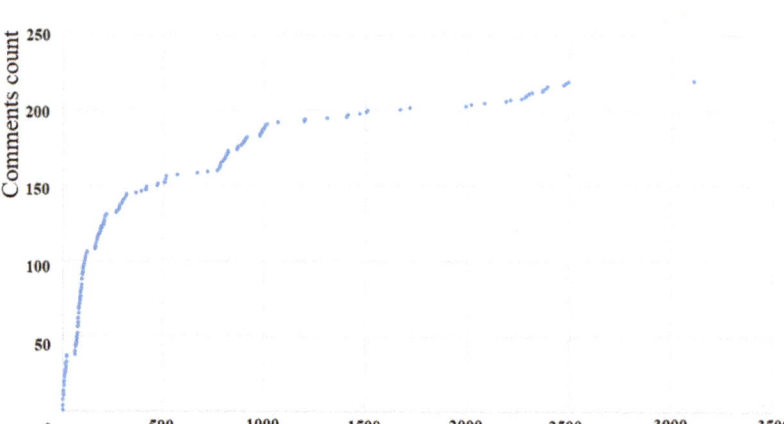

Figure 8. Dynamics of changes over time, the number of comments on a news item of public interest that appeared on the portal https://echo.msk.ru/news/2740844-echo.html on 12 November 2020, after removing the time gaps

The number of comments at the first level (comments on the news itself) was 93, at the second (comments on comments at the first level) 32, at the third 22, and at the fourth and more 73. The average time for second-level comments to appear is about 100 min.

It should be noted that in addition to the two-stage curves (see Figures 6 and 8), in some cases there is an S dynamic for changes in the number of comments (see Figure 9 (without removing the gaps) and Figure 10 (after removing the time gaps) for the news item "Putin has nominated Mishustin for the post of prime Minister" published on the portal https://echo.msk.ru/news/2571431-echo.html (accessed on 21 November 2021) on 15 January 2020 which received 208 comments).

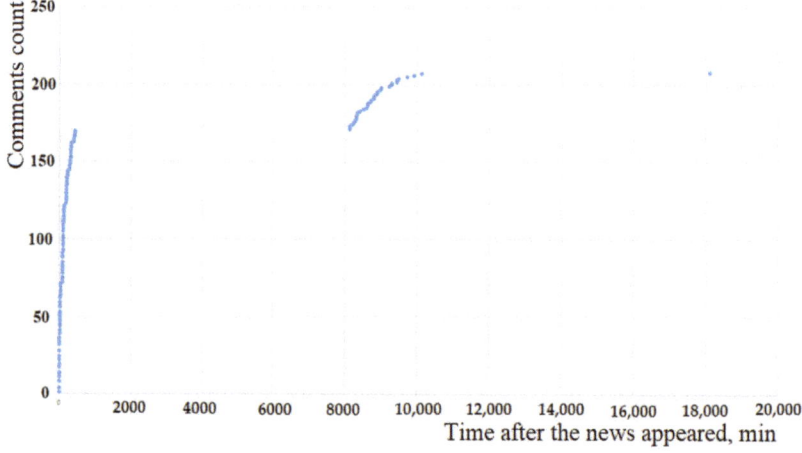

Figure 9. The observed dynamics of change over time, the number of comments on a news item of public interest that appeared on the portal https://echo.msk.ru/news/2571431-echo.html on 15 January 2020.

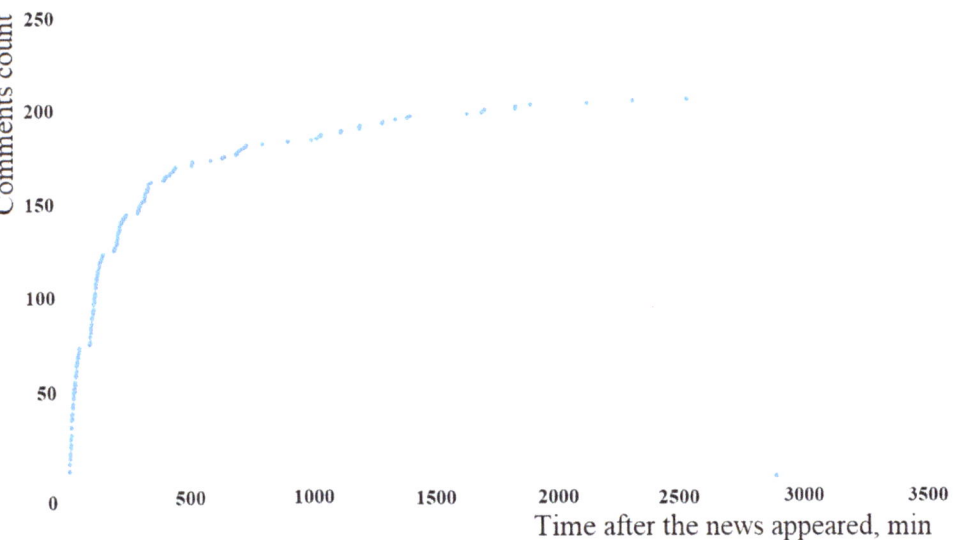

Figure 10. Dynamics of changes over time, the number of comments on a news item of public interest that appeared on the portal https://echo.msk.ru/news/2571431-echo.html on 15 January 2020, after removing the time gaps.

The number of comments at the first level (on the news itself) was 90, at the second (comments on comments at the first level) 38, at the third 14, and at the fourth and more 66. The average time for second-level comments to appear is about 56 min.

Note that the length of the sections of curves 1, 2 and 3 in Figures 6, 8 and 10 may be different, as well as the growth areas of the S-shaped curves.

The dynamics of the appearance of comments for news items: (1) On 16 April 2020: "The Public Council under the Ministry of Defense made a proposal to rename the Prazhskaya metro station in honor of Marshal Konev"; and (2) On 12 November 2020: "Lavrov stated that the Russian Federation has reason to believe that Navalny was poisoned on an airplane or in Germany", have a two-stage character (see Figures 6 and 8). For the news: (3) 15 January 2020: "Putin nominated Mishustin for the post of prime Minister", this is S-shaped (see Figure 10). In our opinion, this may be due to a significant difference in the average time of appearance of second-level comments (the time interval between the appearance of the first-level comment and the comment om this comment). If for the first news and for the second this is about 130 and 100 min, respectively, then for the third it is about 56 min. It should also be noted that the two-stage nature of the dynamics of commenting on the first news item is more evident than for the second, and at the same time the span until the appearance of secondary comments on the second news item is longer. For the other parameters (the total number of comments, the number of comments at the first, second and third levels), the three selected news items are close in quantitative terms.

For further study, the following theoretical research task can be formulated: what is the nature of the processes of commenting on news items and blogs, and what features of these complex social systems lead to the fact that, for the correspondence of the probability density of the distribution of comments by their number, a power law is applied and the dynamics have a complex two-stage character in many cases?

5. Derivation of the Power Law of the Distribution of Comments from the Stationary Fokker-Planck Equation

The Fokker-Planck equation is widely used for the analysis and modeling of non-stationary processes observed in various complex systems and allows the achievement of good agreement with the predicted behavior and observed data. Therefore, as a testable hypothesis, we assume that the Fokker-Planck equation can be used to analyze and model the appearance of comments on newsfeed and blogs.

In general, the Fokker-Planck equation has the form:

$$\frac{\partial \rho(x,t)}{\partial t} = -\frac{\partial}{\partial x}[\mu(x) \cdot \rho(x,t)] + \frac{1}{2}\frac{\partial^2}{\partial x^2}[D(x) \cdot \rho(x,t)] \quad (1)$$

where $\rho(x,t)$ is the time-dependent probability density of the distribution over states x (in our case, state x is the number of comments observed at time t), $D(x)$ is a state-dependent coefficient x that determines a random change in state x, and $\mu(x)$ is a state-dependent coefficient x that determines a purposeful change in state x.

In relation to our model, $D(x)$ can be interpreted as user actions caused by a spontaneous impulse that arose when reading the news or comments on it from other users, when the event described in the newsfeed or blog is not essential, but the user is willing to spend time commenting or responding to another commentator (the user has a spontaneous desire to respond to this news). $\mu(x)$ can be interpreted as purposeful actions caused by the desire to respond to a newsfeed or blog that is essential to the user, as well as to comment on another user's comment if this touches on a topic that is important from the point of view of this user (the user is constantly interested in this topic).

When analyzing the observed data, at first step we will not consider the dynamics of the appearance of comments over time, but take a static picture formed over a certain period of time (when the changes stop), so we can proceed to the stationary Fokker-Planck equation, which has the form:

$$-\frac{d}{dx}[\mu(x) \cdot \rho(x)] + \frac{1}{2}\frac{d^2}{dx^2}[D(x) \cdot \rho(x)] = 0 \quad (2)$$

Calculate the derivatives in Equation (2):

$$-\frac{d}{dx}[\mu(x) \cdot \rho(x)] = -\left[\mu(x) \cdot \frac{d\rho(x)}{dx} + \rho(x) \cdot \frac{d\mu(x)}{dx}\right]$$

$$\frac{d^2}{dx^2}[D(x) \cdot \rho(x)] = \frac{d}{dx}\left[\frac{d}{dx}[D(x) \cdot \rho(x)]\right] = \frac{d}{dx}\left[D(x) \cdot \frac{d\rho(x)}{dx} + \rho(x) \cdot \frac{dD(x)}{dx}\right] =$$

$$= D(x) \cdot \frac{d^2\rho(x)}{dx^2} + 2\frac{dD(x)}{dx} \cdot \frac{d\rho(x)}{dx} + \rho(x) \cdot \frac{d^2D(x)}{dx^2}$$

After substituting the derivatives into Equation (2), we obtain:

$$-\mu(x) \cdot \frac{d\rho(x)}{dx} - \frac{d\mu(x)}{dx} \cdot \rho(x) + \frac{1}{2}D(x) \cdot \frac{d^2\rho(x)}{dx^2} + \frac{dD(x)}{dx} \cdot \frac{d\rho(x)}{dx} + \frac{d^2D(x)}{dx^2} \cdot \rho(x) = 0 \quad (3)$$

Further, to build the model, it is necessary to make assumptions about the dependence of $D(x)$ and $\mu(x)$ on the state of x and consider two conditions. Firstly, we consider the magnitude of the terms included in Equation (3), and secondly, we can assume that with the growth of state x (the increase in the number of possible comments (the significance of a newsfeed or blog), the values $D(x)$ and $\mu(x)$ should also increase). Logic suggests that all terms of Equation (3) should have the same magnitude, which has $p(x)$. Both the first and the second condition will be met if the dependencies $D(x)$ and $\mu(x)$ on the state x have the form: $\mu(x) = \mu_0 \cdot x$ and $D(x) = D_0 \cdot x^2$. In this form, the growth of $D(x)$ and $\mu(x)$

will be ensured with an increase in the state of x, and on the other hand the condition of preserving the magnitude is fulfilled. Substituting $D(x)$ and $\mu(x)$ into Equation (3) gives:

$$-\mu_0 \cdot x \cdot \frac{d\rho(x)}{dx} - \mu_0 \cdot \rho(x) + \frac{1}{2} D_0 \cdot x^2 \cdot \frac{d^2\rho(x)}{dx^2} + 2D_0 \cdot x \cdot \frac{d\rho(x)}{dx} + D_0 \cdot \rho(x) = 0$$

$$x^2 \cdot \frac{d^2\rho(x)}{dx^2} + 2\left[2 - \frac{\mu_0}{D_0}\right] \cdot x \cdot \frac{d\rho(x)}{dx} + 2\left[1 - \frac{\mu_0}{D_0}\right] \rho(x) = 0 \qquad (4)$$

Denote $2\left[1 - \frac{\mu_0}{D_0}\right] = \gamma$, then:

$$x^2 \cdot \frac{d^2\rho(x)}{dx^2} + [2 + \gamma] \cdot x \cdot \frac{d\rho(x)}{dx} + \gamma \cdot \rho(x) = 0 \qquad (5)$$

Equation (5) refers to equations of the Euler equation type and its solution can be found in the form: $\rho(x) = \sum_k C_k x^q$, where C_k are constant coefficients at the corresponding roots of the characteristic equation, which has the form:

$$q(q-1) + [2+\gamma]q + \gamma = 0$$

This equation has two roots: $q_1 = -1$ and $q_2 = -\gamma$. Thus, for $\rho(x)$ we obtain:

$$\rho(x) = C_1 x^{-1} + C_2 x^{-\gamma} \qquad (6)$$

We find the constant coefficients C_1 and C_2 using the normalization condition of the function $\rho(x)$

$$\int_1^\infty \rho(x)dx = C_1 \ln(x)\Big|_1^\infty + C_2 \frac{x^{1-\gamma}}{1-\gamma}\Big|_1^\infty \equiv 1 \qquad (7)$$

Integral (7) is calculated from 1 to ∞, because there may be users who have made a very large number of comments to the news, but there cannot be commentators who have written less than one comment. Given that for $x \to \infty$ $\ln(x)|_\infty = \infty$, then $C_1 = 0$ and, respectively, $C_2 = \gamma - 1$. Finally, we get: $\rho(x) = [\gamma - 1]x^{-\gamma}$.

Let us compare the obtained theoretical result with the observed data (see Figure 5). Linear approximation of the data presented in Figure 5 allowed us to obtain the equation: $y = -1.49 - 1.23z$, which must be compared with the equation:

$$\ln\{\rho(x)\} = \ln\{\gamma - 1\} - \gamma \cdot \ln(x) \qquad (8)$$

If $\gamma = 1.23$, then $\ln(\gamma - 1) = -1.47$, which shows a very good correspondence between the theory and the observed data.

The results obtained show that, with a linear dependence of $\mu(x)$ on the state of x and a quadratic dependence of $D(x)$ on the state of x, the power law of dependence is the probability density of the distribution of comments by their number (states of x). This can be obtained from the solution of the stationary Fokker-Planck equation, and the observed data and theoretical calculations have good agreement with each other.

Special attention should be paid to this result. Its importance lies in the fact that the effects of memory and self-organization play an important role in the dynamics of social processes. However, in this case it turns out that from the Fokker-Planck equation (describing the dynamics as a whole at the macro level), the derivation of which considers a completely stochastic Markov approximation, it is possible to obtain theoretical results that are in good agreement with the observed data. We can make an assumption that the multi-directionality of a multitude of local actions and processes, each of which has both memory and self-organization, leads in the total result to the fact that memory can largely disappear as a result of the multi-direction of the ongoing micro-processes.

6. A Model of the Nonlinear Dynamics of the Appearance of Comments Based on the Fokker-Planck Equation

Since the use of the Fokker-Planck equation and the approach described above allow us to obtain the power law of distribution observed in practice, it is advisable to use this equation to describe the dynamics of the observed processes.

Using the method of Laplace transformations for Equation (1), it is possible to obtain (see Appendix A) the following expression for the distribution function:

$$\rho(x,t) = \int \frac{\left[\frac{[ln(x)]^2}{D_0 t} + \left[\frac{1}{2} - \frac{\mu_0}{D_0}\right]ln(x) - 1\right]}{\sqrt{2\pi D_0 t^3}} e^{-\left[\frac{[ln(x)]^2}{2D_0 t} + \left[\frac{3}{2} - \frac{\mu_0}{D_0}\right]ln(x) + \left[\frac{1}{2} - \frac{\mu_0}{D_0}\right]^2 \frac{D_0 t}{2}\right]} dt \qquad (9)$$

The probability that the number of comments by the time it reaches a certain number L can be found by the formula (10):

$$P(L,t) = 1 - \int_0^L \left[\int \frac{\left[\frac{[ln(x)]^2}{D_0 t} + \left[\frac{1}{2} - \frac{\mu_0}{D_0}\right]ln(x) - 1\right]}{\sqrt{2\pi D_0 t^3}} e^{-\left[\frac{[ln(x)]^2}{2D_0 t} + \left[\frac{3}{2} - \frac{\mu_0}{D_0}\right]ln(x) + \left[\frac{1}{2} - \frac{\mu_0}{D_0}\right]^2 \frac{D_0 t}{2}\right]} dt \right] dx \qquad (10)$$

$$\int_0^L \left[\int \frac{\left[\frac{[ln(x)]^2}{D_0 t} + \left[\frac{1}{2} - \frac{\mu_0}{D_0}\right]ln(x) - 1\right]}{\sqrt{2\pi D_0 t^3}} e^{-\left[\frac{[ln(x)]^2}{2D_0 t} + \left[\frac{3}{2} - \frac{\mu_0}{D_0}\right]ln(x) + \left[\frac{1}{2} - \frac{\mu_0}{D_0}\right]^2 \frac{D_0 t}{2}\right]} dt \right] dx$$

This determines the probability that the threshold L (for example, the maximum possible value of the number of comments) will not be reached by time t. The dependence of the number of comments $N(t)$ on time t will be described by the equation: $N(t) = P(L,t) \cdot L$.

We will conduct simulation modeling and analyze the theoretical results obtained. As an example, we choose $L = 100$ and three sets of values of μ_0 and D_0 ($\mu_0 = 0.45$ и $D_0 = 0.50$ conventional units ($\mu_0 < D_0$ see curve 1 in Figure 11); $\mu_0 = 0.50$ и $D_0 = 0.50$ and $\mu_0 = D_0$ conventional units ($\mu_0 > D_0$ see curve 2 in Figure 11) and $\mu_0 = 0.55$ and $D_0 = 0.50$ conventional units ($\mu_0 > D_0$ see curve 3 in Figure 11)). Figure 11 shows the results of modeling the dynamics of changes over time in the number of comments $N(t)$ at the selected values of the model parameters μ_0, D_0 and L.

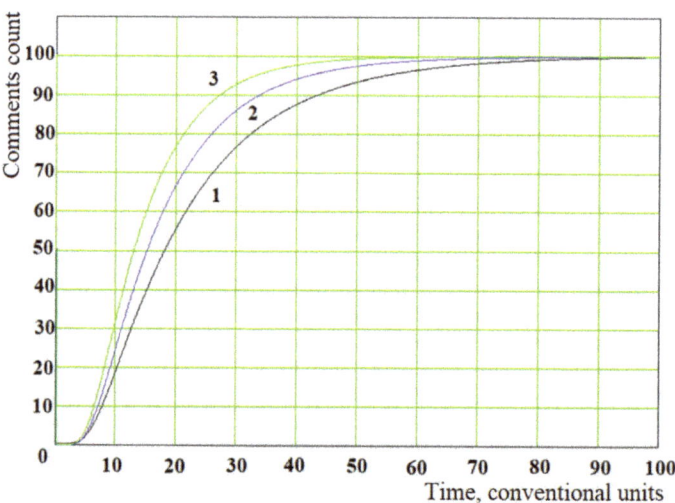

Figure 11. Dynamics of changes over time in the number of comments to the news in a simulation model based on the Fokker-Planck equation.

Theoretical calculations show that, with the growth of μ_0 relative to D_0, the growth rate of the curve increases (see Figure 11).

It is important to note that the model based on the Fokker-Planck equation for all values of the parameters μ_0 and D_0 shows the S-shaped nature of the dynamics of changes in the number of comments to the news over time, which in many cases is not consistent with the observed data (see Figures 6 and 8).

The correspondence of the theoretical model and the observed data (see Figures 6 and 8) can be obtained if we assume that two processes with different μ_0 and D_0 can occur simultaneously. Moreover, the sum of the partial fractions of the processes should be equal to 1, i.e., $P_{total}(L,t) = \alpha_1 \cdot P_1(L,t) + \alpha_2 \cdot P_2(L,t)$, where $\alpha_1 + \alpha_2 = 1$. At the same time, one of the processes is generated by commenting on the newsfeed or blog itself, and the second by commenting on comments. To describe this, we consider the possible time delay in commenting on comments in the model. If we enter the delay time (denote it τ), then the distribution function will take the form:

$$\rho(x, t-\tau) = \int \frac{\left[\frac{[ln(x)]^2}{D_0[t-\tau]} + \left[\frac{1}{2} - \frac{\mu_0}{D_0}\right] ln(x) - 1\right]}{\sqrt{2\pi D_0[t-\tau]^3}} e^{-\left[\frac{[ln(x)]^2}{2D_0[t-\tau]} + \left[\frac{3}{2} - \frac{\mu_0}{D_0}\right] ln(x) + \left[\frac{1}{2} - \frac{\mu_0}{D_0}\right]^2 \frac{D_0[t-\tau]}{2}\right]} dt$$

As we wrote earlier, this may be due to a significant difference in the average time of appearance of second-level comments (the time interval between the appearance of a first-level comment and a comment on this comment), which may lead to the implementation of two-stage dynamics in the appearance of comments.

As an example of modeling, we will choose the following model parameters for the process of commenting on the newsfeed or blog itself: $\mu_{0,1} = 0.55$, $D_{0,1} = 0.50$, and for the second (commenting on comments) $\mu_{0,2} = 0.50$, $D_{0,2} = 0.50$, $\tau = 50$ conventional units, $\alpha_1 = 0.75$, $\alpha_2 = 0.25$ and $L = 100$ ($\mu_{0,1} > \mu_{0,2}$ was chosen based on the assumption that commenting on the news is a more primary process for users than commenting on comments.

Figure 12 shows the results of modeling the dynamics of changes in the number of comments $N(t)$ over time, because two processes can occur in parallel. As can be seen from the simulation results presented in Figure 12, there is a good coincidence of real data (see Figures 6 and 8) and theoretical calculations (curve 1, constructed considering the time delay τ). Without considering the delay, the dynamics of the news commenting process is S-shaped (see curve 2 in Figure 12), which coincides with the observed data presented in Figure 10 and is consistent with a significant difference in the average time of appearance of second-level comments for news items 1, 2 and 3 selected as an example.

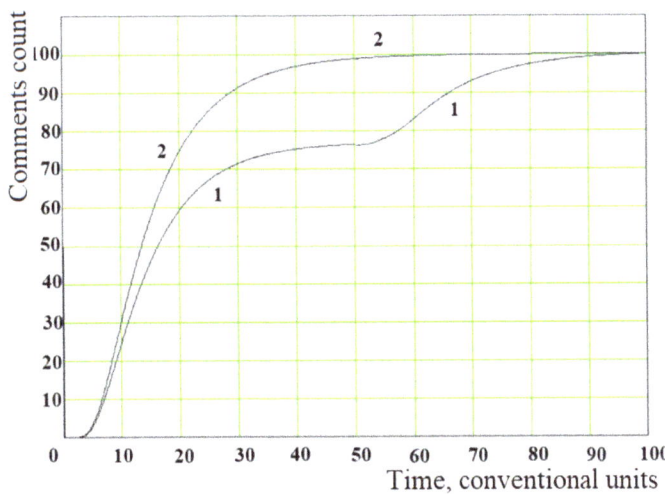

Figure 12. Dynamics of changes over time in the number of comments on the news in the simulation model based on the Fokker-Planck equation, considering two parallel processes.

The parallel flow of the two processes does not violate the integrity of the model, because the stationary solution of the modified Fokker–Planck equation (taking into account the delay by τ) and the usual equation has the same form, which was described in the section "Derivation of the power law of the distribution of comments from the stationary Fokker–Planck equation".

7. Discussion

Firstly, it is possible to analyze the topics of news items that gain the largest number of comments (i.e., have the greatest public interest), make a ranking of their popularity, and study their static distributions. Further, within each group, it is possible to determine the exponent of the power law $\rho(x) = [\gamma - 1]x^{-\gamma}$. Then, considering that $\frac{\mu_0}{D_0} = 1 - \frac{\gamma}{2}$, it is possible to determine the value of $\frac{\mu_0}{D_0}$ by which it is possible to judge for which types of news and messages purposeful commenting is predominant (an increase in the ratio of $\frac{\mu_0}{D_0}$), and for which this is "random" (a decrease in the ratio of $\frac{\mu_0}{D_0}$). This will allow prediction in the future as to what news item may cause what user behavior, and how they may influence public opinion.

Secondly, using the dynamic distribution functions obtained in this work, it is possible to analyze the observed processes of commenting on newsfeed and blogs. Further, based on this, it is possible to determine the parameters of the model μ_0, D_0 and τ for various types of news, which can also allow prediction in the future what news may cause what user behavior, and how this may influence public opinion.

In conclusion, we note that the complex nature of the dynamics of processes in complex social systems can be described, not only based on models created based on the Fokker–Planck equation. For example, in [41–48], models were developed by the authors specifically to describe the stochastic dynamics of changes in the state of complex social systems. These models take into account the processes of self-organization and memory availability. To create this model, graphical diagrams of the probabilities of transitions between possible states of the described systems were considered taking into account previous states. This method allows the taking into account memory, and describes not only Markov but also non-Markov processes. Using this approach, a nonlinear differential equation of the second order was derived, which allows the setting and solution of problems for determining the probability density function of the amplitude of deviations of parameters describing the observed processes of a non-stationary time series, depending on the values of the time interval of its determination and the depth of memory accounting. The differential equation obtained during the study contains not only terms responsible for random change (diffusion) and ordered change (destruction), but also a term that is responsible for the possibility of self-organization, which significantly distinguishes it from the Fokker–Planck equation. Within the framework of the models developed by [41–48], it is possible to describe processes whose dynamics have both an S-shaped character for changes and a two-stage process.

The novelty of our work in comparison with the works of our predecessors is that, by using a stationary version of the Fokker–Planck equation for the data observed in practice, a power law of the distribution of their parameters can be obtained that is consistent with them. In this case, it can be made a pre-position that the multidirectional nature of many local actions and processes, each of which has both memory and self-organization, leads in summary to the fact that memory can largely disappear and the process in a generalized form becomes Markovsky. This allowed us, under certain assumptions for coefficients in the Fokker–Planck equation, to obtain from its stationary form a power law of distribution for the number of comments on news and blogs. As shown in our paper, the theory aligns well with the data observed in reality.

Secondly, assuming that the Fokker–Planck equation under certain circumstances can be applied to describe the dynamics in the systems in question (for example, based on what is described above) we considered the temporal dependencies of the appearance of comments on various news and found that it can be both S-shaped in nature and have a more complex-two-staged form, which can be explained within the framework of using the Fokker–Planck equation only by the presence of two processes and delay time.

8. Conclusions

The results obtained in the work allow us to draw several conclusions:

1. The stationary distribution of news observed in practice by the number of comments to on it corresponds to the power law: $\rho(x) = [\gamma - 1]x^{-\gamma}$, where $\rho(x)$ is the share of news items in their total number having x comments, and γ is the exponent.

2. The dynamics of changes over time in the number of comments to a newsfeed or blog can have both an S-shaped form and a two-stage one, which may be due to a significant difference in the average time of appearance of comments at the second level (the time interval between the appearance of a comment at the first level and a comment on this comment), i.e., the value of the average delay.
3. The power law of dependence observed in practice is the stationary probability density of the distribution of news by the number of comments (states x) which can be obtained from the solution of the stationary Fokker-Planck equation if some assumptions are made during its derivation. We assume that the coefficient $\mu(x)$ responsible in the Fokker-Planck equation for a purposeful change in the state of the system x (x is the current number of comments on the news) linearly depends on the state x, and the coefficient $D(x)$ responsible for a random change depends on x quadratically. All this suggests that the Fokker-Planck equation can be used to describe processes in complex network structures.
4. The solution of the unsteady Fokker-Planck equation under the assumptions of the linear dependence of $\mu(x)$ on the state of x and the quadratic dependence of $D(x)$ on the state of x allows us to obtain an equation for the probability density of transitions between the states of the system per unit of time, which are in good agreement with the observed data, taking into account the effect of the delay time between the appearance of the first level comment and the comment on this comment.
5. The models developed based on the Fokker-Planck equation are in good agreement with the observed data, which makes it possible to create algorithms for monitoring and predicting the evolution of public opinion of users of news information resources.

Author Contributions: D.Z.: conceptualization, formal analysis, writing-review & editing; J.P.: methodology, visualization; V.K.: data curation, writing-original draft. All authors have read and agreed to the published version of the manuscript.

Funding: This research was supported by the Russian Science Foundation (RSF), grant no. 22-21-00109 "Development of the dynamics forecasting models of social moods based on the analysis of text content time series of social networks using the Fokker-Planck and nonlinear diffusion equations".

Institutional Review Board Statement: Not applicable.

Informed Consent Statement: Not applicable.

Data Availability Statement: Not applicable.

Conflicts of Interest: The authors declare no conflict of interest.

Appendix A

One of the solutions of the Fokker-Planck equation can be obtained as follows. Using the method of Laplace transformations for Equation (1), we can write:

$$s\overline{G(s,x)} - \rho(0,x) = -\frac{d}{dx}\left[\mu(x)\cdot\overline{G(s,x)}\right] + \frac{1}{2}\frac{d^2}{dx^2}\left[D(x)\cdot\overline{G(s,x)}\right] \tag{A1}$$

Considering that at time $t = 0$ (the beginning of the process) there are no comments, then: $\rho(0,x) = 0$.

Further, substituting into Equation (A1) the corresponding derivatives and dependencies $\mu(x)$ and $D(x)$ (the choice of which was discussed earlier, and their use leading to the results of the distribution of the number of comments according to the power law observed in reality), we obtain:

$$x^2 \cdot \frac{d^2\overline{G(s,x)}}{dx^2} + 2\left[2 - \frac{\mu_0}{D_0}\right] \cdot x \cdot \frac{d\overline{G(s,x)}}{dx} + 2\left[1 - \frac{\mu_0 + s}{D_0}\right]\overline{G(s,x)} = 0 \tag{A2}$$

We are looking for a solution to this equation in the form: $\overline{G(s,x)} = \sum_k C_k x^q$, where C_k are the coefficients for the roots of the characteristic equation, which has the form: $q(q-1) + 2\left[2 - \frac{\mu_0}{D_0}\right]q + 2\left[1 - \frac{\mu_0+s}{D_0}\right] = 0$. Let us finds the roots of the characteristic equation.

$$q_{1,2} = -\frac{\left[3 - 2\frac{\mu_0}{D_0}\right]}{2} \pm \frac{\sqrt{\left[1 - 2\frac{\mu_0}{D_0}\right]^2 + 8\frac{s}{D_0}}}{2}$$

We write it down as follows:

$$\overline{G(s,x)} = x^{-\frac{[3-2\frac{\mu_0}{D_0}]}{2}} \left\{ C_1 x^{\frac{\sqrt{[1-2\frac{\mu_0}{D_0}]^2 + 8\frac{s}{D_0}}}{2}} + C_2 x^{-\frac{\sqrt{[1-2\frac{\mu_0}{D_0}]^2 + 8\frac{s}{D_0}}}{2}} \right\}$$

Given that $\gamma = 2\left[1 - \frac{\mu_0}{D_0}\right]$ we write:

$$\overline{G(s,x)} = C_1 \cdot x^{-\frac{[\gamma+1]-\sqrt{[\gamma-1]^2 + 8\frac{s}{D_0}}}{2}} + C_2 \cdot x^{-\frac{[\gamma+1]+\sqrt{[\gamma-1]^2 + 8\frac{s}{D_0}}}{2}}$$

For $s \to \infty$ ($t \to 0$) $\rho(x,0)$ for any x must be equal to 0, so C_1 should be put equal to 0 $\frac{-[\gamma+1]+\sqrt{[\gamma-1]^2+8\frac{s}{D_0}}}{2} \to +\infty$ and $x \to +\infty$). Using the normalization condition (for the image, the integral from 1 to ∞ must be equal to $\frac{1}{s}$), we find the coefficient with C_2:

$$\frac{2C_2}{-[\gamma+1]-\sqrt{[\gamma-1]^2+8\frac{s}{D_0}}+2} \cdot x^{-\frac{[\gamma+1]+\sqrt{[\gamma-1]^2+8\frac{s}{D_0}}}{2}+1} \Big|_1^\infty = \frac{1}{s}$$

$$C_2 = \frac{[\gamma-1] + \sqrt{[\gamma-1]^2 + 8\frac{s}{D_0}}}{2s}$$

$$\overline{G(s,x)} = \frac{[\gamma-1] + \sqrt{[\gamma-1]^2 + 8\frac{s}{D_0}}}{2s} \cdot x^{-\frac{[\gamma+1]+\sqrt{[\gamma-1]^2+8\frac{s}{D_0}}}{2}}$$

Substitute γ and get:

$$\alpha = \frac{1 - 2\frac{\mu_0}{D_0}}{2} = \frac{1}{2} - \frac{\mu_0}{D_0}$$

$$\frac{3 - 2\frac{\mu_0}{D_0}}{2} = 1 + \frac{1 - 2\frac{\mu_0}{D_0}}{2} = 1 + \alpha$$

$$\beta = \frac{1}{2}\sqrt{\frac{8}{D_0}} = \sqrt{\frac{2}{D_0}}$$

$$k = \frac{D_0}{8}\left[1 - 2\frac{\mu_0}{D_0}\right]^2 = \frac{D_0}{2}\left[\frac{1}{2} - \frac{\mu_0}{D_0}\right]^2 = \left[\frac{\alpha}{\beta}\right]^2$$

$$x^{-\beta\sqrt{k+s}} = e^{-[\beta \cdot \ln(x)]\sqrt{k+s}}$$

Let us writes this:

$$\overline{G(s,x)} = \left[\alpha \cdot \frac{e^{-[\beta \cdot \ln(x)] \cdot \sqrt{k+s}}}{s} + \beta \cdot \frac{\sqrt{k+s} \cdot e^{-[\beta \cdot \ln(x)] \cdot \sqrt{k+s}}}{s}\right] \cdot x^{-[1+\alpha]}$$

We find the original $\frac{e^{-[\beta \cdot \ln(x)] \cdot \sqrt{k+s}}}{s}$ and the original $\beta \cdot \frac{\sqrt{k+s} \cdot e^{-[\beta \cdot \ln(x)] \cdot \sqrt{k+s}}}{s}$ we find by differentiating the original $\frac{e^{-[\beta \cdot \ln(x)] \cdot \sqrt{k+s}}}{s}$ by $\ln(x)$.

$$\frac{d}{d(\ln(x))}\left[\frac{e^{-[\beta \cdot \ln(x)] \cdot \sqrt{k+s}}}{s}\right] = -\beta \cdot \frac{\sqrt{k+s} \cdot e^{-[\beta \cdot \ln(x)] \cdot \sqrt{k+s}}}{s}$$

$$\overline{G(s,x)} = \left[\alpha \cdot \frac{e^{-[\beta \cdot \ln(x)] \cdot \sqrt{k+s}}}{s} - \frac{d}{d(\ln(x))}\left[\frac{e^{-[\beta \cdot \ln(x)] \cdot \sqrt{k+s}}}{s}\right]\right] \cdot x^{-[1+\alpha]}$$

$\frac{e^{-[\beta \cdot \ln(x)] \cdot \sqrt{k+s}}}{s} = \frac{1}{s} \cdot e^{-y \cdot \sqrt{k+s}}$, where $[\beta \cdot \ln(x)] = y$.

Dividing an image by s is analogous to integrating over t of the original $e^{-y \cdot \sqrt{k+s}}$. Let us find this original:

$$e^{-[\beta \cdot \ln(x)] \cdot \sqrt{k+s}} \risingdotseq \frac{\beta \cdot \ln(x)}{2\sqrt{\pi t^3}} \cdot e^{-\frac{[\beta \cdot \ln(x)]^2}{4t}} \cdot e^{-kt}$$

$$\frac{e^{-[\beta \cdot \ln(x)] \cdot \sqrt{k+s}}}{s} \risingdotseq \int \frac{\beta \cdot \ln(x)}{2\sqrt{\pi t^3}} \cdot e^{-\frac{[\beta \cdot \ln(x)]^2}{4t}} \cdot e^{-kt} dt$$

$$\frac{d}{d(\ln(x))}\left[\frac{e^{-[\beta \cdot \ln(x)]\cdot \sqrt{k+s}}}{s}\right] \doteq \int \frac{\beta \cdot \ln(x)}{2\sqrt{\pi t^3}}\left[1 - \frac{\beta^2}{2t}\cdot \ln(x)\right]\cdot e^{-\frac{[\beta \cdot \ln(x)]^2}{4t}}\cdot e^{-kt}dt$$

After making all the necessary substitutions, we get the following expression for the distribution function:

$$\rho(x,t) = \int \frac{\left[\frac{[\ln(x)]^2}{D_0 t} + \left[\frac{1}{2} - \frac{\mu_0}{D_0}\right]\ln(x) - 1\right]}{\sqrt{2\pi D_0 t^3}} e^{-\left[\frac{[\ln(x)]^2}{2D_0 t} + \left[\frac{3}{2} - \frac{\mu_0}{D_0}\right]\ln(x) + \left[\frac{1}{2} - \frac{\mu_0}{D_0}\right]^2 \frac{D_0 t}{2}\right]} dt \tag{A3}$$

References

1. Gardiner, C. *Stochastic Methods: A Handbook for the Natural and Social Sciences*; Springer: Berlin, Germany, 2009.
2. Lux, T. Inference for systems of stochastic differential equations from discretely sampled data: A numerical maximum likelihood approach. *Ann. Financ.* **2012**, *9*, 217–248. [CrossRef]
3. Hurn, A.; Jeisman, J.; Lindsay, K. Teaching an old dog new tricks: Improved estimation of the parameters of stochastic differential equations by numerical solution of the Fokker-Planck equation. In *Financial Econometrics Handbook*; Gregoriou, G., Pascalau, R., Eds.; Palgrave: London, UK, 2010.
4. Elliott, R.J.; Siu, T.K.; Chan, L. A PDE approach for risk measures for derivatives with regime switching. *Ann. Financ.* **2007**, *4*, 55–74. [CrossRef]
5. Orlov, Y.N.; Fedorov, S.L. Generation of nonstationary time series trajectories based on the Fokker-Planck equation. *WORKS MIPT* **2016**, *8*, 126–133.
6. Chen, Y.; Cosimano, T.F.; Himonas, A.A.; Kelly, P. An Analytic Approach for Stochastic Differential Utility for Endowment and Production Economies. *Comput. Econ.* **2013**, *44*, 397–443. [CrossRef]
7. Savku, E.; Weber, G.-W. Stochastic differential games for optimal investment problems in a Markov regime-switching jump-diffusion market. *Ann. Oper. Res.* **2020**, 1–26. [CrossRef]
8. Andrianova, E.G.; Golovin, S.A.; Zykov, S.V.; Lesko, S.A.; Chukalina, E.R. Review of modern models and methods of analysis of time series of dynamics of processes in social, economic and socio-technical systems. *Russ. Technol. J.* **2020**, *8*, 7–45. [CrossRef]
9. Dorogovtsev, S.N.; Mendes, J.F.F. Evolution of networks. *Adv. Phys.* **2002**, *51*, 1079–1187. [CrossRef]
10. Newman, M.E.J. The structure and function of complex networks. *SIAM Rev.* **2003**, *45*, 167–256. [CrossRef]
11. Dorogovtsev, S.N.; Mendes, J.F.F.; Samukhin, A.N. Generic scale of the scale-free growing networks. *Phys. Rev. E* **2001**, *63*, 062101. [CrossRef]
12. Golder, S.A.; Wilkinson, D.M.; Huberman, B.A. Rhythms of social interaction: Messaging within a massive online network. In *Communities and Technologies 2007*; Steinfield, C., Pentland, B.T., Ackerman, M., Contractor, N., Eds.; Springer: London, UK, 2007; pp. 41–66.
13. Kumar, R.; Novak, J.; Tomkins, A. Structure and evolution of online social networks. In Proceedings of the 12th ACM SIGKDD International Conference on Knowledge Discovery and Data Mining (KDD '06), Philadelphia, PA, USA, 20–23 August 2006; pp. 611–617.
14. Mislove, A.; Marcon, M.; Gummadi, K.P.; Druschel, P.; Bhattacharjee, B. Measurement and analysis of online social networks. In Proceedings of the 7th ACM SIGCOMM Conference on Internet Measurement (IMC '07), San Diego, CA, USA, 24–26 October 2007; pp. 29–42.
15. Pasa, L.; Navarin, N.; Sperdut, A. SOM-based aggregation for graph convolutional neural networks Neural Computing and Applications Neural Comput. *Applic.* **2022**, *34*, 5–24.
16. Pulipati, S.; Somula, R.; Parvathala, B.R. Nature inspired link prediction and community detection algorithms for social networks: A survey. *Int. J. Syst. Assur. Eng. Manag.* **2021**. [CrossRef]
17. Airoldi, E.M.; Blei, D.M.; Fienberg, S.E.; Xing, E.P. Mixed membership stochastic blockmodels. *J. Mach. Learn. Res.* **2008**, *9*, 1981–2014. [PubMed]
18. Cho, Y.-S.; Steeg, G.V.; Galstyan, A. Co-evolution of selection and influence in social networks. In Proceedings of the Twenty-Fifth AAAI Conference on Artificial Intelligence (AAAI 2011), San Francisco, CA, USA, 7–11 August 2011.
19. Sahafizadeh, E.; Ladani, B.T. The impact of group propagation on rumor spreading in mobile social networks. *Phys. A Stat. Mech. Its Appl.* **2018**, *506*, 412–423. [CrossRef]
20. Varma, V.S.; Morarescu, I.C.; Haye, Y. Analysis and control of multi-leveled opinions spreading in social networks. In Proceedings of the American Control Conference (ACC 2018), Milwaukee, WI, USA, 27–29 June 2018; pp. 3404–3409.
21. López-Santamaría, L.-M.; Almanza-Ojeda, D.-L.; Gomez, J.C.; Ibarra-Manzano, M.-A. Age and Gender Identification in Unbalanced Social Media. In Proceedings of the 2019 International Conference on Electronics, Communications and Computers (CONIELECOMP), Cholula, Mexico, 27 February–1 March 2019. [CrossRef]
22. Barberá, P. Less is More? How Demographic Sample Weights Can Improve Public Opinion Estimates Based on Twitter Data. 2016. Available online: http://pablobarbera.com/static/less-is-more.pdf (accessed on 21 December 2021).
23. Luo, F.; Cao, G.; Mulligan, K.; Li, X. Explore Spatiotemporal and Demographic Characteristics of Human Mobility via Twitter: A Case Study of Chicago. *Appl. Geogr.* **2016**, *70*, 11–25. [CrossRef]

24. Sekara, V.; Stopczynski, A.; Lehmann, S. Fundamental structures of dynamic social networks. *Proc. Natl. Acad. Sci. USA* **2016**, 113. [CrossRef]
25. Ubaldi, E.; Vezzani, A.; Karsai, M.; Perra, N.; Burioni, R. Burstiness and tie activation strategies in time-varying social networks. *Sci. Rep.* **2017**, *7*, srep46225. [CrossRef]
26. Yatim, A.F.M.; Wardhana, Y.; Kamal, A.; Soroinda, A.A.R.; Rachim, F.; Wonggo, M.I. A corpus-based lexicon building in Indonesian political context through Indonesian online news media. In Proceedings of the 2016 International Conference on Advanced Computer Science and Information Systems (ICACSIS), Malang, Indonesia, 15–16 October 2016. [CrossRef]
27. Kirn, S.L.; Hinders, M.K. Dynamic wavelet fingerprint for differentiation of tweet storm types. *Soc. Netw. Anal. Min.* **2020**, *10*, 4. [CrossRef]
28. Karami, A.; Elkouri, A. *Political Popularity Analysis in Social Media*; Springer: Berlin, Germany, 2019; pp. 456–465.
29. Koti, P.; Pothula, S.; Dhavachelvan, P. Age Forecasting Analysis—Over Microblogs. In Proceedings of the 2017 Second International Conference on Recent Trends and Challenges in Computational Models (ICRTCCM), Tindivanam, India, 3–4 February 2017; pp. 83–86. [CrossRef]
30. Mukhamediev, R.I.; Yakunin, K.; Mussabayev, R.; Buldybayev, T.; Kuchin, Y.; Murzakhmetov, S.; Yelis, M. Classification of Negative Information on Socially Significant Topics in Mass Media. *Symmetry* **2020**, *12*, 1945. [CrossRef]
31. Ko, H.; Jong, Y.; Sangheon, K.; Libor, M. Human-machine interaction: A case study on fake news detection using a backtracking based on a cognitive system. *Cogn. Syst. Res.* **2019**, *55*, 77–81.
32. Bushman, B.; Whitaker, J. Media Influence on Behavior. Reference Module in: Neuroscience and Biobehavioral Psychology. 2017. Available online: http://scitechconnect.elsevier.com/neurorefmod/ (accessed on 24 November 2020).
33. Bandari, R.; Asur, S.; Huberman, B.A. The Pulse of News in Social Media: Forecasting Popularity. *arXiv* **2012**, arXiv:1202.0332v1. Available online: https://arxiv.org/pdf/1202.0332.pdf (accessed on 21 December 2021).
34. Willaert, T.; Van Eecke, P.; Beuls, K.; Steels, L. Building Social Media Observatories for Monitoring Online Opinion Dynamics. *Soc. Media Soc.* **2020**, *6*. [CrossRef]
35. Tran, C.; Shin, W.-Y.; Spitz, A. Community Detection in Partially Observable Social Networks. *ACM Trans. Knowl. Discov. Data* **2021**, *16*, 1–24. [CrossRef]
36. Chen, Z.; Li, X.; Bruna, J. Supervised community detection with line graph neural networks. In Proceedings of the 7th International Conference on Learning Representations (ICLR 2019), New Orleans, LA, USA, 6–9 May 2019.
37. Hoffmann, T.; Peel, L.; Lambiotte, R.; Jones, N.S. Community detection in networks without observing edges. *Sci. Adv.* **2020**, *6*, eaav1478. [CrossRef]
38. Du, B.; Lian, X.; Cheng, X. Partial differential equation modeling with Dirichlet boundary conditions on social networks. *Bound. Value Probl.* **2018**, *2018*, 50. [CrossRef]
39. Liu, X.; He, D.; Liu, C. Modeling information dissemination and evolution in time-varying online social network based on thermal diffusion motion. *Phys. A Stat. Mech. its Appl.* **2018**, *510*, 456–476. [CrossRef]
40. Bomba, A.; Kunanets, N.; Pasichnyk, V.; Turbal, Y. Mathematical and computer models of message distribution in social networks based on the space modification of Fermi-Pasta-Ulam approach. *Adv. Intell. Syst. Comput.* **2019**, *836*, 257–266.
41. Zhukov, D.; Khvatova, T.; Zaltsman, A. Stochastic Dynamics of Influence Expansion in Social Networks and Managing Users' Transitions from One State to Another. In Proceedings of the 11th European Conference on Information Systems Management (ECISM 2017), Genoa, Italy, 14–15 September 2017; pp. 322–329.
42. Sigov, A.S.; Zhukov, D.O.; Khvatova, T.Y.; Andrianova, E.G. A Model of Forecasting of Information Events on the Basis of the Solution of a Boundary Value Problem for Systems with Memory and Self-Organization. *J. Commun. Technol. Electron.* **2018**, *63*, 1478–1485. [CrossRef]
43. Zhukov, D.; Khvatova, T.; Millar, C.; Zaltcman, A. Modelling the stochastic dynamics of transitions between states in social systems incorporating self-organization and memory. *Technol. Forecast. Soc. Chang.* **2020**, *158*, 120134. [CrossRef]
44. Zhukov, D.; Khvatova, T.; Istratov, L. A stochastic dynamics model for shaping stock indexes using self-organization processes, memory and oscillations. In Proceedings of the European Conference on the Impact of Artificial Intelligence and Robotics (ECIAIR 2019), Oxford, UK, 31 October–1 November 2019; pp. 390–401.
45. Zhukov, D.; Khvatova, T.; Istratov, L. Analysis of non-stationary time series based on modelling stochastic dynamics considering self-organization, memory and oscillations. In Proceedings of the International Conference on Time Series and Forecasting (ITISE 2019), Granada, Spain, 25–27 September 2019; Volume 1, pp. 244–254.
46. Khvatova, T.; Zaltsman, A.; Zhukov, D. Information processes in social networks: Percolation and stochastic dynamics. CEUR Workshop. In *Proceedings of the 2nd International Scientific Conference "Convergent Cognitive Information Technologies"*; Springer: Berlin/Heidelberg, Germany, 2017; Volume 2064, pp. 277–288.
47. Zhukov, D.O.; Lesko, S.A. Stochastic self-organisation of poorly structured data and memory realisation in an information domain when designing news events forecasting models. In Proceedings of the 2nd IEEE International Conference on Big Data Intelligence and Computing, Auckland, New Zealand, 8–12 August 2016. [CrossRef]
48. Zhukov, D.O.; Zaltcman, A.G.; Khvatova, T.Y. Changes in States in Social Networks and Sentiment Security Using the Principles of Percolation Theory and Stochastic Dynamics. In Proceedings of the 2019 IEEE International Conference "Quality Management, Transport and Information Security, Information Technologies" (IT and QM and IS), Sochy, Russia, 23–27 September 2019; pp. 149–153.

Article

Complex Color Space Segmentation to Classify Objects in Urban Environments

Juan-Jose Cardenas-Cornejo [†], Mario-Alberto Ibarra-Manzano [†], Daniel-Alberto Razo-Medina [†] and Dora-Luz Almanza-Ojeda *,[†]

Electronics Engineering Department, DICIS, University of Guanajuato, Carr. Salamanca-Valle de Santiago KM. 3.5 + 1.8 Km., Salamanca 36885, Mexico
* Correspondence: dora.almanza@ugto.mx
† These authors contributed equally to this work.

Abstract: Color image segmentation divides the image into areas that represent different objects and focus points. One of the biggest problems in color image segmentation is the lack of homogeneity in the color of real urban images, which generates areas of over-segmentation when traditional color segmentation techniques are used. This article describes an approach to detecting and classifying objects in urban environments based on a new chromatic segmentation to locate focus points. Based on components a and b on the CIELab space, we define a *chromatic map* on the complex space to determine the highest threshold values by comparing neighboring blocks and thus divide various areas of the image automatically. Even though thresholds can result in broad segmentation areas, they suffice to locate centroids of patches on the color image that are then classified using a convolutional neural network (CNN). Thus, this broadly segmented image helps to crop only outlying areas instead of classifying the entire image. The CNN is trained to use six classes based on the patches drawn from the database of reference images from urban environments. Experimental results show a high score for classification accuracy that confirms the contribution of this segmentation approach.

Keywords: image segmentation; complex numbers; CNN classifier; outdoor environments

MSC: 68T45

Citation: Cardenas-Cornejo, J.-J.; Ibarra-Manzano, M.-A.; Razo-Medina, D.-A.; Almanza-Ojeda, D.-L. Complex Color Space Segmentation to Classify Objects in Urban Environments. *Mathematics* 2022, 10, 3752. https://doi.org/10.3390/math10203752

Academic Editor: Liliya Demidova

Received: 8 September 2022
Accepted: 6 October 2022
Published: 12 October 2022

Publisher's Note: MDPI stays neutral with regard to jurisdictional claims in published maps and institutional affiliations.

Copyright: © 2022 by the authors. Licensee MDPI, Basel, Switzerland. This article is an open access article distributed under the terms and conditions of the Creative Commons Attribution (CC BY) license (https://creativecommons.org/licenses/by/4.0/).

1. Introduction

Autonomous systems need to recognize objects and their position in the real world to interact. Ideally, autonomous systems label objects and regions on an image to understand the environment [1]. Commonly used strategies in smart systems are based on image segmentation and automatic-learning techniques. Image segmentation is a key task in computer vision involving the analysis of standard features, such as texture and color, among others, on the image. However, most models and techniques used in image segmentation are unique, that is to say, only used for a specific purpose, and their performance only differs depending on the color space involved [2]. Therefore, choosing a suitable space to represent color is essential during the segmentation process.

CIELab, HSI [3] or HSV [4] are the most common color spaces used to segment images. Others, such as *Munsel* or *YIQ* spaces [5], are used for several purposes and need specific methodologies to work. The CIELab color space mimics how humans perceive color; it is useful to modify brightness and color values on an image independently [6]. Most processing techniques based on the CIELab color space analyze each plane individually. According to the CIELab theory, chromatic components a and b are orthogonal axes on a 2D plane. Thus, the representation of 2D space on CIELab can be transformed into complex space directly, enabling the possibility of using complex numbers to facilitate algebraic calculations of image data.

A complex number is a pair of real numbers a and b ordered as (a, b), and expressed as $a + bi$ whereby i is the imaginary unit defined as $i^2 = -1$. The symbol z can represent any complex number and is a complex variable subject to operational definitions, such as an addition and a multiplication [7]. Each complex number corresponds to a single point on the complex plane.

On the other hand, automatic learning only extracts data from the most representative objects and regions to classify as segmented images. A good selection of segmentation techniques considers the relevant context, hardware resources, the number of classes, and the size of the dataset [8]. For instance, in classifying the object in the self-driving, hardware resources and the number of classes play a key role because the size of the training data and validation labels could restrict decision-making. A self-driving car that uses deep learning needs to consider hardware resources to process the dataset [9]. A convolutional neural network (CNN) is related to the number of convolutional layers, the kind of layer grouping, the activation function used, the number of fully connected layers, and the size of the image to be processed as well as the techniques used to prevent over adjustment. Even though the training phase of a CNN is computationally costly, these models can reach high classification accuracy levels, making them popular.

This study proposes using a color image segmentation algorithm based on a *chromatic map* defined on a space using complex numbers to analyze the best color distribution. Complex algebra is used spatially to obtain final representative thresholds to segment the image. The segmented images represent similar chromatic values on components a and b of the CIELab space and the image's most relevant areas. Patches from representative areas are extracted based on both aspects. A convolutional neural network (CNN) classifies the extracted patches to label them on the color image. This study's contribution is to propose a new representation of chromatic components based on complex numbers defined as a *chromatic map*. The map can facilitate localizing the most representative areas across the image using fundamental algebra for complex numbers. This segmentation method renders broadly segmented images; however, instead of refining the segmented areas and labeling them, several patches from the color images are extracted using the location of the segmented area as the input for a CNN classifier. Thus, this segmentation strategy is a phase prior to the classifier that looks for similar chromatic patterns that represent the essential content of the image. This approach to segmentation and classification has been tested using urban-context images, and the results include data about the reliability of each predicted image class.

2. Related Works

Labeling segmented areas require high computational resources to recognize objects during the human−machine interaction. Image segmentation is often based on the graphs theory and grouping algorithms. In [10], the authors propose a general scheme of segmentation of scenes based on the spectral grouping algorithm for normalized cuts, fusing geometric and color information on a working frame with no parameters. The study in [11] presents a segmentation scheme to combine color and depth information. Under this scheme, segmentation happens in 3 steps. The study by Karimpoulit [12] identifies the types of rocks using images of rocky settings. Segmentation has been extended to video; for instance, the authors of [13] have developed a method to combine the appearance of an object with the temporal consistency between frames. Using the features of a normalized-color histogram and CNN features, the GrabCut algorithm is applied to different frame boundaries to segment the object in the background. When detecting objects in motion, the background is obtained using videos taken from a static camera. The study presented in [14] suggests the option of a detection and segmentation method based on consecutive stereo images that process dynamic objects found in an urban environment. This is a pixel-by-pixel approach applied to the KITTI dataset [15], and the frame boundaries are generated bearing in mind color and difference data for each moving object.

Unlike object-detection strategies, object recognition focuses on the objectives of the image and provides a specific class for each one [16]. As the objective is better adjusted to the frame boundary, the classification results become more reliable without a background. The fast development of smart vehicles makes object detection and recognition essential in self-driving [1]. In addition, road sign detection provides key information for safe navigation. Often, road detection is based on standard low-profile features used to process the image and isolate the borders. In [17], a real-time two-stage YOLOv2-based road-sign detection system is used. In the first stage, the YOLOv2 detection frame is modified to adapt it to the road-sign detection task and predicts boundary frames, class, and reliability of road signage. In the second stage, an invariant light road-sign transformation network (RM-Net) reclassifies the samples with low accuracy to increase accuracy.

The CNN architectures used for segmentation purposes are usually of three kinds, fully convolutional networks (FCN) [18], coder-decoder networks [19] and "atrous-convolutional" networks [20]. The authors in [21] introduce the Mask R-CNN method, an extension of the Faster R-CNN method [22] to segment images instead of just detecting boundary frames. There are also some approaches whereby Deep Neural Networks are modified, for instance, semantic-aware segmentation [23] to use semantic segmentation and instance segmentation. Recent strategies propose general DWT and IDWT layers to various wavelets and design wavelet integrated CNNs (WaveCNets) for image classification using ImageNet and ImageNet-C, achieving an accuracy of 78.51% [24]. Moreover, a new architecture (VOLO) implements a novel outlook attention operation that dynamically conducts the local feature aggregation mechanism in a sliding window across the input image. This approach uses transformers and CNNs to complement their model and achieves 87.1% using ImageNet-1k [25]. Another natural color image approach is described in [26]. In this approach, the image is split into patches that feed the embedding module to expand the feature dimensions used for image classification [26]. This method achieves 83.9% in the Top-1 accuracy rate.

The main aims of this study are: (1) to develop an automatic strategy to obtain areas on a natural, outdoor image transforming components *a* and *b* of the CIELab image as a complex space to represent image tonality, saturation, and contrast; (2) to build a *chromatic map* that concentrates the distribution of the tone density of pixels from the image using algebra for complex numbers; (3) to provide a strategy that includes sky and road categories, which are usually considered in semantic-based methods but not in object-classifier methods.

3. Image Segmentation Approach

Figure 1 shows an overview of the proposed method to segment images and identify objects. First, input color images are transformed to the CIELab space. Next, chromatic planes *a* and *b* on the CIELab space are used as real and imaginary elements to form complex image *I*. The representative chromatic values of image *I* are calculated using the complex image to build a *chromatic map*. The number of thresholds per image depends on the colors of the image. The segmented areas represent those from images with similar chromatic values without a classification label. The next step consists of extracting several patches from the color image from each segmented area to build a database of images in six categories. A CNN uses the database to train, validate and test the identification of the object on the image. Note that color image patches are the input to the CNN model instead of the segmented areas. The implementation details of the method are shown in the following subsection.

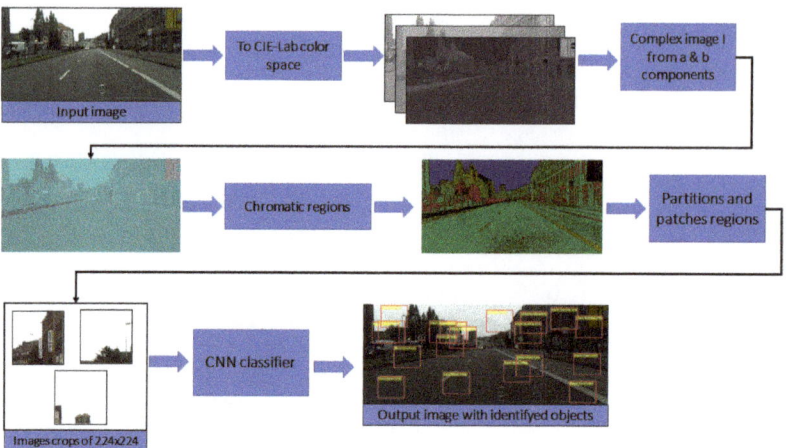

Figure 1. Proposed segmentation method to identify objects.

3.1. Image in the Complex Space

As said earlier, planes a and b on the CIELab space known as imA and imB, are combined to generate complex image I. Figure 2 shows chromatic planes imA and imB to form complex image I for a specific color image. Each pixel on image I is a complex number $z = a + ib$, processed using algebra for complex numbers. In this case, basic operations such as division, modulus, and argument have been used [27], but the division is the main operation used. Each pixel I is divided by a reference point $P_{(r,c)}$; the resulting image is known as the division image and is referred to as D. Image D shows values such as the threshold ones indicated by reference point $P_{(r,c)}$ within boundary ϵ. Thus, the same values as the unit or those close to it point to similar areas as those of the threshold value $P_{(r,c)}$. Equation (1) defines division image D, which is the resulting complex image I size $u \times v$ divided by reference point $P_{(r,c)}$. Values close to the unity in D represent similar pixels as those of $P_{(r,c)}$. Therefore, image D shows the relevance of point $P_{(r,c)}$ on the color image. However, as D is in the complex space, searching for values close to 1 cannot be direct. Using module D, the image of module $|D|$ can generate positive real values.

$$D_{[u \times v]} = \frac{I_{[u \times v]}}{P_{(r,c)}} \tag{1}$$

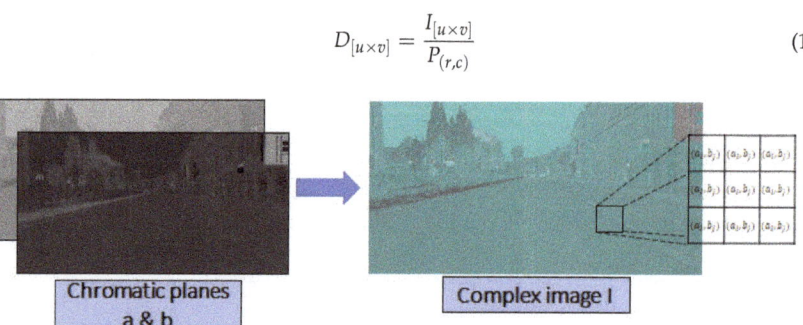

Figure 2. Generating complex image I using the chromatic images imA and imB.

In Equation (2), unitary values in $|D|$ (around an ϵ value) are chosen to obtain the thresholded image F and to highlight areas with a color such as $P_{(r,c)}$. Figure 3 represents the Division image D and the corresponding module $|D|$. $|D|$ shows in white color the areas whose values are similar to $P_{(r,c)}$.

$$F_{[u \times v]} = \begin{cases} 1 & \text{if} \quad 1 - \epsilon \leq \left|D_{[u \times v]}\right| \leq 1 + \epsilon \\ 0 & \text{otherwise} \end{cases} \qquad (2)$$

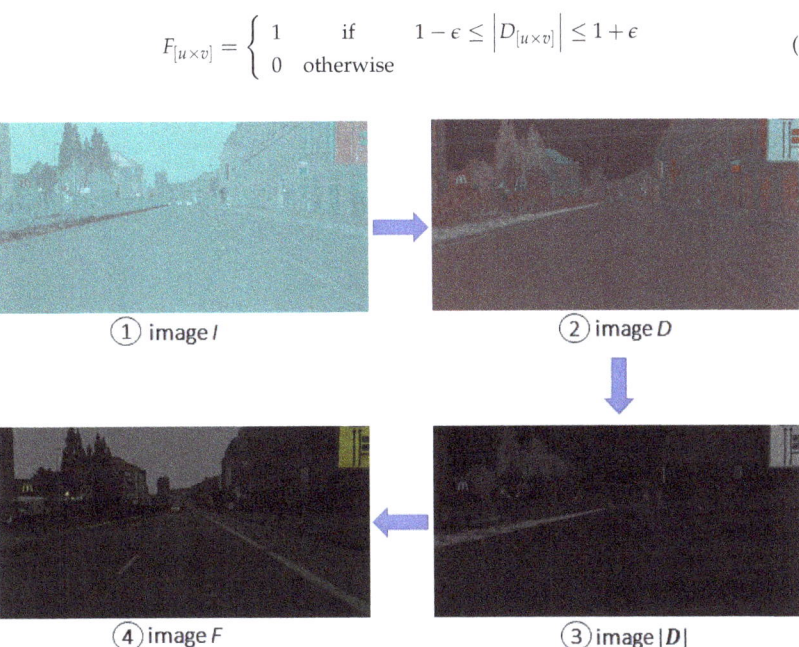

Figure 3. Complex division using a representative chromatic point.

To obtain a final segmented image F, first, representative $P_{(r,c)}$ thresholds must be found. Each threshold requires the division process. A *chromatic map* $\mathbb{AB}$ makes it possible to obtain several thresholds for the image automatically.

3.2. Chromatic Map

Chromatic map $\mathbb{AB}$ can be defined in the context of a bidimensional histogram. Chromatic components a and b on the CIELab space make up the horizontal X_a and vertical Y_b axis on the map $\mathbb{AB}$. This can be illustrated as shown in Figure 4a,c for a real and an artificial image, respectively.

Figure 4d shows five representative points on the *chromatic map* $\mathbb{AB}$, one for each area of the artificial image shown in Figure 4c. These points separate the chromatic components of the image. In the case of images such as those in Figure 4a, chromatic values are calculated by seeking the most representative values, that is to say, the highest density of points. Therefore, *chromatic map* $\mathbb{AB}$ is divided into k-areas, resulting from division m and n on the Y_b and X_a axes, respectively. Thus, the map is divided into $k = m \times n$ areas based on the combinations of m and n within the set of values $\{4, 8, 16, 32\}$. These values reduce the complexity of the power and make the methodology suitable for hardware implementation. For instance, blocks $k = 128$ when dividing the map by $m = 8$ and $n = 16$.

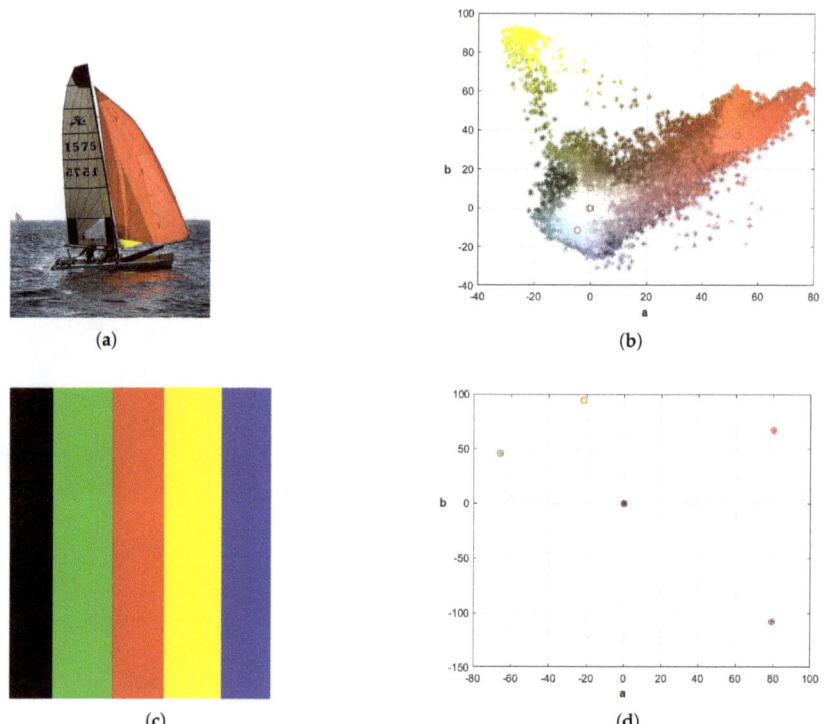

Figure 4. *Chromatic map* $A\mathbb{B}$ for two color images. (**a**) Color image 1. (**b**) *Chromatic map* $A\mathbb{B}$ of image 1. (**c**) Color image 2. (**d**) *Chromatic map* $A\mathbb{B}$ of image 2.

In Equation (3), n_{px} is a percentage based on the total number of pixels on the image, which is used to label blocks as representative. Each block has a chromatic range Δa and Δb defined by Equations (4) and (5). Figure 5 shows the division in k−blocks on a *chromatic map*, whose axes take the chromatic values from planes a and b on the CIELab space used to build complex image I.

$$n_{px} = (u \times v) \cdot \frac{1}{max(m,n)} \tag{3}$$

$$\Delta a = \frac{max(X_a) - min(X_a)}{m} \tag{4}$$

$$\Delta b = \frac{max(Y_b) - min(Y_b)}{n} \tag{5}$$

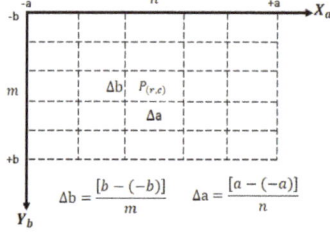

Figure 5. *Chromatic map* $A\mathbb{B}$ divided into $m \times n$ blocks on the chromatic range given by Δa and Δb.

3.3. Segmentation Approach

This study uses complex numbers to segment the complex image I. As shown in the previous subsection, the *chromatic map* $\mathbb{AB}$ represents the pixel density distribution along k-blocks on the complex image. In each block (i, j) on the *chromatic map* $\mathbb{AB}$, density M_μ is calculated by counting the number of pixels M_p and averaging the intensity of each pixel on I, as shown in Equation (6).

$$M_\mu(i,j) = \begin{cases} \dfrac{\sum_{p=1}^{M_p} I_{i,j}(p)}{M_p} & \text{if} \quad M_p > 0 \\ 0 & \text{in another case} \end{cases} \quad (6)$$

Equation (7) calculates indexes ind_{Mp}, showing blocks with a number of pixels greater than n_{px}. In Equation (8), a second criterion is applied to obtain the final vector index $ind_{M\mu}$, which stores the indexes for blocks on M_μ, which also agrees with ind_{Mp}. The number of thresholds n_{th} is used in the segmentation process and is obtained from the cardinality of vector $ind_{M\mu}$ (see Equation (9)).

$$ind_{Mp} = M_p \geq n_{px} \quad (7)$$

$$ind_{M\mu} = M_\mu(ind_{Mp}) \quad (8)$$

$$n_{th} = card(ind_{M\mu}) \quad (9)$$

Vector V_μ is calculated using M_μ and $ind_{M\mu}$, as shown in Equation (10). V_μ is the vector for average values used as thresholds in the segmentation process, which are still represented using complex numbers. The correlation matrix M_{corr} is obtained by dividing each threshold value by all the other values, as shown in Equation (11). Equation (12) represents the areas for average values bound by a circle $|z - z_0| = R$. In this case, areas are defined as being within a unitary circle centered on each threshold value on the matrix M_{corr}.

$$V_\mu = M_\mu(ind_{M\mu}) \quad (10)$$

$$M_{corr}(i,j) = \frac{V_\mu(i)}{V_\mu(j)} \quad i,j = \{1,\ldots,n_{th}\} \quad (11)$$

$$\begin{aligned} M_{r_\mu} &= |1 - |M_{corr}|| \\ &= \left| \begin{pmatrix} 1 - \left|\frac{V_\mu(1)}{V_\mu(1)}\right| & 1 - \left|\frac{V_\mu(1)}{V_\mu(2)}\right| & \cdots & 1 - \left|\frac{V_\mu(1)}{Z_\mu(k)}\right| \\ 1 - \left|\frac{V_\mu(2)}{V_\mu(1)}\right| & 1 - \left|\frac{V_\mu(2)}{V_\mu(2)}\right| & \cdots & 1 - \left|\frac{V_\mu(2)}{V_\mu(k)}\right| \\ \vdots & \vdots & \ddots & \vdots \\ 1 - \left|\frac{V_\mu(k)}{V_\mu(1)}\right| & 1 - \left|\frac{V_\mu(k)}{V_\mu(2)}\right| & \cdots & 1 - \left|\frac{V_\mu(k)}{V_\mu(k)}\right| \end{pmatrix} \right| \end{aligned} \quad (12)$$

The matrix values M_{r_μ} are used to analyze the middle values. Beyond diagonal values, minimization was conducted on matrix M_{r_μ}. Minimum values obtained are then divided by two to ensure there is no overlap between areas centered around average values; this is expressed by $V_{r\mu}$ in Equation (13). n_{th} values are stored in $V_{r\mu}$, which contains the thresholds to conduct color segmentation. Algorithm 1 explains the implementation of the multi-threshold segmentation process on a color image.

$$V_{r_\mu} = \frac{\min\left(M_{r_\mu}(i,j)\right)}{2} \quad \forall i \neq j \tag{13}$$

Algorithm 1 Segmentation method

Input: Input image **im**, number of blocks m, n in the *chromatic map*
Output: Segmented image **imSeg**
1: $n_{px} \leftarrow \frac{(size(\mathbf{im}))}{max(m,n)}$
2: $[imL, imA, imB] \leftarrow$ to_cielab(**im**)
3: $I \leftarrow imA + i\,imB$ %complex image
4: **for** $i = 1$ **to** m **do**
5:     **for** $j = 1$ **to** n **do**
6:         $M_p \leftarrow card(block_{i,j})$
7:         **if** $M_p > 0$ **then**
8:             $M_\mu \leftarrow mean(block_{i,j})$
9:         **end if**
10:     **end for**
11: **end for**
12: $ind_{M_p} \leftarrow (M_p \geq n_{px})$
13: $ind_{M_\mu} \leftarrow M_\mu(ind_{M_p})$;
14: $[V_\mu, n_{th}] \leftarrow [M_\mu\left(ind_{M_\mu}\right), card(ind_{M_\mu})]$
15: **for** $i, j = 1$ **to** n_{th} **do**
16:     $M_{corr}(i,j) \leftarrow \frac{V_\mu(i)}{V_\mu(j)}$
17: **end for**
18: $M_{r_\mu} \leftarrow \mathbf{abs}(1 - \mathbf{abs}(M_{corr}))$
19: $V_{r_\mu} \leftarrow \frac{\min\left(M_{r_\mu}(i,j)\right)}{2}$ for $i \neq j$
20: **for** $k = 1$ **to** n_{th} **do**
21:     **if** $V_{r_\mu}(k) \neq 0$ **then**
22:         $D \leftarrow \frac{I}{V_{r_\mu}(k)}$
23:     **else**
24:         $D \leftarrow \mathbf{abs}(I)$
25:     **end if**
26:     $F \leftarrow \mathbf{abs}(1 - \mathbf{abs}(D))$
27:     $S(:,:,k) \leftarrow k \cdot \left(F < V_{r_\mu}(k)\right)$
28:     $imgSeg(S(:,:,k) \equiv k) \leftarrow k$
29: **end for**

---

4. Results

4.1. Experimental Results

Segmentation and classification results are obtained using Cityscape [28] and CamVid [29] datasets. Similar datasets, i.e., Kitti, Waymo [30], and nuScenes [31], are used for 2D and 3D object detection for self-driving. The Cityscape dataset is divided into 20 folders obtained from several European cities; in this case, the Munster subfolder with 174 images of 1024 × 2048 pixels was chosen. In contrast, the CamVid dataset has 701 images of 720 × 960 pixels. Both datasets showed urban contexts but under different seasonal and lighting conditions.

The color image and the number of blocks on the *chromatic map* are the inputs for the segmentation algorithm. Each input image is processed using 16 different blocks, generating 16 segmented images. Each segmented image is colored by area according to the values of a 256−color map. Figures 6 and 7 show the segmentation results for an image taken from the CamVid dataset, using different block sizes on the *chromatic map*. The validation method used shows that the *chromatic map* for the CamVid dataset produces better results in a (8 × 16) combination, unlike the Cityscape database, which produced better results for (16 × 8) values, as shown in the following subsection.

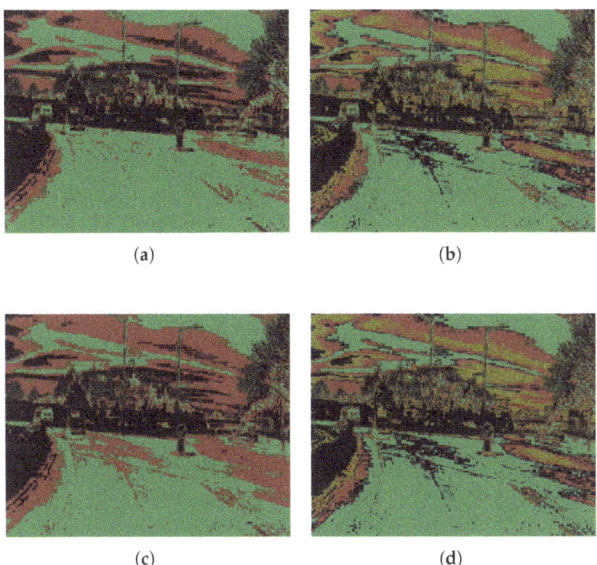

Figure 6. CamVid segmented images for different block sizes. (**a**) Block size 4 × 8. (**b**) Block size 4 × 16. (**c**) Block size 8 × 8. (**d**) Block size 8 × 16.

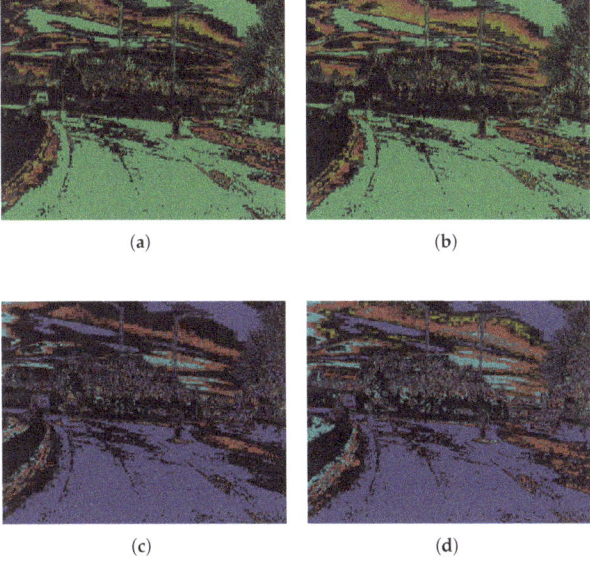

Figure 7. CamVid segmented images for different block sizes. (**a**) Block size 16 × 8. (**b**) Block size 16 × 16. (**c**) Block size 32 × 8. (**d**) Block size 32 × 16.

4.2. Segmentation Performance

The number of representative areas segmented is validated through a quantitative analysis of ground-truth images provided by Cityscape and CamVid datasets. Table 1 shows the number of representative areas n_{th} found by Algorithm 1 for various block sizes on the *chromatic map*. Bear in mind that as the number of blocks on the axes increases, the number of representative areas increases too. Segmented images can be empty in both cases, meaning no representative area was found.

Table 1. Number of representative areas generated by each dataset.

	Cityscape Image				CamVid Image			
Y_b-Axis Blocks	X_a-Axis Blocks				X_a-Axis Blocks			
	4	8	16	32	4	8	16	32
4	3	4	7	11	2	4	6	9
8	4	4	7	11	4	4	5	9
16	6	6	7	13	6	6	6	10
32	12	11	12	12	11	11	10	13

A second validation of segmented images consists of selecting the most common categories and their semantics to compare with the segmented areas. The most common categories from the urban context are enough for a general description of the scene. The selected categories are building, car, pedestrian, road, sky, and tree. Each segmented image is analyzed by area. The results for categories building, pedestrian, and road using the CamVid dataset are shown in Table 2, and those using the Cityscape dataset are shown in Table 3. Both tables show the segmented pixel-by-pixel relationship between the results and the ground-truth images, which makes it possible to consider some criteria to establish block sizes (m, n):

- The percentage of pixel relationship by a class must be at least 50% similar to ground-truth.
- Reject block sizes on m, n where the number of void images is higher than 10%.

Therefore, m, n block sizes where $m \neq n$ are used to comply with the last criterion, and the number of areas are enough to represent the categories.

Table 2. Analysis of segmented image categories for CamVid.

Class	Y_b-Axis Blocks	X_a-Axis Blocks							
		4		8		16		32	
		Pixel Ratio	Void Images	Pixel Ratio	Void Images	Pixel Ratio	Void Images	Pixel Ratio	Void Images
Building	4	0.2049	464	0.4277	227	0.622	28	0.6215	14
	8	0.4415	212	0.4982	162	0.6190	20	0.6050	14
	16	0.5459	15	0.5488	16	0.5397	14	0.5369	14
	32	0.5337	14	0.5358	14	0.5149	14	0.4843	14
Pedestrian	4	0.1984	486	0.3865	267	0.5604	75	0.5437	61
	8	0.4253	249	0.4705	202	0.5572	68	0.5377	61
	16	0.5714	62	0.5736	63	0.5497	61	0.5321	61
	32	0.5551	62	0.5482	61	0.5167	61	0.4812	61
Road	4	0.3461	457	0.6155	214	0.7846	14	0.7546	0
	8	0.6260	202	0.6697	150	0.7521	7	0.7155	0
	16	0.7147	1	0.6807	2	0.6488	0	0.6048	0
	32	0.6058	0	0.6056	0	0.5788	0	0.5591	0

Table 3. Analysis of segmented image categories for CityScape.

Class	Y_b-Axis Blocks	X_a-Axis Blocks							
		4		8		16		32	
		Pixel Ratio	Void Images	Pixel Ratio	Void Images	Pixel Ratio	Void Images	Pixel Ratio	Void Images
Building	4	0.1427	130	0.3275	73	0.4355	4	0.4390	4
	8	0.5105	45	0.4697	47	0.4903	4	0.4620	4
	16	0.6817	4	0.6406	4	0.5418	4	0.4652	4
	32	0.7239	4	0.6817	4	0.5853	4	0.4850	4
Pedestrian	4	0.0885	139	0.2179	94	0.2982	38	0.3068	38
	8	0.4251	71	0.3635	73	0.3843	38	0.4253	38
	16	0.5761	38	0.5494	38	0.4741	38	0.4704	38
	32	0.6114	38	0.5885	38	0.5278	38	0.4439	38
Road	4	0.2277	128	0.4983	71	0.7376	2	0.6822	2
	8	0.6493	43	0.6222	45	0.7327	2	0.6284	2
	16	0.8533	2	0.8310	2	0.7321	2	0.5709	2
	32	0.8346	2	0.8063	2	0.7089	2	0.6295	2

4.3. Cnn Architecture

Figure 8 shows network architecture based on VGG-16 [32] used in this study. This architecture has 16 layers to train about 138 million of parameters. The network consists of five blocks of convolutional layers. Each block consists of two or three convolutional layers followed by a groping layer. The number of filters increases by 2, from 64 to 512. The *Dropout* layers are added between one block and the next to avoid over-adjustment [33]. Each *Dropout* layer reduces the connection between one block and the next. The flat layer connects convolutional blocks with the fully connected layer. The fully connected layers have 4096 neurons, including "bias" and the activation function, a ReLU in this case. The last fully connected layer is the output from the network. The number of neurons on this layer is the same as the number of categories. The activation function associated with the last fully connected layer is the Softmax or normalized exponential function for a multi-class problem.

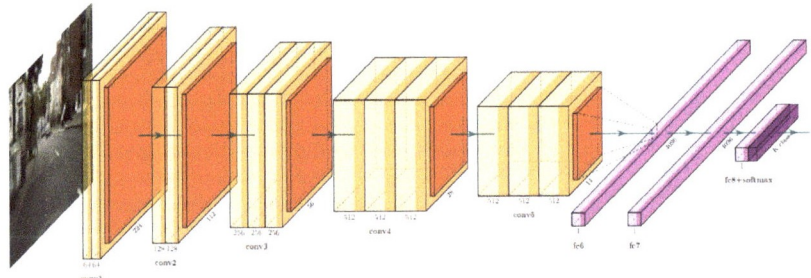

Figure 8. Modified convolutional neural network VGG-16.

Algorithm 1 calculates the segmentation of input images used to process the training and validation dataset. This process is illustrated in Figure 9. A binary mask per category, known as *class mask*, is generated for each image on the dataset. The *class mask* is then used to crop p patches randomly sized $[lu \times lv] = [60 \times 80]$ for each category. About 30,000 patches were generated for all the classes using the Cityscape database, with approximately 3000 images.

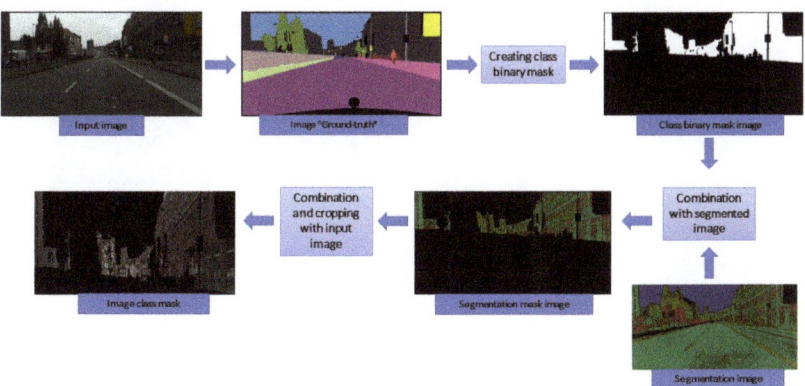

Figure 9. *Class mask* obtained from a segmented image to generate patches for the category *building*. A similar process is followed for all the categories to process the training dataset.

All patches were resized to [96 × 96], [128 × 128] and [224 × 224] for use on the CNN. Figure 10a,b show the accuracy and loss chart, respectively, for training of 100 epochs using an image size of (224 × 224).

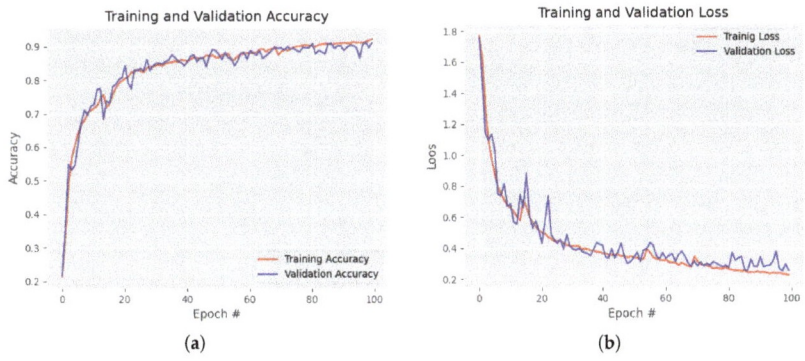

Figure 10. Results from training the CNN using 224 × 224 images. (**a**) Accuracy graph. (**b**) Loss graph.

The *SmallVGG* network model was also used to optimize its resources and keep performance results optimal. This network model reduces the original architecture presented in this study [32]. Even though the VGG-16 model for a resized 96 × 96 path shows greater accuracy than the results shown in Table 4, 224 × 224 images have had a more stable performance during the training and validation phase.

Table 4. CNN accuracy results for different image sizes.

Architecture	Image Size (in Pixels)		
	96 × 96	128 × 128	224 × 224
SmallVGG	0.73	0.82	0.87
VGG16-Modified	0.92	0.90	0.91
ResNet150	0.26	0.81	0.94

Additional experimental tests were performed using the ResNet CNN model, and the results are included in Table 4. In [34], the authors describe the residual blocks used for training deeper layers in the network. Using skip connections, it is possible to activate one layer and relocate its output to feed deeper layers in the network. ResNet CNN architectures are built by grouping a set of residual blocks. It is important to point out that the adder in the residual block can only be performed if both layers have the same dimension. For six categories and three different sizes of patches, we obtained an accuracy of 94% for 224 × 224 image patches.

The network model is validated using a training dataset from segmented images. Ground-truth information is not used with the validation dataset, and therefore, patches generated depend only on the areas obtained from the segmented image and the equivalent input color image. Unlike the training dataset, these patches are chosen randomly by area and do not have a predetermined category. This is represented visually in Figure 11. The patches are cropped from the color image using a fixed size $[lu \times lv] = [224 \times 224]$, which is the classifier input size. A different number of patches is cropped for each segmented area depending on the size and the number of regions obtained. The fixed size of bounding boxes allows the classification of undefined categories, such as sky and road, which most object-detect methodologies cannot detect and classify. This is one of our contributions to classifiers in urban environments.

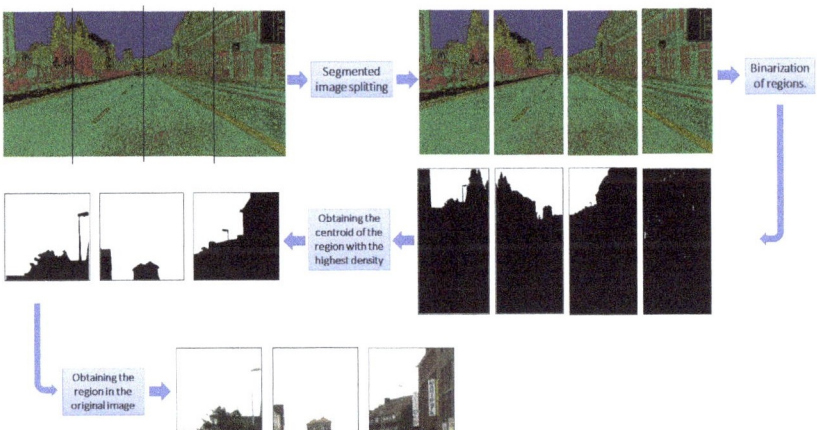

Figure 11. Image patches generated to validate the classifier.

Experimental tests to validate this approach use patches generated using the CamVid dataset. The classifier assigns a label and a reliability label to each patch. The output image shows different boundary frames with the brand and the reliability value corresponding to each image patch. Some results are shown in Figure 12. The CNN architecture was trained using the CityScape dataset, which has bigger images, and therefore, the process of generating patches was more straightforward.

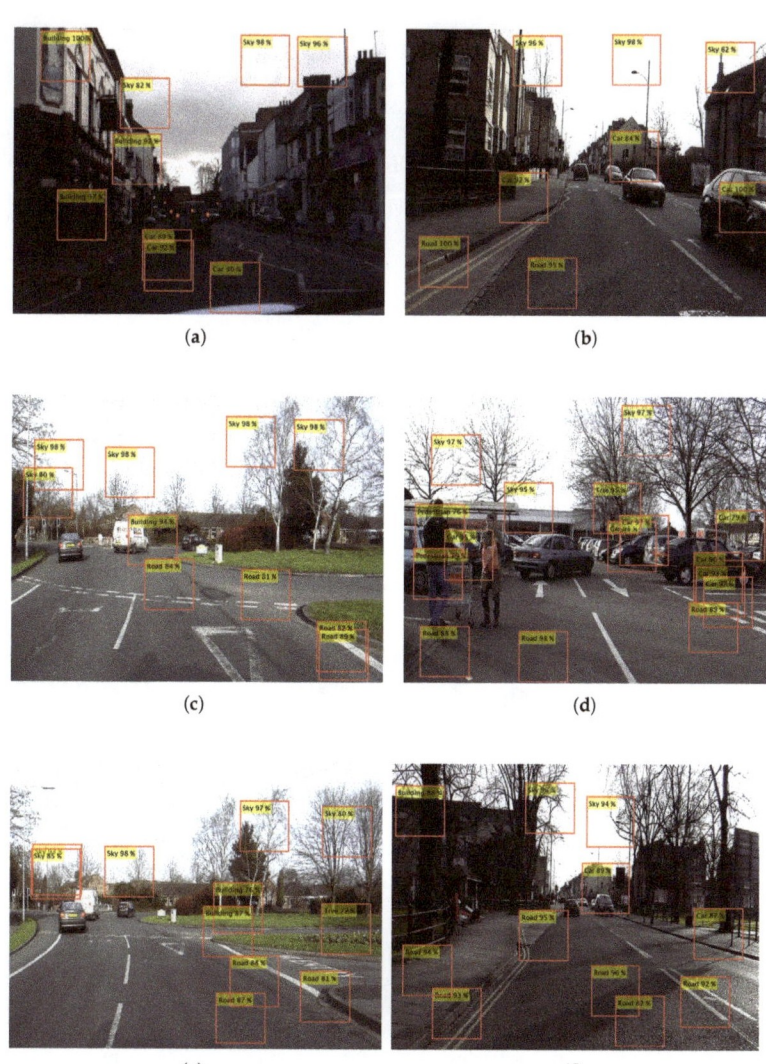

Figure 12. Classification of objects using CamVid. (**a**) Test image #1. (**b**) Test image #2. (**c**) Test image #3. (**d**) Test image #4. (**e**) Test image #5. (**f**) Test image #6.

Experimental tests were conducted using a PC with Intel Core i5 9th generation, 32 GB of RAM, and an NVIDIA GeForce GTX 1650 graphics card. Table 5 shows the time for the segmentation algorithm.

Table 5. Execution time for the segmentation algorithm.

Dataset	Execution Time (in Seconds)	
	Per Image	Total No. of Images Per Dataset
CamVid	0.83187	394.0215
Cityscape	3.07230	4662.554

Bear in mind that the time presented in Table 5 depends on the number of areas on the segmented image and their sizes. When a patch for an area cannot be obtained, this increases processing time significantly. To limit the execution time, a maximal number of tries to generate the patches has been established. In addition, the number of patches per image depends on the number of representative areas obtained by the segmentation algorithm for each image divided into four partitions (see Figure 11). Thus, the number of patches changes from image to image, and so does the total processing time. Processing times were analyzed, including those recorded in the classification phase. Table 6 shows the number of patches generated and the time. A general processing time per image can be produced by adding the segmentation and classification times. For instance, the time for the CamVid dataset is 4 seconds; for the CityScape image, it is twice as long.

Table 6. Classification execution time.

Dataset	Number of Patches Generated	Execution Time (in Seconds)	
		Per Image	Total No. of Images on Dataset
CamVid	11,660	2.9092	889.5841
Cityscape	2883	5.2499	245.0659

5. Discussion

Table 7 shows a comparison between our proposal and other methodologies in the literature. Using ResNet, we achieve 94% accuracy, whereas YOLOv3 [35] and YOLOv4 [36] architecture achieve over 95% accuracy for the ImageNet dataset. Different approaches compared were VOLO [25] and SPPNet [37], which also achieved good accuracy in the top rate. Even if our classification accuracy is lower, in this work, we provide an alternative method to classify image content without performing a whole refined segmentation of the image and without using semantic image information. Therefore, sky and road classes have been included as categories. In contrast, YOLO or other object classification architectures do not consider it because a bounding box cannot be defined for both categories.

Our accuracy results also depend on the bounding-boxes size extracted from the image; note in Table 4 that our accuracy increases as this selected size does. Our methodology is an alternative region-based approach that has been trained with one dataset and validated with another. Both datasets only have the urban context in common, but resolution and illumination are different, becoming more difficult for the validation task.

Table 7. Comparison with related works.

Work	Methodology	Dataset	Accuracy
YOLOv3 [35] YOLOv4 [36]	An integrated CNN's used for feature extraction and object classification in real-time.	ImageNet	93.8% 94.8% Top-5 accuracy rate
VOLO [25]	A new architecture that implements a novel outlook attention operation that dynamically conducts the local feature aggregation mechanism in a sliding window manner across the input image.	ImageNet	87.1% Top-1 accuracy rate
SPPNet [37]	Strategy of spatial pyramid pooling to construct a network structure called SPP-net for image classification.	Caltech101	93.42%
Our approach	Selection of region chromatic based on complex numbers with CNN to object detection.	Cityscapes and Camvid	94% for 6 classes

A final experimental test was performed by training boosted trees and several machine learning classifiers using the patches extracted from our method; the obtained results are illustrated in Table 8. For six categories and three different sizes, the highest accuracy was 79.80%, achieved by the Bagged Trees classifier. Considering that CNN architectures extract the main and representative features through the layers, machine learning-based classifiers require a more careful feature extractor strategy to improve their classification accuracy.

Table 8. Classification result using machine learning approaches.

Classification Learner	Patches Sizes (in Pixels)		
	96 × 96	128 × 128	224 × 224
Quadratic SVM	78.10%	78.30%	78.90%
Cubic SVM	78.50%	79.10%	80.10%
Fine Gaussian SVM	67.30%	70.20%	74.10%
Medium Gaussian SVM	77.80%	77.80%	77.40%
Bagged Trees	79.20%	79.40%	79.80%
Narrow Neural Network	72.90%	74.20%	76.20%
Medium Neural Network	74.60%	76.60%	78.70%
Bilayered Neural Network	72.90%	74.20%	77.00%
Trilayered Neural Network	73.70%	74.60%	76.10%

6. Conclusions

This study shows a new approach to image segmentation to identify objects in structured outdoor spaces. The approach extracts representative features based on combining algebra for complex numbers on planes a and b on the CIELab color space. The complex image makes it possible to develop and implement a multi-threshold segmentation algorithm. The methodology follows a typical automatic learning technique. The required features to input the classifier are chosen from specific areas on the segmented image. Despite light and overcrowding issues in outdoor environments, the number of classes and images used in the training and validation phases of the model are enough to execute the identification of objects.

The multi-threshold segmentation algorithm produces different execution time lapses depending on the image features to be processed. This is also dependent on the computing power available. In addition, the different sets of images used for CNN training and validation are created using random conditions. The execution time results for the multi-threshold segmentation algorithm depend on the size and features of the image. Thus far, this approach cannot be used in real-time conditions that require execution speeds of milliseconds. However, a dispersal strategy to select different areas on the scene could provide lighter techniques for classification purposes. Given the modular nature of the methodology, modifications to increase hardware performance are possible.

The VGG-16 network responds well to conditions such as those in this study, showing a uniform and flexible architecture; however, better accuracy results were achieved using the ResNet-150 network. Execution times for classification purposes are affected by the various phases in the methodology and the different features of the images from the databases. Hence, the decision to train the CNN architecture using the Cityscape dataset and validate it using the CamVid dataset shows similar outdoor and urban environments.

Finally, this study has focused on a less computationally intensive alternative to conducting color segmentation and object detection tasks, with the flexibility of adapting to different hardware architectures and scenarios.

Author Contributions: Conceptualization, D.-L.A.-O. and M.-A.I.-M.; methodology, D.-A.R.-M. and D.-L.A.-O.; software, J.-J.C.-C. and M.-A.I.-M.; validation, J.-J.C.-C. and D.-A.R.-M.; formal analysis, J.-J.C.-C., D.-L.A.-O. and M.-A.I.-M.; investigation, J.-J.C.-C. and D.-A.R.-M.; data curation, J.-J.C.-C. and D.-L.A.-O.; writing—original draft preparation, J.-J.C.-C.; writing—review and editing, D.-L.A.-O. and M.-A.I.-M.; visualization, D.-L.A.-O., D.-A.R.-M. and M.-A.I.-M.; project administration, D.-L.A.-O. All authors have read and agreed to the published version of the manuscript.

Funding: This study was conducted as part of the doctoral studies of Juan-Jose Cardenas-Cornejo, funded through scholarship number 2021-000018-02NACF-07210, awarded by CONACYT.

Data Availability Statement: Not applicable.

Acknowledgments: The authors are grateful to the University of Guanajuato. The authors would like special thanks to Carlos Montoro for his technical support in the English revision of the manuscript.

Conflicts of Interest: The authors declare no conflict of interest.

References

1. Yurtsever, E.; Lambert, J.; Carballo, A.; Takeda, K. A Survey of Autonomous Driving: Common Practices and Emerging Technologies. *IEEE Access* **2020**, *8*, 58443–58469. [CrossRef]
2. Narkhede, P.R.; Gokhale, A.V. Color image segmentation using edge detection and seeded region growing approach for CIELab and HSV color spaces. In Proceedings of the 2015 International Conference on Industrial Instrumentation and Control (ICIC), Pune, India, 28–30 May 2015. [CrossRef]
3. Xu, Y.; Shen, B.; Zhao, M.; Luo, S. An Adaptive Robot Soccer Image Segmentation Based on HSI Color Space and Histogram Analysis. *J. Comput.* **2019**, *30*, 290–303.
4. Smith, A.R. Color gamut transform pairs. In Proceedings of the SIGGRAPH '78, Atlanta, GA, USA, 23–25 August 1978.
5. Cheng, H.D.; Jiang, X.H.; Sun, Y.; Wang, J. Color Image Segmentation: Advances and Prospects. *Pattern Recognit.* **2001**, *34*, 2259–2281. [CrossRef]
6. Bansal, S.; Aggarwal, D. Color image segmentation using CIELab color space using ant colony optimization. *Int. J. Comput. Appl. Citeseer* **2011**, *29*, 28–34. [CrossRef]
7. Murray, R. Spiegel, Seymour Lipschutz, J.J.S.; Spellman, D. *Complex Variables: With an Introduction to Conformal Mapping and Its Applications*, 2nd ed.; Schaum's Outlines Series; McGraw-Hill: New York, NY, USA, 2009.
8. Fujiyoshi, H.; Hirakawa, T.; Yamashita, T. Deep learning-based image recognition for autonomous driving. *IATSS Res.* **2019**, *43*, 244–252. [CrossRef]
9. Xu, H.; Gao, Y.; Yu, F.; Darrell, T. End-To-End Learning of Driving Models From Large-Scale Video Datasets. In Proceedings of the IEEE Conference on Computer Vision and Pattern Recognition (CVPR), Honolulu, HI, USA, 21–26 July 2017.
10. Dal Mutto, C.; Zanuttigh, P.; Cortelazzo, G.M. Fusion of geometry and color information for scene segmentation. *IEEE J. Sel. Top. Signal Process.* **2012**, *6*, 505–521. [CrossRef]
11. Pagnutti, G.; Zanuttigh, P. Joint segmentation of color and depth data based on splitting and merging driven by surface fitting. *Image Vis. Comput.* **2018**, *70*, 21–31. [CrossRef]
12. Karimpouli, S.; Tahmasebi, P. Segmentation of digital rock images using deep convolutional autoencoder networks. *Comput. Geosci.* **2019**, *126*, 142–150. [CrossRef]
13. Rochan, M.; Rahman, S.; Bruce, N.D.; Wang, Y. Weakly supervised object localization and segmentation in videos. *Image Vis. Comput.* **2016**, *56*, 1–12. [CrossRef]
14. Zhou, D.; Frémont, V.; Quost, B.; Dai, Y.; Li, H. Moving object detection and segmentation in urban environments from a moving platform. *Image Vis. Comput.* **2017**, *68*, 76–87. [CrossRef]
15. Xie, J.; Kiefel, M.; Sun, M.T.; Geiger, A. Semantic Instance Annotation of Street Scenes by 3D to 2D Label Transfer. In Proceedings of the Conference on Computer Vision and Pattern Recognition (CVPR), Las Vegas, NV, USA, 27–30 June 2016.
16. Kaushik, R.; Kumar, S. Image Segmentation Using Convolutional Neural Network. *Int. J. Sci. Technol. Res.* **2019**, *8*, 667–675.
17. Ye, X.Y.; Hong, D.S.; Chen, H.H.; Hsiao, P.Y.; Fu, L.C. A two-stage real-time YOLOv2-based road marking detector with lightweight spatial transformation-invariant classification. *Image Vis. Comput.* **2020**, *102*, 103978. [CrossRef]
18. Long, J.; Shelhamer, E.; Darrell, T. Fully convolutional networks for semantic segmentation. In Proceedings of the IEEE Conference on Computer Vision and Pattern Recognition, Boston, MA, USA, 7–12 June 2015; pp. 3431–3440.
19. Noh, H.; Hong, S.; Han, B. Learning Deconvolution Network for Semantic Segmentation. In Proceedings of the IEEE International Conference on Computer Vision (ICCV), Santiago, Chile, 7–13 December 2015.
20. Chen, L.C.; Papandreou, G.; Kokkinos, I.; Murphy, K.; Yuille, A.L. Deeplab: Semantic image segmentation with deep convolutional nets, atrous convolution, and fully connected crfs. *IEEE Trans. Pattern Anal. Mach. Intell.* **2017**, *40*, 834–848. [CrossRef]
21. He, K.; Gkioxari, G.; Dollár, P.; Girshick, R. Mask r-cnn. In Proceedings of the IEEE International Conference on Computer Vision, Venice, Italy, 22–29 October 2017; pp. 2961–2969.
22. Ren, S.; He, K.; Girshick, R.; Sun, J. Faster R-CNN: Towards Real-Time Object Detection with Region Proposal Networks. *IEEE Trans. Pattern Anal. Mach. Intell.* **2017**, *39*, 1137–1149. [CrossRef] [PubMed]
23. Rehman, S.; Ajmal, H.; Farooq, U.; Ain, Q.U.; Riaz, F.; Hassan, A. Convolutional neural network based image segmentation: A review. In Proceedings of the Pattern Recognition and Tracking XXIX, Orlando, FL, USA, 15–19 April 2018; [CrossRef]
24. Li, Q.; Shen, L.; Guo, S.; Lai, Z. Wavelet integrated CNNs for noise-robust image classification. In Proceedings of the IEEE/CVF Conference on Computer Vision and Pattern Recognition, Seattle, WA, USA, 13–19 June 2020; pp. 7245–7254.
25. Yuan, L.; Hou, Q.; Jiang, Z.; Feng, J.; Yan, S. Volo: Vision outlooker for visual recognition. *IEEE Trans. Pattern Anal. Mach. Intell.* **2022**, 1–13. [CrossRef] [PubMed]

26. Wu, Y.H.; Liu, Y.; Zhan, X.; Cheng, M.M. P2T: Pyramid pooling transformer for scene understanding. *IEEE Trans. Pattern Anal. Mach. Intell.* **2022**, 1–12. [CrossRef] [PubMed]
27. Churchill, R.V.; Brown, J.W. *Variable Compleja y Aplicaciones*, 5th ed.; McGraw-Hill-Interamericana: Madrid, Spain, 1996.
28. Cordts, M.; Omran, M.; Ramos, S.; Rehfeld, T.; Enzweiler, M.; Benenson, R.; Franke, U.; Roth, S.; Schiele, B. The Cityscapes Dataset for Semantic Urban Scene Understanding. In Proceedings of the IEEE Conference on Computer Vision and Pattern Recognition (CVPR), Las Vegas, NV, USA, 27–30 June 2016; pp. 3213–3223.
29. Brostow, G.J.; Fauqueur, J.; Cipolla, R. Semantic object classes in video: A high-definition ground truth database. *Pattern Recognit. Lett.* **2009**, *30*, 88–97. [CrossRef]
30. Sun, P.; Kretzschmar, H.; Dotiwalla, X.; Chouard, A.; Patnaik, V.; Tsui, P.; Guo, J.; Zhou, Y.; Chai, Y.; Caine, B.; et al. Scalability in Perception for Autonomous Driving: Waymo Open Dataset. In Proceedings of the IEEE/CVF Conference on Computer Vision and Pattern Recognition (CVPR), Seattle, WA, USA, 13–19 June 2020; pp. 2446–2454
31. Caesar, H.; Bankiti, V.; Lang, A.H.; Vora, S.; Liong, V.E.; Xu, Q.; Krishnan, A.; Pan, Y.; Baldan, G.; Beijbom, O. nuScenes: A multimodal dataset for autonomous driving. In Proceedings of the CVPR, Seattle, WA, USA, 13–19 June 2020; pp. 11621–11631.
32. Simonyan, K.; Zisserman, A. Very deep convolutional networks for large-scale image recognition. In Proceedings of the 3rd International Conference on Learning Representations, ICLR 2015—Conference Track Proceedings, San Diego, CA, USA, 7–9 May 2015; pp. 1–14.
33. Srivastava, N.; Hinton, G.; Krizhevsky, A.; Sutskever, I.; Salakhutdinov, R. Dropout: A simple way to prevent neural networks from overfitting. *J. Mach. Learn. Res. JMLR. Org.* **2014**, *15*, 1929–1958.
34. He, K.; Zhang, X.; Ren, S.; Sun, J. Deep residual learning for image recognition. In Proceedings of the IEEE Conference on Computer Vision and Pattern Recognition, Las Vegas, NV, USA, 27–30 June 2016; pp. 770–778.
35. Redmon, J.; Farhadi, A. Yolov3: An incremental improvement. *arXiv* **2018**, arXiv:1804.02767.
36. Bochkovskiy, A.; Wang, C.Y.; Liao, H.Y.M. Yolov4: Optimal speed and accuracy of object detection. *arXiv* **2020**, arXiv:2004.10934.
37. He, K.; Zhang, X.; Ren, S.; Sun, J. Spatial pyramid pooling in deep convolutional networks for visual recognition. *IEEE Trans. Pattern Anal. Mach. Intell.* **2015**, *37*, 1904–1916. [CrossRef]

Article

Relaxation Subgradient Algorithms with Machine Learning Procedures †

Vladimir Krutikov [1], Svetlana Gutova [1], Elena Tovbis [2], Lev Kazakovtsev [2] and Eugene Semenkin [2,*]

[1] Department of Applied Mathematics, Kemerovo State University, Krasnaya Street 6, Kemerovo 650043, Russia
[2] Institute of Informatics and Telecommunications, Reshetnev Siberian State University of Science and Technology, Prosp. Krasnoyarskiy Rabochiy 31, Krasnoyarsk 660031, Russia
* Correspondence: eugenesemenkin@yandex.ru
† This paper is an extended version of our paper published in Mathematical Optimization Theory and Operations Research MOTOR 2021 Conference, Irkutsk, Russia, 5–10 July 2021; pp. 477–492.

Abstract: In the modern digital economy, optimal decision support systems, as well as machine learning systems, are becoming an integral part of production processes. Artificial neural network training as well as other engineering problems generate such problems of high dimension that are difficult to solve with traditional gradient or conjugate gradient methods. Relaxation subgradient minimization methods (RSMMs) construct a descent direction that forms an obtuse angle with all subgradients of the current minimum neighborhood, which reduces to the problem of solving systems of inequalities. Having formalized the model and taking into account the specific features of subgradient sets, we reduced the problem of solving a system of inequalities to an approximation problem and obtained an efficient rapidly converging iterative learning algorithm for finding the direction of descent, conceptually similar to the iterative least squares method. The new algorithm is theoretically substantiated, and an estimate of its convergence rate is obtained depending on the parameters of the subgradient set. On this basis, we have developed and substantiated a new RSMM, which has the properties of the conjugate gradient method on quadratic functions. We have developed a practically realizable version of the minimization algorithm that uses a rough one-dimensional search. A computational experiment on complex functions in a space of high dimension confirms the effectiveness of the proposed algorithm. In the problems of training neural network models, where it is required to remove insignificant variables or neurons using methods such as the Tibshirani LASSO, our new algorithm outperforms known methods.

Keywords: relaxation subgradient methods; space dilation; nonsmooth minimization methods; machine learning algorithm

MSC: 49M20; 65K10; 68T20

1. Introduction

In this study, which is an extension of previous work [1], a problem of minimizing a convex, not necessarily differentiable function $f(x)$, $x \in \mathbb{R}^n$ (where $\mathbb{R}^n$ is a finite-dimensional Euclidean space) is discovered. Such a problem is quite common in the field of machine learning (ML), where optimization methods, in particular, gradient descent, are widely used to minimize the loss function during training stage. In the era of the digital economy, such functions arise in many engineering applications. First of all, training and regularizing the artificial neural networks of a simple structure (e.g., radial or sigmoidal) may lead to the application of a loss function in a high-dimensional space, which are often non-smooth. When working with more complex networks, such functions can be non-convex.

While a number of efficient machine learning tools exist to learn smooth functions with high accuracy from a finite data sample, the accuracy of these approaches becomes less satisfactory for nonsmooth objective functions [2]. In a machine learning context, it is quite common to have an objective function with a penalty term that is non-smooth such as the Lasso [3] or Elastic Net [4] linear regression models. Common loss functions, such as the hinge loss [5] for binary classification, or more advanced loss functions, such as the one arising in classification with a reject option, are also nonsmooth [6], as well as some widely used activation functions (ReLU) [7] in the field of deep learning. Modern convolutional networks, incorporating rectifiers and max-pooling, are neither smooth nor convex. However, the absence of differentiability creates serious theoretical difficulties on different levels (optimality conditions, definition and computation of search directions, etc.) [8].

Modern literature offers two main approaches to building nonsmooth optimization methods. The first is based on creating smooth approximations for nonsmooth functions [9–13]. On this basis, various methods intended for solving convex optimization problems, problems of composite and stochastic composite optimization [9–11,14] were theoretically substantiated.

The second approach is based on subgradient methods that have their origins in the works of N. Z. Shor [15] and B.T. Polyak [16], the results of which can be found in [17]. Initially, relaxation subgradient minimization methods (RSMMs) were considered in [18–20]. They were later developed into a number of effective approaches such as the subgradient method with space dilation in the subgradient direction [21,22] that involve relaxation by distance to the extremum [17,23,24]. The idea of space dilation is to change the metric of the space at each iteration with a linear transformation and to use the direction opposite to that of the subgradient in the space with the transformed metric.

Embedding the ideas of machine learning theory [25] into such optimization methods made it possible to identify the principles of organizing RSMM with space dilation [26–29]. The problem of finding the descent direction in the RSMM can be reduced to the problem of solving a system of inequalities on subgradient sets, mathematically formulated as a problem of minimizing a quality functional. This means that a new learning algorithm is embedded into the basis of some new RSMM algorithm. Thus, the convergence rate of the minimization method is determined by the properties of the learning algorithm.

Rigorous investigation of the approximation capabilities of various neural networks has received much research interest [30–36] and is widely applied to problems of system identification, signal processing, control, pattern recognition and many others [37]. Due to universal approximation theorem [30], a feedforward network with a single hidden layer and a sigmoidal activation function can arbitrarily well approximate any continuous function on a compact set [38]. The studies of learning theory on unbounded sets can be found in [39–41].

The stability of the neural network solutions can be improved by introducing a regularizing term in the minimized functional [42], which stabilizes the solution using some auxiliary non-negative function carrying information on the solution obtained earlier (a priori information). The most common form of a priori information is the assumption of the function smoothness in the sense that the same input signal corresponds to the same output. Commonly used regularization types include:

1. Quadratic Tikhonov regularization (or ridge regression, R_2). In the case of approximation by a linear model, the Tikhonov regularizer [42] is used:

$$R_2(U) = \sum_{i=1}^{k} u_i^2, \qquad (1)$$

where parameters of the linear part of the model are included, and k is the number of vector U components. The regularizer R_2 is mainly used to suppress large components of the vector U to prevent overfitting the model.

2. Modular linear regularization (Tibshirani Lasso, R_1). The regularizer proposed in [3] is mainly used to suppress large and small components of the vector U:

$$R_1(U) = \sum_{i=1}^{k} |u_i|. \qquad (2)$$

3. Non-smooth regularization (R_γ) [3,43]:

$$R_\gamma(U) = \sum_{i=1}^{k} (|u_i| + \varepsilon)^\gamma, \varepsilon = 10^{-6}, \gamma = 0.7. \qquad (3)$$

The use of R_γ led to the suppression of small ("weak") components of the vector U. This property of R_γ enables us to reduce to zero weak components that are not essential for the description of data.

The aim of our work is to outline an approach to accelerating the convergence of learning algorithms in RSMM with space dilation and to give an example of the implementation of such an algorithm, confirming the effectiveness of theoretical constructions.

In the RSMM, successive approximations [18–20,26,28,44] are:

$$x_{k+1} = x_k - \gamma_k s_{k+1}, \ \gamma_k = \arg\min_{\gamma} f(x_k - \gamma s_{k+1}), \qquad (4)$$

where k is the iteration number, γ_k is the stepsize, x_0 is a given starting point, and the descent direction s_{k+1} is a solution of a system of inequalities on $s \in \mathbb{R}^n$ [20]:

$$(s, g) > 0, \ \forall g \in G. \qquad (5)$$

Hereinafter, (s, g) is a dot product of vectors, and G is a set of subgradients calculated on the descent trajectory of the algorithm at a point x_k.

Denote as (s, g) a set of solutions to inequality (5), as $\partial f(x)$ is a subgradient set at point x. If the function is convex and $G = \partial_\varepsilon f(x_k)$ is an ε-subgradient set at point x_k, and s_{k+1} is an arbitrary solution of system (5), then the function will be reduced by at least ε after iteration (4) [20].

Since there is no explicit specification of ε-subgradient sets, the subgradients $g_k \in \partial f(x_k)$ are used as elements of the set G, calculated on the descent trajectory of the minimization algorithm. These vectors must satisfy the condition:

$$(s_k, g_k) \leq 0. \qquad (6)$$

Inequality (6) means that for the vectors used, condition (5) is not satisfied. The choice of learning vectors is made according to this principle in the perceptron method [25,45], for instance.

A sequence of vectors $g_k \in \partial f(x_k)$, $k = 0, 1, \ldots$ is not predetermined, but determined during minimization (4) with a built-in method for finding the vector s_{k+1} at each iteration of minimization by a ML algorithm.

Let vector s_{k+1} be a solution of the system of inequalities (5) for the subgradient set of some neighborhood of the current minimum x_k. Then, as a result of iteration (4), we go beyond this neighborhood with a simultaneous function decrease, since vector s_{k+1} forms an acute angle with each of the subgradients of the set.

In this work, we present a formalized model of subgradient sets, which enables us, taking into account their specificity, to formulate stronger learning relations and quality functionals, which leads to acceleration in the convergence rate of learning algorithms designed to form the direction of descent in the RSMM.

As a result of theoretical analysis, an effective learning algorithm has been developed. For the proposed ML algorithm, the convergence in a finite number of iterations is proved when solving problem (5) on separable sets. Based on the learning algorithm, we proposed a method for minimizing nonsmooth functions. Its convergence on convex functions was substantiated. It is shown that on quadratic functions, the minimization method generates a sequence of minimum approximations identical to the sequence of the conjugate gradient method. We also proposed a minimization algorithm with a specific one-dimensional search method. A computational experiment confirmed its effectiveness for problems of neural network approximations, where the technology of uninformative model component suppression with regularizers similar to the Tibshirani LASSO was used [46]. The result of our work is an optimization algorithm applicable for solving neuron network regularization and other machine learning problems which, in turn, contains an embedded machine learning algorithm for finding the most promising descent direction. In the problems used for comparison, the objective function forms an elongated multidimensional ravine. As with other subgradient algorithms, our new algorithm proved to be efficient for such problems. Moreover, the new algorithm outperforms known relaxation subgradient and quasi-Newtonian algorithms.

The rest of this article is organized as follows. In Section 2, we consider a problem of acceleration of the learning algorithms convergence using relaxation subgradient methods. In Section 3, we make assumptions regarding the parameters of subgradient sets that affect the convergence rate of the proposed learning algorithm. In Section 4, we formulate and justify a machine learning algorithm for finding the descent direction in the subgadient method. In Section 5, we give a description of the minimization method. In Section 6, we establish the identity of the sequences generated by the conjugate gradient method and the relaxation subgradient method with space dilation on the minimization of quadratic functions. In Sections 7 and 8, we consider a one-dimensional minimization algorithm and its implementation, respectively. In Sections 9 and 10, we present experimental results for the considered algorithms. In Section 9, we show a computational experiment on complex large-sized function minimization. In Section 10, we consider experiments with training neural network models, where it is required to remove insignificant neurons. Section 11 contains a summary of the work.

2. Acceleration of the Learning Algorithm's Convergence in Relaxation Subgradient Methods

To use more efficient learning algorithms, a relation stronger than (5) can be written for the descent direction. We make an additional assumption about the properties of the set G.

Assumption 1. *Let a convex set $G \subset \mathbb{R}^n$ belong to a hyperplane; its minimal length vector η is also the minimal length vector of this hyperplane. Then, a solution of the system $(s, g) = 1 \; \forall g \in G$ is also a solution of (5) [26]. It can be found as a solution to a system of equations using a sequence of vectors from G [26]:*

$$(s, g_i) = q_i = 1, \; g_i \in G, \; i = 0, 1, \ldots k. \tag{7}$$

It is easy to see that the solution to system (7) in s is the vector $s^* = \eta / ||\eta||^2$. Figure 1 shows the subgradient set in the form of a segment lying on a straight line. Equalities (7) can be solved by a least squares method. For example, using the quadratic quality functional

$$Q_k(s) = \frac{1}{2}(1 - (s, g_k))^2,$$

it is possible to implement a gradient machine learning algorithm,

$$s_{k+1} = s_k - \beta_k \nabla Q_k(s_k),$$

where β_k is a gradient method step. Hence, when choosing $\beta_k = 1/(g_k, g_k)$, we obtain the well-known Kaczmarz algorithm [47],

$$s_{k+1} = s_k + \frac{1 - (s_k, g_k)}{(g_k, g_k)} g_k. \tag{8}$$

The found direction s_k satisfies the learning equality $(s_{k+1}, g_k) = 1$. To ensure the possibility of decreasing the function as a result of iteration (4), the new descent direction in the minimization method must be consistent with the current subgradient, i.e., satisfy inequality $(s_{k+1}, g_k) > 0$. Process (8) corresponds to this condition.

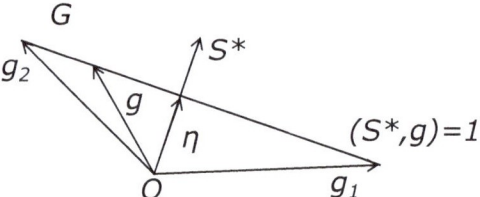

Figure 1. Set G belongs to a hyperplane.

To propose a faster algorithm, consider the interpretation of process (8). Let Assumption 1 be fulfilled. The step of process (8) is equivalent to the step of one-dimensional minimization of the function

$$E(s) = \frac{(s - s^*, s - s^*)}{2}$$

from point s_k in the direction g_k. Let the current approximation s_k be obtained using a vector g_{k-1} and satisfy the condition $(s_k, g_{k-1}) = 1$. Figure 2 shows the projections of the current approximation s_k and the required vector s^* on the plane of vectors g_{k-1}, g_k. Straight lines W_1 and Z_1 are hyperplane projections for vectors s, given by the equalities $(s, g_{k-1}) = 1$ and $(s, g_k) = 1$. Vector s^1_{k+1} is a projection of the approximation obtained from the iteration (8).

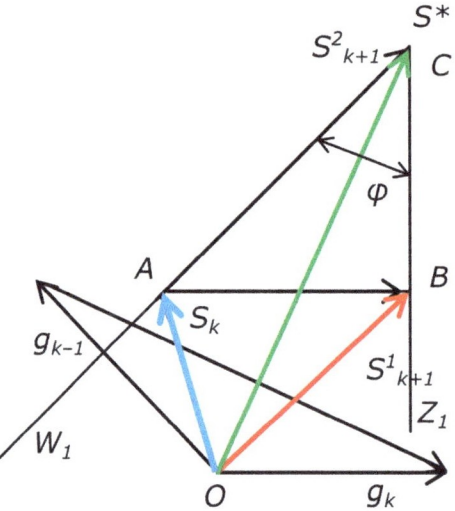

Figure 2. Projections of approximations s_{k+1} in the plane of vectors g_k, g_{k-1}.

If $(g_k, g_{k-1}) \leq 0$, then the angle between subgradients is obtuse, and the angle φ is acute (Figure 2). In this case, it is possible to completely extinguish the projection of the residual between s_k and s^* in the plane of vectors g_{k-1}, g_k, passing from point A to point C along vector AC, perpendicular to the vector g_{k-1}, i.e., along vector p_k:

$$p_k = g_k - g_{k-1}\frac{(g_k, g_{k-1})}{(g_{k-1}, g_{k-1})}. \tag{9}$$

In this case, the iteration has the form

$$s_{k+1} = s_k + p_k \frac{1 - (s_k, g_k)}{(g_k, p_k)}. \tag{10}$$

In Figure 2, this vector is denoted as s_{k+1}^2. The vector s_{k+1}, obtained by formula (10), satisfies the equalities $(s_{k+1}, g_{k-1}) = 1$, $(s_{k+1}, g_k) = 1$ and coincides with the projection s^* of the optimum of the function $E(s)$. At small angles ϕ between the straight lines W_1 and Z_1, the acceleration of convergence for process (10) becomes essential. In this work, process (10) will be used to accelerate the convergence in the metric of the iterative least squares method.

Using learning information (7), one of the possible solutions to the system of inequalities (5) can be found in the form $s_{k+1} = \arg\min_s F_k(s)$, where

$$F_k(s) = \sum_{i=0}^{k} w_i Q_i(s) + \frac{1}{2}\sum_{i=1}^{n} s_i^2, \quad Q_i(s) = \frac{1}{2}(q_i - (s, g_i))^2.$$

Such a solution can be obtained by the iterative least squares method (ILS). With weight factors $w_i = 1$, after the arrival of new data q_k, g_k, the transition from the previously found solution s_k to a new solution s_{k+1} in ILS is made as follows:

$$s_{k+1} = s_k + \frac{H_k g_k(q_k - (s_k, g_k))}{1 + (H_k g_k, g_k)}, \quad s_0 = 0, \tag{11}$$

$$H_{k+1} = H_k - \frac{H_k g_k g_k^T H_k^T}{1 + (g_k, H_k g_k)}, \quad H_0 = I. \tag{12}$$

Note that, in contrast to the usual ILS, there is a regularizing component $\sum_{i=1}^{n} s_i^2/2$ in $F_k(s)$, which allows us to use transformations (11) and (12) from the initial iteration, setting $s_0 = 0$ and $H_0 = I$.

In [26], based on ILS (11) and (12), an iterative process is proposed for solving the system of inequalities (5) using learning information (7):

$$s_{k+1} = s_k + \frac{H_k g_k[1 - (s_k, g_k)]}{(g_k, H_k g_k)}, \quad s_0 = 0, \tag{13}$$

$$H_{k+1} = H_k - (1 - \frac{1}{\alpha_k^2})\frac{H_k g_k g_k^T H_k^T}{(g_k, H_k g_k)}, \quad H_0 = I. \tag{14}$$

Here, $\alpha_k > 1$ is a space dilation parameter.

Consider the rationale for the method of obtaining formulas (13) and (14). Using processes (11) and (12) for scaled data, we obtain

$$\hat{g}_k = g_k[q(g_k, H_k g_k)]^{-0.5}, \quad \hat{q}_k = q_k[q(g_k, H_k g_k)]^{-0.5},$$

where scaling factor $q > 0$. The latter is equivalent to introducing the weight factors $w_k = 1/[q(g_k, H_k g_k)]$ in $F(s)$. Then, after returning to the original data g_k, y_k, we obtain the expressions:

$$s_{k+1} = s_k + \frac{H_k g_k [q_k - (s_k, g_k)]}{(1+q)(g_k, H_k g_k)}, \quad s_0 = 0, \tag{15}$$

$$H_{k+1} = H_k - \frac{H_k g_k g_k^T H_k^T}{(1+q)(g_k, H_k g_k)}, \quad H_0 = I. \tag{16}$$

The transformation of matrices (16) is practically equivalent to (14) after the appropriate choice of the parameter q. For transformation (15), the condition $(s_{k+1}, g_k) > 0$ providing the condition for the possibility of decreasing the function in the course of iteration (4) along the direction s_{k+1} may not be satisfied. Therefore, the transformation (13) is used with $q_k = 1$, which ensures equality $(s_{k+1}, g_k) = 1 > 0$. Transformation (13) can be interpreted as the Kaczmarz algorithm in the corresponding metric. As a result, we obtain processes (13) and (14). Methods [18–20] of the class under consideration possess the properties of the conjugate gradient method. The noted properties expand the area of effective application of such methods.

The higher the convergence rate of processes (13) and (14), the greater the value of the permissible value α_k in (14) [26], which depends on the set G's characteristics. In algorithms (13) and (14), we distinguish 2 stages: the correction stage (13). reducing the residual between the optimal solution s^* and the current approximation s_k, and the space dilation stage (14), resulting in the increase in the residual in the transformed space without exceeding its initial value, which limits the magnitude of the space dilation parameter. To create more efficient algorithms for solving systems of inequalities, we have to choose the direction of correction in such a way that the reduction of the residual is higher than that of process (13). The direction of space dilation should be chosen so that it becomes possible to increase the space dilation parameter value due to this choice.

This paper presents one of the special cases of the implementation of the correction stage and space dilation stage. It was proposed to use linear combinations of vectors g_{k-1}, g_k in transformation (13) instead of a vector g_k when it is appropriate:

$$p_k = g_k - g_{k-1} \frac{(g_k, H_k g_{k-1})}{(g_{k-1}, H_k g_{k-1})}, \tag{17}$$

$$s_{k+1} = s_k + H_k p_k \frac{1 - (s_k, g_k)}{(g_k, H_k p_k)}. \tag{18}$$

Transformations (17) and (18) are similar to the previously discussed transformations (9) and (10) carried out in the transformed space.

In the matrix transformation, we use equation (14) instead of vector g_k. We also use vector
$y_k = g_k - g_{k-1}$ such that

$$H_{k+1} = H_k - (1 - \frac{1}{\alpha_k^2}) \frac{H_k y_k y_k^T H_k^T}{(y_k, H_k y_k)}. \tag{19}$$

As shown below, the discrepancy between the optimal solution s^* and the current approximation s_{k+1} along the vector y_k is small, which makes it possible to use large parameters of space dilation α_k in (19). Iterations (18) and (19) are conducted under the condition:

$$(g_k, H_k g_{k-1}) \leq 0. \tag{20}$$

In the next section, assumptions will be made regarding the parameters of subgradient sets that affect the convergence rate of the proposed learning algorithm and determine the permissible parameters of space dilation. This allows us to formulate and justify a machine learning algorithm for finding the descent direction in the subgradient method.

Note that the described parameterization of the sets does not impose any restrictions on the subgradient sets but is used only for the purpose of developing constraints on the learning algorithm parameters.

3. Formalization of the Separable Sets Model

In this section, we will use the following notation (as earlier, vector η is the shortest vector from G):

(1) $\rho = ||\eta||$ is the length of the minimal vector of the set;
(2) $R = \max_{g \in G} ||g||$ is the length of the maximal vector of the set;
(3) $\mu = \eta/\rho$ is the normalized vector η;
(4) $s^* = \mu/\rho$ is a vector associated with the sought solution of systems (5) and (7) when analyzing the ML algorithm;
(5) $R_s = \max_{g \in G}(\mu, g)$ is an upper-bound value of the set G in the direction μ;
(6) $M = R_s/\rho$ is the ratio of the upper and lower bounds of the set along μ, $r = \rho/R_s = M^{-1}$;
(7) $V = \rho/R$ is the ratio of the minimal and maximal vectors of the set.

For some set Q, we will use the noted characteristics indicating the set as an argument; for example, $\eta(Q), r(Q)$.

We assume that set G satisfies the assumption:

Assumption 2 ([1]). *Set G is convex, closed, limited ($R < \infty$) and satisfies the separability condition, i.e., $\rho > 0$.*

Vector s^* is a solution to the system of inequalities (5), and ρ and R_s describe the thickness of the set G in the direction μ:

$$\rho \leq (\mu, g) \leq R_s, \quad \forall g \in G. \tag{21}$$

Due to (21) and the form of s^*:

$$1 \leq (s^*, g) \leq R_s/\rho = M, \quad \forall g \in G. \tag{22}$$

R_s, according to its definition, satisfies the constraints:

$$\rho \leq R_s \leq ||\mu|| \max_{g \in G} ||g|| \leq R.$$

Figure 3 shows a separable set and its characteristics. The R_s characteristic determines the thickness of the set G and significantly affects the convergence rate of learning algorithms with space dilation. When the thickness of the set is equal to zero, $R_s = \rho$ and a flat set takes place (Figure 1). Set G and its characteristics with boundaries (22) are shown in Figure 3.

For example, consider the function

$$f(x) = \sum_{i=1}^{n} |x_i| a_i, \ a_i \geq 0, \ i = 1, ..., n, \ x^0 = (b_1, ..., b_m, 0, ..., 0). \tag{23}$$

The point x^0 is located at the bottom of a multidimensional ravine. Let us study its subgradient set at point x^0. As earlier, $g(x^0)$ is subgradient of a function. Components of subgradient vectors at non-zero values x_i are as follows: $g_i(x) = sign(x_i)a_i$. For zero x_i, the components of the subgradient vectors belong to the set $g_i(x) \in [-a_i, a_i]$, where the zero component $g_i(x) = 0$ exists. Hence, it follows that the subgradient of the minimum length of function (23) at point x^0 has the form

$$\eta = g_{min}^0 = (sign(b_1)a_1, \ldots, sign(b_m)a_m, 0, \ldots, 0).$$

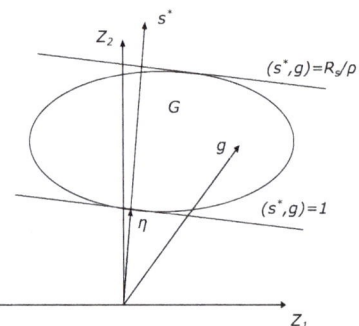

Figure 3. The set G and its characteristics.

Maximum length subgradients are specified by a set of subgradients

$$g^0_{max} \in G = \{(sign(b_1)a_1, \ldots, sign(b_m)a_m, \pm a_{m+1}, \ldots, \pm a_n)\}.$$

It is easy to verify that the projections of arbitrary subgradients at the point x_0 onto vector g^0_{min} are the same. Therefore, the thickness of the subgradient set is zero. In a sufficiently small neighborhood of the point x^0, the union of the subgradient sets of function (23) coincides with the subgradient set at the point x^0. Consequently, the descent direction in the form of a solution to the system of inequalities (7) enables us to go beyond this neighborhood.

Figure 4 shows a representation of the subgradient set of a two-dimensional piecewise linear function

$$f(x) = |x_1| + |x_2|a, \ a > 1, \ x^0 = (b_1, 0). \tag{24}$$

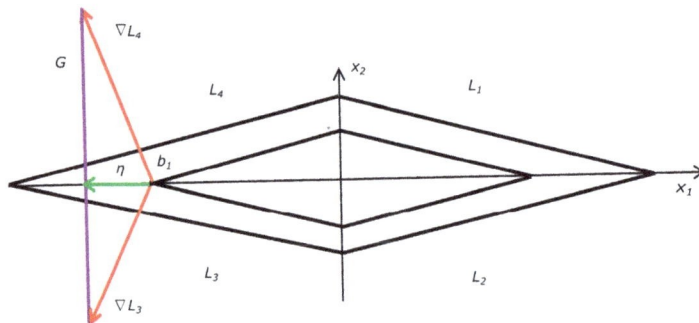

Figure 4. Level lines, subgradient set and minimum length vector.

In quadrants, the function has the form

$$L_1(x) = x_1 + x_2a, \ L_2(x) = x_1 - x_2a, \ L_3(x) = -x_1 - x_2a, \ L_4(x) = -x_1 + x_2a.$$

Its subgradients at point x^0 are given as follows:

$$g_1(x^0) = \nabla L_3(x^0) = (-1, -a)^T, \ g_2(x^0) = \nabla L_4(x^0) = (-1, a)^T.$$

Minimum length vector $\eta = (-1, 0)^T$.

For large values of the parameter a in (24), the complexity of solving the minimization problem increases significantly.

4. Machine Learning Algorithm with Space Dilation for Solving Systems of Inequalities on Separable Sets

In this section, we briefly introduce an algorithm for solving systems of inequalities from [1] and theoretically justify iterations (18) and (19). Specific operators will be used for transformations (13), (14) and (17)–(19). Denote by $S(s, g, p, H)$ transformation (18)'s operator, where the correspondence is used for the eponymous components. Then, for example, Formula (13) can be represented as $s_{k+1} = S(s_k, g_k, g_k, H_k)$. Similarly, for (14) and (19), we introduce the operator $H(H, \alpha, g)$. Formula (19) can be represented as $H_{k+1} = H(H_k, \alpha_k, y_k)$.

For a chain of approximations s_k, we form the residual vector $\Delta_k = s^* - s_k$. Until vector s_k is not a solution to (5), for vectors g_k selected at step 2 of Algorithm 1, from (6) and (22), the following inequality holds:

$$(\Delta_k, g_k) = (s^* - s_k, g_k) = (s^*, g_k) - (s_k, g_k) \geq 1 - (s_k, g_k) \geq 1. \tag{25}$$

The transformation equation for matrix A_k is as follows [1]:

$$A_{k+1} = A_k + (\alpha^2 - 1)\frac{g_k g_k^T}{(g_k, H_k g_k)}, \tag{26}$$

$$A_{k+1} = A_k + (\alpha_k^2 - 1)\frac{y_k y_k^T}{(y_k, H_k y_k)}, \tag{27}$$

where $A_k = H_k^{-1}$. For vectors s_k and g_k of Algorithm 1:

$$1 \leq (\Delta_k, g_k)^2 = (\Delta_k, A_k^{1/2} H_k^{1/2} g_k)^2 \leq (\Delta_k, A_k \Delta_k)(g_k, H_k g_k), \tag{28}$$

where $A^{1/2} A^{1/2} = A$, and $A > 0$ is a symmetric, strictly positive, definite matrix.

Algorithm 1 Method for solving systems of inequalities.

1: Set $k = 0$, $s_0 = 0$, $g_{-1} = 0$, $H_0 = I$. Set $\alpha > 1$ as the limit for choosing the admissible value of the parameter α_k for transformations (13) and (14)
2: Find $g_k \in G$, satisfying the condition (6) $(s_k, g_k) \leq 0$
3: **If** such a vector does not exist, **then**
   solution $s_k \in S(G)$ is found; stop the algorithm.
   end if
4: **If** $k = 0$ or condition (20) $(g_k, H_k g_{k-1}) \leq 0$ is not satisfied, **then**
   go to step 7
   end if
5: Compute vector $p_k = g_k - g_{k-1}(g_k, H_k g_{k-1})/(g_{k-1}, H_k g_{k-1})$ and perform transformation (18) $s_{k+1} = S(s_k, g_k, p_k, H_k)$. Compute the limit of the admissible values of the space dilation parameter α_{yk} for the combination of transformations (18) and (19)
6: **If** $\alpha_{yk}^2 \geq \alpha^2$, **then**
   set α_k satisfying the inequalities $\alpha^2 \leq \alpha_k^2 \leq \alpha_{yk}^2$ and perform transformation (19) $H_{k+1} = H(H_k, \alpha_k, y_k)$,
   else
   compute the limit of the admissible values of the space dilation parameter α_{gk} for the combination of transformations (18), (14); set α_k satisfying the inequalities $\alpha^2 \leq \alpha_k^2 \leq \alpha_{gk}^2$ and perform transformation (14) $H_{k+1} = H(H_k, \alpha_k, g_k)$. Go to step 8
   end if
7: Set $\alpha_k^2 = \alpha^2$ and perform transformations (13), (14) $s_{k+1} = S(s_k, g_k, g_k, H_k)$, $H_{k+1} = H(H_k, \alpha_k, g_k)$
8: Increase k by one and go to step 2

Inequality (28) is essential in justifying the convergence rate of the methods we study for solving systems of inequalities (5). The main idea of the algorithm formation is the point that the values of $(\Delta_k, A_k\Delta_k)$ do not increase when the values of $(g_k, H_k g_k)$ decrease with a geometric progression speed. In such a case, after a finite number of iterations, the right side of (28) becomes less than one. The resulting contradiction means that problem (5) is solved, and there is no more possibility of finding a vector g_k satisfying condition (6).

For the decreasing rate of the sequence $\{\tau_k\}$, $\tau_k = \min_{0 \leq j \leq k-1}[(g_j, H_j g_j)/(g_j, g_j)]$, the following theorem is known [26].

Theorem 1. *Let a sequence $\{H_k\}$ be a transformation (14) result with $H_0 = I$, $\alpha_k = \alpha > 1$ and arbitrary $g_k \in \mathbb{R}^n$, $g_k \neq 0$, $k = 0,1,2,\ldots$. Then*

$$\tau_k \leq k(\alpha^2 - 1)/n(\alpha^{2k/n} - 1), \quad k \geq 1. \tag{29}$$

This theorem does not impose restrictions on the choice of vectors g_k. Therefore, regardless of which of equations (14) or (19) is used to transform the matrices, the result (29) is valid for a sequence of vectors composed of g_k or y_k, depending on which one of them is used to transform the matrices. Let us show that for Algorithm 1 with fixed values of parameter α_k, estimates similar to (29) are valid, and we obtain expressions for the admissible parameters α_k in (14), (19), at which the values $(\Delta_k, A_k\Delta_k)$ do not increase.

In order to obtain the visually analyzed operation of the algorithm, similarly to the analysis of iterations of the process (9), (10) carried out on the basis of Figure 2, we pass to the coordinate system $\hat{s} = A_k^{1/2} s$. In this new coordinate system, corresponding vectors and matrices of iterations (13), (14) and (18), (19) are transformed as follows [1]:

$$\hat{s} = A_k^{1/2} s, \ \hat{g} = H_k^{1/2} g, \ \hat{A}_k = H_k^{1/2} A_k H_k^{1/2} = I, \ \hat{H}_k = A_k^{1/2} H_k A_k^{1/2} = I.$$

$$\hat{s}_{k+1} = \hat{s}_k + \frac{\hat{g}_k[1 - (\hat{s}_k, \hat{g}_k)]}{(\hat{g}_k, \hat{g}_k)}, \tag{30}$$

$$\hat{H}_{k+1} = I - (1 - \frac{1}{\alpha_k^2}) \frac{\hat{g}_k \hat{g}_k^T}{(\hat{g}_k, \hat{g}_k)}, \tag{31}$$

$$\hat{A}_{k+1} = I + (\alpha_k^2 - 1) \frac{\hat{g}_k \hat{g}_k^T}{(\hat{g}_k, \hat{g}_k)}. \tag{32}$$

For expressions (17), (18) and (27):

$$\hat{s}_{k+1} = \hat{s}_k + \frac{\hat{p}_k[1 - (\hat{s}_k, \hat{g}_k)]}{(\hat{g}_k, \hat{p}_k)}, \tag{33}$$

$$\hat{H}_{k+1} = I - (1 - \frac{1}{\alpha_k^2}) \frac{\hat{y}_k \hat{y}_k^T}{(\hat{y}_k, \hat{y}_k)}, \tag{34}$$

$$\hat{y}_k = \hat{g}_k - \hat{g}_{k-1}, \ \hat{p}_k = \hat{g}_k - \frac{\hat{g}_{k-1}(\hat{g}_k, \hat{g}_{k-1})}{(\hat{g}_{k-1}, \hat{g}_{k-1})}, \tag{35}$$

$$\hat{A}_{k+1} = I + (\alpha_k^2 - 1) \frac{\hat{y}_k \hat{y}_k^T}{(\hat{y}_k, \hat{y}_k)}. \tag{36}$$

Inequality (22) for new variables is:

$$1 \leq (\hat{s}^*, \hat{g}) \leq R_s/\rho = M, \ \forall \hat{g} \in \hat{G}. \tag{37}$$

In Figure 5, characteristics of set $\hat{G}$ in the plane Z formed by the vectors $\tilde{g}_k$, $\tilde{g}_{k-1}$ are shown. Straight lines W_1, W_M are projections of hyperplanes, i.e., corresponding inequality (37) boundaries for possible positions of the vector $\hat{s}^*$ projections defined by the normal $\tilde{g}_{k-1}$. Straight lines Z_1, Z_M are boundaries of inequality (37) for vector $\hat{s}^*$ possible projection positions defined by the normal $\tilde{g}_k$.

Let ψ be the angle between vectors $\tilde{g}_k$ and $\tilde{g}_{k-1}$. Since in Figure 5, this angle is obtuse, then condition (20) holds:

$$(g_k, H_k g_{k-1}) = (\tilde{g}_k, \tilde{g}_{k-1}) \leq 0.$$

Consequently, angle φ in Figure 5 is acute. Due to the fact that vectors $\tilde{g}_k$, $\tilde{g}_{k-1}$ are normals for the straight lines W_1 and Z_1, we obtain the relations [1]:

$$\sin^2 \varphi = \sin^2(\pi - \psi) = \sin^2 \psi = 1 - \cos^2 \psi, \quad \cos^2 \varphi = \cos^2 \psi. \tag{38}$$

$$\cos^2 \varphi = \cos^2 \psi = \frac{(\tilde{g}_k, \tilde{g}_{k-1})^2}{(\tilde{g}_k, \tilde{g}_k)(\tilde{g}_{k-1}, \tilde{g}_{k-1})} = \frac{(g_k, H_k g_{k-1})^2}{(g_k, H_k g_k)(g_{k-1}, H_k g_{k-1})}. \tag{39}$$

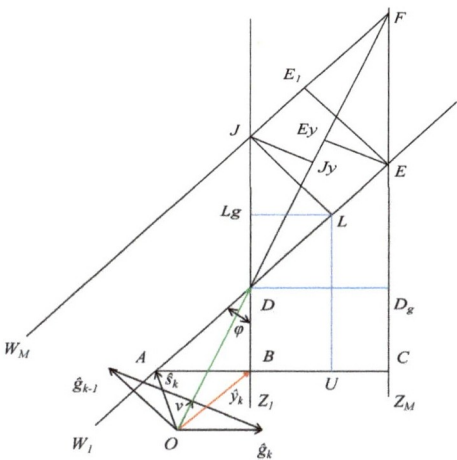

Figure 5. Characteristics of the set G in the plane of vectors $\tilde{g}_k$, $\tilde{g}_{k-1}$.

The following lemmas [1] allow us to estimate the admissible values of space dilation parameters.

Lemma 1. *Let the values a, b, c, β satisfy the constraints $a \geq a_m \geq 0$, $b > 0$, $c > 0$ and $0 \leq \beta \leq 1$; then:*

$$\min_{\alpha, \beta} \left(\frac{(a + \beta b)^2 - \beta^2 b^2}{\beta^2 c^2} \right) = \frac{a_m^2 + 2 a_m b}{c^2} = \frac{(a_m + b)^2 - b^2}{c^2}. \tag{40}$$

The proofs of Lemmas 1–6, as well as the proofs of Theorems 2–5, can be found in [1].

Lemma 2. *Let vectors p_1, p_2 and g be linked by equalities $(p_1, g) = a$, $(p_2, g) = b$. Let the difference of vectors $p_2 - p_1$ be collinear to the vector p, and let ζ be an angle between vectors p and g; then:*

$$\|p_1 - p_2\|^2 = \frac{(a-b)^2}{(g,p)^2} \|p\|^2 = \frac{(a-b)^2}{\|g\|^2 \cos^2 \zeta}. \tag{41}$$

Lemma 3. *As a result of transformation (13) at step 7 of Algorithm 1, the following equality holds:*

$$(s_{k+1}, g_k) = (\hat{s}_{k+1}, \hat{g}_k) = 1, \tag{42}$$

and as a result of (18) at step 5, (42) will hold, and the equality is as follows:

$$(s_{k+1}, g_{k-1}) = (\hat{s}_{k+1}, \hat{g}_{k-1}) = 1. \tag{43}$$

Lemma 4. *Let set G satisfy Assumption 2. Then, the limit α of the admissible parameter value $\alpha_k \leq \alpha$ in Algorithm 1 providing inequality $(\Delta_{k+1}, A_{k+1}\Delta_{k+1}) \leq (\Delta_k, A_k\Delta_k)$ in the case of transformations (13) and (14) is*

$$\alpha^2 = \frac{M^2}{(M-1)^2} = \frac{1}{(1-r)^2}. \tag{44}$$

Lemma 5. *Let set G satisfy Assumption 2. Then, the limit α_{gk} of the admissible parameter value α_k at step 5 of Algorithm 1, providing inequality $(\Delta_{k+1}, A_{k+1}\Delta_{k+1}) \leq (\Delta_k, A_k\Delta_k)$ in the case of transformations (18), (14) is given by the equation:*

$$\alpha_{gk}^2 = 1 + \frac{M^2 - (M-1)^2}{(M-1)^2 \sin^2 \varphi} = 1 + \frac{2M-1}{(M-1)^2 \sin^2 \varphi}, \tag{45}$$

where

$$\sin^2 \varphi = 1 - \frac{(g_k, H_k g_{k-1})^2}{(g_k, H_k g_k)(g_{k-1}, H_k g_{k-1})}. \tag{46}$$

Lemma 6. *Let set G satisfy Assumption 2. Then, the limit α_{yk} for the admissible value of parameter α_k at step 5 of Algorithm 1 providing inequality $(\Delta_{k+1}, A_{k+1}\Delta_{k+1}) \leq (\Delta_k, A_k\Delta_k)$ in the case of transformations (18) and (19) is given as*

$$\alpha_{yk}^2 = \min\{\alpha_{Ek}^2, \alpha_{Jk}^2\}, \tag{47}$$

where

$$\alpha_{Ek}^2 = 1 + \frac{(2M-1)(y_k, H_k y_k)}{(M-1)^2 (g_k, H_k g_k) \sin^2 \varphi}, \tag{48}$$

$$\alpha_{Jk}^2 = 1 + \frac{(y_k, H_k y_k)}{(M-1)^2 (g_k, H_k g_k) \sin^2 \varphi} \left(1 + \frac{2(M-1)(g_k, H_k g_k)^{1/2} \cos \varphi}{(g_{k-1}, H_k g_{k-1})^{1/2}} \right), \tag{49}$$

The value $\cos^2 \varphi$ is defined in (39), and $\sin^2 \varphi = 1 - \cos^2 \varphi$.

In matrix transformations (14) and (19) of Algorithm 1, vectors g_k and y_k are used, which does not allow for directly using estimate (29) of Theorem 1 in the case when expression τ_k involves some vector y_m, $m < k$. In the next theorem, an estimate similar to (29) is obtained directly for subgradients g_k generated by Algorithm 1.

Theorem 2. *Let set G satisfy Assumption 1 and let the sequence $\{\pi_k = \min_{0 \leq j \leq k-1}(g_j, H_j g_j) = (g_{Jk}, H_{Jk} g_{Jk})\}$ be calculated based on the characteristics of Algorithm 1 for fixed values of the space dilation parameters $\alpha_k^2 = \alpha^2$ specified at steps 5 and 6, where parameter α is specified according to (44). Then:*

$$\pi_k = (g_m, H_m g_m) \leq \frac{4R^2 k(\alpha^2 - 1)}{n[\alpha^{2k/n} - 1]}, \; k \geq 1, \tag{50}$$

where $m = \arg\min_{0 \leq j \leq k-1}(g_j, H_j g_j)$.

Theorem 3. *Let set G satisfy Assumption 1 and let the sequence $\{(\Delta_k, A_k\Delta_k)\}$ be calculated based on the characteristics of Algorithm 1. Let dilation parameter α satisfy constraint (44) and let the admissible value α_{yk}^2 be given by (47). Then:*

$$(\Delta_{k+1}, A_{k+1}\Delta_{k+1}) \leq (\Delta_k, A_k\Delta_k) \leq (\Delta_0, A_0) = \rho^{-2}, \; k = 0, 1, 2\ldots \tag{51}$$

For fixed values of the space dilation parameter with respect to the convergence of Algorithm 1, the following theorem holds.

Theorem 4. *Let set G satisfy Assumption 2. Let the values of the space dilation parameters in Algorithm 1 specified at steps 5 and 6 be fixed as $\alpha_k^2 = \alpha^2$, and let parameter α be given according to constraint (44). Then, the solution to system (5) will be found by Algorithm 1 in a finite number of iterations, which does not exceed K_0, the minimum integer number k satisfying the inequality*

$$\frac{4kR^2(\alpha^2-1)}{n\rho^2[\alpha^{2k/n}-1]} = \frac{4k(\alpha^2-1)}{nV^2[\alpha^{2k/n}-1]} < 1. \tag{52}$$

Herewith, until a solution $s_k \notin S(G)$ is found, and the following inequalities hold:

$$(g_k, H_k g_k) \geq \rho^2, \tag{53}$$

$$\frac{(g_k, H_k g_k)}{(g_k, g_k)} \geq \frac{\rho^2}{R^2} = V^2. \tag{54}$$

According to (21), parameters ρ and R_s characterize the deviation of the component vectors $g \in G$ along the vector μ. If $\rho = R_s$, there is a set G in plane with normal μ. Such a structure of the set G allows one to specify large values of the parameter α (44) in Algorithm 1 and, according to (52), to obtain a solution in a small number of iterations.

In the minimization algorithm (4) on the descent trajectory, due to the exact one-dimensional search, it is always possible to choose a subgradient from the subgradient set satisfying condition (6), including at the minimum point. Therefore, we will impose constraints on the subgradient sets of functions to be minimized, similar to those for the set G. Due to the biases in the minimization algorithm, we need to define the constraints, taking into account the union of subgradient sets in the neighborhood of the current minimum point x_k, and use these characteristics based on Theorem 4 results to develop a stopping criterion for the algorithm for solving systems of inequalities.

5. Minimization Algorithm

Since in the subgradient set at point x_{k+1} an exact one-dimensional search is performed, there is always a subgradient satisfying condition (6): $(s_{k+1}, g_{k+1}) \leq 0$. For example, for smooth functions, the equality $(s_{k+1}, g_{k+1}) = 0$ holds. Therefore, vector g_{k+1} can be used in Algorithm 1 to find a new descent vector approximation. In the built-in algorithm for solving systems of inequalities, the dilation parameter is chosen to solve the system of inequalities for the union of subgradient sets in some neighborhood of current approximation x_k. This allows the minimization algorithm to leave the neighborhood after a finite number of iterations.

Due to possible significant biases during the operation of the minimization algorithm, the shell of the subgradient set involved in the learning may contain a zero vector. To avoid situations when there is no solution similar to (5) for the subgradient set from the operational area of the algorithm, we introduce an update to the algorithm of solving systems of inequalities. To track the updates, we used a stopping criterion, formulated based on Theorem 4's results.

To accurately determine the parameters of the algorithm involved in the calculation of the dilation parameters α_{yk} and α_{gk}, we define their calculation in the form of operators. Denote by $AL_g^2(M, H, g_{-1}, g)$ the operator of calculation α_{gk}^2 according to (45) and (46) in Lemma 5, which is $\alpha_{gk}^2 = AL_{yg}^2(M, H_k, g_{k-1}, g_k)$. For α_{yk}^2's calculation according to expressions (47)–(49) in Lemma 6, we introduce operator $AL_{yg}^2(M, H, g_{-1}, g)$, where parameters H, g_{-1}, g correspond to set H_k, g_{k-1}, g_k.

A description of the minimization method is given in Algorithm 2.

Algorithm 2 $RA(\alpha)$.

1: Set $x_0 \in \mathbb{R}^n$, $w_0 = x_0$, $k = q = l = 0$, $s_0 = 0$, $H_0 = I$. Set $\sigma > 0$, parameters $M > 0$, $r = 1/M$ and the limit α for the dilation parameter according to equality (44). Compute $g_0 \in \partial f(x_0)$.
2: **If** $g_k = 0$ **then**
   stop the algorithm
   end if
3: **If** $(g_k, H_k g_k)/(g_k, g_k) < \sigma$ **then**
   update $q = q + 1$, $w_q = x_k$, $l = 0$, $H_k = I$, $s_k = 0$
   end if
4: **If** $l = 0$ or $(g_k, H_k g_{k-1}) > 0$ **then**
   go to step 7
   end if
5: Compute vector $p_k = g_k - g_{k-1}(g_k, H_k g_{k-1})/(g_{k-1}, H_k g_{k-1})$ and perform transformation (18) $s_{k+1} = S(s_k, g_k, p_k, H_k)$. Compute the limit of the admissible value of the dilation parameter $\alpha_{yk}^2 = AL_y^2(M, H_k, g_{k-1}, g_k)$ for the combination of transformations (18) and (19).
6: **If** $\alpha_{yk}^2 \geq \alpha^2$ **then**
   set α_k satisfying the inequalities $\alpha^2 \leq \alpha_k^2 \leq \alpha_{yk}^2$ and perform transformation (19)
   $H_{k+1} = H(H_k, \alpha_k, y_k)$
   else
   compute the limit of the admissible value of the dilation parameter
   $\alpha_{gk}^2 = AL_g^2(M, H_k, g_{k-1}, g_k)$ for the combination of transformations (18) and (14), set
   α_k satisfying the inequalities $\alpha^2 \leq \alpha_k^2 \leq \alpha_{gk}^2$ and perform transformation (14)
   $H_{k+1} = H(H_k, \alpha_k, g_k)$. Go to step 8
   end if
7: Set $\alpha_k^2 = \alpha^2$ and perform transformations (13), (14) $s_{k+1} = S(s_k, g_k, g_k, H_k)$, $H_{k+1} = H(H_k, \alpha_k, g_k)$
8: Find a new approximation of the minimum point $x_{k+1} = x_k - \gamma_k s_{k+1}$, $\gamma_k = \arg\min_\gamma f(x_k - \gamma s_{k+1})$
9: Compute subgradient $g_{k+1} \in \partial f(x_{k+1})$, based on the condition $(g_{k+1}, s_{k+1}) \leq 0$.
10: Increase k and l by one and go to step 2

At step 9, due to the condition of the exact one-dimensional descent at step 8, the sought subgradient always exists. This follows from the condition for the extremum of the one-dimensional function. For the sequence of approximations of the algorithm, due to the exact one-dimensional descent at step 8, the following lemma holds [20].

Lemma 7. *Let function $f(x)$ be strictly convex on $\mathbb{R}^n$, let set $D(x_0)$ be limited, and let the sequence $\{x_k\}_{k=0}^\infty$ be such that $f(x_{k+1}) = \min_{\gamma \in [0,1]} f(x_k + \gamma(x_{k+1} - x_k))$. Then, $\lim_{k \to \infty} \|x_{k+1} - x_k\| = 0$.*

Denote $D(z) = \{x \in \mathbb{R}^n \mid f(x) \leq f(z)\}$. Let x_* be a minimum point of function and let x^* be limit points of the sequence $\{w_q\}$ generated by Algorithm 2 ($RA(\alpha)$). The existence of limit points of a sequence $\{w_q\}$ when the set $D(x_0)$ is bounded follows from $w_q \in D(x_0)$. Concerning the convergence of the algorithm, we formulate the following theorem [1].

Theorem 5. *Let function $f(x)$ be strictly convex on $\mathbb{R}^n$; let set $D(x_0)$ be bounded, and for $x \neq x_*$,*

$$r(\partial f(x)) \geq r_0 > 0, \tag{55}$$

$$V(\partial f(x)) \geq V_0 > 0, \tag{56}$$

where parameters M, r and α of Algorithm 2 are given according to the equalities

$$M = \frac{4}{3}r_0, \ r = \frac{3}{4}r_0, \ \alpha = \frac{1}{1 - 3r_0/4'} \tag{57}$$

and parameters α_k, set at steps 5 and 7, are fixed as $\alpha_k = \alpha$. In this case, if $\sigma = (3V_0/4)^2$, then any limit point of the sequence $\{w_q\}$ generated by Algorithm 2 ($RA(\alpha)$) is a minimum point on $\mathbb{R}^n$.

6. Relationship between the Relaxation Subgradient Method and the Conjugate Gradient Method

Let us establish the identity of the sequences generated by the conjugate gradient method and the relaxation subgradient method with space dilation on the minimization of quadratic functions:

$$f(x) = \frac{1}{2}(x, Ax) + (b, x) + c, \ A \in \mathbb{R}^{n \times n}, \ A > 0, \ b \in \mathbb{R}^n.$$

Suppose that the number of iterations without updating the relaxation subgradient method and the conjugate gradient method is the same and equal to $m \leq n$. Denote by $\nabla f(x)$ the function gradient at point x. Denote by $g_k = \nabla f(x_k)$ the gradients at the points of the current minimum approximation x_k and denote by $x_0 \in \mathbb{R}^n$ the initial point. Iterations of the subgradient method for the purposes of its comparison with the conjugate gradient method are briefly represented in Algorithm 3 (SSG).

As we will see below, metric transformations for establishing the identity of the approximation sequences of the subgradient method and the method of conjugate gradients on quadratic functions are not essential. Therefore, in this scheme, there are no details of the choice of space dilation transformations and their parameters.

Algorithm 3 SSG

1: Set initial point $x_0 \in \mathbb{R}^n$, $s_0 = 0$, $H_0 = I$.
2: **For** $k = 0, 1, ..., m < n$ **do**
   2.1 Compute s_{k+1} as:

$$s_{k+1} = s_k + H_k p_k \frac{1 - (s_k, g_k)}{(g_k, H_k p_k)}, \tag{58}$$

   where

$$p_k = \begin{cases} g_k, & \text{if } (k \geq 1 \text{ and } (g_{k-1}, H_k g_{k-1}) > 0) \text{ or } k = 0, \\ g_k - \frac{g_{k-1}(g_k, H_k g_{k-1})}{(g_{k-1}, H_k g_{k-1})}, & \text{otherwise.} \end{cases} \tag{59}$$

   2.2 Perform metric transformation according to one of the formulas (14) or (19) according to Algorithm 2 ($RA(\alpha)$):

$$H_{k+1} = H_k - (1 - \frac{1}{\alpha_k^2}) \frac{H_k z_k z_k^T H_k^T}{(z_k, H_k z_k)}, \tag{60}$$

   where $z_k = g_k$ in the case of transformation (14) and $z_k = g_k - g_{k-1}$ in the case of transformation (19)
   2.3 Execute the descent step: $x_{k+1} = x_k - \gamma_k s_{k+1}$, $\gamma_k = \arg\min_\gamma f(x_k - \gamma s_{k+1})$
endfor

Iterations of the conjugate gradient method are carried out according to the Algorithm 4 scheme (see, for instance, [17]):

Algorithm 4 SG

1: Set initial point $\tilde{x}_0 \in \mathbb{R}^n$
2: **For** $k = 0, 1, \ldots, m < n$ **do**
    2.1 Compute $\tilde{x}_{k+1} = \tilde{x}_k - \tilde{\gamma}_k \tilde{s}_{k+1}$, $\tilde{\gamma}_k = \arg\min_{\tilde{\gamma}} f(\tilde{x}_k - \tilde{\gamma}\tilde{s}_{k+1})$
    where

$$\tilde{s}_k = \tilde{g}_k + \beta_k \tilde{s}_{k-1}, \; \tilde{g}_k = \nabla f(\tilde{x}_k), \tag{61}$$

$$\beta_k = \begin{cases} 0, & \text{if } k = 0, \\ \frac{(\tilde{g}_k, \tilde{g}_k)}{(\tilde{g}_{k-1}, \tilde{g}_{k-1})}, & \text{otherwise.} \end{cases}$$

endfor

The following theorem gives conditions for the equivalence of methods for minimizing quadratic functions:

Theorem 6. *Let function $f(x)$ be quadratic, and for the SSG process matrix $H_0 = I$, $\alpha_k \geq 1$. Then, if the initial points for the SSG and SG processes coincide, $x_0 = \tilde{x}_0$, and for any $m > k \geq 0$, until a solution is found, the following sequences coincide:*

$$x_k = \tilde{x}_k \tag{62}$$

$$s_k = \frac{\tilde{s}_k}{(\tilde{g}_k, \tilde{g}_k)}, \tag{63}$$

i.e., both processes generate coincident successive approximations.

Proof. We carry out the proof by induction. With $k = 0$, Equalities (62) and (63) hold, since, according to (59), $p_k = g_k$, taking into account $s_0 = 0$, we obtain:

$$s_1 = s_0 + I g_0 \frac{1 - (s_0, g_0)}{(g_0, I g_0)} = \frac{g_0}{(g_0, g_0)}.$$

According to (61) with $\beta_0 = 0$, we have $\tilde{s}_0 = \tilde{g}_0 = g_0$.

Assume that equalities (62) and (63) are satisfied for $k = 0, 1, \ldots, l$, where $l > 0$. Let us show that they are satisfied for $k = l + 1$.

Since $x_l = \tilde{x}_l$, vectors s_l and $\tilde{s}_l$ are collinear, then by virtue of the condition of exact one-dimensional descent $\tilde{x}_{l+1} = x_{l+1}$. For the conjugate gradient method, the gradient vectors calculated during the operation of the algorithm are mutually orthogonal [17]. Therefore, by virtue of (62), all of the vectors $g_0, g_1, \ldots, g_l$ will be mutually orthogonal. Using the recursive transformation of inverse matrices for (60),

$$A_{k+1} = A_k + (\alpha_k^2 - 1) \frac{z_k z_k^T}{(z_k, H_k z_k)},$$

we obtain an expression for the matrix A_l,

$$A_l = I + \sum_{k=0}^{l-1} (\alpha_k^2 - 1) \frac{z_k z_k^T}{(z_k, H_k z_k)}.$$

Since in (60), vectors $z_k = g_k$ or $z_k = g_k - g_{k-1}$, then, in this expression, all vectors z_k, $k = 0, 1, \ldots, l-1$ participating in the formation of matrix A_l are orthogonal to vector g_l. Therefore, $A_l g_l = g_l$. This implies the equality $H_l g_l = g_l$. Due to the orthogonality of the vectors g_l, g_{l-1}, according to (59), equality $p_l = g_l$ holds. By virtue of the condition of the exact one-dimensional descent, $(s_l, g_l) = 0$. In view of the above, from (58), we obtain:

$$s_{l+1} = s_l + \frac{H_l g_l}{(g_l, H_l g_l)} = \frac{\bar{s}_l}{(g_{l-1}, g_{l-1})} + \frac{g_l}{(g_l, g_l)}.$$

Multiplying the last equality by (g_l, g_l), we obtain a proof of equality (63) for $k = l + 1$:

$$s_{l+1}(g_l, g_l) = \bar{s}_l \frac{(g_l, g_l)}{(g_{l-1}, g_{l-1})} + g_l = \bar{s}_{l+1}.$$

□

Note. For an arbitrary initial matrix $H_0 > 0$, one should pass to the coordinate system, where the initial matrix $\tilde{H}_0 = I$, and in the new coordinate system, one should use the results of Theorem 6.

The presented RSMM with space dilation in an exact one-dimensional search has the properties of the conjugate gradient method. On a quadratic function, it is equivalent to the conjugate gradient method.

7. One-Dimensional Search Algorithm

Consider a one-dimensional minimization algorithm for process (4). Computational experience shows that the one-dimensional search algorithm in relaxation subgradient methods should have the following properties:

1. An overly accurate one-dimensional search in subgradient methods leads to poor convergence. The search should be adequately rough.
2. At the iteration of the method, the search step should be large enough to leave a sufficiently large neighborhood of the current minimum.
3. To ensure the position of the previous paragraph, it should be possible to increase the search step faster than the possibilities of decreasing it.
4. In PCM, a one-dimensional search should provide over-relaxation, that is, overshoot the point of a one-dimensional minimum along the direction of descent when implementing iteration (4). This provides condition (6), which is necessary for the learning process.
5. When implementing one-dimensional descent along the direction at iteration (4), as a new approximation of the minimum, one can take the points with the smallest value of the function, and for training, one can take the points that ensure condition (6).

We use the implementation of the one-dimensional minimization procedure proposed in [26]. The set of input parameters is $\{x, s, g_x, f_x, h_0\}$, where x is the current minimum approximation point, s is the descent direction, h_0 is the initial search step, and $f_x = f(x)$, $g_x \in \partial f(x)$; moreover, the necessary condition for the possibility of decreasing the function along the direction $(g_x, s) > 0$ must be satisfied. Its output parameters are $\{\gamma_m, f_m, g_m, \gamma_1, g_1, h_1\}$. Here, γ_m is a step to the new minimum approximation point

$$x^+ = x - \gamma_m s, \quad f_m = f(x^+), \quad g_m \in \partial f(x^+),$$

where γ_1 is a step along s, such that at the point $z^+ = x - \gamma_1 s$ for subgradient $g_0 \in \partial f(z^+)$, inequality $(g_0, s) \leq 0$ holds. This subgradient is used in the learning algorithm. The output parameter h_1 is the initial descent step for the next iteration. Step h_1 is adjusted in order to reduce the number of calls to the procedure for calculating the function and the subgradient.

In the minimization algorithm, vector $g_0 \in \partial f(z^+)$ is used to solve the system of inequalities, and point $x^+ = x - \gamma_m s$ is a new minimum approximation point.

Denote the call to the procedure of one-dimensional minimization as $OM(\{x, s, g_x, f_x, h_0\}; \{\gamma_m, f_m, g_m, \gamma_0, g_0, h_1\})$. Here is a brief description of it. We introduce the one-dimensional function $\varphi(\beta) = f(x - \beta s)$. To localize its minimum, we take an increasing sequence $\beta_0 = 0$ and $\beta_i h_0 q_M^{i-1}$ with $i \geq 1$. Here, $q_M > 1$ is step increase parameter. In most cases, $q_M = 3$ is set. Denote $z_i = x - \beta_i s$, $r_i \in \partial f(z_i)$, $i = 0, 1, 2, \ldots$; l is the number i at which the relation $(r_i, s) = 0$ holds. Let us determine the parameters of the localization segment $[\gamma_0, \gamma_1]$ of the one-dimensional minimum $\gamma_0 = \beta_{l-1}$, $f_0 = f(z_{l-1})$, $g_0 = r_{l-1}$, $\gamma_1 = \beta_l$, $f_1 = f(z_l)$, $g_0 = r_l$ and find the minimum point γ^* using a cubic approximation of function [48] on the localization segment using the values of the one-dimensional function and its derivative. Compute

$$\gamma_m = \begin{cases} 0.1\gamma_1, & \text{if } l = 1 \text{ and } \gamma^* \leq 0.1\gamma_1, \\ \gamma_1, & \text{if } \gamma_1 - \gamma^* \leq 0.2(\gamma_1 - \gamma_0), \\ \gamma_0, & \text{if } l > 1 \text{ and } \gamma^* - \gamma_0 \leq 0.2(\gamma_1 - \gamma_0), \\ \gamma^*, & \text{otherwise.} \end{cases}$$

The initial descent step for the next iteration is defined by the rule $h_1 = q_m h_0 (\gamma_1/h_0)^{1/2}$. Here, $q_m < 1$ is the parameter of the descent step decrease, which, in most cases, is given as $q_m = 0.8$. In the overwhelming majority, when solving applied problems, the set of parameters $\{q_M = 3, q_m = 0.8\}$ is satisfactory. When solving complex problems with a high degree of level surface elongation, the parameter $q_m \to 1$ should be increased.

8. Implementation of the Minimization Algorithm

Algorithm 2 ($RA(\alpha)$), as a result of updates at step 3, loses information about the space metric. In the proposed algorithm, the matrix update is replaced by the correction of the diagonal elements, and exact one-dimensional descent by approximate. Denote by $Sp(H)$ the matrix H's trace and denote by ε_H the limit of admissible decrease in the matrix H's trace. The algorithm sets the initial metric matrix $H_0 = I$. Since, as a result of transformations, the elements of the matrix decrease, then when the trace of the matrix decreases, $Sp(H) \leq \varepsilon_H$, it is corrected using the transformation $H^+ = nH/Sp(H)$, where ε_H is a lower bound for trace reduction, and n is the space dimension. As an indicator of matrix degeneracy, we use the cosine of the angle between vectors g and Hg. When it decreases to a certain value ε_λ, which can be done by checking $(g, Hg) \leq \varepsilon_\lambda ||g|| ||Hg||$, transformation $H^+ = H + 10\varepsilon_\lambda I$ is performed. Here, I is the identity matrix and ε_λ is the cosine angle limit. To describe the algorithm, we will use the previously introduced operators.

Let us explain the actions of the algorithm. Since $s_0 = 0$, then at $k = 0$, condition (6) is satisfied, and $(s_k, g_k) \leq 0$ and $g_0^O = g_0$. Therefore, at step 8, learning iterations (13) and (14) will be implemented. According to the algorithm of the OM procedure, the subgradient g_{k+1}^O obtained at step 10 of the algorithm satisfies the condition (6): $(g_{k+1}^O, s_{k+1}) \leq 0$. Therefore, at the next iteration, it is used in learning in steps 6–8.

At step 9, an additional correction of the descent direction is made in order to provide the necessary condition $(g_k, s_{k+1}) > 0$ for the possibility of descent in the direction opposite to s_{k+1}. From the point of view of solving the system of inequalities, this correction also improves the descent vector, which can be shown using Figure 5. Here, as under the conditions of Lemma 4, the movement is made in the direction AB, not from point A, but from some point of the segment AB, where $(s_{k+1}^{1/2}, g_k) < 1$. Since the projection of the optimal solution is in the area between the straight lines Z_1, Z_M, the shift to point B, where $(s_{k+1}, g_k) = 1$, reduces the distance to the optimal vector.

An effective set of parameters for the OM in the minimization algorithm is $\{q_m = 0.8, q_M = 3\}$. The next section presents the results of numerical studies of the presented Algorithm 5.

Algorithm 5 $RA_{OM}(\alpha)$

1: Set $x_0 \in \mathbb{R}^n$, $w_0 = x_0$, $k = 0$, $s_0 = 0$, $H_0 = I$. Set $\varepsilon_H > 0$, $\varepsilon_\lambda > 0$, $M > 0$, $r = 1/M$ and the limit α for the dilation parameter according to equality (44) $\alpha^2 = M^2/(M-1)^2$. Compute $f_k = f(x_0)$. Set $g_0^O = g_0$, $f_k^{min} = f_0$, $x_k^{min} = x_0$.
2: **If** $g_k = 0$ **then**
   stop the algorithm
3: **If** $(g_k, H_k g_k) \leq \varepsilon_\lambda ||g_k|| ||H_k g_k||$ **then**
   $H_k = nH_k/Sp(H_k)$
4: **If** $Sp(H_k) \leq \varepsilon_H$ **then**
   $H_k = H_k + 10\varepsilon_\lambda I$
5: **If** $k = 0$ or $(g_k, H_k g_{k-1}) > 0$ **then**
   go to step 8
6: Perform transformations (17) and (18) for the training system of subgradients: $p_k = g_k^O - g_{k-1}(g_k^O, H_k g_{k-1})/(g_{k-1}, H_k g_{k-1})$, $s_{k+1}^{1/2} = S(s_k, g_k^O, p_k, H_k)$. Compute the limit of the dilation parameter $\alpha_{yk}^2 = AL_y^2(M, H_k, g_{k-1}, g_k^O)$ for the combination of transformations (18) and (19)
7: **If** $\alpha_{yk}^2 \geq \alpha^2$ **then**
   set α_k satisfying the inequalities $\alpha^2 \leq \alpha_k^2 \leq \alpha_{yk}^2$ and perform transformation (19)
   $H_{k+1} = H(H_k, \alpha_k, y_k)$ with $y_k = g_k^O - g_{k-1}$
   else
   compute the limit of the dilation parameter $\alpha_{gk}^2 = AL_g^2(M, H_k, g_{k-1}, g_k^O)$
   for the combination of transformations (18), (14), set α_k satisfying the inequalities $\alpha^2 \leq \alpha_k^2 \leq \alpha_{gk}^2$ and perform transformation (14) $H_{k+1} = H(H_k, \alpha_k, g_k^O)$.
   Go to step 9
8: Set $\alpha_k^2 = \alpha^2$ and perform transformations (13), (14) $s_{k+1}^{1/2} = S(s_k, g_k^O, g_k^O, H_k)$, $H_{k+1} = H(H_k, \alpha_k, g_k^O)$
9: **If** $(s_{k+1}^{1/2}, g_k) < 1$ **then**
   perform transformation $s_{k+1} = S(s_{k+1}^{1/2}, g_k, g_k, H_{k+1})$
   else
   $s_{k+1} = s_{k+1}^{1/2}$
10: Perform one-dimensional minimization $OM(\{x_k, s_k, g_{k+1}, f_k, h_k\}$; $\{\gamma_{k+1}, f_{k+1}, g_{k+1}, g_{k+1}^O, h_{k+1}\})$ and compute a new approximation of the minimum point $x_{k+1} = x_k - \gamma_{k+1} s_{k+1}$
11: **If** $f_k^{min} > f_{k+1}$ **then**
   set $f_{k+1}^{min} = f_{k+1}$, $x_{k+1}^{min} = x_{k+1}$
   else
   set $f_{k+1}^{min} = f_k^{min}$, $x_{k+1}^{min} = x_k^{min}$
   Here, the subgradient $g_{k+1} \in \partial f(x_{k+1})$ is obtained in the OM procedure and is used as the current approximation of the minimum. Subgradient g_{k+1}^O is also obtained in the OM procedure. It satisfies condition (6) $(g_{k+1}^O, s_{k+1}) \leq 0$ and is further used in training
12: **If** $||x_{k+1} - x_k|| \leq \varepsilon_x$ **then**
   stop the algorithm
   else
   increase k by one and go to step 2

9. Computational Experiment Results

In this section, we conduct a computational experiment on minimizing test functions using the following methods: (1) the relaxation method with space dilation in the direction of the subgradient (RSD) [26]; (2) the r-algorithm ($r_{OM}(\alpha)$) [22,26]; (3) the quasi-Newtonian method (QN) implemented with the matrix transformation formula BFGS; (4) algorithm $RA(\alpha)$ with the fixed parameter ($RA(\alpha = const)$), where $\alpha^2 = 6$; (5) an algorithm with a dynamic way to select the space dilation parameter ($RA(\alpha_k)$), where $\alpha^2 = 6$.

As test functions, we took functions with a high degree of level surface elongation, which increases with the dimension:

(1) $f_1(x) = \sum_{i=1}^{n} x_i^2 i^6$, $x_0 = (10/1, 10/2, \ldots, 10/n)$, $\varepsilon = 10^{-10}$;
(2) $f_2(x) = \sum_{i=1}^{n} x_i^2 (n/i)^6$, $x_0 = (10/1, 10/2, \ldots, 10/n)$, $\varepsilon = 10^{-10}$;
(3) $f_3(x) = (\sum_{i=1}^{n} x_i^2 i)^r$, $x_0 = (1, 1, \ldots, 1)$, $r = 2$, $\varepsilon = 10^{-10}$;
(4) $f_4(x) = \sum_{i=1}^{n} |x_i| i^3$, $x_0 = (10/1, 10/2, \ldots, 10/n)$, $\varepsilon = 10^{-4}$;
(5) $f_5(x) = \max_{1 \leq i \leq n}(|x_i| i^3)$, $x_0 = (10/1, 10/2, \ldots, 10/n)$, $\varepsilon = 10^{-4}$.

When testing the methods, the values of the function and the subgradient were computed simultaneously. Parameter ε for quadratic functions was chosen as a sufficiently small value (10^{-10}); for non-smooth functions, it was chosen so that the accuracies in terms of variables are approximately the same for different types of functions. Tables 1–6 show the number of calculations of the function values and the subgradient values necessary for achieving the required accuracy for the function $f(x_k) - f^* \leq \varepsilon$. The initial point of minimization x_0 and the value ε are given in the description of the function.

The test case contains quadratic and piecewise linear functions. Due to their simplicity and unambiguity, an analysis of the level surface elongation can be carried out easily. This choice of functions is due to the fact that, during minimization, the local representation in the current minimization area, as a rule, has either a quadratic or piecewise linear representation.

Functions 1 and 2 are quadratic, where the ratio of the minimum to maximum eigenvalue is $1/n^6$. The ratio of the level surface range along the coordinate axes of the minimum to the maximum is equal to $1/n^3$. Function 2, in comparison with function 1, has a higher density of eigenvalues in the region of small values. Function 3 is smooth with a low degree of variation of the level surface elongation. Its complexity is due to the degree above quadratic. Functions 4 and 5 are piecewise. For these functions, the ratio of the level surface range along the coordinate axes of the minimum to the maximum is equal to $1/n^3$. the same as for quadratic functions 1 and 2. It is of interest to compare the complexity of minimizing smooth and nonsmooth functions by nonsmooth optimization methods provided that their ratios of the surface range are identical.

None of problems 1, 2, 4 and 5 can be solved by the multistep minimization method [24] for $n \geq 100$, which emphasizes the relevance of methods with a change in the space metric, in particular, space dilation minimization algorithms capable of solving nonsmooth minimization problems with a high degree of level surface elongation.

In order to identify the least costly one-dimensional search in the quasi-Newtonian method, it was implemented in various ways when specifying the initial unit step. Due to the high degree of condition number for functions 1 and 2, for the best of them, the costs of localizing a one-dimensional minimum when minimizing function 1 include about 2–4 steps. This, together with the final iteration of the approximation and finding the minimum on the localized segment, adds up to 3–5 calculations of the function and the gradient. For function 2, the total iteration costs are 5–10 calculations of the function and the gradient. Tables 1–3 for the QN method show only the number of iterations required to solve the problem.

Table 1. Function $f_1(x)$ minimization results.

n	$RA(\alpha_k)$	$RA(\alpha = const)$	RSD	$r_{OM}(\alpha)$	QN
100	1494	1834	2127	2333	107
200	3474	3896	4585	5244	216
300	5507	6317	7117	8480	324
400	7690	8548	9791	11,773	432
500	9760	11,510	12,366	15,281	542
600	12,133	13,889	15,537	19,073	650
700	13,933	16,394	18,450	22,500	757
800	16,492	18,721	21,387	26,096	867
900	17,774	21,606	24,671	30,233	975
1000	20,324	24,206	27,447	34,702	1084

Table 2. Function $f_2(x)$ minimization results.

n	$RA(\alpha_k)$	$RA(\alpha = const)$	RSD	$r_{OM}(\alpha)$	QN
100	304	381	480	482	124
200	525	621	788	852	239
300	715	842	1063	1223	336
400	869	1015	1307	1587	423
500	1065	1241	1497	1900	504
600	1217	1368	1742	2188	582
700	1366	1527	1898	2512	658
800	1465	1721	2095	2829	733
900	1602	1885	2293	3101	855
1000	1791	2019	2555	3300	1022

According to the results of Tables 1 and 2, the $RA(\alpha = const)$ algorithm outperforms the RSD and $r_{OM}(\alpha)$ methods on smooth functions. Therefore, the changes in the directions of correction and space dilation have a positive effect on the convergence rate of the new algorithm. In the $RA(\alpha_k)$ algorithm, compared to $RA(\alpha = const)$, an additional factor of convergence acceleration is involved due to an increase in the space dilation parameter, which, according to the results of Tables 1 and 2, led to an increase in the $RA(\alpha = const)$ algorithm's convergence rate.

For function 2, the eigenvalues of the Hessian are shifted to the small values area, which has a positive effect on the convergence rate of subgradient methods. Here, the quasi-Newtonian method QN, taking into account the costs of localizing the minimum in a one-dimensional search, required a larger number of calculations of the function and gradient.

Table 3. Function $f_3(x)$ minimization results.

n	$RA(\alpha_k)$	$RA(\alpha = const)$	RSD	$r_{OM}(\alpha)$	QN
200	159	148	365	295	440
400	221	200	395	505	638
600	258	248	409	702	833
800	295	280	421	900	1030
1000	336	317	433	1094	1205

For function 3, the number of iterations of the quasi-Newtonian method turned out to be higher than the number of calculations of the function and the gradient of subgradient methods. Based on the results of minimizing functions 1–3, we can conclude that subgradient methods with space dilation can also be useful in minimizing smooth functions. New methods $RA(\alpha_k)$ and $RA(\alpha = const)$ show better results here than other algorithms with space dilation.

Table 4. Function $f_4(x)$ minimization results.

n	$RA(\alpha_k)$	$RA(\alpha = const)$	RSD	$r_{OM}(\alpha)$
100	2248	2714	4214	3505
200	4988	6010	9087	8826
300	7680	9301	11,144	14,018
400	10,625	12,808	23,687	19,549
500	13,490	16,656	28,037	24,865
600	16,466	20,207	39,703	31,502
700	20,122	22,850	44,573	38,796
800	23,016	27,653	52,380	44,200
900	25,913	31,982	61,631	43,502
1000	28,962	35,792	72,175	49,050

Table 5. Function $f_4(x)$ minimization results with subgradient distortion.

n	$RA(\alpha_k)$	$RA(\alpha = const)$	RSD	$r_{OM}(\alpha)$
100	2505	3135	5739	4777
200	5538	7393	13,364	10,665
300	9033	11,646	20,589	16,889
400	12,886	18,705	30,132	23,397
500	18,490	22,059	35,544	30.015
600	20,742	29,976	47,664	36,749
700	25,524	39,258	54,768	43,589
800	30,462	43,961	68,944	50,737
900	33,570	44,089	78,697	57,817
1000	39,764	49,772	82,490	64,777

According to the ratio of the level surface range along the coordinate axes, functions 1, 2, and 4 are similar. Function 4 is difficult to minimize by subgradient methods. Comparing the results of Tables 1 and 4, we can note insignificant differences in the convergence rate of subgradient methods on these functions, which is additional evidence of the method's effectiveness in solving nonsmooth optimization problems.

To simulate the presence of the thickness of the subgradient set when minimizing function 4, the subgradients $g(x) \in \partial f(x)$ in the process of minimization were generated with interference according to the $g(x) \in (1 + \xi)\partial f(x)$, where $\xi \in [0,1]$ is a uniformly distributed random number. The interference negatively affects both the quality of the one-dimensional search and the quality of the descent direction. The results are shown in Table 5. Here, the maximum possible value of the characteristic of a subgradient set $M = R_s/\rho = 2$. Due to the random nature of the quantities $\xi \in [0,1]$, the value of M for a set of subgradients on a certain time interval of minimization may have smaller values. According to the results of Lemma 4, the admissible value is $\alpha^2 = M^2/(M-1)^2 = 4$. The calculations were carried out at large values of the space dilation parameter $\alpha^2 = 6$. The proposed methods also show significantly better results here.

The ratios of the level surface range along the coordinate axes for functions 5 and 1 are similar. The results for function 5 are shown in Table 6. Here, the RSD method has an advantage due to the fact that the function is separable and all of its subgradients calculated in the minimization procedure are directed along the coordinate axes. Space dilations occur along the coordinate axes, which does not change the eigenvectors of the metric matrix directed along the coordinate axes.

Table 6. Function $f_5(x)$ minimization results.

n	$RA(\alpha_k)$	$RA(\alpha = const)$	RSD	$r_{OM}(\alpha)$
200	3401	3551	3151	6906
400	7483	7707	6431	14,596
600	11,678	11,851	10,280	22,853
800	15,868	16,088	14,020	31,259
1000	19,893	20,867	17,707	39,275

To simulate the presence of the thickness of the subgradient set when minimizing function 5, the subgradients $g(x) \in \partial f(x)$ in the process of minimization were generated with interference according to the $g(x) \in (1 + \xi)\partial f(x)$, where $\xi \in [0,1]$ is uniformly distributed random number. The results for function 5 with subgraduient distortion are shown in Table 7. Here, the maximum possible value of the characteristic of a subgradient set $M = R_s/\rho = 2$. The proposed methods show better results here than the RSD and $r_{OM}(\alpha)$ methods.

Table 7. Function $f_5(x)$ minimization results with subgradient distortion.

n	$RA(\alpha_k)$	$RA(\alpha = const)$	RSD	$r_{OM}(\alpha)$
200	3773	3816	6805	7463
400	7976	8370	16,188	15,246
600	12,654	13,548	24,873	24,542
800	17,286	18,411	35,251	33,600
1000	22,344	23,559	46,873	41,773

A number of conclusions can be drawn regarding the convergence rate of the presented methods:

1. Functions 1, 2, 4, 5 have a significant degree of level surface elongation. The problems of minimizing these functions could not be solved by the multistep minimization methods investigated in [24], which emphasize the relevance of developing methods with a change in the space metric, in particular, space dilation minimization algorithms capable of solving nonsmooth minimization problems with a high degree of level surface elongation.
2. Based on the results of minimizing smooth functions 1–3, we can conclude that subgradient methods with space dilation can also be useful in minimizing smooth functions. At the same time, the new algorithms $RA(\alpha_k)$ and $RA(\alpha = const)$ also show significantly better results on smooth functions than other subgradient RSD and $r_{OM}(\alpha)$ methods.
3. The new methods $RA(\alpha_k)$ and $RA(\alpha = const)$ significantly outperform the RSD and $r_{OM}(\alpha)$ methods when minimizing nonsmooth functions. In the $RA(\alpha_k)$ algorithm, in comparison with the $RA(\alpha = const)$ algorithm, an additional factor of convergence acceleration is involved due to an increase in the space dilation parameter, which also leads to a significant increase in the convergence rate.

10. Computational Experiment Results in Approximation by Neural Networks

The purpose of this section is to demonstrate the usefulness of applying the methods of nonsmooth regularization (for example, the "Tibshirani lasso" [3]) to the problems of the elimination of uninformative variables when constructing mathematical models, where a necessary element of the technology is rapidly converging nonsmooth optimization methods applicable to minimize nonsmooth nonconvex functions. In this section, we will give several examples of approximation by artificial neural networks (ANN) using nonsmooth regularization to remove uninformative neurons. To assess the quality of this approximation technology using nonsmooth regularization, the obtained approximation results are compared with the previously known results. In each of the examples, a study of the effectiveness of the presented nonsmooth optimization methods will be carried out.

Consider the approximation problem

$$w^* = \arg\min_w E(\alpha, w, D), \tag{64}$$

$$E(\alpha, w, D) = \sum_{x,y \in D} (y - f(x,w))^2 + \alpha R_i(w),$$

where $D = \{(x^i, y_i) | x^i \in \mathbb{R}^p, \, y_i \in \mathbb{R}^1\}, \, i = 1, \ldots, N$ are observational data, $R_i(w)$ are different kinds of regularizers, α are regularization parameters, $f(x, w)$ is an approximating function, $x \in \mathbb{R}^p$ is a data vector, $w \in \mathbb{R}^n$ is a vector of the tunable parameters, and p and n are their dimensions. Formulas (1)–(3) can be used as regularizers.

Suppose that in the problem of approximation by a feedforward network, it is required to train a two-layer sigmoidal neural network of the following form using data D (i.e., evaluate its unknown parameters w)

$$f(x,w) = w_0^{(2)} + \sum_{i=1}^{m} w_i^{(2)} \varphi(s_i), \; \varphi(s) = 1/(1+e^{-s}). \tag{65}$$

For the sigmoidal network

$$s_i = w_{i0}^{(1)} + \sum_{j=1}^{p} x_j w_{ij}^{(1)}, \; i = 1,2,\ldots,m, \tag{66}$$

where x_j are components of vector $x \in \mathbb{R}^p$, $w = ((w_i^{(2)}, i=0,\ldots,m), (w_{ij}^{(1)}, j=0,\ldots,p, i=1,\ldots,n))$ is a set of parameters, the total number of which is denoted by n, $\varphi(s)$ is a neuron activation function, and m is the number of neurons. The unknown parameters w must be estimated by the least squares method (64) using one of the regularizers $R_i(w)$. To solve problem (64), we use subgradient methods.

In a radial basis function (RBF) network, we will use the following representation of a neuron

$$s_i = \sum_{j=1}^{p} (w_{ij}^{(1)}(x_j - c_{ij}))^2, \; i = 1,2,\ldots,m, \tag{67}$$

where x_j are components of vector $x \in \mathbb{R}^p$, and the network parameters will be as follows:

$w = ((w_i^{(2)}, i=0,\ldots,m), (w_{ij}^{(1)}, j=0,\ldots,p, i=1,\ldots,m), (w_{ij}^{(0)} = c_{ij}, j=0,\ldots,p, i=1,\ldots,m)).$

One of the goals of our study is to compare the effectiveness of subgradient methods in solving the problem of approximating a two-layer sigmoidal ANN under conditions of reducing the number of excess neurons using various regularization functionals. To assess the quality of the solution, we will use the value of the root-mean-square error:

$$S(D,f) = \sum_{x,y \in D} (y - f(x,w))^2 / N$$

on a test sample of data $D = DT_{10.000}$ uniformly distributed in Ω.

In the algorithm we use (Algorithm 6), at the initial stage, an approximation of the ANN is found with a fixed position of the neurons' working areas using the specified centers $c_i \in \mathbb{R}^p$, $i = 1,2,\ldots,m$ in the approximation area defined by the data. By neuron working area, we mean the area of significant changes in the neuron activation function. The need for fixation arises due to the possible displacement of the working areas of neurons outside the data area. As a result, the neuron in the data area turns into a constant. For the RBF networks (65) and (67), this is easy to do, since the parameters of the centers are present in expression (67). For RBF networks (65) and (66), instead of (66), the following expression will be used:

$$s_i = \sum_{j=1}^{p} (x_j - c_{ij}) w_{ij}^{(1)}, \; i = 1,2,\ldots,m, \tag{68}$$

where vector w components do not contain free members. In this case, some center c_i is located on the central hyperplane of the working band of a sigmoidal neuron. Centers c_i inside the data area can be found by some data clustering algorithm $x^i \in \mathbb{R}^p$, $i = 1,\ldots,N$, which will ensure that neurons are located in areas with high data density. We use the maximin algorithm [45] in which two data points that are maximally distant from each other are selected as the first two centers. Each new center is obtained by choosing data point x^i, the distance from which to the nearest known center is at its maximum. The resulting centers are mainly located on the edges of the data area. Computational experience shows that the use of the k-means method turns out to be ineffective, or effective with a small number of iterations.

Algorithm 6 Training Algorithm

1: On the data D, using the maximin algorithm, form the centers $c_i \in \mathbb{R}^p$, $i = 1, 2, \ldots, m$, where m is the initial number of neurons. Set the regularization parameter α and the type of regularizer $R_i(w)$. Using a generator of uniformly distributed random numbers for each neuron, determine the initial parameters of the ANN.

2: Solve the problem of estimating the parameters W of the neural network (64) for an ANN at fixed centers $c_i \in \mathbb{R}^p$, $i = 1, 2, \ldots, m$ with a regularizer $R_i(w)$. Create an initial set of parameters for solving the problem of estimating network parameters (64) without fixing the centers of neurons. The resulting set of parameters is denoted by W^0.

3: **For** $k = 0, 1, \ldots$ **do**

    3.1 Set $S_0 = S(D, f^k)$, where f^k is a neural network obtained as a result of solving problem (64) at the current iteration. Perform sequential removal of all neurons for

    which, after removal, inequality $S(D, \tilde{f}^k) \leq (1 + eps)S_0$ is satisfied, where $eps = 0.1$,

    $\tilde{f}^k$ is a neural network with removed neurons. If none of the neurons could be removed,

    then the neuron is removed, leading to the smallest increase in the value $S(D, \tilde{f}^k)$.

    3.2 **If** the number of neurons is less than three, **then**

        stop the algorithm

    endif

    3.3 Using the neural network parameters for the remaining neurons as initial values, obtain

        a new approximation W^{k+1}, solving problem (64) for the ANN with regularizer $R_i(w)$

endfor

Initially, problem (64) is solved with an excess number of neurons at fixed centers $c_i \in \mathbb{R}^p$, $i = 1, \ldots, m$ for the RBF network in the forms (65) and (67) or for a sigmoidal network in the forms (65) and (68). Regularization even with an excessive number of parameters in comparison with the amount of data allows, at this stage, to obtain an acceptable solution.

After solving problem (4) with fixed centers, it is necessary to return to the original description for the sigmoidal network in the forms (65) and (66). This can be done through the formation of a free member of the neuron

$$w_{i0}^{(1)} = -\sum_{j=1}^{p} c_{ij} w_{ij}^{(1)}, \; i = 1, 2, \ldots, m,$$

while leaving the other parameters unchanged. Such an algorithm for finding the initial approximation of the sigmoidal ANN guarantees that the data area will be covered by the working areas of neurons.

Here is a brief description of the algorithm for constructing an ANN. The algorithm first finds the initial approximation for fixed working areas of neurons and then iterates the removal of insignificant neurons, which is followed by training the trimmed network.

With a limited number of data, ANN $f(x, W^k)$ with a number of parameters n not exceeding N and the smallest value of $S_k = S(D, f^k)$ is selected as the final approximation model.

Consider examples of solving approximation problems. Tables 8–10 show the value of $S(DT_{10.000,f})$ calculated during the operation of the network learning algorithm with the sequential removal of insignificant neurons after network training at step 3.3. The first row of each table contains the function $f_i(x)$ to be approximated, the initial number of neurons $m0$, number of training data $N0$, the type of regularizer, the regularization parameter α, and the index deduced by rows. The first two columns indicate the number of neurons and the number of ANN parameters. The remaining columns show the values of the index for the tested methods. The values of the index with the limiting order of accuracy are highlighted in bold. This allows one to see a segment of maintaining a high quality of the network with a decrease in the number of neurons for each of the presented minimization algorithms. For some of the tables, the last row contains the minimum value of the maximum network deviation for the constructed models on the test data Δ_{min}. The dimensions of problems where the number of model variables exceeds the number of data are underlined. Standard least squares practice recommends having more data than the parameters to be estimated. Good values of the index for this case emphasize the role of regularization in approximation by neural networks.

In [49], in the domain $\Omega = [-1,1] \times [-1,1]$ the function

$$f_6(x) = \sin(\pi x_1^2)\sin(2\pi x_2)/2$$

was approximated by the cascade correlation method using data uniformly distributed at $N = 500$. The maximum deviation of the ANN obtained in [49] with the number of neurons $m = 41$ on the test sample of 1000 data was $\Delta \approx 0.15$. Such a result is practically very difficult to obtain using the standard ANN learning apparatus. The authors in [49] did not succeed in obtaining such a result without first fixing the position of the working areas of neurons at the initial stage of the approximation algorithm. In our work, we obtained a series of ANN models with a smaller number of network training data $N = 150$ and with an assessment of the results on a test sample $DT_{10.000}$ consisting of 10.000 data with good approximation quality ($\Delta < 0.09$ for selected index values). For example, for some of the constructed models, $\Delta \approx 0.02$, which is almost an order of magnitude less than the result from [49].

Table 8 shows the results of the approximation of the function $f_6(x)$ using a smooth regularizer $R_2(w)$. The quasi-Newtonian method (QN) was also used here. Using the $RA(\alpha_k)$, $RA(\alpha = const)$ and RSD methods, it is possible to obtain a better quality approximation with a smaller number of neurons. The QN method is inferior in approximation quality to subgradient methods. Note that in some cases, the number of network parameters exceeds the number of data. At the same time, the network quality index is not worse than in the area with $m < 38$. For the methods $r_{OM}(\alpha)$ and QN, the best indexes are in the $m > 37$ area.

Table 8. Results of function $f_6(x)$ approximation by a sigmoidal ANN with a regularizer $R_2(w)$, $m0 = 50$, $N0 = 150$, $\alpha = 10^{-7}$, $S(DT_{10.000,f})$. The values with the limiting order of accuracy are given in bold. The dimensions of problems where the number of variables exceeds the number of data are given in underline.

m	n	$RA(\alpha_k)$	$RA(\alpha = const)$	$r_{OM}(\alpha)$	RSD	QN
50	151	0.000271	0.000807	0.000446	0.000389	0.00126
49	<u>197</u>	0.0000228	0.0000699	0.0000153	0.0000601	0.000259
48	<u>193</u>	0.0000171	0.000057	0.0000106	0.0000242	0.00014
47	<u>189</u>	0.00002	0.0000188	0.0000148	0.0000274	0.000129
46	<u>185</u>	0.0000190	0.0000268	0.0000173	0.0000194	0.000693
45	<u>181</u>	0.0000166	0.0000253	0.0000477	0.0000158	0.000774
44	<u>177</u>	0.0000142	0.0000201	0.0000796	0.0000222	0.00442
43	<u>173</u>	0.0000158	0.0000213	0.0000556	0.0000275	0.0038
42	<u>169</u>	0.0000158	0.0000966	0.0000260	0.0000260	0.064
41	<u>165</u>	0.0000168E	0.0000183	0.00022	0.0000384	0.0906
40	<u>161</u>	0.0000289	0.0000673	0.000107	**0.00127**	0.039
39	<u>157</u>	0.00006	0.0000507	0.000367	0.0000249	0.0597
38	<u>153</u>	0.000036	0.0000656	0.00114	0.0000461	0.0544
37	149	0.0000305	0.0000298	0.000261	0.0000298	0,437
36	145	0.000037	0.0000794	0.00203	0.0000323	0,16
35	141	0.0000437	0.0000294	0.00115	0.0000366	0,256
34	137	0.0000171	0.0000315	0.000965	0.00012	1,82
33	133	0.0000655	0.0000239	0.000547	0.0000886	0,459
32	129	0.000468	0.000014	0.00315	0.000882	2,91
31	125	0.000215	0.000153	0.0115	0.00051	2,22
30	121	0.000175	0.0000624	0.00139	0.003	14,7
Δ_{min}		0.0234	0.0236	0.0263	0.0287	0,9

Table 9 shows the results of approximating function $f_6(x)$ by the sigmoidal ANN using a nonsmooth regularizer $R_1(w)$ ("Tibshirani lasso" technique [3]). Here, the trend in the relative efficiency of the methods continues. Using the $RA(\alpha_k)$, $RA(\alpha = const)$ and RSD methods, it is possible to obtain a better-quality approximation with a smaller number of neurons.

Table 9. Results of function $f_6(x)$ approximation by a sigmoidal ANN with a regularizer $R_1(w)$, $m0 = 50$, $N0 = 150$, $\alpha = 10^{-7}$, $S(DT_{10000,f})$. The values with the limiting order of accuracy are given in bold. The dimensions of problems where the number of variables exceeds the number of data are given in underline.

m	n	$RA(\alpha_k)$	$RA(\alpha = const)$	$r_{OM}(\alpha)$	RSD
50	151	0.000271	0.000807	0.000446	0.000389
49	197	0.0000214	0.0000158	0.0000182	0.0000315
48	193	0.0000339	0.0000057	0.0000307	0.0000211
47	189	0.0000287	0.00000842	0.0000547	0.0000368
46	185	0.0000139	0.0000106	0.0000341	0.0000443
45	181	0.0000161	0.0000372	0.000103	0.0000371
44	177	0.0000142	**0.000008**	0.000263	0.0000226
43	173	0.0000232	0.0000139	0.000455	0.0000389
42	169	0.0000317	0.0000348	0.00127	0.0000154
41	165	0.0000259	0.0000657	0.00127	0.000183
40	161	0.0000179	0.0000593	0.00357	0.0000189
39	157	0.0000209	0.000784	0.00163	0.00148
38	153	0.0000239	0.000977	0.000139	0.00537
37	149	0.0000245	0.000478	0.000404	0.000232
36	145	0.0000157	0.000605	0.00042	0.00189
35	141	0.0000148	0.000272	0.00415	0.000476
34	137	0.0000168	0.000353	0.00362	0.000549
33	133	0.0000162	0.00185	0.00246	0.00324
32	129	0.00024	0.000263	0.0019	0.00498
31	125	0.0000891	0.000844	0.000925	0.0134
Δ_{min}		0.02	0.025	0.0373	0.03

Table 10 shows the results of approximating function $f_6(x)$ by the sigmoidal ANN using a nonsmooth regularizer $R_\gamma(w)$. Using the $RA(\alpha_k)$, $RA(\alpha = const)$ and RSD methods, it is possible to obtain a better quality approximation with a smaller number of neurons. When using a nonsmooth regularizer to approximate a function, it is possible to obtain an ANN with good approximation quality characteristics with a smaller number of neurons.

Based on the results of Tables 8–10, it can be concluded that the use of regularizers makes it possible to obtain a qualitative approximation in the case when the number of parameters of the neural network function exceeds the number of data.

In [49], on the data at $N = 625$, formed in the domain $\Omega = [-3,3] \times [-3,3]$, the generator of uniform random numbers approximated the function:

$$f_7(x_1, x_2) = 3(1-x_1)^2 e^{-x_1^2-(x_2+1)} - 10(\frac{x_1}{5} - x_1^3 - x_2^5)e^{x_1^2-x_2^2} - \frac{e^{-(x_1+1)-x_2^2}}{3}.$$

The maximum deviation of the ANN constructed in [49], based on RBF, on a test sample of 1000 data was $\Delta_1000 = 0.06$. Function f_3 is a typical example of a convenient radial basis function for approximating a network. In this work, we obtained a series of ANN models based on RBF with a smaller number of network training data $N = 150$ and with an assessment of the results on the test sample $DT_{10.000}$ consisting of 10.000 data, with good quality of approximation. For example, several of the constructed models give a value that is an order of magnitude smaller: $\Delta_{10.000} = 0.0024$ (see Table 11).

Table 11 shows the value of the index $S(DT_{10.000}, f)$ calculated during the operation of the network learning algorithm with the sequential removal of insignificant neurons after training the network at step 3.3. The initial number of neurons is 36. The first two columns indicate the number of neurons and the number of ANN parameters. The last row of the tables shows the maximum deviation of the network for the constructed models on the test data Δ_{min}. On this function, the methods $RA(\alpha_k)$, $RA(\alpha = const)$ and RSD turned out to be equivalent in quality of approximation.

Table 10. Results of function $f_6(x)$ approximation by a sigmoidal ANN with a regularizer $R_\gamma(w)$, $m0 = 50$, $N0 = 150$, $\alpha = 10^{-7}$, $S(DT_{10.000,f})$. The values with the limiting order of accuracy are given in bold. The dimensions of problems where the number of variables exceeds the number of data are given in underline.

m	n	$RA(\alpha_k)$	$RA(\alpha = const)$	$r_{OM}(\alpha)$	RSD
50	<u>151</u>	0.000271	0.000807	0.000446	0.0000389
49	<u>197</u>	0.0000195	0.0000263	0.0000327	0.0000108
48	<u>193</u>	0.0000292	0.0000272	0.0000207	0.000023
47	<u>189</u>	0.0000257	0.0000134	0.0000981	0.0000355
46	<u>185</u>	0.0000294	0.0000146	0.000906	0.0000502
45	<u>181</u>	0.0000264	0.0000227	0.00031	0.0000761
44	<u>177</u>	0.000032	0.0000331	0.0000578	0.0000773
43	<u>173</u>	0.0000332	0.0000335	0.000986	0.000079
42	<u>169</u>	0.0000307	0.000044	0.000887	0.000079
41	<u>165</u>	0.0000307	0.000044	0.00174	0.000079
40	<u>161</u>	0.000042	0.000044	0.00174	0.000079
39	<u>157</u>	0.0000406	0.000044	0.00126	0.000079
38	<u>153</u>	0.0000241	0.0000466	0.000242	0.0000778
37	149	0.0000477	0.0000407	0.000169	0.0000596
36	145	0.0000267	0.0000571	0.00115	0.0000455
35	141	0.0000297	0.0000286	0.000335	0.0000588
34	137	0.0000185	0.0000192	0.000689	0.000057
33	133	0.0000177	0.000018	0.000598	0.0000593
32	129	0.0000142	0.0000129	0.000795	0.0000464
31	125	0.0000171	0.0000319	0.000402	0.0000608
30	121	0.0000153	0.000168	0.000669	0.0000681
29	117	0.0000138	0.000312	0.00301	0.0000502
28	113	0.0000384	0.000106	0.00117	0.0000405
27	109	0.0000346	0.001	0.00255	0.0000519
26	105	0.0000288	0.000487	0.00374	0.0000674
Δ_{min}		0.02	0.026	0.036	0.028

Table 11. Results of function $f_7(x)$ approximation by RBF ANN with a regularizer $R_\gamma(w)$, $m0 = 36$, $N0 = 150$, $\alpha = 10^{-7}$, $S(DT_{10.000,f})$. The values with the limiting order of accuracy are given in bold. The dimensions of problems where the number of variables exceeds the number of data are given in underline.

m	n	$RA(\alpha_k)$	$RA(\alpha = const)$	$r_{OM}(\alpha)$	RSD
36	109	0.0706	0.037	0,244	0.0596
35	<u>176</u>	0.000196	0.00214	0.000304	0.000165
34	<u>171</u>	0.00000852	0.000000616	0.0000287	0.00000127
33	<u>166</u>	0.000000445	0.000000128	0.00000736	0.0000000735
32	<u>161</u>	0.000000601	0.000000169	0.00000929	0.000000192
31	<u>156</u>	0.000000229	0.00000017	0.00000491	0.000000193
30	<u>151</u>	0.000000323	0.000000168	0.00000208	0.000000191
29	146	0.000000304	0.000000167	0.00000219	0.00000019
28	136	0.000000273	0.000000168	0.00000102	0.000000192
27	136	0.000000273	0.000000168	0.000000523	0.000000193
26	131	0.000000558	0.000000168	0.00000518	0.000000291
25	126	0.000000187	0.000000166	0.00000046	0.000000291
24	121	0.000000523	0.000000324	0.000000502	0.000000293
23	116	0.000000397	0.000000323	0.00000052	0.000000288
22	116	0.000000397	0.000000319	0.00000052	0.000000214
21	116	0.000000397	0.000000325	0.00000035	0.000000205
20	116	0.000000397	0.000000192	0.000000496	0.000000203
19	96	0.000000521	0.000000195	0.000000529	0.000000161
18	91	0.000000613	0.0000000755	0.000000596	0.000000148
17	86	0.000000747	0.000000103	0.000000392	0.000000138
16	81	0.000000152	0.000000163	0.000181	0.00000014
15	76	0.000000124	0.00000017	0.0000167	0.000000144
Δ_{min}		0.0024	0.0024	0.005	0.0025

In [50], for testing purposes, an RBF ANN was built on data uniformly distributed in the domain $\Omega = [-3, 3] \times [-3, 3]$ for function

$$f_8(x_1, x_2) = x_1^2 + x_2^2$$

with the number of data $N = 100$. In this case, the achieved value of the root-mean-square error on the training sample is $S(D_{100}, f) = 10^{-6}$ [50]. We have built a number of sigmoidal ANNs with several orders of magnitude lower value of the quality index on a test sample. The values of the index $S(D_{10.000}, f) = 10^{-6}$ on the test sample, depending on the number of neurons in the ANN, are given in Table 12. Here, as earlier, algorithms $RA(\alpha_k)$ and $RA(\alpha = const)$ manage to obtain a longer series of ANN models with good quality of approximation.

Table 12. Results of function $f_8(x)$ approximation by a sigmoidal ANN with a regularizer $R_\gamma(w)$, $m0 = 30$, $N0 = 100$, $\alpha = 10^{-7}$, $S(DT_{10.000,f})$. The values with the limiting order of accuracy are given in bold. The dimensions of problems where the number of variables exceeds the number of data are given in underline.

m	n	$RA(\alpha_k)$	$RA(\alpha = const)$	$r_{OM}(\alpha)$	RSD
30	91	0.000378	0.00135	0.000179	0.000464
29	<u>117</u>	0.000000041	0.000000437	0.00000121	0.0000112
28	<u>113</u>	0.000000041	0.00000000794	0.00000000707	0.000000866
27	<u>109</u>	**0.000000000862**	0.00000000343	0.00000000372	0.000000089
26	<u>105</u>	**0.000000000711**	0.00000000152	0.00000000105	0.00000018
25	<u>101</u>	**0.000000000685**	0.00000000115	0.00000000341	0.00000000607
24	97	0.00000000567	0.000000000798	0.00000000154	0.00000000091
23	93	0.00000000156	0.000000000717	0.00000000315	0.000000000333
22	89	0.00000000378	0.000000000572	0.00000000435	0.00000000128
21	85	0.00000000272	0.000000000291	0.00000000847	0.00000000127
20	81	0.0000000026	0.000000000246	0.000000108	0.00000000162
19	77	0.000000000888	0.000000000612	0.000000396	0.00000000775
18	73	0.0000000345	0.0000000326	0.0000000162	0.0000000136
17	69	0.00000000114	0.00000000296	0.000000105	0.0000000181
16	65	0.00000000413	0.00000000747	0.000000113	0.000000168
15	61	0.0000000395	0.0000000982	0.0000000495	0.000000054
14	57	0.00000000245	0.0000000221	0.000000328	0.0000000475
Δ_{min}		0.000244	0.000293	0.000331	0.000301

In this section, the ANN training technology was presented, where nonsmooth optimization methods are its integral component. A specific feature of the ANN approximation problems is the absence of convexity of the minimized functions. The fastest methods $RA(\alpha_k)$ and $RA(\alpha = const)$ turn out to be more effective in solving problems of ANN approximation and make it possible to obtain models with a smaller number of neurons. Nevertheless, the experience of solving similar problems of approximation suggests that when solving an applied problem, it is better to have several alternatives for choosing a minimization method.

11. Conclusions

The statement of the problem consisted in the construction of a rapidly converging algorithm for finding the descent direction in the minimization method, which forms an obtuse angle with all subgradients of some neighborhood of the current minimum, forming a separable set. Minimization along such a direction allows the algorithm to go beyond this neighborhood. This is the problem of constructing a separating hyperplane between the origin and a separable set, the normal of which is the desired direction. As a result, we have a problem of solving a system of inequalities, for the solution of which learning algorithms can be applied, for example, the perceptron learning algorithm [45].

Formalization of the subgradient sets model made it possible to reduce the problem of solving a system of inequalities to an approximation problem, for the solution of which an algorithm with space dilation was proposed, which is ideologically close to the iterative least squares method. Taking into account the peculiarities of subgradient sets makes it possible to improve the standard ILS scheme and obtain an effective rapidly converging iterative method for finding the descent direction in the minimization method based on subgradients obtained in the process of the one-dimensional search.

The new algorithm for solving inequalities was theoretically substantiated, and an estimate of its convergence rate was obtained depending on the parameters of the subgradient set. On this basis, a new subgradient minimization method was developed and justified. On quadratic functions, the proposed method has the properties of the conjugate gradient method. The outlined approach to creating learning algorithms can be used to develop new learning algorithms with space dilation for relaxation subgradient minimization.

A practically implementable version of the minimization algorithm has been developed, which uses a rough one-dimensional search. The performed computational experiment on complex large-sized functions confirms the effectiveness of the proposed relaxation subgradient minimization method.

The possibility of using the relaxation subgradient minimization method in solving nonsmooth non-convex optimization problems makes it possible to use it in problems of neural network training, where it is required to remove insignificant variables or neurons by methods similar to the Tibshirani lasso. Algorithms of this type are of great practical importance due to their high convergence rate and the possibility of using them to minimize non-convex functions, for example, when estimating the parameters of mathematical models under conditions of nonsmooth regularization, used for the purpose of model feature reduction [3,29,46]. The effectiveness of using the proposed relaxation subgradient minimization method in one of these technologies has been demonstrated in the present work.

Author Contributions: Conceptualization, V.K. and L.K.; methodology, V.K., S.G. and L.K.; software, S.G.; validation, E.T. and E.S.; formal analysis, E.S.; investigation, L.K. and E.S.; resources, L.K. and E.S.; data curation, V.K.; writing—original draft preparation, V.K., S.G., E.T. and L.K; writing—review and editing, E.T. and L.K.; visualization, V.K. and E.T.; supervision, E.S.; project administration, L.K.; funding acquisition, L.K. and E.S. All authors have read and agreed to the published version of the manuscript.

Funding: This work was supported by the Ministry of Science and Higher Education of the Russian Federation (Project FEFE-2020-0013).

Institutional Review Board Statement: Not applicable.

Informed Consent Statement: Not applicable.

Data Availability Statement: Not applicable.

Conflicts of Interest: The authors declare no conflict of interest.

References

1. Krutikov, V.; Meshechkin, V.; Kagan, E.; Kazakovtsev, L. Machine Learning Algorithms of Relaxation Subgradient Method with Space Extension. In *Mathematical Optimization Theory and Operations Research: MOTOR 2021*; Lecture Notes in Computer Science; Pardalos, P., Khachay, M., Kazakov, A., Eds.; Springer: Berlin/Heidelberg, Germany, 2021; Volume 12755, pp. 477–492.
2. Lauer, F.; Le, V.; Bloch, G. Learning smooth models of nonsmooth functions via convex optimization. In Proceedings of the 2012 IEEE International Workshop on Machine Learning for Signal Processing, Santander, Spain, 23–26 September 2012; Volume 1, pp. 1–6.
3. Tibshirani, R. Regression shrinkage and selection via the lasso. *J. R. Stat. Soc.* **1996**, *58*, 267–288. [CrossRef]
4. Friedman, J.; Hastie, T.; Tibshirani, R.J. Regularization paths for generalized linear models via coordinate descent. *J. Stat. Softw.* **2010**, *33*, 1–22. [CrossRef] [PubMed]
5. Chang, K.; Hsieh, C.; Lin, C. Coordinate descent method for largescale l2-loss linear support vector machines. *J. Mach. Learn. Res.* **2008**, *9*, 1369–1398.
6. Pierucci, F. Nonsmooth Optimization for Statistical Learning with Structured Matrix Regularization. Ph.D Thesis, Université Grenoble Alpes, Grenoble, France, 2017.
7. Hahnloser, R.; Sarpeshkar, R.; Mahowald, M.; Douglas, R.; Seung, H. Digital selection and analogue amplification coexist in a cortex-inspired silicon circuit. *Nature* **2000**, *405*, 947–951. [CrossRef]

8. Nesterov, Y. *Subgradient Optimization*; John Wiley and Sons, Inc.: Hoboken, NJ, USA, 2009.
9. Golshtein, E.; Nemirovsky, A.; Nesterov, Y. Level method, its generalizations and applications. *Econ. Math. Methods* **1995**, *31*, 164–180.
10. Nesterov, Y. Universal gradient methods for convex optimization problems. *Math. Program. Ser. A* **2015**, *152*, 381–404. [CrossRef]
11. Gasnikov, A.; Nesterov, Y. Universal method for stochastic composite optimization problems. *Comput. Math. Math. Phys.* **2018**, *58*, 48–64. [CrossRef]
12. Nesterov, Y. Smooth minimization of nonsmooth functions. *Math. Program.* **2005**, *103*, 127–152. [CrossRef]
13. Ouyang, H.; Gray, A. Stochastic smoothing for nonsmooth minimizations: Accelerating SGD by exploiting structure. In Proceedings of the 29th International Conference on Machine Learning (ICML), Edinburgh, UK, 26 June–1 July 2012; Volume 1, pp. 33–40.
14. Gasnikov, A.; Lagunovskaya, A.; Usmanova, I.; Fedorenko, F. Gradient-free proximal methods with inexact oracle for convex stochastic nonsmooth optimization problems on the simplex. *Autom. Remote Control* **2016**, *77*, 2018–2034. [CrossRef]
15. Shor, N.Z. Applying the gradient descent method to solve transportation network problem. In *Issues in Cybernetics and Operational Research*; Scientific Council on Cybernetics AS UkrSSR: Kyiv, Ukraine, 1962; pp. 9–17.
16. Polyak, B. A general method for solving extremum problems. *Sov. Math. Dokl.* **1967**, *8*, 593–597.
17. Polyak, B. *Introduction to Optimization*; Optimization Software: New York, NY, USA, 1987.
18. Wolfe, P. Note on a method of conjugate subgradients for minimizing nondifferentiable functions. *Math. Program.* **1974**, *7*, 380–383. [CrossRef]
19. Lemarechal, C. An extension of Davidon methods to non-differentiable problems. *Math. Program. Study* **1975**, *3*, 95–109.
20. Demyanov, V. Nonsmooth Optimization. In *Nonlinear Optimization*; Lecture Notes in Mathematics; Di Pillo, G., Schoen, F., Eds.; Springer: Berlin/Heidelberg, Germany, 2010; Volume 1989, pp. 55–163.
21. Nemirovsky, A.; Yudin, D. *Problem Complexity and Method Efficiency in Optimization*; Wiley: Chichester, UK, 1983.
22. Shor, N. *Minimization Methods for Nondifferentiable Functions*; Springer: Berlin/Heidelberg, Germany, 1985.
23. Polyak, B. Optimization of non-smooth composed functions. *USSR Comput. Math. Math. Phys.* **1969**, *9*, 507–521.
24. Krutikov, V.; Samoilenko, N.; Meshechkin, V. On the properties of the method of minimization for convex functions with relaxation on the distance to extremum. *Autom. Remote Control* **2019**, *80*, 102–111. [CrossRef]
25. Tsypkin, Y.Z. *Foundations of the Theory of Learning Systems*; Academic Press: New York, NY, USA, 1973.
26. Krutikov, V.N.; Petrova, T. Relaxation method of minimization with space extension in the subgradient direction. *Ekon. Mat. Met.* **2003**, *39*, 106–119.
27. Cao, H.; Song, Y.; Khan, K. Convergence of Subtangent-Based Relaxations of Nonlinear Programs. *Processes* **2019**, *7*, 221. [CrossRef]
28. Krutikov, V.N.; Gorskaya, T. A family of subgradient relaxation methods with rank 2 correction of metric matrices. *Ekon. Mat. Met.* **2009**, *45*, 37–80.
29. Krutikov, V.; Meshechkin, V.; Kagan, E.; Kazakovtsev, L. Approximation Capability to Compact Sets of Functions and Operators by Feedforward Neural Networks. In *Mathematical Optimization Theory and Operations Research*; Lecture Notes in Computer Science; Pardalos, P., Khachay, M., Kazakov, A., Eds.; Springer: Berlin/Heidelberg, Germany, 2021; Volume 12755, pp. 477–493.
30. Cybenko, G. Approximation by superpositions of a sigmoidal function. *Math. Control Signals Syst.* **1989**, *2*, 303–314. [CrossRef]
31. Funahashi, K.I. On the approximate realization of continuous mappings by neural networks. *Neural Netw.* **1989**, *2*, 183–192. [CrossRef]
32. Hornik, K. Approximation capabilities of multilayer feedforward networks. *Neural Netw.* **1991**, *4*, 251–257. [CrossRef]
33. Guliyev, N.J.; Ismailov, V.E. Approximation capability of two hidden layer feedforward neural networks with fixed weights. *Neurocomputing* **2018**, *316*, 262–269. [CrossRef]
34. Hanin, B.; Sellke, M. Approximating continuous functions by ReLU nets of minimal width. *arXiv* **2017**, arXiv:1710.11278.
35. Petersen, P.; Voigtlaender, F. Optimal approximation of piecewise smooth functions using deep ReLU neural networks. *Neural Netw.* **2018**, *108*, 296–330. [CrossRef] [PubMed]
36. Yarotsky, D. Error bounds for approximations with deep ReLU networks. *Neural Netw.* **2017**, *94*, 103–114. [CrossRef]
37. Tsypkin, Y.Z.; Gupta, M.; Jin, L.; Homma, N. *Static and Dynamic Neural Networks: From Fundamentals to Advanced Theory*; John Wiley and Sons: Hoboken, NJ, USA, 2003.
38. Wei, W.; Nan, D.; Li, Z.; Long, J.; Wang, J. Approximation Capability to Compact Sets of Functions and Operators by Feedforward Neural Networks. In Proceedings of the 2007 Second International Conference on Bio-Inspired Computing: Theories and Applications, Zhengzhou, China, 14–17 September 2007; pp. 82–86.
39. Gribonval, R.; Kutyniok, G.; Nielsen, M.; Voigtlaender, F. Approximation spaces of deep neural networks. *arXiv* **2020**, arXiv:1905.01208.
40. Liu, Z.; Tilman, H.; Masahito, U. Neural networks fail to learn periodic functions and how to fix it. In Proceedings of the 34th Conference on Neural Information Processing Systems (NeurIPS 2020), Vancouver, BC, Canada, 6–12 December 2020; pp. 1583–1594.
41. Wang, M.X.; Qu, W. Approximation capabilities of neural networks on unbounded domains. *Neural Netw.* **2022**, *145*, 56–67. [CrossRef]
42. Tikhonov, A.; Arsenin, V. *Solutions of Ill-Posed Problems*; John Wiley and Sons: New York, NY, USA, 1977.

43. Krutikov, V.; Samoilenko, N.; Nasyrov, I.; Kazakovtsev, L. On the applicability of non-smooth regularization in construction of radial artificial neural networks. *Control Syst. Inf. Technol.* **2018**, *2*, 70–75.
44. Nurminskii, E.; Thien, D. Method of conjugate subgradients with constrained memory. *Autom. Remote Control* **2014**, *75*, 646–656. [CrossRef]
45. Neimark, J. *Perceptron and Pattern Recognition*; Springer: Berlin/Heidelberg, Germany, 2003.
46. Krutikov, V.; Kazakovtsev, L.; Shkaberina, G.; Kazakovtsev, V. New method of training two-layer sigmoid neural networks using regularization. *IOP Conf. Ser. Mater. Sci. Eng.* **2019**, *537*, 042055. [CrossRef]
47. Kaczmarz, S. Approximate solution of systems of linear equations. *Int. J. Control* **1993**, *57*, 1269–1271. [CrossRef]
48. Lorentz, G. *Approximation of Functions*; American Mathematical Society: Providence, RI, USA, 2005.
49. Osovski, S. *Neural Networks for Information Processing*; Hot Line-Telecom: Moscow, Russia, 2016.
50. Filippov, V.; Elisov, L.; Gorbachenko, V. Radial basis function networks learning to solve approximation problems. *Int. J. Civ. Eng. Technol.* **2019**, *10*, 872–881.

Article

Machine Learning Feedback Control Approach Based on Symbolic Regression for Robotic Systems

Askhat Diveev * and Elizaveta Shmalko

Federal Research Center "Computer Science and Control", the Russian Academy of Sciences, 119333 Moscow, Russia
* Correspondence: aidiveev@mail.ru

Abstract: A control system of an autonomous robot produces a control signal based on feedback. This type of control implies the control of an object according to its state that is mathematically the control synthesis problem. Today there are no universal analytical methods for solving the general synthesis problem, and it is solved by certain particular approaches depending on the type of control object. In this paper, we propose a universal numerical approach to solving the problem of optimal control with feedback using machine learning methods based on symbolic regression. The approach is universal and can be applied to various objects. However, the use of machine learning methods imposes two aspects. First, when using them, it is necessary to reduce the requirements for optimality. In machine learning, optimization algorithms are used, but strictly optimal solutions are not sought. Secondly, in machine learning, analytical proofs of the received properties of solutions are not required. In machine methods, a set of tests is carried out and it is shown that this is sufficient to achieve the required properties. Thus, in this article, we initially introduce the fundamentals of machine learning control, introduce the basic concepts, properties and machine criteria for application of this technique. Then, with regard to the introduced notations, the feedback optimal control problem is considered and reformulated in order to add to the problem statement that such a property adjusts both the requirements of stability and optimality. Next, a description of the proposed approach is presented, theoretical formulations are given, and its efficiency is demonstrated on the computational examples in mobile robot control tasks.

Keywords: control synthesis; optimal control; stabilization; symbolic regression; machine learning; evolutionary algorithm; mobile robot

MSC: 49M25; 68T05

Citation: Diveev, A.; Shmalko, E. Machine Learning Feedback Control Approach Based on Symbolic Regression for Robotic Systems. *Mathematics* **2022**, *10*, 4100. https://doi.org/10.3390/math10214100

Academic Editor: Liliya Demidova

Received: 9 October 2022
Accepted: 31 October 2022
Published: 3 November 2022

Publisher's Note: MDPI stays neutral with regard to jurisdictional claims in published maps and institutional affiliations.

Copyright: © 2022 by the authors. Licensee MDPI, Basel, Switzerland. This article is an open access article distributed under the terms and conditions of the Creative Commons Attribution (CC BY) license (https://creativecommons.org/licenses/by/4.0/).

1. Introduction

Aiming at the automation of processes, we intend to automate the very process of control systems development in order to make it fast and generic. This sounds especially relevant in the context of ever-increasing robotization and the emergence of a variety of robots as control objects. To reach this goal of all-round automation, it is necessary to generalize the needed tasks, that is, to formulate them in general mathematical statements, and then develop universal methods for solving them. However, the problem here is that despite the extensive theoretical background of control theory, today, there is a wide range of applied problems that do not have exact analytical solutions. At the same time, there is an objective need for solving them.

In fact, in robotics, most modern control systems for robots are programmed by hand, and engineers do not even set the general problems because there are no general ways to solve them. The developer, based on his experience, sets the structure of the control system, determines the control channels, types of regulators, and then adjusts the parameters of the given system so that they meet certain requirements [1]. However, every problem can and should be considered an optimal one, defining not only the parameters, but also the structure of the control system optimally and, again, automatically.

If a robot has to perform rather simple actions, for example, moving from one point to another and going around some obstacles, then the program of its control system contains supposedly several hundreds of lines. In more complex control tasks, the programs that must control robots can include several tens or hundreds of thousands of lines. These programs will grow as the tasks or the robots structure become more complex. One can assume that a control system for a robot that repeats the actions of a fly must contain some millions of lines. It follows from that stated above that the manual creation of the robot control system is an unpromising direction. It is necessary to automate this process.

Any problem for robots, as well as any other control objects, can be formulated as a mathematical optimization problem, such as a problem of providing stability, an optimal control problem for finding optimal path in current real conditions, a problem of stabilization of movement along of the optimal path, a problem of avoiding collisions with static and dynamic obstacles, the problem of interaction with other control objects, the problem of precise achievement of some given terminal conditions and so on. The most general problem in robotics is feedback control synthesis. It assumes that a control system that makes the object reach its goal is designed as a function of the object state optimally according to given criteria. Even if the optimal control problem is solved and the optimal path is found, we must further ensure the movement of the object along the obtained trajectory to compensate for possible ever-existing uncertainties.

The general synthesis problem was formulated back in the early 1960s by Bellman [2,3], where the continuous-time nonlinear optimal control problem was solved through the Hamilton–Jacobi–Bellman equation, which is a nonlinear partial differential equation. Even in simple cases, the HJB equation may not have global analytic solutions. Various numerical methods based on dynamic programming have been proposed in the literature [4–7], including the modern adaptive dynamic programming technique [8–10] and reinforcement learning [11–13]. However, the main drawback of dynamic programming methods today is still the computational complexity required to describe the value function, which grows exponentially with the dimension of its domain.

A different way to construct a feedback optimal control is firstly to solve an optimal control problem by direct methods of nonlinear programming or by the indirect approach of the Pontryagin maximum principle and then to synthesize a feedback stabilization system in order to supply movement along the received optimal trajectory. For example, in [14], points are placed on the trajectory, and the object is stabilized at these points. This is the most popular practical approach to feedback optimal control system design.

However, concerning the optimality criterion, this approach is not correct since it turns out that the optimal path is considered for one control object, and the introduced stabilization system changes the object so that the calculated path may not be optimal for the modified object model. In addition, when approaching a given point on the path, the system slows down, so it is necessary to carry out additional estimates in each specific task, according to the optimal moments of points switching.

In this work, we propose an inverse approach to feedback optimal control system synthesis. The general idea is the following. We firstly stabilize an object according to some point in the state space by solving the stabilization system synthesis problem. Note that this problem is computationally easier than the general synthesis problem. The stabilization task can be solved by a plain variety of methods depending on the complexity of the object model, particularly analytical methods of backstepping [15,16] or the analytical design of aggregated controllers [17], or synthesis based on the application of the Lyapunov function [18,19], as well as any classical methods for liner systems, such as modal control [20], differently tuned PID controllers [21], and fuzzy [22] and neural network [23] controllers. In the overwhelming majority of cases, the control synthesis problem is solved analytically or technically by taking into account the specific properties of the mathematical model. Today, modern numerical machine learning methods can be applied to find a solution for generic dynamic objects [24].

This new paradigm of machine learning control [25,26] allows to find some good near optimal solutions in a limited amount of time. However, due to the novelty of these methods, it becomes necessary to substantiate the results obtained by machine learning. In this paper, we introduce definitions of some machine properties of the system. We introduce the definition of machine learning control from our point of view, give machine proof of the existence of a specific property in some mathematical model, refine the definition of the feasibility property of the mathematical model of the control object and present the extended statement of the optimal control problem.

The addition of the stabilization system into the object model gives it a new property: at each moment of time, the object has a point of equilibrium. Thus, in the synthesized optimal control approach, the uncertainty in the right parts is compensated by the stability of the system relative to a point in the state space. Near the equilibrium point, all solutions converge. Now, we can solve the problem of optimal control through the optimal position of the equilibrium point. The found synthesized optimal control can be realized in the real object directly without additional feedback stabilization loops.

The paper is structured in the following order. After the introduction, the theoretical base of machine learning control is presented in Section 2, introducing the main definitions and machine criteria for justification of the results received by machine numerical methods. Next, in Section 3, we formulate the mathematical statement of the problem of feedback machine learning control, extending the optimal control problem statement with additional requirements. Then in Section 4, the paper proposes a synthesized approach to the solution of the stated feedback optimal control problem. Algorithms for its solution are considered in Sections 5 and 6, and computational examples of solving control problems for mobile robots are presented in Section 7. In the experimental part, the computational examples of synthesized control application for solving feedback control problems in the class of feasible controls for mobile robots are presented.

2. Theoretical Base of Machine Learning Control

Summarizing various definitions of machine learning [27–29], we can conclude that machine learning is an inexact numerical solution of some mathematical optimization problem, that is, the solution obtained by machine learning differs from the exact one by some known value but satisfies the researcher, and it can be improved with continuing learning. In all cases, different optimization algorithms are used for machine learning, but for these algorithms, it is enough to find a near optimal solution.

Let us introduce some definitions.

Definition 1. *The machine learning problem is a search of an unknown function.*

$$\mathbf{y} = \alpha(\mathbf{x}, \mathbf{q}), \tag{1}$$

where $\mathbf{y}$ is a vector of function values, $\mathbf{y} \in \mathbb{R}^r$, $\mathbf{x}$ is a vector of arguments, $\mathbf{x} \in \mathbb{R}^n$, $\mathbf{q}$ is a vector of constant parameters, $\mathbf{q} \in Q \subseteq \mathbb{R}^p$,

$$\alpha(\mathbf{x}, \mathbf{q}) : \mathbb{R}^n \times \mathbb{R}^p \to \mathbb{R}^r. \tag{2}$$

This function during training approximates some data set, which is called the training sample:

$$J = \sum_{i=0}^{N} \|\hat{\mathbf{y}}^i - \alpha(\mathbf{x}^i, \mathbf{q})\|, \tag{3}$$

where $\hat{Y} = \{\hat{\mathbf{y}}^1, \ldots, \hat{\mathbf{y}}^N\}$ is a training sample.

With unsupervised learning, this function is used for the minimization of some functional

$$J = \int_0^{t_f} f_0(\mathbf{x}(t), \alpha(\mathbf{x}(t), \mathbf{q})) dt, \tag{4}$$

where t_f is the goal achievement time.

Definition 2. *Machine learning is finding a solution of the optimization problem in the given Δ neighborhood of the optimal solution.*

The peculiarity of machine learning is that learning does not require the exact achievement of minimum criterion (3) or (4):

$$J_1 \leq \min J + \Delta^*, \tag{5}$$

where Δ^* is a given positive value determining a functional value achievable during learning. For criterion (3), a minimum value is equal to zero. For criterion (4), the minimal value can be unknown. Then, the limit minimum value can be used instead:

$$J_1 = J^- + \Delta^*, \tag{6}$$

where $J^- \leq \min J$.

If, as a result of learning, the found function (1) must acquire some properties, then the proof of the presence of these properties is confirmed by simulation.

$$J_2 = \sum_{i=0}^{K} \vartheta(\phi(\alpha(\mathbf{x}^i, \mathbf{q}))), \tag{7}$$

where $\vartheta(z)$ is the Heaviside function

$$\vartheta(z) = \begin{cases} 1, \text{ if } z > 0 \\ 0, \text{ otherwise} \end{cases}, \tag{8}$$

$\phi(\mathbf{x}, \mathbf{q})$ is a condition that determines whether a function property exists

$$\phi(\mathbf{x}, \mathbf{q}) \leq 0, \tag{9}$$

where K is a number of consecutive experiments performed with a positive result (9), set to prove the presence of a property.

Definition 3. *Machine learning control is a search of control function.*

Machine learning searches for a function that, for some sets of arguments, returns the required values. Note that there can be many such functions, and all they can have various structures and parameter values.

According to the introduced Definitions 1–3, an optimization problem of the control function search must be formulated for machine learning control. A solution of this problem is not optimal, as the found function gives a value of the quality criterion close to optimal one. On the one hand, this might reduce the importance of the solution found, but on the other hand, it allows for solving very complex problems.

Let us be given a mathematical model of a control object. This model can be derived from physical laws or identified by some machine learning technique [30,31]. Generally, this model is described by a system of ordinary differential equations with a free control vector in the right-hand side:

$$\dot{\mathbf{x}} = \mathbf{f}(\mathbf{x}, \mathbf{u}), \tag{10}$$

where $\mathbf{x}$ is a state vector, $\mathbf{u}$ is a control vector,

$$\begin{aligned} \mathbf{x} &= [x_1 \ldots x_n]^T, \\ \mathbf{u} &= [u_1 \ldots u_m]^T,\ m \le n, \\ \mathbf{f}(\mathbf{x}, \mathbf{u}) &= [f_1(\mathbf{x}, \mathbf{u}) \ldots f_n(\mathbf{x}, \mathbf{u})]^T. \end{aligned} \tag{11}$$

The problem of control, including machine learning control, is to find a control function instead of the control vector

$$\mathbf{u} = \mathbf{h}(\mathbf{x}), \tag{12}$$

to make the differential equation system

$$\dot{\mathbf{x}} = \mathbf{f}(\mathbf{x}, \mathbf{h}(\mathbf{x})), \tag{13}$$

acquire some new properties. For example, these can be such properties as stability, the optimality of solutions, and others.

In machine learning, the control function of these new properties of the control object has to be checked by a computer as well.

When the control function is derived analytically, then the system is guaranteed to have the desired property. In the case of machine learning control, events occur when the system does not have the desired property. Let us call them bad events. For example, the robot reaches the terminal position from almost all initial conditions, but does not reach it from some other initial condition. Although such events are rare with good training, they can occur, and the probability of its occurrence is not known. We also need to introduce some estimate when we can consider that the probability of the bad event is small, and we can consider learning to be successful, i.e., assume that the system has obtained the desired property.

The appearance of bad events is due to the presence of various uncertainties and disturbances in the system. According to Lyapunov [32], the existing uncertainties can be considered uncertainties in the initial conditions.

Let us formulate a machine criterion of obtaining some property by a differential equation system. To define the property of the whole system (13), it is enough to set a quantity K of partial solutions that obtain this property.

Definition 4. *If D experiments are carried out and in every i experiment, K_i partial solutions of the differential equation perform the required property from any $M_i \ge K_i$ randomly selected initial conditions from the initial domain, and*

$$\lim_{D \to \infty} \sum_{i=1}^{D} \frac{K_i}{M_i} \to 1, \tag{14}$$

the existence of this property for the differential equation in this domain is proven by machine.

In other words, as the number of experiments increases, the probability of such a bad event, when the system does not have the desired property, tends to zero. From a mathematical point of view, this means that all private solutions for the domain of initial conditions have this property, except solutions for a subset of a zero measure.

Now we can redefine some properties of differential equations into appropriate machine properties.

Let the computer check the new properties in terminal time interval, $(0; t^+)$.

Let, in the state space of differential equation system (13), a manifold of the dimension $n - s$ be defined by

$$\phi_i(\mathbf{x}) = 0,\ i = 1, \ldots, s. \tag{15}$$

Definition 5. In some domain $X \in \mathbb{R}^n$, the following properties are performed: for given quantity K of initial conditions $\mathbf{x}^{0,i} \in X$, $i = 1, \ldots, K$ for the partial solution $\mathbf{x}(t, \mathbf{x}^{0,i})$ of differential Equation (13) $\exists t'$, $0 < t' \leq t^+$. Then,

$$\|\phi(\mathbf{x}(t', \mathbf{x}^{0,i}))\| \leq \Delta, \ i = 1, \ldots, K, \tag{16}$$

where $\phi(\mathbf{x}) = [\phi_1(\mathbf{x}) \ldots \phi_s(\mathbf{x})]^T$, and $\forall t' < t \leq t^+$

$$\|\phi(\mathbf{x}(t, \mathbf{x}^{0,i}))\| < \Delta, \ i = 1, \ldots, K. \tag{17}$$

Then, differential equation system (13) is machine stable on a bound time interval $(0; t^+)$ relative to the manifold (15).

If a dimension of the manifold equals to 0, then a machine stable equilibrium point is obtained. Coordinates of this point in the state space are determined from solving the algebraic equation system,

$$\phi_i(\mathbf{x}) = 0, \ i = 1, \ldots, n. \tag{18}$$

The definition of machine stability uses a manifold (15) that can be expressed from the partial solution. Let $\mathbf{x}(t, \mathbf{x}^0)$ be a partial solution of differential Equation (13):

$$\mathbf{x}(t, \mathbf{x}^0) = [\tilde{x}_1(t) \ldots \tilde{x}_n(t)]^T. \tag{19}$$

Let us solve one component (19) relative to t. Let it be the last component:

$$t = \omega(\tilde{x}_n). \tag{20}$$

After inserting Equation (20) in solution (19), a one-dimensional manifold is received:

$$x_i(\omega(\tilde{x}_n), \mathbf{x}^0) - \tilde{x}_i(\omega(\tilde{x}_n)) = 0, \ i = 1, \ldots, n-1. \tag{21}$$

Machine stability relative to the manifold (21) is the machine stability of solution (19) of differential Equation (13).

Now consider the equilibrium points of some generic differential equation:

$$\dot{\mathbf{x}} = \mathbf{w}(\mathbf{x}), \tag{22}$$

where $\mathbf{x} \in \mathbb{R}^n$, $\mathbf{w}(\mathbf{x}) : \mathbb{R}^n \to \mathbb{R}^n$.

Analytically, the equilibrium points are defined as solutions of the system of algebraic equations:

$$\mathbf{w}(\mathbf{x}) = 0. \tag{23}$$

Machine-determined equilibrium points $\tilde{\mathbf{x}}^1, \ldots, \tilde{\mathbf{x}}^K$ are the points that satisfy the following condition:

$$\|\mathbf{w}(\tilde{\mathbf{x}}^i)\| \leq \varepsilon_1 \tag{24}$$

and $\forall \tilde{\mathbf{x}}^i, \tilde{\mathbf{x}}^j, i \neq j$,

$$\|\tilde{\mathbf{x}}^i - \tilde{\mathbf{x}}^j\| > \varepsilon_1, i, j \in \{1, \ldots, K\}, \tag{25}$$

where ε_1 is a given small positive number.

Definition 6. An equilibrium point $\tilde{\mathbf{x}} \in \mathbb{R}^n$ of differential Equation (22) is stable if there is a domain $X_0 \subseteq \mathbb{R}^n$, $\tilde{\mathbf{x}} \subset X_0$ such that it contains a sphere S

$$\sum_{i=1}^{n}(x_i - \tilde{x}_i)^2 = r^2, \tag{26}$$

where $r > \varepsilon_1$ is located completely in this domain $X_0 \, S \subset X_0$, and $\forall \mathbf{x}^0 \in S$, a partial solution $\mathbf{x}(t, \mathbf{x}^0)$ of differential Equation (22), will reach the point $\mathbf{x} \in S$ for limited time

$$\|\mathbf{x}(t_f, \mathbf{x}^0) - \tilde{\mathbf{x}}\| \leq \varepsilon_1, \tag{27}$$

where $t_f < t^+ < \infty$.

The sphere is introduced here in order to guarantee that the equilibrium point is inside the region and exclude it from falling on the boundary.

The introduced machine interpretations of the known properties of objects eliminate the need to analytically prove the existence of these properties for an object since this is often very laborious or completely impossible. This allows further solving complex technical problems by machine methods and checking the achievement of the required properties by machine.

3. Machine Learning Feedback Control

Recall our goal. We want to automate the design of an automatic control system. For this purpose, it is necessary to formulate for the computer the control problem and make the computer solve it automatically and design a control system for a control object without human.

To do this, let us formulate the problem in a general mathematical setting of optimal control.

The mathematical model of the control object is given in the form of differential equation system (10).

The initial condition is given:

$$\mathbf{x}(0) = \mathbf{x}^0 \in \mathbb{R}^n. \tag{28}$$

Given the terminal position as a goal,

$$\mathbf{x}^f = [x_1^f \ldots x_n^f]^T. \tag{29}$$

The quality criterion is given in the form of an integral functional:

$$J_1 = \int_0^{t_f} f_0(\mathbf{x}, \mathbf{u}) dt \to \min. \tag{30}$$

It is necessary to find a control function in the form

$$\mathbf{u} = \mathbf{g}(\mathbf{x}, t). \tag{31}$$

where $\mathbf{g}(\mathbf{x}, t) = [g_1(\mathbf{x}, 1) \ldots g_m(\mathbf{x}, t)]^T$, which makes object (10) achieve given goal (29) with the optimal value of quality criterion (30). A found control function (31) has to satisfy the boundaries:

$$u_i^- \leq g_i(\mathbf{x}, t) \leq u_i^+, \quad i = 1, \ldots, m. \tag{32}$$

We are looking for control as a function of the state of the object, which corresponds to the principle of feedback control. It is generally accepted that this type of control is implemented in real systems since it allows leveling the inaccuracies of the model.

Definition 7. *For a mathematical model to correspond to a dynamic real object, it is necessary and sufficient that the mathematical estimation error of the real object state does not increase over time.*

That is, the introduction of the feedback control to the differential equation system gives the system some property that allows the object to achieve the goal with the optimal quality value, that is, to be feasible. The question is, what is this property?

It is clear that not all control systems are feasible. For example, optimal but open-loop control systems do not have the feasibility property. Conversely, Lyapunov-stable systems are feasible. However, there are examples when the solution is not Lyapunov stable but at the same time it is feasible [32]. For example, when moving through points, the movement itself to a point is Lyapunov stable, but movement along a trajectory consisting of points is not Lyapunov stable, but this control is now most often implemented. Thus, it becomes necessary to formulate a property that makes it possible to determine the feasibility of the system.

In fact, by introducing a feedback system, we change the differential equations of the system so that a certain area appears around some particular solution of the system (the optimal trajectory) such that other trajectories that fall into this area will not leave it.

This trajectory is a partial solution of differential equation

$$\dot{\mathbf{x}} = \mathbf{f}(\mathbf{x}, \mathbf{g}(\mathbf{x}, t)) \tag{33}$$

for the found optimal control.

Definition 8. *The partial solution* $\mathbf{x}(t, \mathbf{x}^0)$ *of differential Equation (22) has a compressibility property if, for any other partial solution* $\mathbf{x}(t, \mathbf{x}^*)$, *the following conditions are performed.*
If

$$\|\mathbf{x}(t', \mathbf{x}^0) - \mathbf{x}(t', \mathbf{x}^*)\| \leq \sigma, \tag{34}$$

where $t' > 0$, $\sigma > 0$, *then* $\exists \alpha > 0$ *such, that for any* $\varepsilon^+ > 0$

$$\|\mathbf{x}(t' + \alpha, \mathbf{x}^0) - \mathbf{x}(t' + \alpha, \mathbf{x}^*)\| \leq \varepsilon^+. \tag{35}$$

Hypothesis 1. *To realize the found optimal control function (31) in the real control object, the optimal trajectory must compressibility properties (34) and (35).*

Obviously, if a control function provides performing properties (34) and (35), then this control function according to Definition 8 can be realized in the real object directly. According to Definition 8, an unstable differential equation cannot be realized. Highly unstable systems exist, but they cannot be described by unstable differential equations because these differential equations cannot estimate the state of unstable objects in time. Any small error in the initial conditions for the unstable differential equation of a mathematical model will be increasing over time. To estimate the state of an unstable object, it is necessary to use a stable differential equation.

Thus, to solve the stated feedback optimal control problem, it is necessary to construct such a control function (31) that makes the object (10) achieve given goal (29) with the optimal value of quality criterion (30) and obtain required properties (34) and (35).

4. Synthesized Optimal Control Approach for the Solution of the Stated Problem

In this section, we propose our synthesized optimal control approach [33] that completely satisfies requirements (34) and (35) in the construction of optimal control (31).

The idea of the approach consists in providing the object with the existence of some equilibrium point in the state space and then constructing such a control function that controls the position of the equilibrium point in order to make the object reach the goal with the optimal value of the quality criterion.

Initially, the control synthesis problem is solved to provide the existence of the equilibrium point. As a result, the control function in the following form is found:

$$u = h(x^* - x), \qquad (36)$$

where x^* in each fixed moment of time is some point in the state space that affects the position of the equilibrium point of the differential equation:

$$\dot{x} = f(x, h(x^* - x)), \qquad (37)$$

$$h(x^* - x) = [h_1(x^* - x) \ldots h_m(x^* - x)]^T. \qquad (38)$$

The control function (38) must satisfy restrictions for any position of the point x^*

$$u_i^- \leq h_i(x^* - x) \leq u_i^+, \quad i = 1, \ldots, m. \qquad (39)$$

For any value x^*, the differential equation system (37) has an equilibrium point $\tilde{x}(x^*)$:

$$f(\tilde{x}(x^*), h(x^* - \tilde{x}(x^*))) = 0. \qquad (40)$$

A matrix of Jacobi

$$A(x^*) = \frac{\partial f(x, x^* - x)}{\partial x}, \qquad (41)$$

computed in the equilibrium point $\tilde{x}(x^*)$ has all eigenvalues in the left part of the complex plane.

$$\det(A(x^*) - \lambda E) = \prod_{i=1}^{n}(\lambda - \lambda_j) = 0, \qquad (42)$$

where

$$\lambda_j = \alpha_j + i\beta_j, \qquad (43)$$

$\alpha_j < 0, j = 1, \ldots, n, i = \sqrt{-1}$.

In many cases, the equilibrium point $\tilde{x}$ coincides with the point x^*, but in some cases, it is impossible. For example, if the differential equation system includes an equation $\dot{x}_k = x_l$, then the component x_k of the equilibrium point will have only value 0 for any values of components x_k^*.

Note that when this control synthesis problem is solved by some machine learning method, conditions (41) and (42) cannot be checked for each mathematical expression $h(x^* - x)$ of the control function because these are very time-consuming procedures. In machine learning control, to prove the stability in an equilibrium point, Definition 6 is used.

To synthesize control function (36), it is necessary to determine domain $X \in \mathbb{R}^n$ and then to determine equilibrium point $\tilde{x}$. If the equilibrium point is equal to point x^*, then the control function is searched in the form of (36), where $x^* = \tilde{x}$.

Computationally, to provide a stable property of equilibrium point $\tilde{x}$, the synthesis problem (10)–(12) is solved with the terminal point $x^f = \tilde{x}$, the initial domain $X_0 \subset X$, and the quality criterion

$$J = \max\{t_{f,1}, \ldots, t_{f,K}\} + a_1 \sum_{i=1}^{K} \Delta_{f,i} \to \min, \qquad (44)$$

where a_1 is the weight coefficient,

$$\Delta_{f,i} = \left\| x^f - x(t_{f,i}, x^{0,i}) \right\|, \qquad (45)$$

where $t_{f,i}$ is the time of achievement of the terminal position (29) from the initial condition $x^{0,i}$ of the set of initial conditions $X_0 = \{x^{0,1}, \ldots, x^{0,K}\}, i \in \{1, \ldots, K\}$,

$$t_{f,i} = \begin{cases} t, & \text{if } t < t^+ \text{ and } \Delta_{f,i} \leq \varepsilon \\ t^+ & \text{otherwise} \end{cases}, \tag{46}$$

where t^+ and ε are given positive values, $\mathbf{x}(t, \mathbf{x}^{0,i})$ is a partial solution of the system

$$\dot{\mathbf{x}} = \mathbf{f}(\mathbf{x}, \mathbf{h}(\mathbf{x}^f - \mathbf{x})), \tag{47}$$

for initial conditions $\mathbf{x}(t_0) = \mathbf{x}^{0,i}, i \in \{1, \ldots, K\}$,

$$\left\| \mathbf{x}^f - \mathbf{x} \right\| = \sqrt{\sum_{i=1}^{n} (x_i^f - x_i)^2}. \tag{48}$$

In the second stage, the following optimal control problem is solved. The mathematical model of the control object is given in the form of (37), and the initial conditions are given as (28). It is necessary to find control as a function of time:

$$\mathbf{x}^* = \mathbf{v}^*(t), \tag{49}$$

in order to minimize the functional

$$J_2 = \int_0^{t_f} f_0(\mathbf{x}, \mathbf{x}^* - \mathbf{x}) dt \to \min_{\mathbf{x}^* \in X}. \tag{50}$$

The obtained control

$$\mathbf{u} = \mathbf{g}(\mathbf{x}, t) = \mathbf{h}(\mathbf{v}^*(t) - \mathbf{x}) \tag{51}$$

allows performing conditions (34) and (35); therefore, it can be realized in the real object.

Further in the paper, we discuss the machine learning methods appropriate to solve the described problems and show the examples of applying the proposed approach to the solution of two different robotic tasks.

5. Symbolic Regression for Machine Learning

According to the introduced Definitions 1, 2 and 3, the task of searching for the needed control function (36) in the first step is to be considered a machine learning task.

A search of an unknown function consists in searching for the structure and parameters of this function. Usually structures of the functions are set by a researcher on the base of data analysis, experience, or intuition. Today different universal structures become popular such as various mathematical series and artificial neural networks. If a structure of the needed function is set, then machine learning searches for the optimal values of parameters according to some criterion [34].

An ML technique such as symbolic regression allows to look for the optimal structure of the needed function and parameters as well [35].

Symbolic regression methods have made huge strides over the past decade and recently, the importance of interpretable machine learning has been recognized by the wider scientific community. However, to a greater extent, symbolic regression methods are used for so-called supervised machine learning, when there are some data that need to be approximated [36–39].

The considered problem of machine learning for control does not have a training set, and the search for a control function must be based on minimizing the quality criterion. This approach, in conventional terminology, refers to unsupervised learning. In this direction, there are much fewer examples due to the complexity of the search. In [40–42], the control functions are searched as linear combinations of basic functions, and mainly smooth functions are used as basic functions. We perform the control function search [43,44] in the form of function nesting, which allows to obtain more complex mathematical expressions, and also use a wider set of basic functions, including discontinuous functions.

All symbolic regression methods code the searched mathematical expression in the form of special code and search for the optimal solutionon the space of codes by a special genetic algorithm. For this purpose, a special crossover operation is developed. The application of a special crossover operation for two codes of parents allows to receive two new codes of child chromosomes. Different crossover operations are used for different code forms.

A complex crossover operation in symbolic regression methods, in our opinion, makes it difficult to find a solution. Creating new possible solutions as a result of a complex crossover operation is similar to generating new possible solutions. Therefore, the search process does not use the properties of evolution and is more like a random search. In order for the search algorithms of symbolic regression methods to have metaheuristic evolutionary properties, it is necessary that new possible solutions obtained by transforming existing possible solutions have the property of inheritance.

Definition 9. *The evolutionary algorithm has an inheritance property, if among the new possible solutions obtained, as a result of the evolutionary transformations of existing possible solutions, named parents, at least a given part of the new possible solutions have functional values, which differ from the functional values of the parents by not more than a given value.*

A universal approach to provide the inheritance property to any symbolic regression algorithm is using the principle of small variations of the basic solution [45]. The application of this principle makes it possible to find solutions that are close to optimal in a reasonable time.

In [24], this principle was applied to Cartesian genetic programming, and it improved the search process of the optimal solution. In the present paper, in the experimental part, the network operator method [46] is used, which was developed exactly for the solution of the control synthesis problem and was the first method where the principle of small variations was applied.

6. Hybrid Algorithm for Optimal Control Problem

The second step of the proposed approach (49) is essentially a pure optimization problem. Today, most generic optimization algorithms are based on population search [47], and so we also use them as a main technique, but according to the task, any other optimization algorithm can also be appropriate.

For the most complex optimal control problems with complex phase constraints, we propose to use a hybrid algorithm that combines GA [48], GWO [49] and PSO [50]. As we experimentally noticed, such a combination of the evolutionary algorithms allows to avoid the local minimum in complex tasks. A pseudocode of the algorithm can be found in Appendix A.

7. Computational Experiment

To demonstrate the proposed synthesized approach for the machine learning feedback control problem solution, let us consider two different optimal control tasks with mobile robots in complex environments with phase constraints.

7.1. Two Mobile Robots with Bottlenecks Phase Constraints

The first task we considered was to make two robots switch places with each other while accurately passing through the given areas, as if through bottlenecks.

The mathematical model of the control object has the following form:

$$\begin{aligned}
\dot{x}_1 &= 0.5(u_1 + u_2)\cos(x_3), \\
\dot{x}_2 &= 0.5(u_1 + u_2)\sin(x_3), \\
\dot{x}_3 &= 0.5(u_1 - u_2), \\
\dot{x}_4 &= 0.5(u_3 + u_4)\cos(x_6), \\
\dot{x}_5 &= 0.5(u_3 + u_4)\sin(x_6), \\
\dot{x}_6 &= 0.5(u_3 - u_4),
\end{aligned} \qquad (52)$$

where x_1, x_2, and x_3 are coordinates of the state vector of the first mobile robot, x_4, x_5, and x_6 are coordinates of the state vector of the second mobile robot, u_1 and u_2 are components of the control vector for the first robot, and u_3 and u_4 are components of the control vector for the second robot.

The values of control are limited:

$$-10 = u_i^- \le u_i \le u_i^+ = 10, \quad i = 1, 2, 3, 4. \qquad (53)$$

The initial and terminal conditions are given:

$$\mathbf{x}(0) = \mathbf{x}^0 = [0\ 0\ 0\ 10\ 10\ 0]^T, \qquad (54)$$

$$\mathbf{x}(t_f) = \mathbf{x}^f = [10\ 10\ 0\ 0\ 0\ 0]^T. \qquad (55)$$

The quality functional is given:

$$J_3 = t_f + p_1 \|\mathbf{x}^f - \mathbf{x}(t_f)\| + p_2 \int_0^{t_f} \vartheta(\chi(\mathbf{x}))dt + p_3 \sum_{i=1}^{k_g} \sum_{j=1}^{2} \vartheta(\Delta_{i,j} - \varepsilon_i) \to \min, \qquad (56)$$

where

$$t_f = \begin{cases} t, \text{ if } t < t^+, \text{ and } \|\mathbf{x}^f - \mathbf{x}(t_f)\| < \varepsilon_0 \\ t^+, \text{ otherwise} \end{cases}, \qquad (57)$$

$$\chi(\mathbf{x}) = r_0 - \sqrt{(x_1 - x_4)^2 + (x_2 - x_5)^2}, \qquad (58)$$

$\vartheta(\alpha)$ is a Heaviside step function

$$\vartheta(\alpha) = \begin{cases} 1, \text{ if } \alpha \ge 0 \\ 0, \text{ otherwise} \end{cases}, \qquad (59)$$

$$\Delta_{i,j} = \min_t \sqrt{(x_{1+(j-1)3} - y_1^i)^2 + (x_{2+(j-1)3} - y_2^i)^2}, \qquad (60)$$

$r_0 = 2$, $k_g = 4$, $\varepsilon_i = 0.1$, $i = 1,2,3,4$, $y_1^1 = 4$, $y_2^1 = 2$, $y_1^2 = 6$, $y_2^2 = 4$, $y_1^3 = 4$, $y_2^3 = 6$, $y_1^4 = 6$, $y_2^4 = 8$, $p_1 = 4$, $p_2 = 3$, $p_3 = 4$, $\varepsilon_0 = 0.01$, $t^+ = 4.8$.

In the first stage, according to the proposed approach, the control synthesis problem is solved in order to provide the existence of the equilibrium point.

The stabilization system was received by the network operator method. As far as the received expressions of the control function, both the encoded and decoded forms are too long, so we place them into the Appendix B.

In the second stage, it is necessary to solve the optimal control problem and to find the control function in the form of piece-wise constant control function

$$\mathbf{x}^* = \mathbf{x}^{*,i}, \ (i-1)\Delta t \le t < i\Delta t, \tag{61}$$

where $i = 1, \ldots, K$, Δt is a time interval, $\Delta t = 0.6$, and K is the number of time intervals

$$K = \left\lfloor \frac{t^+}{\Delta t} \right\rfloor = \left\lfloor \frac{4.8}{0.6} \right\rfloor = 8. \tag{62}$$

To solve the optimal control problem and find $\mathbf{x}^{*,i}, i = 1, \ldots, 8$, the described hybrid algorithm was used. The following optimal solution was found:

$$\begin{aligned}
\mathbf{x}^{*,1} &= [5.4629\ 0.8503\ -0.0834\ 5.5730\ 7.4134\ -0.2191]^T, \\
\mathbf{x}^{*,2} &= [8.0879\ 4.6283\ -0.1367\ 2.7272\ 4.3233\ -04311]^T, \\
\mathbf{x}^{*,3} &= [6.6929\ 4.2258\ -1.4392\ 1.1911\ 7.7361\ 0.2100]^T, \\
\mathbf{x}^{*,4} &= [1.8651\ 7.0765\ -0.0173\ 6.6029\ 2.6080\ 0.1310]^T, \\
\mathbf{x}^{*,5} &= [3.6284\ 4.0688\ 0.3204\ 0.7814\ 9.4491\ -0.1612]^T, \\
\mathbf{x}^{*,6} &= [8.4951\ 8.4002\ 0.3134\ 1.0557\ 0.7920\ 0.7306]^T, \\
\mathbf{x}^{*,7} &= [7.7752\ 9.9316\ -0.0237\ 1.6134\ 1.9251\ 0.0495]^T, \\
\mathbf{x}^{*,8} &= [10.0465\ 9.8035\ 0.1303\ -1.0000\ 0.0051\ 0.2369]^T.
\end{aligned} \tag{63}$$

Optimal trajectories on horizontal plane for robots are presented in Figure 1.

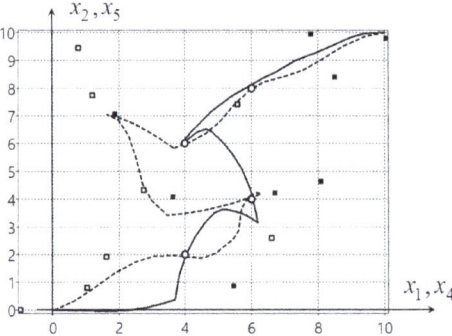

Figure 1. Optimal trajectories of robots for synthesized control

In the Figure 1 the solid black line is a trajectory of the first robot, the dash line is a trajectory of the second robot, the small circles are the bottlenecks, the small black squares are the optimal control points (63) for the first robot, and the small white squares are the optimal control points (63) for the second robot. The optimal value of the functional (56) is 4.8347.

For comparison, the optimal control problem (52)–(60) was solved by the direct approach of optimal control. For this purpose, the time axis was divided on $\tilde{K}$ intervals. The control function is found in the form of the piece-wise linear function

$$u_j = \begin{cases} u_j^+ = 10, & \text{if } \hat{u}_i > u_i^+ \\ u_j^- = -10, & \text{if } \hat{u}_i < u_i^- \\ \hat{u}_j, & \text{otherwise} \end{cases}, j = 1,2,3,4, \tag{64}$$

where

$$\hat{u}_j = (q_{i+(j-1)\tilde{K}+1} - q_{i+(j-1)\tilde{K}}) \frac{t - (i-1)\tilde{\Delta} t}{\tilde{\Delta} t} + q_{i+(j-1)\tilde{K}} \tag{65}$$

where $j = 1, 2, 3, 4$, $j = 1, \ldots, \tilde{K}$, $\tilde{\Delta}t$ is a time interval, $\tilde{\Delta}t = 0.2$,

$$\tilde{K} = \left\lfloor \frac{t^+}{\tilde{\Delta}t} \right\rfloor = \left\lfloor \frac{4.8}{0.2} \right\rfloor = 24. \tag{66}$$

In total, it is necessary to find 96 parameters, $\mathbf{q} = [q_1 \ldots q_{96}]^T$. The problem was very difficult for many evolutionary algorithms. The most successful in solving this problem was the described hybrid evolutionary algorithm.

In the result, the following solution was obtained:

$$\begin{aligned}\mathbf{q} = &\ [3.6515\ -5.6155\ -5.8103\ -4.1722\ -3.1398\ -5.4711\ 0.0936\\ &\ 6.6150\ 2.6432\ -8.8133\ -2.4498\ -18.5059\ -9.5896\ 0.1931\\ &\ -5.5797\ -14.2516\ 9.5304\ 0.2181\ 0.6002\ -11.9435\ -12.2196\\ &\ -0.0127\ -19.4712\ 8.8589\ 5.5695\ 8.4877\ 5.6459\ 0.7054\ -3.6582\\ &\ -8.0966\ -0.6840\ -8.6774\ 7.7892\ -5.6366\ -5.3715\ -4.8317\\ &\ -16.6047\ -19.8104\ -14.9474\ 7.6756\ 4.7000\ 9.7919\ -14.6483\\ &\ -3.5860\ -3.1178\ -9.7188\ -16.2048\ -15.9328\ -1.3150\ 1.9570\\ &\ -10.2673\ -0.5094\ -6.4163\ -4.9303\ -3.7649\ -6.3955\\ &\ -5.8384\ -15.8273\ -9.2860\ -0.1217\ 9.0490\ -3.0543\ 0.8906\\ &\ 7.6340\ 10.8459\ 10.2492\ 3.4207\ -10.6311\ -4.9477\ -3.4041\\ &\ -13.6140\ -15.2029\ 4.8782\ -10.4763\ -10.5894\ 6.4966\ -4.2872\\ &\ -12.7573\ -8.2174\ -0.8267\ -14.1822\ -1.6810\ -15.3973\ 12.1957\\ &\ 15.4694\ 10.3573\ -12.7840\ 7.9684\ -6.3937\ 17.4171\ -6.6234\ 1.3378\\ &\ -8.2870\ -0.2343\ -18.0791\ -5.3433]^T.\end{aligned} \tag{67}$$

The functional value is 4.8132. The optimal trajectories on the horizontal plane are presented in Figure 2.

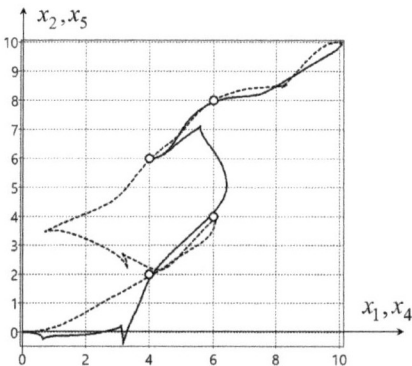

Figure 2. Optimal trajectories of robots for direct control.

To analyze the received results, these optimal control functions were tested for the mathematical model with perturbations:

$$\begin{aligned}\dot{x}_1 &= 0.5(u_1 + u_2)\cos(x_3) + \beta\xi(t),\\ \dot{x}_2 &= 0.5(u_1 + u_2)\sin(x_3) + \beta\xi(t),\\ \dot{x}_3 &= 0.5(u_1 - u_2) + \beta\xi(t),\\ \dot{x}_4 &= 0.5(u_3 + u_4)\cos(x_6) + \beta\xi(t),\\ \dot{x}_5 &= 0.5(u_3 + u_4)\sin(x_6) + \beta\xi(t),\\ \dot{x}_6 &= 0.5(u_3 - u_4) + \beta\xi(t),\end{aligned} \tag{68}$$

where $\xi(t)$ is a function that returns a random number from diapason $(-1;\ 1)$ at every call, and β is a constant value.

For the system (68), disturbances were also introduced into the initial conditions

$$x_i(0) = x_i^0 + \beta_0 \xi, \ i = 1, \ldots, 6, \quad (69)$$

where β_0 is a constant value. The results of the tests are presented in Table 1. For every disturbance, 10 tests were performed. In Table 1, J_3 is an average functional value for synthesized control, $\sigma(J_3)$ is a standard deviation for values J_3, J_4 is an average functional value for direct control, and $\sigma(J_4)$ is a standard deviation for values J_4.

Table 1. Functional values for perturbed control object model.

β_0	β	J_3	$\sigma(J_3)$	J_4	$\sigma(J_4)$
0	0	4.8347	0	4.8132	0
0	0.01	4.9999	0.1989	4.9267	0.1462
0	0.02	5.0868	0.288	5.1706	0.2559
0	0.05	5.3896	0.2087	6.1610	1.0704
0.01	0	5.2286	0.2053	6.5891	0.9445
0.02	0	5.4569	0.266	7.2853	1.6878
0.05	0	5.7369	0.6871	13.4286	3.5257
0.01	0.01	5.2365	0.2861	6.4381	0.9502
0.1	0	6.2945	0.7365	19.8192	8.0565

As the test results show, synthesized control is much less susceptible to perturbations of the mathematical model and the initial conditions than direct control. Direct optimal control is the most sensitive to disturbances of initial conditions. Even the smallest disturbances of the initial conditions make direct control unacceptable. The results show that the synthesized control obtains the compression property, and it is feasible in real systems.

7.2. Synthesized Control for Omni-Mecanum-Wheeled Robot

A mecanum robot has special wheels that allow it to move under a direct angle to its direction of axis without any turns [51]. In Figure 3, an example of a mecanum robot is shown.

Figure 3. Omni-mecanum-wheeled robot.

Consider the optimal control problem, where two identical mecanum robots have to swap their places in some area with obstacles and without collisions for a minimal amount of time.

The mathematical model of the control object is the following:

$$\begin{aligned}
\dot{x}_1 &= 0.25((u_1+u_4)(\cos(x_3)+\sin(x_3))+(u_2+u_3)(\cos(x_3)-\sin(x_3))), \\
\dot{x}_2 &= 0.25((u_1+u_4)(\sin(x_3)-\cos(x_3))+(u_2+u_3)(\cos(x_3)+\sin(x_3))), \\
\dot{x}_3 &= 0.25(-u_1+u_2-u_3+u_4)/(L_0+H_0), \\
\dot{x}_4 &= 0.25((u_5+u_8)(\cos(x_6)+\sin(x_6))+(u_6+u_7)(\cos(x_6)-\sin(x_6))), \\
\dot{x}_5 &= 0.25((u_5+u_8)(\sin(x_6)-\cos(x_6))+(u_6+u_7)(\cos(x_6)+\sin(x_6))), \\
\dot{x}_6 &= 0.25(-u_5+u_6-u_7+u_8)/(L_0+H_0),
\end{aligned} \qquad (70)$$

where x_1, x_2, and x_3 are the state vector coordinates of the first mecanum robot, x_4, x_5, and x_6 are the state vector coordinates of the second mecanum robot, u_1, u_2, u_3, and u_4 are components of the control vector of the first mecanum robot, u_5, u_6, u_7, and u_8 are components of the control vector of the first mecanum robot, and L_0 and H_0 are geometric parameters of the robots, $L_0 = 2$, $H_0 = 1$.

The control is restricted:

$$-10 = u_i^- \leq u_i \leq u_i^+ = 10, \ i=1,\ldots,8, \qquad (71)$$

where u_i^- and u_i^+ are given lower and upper limits for values of control, respectively, $i=1,\ldots,8$.

The initial state is given:

$$x(0) = x^0 = [0\ 0\ 0\ 10\ 10\ 0]^T. \qquad (72)$$

The terminal state is given:

$$x(t_f) = x^f = [10\ 10\ 0\ 0\ 0\ 0]^T, \qquad (73)$$

where t_f is the time of achievement of the terminal state. It is determined by Equation (57) with $\varepsilon_0 = 0.05$, $t^+ = 1.9$.

The quality criterion includes phase constraints and the accuracy of the terminal state achievement.

$$J = p_1 \|x^f - x(t_f)\| + \sum_{i=1}^{K} w_i \int_0^{t_f} \vartheta(\phi_i(x))dt + p_2 \int_0^{t_f} \vartheta(\chi(x))dt + t_f \to \min_{u}, \qquad (74)$$

where p_1 and p_1 are the penalty coefficient, where $p_1 = 3$ and $p_2 = 3$, w_i is a weight coefficient, $i=1,\ldots,K$, $K=8$, $\vartheta(\alpha)$ is a Heaviside step function (59), and $\chi(x)$ is determined by Equation (58):

$$\phi_i(x) = r_i - \sqrt{(x_1)-x_{1,i})^2 + (x_2-x_{2,i})^2}, \ i=1,2,3,4, \qquad (75)$$

$$\phi_i(x) = r_{i-4} - \sqrt{(x_4)-x_{1,i-4})^2 + (x_5-x_{2,i-4})^2}, \ i=5,6,7,8, \qquad (76)$$

$r_1 = 2$, $r_2 = 2.5$, $r_3 = 2.5$, $r_4 = 2$, $x_{1,1} = 2$, $x_{2,1} = 2$, $x_{1,2} = 8$, $x_{2,2} = 2$, $x_{1,3} = 2$, $x_{2,3} = 8$, $x_{1,4} = 8$, $x_{2,4} = 8$, $r_0 = 1$.

According to the synthesized method, initially, the feedback control synthesis problem is solved, such that the closed-loop control system is stable relative to some equilibrium point in the state space. For this purpose, again, the network operator method is used.

Since the robots are the same, we make the synthesis of the stabilization system for one robot, for example, the first robot.

In the result, the network operator method found the following control function:

$$u_i = \begin{cases} u_i^+, \text{ if } \tilde{u}_i \geq u_i^+ \\ u_i^-, \text{ if } \tilde{u}_i \leq u_i^- \\ \tilde{u}_i \text{otherwise} \end{cases}, \tag{77}$$

where

$$\tilde{u}_1 = D + \arctan(q_1 \Delta_1), \tag{78}$$

$$\tilde{u}_2 = \rho_{19}(\tilde{u}_1) + \rho_4(C) + \rho_{17}(B) + \text{sgn}(q_2\Delta_2 + q_1\Delta_1 + q_3\sqrt[3]{\Delta_3}) + \rho_{18}(q_2\Delta_2) + q_1\Delta_1 - (q_1\Delta_1)^3, \tag{79}$$

$$\tilde{u}_3 = \tilde{u}_2 + C^3 + A + \arctan(q_1) - (A + \arctan(q_1))^3 + \Delta_2^{-1}, \tag{80}$$

$$\tilde{u}_4 = \sin(\tilde{u}_3) + \rho_{16}(\tilde{u}_2) + (C + \sqrt[3]{\Delta_1})^3 + B + \vartheta(q_2\Delta_2 + q_1\Delta_1) + q_3\sqrt[3]{\Delta_3}, \tag{81}$$

$$A = \text{sgn}(q_2\Delta_2 + q_1\Delta_1 + q_3\sqrt[3]{\Delta_3}) + \vartheta(q_2\Delta_2 + q_1\Delta_1),$$

$$B = A + \arctan(q_1) + \text{sgn}(q_2\Delta_2 + q_1\Delta_1) + \arctan(q_1\Delta_1),$$

$$C = \cos(B) + \rho_4(q_2\Delta_2 + q_1\Delta_1) + \rho_{16}(\Delta_1) + \rho_{19}(q_1\Delta_1 + q_2\Delta_2) + \exp(q_1\Delta_1),$$

$$D = C + \sqrt[3]{\Delta_1} + C^3 + \rho_B - A - \arctan(q_1) + \rho_{16}(q_1\Delta_1),$$

$\Delta_1 = x_1^* - x_1, \Delta_2 = x_2^* - x_2, \Delta_3 = x_3^* - x_3, q_1 = 11.89282, q_2 = 10.15381, q_3 = 15.25903,$

$$\rho_4(\alpha) = \text{sgn}(\alpha)\sqrt{|\alpha|}, \rho_{16}(\alpha) = \begin{cases} \alpha, \text{ if } |\alpha| < 1 \\ \text{sgn}(\alpha), \text{ otherwise} \end{cases},$$

$$\rho_{17}(\alpha) = \text{sgn}(\alpha)\ln(|\alpha| + 1), \rho_{18}(\alpha) = \text{sgn}(\alpha)(\exp(|\alpha|) - 1),$$

$$\rho_{19}(\alpha) = \text{sgn}(\alpha)\exp(-|\alpha|).$$

For the second robot in the control function (77), it is necessary to replace $x_i, i = 1, 2, 3$ with $x_i, i = 4, 5, 6$, and $x_i^*, i = 1, 2, 3$, with $x_i^*, i = 4, 5, 6$, respectively.

Plots of the trajectories of the robot movement from four initial states are presented in Figure 4.

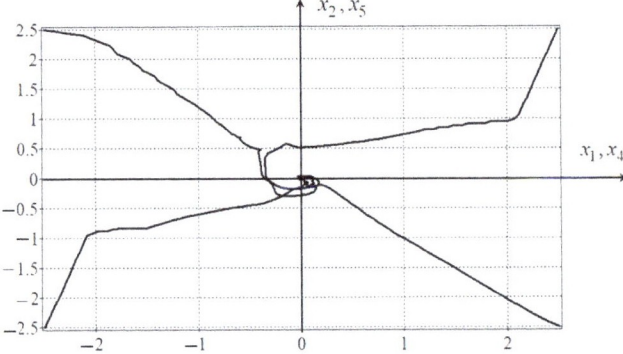

Figure 4. Trajectories on the horizontal plane for four initial states.

On the second stage, the optimal control problem (70)–(74) is solved for the closed loop control system with the control function (77). A control on the second stage is vector **x***, determining the position of the stable equilibrium point in the state space. For solving the optimal control problem, the time axis is divided on the intervals, and in each interval, a control function is approximated by a piece-wise constant function. The value of the interval is equal to $\Delta t = 0.19$.

$$x_i^* = x_i(t_j) = q_{i+(j-1)6}, \tag{82}$$

where $i = 1, \ldots, 6$, $t_j = (j-1)\Delta t$ $j = 1, \ldots, D$, D is the number of intervals,

$$D = \frac{t^+}{\Delta t} = \frac{1.9}{0.19} = 10. \tag{83}$$

In total, it was necessary to find an optimal vector with $10 \cdot 6 = 60$ parameters:

$$\mathbf{q} = [q_1 \ldots q_{60}]^T.$$

For solving the problem, the hybrid evolutionary algorithm was applied. The values of the parameters were restricted:

$$\begin{aligned}
-2.5 &= q_1^+ \leq q_{1+3(k-1)} \leq q_1^- = 2.5 \\
-2.5 &= q_2^+ \leq q_{2+3(k-1)} \leq q_2^- = 2.5 \\
-5\pi/12 &= q_2^+ \leq q_{3+3(k-1)} \leq q_2^- = 5\pi/12
\end{aligned}, \tag{84}$$

where $k = 1, \ldots, 20$.

The following solution was obtained:

$$\begin{aligned}
\mathbf{q} = [&-2.4862\ 2.0000\ 0.6231\ -2.1975\ -1.3799\ 0.7058\ -2.5000\ 1.9421 \\
&1.2094\ -0.6933\ -2.0088\ -0.3378\ 0.1956\ 1.7643\ 0.6378\ 1.4052 \\
&-2.4611\ -0.3230\ 1.7245\ 2.0000\ 0.8872\ 1.6769\ -1.2832\ -0.4372 \\
&0.5624\ 1.9987\ -1.1601\ 1.9452\ -1.8859\ 0.7357\ 1.6876\ 1.5024 \\
&0.0997\ 1.1642\ -1.3678\ 0.5321\ 1.6945\ 1.9946\ 0.5580\ 0.7886 \\
&-1.6027\ 1.3090\ 1.1795\ 1.5385\ -1.0798\ 0.6781\ -1.9975\ 0.0204 \\
&-0.8939\ 1.0578\ -0.4106\ -2.1003\ -1.2544\ -1.3090\ -2.5000\ 1.0746 \\
&-1.2216\ -2.0840\ -1.3344\ -0.8913]^T.
\end{aligned} \tag{85}$$

The optimal value of the functional (74) is $J = 1.923$.

Optimal trajectories on the horizontal plane of two robots are presented in Figure 5. The solid line is the trajectory of the first robot, the dash line is the trajectory of the second robot, the red circles are the phase constraints, the black small squares are projections of control **x*** on the horizontal plane for the first robot, and the white small squares are projections of control **x*** on the horizontal plane for the second robot.

Figure 5 shows very clearly, as in the previous example with bottlenecks, that the equilibrium points are located not on the trajectory of the robot, as is done with conventional stabilization, but outside the trajectory. By placing points on the trajectory, we can lose quality because when approaching the equilibrium point, the robot must slow down. Such an optimal arrangement of points ensures the optimal value of the functional.

In this example, we would like to note the following. It occurs that two components of the control vector are enough to control the mecanum robot. The other two components have limit values and do not change during the control process. This can be seen in the additional control plots presented in Appendix C. However, indeed, we noted that in the mathematical model of the mecanum robot (70), the control was redundant, $m > n$. So, the computer itself found a solution for how to proceed in this case, and in the solution found, the two components of control, in fact, do not participate in the search for the optimal solution. This is one of the more successful demonstrations of intelligent machine automation of the process of creating control systems.

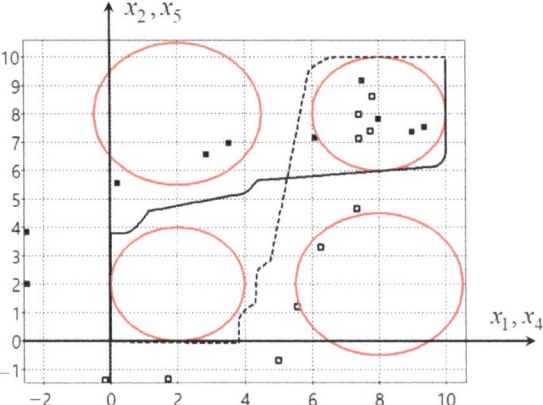

Figure 5. Optimal trajectories on the horizontal plane.

8. Discussion

In this work, we are laying the theoretical foundations of machine learning control. The main feature is that the machine proof of various properties is implemented experimentally basing on examples. In particular, this is what happens in neural networks, when experiments are carried out on a test sample to check whether the system achieves certain properties. We formulate several machine properties in the control system design. In the future, the proposed formal descriptions can be developed, new properties of systems can be considered, and quantitative probabilistic estimates can be given based on positive test results.

An important result of the work is the expansion of the formulation of the optimal control problem and the introduction of additional requirements for the required control. Ensuring the introduced conditions additionally requires the introduction of feedback. The paper presents the approach of synthesized optimal control, which allows implementing optimal control systems, taking into account the introduced additional requirement. In this case, other approaches can be considered and proposed.

9. Conclusions

A general machine learning approach for the automatic design of feedback control systems for any dynamical nonlinear control objects is considered. The main perspective is the machine-automated development of control systems. According to this trend, the control system is obtained as a result of a machine solution of some formal mathematical control problem and it is to be implemented in the real object directly.

Since the control system is created by machine learning, the paper formulates a machine check of all the properties required from the control system. Mathematical statements of control problems and some theoretical justifications for solution of these problems by machine methods are presented. The paper introduces and discusses such notions as machine learning control, stability, optimality and feasibility of machine-made control systems. In this regard, substantiations are introduced for the machine learning feedback control approach based on symbolic regression and evolutionary algorithms.

Thus, the feedback control design is generalized and automated with a generic approach applicable to any nonlinear models, including machine-learning-identified models. It is shown that with this approach, the computer is able to propose interesting outstanding solutions, which sometimes an engineer cannot even suppose.

There is another feature in the proposed approach that can be developed in a good direction. It is possible to control an object by controlling the position of the equilibrium point both offline under predetermined operating conditions, and online, when the positions of the points can be optimally planned for some short term and then adjusted according to the situation. This is one more direction for further research and application of the presented approach.

Author Contributions: Conceptualization, A.D. and E.S.; methodology, A.D. and E.S.; software, A.D. and E.S.; validation, A.D. and E.S.; formal analysis, A.D.; investigation, E.S.; writing—original draft preparation, A.D. and E.S.; writing—review and editing, E.S.; supervision, A.D. All authors have read and agreed to the published version of the manuscript.

Funding: This research is supported by the Ministry of Science and Higher Education of the Russian Federation, project No. 075-15-2020-799.

Data Availability Statement: Not applicable.

Conflicts of Interest: The authors declare no conflict of interest.

Abbreviations

The following abbreviations are used in this manuscript:

HJB	Hamilton–Jacobi–Bellman Equation
PID	Proportional–Integral–Derivative Controller
ML	Machine Learning
SR	Symbolic Regression
GA	Genetic Algorithm
GWO	Grey Wolf Optimizer
PSO	Particle Swarm Optimization

Appendix A. Hybrid Evolutionary Algorithm

During the experiments, we noticed that evolutionary algorithms work faster if they use as much information as possible about the goal function values in the space of search at the evolutionary transformation of each possible solution. The PSO algorithm at the construction of new possible solutions uses information about the current best possible solution, about the best possible solution among random selected informants, and about previous goal function values for each possible solution. The GWO algorithm uses information about some current best possible solutions. Therefore, these algorithms work well.

However, when the goal function has a complex form, or it includes many complex constraints, then these algorithms stop at some points of the local minimum. The GA in these cases begins to work better than other evolutionary algorithms. The GA often can shift the search from the current local minimum.

We propose a hybrid algorithm that includes all three listed above algorithms.

Initially, all arrays are created, and the type of evolutionary transformation is randomly chosen: GA, GWO or PSO. In each generation, the number of transformations of every algorithms is approximately the same. A pseudocode of the algorithm can be found in the Algorithms A1–A4. We proposed that the hybrid algorithm worked better than GA, PSO and GWO individually.

Here is the description of the proposed hybrid algorithm.

In the description of the algorithm, a function $Goal(\mathbf{q})$ returns the goal function value for the vector of parameters $\mathbf{q}$. Procedure $NumbertoGray(a, \mathbf{y})$ converts the real number a to Gray code $\mathbf{y}$. Procedure $GraytoNumber(\mathbf{y}, a)$, on the contrary, converts Gray code to a real number a. Procedure $Sort(I, F, k)$ sorts the first k elements in array F and sets the first indexes in the array of index I.

Algorithm A1 Hybrid algorithm.

Require: $H > 0$ is a number of possible solutions in the initial population, $G > 0$ is the number of generations, $R > 0$ is the number of evolutionary changes in one generation, p is the number of searched parameters, $q_i^+ > q_i^-$, $i = 1, \ldots, p$, are restrictions on the parameters, c is the number bits in the integer part of the parameter, d is the number of bits in the fractional part of the parameter, $\alpha, \beta, \gamma, \sigma, k_0$ are parameters for the PSO algorithm, and k_w is the number of leaders for the GWO algorithm.

Ensure: $\tilde{\mathbf{q}} = [\tilde{q}_1 \ldots \tilde{q}_p]^T$ is the optimal vector of parameters

$q_j^0 = \tilde{q}_j\, j = 1, \ldots, p,$
$q_j^i \leftarrow (q_j^+ - q_j^-)\xi + q_j^-, j = 1, \ldots, p, i = 1, \ldots, H-1$
$v_j^i \leftarrow 0, j = 1, \ldots, p, i = 0, \ldots, H-1$
$F_j \leftarrow Goal(\mathbf{q}^j), j = 0, \ldots, H-1$
$I_j = j, \tilde{F}_j = F_j, j = 0, \ldots, H-1$
$t \leftarrow 0$
while $t < G$ **do**
    $j_- \leftarrow 0, F_- \leftarrow F_0, j \leftarrow 1$
    while $j < H$ **do**
        if $F_j < F_{j_-}$ **then**
            $j_- \leftarrow j,$
            $F_{j_-} \leftarrow F_j$
        end if
        $j \leftarrow j+1$
    end while
    $Sort(I, \tilde{F}, k_w)$
    $s \leftarrow 0$
    while $s < R$ **do**
        $k_a \leftarrow \xi(3)$
        if $k_a = 0$ **then**
            GWO transformations
        end if
        if $k_a = 1$ **then**
            GA transformation
        end if
        if $k_a = 2$ **then**
            PSO transformation
        end if
        $s \leftarrow s+1$
    end while
    $t \leftarrow t+1$
end while
$j_- \leftarrow 0, F_- \leftarrow F_0, j \leftarrow 1$
while $j < H$ **do**
    if $F_j < F_{j_-}$ **then**
        $j_- \leftarrow j,$
        $F_{j_-} \leftarrow F_j$
    end if
    $j \leftarrow j+1$
end while
$\tilde{\mathbf{q}} \leftarrow \mathbf{q}^{j_-}$

Algorithm A2 GWO transformation.

$L \leftarrow 2 - t(2/G)$
$i \leftarrow \xi(H)$
$j \leftarrow 0$
while $j < p$ **do**
    $\alpha_x \leftarrow 0$
    $k \leftarrow 0$
    while $k < k_w$ **do**
        $g_A \leftarrow 2L\xi - L$
        $g_C \leftarrow 2\xi$
        $\alpha_D \leftarrow |g_C q_j^{I_k} - q_j^i|$
        $\alpha_x \leftarrow \alpha_x + q_j^{I_k} - g_A \alpha_D$
        $k \leftarrow k + 1$
    end while
    $\hat{q}_j \leftarrow \alpha_x / k_w$
    if $\hat{q}_j > q_j^+$ **then**
        $\hat{q}_j \leftarrow q_j^+$
    end if
    if $\hat{q}_j < q_j^-$ **then**
        $\hat{q}_j \leftarrow q_j^-$
    end if
    $j \leftarrow j + 1$
end while
$\hat{F} \leftarrow Goal(\hat{\mathbf{q}})$
if $\hat{F} < F_i$ **then**
    $F_i \leftarrow \hat{F}$
    $\mathbf{q}^i \leftarrow \hat{\mathbf{q}}$
    $Sort(I, F, k_w)$
end if

Algorithm A3 GA transformation.

$k_1 \leftarrow \xi(H), k_2 \leftarrow \xi(H)$
$d \leftarrow \xi$
if $d > F_{j_-}/F_{k_1}$ or $d > F_{j_-}/F_{k_2}$ **then**
    $k_s \leftarrow \xi(p)$
    $NumbertoGray(q_{k_s}^{k_1}, \mathbf{y}^1)$
    $NumbertoGray(q_{k_s}^{k_2}, \mathbf{y}^2)$
    $k_c \leftarrow \xi(c+d)$
    $j \leftarrow 0$
    while $j < k_c$ **do**
        $Sony_j^1 \leftarrow y_j^1, Sony_j^2 \leftarrow y_j^2, j \leftarrow j+1$
    end while
    $j \leftarrow k_c$
    while $j < c+d$ **do**
        $Sony_j^1 \leftarrow y_j^2, Sony_j^2 \leftarrow y_j^1, j \leftarrow j+1$
    end while
    $i \leftarrow 0$
    while $i < k_s$ **do**
        $Son_i^1 \leftarrow q_i^{k_1}, Son_i^2 \leftarrow q_i^{k_2}, i \leftarrow i+1$
    end while
    $i \leftarrow k_s + 1$
    while $i < p$ **do**
        $Son_i^1 \leftarrow q_i^{k_2}, Son_i^2 \leftarrow q_i^{k_1}, i \leftarrow i+1$
    end while
    $GraytoNumber(Sony^1, Son_{k_s}^1)$
    $GraytoNumber(Sony^2, Son_{k_s}^2)$
    $j \leftarrow 1$
    while $j \leq 2$ **do**
        if $Son_{k_s}^j > q_{k_s}^+$ **then**
            $Son_{k_s}^j \leftarrow q_{k_s}^+$
        else if $Son_{k_s}^j < q_{k_s}^-$ **then**
            $Son_{k_s}^j \leftarrow q_{k_s}^-$
        end if
        $\hat{F} \leftarrow Goal(Son^j)$
        $i_+ \leftarrow 0, i \leftarrow 1$
        while $i < H$ **do**
            if $F_i > F_{i_+}$ **then**
                $i_+ \leftarrow i$
            end if
        end while
        if $\hat{F} < F_{i_+}$ **then**
            $\mathbf{q}^{i_+} \leftarrow Son^j$
            $F_{i_+} \leftarrow \hat{F}$
        end if
        $j \leftarrow j+1$
    end while
end if

Algorithm A4 PSO transformation.

$j \leftarrow \xi(H)$
$k \leftarrow \xi(H)$
$i \leftarrow 0$
while $i < k_0$ **do**
    $l \leftarrow \xi(H)$
    if $F_l < F_k$ **then**
        $k \leftarrow l$
    end if
end while
$i \leftarrow 0$
while $i < p$ **do**
    $v_i^j \leftarrow \alpha v_i^j + \xi \beta (q_i^k - q_i^j) + \xi \gamma (q_i^{j-} - q_i^j)$
    $\hat{q}_i \leftarrow q_i^j + \sigma v_i^j$
    if $\hat{q}_i > q_i^+$ **then**
        $\hat{q}_i \leftarrow q_i^+$
    else if $\hat{q}_i < q_i^-$ **then**
        $\hat{q}_i \leftarrow q_i^-$
    end if
    $i \leftarrow i + 1$
end while
$\hat{F} \leftarrow Goal(\hat{\mathbf{q}})$
if $\hat{F} < F_j$ **then**
    $F_j \leftarrow \hat{F}$
    $\mathbf{q}^j \leftarrow \hat{\mathbf{q}}$
end if

Appendix B. Stabilization System of the Mobile Robot

$$\Psi = \begin{bmatrix} \Psi_{1,1} & \Psi_{1,2} \\ 0_{12 \times 12} & \Psi_{2,2} \end{bmatrix} \tag{A1}$$

$$\Psi_{1,1} = \begin{bmatrix} 0 & 0 & 0 & 0 & 0 & 0 & 1 & 1 & 0 & 0 & 0 & 12 & 1 \\ 0 & 0 & 0 & 0 & 0 & 0 & 0 & 1 & 0 & 0 & 0 & 0 \\ 0 & 0 & 0 & 0 & 0 & 0 & 0 & 0 & 1 & 0 & 0 & 0 \\ 0 & 0 & 0 & 0 & 0 & 0 & 1 & 0 & 0 & 0 & 0 & 0 \\ 0 & 0 & 0 & 0 & 0 & 0 & 0 & 1 & 0 & 0 & 0 & 0 \\ 0 & 0 & 0 & 0 & 0 & 0 & 0 & 0 & 1 & 0 & 0 & 0 \\ 0 & 0 & 0 & 0 & 0 & 2 & 0 & 0 & 8 & 0 & 0 \\ 0 & 0 & 0 & 0 & 0 & 0 & 0 & 2 & 0 & 1 & 19 & 0 \\ 0 & 0 & 0 & 0 & 0 & 0 & 0 & 0 & 2 & 1 & 0 & 0 \\ 0 & 0 & 0 & 0 & 0 & 0 & 0 & 0 & 0 & 1 & 1 & 8 \\ 0 & 0 & 0 & 0 & 0 & 0 & 0 & 0 & 0 & 0 & 1 & 1 \\ 0 & 0 & 0 & 0 & 0 & 0 & 0 & 0 & 0 & 0 & 0 & 1 \end{bmatrix} \tag{A2}$$

$$\Psi_{1,2} = \begin{bmatrix} 15 & 0 & 0 & 0 & 0 & 0 & 0 & 0 & 0 & 0 & 0 & 10 \\ 0 & 0 & 0 & 0 & 0 & 0 & 0 & 0 & 0 & 0 & 0 & 0 \\ 0 & 0 & 0 & 9 & 0 & 0 & 0 & 0 & 10 & 0 & 0 & 0 \\ 0 & 0 & 0 & 13 & 0 & 0 & 0 & 0 & 0 & 0 & 0 & 0 \\ 0 & 0 & 0 & 0 & 0 & 0 & 0 & 0 & 0 & 0 & 0 & 0 \\ 0 & 0 & 0 & 0 & 0 & 0 & 0 & 0 & 0 & 0 & 0 & 0 \\ 0 & 4 & 13 & 10 & 0 & 0 & 0 & 0 & 0 & 0 & 0 & 0 \\ 0 & 0 & 0 & 0 & 0 & 0 & 0 & 0 & 0 & 0 & 0 & 0 \\ 0 & 0 & 0 & 0 & 12 & 0 & 0 & 0 & 19 & 0 & 0 & 0 \\ 0 & 1 & 0 & 0 & 0 & 0 & 0 & 0 & 0 & 0 & 0 & 0 \\ 0 & 0 & 4 & 23 & 1 & 0 & 0 & 0 & 0 & 0 & 0 & 23 \\ 1 & 10 & 10 & 0 & 0 & 0 & 0 & 23 & 0 & 16 & 0 & 16 \end{bmatrix} \quad (A3)$$

$$\Psi_{2,2} = \begin{bmatrix} 1 & 1 & 15 & 0 & 14 & 0 & 0 & 0 & 0 & 0 & 0 & 0 \\ 0 & 1 & 1 & 0 & 0 & 0 & 0 & 0 & 0 & 0 & 0 & 0 \\ 0 & 0 & 1 & 1 & 0 & 0 & 0 & 0 & 0 & 0 & 0 & 13 \\ 0 & 0 & 0 & 1 & 8 & 0 & 0 & 0 & 0 & 0 & 0 & 0 \\ 0 & 0 & 0 & 0 & 1 & 1 & 0 & 0 & 0 & 0 & 0 & 0 \\ 0 & 0 & 0 & 0 & 0 & 2 & 1 & 0 & 15 & 0 & 0 & 0 \\ 0 & 0 & 0 & 0 & 0 & 0 & 1 & 1 & 0 & 0 & 0 & 0 \\ 0 & 0 & 0 & 0 & 0 & 0 & 0 & 1 & 5 & 0 & 0 & 0 \\ 0 & 0 & 0 & 0 & 0 & 0 & 0 & 0 & 1 & 1 & 0 & 0 \\ 0 & 0 & 0 & 0 & 0 & 0 & 0 & 0 & 0 & 1 & 1 & 12 \\ 0 & 0 & 0 & 0 & 0 & 0 & 0 & 0 & 0 & 0 & 2 & 1 \\ 0 & 0 & 0 & 0 & 0 & 0 & 0 & 0 & 0 & 0 & 0 & 1 \end{bmatrix} \quad (A4)$$

In the matrices, the numbers correspond to the functions with one and two arguments according to [46].

The mathematical expression for the found control function described by these matrices has the following form and parameters:

$$u_{i+(j-1)2} = \begin{cases} u^+_{i+(j-1)2} & \text{if } \tilde{u}_{i+(j-1)2} > u^+_{i+(j-1)2} \\ u^-_{i+(j-1)2} & \text{if } \tilde{u}_{i+(j-1)2} < u^-_{i+(j-1)2} \\ \tilde{u}_{i+(j-1)2} & \text{otherwise} \end{cases}, \quad (A5)$$

where $i = 1, 2, j = 1, 2$,

$$\tilde{u}_{1+(j-1)2} = \text{sgn}(q_3(x^*_{3+(j-1)3} - x_{3+(j-1)3})) \exp(-|q_3(x^*_{3+(j-1)3} - x_{3+(j-1)3})|) +$$

$$a^{-1} + \sqrt[3]{a} + \text{sgn}(x^*_{3+(j-1)3} - x_{3+(j-1)3}) + \mu(b), \quad (A6)$$

$$\tilde{u}_{2+(j-1)2} = \tilde{u}_{1+(j-1)2} + \sin(\tilde{u}_{1+(j-1)2}) + \arctan(h) + \mu(b) + c - c^3, \quad (A7)$$

$$a = \tanh(d) + \left(b + \sqrt[3]{x^*_{1+(j-1)3} - x_{1+(j-1)3}}\right)^3 +$$

$$c + \sin(q_3(x^*_{3+(j-1)3} - x_{3+(j-1)3})),$$

$$b = g + \text{sgn}(\text{sgn}(x^*_{1+(j-1)3} - x_{1+(j-1)3})q_2(x^*_{2+(j-1)3} - x_{2+(j-1)3})) \times$$

$$\exp(-|\text{sgn}(x^*_{1+(j-1)3} - x_{1+(j-1)3})q_2(x^*_{2+(j-1)3} - x_{2+(j-1)3})|) +$$

$$\sin(x^*_{1+(j-1)3} - x_{1+(j-1)3}) + \tanh(g) + x^*_{1+(j-1)3} - x_{1+(j-1)3},$$

$$c = g + \text{sgn}(\text{sgn}(x^*_{1+(j-1)3} - x_{1+(j-1)3})q_2(x^*_{2+(j-1)3} - x_{2+(j-1)3})) \times$$

$$\exp(-|\text{sgn}(x^*_{1+(j-1)3} - x_{1+(j-1)3})q_2(x^*_{2+(j-1)3} - x_{2+(j-1)3})|) +$$

$$\sin(x^*_{1+(j-1)3} - x_{1+(j-1)3}),$$
$$d = h + c - c^3 + \text{sgn}(q_1(x^*_{1+(j-1)3} - x_{1+(j-1)3})) +$$
$$\arctan(q_1) + \vartheta(x^*_{3+(j-1)3} - x_{3+(j-1)3}),$$
$$g = \text{sgn}(x^*_{1+(j-1)3} - x_{1+(j-1)3})q_2(x^*_{2+(j-1)3} - x_{2+(j-1)2}) +$$
$$q_3(x^*_{3+(j-1)3} - x_{3+(j-1)3}) + \tanh(q_1(x^*_{1+(j-1)3} - x_{1+(j-1)3})),$$
$$h = \arctan(q_1(x^*_{1+(j-1)3} - x_{1+(j-1)3})) +$$
$$\text{sgn}(w)\sqrt{|w|} + w + v + 2\text{sgn}(w + \tanh(v)) +$$
$$\sqrt[3]{w + \tanh(v)} + \sqrt[3]{x^*_{1+(j-1)3} - x_{1+(j-1)3}} +$$
$$\text{sgn}(x^*_{1+(j-1)3} - x_{1+(j-1)3})\sqrt{|x^*_{1+(j-1)3} - x_{1+(j-1)3}|} +$$
$$\sqrt[3]{x^*_1 - x_1} + \tanh(v),$$
$$w = \text{sgn}(x^*_{1+(j-1)3} - x_{1+(j-1)3}) +$$
$$\text{sgn}(q_2(x^*_{2+(j-1)3} - x_{2+(j-1)3}))\text{sgn}(x^*_{1+(j-1)3} - x_{1+(j-1)3}) \times$$
$$\tanh(x^*_{1+(j-1)3} - x_{1+(j-1)3}),$$
$$v = q_3(x^*_{3+(j-1)3} - x_{3+(j-1)3}) + \text{sgn}(x^*_{1+(j-1)3} - x_{1+(j-1)3})q_2 \times$$
$$(x^*_{2+(j-1)3} - x_{2+(j-1)3}) + \tanh(x^*_{1+(j-1)3} - x_{1+(j-1)3}),$$
$$\mu(\alpha) = \text{sgn}(\alpha)\min\{1, |\alpha|\}, \quad \tanh(\alpha) = \frac{1 - \exp(-2\alpha)}{1 + \exp(-2\alpha)},$$
$$j = 1, 2, q_1 = 14.7288, q_2 = 2.0271, q_3 = 4.0222.$$

Appendix C. Plots for Mecanum Robot

Figures A1–A6 demonstrate the plots of optimal values of the state-space vector components (black lines) and the corresponding values of the vector **x*** (red lines).

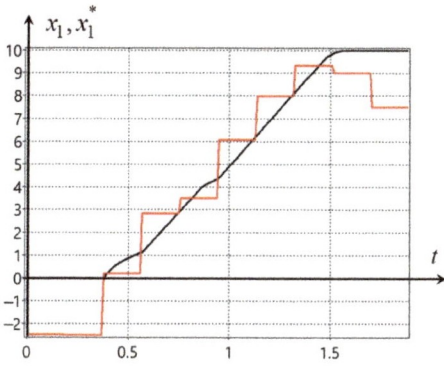

Figure A1. Plots of optimal x_1 and x_1*.

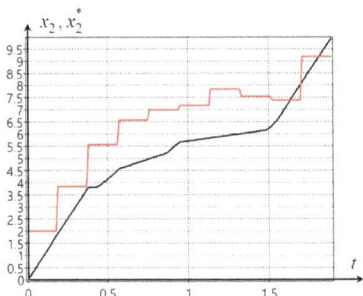

Figure A2. Plots of optimal x_2 and x_2^*.

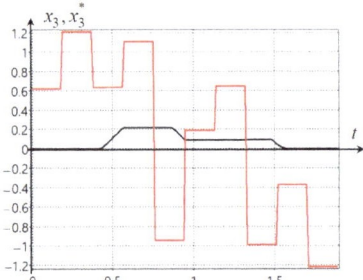

Figure A3. Plots of optimal x_3 and x_3^*.

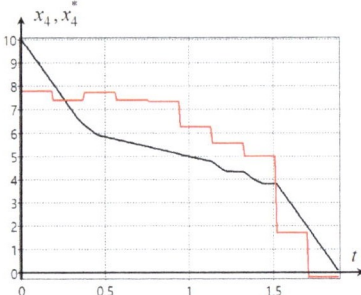

Figure A4. Plots of optimal x_4 and x_4^*.

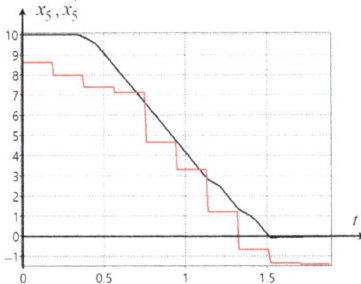

Figure A5. Plots of optimal x_5 and x_5^*.

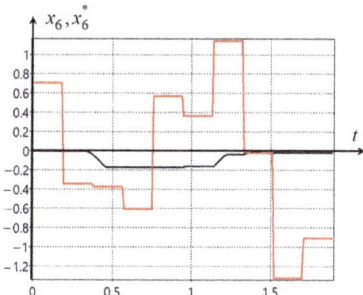

Figure A6. Plots of optimal x_6 and $x_6{}^*$.

In Figures A7–A14, the plots of optimal values of the control vector components are presented.

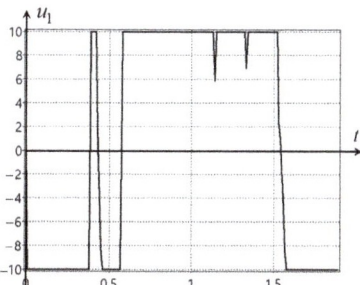

Figure A7. Plot of optimal values of control component u_1.

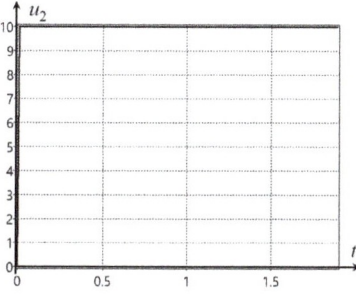

Figure A8. Plot of optimal values of control component u_2.

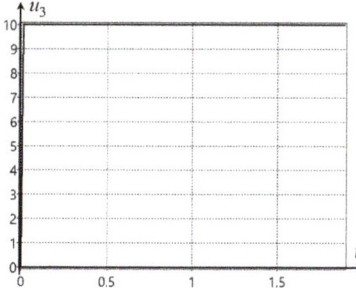

Figure A9. Plot of optimal values of control component u_3.

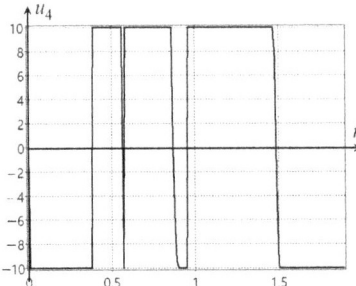

Figure A10. Plot of optimal values of control component u_4.

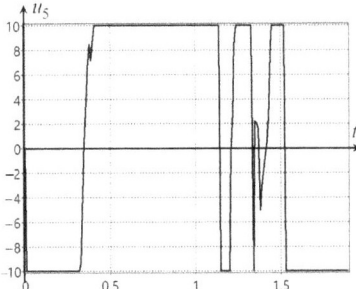

Figure A11. Plot of optimal values of control component u_5.

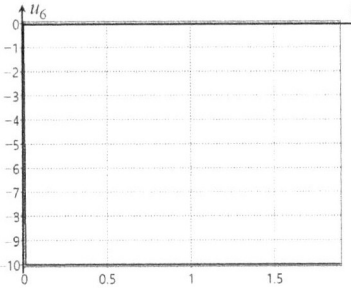

Figure A12. Plot of optimal values of control component u_6.

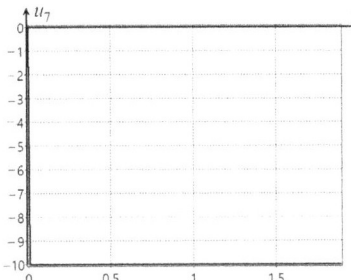

Figure A13. Plot of optimal values of control component u_7.

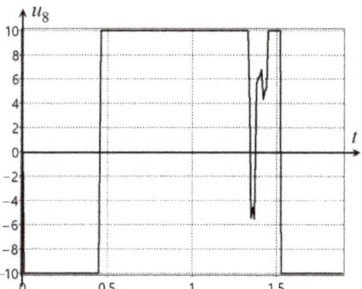

Figure A14. Plot of optimal values of control component u_8.

References

1. Egerstedt, M. Motion Planning and Control of Mobile Robots. Ph.D. Thesis, Royal Institute of Technology, Stockholm, Sweden, 2000.
2. Bellman, R. Dynamic programming. *Science* **1966**, *153*, 34–37. [CrossRef] [PubMed]
3. Jones, M.; Peet, M.M. A generalization of Bellmans equation with application to path planning, obstacle avoidance and invariant set estimation. *Automatica* **2021**, *127*, 109510. [CrossRef]
4. Aguilar, C.O.; Krener, A.J. Numerical solutions to the Bellman equation of optimal control. *J. Optim. Theory Appl.* **2014**, *160*, 527–552. [CrossRef]
5. Aliyu, M.D.S. An iterative relaxation approach to the solution of the Hamilton-Jacobi-Bellman-Isaacs equation in nonlinear optimal control. *IEEE/CAA J. Autom. Sin.* **2018**, *5*, 360–366. [CrossRef]
6. Fraga, S.L.; Pereira, F.L. Hamilton-Jacobi-Bellman Equation and Feedback Synthesis for Impulsive Control. *IEEE Trans. Autom. Control* **2012**, *57*, 244–249. [CrossRef]
7. Liu, D.; Wang, D.; Wang, F.; Li, H.; Yang, X. Neural-Network-Based Online HJB Solution for Optimal Robust Guaranteed Cost Control of Continuous-Time Uncertain Nonlinear Systems. *IEEE Trans. Cybern.* **2014**, *44*, 2834–2847. [CrossRef]
8. Wei, Q.; Liu, D.; Lin, H. Value Iteration Adaptive Dynamic Programming for Optimal Control of Discrete-Time Nonlinear Systems. *IEEE Trans. Cybern.* **2016**, *46*, 840–853. [CrossRef]
9. Liu, D.; Xue, S.; Zhao, B.; Luo, B.; Wei, Q. Adaptive Dynamic Programming for Control: A Survey and Recent Advances. *IEEE Trans. Syst. Man Cybern. Syst.* **2021**, *51*, 142–160. [CrossRef]
10. Lu, J.; Wei, Q.; Wang, F.-Y. Parallel control for optimal tracking via adaptive dynamic programming. *IEEE/CAA J. Autom. Sin.* **2020**, *7*, 1662–1674. [CrossRef]
11. Lewis, F.L.; Vrabie, D.; Vamvoudakis, K.G. Reinforcement learning and feedback control: Using natural decision methods to design optimal adaptive controllers. *IEEE Control Syst.* **2012**, *32*, 76–105.
12. Wen, G.; Chen, C.L.P.; Ge, S.S. Simplified Optimized Backstepping Control for a Class of Nonlinear Strict-Feedback Systems With Unknown Dynamic Functions. *IEEE Trans. Cybern.* **2021**, *51*, 4567–4580. [CrossRef] [PubMed]
13. Kim, J.; Shin, J.; Yang, I. Hamilton-Jacobi Deep Q-Learning for Deterministic Continuous-Time Systems with Lipschitz Continuous Controls. *J. Mach. Learn. Res.* **2021**, *22*, 1–34.
14. Walsh, G.; Tilbury, D.; Sastry, S.; Murray, R.; Laumond, J.P. Stabilization of trajectories for systems with nonholonomic constraints. *IEEE Trans. Autom. Control* **1994**, *39*, 216–222. [CrossRef]
15. Wang, S.; Dai, M.; Wang, Y. Robust Adaptive Backstepping Sliding Mode Control for a Class of Uncertain Nonlinear System. In Proceedings of the 2018 Chinese Automation Congress (CAC), Xi'an, China, 30 November–2 December 2018; pp. 3534–3538. [CrossRef]
16. Zhao, X.; Wang, X.; Zhang, S.; Zong, G. Adaptive Neural Backstepping Control Design for A Class of Nonsmooth Nonlinear Systems. *IEEE Trans. Syst. Man Cybern. Syst.* **2019**, *49*, 1820–1831. [CrossRef]
17. Tyutikov, V.V.; Panteleev, E.R.; Zhilnikova, Y.F. Analysing Impact of Transfer Function Zeros in Controlled Object on Parametric Sensitivity of Systems Synthesized by Method of Aggregated Controller Analytical Design (ACAD). In Proceedings of the 2020 International Conference on Industrial Engineering, Applications and Manufacturing (ICIEAM), Sochi, Russia, 18–22 May 2020; pp. 1–6. [CrossRef]
18. Clarke, F. Lyapunov Functions and Feedback in Nonlinear Control. In *Optimal Control, Stabilization and Nonsmooth Analysis*; de Queiroz, M.S., Malisoff, M., Wolenski, P., Eds.; LNCIS 301; Springer: Berlin/Heidelberg, Germany, 2004; pp. 267–282.
19. Benzaouia, A.; Hmamed, A.; Mesquine, F.; Benhayoun, M.; Tadeo, F. Stabilization of Continuous-Time Fractional Positive Systems by Using a Lyapunov Function. *IEEE Trans. Autom. Control* **2014**, *59*, 2203–2208. [CrossRef]
20. Simon, J.D.; Mitter, S.K. A theory of modal control. *Inf. Control* **1968**, *13*, 316–353. [CrossRef]
21. Tousi, S.M.A.; Mostafanasab, A.; Teshnehlab, M. Design of Self Tuning PID Controller Based on Competitional PSO. In Proceedings of the 2020 4th Conference on Swarm Intelligence and Evolutionary Computation (CSIEC), Mashhad, Iran, 2–4 September 2020; pp. 22–26. [CrossRef]

22. Cherroun, L.; Nadour, M.; Kouzou, A. Type-1 and Type-2 Fuzzy Logic Controllers for Autonomous Robotic Motion. In Proceedings of the 2019 International Conference on Applied Automation and Industrial Diagnostics (ICAAID), Elazig, Turkey, 25–27 September 2019; pp. 1–5. [CrossRef]
23. Ahmed, A.A.; Alshandoli, A.F.S. On replacing a PID controller with Neural Network controller for Segway. In Proceedings of the 2020 International Conference on Electrical Engineering (ICEE), Takamatsu, Japan, 28 June–2 July 2020; pp. 1–4. [CrossRef]
24. Diveev, A.I.; Shmalko, E.Y. Machine-Made Synthesis of Stabilization System by Modified Cartesian Genetic Programming. *IEEE Trans. Cybern.* **2022**, *52*, 6627–6637. [CrossRef]
25. Duriez, T.; Brunton, S.L.; Noack, B.R. *Machine Learning Control—Taming Nonlinear Dynamics and Turbulence*; Springer International Publishing: Cham, Switzerland, 2017.
26. Moe, S.; Rustad, A.M.; Hanssen, K.G. Machine Learning in Control Systems: An Overview of the State of the Art. In *Artificial Intelligence XXXV, Proceedings of the 38th SGAI International Conference on Artificial Intelligence, AI 2018, Cambridge, UK, 11–13 December 2018*; Bramer, M., Petridis, M., Eds.; LNCS; Springer: Cham, Switzerland, 2018.
27. Deisenroth, M.P.; Faisal, A.A.; Ong, C.S. *Mathematics for Machine Learning*; Cambridge University Press: Cambridge, UK, 2020. [CrossRef]
28. Burkov, A. *The Hundred-Page Machine Learning Book*; Andriy Burkov: Quebec City, QC, Canada, 2019; 160p.
29. Géron, A. *Hands-On Machine Learning with Scikit-Learn, Keras, and TensorFlow: Concepts, Tools, and Techniques to Build Intelligent Systems*; O'Reilly Media, Inc.: Sebastopol, CA, USA, 2019; 856p.
30. Brunton, S.L.; Proctor, J.L.; Kutz, J.N. Discovering governing equations from data: Sparse identification of nonlinear dynamical systems. *Proc. Natl. Acad. Sci. USA* **2015**, *113*, 3932–3937. [CrossRef]
31. Shmalko, E.; Rumyantsev, Y.; Baynazarov, R.; Yamshanov, K. Identification of Neural Network Model of Robot to Solve the Optimal Control Problem. *Inform. Autom.* **2021**, *20*, 1254–1278. [CrossRef]
32. Malkin, I.G. *Theory of Motion Stability*; Nauka: Moscow, Russia, 1966.
33. Diveev, A.; Shmalko, E.; Serebrenny, V.; Zentay, P. Fundamentals of Synthesized Optimal Control. *Mathematics* **2021**, *9*, 21. [CrossRef]
34. Sun, S.; Cao, Z.; Zhu, H.; Zhao, J. A Survey of Optimization Methods From a Machine Learning Perspective. *IEEE Trans. Cybern.* **2020**, *50*, 3668–3681. [CrossRef] [PubMed]
35. Diveev, A.; Shmalko, E. *Machine Learning Control by Symbolic Regression*; Springer International Publishing: Cham, Switzerland, 2021.
36. Silviu-Marian, U.; Max, T. AI Feynman: A physics-inspired method for symbolic regression. *Sci. Adv.* **2020**, *6*, eaay2631. [CrossRef]
37. Jin, Y.; Fu, W.; Kang, J.; Guo, J.; Guo, J. Bayesian Symbolic Regression. *arXiv* **2019**, arXiv:1910.08892.
38. La Cava, W.; Moore, J.H. Learning feature spaces for regression with genetic programming. *Genet. Program. Evolvable Mach.* **2022**, *21*, 433–467. [CrossRef] [PubMed]
39. Petersen, B.K.; Larma, M.L.; Mundhenk, T.N.; Santiago, C.P.; Kim, S.K.; Kim, J.T. Deep symbolic regression: Recovering mathematical expressions from data via risk-seeking policy gradients. In Proceedings of the International Conference on Learning Representations, Virtual, 3–7 May 2021.
40. Derner, E.; Kubalík, J.; Ancona, N.; Babuška, R. Symbolic Regression for Constructing Analytic Models in Reinforcement Learning. *Appl. Soft Comput.* **2020**, *94*, 106432. [CrossRef]
41. Alibekov, E.; Kubalık, J.; Babuska, R. Symbolic Method for Deriving Policy in Reinforcement Learning. In Proceedings of the 2016 IEEE 55th Conference on Decision and Control (CDC), Las Vegas, NV, USA, 12–14 December 2016; pp. 2789–2795. [CrossRef]
42. Derner, E.; Kubalík, J.; Babuška, R. Reinforcement Learning with Symbolic Input-Output Models. In Proceedings of the 2018 IEEE/RSJ International Conference on Intelligent Robots and Systems (IROS), Madrid, Spain, 1–5 October 2018; pp. 3004–3009. [CrossRef]
43. Diveev, A.I.; Shmalko, E.Yu. Evolutionary computations for synthesis of control system of group of robots and the optimum choice of trajectories for their movement. In Proceedings of the CEUR Workshop Proceedings: VIII International Conference on Optimization and Applications (OPTIMA-2017), Petrovac, Montenegro, 2–7 October 2017; pp. 158–165.
44. Shmalko, E.; Diveev, A. Control Synthesis as Machine Learning Control by Symbolic Regression Methods. *Appl. Sci.* **2021**, *11*, 5468. [CrossRef]
45. Diveev, A.I. Small Variations of Basic Solution Method for Non-numerical Optimization. *IFAC-PapersOnLine* **2015**, *48*, 28–33. [CrossRef]
46. Diveev, A.I. Numerical method for network operator for synthesis of a control system with uncertain initial values. *J. Comp. Syst. Sci. Int.* **2012**, *51*, 228–243. [CrossRef]
47. Diveev, A.I.; Konstantinov, S.V. Study of the Practical Convergence of Evolutionary Algorithms for the Optimal Program Control of a Wheeled Robot. *J. Comput. Syst. Sci. Int.* **2018**, *57*, 561–580. [CrossRef]
48. Goldberg, D. *Genetic Algorithms in Search, Optimization and Machine Learning*; Addison-Wesley Professional: Reading, MA, USA, 1989.
49. Mirjalili, S.; Mirjalili, S.M.; Lewis, A. Grey Wolf Optimizer. *Adv. Eng. Softw.* **2014**, *69*, 46–61. [CrossRef]

50. Kennedy, J.; Eberhart, R. Particle swarm optimization. In Proceedings of the ICNN'95–International Conference on Neural Networks, Perth, Australia, 27 November–1 December 1995; pp. 1942–1948. [CrossRef]
51. Huang, H.-C.; Tao, C.-W.; Chuang, C.-C.; Xu, J.-J. FPGA-Based Mechatronic Design and Real-Time Fuzzy Control with Computational Intelligence Optimization for Omni-Mecanum-Wheeled Autonomous Vehicles. *Electronics* **2019**, *8*, 1328. [CrossRef]

Article

On Improving Adaptive Problem Decomposition Using Differential Evolution for Large-Scale Optimization Problems

Aleksei Vakhnin, Evgenii Sopov and Eugene Semenkin *

Department of System Analysis and Operations Research, Reshetnev Siberian State University of Science and Technology, Krasnoyarsk 660037, Russia
* Correspondence: eugenesemenkin@yandex.ru

Abstract: Modern computational mathematics and informatics for Digital Environments deal with the high dimensionality when designing and optimizing models for various real-world phenomena. Large-scale global black-box optimization (LSGO) is still a hard problem for search metaheuristics, including bio-inspired algorithms. Such optimization problems are usually extremely multi-modal, and require significant computing resources for discovering and converging to the global optimum. The majority of state-of-the-art LSGO algorithms are based on problem decomposition with the cooperative co-evolution (CC) approach, which divides the search space into a set of lower dimensional subspaces (or subcomponents), which are expected to be easier to explore independently by an optimization algorithm. The question of the choice of the decomposition method remains open, and an adaptive decomposition looks more promising. As we can see from the most recent LSGO competitions, winner-approaches are focused on modifying advanced DE algorithms through integrating them with local search techniques. In this study, an approach that combines multiple ideas from state-of-the-art algorithms and implements Coordination of Self-adaptive Cooperative Co-evolution algorithms with Local Search (COSACC-LS1) is proposed. The self-adaptation method tunes both the structure of the complete approach and the parameters of each algorithm in the cooperation. The performance of COSACC-LS1 has been investigated using the CEC LSGO 2013 benchmark and the experimental results has been compared with leading LSGO approaches. The main contribution of the study is a new self-adaptive approach that is preferable for solving hard real-world problems because it is not overfitted with the LSGO benchmark due to self-adaptation during the search process instead of a manual benchmark-specific fine-tuning.

Keywords: problem decomposition; large-scale global optimization; self-adaptive differential evolution; memetic algorithm; cooperative co-evolution.

MSC: 90C06; 90C26; 68W50; 49M27

1. Introduction

Modern numerical continuous global optimization problems deal with high dimensionality and the number of decision variables is still increasing because of the need to take into account more internal and external factors when designing and analyzing complex systems. This is also facilitated by the development of high-performance hardware and algorithms. "Black-box" large-scale global optimization (LSGO) is one of the most important and hardest types of optimization problems. The search space of LSGO problems exponentially grows and many state-of-the-art optimization algorithms, including evolutionary algorithms, lose their efficiency. However, the issue cannot be solved by straightforward increasing the number of objective function evaluations.

Many researchers note that the definition of a LSGO problem depends on the nature of the problem and changes over time and with the development of optimization approaches. For example, the global optimization of Morse clusters is known as a hard real-world optimization problem. The best-found solutions for Morse clusters are collected in the Cambridge Energy Landscape Database [1]. At the moment, the database contains the highest value equal to 147 atoms, which corresponds to 441 continuous decision variables only. The most popular LSGO benchmark was proposed within the IEEE Congress on Evolutionary Computation and is used for the estimation and comparison of new LSGO approaches. The benchmark contains 1000-dimensional LSGO problems. There exist solutions for real-world problems with many thousands of decision variables.

The general LSGO optimization problem is defined as (1):

$$f(x_1, x_2, \ldots, x_n) \to \min_{x \in R^n}, f : R^n \to R^1, \tag{1}$$

here f is an objective function, x_i are box-constrained decision variables. We do not impose any restrictions on the type of the objective function, such as linearity, continuity, convexity, and the need to be defined at all points requested by the search algorithm. In the general case, the objective function is defined algorithmically, there is no information about the properties of its landscape, thus the objective function is a "black-box" model.

As previously mentioned, the performance of many black-box global optimization algorithms cannot be improved by only increasing the budget of function evaluations when solving LSGO problems. One of challenges for researchers in the LSGO field is the development of new approaches, which can deal with the high dimensionality. Various LSGO algorithms that use fundamentally different ideas and demonstrate different performances for different classes of LSGO problems have been proposed. When solving a specific LSGO problem, a researcher must choose an appropriate LSGO algorithm and fine-tune its parameters. Moreover, the algorithm can require different settings at different states of the optimization process (for example, at exploration and exploitation stages). Thus, the development of self-adaptive approaches for solving hard LSGO problem is an actual research task.

In this study, an adaptive hybrid approach that combines three general conceptions, such as problem decomposition using cooperative co-evolution (CC), global search based on differential evolution (DE), and local search is proposed. This approach demonstrates performance comparable with LSGO competition winners and outperforms most of them. At the same time, it demonstrates the same high efficiency for different classes of LSGO problems, which makes the proposed approach preferable for "black-box" LSGO problems when it is not possible to prove the choice of an appropriate search algorithm.

The rest of the paper is organized as follows. Section 2 presents the related works for reviewing state-of-the-art in the field of LSGO and motivates designing a hybrid approach. Sections 3 and 4 describe the proposed approach, experimental setups, some general top-level settings, and implementation. In Section 5, the experimental results, analysis, and discussion of the algorithm dynamics and convergence, and the comparison of the results with state-of-the-art and competition-winner approaches are presented. In conclusion, the proposed methods and the obtained results are summarized and some further ideas are suggested.

2. Related Work

The complexity of real-world optimization problems has grown in recent years and is still growing. The class of global "black-box" optimization problems for which the high dimensionally causes the loss in the performance of a search algorithm is known as Large Scale Global Optimization or LSGO. Well-known experts in the field of LSGO, Mohammad Nabi Omidvar and Xiaodong Li, note that the term "large scale" is not definitively determined because the dimensionality of problems in LSGO grows over time, and it can also be different in different application areas. Many modern metaheuristics, including EAs, consider LSGO problems with 1000 real variables.

One of the first discussions on LSGO have been proposed within the special session of the IEEE CEC conference in 2008 [2,3]. Since 2008, the LSGO scientific community has proposed the LSGO benchmark for evaluating and comparing LSGO algorithms. The first benchmark in 2008 had only 7 test problems, including 2 unimodal and 5 multimodal optimization problems [2]. The CEC LSGO 2010 benchmark was extended with test problems grouped by the separability property and contained 20 optimization problems, including 3 fully separable, 15 partially non-separable, and 2 fully non-separable functions [4]. Finally, within the IEEE CEC 2013 special session and completion, a new benchmark has been proposed, and it is still used today and is known as a hard benchmark set for many state-of-the-art LSGO techniques [5]. The CEC LSGO 2013 benchmark contains 3 fully separable, 8 partially additive non-separable functions, 3 functions with overlapping components, and 1 fully non-separable function. In 2018, a new online Toolkit for Automatic Comparison of Optimizers (TACO) has been proposed for a fair independent comparison of LSGO algorithms [6]. In 2021, the TACO database includes the results of 25 leading and competition-winner LSGO algorithms.

Some extensive studies with surveys of the current state of LSGO and systematizations of LSGO techniques have been proposed in [7,8]. In [9], LSGO is highlighted as one of the urgent domains of bio-inspired computation. The recent work on the LSGO review proposes a large summary of the state of affairs and accumulated experience [10,11]. Within the proposed systematizations, the following main approaches are developing:

- Random (static or dynamic) problem decomposition using cooperative co-evolution,
- Learning-based decomposition using cooperative co-evolution,
- Modifications of the standard evolutionary algorithms without problem decomposition, including hybrid memetic approaches.

The first group of approaches is the largest one. Decomposition divides the search space into a set of lower-dimensional subspaces by grouping decision variables (or subcomponents), which are expected to be easier to explore independently by an optimization algorithm. For aggregating the whole candidate-solution from subcomponents, the cooperative co-evolution framework is used. Therefore, a decomposition-based approach involves three general components, namely, a decomposition algorithm, a subcomponent optimizer, and a cooperative co-evolution technique. The number of subcomponents and appropriate decomposition depend on the properties of the objective function and are unknown beforehand. Thus, decomposition mechanisms are also a part of the search approach and must be adaptive. Despite the fact that we optimize lower-dimensional subproblems, each decomposition can generate a complex landscape, and the subcomponent optimizer should be also adaptive for demonstrating the high performance for any decomposition. The standard co-evolution framework is also a subject for modification. Nevertheless, the decomposition-based approaches demonstrate high performance for a wide range of LSGO problems.

Learning-based techniques are aimed to identify the interaction of variables and to group them into separable subcomponents. The approaches usually perform well with fully separable and partially non-separable problems only. At the same time, some recent algorithms can also efficiently deal with overlapping components, but still demonstrate poor performance with fully non-separable problems (for example, CC-RDG3, who is the 2019 LSGO competition winner [12]).

Hybrid memetic approaches usually demonstrate high performance for all types of LSGO problems (for example, SHADE-ILS, the 2018 LSGO competition winner [13]). It is worth noting the Multiple Offspring Sampling (MOS) algorithm [14], which was the LSGO competition winner for 5 years (2013–2018). MOS proposes a high-level relay hybrid approach for adaptive switching between global and local search algorithms (one of the modifications uses switching only between multiple local search algorithms).

We will briefly review some state-of-the-art and competition-winner LSGO algorithms for analyzing the general approaches implemented in the algorithms.

2.1. Approaches without Problem Decomposition

Dynamic Multi-Swarm Particle Swarm Optimizer (DMS-PSO) [15] is one of the early approaches investigated using the CEC LSGO 2008 benchmark. DMS-PSO uses a multi-population scheme and combines PSO with a modified neighborhood topology [16] and the BFGS Quasi-Newton method for local search. Canonical Differential Evolutionary Particle Swarm Optimization (C-DEEPSO) [17] is based on a combination of DE and PSO algorithms. Variable Mesh Optimization Differential Evolution (VMODE) [18] uses the standard DE as the core optimizer and the population distributed in nodes of a mesh. The mesh nodes can be redistributed for maintaining diversity and for guiding the optimizer to the best-found solutions.

Multi-trajectory Search (MTS) [19] uses a combination of coordinate-wise random searches titled MTS-LS1, MTS-LS2, and MTS-LS3. On each iteration, coordinates are ranked based on the objective improvements, the next step starts with the coordinate that has provided the highest increment of the objective function. Despite the simple idea, MTS demonstrates high performance with LSGO problems and is used as the main local search algorithm in many hybrid memetic approaches.

Iterative Hybridization of Differential Evolution with Local Search (IHDELS) [20] is one of the first competition-winner memetic evolutionary algorithms (the 2nd place in the 2015 IEEE CEC LSGO competition). IHDELS uses self-adaptive DE (SaDE) [21] and two local search algorithms: L-BFGSB [22] and MTS-LS1 [19].

Multiple Offspring Sampling (MOS) in the original paper used a combination of Restart Covariance Matrix Adaptation Evolution Strategy With Increasing Population Size (IPOPCMA-ES) [23] with a restart and variable population size and the standard DE [24]. The 2013 version of MOS [25] uses a hybridization of 3 algorithms: MTS LS1, Solis and Wets, and GA.

Success-History Based Parameter Adaptation for Differential Evolution with Iterative Local Search (SHADE-ILS) [13] is the winner of the 2018 competition. SHADE-ILS combines SHADE [26] for global search, MTS LS1 and L-BFGS-B for local search, and restart strategies.

Hybrid of Minimum Population Search and Covariance Matrix Adaptation Evolution Strategy (MPS-CMA-ES) [27,28] has taken second place in the 2019 competition.

The most recent algorithm selection wizard, titled as automated black-box optimization (ABBO), can select one or several optimization algorithms from a very large number of base algorithms based on some input information about the considered optimization problem [29]. ABBO uses three types of selection techniques: passive algorithm selection, active algorithm selection, and chaining (several algorithms run in turn). ABBO outperforms many state-of-the-art algorithms on LSGO benchmarks.

2.2. Decomposition-Based Approaches with Static Grouping

A Cooperative Co-evolutionary approach for Genetic Algorithm (CCGA-1 and CCGA-2) [30] is the first attempt for improving the standard EA (namely, a binary GA) using the coordinate-wise decomposition. In [31,32], CC was implemented for improving evolution programming (Fast Evolutionary Programming with Cooperative Co-evolution, FEPCC). In Cooperative Co-evolutionary Differential Evolution (CCDE) [33], the approach was modified for using subcomponents with many variables. There were proposed two modifications: CCDE-H with 2 subcomponents and CCDE-O with the number of subcomponents equal to the number of variables.

Some more complicated decompositions have been proposed for PSO algorithms. Cooperative Approach to Particle Swarm Optimization (CPSO) [34] performed grouping into k subcomponents (CPSO-Sk) or combined CPSO-Sk with the standard PSO (CPSO-Hk). A similar idea was used in Cooperative Bacterial Foraging Optimization (CBFO) [35] and Cooperative Artificial Bee Colony (CABC) [36]. Both approaches had two modifications: CBFO-S, CBFO-H, CABC-H, and CABC-S.

2.3. Decomposition-Based Approaches with Random Grouping

In random grouping approaches, subcomponents vary during the search process. One of the first approaches DECC-G [37] has proposed a combination of random grouping and Self-adaptive Differential Evolution with Neighborhood Search (SaNSDE) [38] that demonstrates high performance for LSGO benchmarks and is still used as a base-line for evaluating and comparing new LSGO approaches.

In Multilevel Cooperative Co-evolution (MLCC) [39], SaNSDE is combined with modified random grouping, which uses a distribution of probabilities for choosing subcomponents from a decomposition pool based on the success of the previous choices. In DECC-ML, a modification of MLCC with a better optimizer for the more frequent random grouping was proposed [40]. Cooperatively Co-evolving Particle Swarms algorithms (CCPSO and CCPSO2) [41,42] use random grouping with PSO. CCPSO2 applies a random search for dynamic regrouping variables. In Cooperative Co-evolution Orthogonal Artificial Bee Colony (CCOABC) [43], random grouping is combined with the ABC algorithm.

Memetic Framework for Solving Large-scale Optimization Problems (MLSHADE-SPA) [44] is a multi-algorithms approach, which iteratively applies Success History-based Differential Evolution with Linear Population Size Reduction (L-SHADE) [45], two self-adaptive DE algorithms, and a modified version of MTS. All algorithms are applied for the whole optimization problem and for subcomponents. MLSHADE-SPA has taken second place in the 2018 IEEE CEC LSGO competition.

2.4. Learning-Based Grouping Approaches

The idea behind algorithms of this type is to identify the interaction of decision variables and group them into the same subcomponent. For some separable test problems, the algorithms can identify true subcomponents.

Correlation-based Adaptive Variable Partitioning (CCEA-AVP) [46] evaluates the correlation matrix for the best solutions (in the original algorithm, half of the population is used). Variables for which values of the correlation coefficient are greater than a threshold are placed in one group. In [47], CCEA-AVP uses NSGA-2 as the core optimizer. Contribution Based Cooperative Co-evolution (CBCC) applies SaNSDE with Delta Grouping and Ideal Grouping algorithms [48]. Each subcomponent is optimized using the number of function evaluations based on the improvement of the objective function obtained by this component. The delta grouping approach is also applied in Cooperative Co-evolution with Delta Grouping (DECC-DML) [49]. In Cooperative Co-evolution with Variable Interaction Learning (CCVIL) [50], groups are formed iteratively starting with one-dimensional subcomponents, which are combined if the interaction between them is detected. CCVIL uses JADE [51] for optimizing subcomponents. Dependency Identification with Memetic Algorithm (DIMA) [52] applies the local search algorithm proposed in [53] for detecting the interaction of variables.

Differential grouping is based on the mathematical definition of a partially additively separable function that is used for the identification of the interaction of variables. Cooperative Co-Evolution with Differential Grouping (DECC-DG) [54], Extended Differential Grouping (DECC-XDG) [55], and modified DECC-DG2 [56] use the SaNSDE algorithm for evolving subcomponents. A competitive divide and-conquer algorithm (CC-GDG-CMAES) [57] combines differential grouping with the CMA-ES optimizer. In Differential Grouping with Spectral Clustering (DGSC) [58], SaNSDE is applied for subcomponents discovered using clustering of the identified interactions in variables.

Some original approaches are proposed in Scaling Up Covariance Matrix Adaptation Evolution Strategy (CC-CMA-ES) [59], Cooperative co-evolution with Sensitivity Analysis-based Budget Assignment Strategy (SACC) [60], Bi-space Interactive Cooperative Co-evolutionary Algorithm (BICCA) [61], and Cooperative Co-evolution with Soft Grouping (SGCC) [62]. All approaches, except CC-CMA-ES, use self-adaptive DE algorithms.

A recursive decomposition method (RDG) [63] proposes a new approach for better differential grouping. CC-RDG3 [12] combines CMA-ES with RDG for the efficient identification of overlapping subcomponents. Authors have shown that CC-RDG3 can greatly improve LSGO algorithms. CC-RDG3 has taken first place in the 2019 IEEE CEC LSGO competition and it is still the leading LSGO approach. An Incremental Recursive Ranking Grouping (IRRG) is one of the recent approaches that uses monotonicity checking for more accurate identification of variable linkages [64]. IRRG requires more fitness function evaluations than RDG3, but never reports false linkages.

2.5. LSGO State-of-the-Art Algorithms

We have summarized all approaches mentioned above in Table 1 to highlight their main features, such as the type of decomposition, and the global and local search algorithms used. As we can see from the proposed review, many state-of-the-art LSGO algorithms contain, in different combinations, three main components: problem decomposition with cooperative co-evolution, a global optimizer, and a local search algorithm. The majority of the algorithms apply a self-adaptive DE as the global search technique. In Table 2, all participants of the IEEE CEC LSGO competitions of different years are collected. In the table, one can find out the winners of the competitions and what components (CC, DE, and LS) are implemented in the algorithms (a "plus" sign indicates that the corresponding components are used).

Table 1. The summary of the reviewed LSGO approaches.

Approach	Decomposition Type	Global Search	Local Search
ABBO [29]	No	miniLHSDE	No
BICCA [61]	Learning	L-SHADE	No
CBCC [48]	Learning	SaNSDE	No
CC-CMA-ES [59]	Learning	CMA-ES	No
CCDE-H [33]	Static	DE	No
CCDE-O [33]	Static	DE	No
CCEA-AVP [46]	Learning	NSGA-2	No
CCGA [30]	Static	GA	No
CC-GDG-CMAES [57]	Learning	CMA-ES	No
CC-RDG3 [12]	Learning	CMA-ES	No
CCVIL [50]	Learning	JADE	No
C-DEEPSO [17]	Random	EP, PSO, and DE	No
DECC-DG [54]	Learning	SaNSDE	No
DECC-DG2 [56]	Learning	SaNSDE	No
DECC-DML [49]	Learning	SaNSDE	No
DECC-G [37]	Random	SaNSDE	No
DECC-XDG [55]	Learning	SaNSDE	No
DGSC [58]	Learning	SaNSDE	No
DIMA [52]	Learning	GA	Self-directed Local Search
DMS-PSO [15]	No	PSO	Quasi-Newton method
IHDELS [20]	No	SaDE	MTS-LS1, L-BFGS-B
IPOPCMA-ES [23]	No	CMA-ES	No
IRRG [64]	Learning	CMA-ES	No
MLCC [39]	Random	SaNSDE	No
MLSHADE-SPA [44]	Random	L-SHADE	MTS-LS1
MOS [14]	No	No	Solis and Wets, MTS-LS1
MOS 2013 [25]	No	GA	Solis Wets, MTS-LS1
MPS-CMA-ES [27]	No	CMA-ES	No
MTS [19]	No	No	MTS-LS1, MTS-LS2, MTS-LS3
SACC [60]	Learning	SaNSDE	No
SGCC [62]	Learning	SaNSDE	No
SHADE-ILS [13]	No	SHADE	MTS-LS1, L-BFGS-B
VMODE [18]	Static	DE	No

Table 2. LSGO state-of-the-art algorithms.

Algorithm	Year	Winner	2nd	3rd	CC	DE	LS
CC-CMA-ES	2015			2015	+	−	−
DEEPSO	2015				−	+	−
IHDELS	2015		2015		−	+	+
SACC	2015				+	+	+
VMODE	2015				−	+	−
BICCA	2018				+	−	−
MPS	2019		2019		−	−	−
SGCC	2019			2019	+	+	−
DECC-G	2015, 2018				+	+	−
MOS	2015, 2018	2015		2018	−	+	+
MLSHADE-SPA	2018		2018		−	+	+
SHADE-ILS	2018	2018			−	+	+
CC-RDG3	2019	2019			+	−	−
DGSC	2019				+	+	−

As we can see from Table 2, 10 of 14 participants use DE as a core global optimizer, 7 algorithms apply problem decomposition with CC, and 5 algorithms are memetic. All winners use DE and all winners, except CC-RDG3, use local search. The current leader, CC-RDG3, applies problem decomposition with CC. From a historical perspective, we can notice that leading approaches improve global and local algorithms and develop more advanced frameworks for problem decomposition and adaptive control of the interaction of global and local search. This fact motivates us to design new approaches that combine all 3 components.

3. The Proposed Approach

As we can see from the review in the previous section, the majority of state-of-the-art approaches use CC. At the same time, many CC approaches apply an additional learning stage before the main subcomponents' optimization stage. The learning stage is used for identifying interconnected and independent variables. The identification of non-separable groups of variables usually takes a sufficiently large number of function evaluations (FEVs), which could be utilized for the main optimization process. However, the finding of all non-separable groups does not guarantee the high efficiency of solving the obtained optimization sub-problems.

The proposed approach uses an adaptive change of the number of subcomponents, which leads to a dynamic redistribution of the use of computational resources. The set of values of the number of subcomponents is predefined and it is a parameter of the algorithm, which can be set based on the limitations of FEVs. As it was shown in [65,66], it is better to use different decompositions for different stages of the optimization process while exploring different regions of the search space instead of using the only decomposition even it is correct. We have discovered that, in general, an optimizer better operates small subcomponents at the early stages and the whole solution vector at the final stage, when a basin of a global optimum is discovered. Additionally, the way of adaptive changing the number of subcomponents can vary for different types of LSGO problems.

We will use the following algorithm for adaptive change of the number of subcomponents. We will run many optimizers, which use decompositions with subcomponents of different sizes. Each algorithm uses its number of FEVs based on its success in the previous generations. Thus, we dynamically redistribute resources in favor of a more preferable decomposition variant.

A set of M values of the number of subcomponents is defined as $\{CC_1, CC_2, \ldots, CC_M\}$, where all elements should be different, i.e., $CC_1 \neq CC_2 \neq \ldots \neq CC_M$. At the initialization stage, for each of M algorithms, we assign equal resources defined as the number of generations ($G_i, i = 1, \ldots, M$). After all resources are exhausted by algorithms, we start a new cycle by redistributing the resources. In each cycle, algorithms are applied consequently in random order.

At the end of the run of each algorithm, we evaluate the improvement rate (2):

$$improvment\_rate_i = \frac{(best\_found_{before} - best\_found_{after})}{best\_found_{after}}, \quad (2)$$

here $best\_found_{before}$ is the best-found solution before the run, and $best\_found_{after}$ is the best-found solution after the run, and $i = 1, \ldots, M$.

After each cycle, all algorithms are ranked by their improvement rates. The best algorithm increases its resource by G_{win} generations, which is a sum of G_{lose} generations subtracted from resources of all the rest algorithms. For all algorithms, we define G_{min} for preventing the situation when the current-winner algorithm takes all resources and eliminates all other participants.

In the proposed approach, we will run the MTS-LS1 algorithm after CC-based SHADE. Usually, MTS-LS1 can find a new best-found solution that becomes far from other individuals in the population. In this case, SHADE cannot improve the best-found solution for a long time but improves the average fitness in the population. Criterion (2) becomes insensitive to differences in the behavior of algorithms if the improving rate is calculated using the best-found solution. To overcome this difficulty, we will calculate the improving rate using the median fitness before and after an algorithm run using (3) instead of (2).

$$improving\_rate_i = \frac{medianFitness_{before} - medianFitness_{after}}{medianFitness_{after}}, \quad (3)$$

here $medianFitness$ is the median fitness of individuals in the population, and $i = 1, \ldots, M$.

We will use the following approach for changing the number of generations assigned for each algorithm in the cooperation (4)–(8):

$$IR = \left\{ i : improvment\_rate_i = \max_{j=1,\ldots,M} \{improvment\_rate_j\} \right\} \quad (4)$$

$$NI = |IR| \quad (5)$$

$$pool = \sum_{j=1}^{M} \begin{cases} G_{lose}, & \text{if } (G_i - G_{lose} \geq G_{min}) \wedge i \notin IR \\ 0, & \text{otherwise} \end{cases} \quad (6)$$

$$G_{win} = \left\lfloor \frac{pool}{NI} \right\rfloor \quad (7)$$

$$G_i = \begin{cases} G_i + G_{win}, & \text{if } i \in IR \\ G_i - G_{lose}, & \text{if } (G_i - G_{lose} \geq G_{min}) \wedge i \notin IR \\ G_{min}, & \text{if } (G_i - G_{lose} < G_{min}) \wedge i \notin IR \end{cases} \quad (8)$$

here IR is a set of indexes of algorithms with the best improving rate, NI is the number of algorithms with the best improving rate, $pool$ is a pool of resources for redistribution, and $i = 1, \ldots, M$.

We will use SHADE as a core optimizer for subcomponents in CC-based algorithms. In our review, we have shown that almost all competition winners and state-of-the-art algorithms use one of the modifications of DE. The main benefit of the SHADE algorithm in solving "black-box" optimization problems is that it has only two control parameters, which can be automatically tuned during the optimization process [67].

The main parameters of DE (scale factor F and crossover rate Cr) in SHADE are self-configuring. SHADE uses a historical memory, which contains H pairs of the parameters from the previous generations. A mutant vector is created using a random pair of the parameters from the historical memory. When applying SHADE with CC, we will use specific parameters Cr and F for each subcomponent.

SHADE, like many other DE algorithms, uses an external archive for saving some promising solutions from the previous generations. SHADE records the parameter values and the corresponding function increments when a better solution is found. After each generation, SHADE calculates new values of the control parameters using the weighted Lehmer mean [67]. New calculated values of Cr and F are placed in the historical memory.

SHADE uses the *current-to-pbest/1* mutation scheme. The archived solutions can be chosen and reused at the mutation stage for maintaining the population diversity.

Our experimental results have shown that the use of independent populations and archives for each of the algorithms does not increase the overall performance of the proposed approach. In this work, all algorithms in the cooperation use the same population and archive.

One of the important control parameters of EA-based algorithms is the population size. A large population is more preferable at the exploration stage, when the algorithm converges, it loses the population diversity and the population size can be increased. If the variance of coordinates is high (individuals are well distributed in the search space), we reduce the population size and drop out randomly chosen solutions except the best one. We will use an adaptive size of the population based on the analysis of the diversity. The following diversity measure (9) is used [68]:

$$DI = \sqrt{\frac{1}{NP} \sum_{i=1}^{NP} \sum_{j=1}^{n} (x_{ij} - \bar{x}_j)^2}, k = 1, \ldots, M, \quad (9)$$

here NP is the population size, n is the dimensionality of the objective function, $\bar{x}_j$ is the average value of the j-th variable of all individuals in the population.

After each cycle, we define a new population size for each algorithm using (10)–(13).

$$RD = \frac{DI}{DI_{init}} \quad (10)$$

$$RFES = \frac{FEVs}{maxFEVs} \quad (11)$$

$$rRD = 1 - \frac{RFES}{0.9} \quad (12)$$

$$NP = \begin{cases} NP+1, & \text{if } (NP+1 \leq maxNP) \land (RD < 0.9 \cdot rRD) \\ NP-1, & \text{if } (NP-1 \geq minNP) \land (RD > 1.1 \cdot rRD) \\ NP, & \text{otherwise} \end{cases} \quad (13)$$

here RD is relative diversity, $RFES$ is a relative spend of the FEV budget ($maxFEVs$), rRD is the required value of RD, $minNP$, and $maxNP$ are low and upper bounds for the population size.

The relationship between RD and $RFES$ is presented in Figure 1.

If the variance of coordinates is high (individuals are well distributed in the search space), we reduce the population size and drop out randomly chosen solutions except the best one. If the variance is low (individuals are concentrated in some region of the search space), we increase the population size by adding new random solutions. The approach tries to keep relative diversity close to rRD, which linearly decreases with spending FEVs.

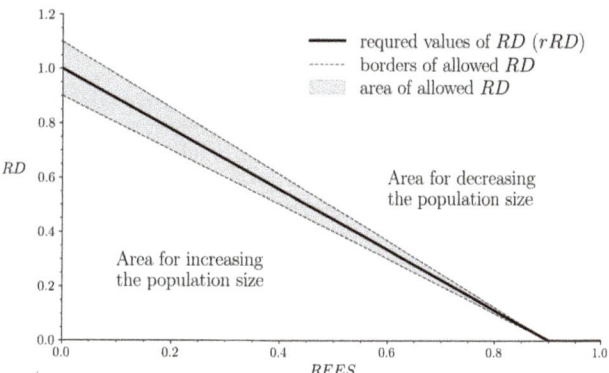

Figure 1. Diversity-based mechanism of population size adaptation.

The proposed above ideas are implemented in our new algorithm titled COSACC-LS1. One of the hyper-parameters of COSACC-LS1 is the number of algorithms with different subcomponents (M). Because of the high computational cost of LSGO experiments, in this research we have tried $M = 3$ and the following combinations of the number of subcomponents: $\{1,2,4\}$, $\{1,2,8\}$, $\{1,2,10\}$, $\{1,4,8\}$, $\{1,4,10\}$, $\{1,8,10\}$, $\{2,4,8\}$, and $\{2,4,10\}$. Thereafter, we will use the notation "COSACC-LS1 $\{x,y,z\}$", where x, y, and z stands for the number of subcomponents, which are used in three DE algorithms: CC-SHADE(x), CC-SHADE(y), and CC-SHADE(z).

We have tried different mutation schemes and have obtained that the best performance of COSACC-LS1 is reached using the following scheme (14):

$$u_i = x_i + F_i \cdot \left(x_{pbest} - x_i\right) + F_i \cdot (x_t - x_r), i = 1, \ldots, NP, \quad (14)$$

here, u_i is a mutant vector, F_i is the scale factor, x_{pbest} is a random solution chosen from the p best solutions, x_t is an individual chosen using the tournament selection from the population (the tournament size is 2), x_r is a random solution chosen from the union of the current population and the archive, and all solutions chosen for performing mutation must be different, i.e., $i \neq pbest \neq t \neq r$.

The size of the archive is set two times larger than the initial population size. The size of historical memory in SHADE is set to 6 (the value is defined using grid search).

We have chosen MTS-LS1 for implementing local search in COSACC, because it demonstrates high performance in solving LSGO problems both alone and when applied with a global search algorithm [19]. We use the following settings for MTS-LS1. The maximum number of FEVs is 25000 (the value is defined by numerical experiments). MTS-LS1 searches along each i-th coordinate using the search range $SR[i]$. The initialization of $SR[i]$ is the same as in the original MTS: ($SR[i] = (b-a) \cdot 0.4$), where $[a,b]$ is low and high bounds for the i-th variable. If a better solution is not found using the current value of $SR[i]$, it is reduced ($SR[i] = SR[i]/2$). If $SR[i]$ becomes less than 1E-18 (the original threshold was 1E-15), the value is reinitialized.

MTS-LS1 is applied after each main cycle starting with the current best-found solution until maximum FEVs are reached.

The initial number of generations for all algorithms is 15, the minimum value is 5, respectively. After a cycle, we will add $(M-1)$ generation to G for the algorithm with the highest improving rate. All other algorithms will reduce the number of generations by one. The initial population size is 100, minimum and maximum values are 25 and 200, respectively. After the algorithm spends 90% of its computational resource, the population size is set to its minimum value as proposed in [68] (in this work the value is 25).

The whole implementation scheme for the proposed approach is presented using pseudocode in Algorithm 1.

Algorithm 1 The general scheme of COSACC-LS1

Require: The number of algorithms M in CC, the number of subcomponents for each algorithm, n, NP, $minNP$, $maxNP$, G_{init}, G_{lose}, G_{min}, $maxFEVs$.
Ensure:
  $population \leftarrow RandomPopulation(n, NP)$
  $DI_{init} \leftarrow CalculateDiversity(population)$ ▷ Using Equation (9)
  for all $i = 1, \ldots, M$ **do**
    $G_i \leftarrow G_{init}$
  end for
  while $FEVs < maxFEVs$ **do**
    for all $i \in RandomPermutation(1, \ldots, M)$ **do**
      $medianFitness\_before \leftarrow GetMedianFitness(population)$
      for $g \leftarrow 1, G_i$ **do**
        $best\_found \leftarrow CC\text{-}SHADE(population, NP, i)$
        $RD \leftarrow EvalRD(DI_{init}, population, NP)$ ▷ Equation (10)
        $NP \leftarrow EvalPopsize(RD, maxFEVs, NP, maxNP)$ ▷ Equation (13)
      end for
      $medianFitness\_after \leftarrow GetMedianFitness(population)$
      $improving\_rate_i \leftarrow \frac{medianFitness\_before - medianFitness\_after}{medianFitness\_after}$
    end for
    for all $i = 1, \ldots, M$ **do**
      $G_i \leftarrow EvalNumGenerations(improving\_rate_i)$ ▷ Equation (8)
    end for
    $best\_found \leftarrow GetBestFound(population)$
    $best\_found \leftarrow MTS\text{-}LS1(best\_found)$
  end while

---

4. Experimental Setups and Implementation

We have investigated the performance of COSACC-LS1 and have compared the results with other state-of-the-art approaches using the actual LSGO benchmark, proposed at the special session of IEEE Congress on Evolutionary Computation in 2013 [5]. The benchmark proposes 15 "black-box" real-valued LSGO problems. There are 4 types of problems, namely fully-separable functions (F1–F3), partially separable functions (F4–F11), functions with overlapping subcomponents (F12–F14), and fully-nonseparable functions (F15). The functions have many features, which complicate solving the problems using standard EAs and other metaheuristics. Some of the features are non-uniform subcomponent sizes, imbalance in the contribution of subcomponents, overlapping subcomponents, transformations to the base functions, ill-conditioning, symmetry breaking, and irregularities [48,69].

The performance measure for LSGO algorithms is the error of the best-found solution averaged over 25 independent runs. The error is an absolute difference between the best-found solution and the true value of a global optimum. The maximum FEVs in a run is 3.0E+06. Based on the benchmark rules, the following additional data is collected: for each problem, the best-found fitness values averaged over 25 runs are saved after 1.2E+05, 6.0E+05, and 3.0E+06 FEVs. We also will estimate the variance of the results using the best, median, worst, mean, and standard deviation of the results.

Authors of the LSGO CEC 2013 benchmark propose software implementation using C++, Java, and Python programming languages. For a fair comparison of the results with other state-of-the-art algorithms, the Toolkit for Automatic Comparison of Optimizers (TACO) [6,70] is used. TACO is an online database, which proposes the automatic comparison of the results uploaded by users with the results of selected LSGO algorithms stored in the database. TACO presents reports of the results of ranking the selected algorithms based on the Formula 1 ranking system. The ranking is presented for the whole benchmark and each of the 4 types of problems.

Experimental analysis of new LSGO approaches is very expensive in terms of computational time. For all computational experiments, the proposed approach has been implemented using C++. The C++ language usually demonstrates higher computing speed and has wide possibilities for parallelization using many computers with many CPU cores. We have designed and assembled our computational cluster based on 8 AMD Ryzen Pro CPUs, which, in total, supply 128 threads for parallel computing. The MPICH2 (Message Passing Interface Chameleon) framework for connecting all PCs in the cluster is used. The Master–Slave communication scheme with the queue is applied. The operating system is Ubuntu LTS 20.04. One series of experiments using the LSGO benchmark using the cluster takes about 2 h compared to 265 h when using a single computer with regular sequential computing. The source codes and additional information on our cluster are available on https://github.com/VakhninAleksei/COSACC-LS1 (accessed on 01 September 2022).

5. The Experimental Results

The results of evaluating COSACC-LS1 with the best configuration $\{1, 2, 4\}$ on the IEEE CEC LSGO benchmark are presented in Table 3. The results contain the best, median, worst, mean, and standard deviation values of the best-found solutions from 25 independent runs after 1.2E+05, 6.0E+05, and 3.0E+06 FEVs (following the benchmark rules).

Table 3. The experimental results on the IEEE CEC 2013 LSGO benchmark.

Problems:		F1	F2	F3	F4	F5	F6	F7	F8
1.20E+05	Best	2.82E−06	1.02E+03	2.00E+01	1.28E+10	1.55E+06	1.04E+06	1.14E+09	6.24E+14
	Median	5.13E−06	1.14E+03	2.00E+01	1.23E+11	3.06E+06	1.05E+06	2.33E+09	2.05E+15
	Worst	1.05E−05	1.29E+03	2.00E+01	2.52E+11	4.88E+06	1.06E+06	4.86E+09	1.24E+16
	Mean	5.68E−06	1.14E+03	2.00E+01	1.32E+11	3.34E+06	1.05E+06	2.51E+09	2.92E+15
	StDev	2.10E−06	7.60E+01	1.91E−04	5.99E+10	9.76E+05	4.11E+03	9.57E+08	2.48E+15
6.00E+05	Best	0.00E+00	1.00E+03	2.00E+01	2.33E+09	9.08E+05	1.04E+06	2.62E+07	5.97E+13
	Median	0.00E+00	1.12E+03	2.00E+01	8.63E+09	1.07E+06	1.04E+06	6.26E+07	2.94E+14
	Worst	6.53E−24	1.24E+03	2.00E+01	3.95E+10	1.76E+06	1.05E+06	1.50E+08	7.11E+14
	Mean	2.61E−25	1.12E+03	2.00E+01	1.34E+10	1.13E+06	1.05E+06	6.74E+07	3.04E+14
	StDev	1.31E−24	7.42E+01	1.91E−04	1.09E+10	2.15E+05	3.34E+03	2.94E+07	1.69E+14
3.00E+06	Best	0.00E+00	1.00E+03	2.00E+01	1.21E+08	9.08E+05	1.04E+06	2.00E+02	1.36E+13
	Median	0.00E+00	1.11E+03	2.00E+01	1.27E+09	1.07E+06	1.04E+06	1.00E+04	6.58E+13
	Worst	0.00E+00	1.22E+03	2.00E+01	7.76E+09	1.76E+06	1.05E+06	1.80E+05	2.99E+14
	Mean	0.00E+00	1.11E+03	2.00E+01	2.17E+09	1.13E+06	1.04E+06	3.16E+04	8.02E+13
	StDev	0.00E+00	7.29E+01	1.57E−04	2.07E+09	2.15E+05	1.80E+03	5.38E+04	6.86E+13
		F9	F10	F11	F12	F13	F14	F15	
1.20E+05	Best	1.78E+08	9.26E+07	2.35E+10	9.62E+02	3.22E+09	1.62E+11	6.37E+07	
	Median	3.36E+08	9.38E+07	1.15E+11	1.95E+03	2.66E+10	3.55E+11	1.10E+08	
	Worst	4.30E+08	9.47E+07	3.11E+11	8.24E+03	4.65E+10	6.76E+11	2.21E+08	
	Mean	3.22E+08	9.38E+07	1.21E+11	2.48E+03	2.84E+10	3.87E+11	1.16E+08	
	StDev	6.69E+07	5.68E+05	8.24E+10	1.92E+03	8.76E+09	1.49E+11	3.84E+07	
6.00E+05	Best	8.42E+07	9.23E+07	7.22E+08	1.43E+02	1.09E+08	7.61E+08	1.11E+07	
	Median	1.23E+08	9.32E+07	1.34E+09	7.37E+02	1.90E+09	6.60E+09	1.54E+07	
	Worst	1.62E+08	9.38E+07	1.18E+10	1.62E+03	3.09E+09	2.68E+10	2.86E+07	
	Mean	1.25E+08	9.31E+07	1.71E+09	7.13E+02	1.97E+09	8.37E+09	1.67E+07	
	StDev	2.09E+07	4.27E+05	2.15E+09	3.23E+02	6.42E+08	6.58E+09	4.69E+06	
3.00E+06	Best	8.42E+07	9.23E+07	1.34E+06	7.72E−09	5.52E+04	6.53E+06	1.10E+06	
	Median	1.23E+08	9.27E+07	2.69E+06	1.20E+01	1.42E+06	9.11E+06	1.48E+06	
	Worst	1.62E+08	9.32E+07	3.70E+07	2.58E+02	2.60E+06	1.61E+07	2.26E+06	
	Mean	1.25E+08	9.27E+07	6.74E+06	5.02E+01	1.42E+06	9.25E+06	1.52E+06	
	StDev	2.10E+07	2.17E+05	1.06E+07	7.25E+01	6.37E+05	2.07E+06	2.94E+05	

At first, the results of COSACC-LS1 have been compered with its component algorithms, COSACC and LS1, to prove the benefits of their cooperation. Both component algorithms have been evaluated using their best settings obtained with the grid search. All comparisons have been performed using the median of the best-found solutions in the runs after spending the full FEVs budget. Table 4 contains the medians and the results of the Mann–Whitney–Wilcoxon (MWW) tests and ranking. High values of ranks are better. When the difference in the results is not statistically significant, algorithms share ranks. The average ranks are presented in Figure 2.

Table 4. The comparison of algorithms.

Problems:	F1	F2	F3	F4	F5	F6	F7	F8
				The median of the best-found solution				
COSACC (A1)	2.22E-14	6.70E+03	2.02E+01	3.02E+09	1.31E+06	1.06E+06	7.46E+05	3.04E+13
LS1 (A2)	0.00E+00	1.10E+03	2.00E+01	1.21E+11	2.05E+07	1.05E+06	1.44E+09	1.07E+16
COSACC-LS1 (A3)	0.00E+00	1.11E+03	2.00E+01	2.17E+09	1.13E+06	1.04E+06	3.16E+04	8.02E+13
				The MWW test				
A1 vs. A3, p-value	5.96E-08	5.96E-08	5.96E-08	1.34E-01	2.36E-02	5.96E-08	5.96E-08	1.40E-04
A1 vs. A2, p-value	5.96E-08	5.96E-08	5.96E-08	5.96E-08	5.96E-08	5.96E-08	5.96E-08	5.96E-08
A2 vs. A3, p-value	0.00E+00	3.25E-01	5.49E-02	5.96E-08	5.96E-08	7.50E-05	5.96E-08	5.96E-08
				The ranking of algorithms				
COSACC (A1)	1	1	1	2.5	2	1	2	3
LS1 (A2)	2.5	2.5	2.5	1	1	2	1	1
COSACC-LS1 (A3)	2.5	2.5	2.5	2.5	3	3	3	2
	F9	F10	F11	F12	F13	F14	F15	
				The median of the best-found solution				
COSACC (A1)	1.38E+08	9.39E+07	1.18E+07	1.85E+03	8.23E+06	2.07E+07	4.51E+05	
LS1 (A2)	1.76E+09	9.42E+07	2.21E+11	1.23E+03	1.35E+10	3.20E+11	7.59E+07	
COSACC-LS1 (A3)	1.25E+08	9.27E+07	6.74E+06	5.02E+01	1.42E+06	9.25E+06	1.52E+06	
				The MWW test				
A1 vs. A3, p-value	9.03E-02	5.96E-08	1.05E-02	5.96E-08	5.96E-08	2.98E-07	5.96E-08	
A1 vs. A2, p-value	5.96E-08	7.55E-02	5.96E-08	1.36E-02	5.96E-08	5.96E-08	5.96E-08	
A2 vs. A3, p-value	5.96E-08	5.96E-08	5.96E-08	5.96E-08	5.96E-08	5.96E-08	5.96E-08	
				The ranking of algorithms				
COSACC (A1)	2.5	1.5	2	1	2	2	3	
LS1 (A2)	1	1.5	1	2	1	1	1	
COSACC-LS1 (A3)	2.5	3	3	3	3	3	2	

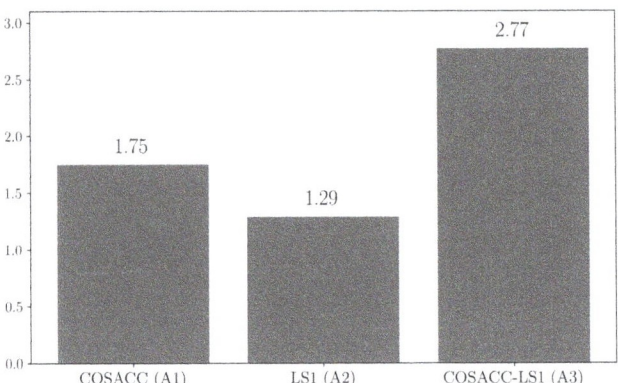

Figure 2. Average ranks of COSACC, LS1, and COSACC-LS1 algorithms.

As we can see from the results, COSACC-LS1 has won 8 times, 5 times has shared first place with a component algorithm, and 2 times has taken second place. On easy separable problems (F1–F6), single COSACC yields to both algorithms, because it spends the budget for exploration of the search space while LS1 greedy converges to an optimum. On average,

COSACC-LS1 obtains the best ranks, thus, in the case of black-box LSGO problems, the choice of the hybrid approach is preferable.

The following statistical data for each benchmark problem collected during independent runs of COSACC-LS1 have been visualized: convergence, dynamics of the population size, and redistribution of the computational resources for algorithms with the different number of subcomponents. Each plot presents the mean and standard deviation of 25 runs. The whole set of plots is presented in Appendix A (Figures A1–A15).

6. Discussion

In this section, we have analyzed 3 general situations in the algorithm behavior based on plots for F3, F8, and F10 problems.

LSGO problems are hard for many search techniques when they optimize the complete solution vector, and the problem decomposition can ease this issue. In our previous studies, we have discovered that the cooperation of multiple algorithms with a different number of subcomponents usually demonstrates the following usage of decompositions. At the initial generations, the best performance is obtained using many subcomponents of small sizes. Such component-wise search performs the exploration strategy. After that, the approach usually chooses algorithms with a smaller number of subcomponents and at the final generations, it optimizes the complete solution vector. Optimization without decomposition tries to improve the final solution and performs the exploitation strategy [65]. A similar behavior we can see for COSACC-LS1.

Figure A3 (see Appendix A) shows the dynamics of the algorithms on the F3 problem. F3 is a fully separable problem based on the Ackley function. At the same time, the problem is one of the hardest in the benchmark. The basin of global optimum is narrow. F3 has a huge number of local optima with almost the same values, which cover most of the search space.

As we can see in Figure A3a, the algorithm demonstrates fast convergence at the initial generations and after that, there are no significant improvements in the best-found value. The population size at the initial generations is big because the population diversity (DI) becomes less than the required relative diversity (rRD). This is the result of the fast convergence, and the algorithm tries to increase the population size up to the threshold value (Figure A3b). When the algorithm falls into stagnation, individuals save their positions, and the diversity becomes greater than rRD, thus the population size decreases. As we can see from low STD values, the situation is repeated in every run. The resource redistribution plots (Figure A3c) show that at the initial generations the algorithm prefers to use many subcomponents, but when it falls into stagnation, the algorithm takes this as the end of the exploration and gives resources for optimizing the complete solution vector.

Figure A8 shows the dynamics of the algorithms on the F8 problem, which is a combination of 20 non-separable shifted and rotated elliptic functions. The problem is assumed to be a good test function for decomposition-based approaches, but each subcomponent is a hard optimization problem, which is non-separable and has local irregularities.

As we can see in Figure A8a, the proposed approach demonstrates good convergence at the beginning of the optimization process and then stagnates. Figure A8b shows that the fast convergence leads to a loss in diversity (DI) and the algorithm increases the population size until 50% of FEVs is reached. In the middle of the budget spend, individuals have almost the same fitness values and do not improve the best-found value (plateau area in Figure A8b). Finally, the diversity (DI) becomes less than the required relative diversity (rRD) and the population size decreases. In contrast with the results on F3, before the algorithm falls into stagnation, the fast improvements in the objective lead to an increase in the population size for preventing local convergence.

Figure A8c shows that the algorithm distributes computational resources almost in equal portions on average. We can see an example of the true cooperative search when all component algorithms support each other. The standard deviation of the redistribution is high because the algorithm permanently adapts G_i values in the run.

Figure A10 presents the convergence on the F10 problem. F10 is a combination of 20 non-separable shifted and rotated Ackey's functions. As it was said previously, the Ackley function is one of the hardest in the benchmark and all Ackley-based problems are also very challenging tasks for LSGO approaches.

As we can in Figure A10a, the algorithm improves the fitness value permanently during the run. At the same time, the relative value of the improvements is low, and coordinates of individuals remain almost the same. The DI value becomes less than rRD at the early generations and the algorithm decreases the population size (Figure A10b). As we have mentioned previously, slow convergence and stagnation usually are the result of the end of the exploration stage and the algorithm prefers to optimize the complete solution vector instead of decomposition-based subcomponents. As we can see in Figure A10c, COSACC-LS1 gives all resources to the component algorithm with no decomposition.

Here it should be noted that in all experiments all component algorithms have a minimum guarantee amount of the computational resource. Even when one of the algorithms is leading, this can still be the result of the cooperation of multiple decompositions, and their small contribution essentially increases the performance of the leading algorithm.

As we can see from the presented convergence plots, COSACC-LS1 demonstrates the self-configuration capability. The approach can adaptively select the best decomposition option using redistribution of the computational resource. Different behavior for different LSGO problems ensures that COSACC-LS1 adapts to the topology of the given objective function. Another feature of the proposed approach is the adaptive control of the population size that maintains the population diversity and prevents the premature convergence.

Finally, the results of COSACC-LS1 have been compared with state-of-the-art approaches using the TACO online database. For the comparison, we have selected all algorithms, which were winners and prize-winners of all previous IEEE CEC LSGO competitions: CC-CMA-ES, CC-RDG3, IHDELS, MLSHADE-SPA, MOS, MPS, SGCC, and SHADEILS (see Table 2). Additionally, we have added DECC-G as it is used as a baseline in the majority of studies and experimental comparisons. Table 5 and Figure 3 show the results of the comparison. For all algorithms, we can see the sum of scores obtained on all benchmark problems and the sum of scores for each type of LSGO problems. The following notation for classes of LSGO problems is used: non-separable functions (Class 1), overlapping functions (Class 2), functions with no separable subcomponents (Class 3), functions with a separable subcomponent (Class 4), and fully-separable functions (Class 5).

Table 5. Comparison of state-of-the-art algorithms.

	Class 1	Class 2	Class 3	Class 4	Class 5	Sum	Mean	Std
SHADEILS	25	61	49	57	33	225	45	15.49
COSACC-LS1	15	58	48	45	43	209	41.8	16.05
CC-RDG3	12	35	76	68	14	205	41	29.83
MLSHADE-SPA	4	36	56	48	60	204	40.8	22.52
MOS	10	32	37	46	58	183	36.6	17.85
IHDELS	8	32	33	28	27	128	25.6	10.16
MPS	6	7	28	46	13	100	20	16.99
SGCC	18	20	33	23	4	98	19.6	10.45
CC-CMA-ES	2	14	32	19	28	95	19	11.87
DECC-G	1	8	15	24	30	78	15.6	11.72

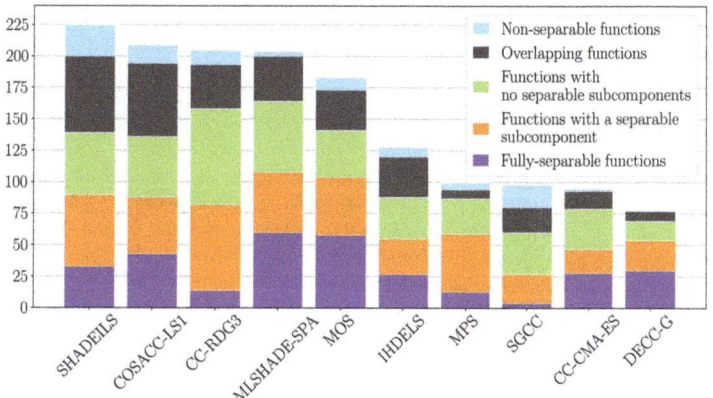

Figure 3. Summary scores of state-of-the-art algorithms.

The LSGO benchmark contains only one fully non-separable problem and three problems with overlapping components, which are the hardest problems. At the same time, an algorithm can obtain high summary scores if it has high scores for the type of LSGO problem, which contains many problems.

As we can see from the comparison, CC-RDG3, SHADE-SPA, and MOS have average scores for non-separable and overlapping problems but perform well for other types of LSGO problems. SGCC is the second-best in solving non-separable problems and yields in solving all the rest. SHADEILS is still the competition winner, but it demonstrates low performance when solving fully separable problems because it does not use any decomposition approach that can improve the results for this type.

To better investigate the results for each class of LSGO problems, we have adjusted the given scores by the number of problems of each class. Table 6 shows the results adjusted for the number of problems in each class. Figure 4 demonstrates the variance of scores for the 5 best algorithms. MLSHADE-SPA and MOS obtain high scores for fully-separable functions (outliers in Figure 4), although the results for all other classes have low variance, they are below median values of leading approaches. Median values of SHADEILS and COSACC-LS1 are close, but, as we can see, COSACC-LS1 has less variance thus the results are more stable. We can see that the variance in SHADEILS is towards larger ranks, at the same time this is true only with this benchmark set, because the approach is fine-tuned for the benchmark.

Table 6. Comparison of state-of-the-art algorithms.

	Class 1	Class 2	Class 3	Class 4	Class 5	Sum	Mean	Std
SHADEILS	25	20.33	12.25	14.25	11	82.83	16.57	5.92
COSACC-LS1	15	19.33	12	11.25	14.33	71.92	14.38	3.18
CC-RDG3	12	11.67	19	17	4.67	64.33	12.87	5.57
MLSHADE-SPA	4	12	14	12	20	62	12.4	5.73
MOS	10	10.67	9.25	11.5	19.33	60.75	12.15	4.1
IHDELS	8	10.67	8.25	7	9	42.92	8.58	1.37
SGCC	18	6.67	8.25	5.75	1.33	40	8	6.15
MPS	6	2.33	7	11.5	4.33	31.17	6.23	3.44
CC-CMA-ES	2	4.67	8	4.75	9.33	28.75	5.75	2.92
DECC-G	1	2.67	3.75	6	10	23.42	4.68	3.48

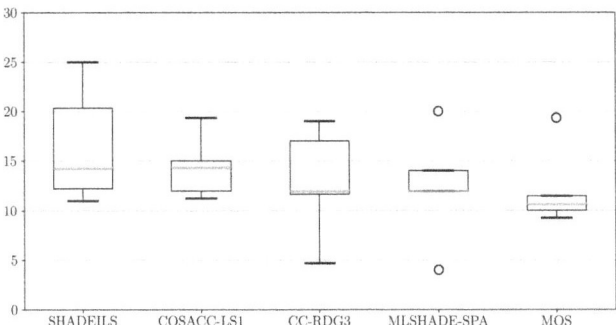

Figure 4. Variance of the adjusted scores.

Taking into account the number of problems of each type, we can conclude that the proposed algorithm performs well with all types of LSGO problems. This fact makes COSACC-LS1 preferable in solving "black-box" LSGO problems when information on the problem type is not available. At the same time, COSACC-LS1 proposes a general framework for hybridization of multiple problem decomposition schemes, a global optimizer, and a local search algorithm, thus it has great potential for further improving its performance by applying other component approaches.

7. Conclusions

In this paper, a framework for solving LSGO problems has been proposed and a new optimization algorithm COSACC-LS1 based on the framework has been designed and investigated. The performance of COSACC-LS1 has been evaluated and compared with state-of-the-art approaches using the IEEE CEC LSGO 2013 benchmark and the TACO database. The proposed approach outperforms all LSGO competition winners except for one approach—SHADEILS. At the same time, COSACC-LS1 performs well with all types of LSGO problems, while SHADEILS shows poor results on fully-separable problems.

COSACC-LS1 proposed an original hybridization of three main LSGO techniques: CC, DE, and LS. In this work, we have applied SHADE as a DE component, MTS LS1 as LS, and a new approach for the adaptive selection of problem decomposition (several variants with different sizes of subcomponents). The proposed framework does not specify the exact choice of component algorithms, and the user may apply any global and local search algorithm. In that sense, the proposed approach has potential for improvement. In our further research we will examine the proposed framework with other stochastic population-based metaheuristics.

Interaction of three CC-based algorithms demonstrates high performance due to adaptive redistribution of computational resources. We have visualized the redistribution and have found that the approach can adapt to a new environment (new landscape of a LSGO problem). Instead of selecting one variant of decomposition, the interaction allows the component algorithm with the least amount of resources to still participate in the optimization process, and we can see that the algorithm contributes to the optimization process in some regions of the search space.

The well-known "No free lunch" theorem says that it is not possible to choose one optimization algorithm that performs well for all types and instances of optimization problems. At the same time, we can relax the theorem by introducing self-adaptive control of multiple approaches. The approach can adaptively design an effective algorithm (by giving more computations to the best component algorithm) for a specific optimization problem, as well as for a specific region of the search space within the optimization process.

Even though the LSGO benchmark contains many types of LSGO problems, many real-world optimization problems are not well studied and can require fine adjustment of some COSACC-LS1 parameters. In further work, we will address the issue of developing an approach for online adaptation of the internal parameters of the subcomponent optimizers.

Author Contributions: A.V.: methodology, software, validation, investigation, resources, writing—original draft preparation, visualization; E.S. (Evgenii Sopov): conceptualization, methodology, formal analysis, writing—review and editing, visualization, supervision; E.S. (Eugene Semenkin): conceptualization, formal analysis, writing—review and editing, supervision, funding acquisition. All authors have read and agreed to the published version of the manuscript.

Funding: This work was supported by the Ministry of Science and Higher Education of the Russian Federation within limits of state contract No. FEFE-2020-0013.

Institutional Review Board Statement: Not applicable.

Informed Consent Statement: Not applicable.

Data Availability Statement: Not applicable.

Conflicts of Interest: The authors declare no conflict of interest.

Nomenclature

The following abbreviations are used in this manuscript:

$best\_found_{before}$	The best found solution before an optimization cycle
$best\_found_{after}$	The best found solution after an optimization cycle
$CalculateDiversity(population)$	Function for calculating the diversity of the population
CC_i	The number of subcomponents of the i-th algorithm
$CC-SHADE(population, NP, i)$	Function for evolving the population using the cooperative coevolution algorithm with NP individuals and i subcomponents
Cr	Crossover rate
$current - to - pbest/1$	Mutation scheme in SHADE
DI	Population diversity
$EvalNumGenerations$	Function for calculating a new number of generations
$EvalPopsize$	Function for calculating a new value of the population size
$EvalRD$	Function for calculating relative diversity of the population
F	Scale factor
FEV	The number of function evaluations
G_i	The number of generations of the i-th algorithm
G_{lose}	The minimal number of generations
G_{lose}	The number of generations by which the budget of algorithms is reduced
G_{win}	The number of generations by which the budget of algorithms is increases
$GetBestFound$	Function that returns the best-found solution from the population
$GetMedianFitness(population)$	Function that returns the median fitness value in the population
H	The number of F and Cr pairs in SHADE
$improvment\_rate_i$	The change of the best-found fitness of the i-th algorithm in an optimization cycle
IR	A set of indexes of algorithms with the best improvement rate
M	The number of algorithms
$maxFEVs$	The maximum number of fitness function evaluations
$maxNP$	The upper bound for the population size
$minNP$	The lower bound for the population size
$medianFitness_{before}$	The median fitness in the population before an optimization cycle
$medianFitness_{after}$	The median fitness in the population after an optimization cycle
n	The number of decision variables
NI	The number of algorithms with the best improvement rate
NP	The population size
$pool$	The number of generations for redistribution

$RandomPermutation$	Function that randomly permutes values of a vector
$RandomPopulation(n, NP)$	Function that generates a random population with NP individuals of n variables
RD	The relative diversity
$RFES$	The relative spend of the FEV budget
rRD	The required value of RD
$SR[i]$	A search range for the i-th coordinate in MTS-LS1
STD	The standard deviation
u	A mutant vector
x_{pbest}	A random solution chosen from the p best individuals
x_t	An individual chosen using the tournament selection

Acronyms

The following acronyms are used in this manuscript:

ABBO	Automated Black-box Optimization
BICCA	Bi-space Interactive Cooperative Co-evolutionary Algorithm
CABC	Cooperative Artificial Bee Colony
CBCC	Contribution Based Cooperative Co-evolution
CBFO	Cooperative Bacterial Foraging Optimization
CC	Cooperative Co-evolution
CC-CMA-ES	Scaling up Covariance Matrix Adaptation Evolution Strategy
CCDE	Cooperative Co-evolutionary Differential Evolution
CCEA-AVP	Correlation-based Adaptive Variable Partitioning
CCFR2	Extended Cooperative Co-evolution Framework
CCGA	Cooperative Co-evolutionary Approach for Genetic Algorithm
CC-GDG-CMAES	Competitive Divide-and-conquer Algorithm Covariance Matrix Adaptation Evolution Strategy
CCOABC	Cooperative Co-evolution Orthogonal Artificial Bee Colony
CCPSO	Cooperatively Co-evolving Particle Swarms Algorithm
CC-RDG3	Cooperative Co-evolution Recursive Differential Grouping
CCVIL	Cooperative Co-evolution with Variable Interaction Learning
C-DEEPSO	Canonical Differential Evolutionary Particle Swarm Optimization
CEC	IEEE Congress on Evolutionary Computation
COSACC-LS1	Coordination of Self-adaptive Cooperative Co-evolution Algorithms with Local Search
CPSO	Cooperative Approach to Particle Swarm Optimization
CPSO-Hk	Combination of Cooperative Approach to Particle Swarm Optimization with k Subcomponents with the Standard Particle Swarm Optimization
CPSO-Sk	Cooperative Approach to Particle Swarm Optimization with k Subcomponents
CPU	Central Processing Unit
DE	Differential Evolution
DECC-DG	Cooperative Co-Evolution with Differential Grouping
DECC-DG2	Cooperative Co-Evolution with A Faster and More Accurate Differential Grouping
DECC-DML	Cooperative Co-evolution with Delta Grouping
DECC-G	Self-Adaptive Differential Evolution with Neighborhood Search with Cooperative Co-evolution
DECC-ML	Multilevel Cooperative Co-evolution with More Frequent Random Grouping
DECC-XDG	Cooperative Co-Evolution with Extended Differential Grouping
DGSC	Differential Grouping with Spectral Clustering
DIMA	Dependency Identification with Memetic Algorithm
DMS-PSO	Dynamic Multi-Swarm Particle Swarm Optimizer
EA	Evolutionary Algorithm
FEPCC	Fast Evolutionary Programming with Cooperative Co-evolution
GA	Genetic Algorithm

IHDELS	Iterative Hybridization of Differential Evolution with Local Search
IPOPCMA-ES	Restart Covariance Matrix Adaptation Evolution Strategy with Increasing Population Size
IRRG	Incremental Recursive Ranking Grouping
JADE	Adaptive Differential Evolution with Optional External Archive
L-BFGSB	Limited-memory the Broyden–Fletcher–Goldfarb–Shanno algorithm
LSGO	Large-Scale Global Optimization
L-SHADE	Iteratively Applies Success History-Based Differential Evolution with Linear Population Size Reduction
MLCC	Multilevel Cooperative Co-evolution
MLSHADE-SPA	Memetic Framework for Solving Large-scale Optimization Problems
MOS	Multiple Offspring Sampling
MPICH2	Message Passing Interface Chameleon
MPS-CMA-ES	Hybrid of Minimum Population Search and Covariance Matrix Adaptation Evolution Strategy
MTS	Multi-trajectory Search
MWW	Mann-Whitney-Wilcoxon
NSGA-2	Non-dominated Sorting Genetic Algorithm
PSO	Particle Swarm Optimization
SACC	Cooperative Co-evolution with Sensitivity Analysis-based Budget Assignment Strategy
SaDE	Self-Adaptive Differential Evolution
SaNSDE	Self-Adaptive Differential Evolution with Neighborhood Search
SGCC	Cooperative Co-evolution with Soft Grouping
SHADE-ILS	Success-History Based Parameter Adaptation for Differential Evolution with Iterative Local Search
TACO	Toolkit for Automatic Comparison of Optimizers
VMODE	Variable Mesh Optimization Differential Evolution

Appendix A. Plots of Convergence, the Population Size, and Redistribution of the Computational Resources

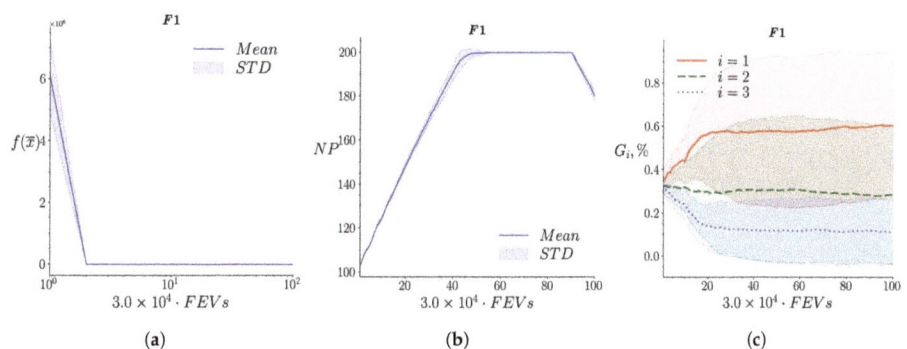

Figure A1. The dynamics of COSACC-LS1 on the F1 problem: (**a**) Convergence; (**b**) Population size; (**c**) Redistribution of resources.

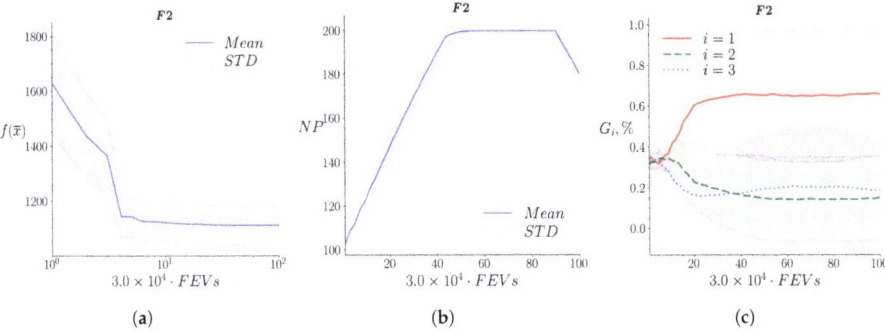

Figure A2. The dynamics of COSACC-LS1 on the F2 problem: (**a**) Convergence; (**b**) Population size; (**c**) Redistribution of resources.

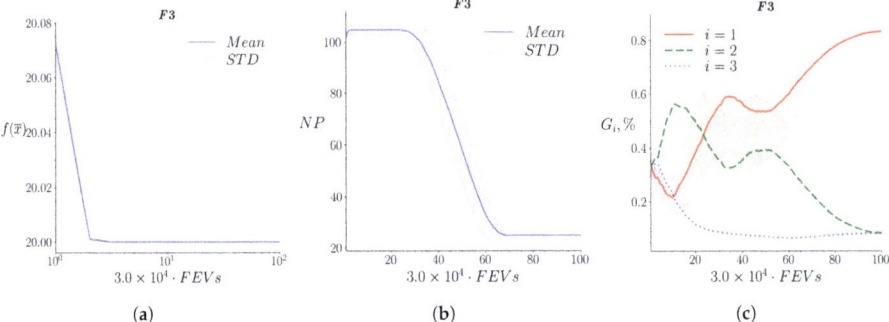

Figure A3. The dynamics of COSACC-LS1 on the F3 problem: (**a**) Convergence; (**b**) Population size; (**c**) Redistribution of resources.

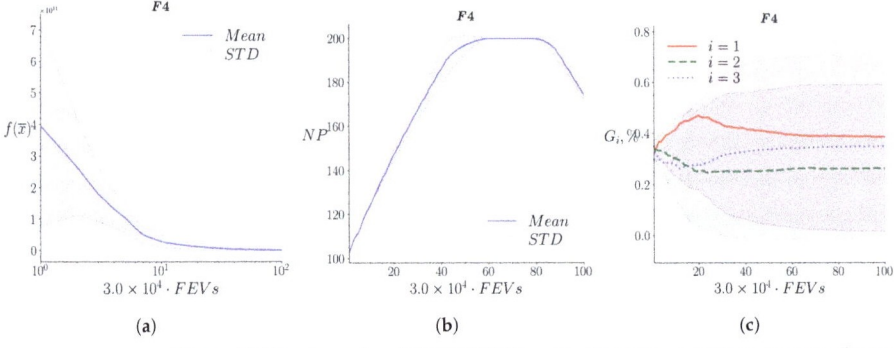

Figure A4. The dynamics of COSACC-LS1 on the F4 problem: (**a**) Convergence; (**b**) Population size; (**c**) Redistribution of resources.

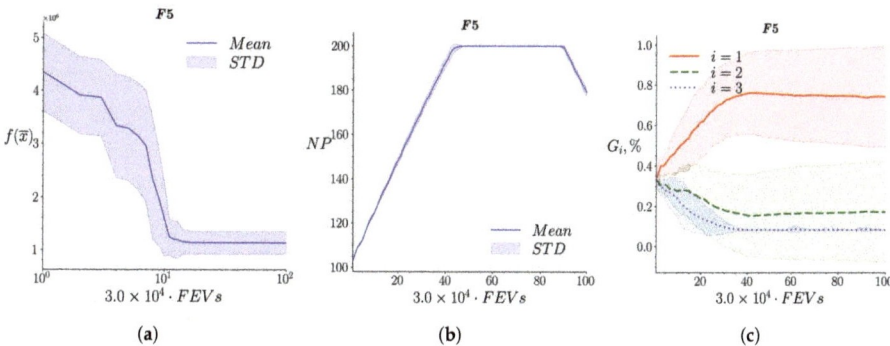

Figure A5. The dynamics of COSACC-LS1 on the F5 problem: (**a**) Convergence; (**b**) Population size; (**c**) Redistribution of resources.

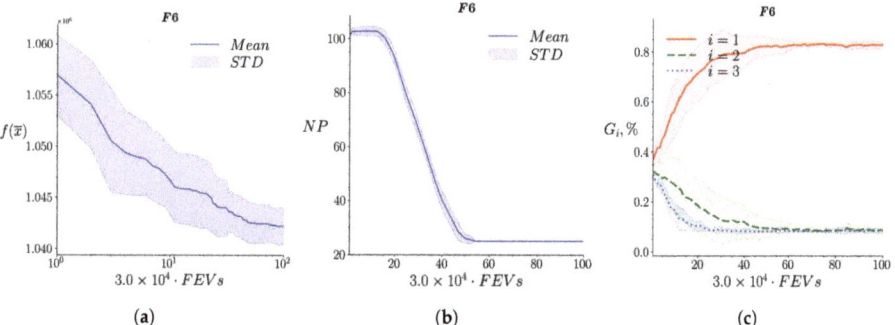

Figure A6. The dynamics of COSACC-LS1 on the F6 problem: (**a**) Convergence; (**b**) Population size; (**c**) Redistribution of resources.

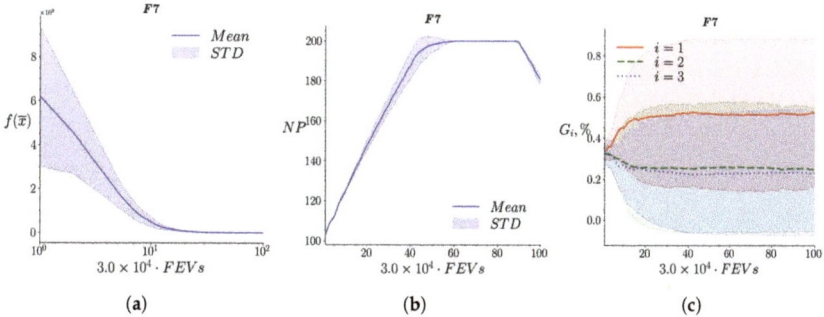

Figure A7. The dynamics of COSACC-LS1 on the F7 problem: (**a**) Convergence; (**b**) Population size; (**c**) Redistribution of resources.

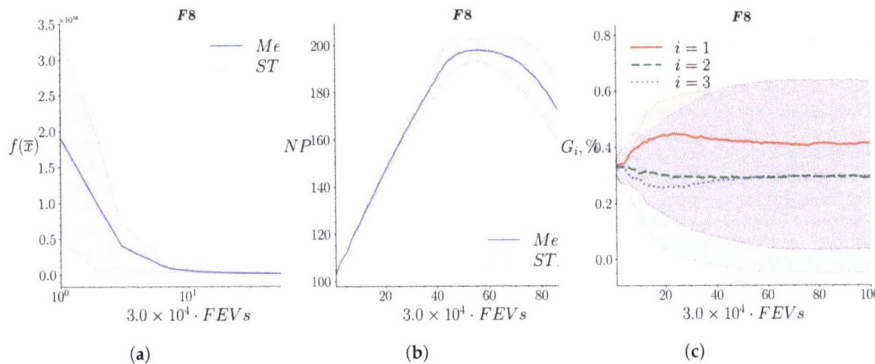

Figure A8. The dynamics of COSACC-LS1 on the F8 problem: (**a**) Convergence; (**b**) Population size; (**c**) Redistribution of resources.

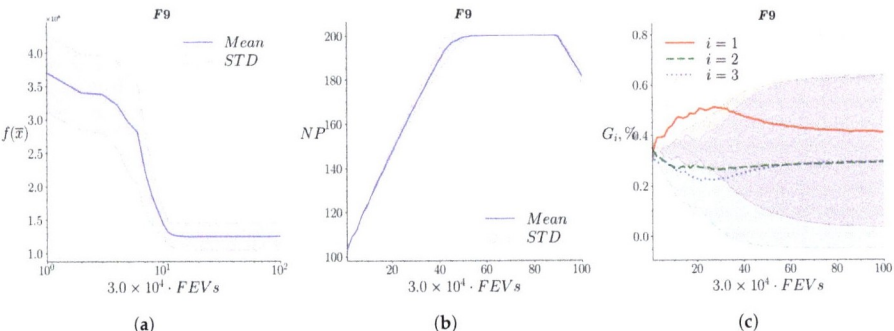

Figure A9. The dynamics of COSACC-LS1 on the F9 problem: (**a**) Convergence; (**b**) Population size; (**c**) Redistribution of resources.

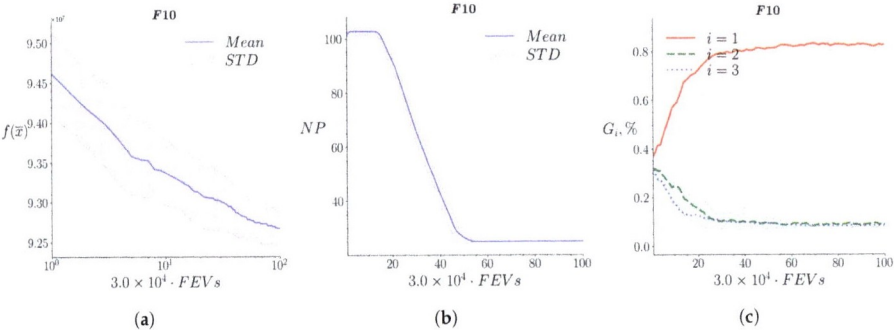

Figure A10. The dynamics of COSACC-LS1 on the F10 problem: (**a**) Convergence; (**b**) Population size; (**c**) Redistribution of resources.

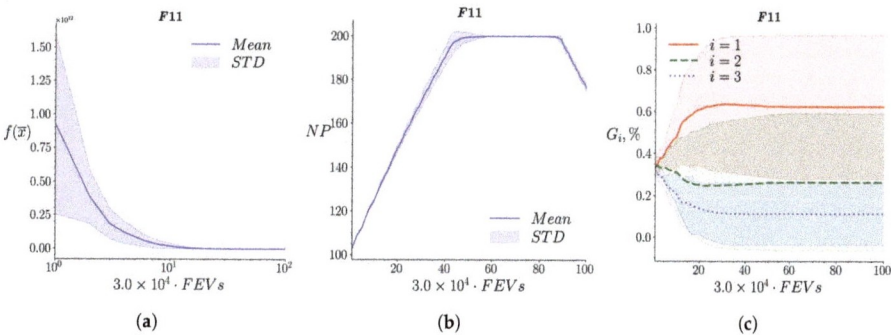

Figure A11. The dynamics of COSACC-LS1 on the F11 problem: (**a**) Convergence; (**b**) Population size; (**c**) Redistribution of resources.

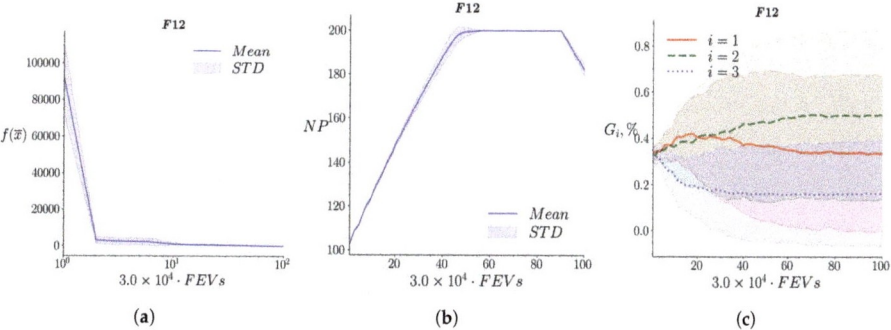

Figure A12. The dynamics of COSACC-LS1 on the F12 problem: (**a**) Convergence; (**b**) Population size; (**c**) Redistribution of resources.

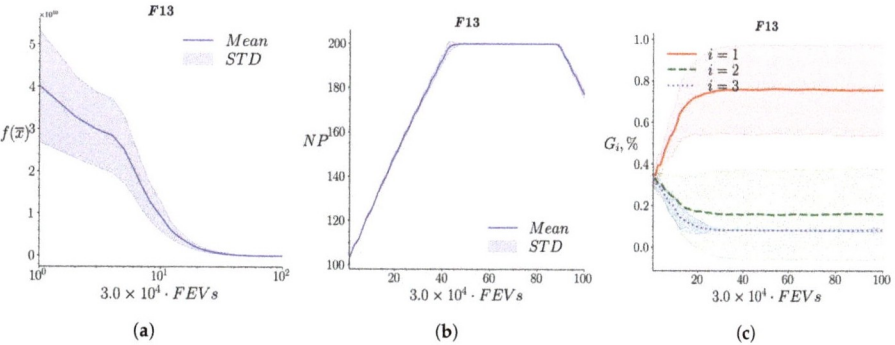

Figure A13. The dynamics of COSACC-LS1 on the F13 problem: (**a**) Convergence; (**b**) Population size; (**c**) Redistribution of resources.

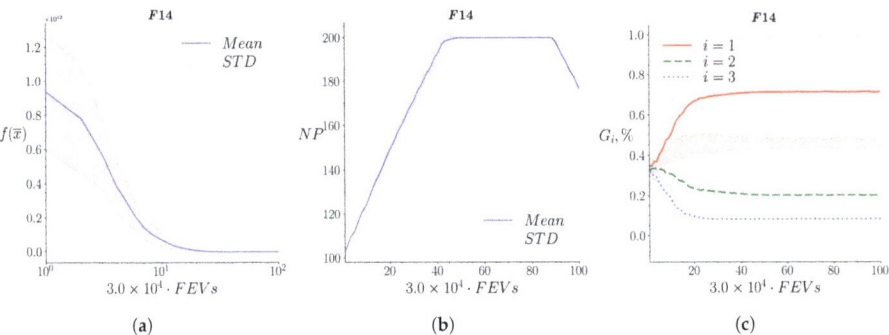

Figure A14. The dynamics of COSACC-LS1 on the F14 problem: (**a**) Convergence; (**b**) Population size; (**c**) Redistribution of resources.

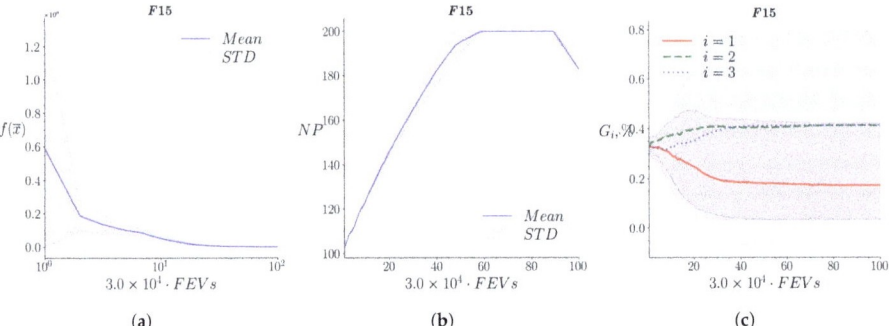

Figure A15. The dynamics of COSACC-LS1 on the F15 problem: (**a**) Convergence; (**b**) Population size; (**c**) Redistribution of resources.

References

1. The Cambridge Energy Landscape Database. Available online: https://www-wales.ch.cam.ac.uk/CCD.html (accessed on 31 January 2022).
2. Tang, K.; Yao, X.; Suganthan, P.N.; Macnish, C.; Chen, Y.P.; Chen, C.M.; Yang, Z. *Benchmark Functions for the CEC'2008 Special Session and Competition on Large Scale Global Optimization*; Technical Report; Nature Inspired Computation and Application Laboratory, USTC: Hefei, China, 2007.
3. Tang, K. *Summary of Results on CEC'08 Competition on Large Scale Global Optimization*; Technical Report; Nature Inspired Computation and Application Laboratory, USTC: Hefei, China, 2008.
4. Tang, K.; Li, X.; Suganthan, P.N.; Yang, Z.; Weise, T. *Benchmark Functions for the CEC'2010 Special Session and Competition on Large-Scale Global Optimization*; Technical Report; Nature Inspired Computation and Applications Laboratory; USTC: Hefei, China, 2009.
5. Li, X.; Tang, K.; Omidvar, M.N.; Yang, Z.; Qin, K. *Benchmark Functions for the CEC'2013 Special Session and Competition on Large-Scale Global Optimization*; Technical Report; RMIT University: Melbourne, Australia, 2013.
6. Molina, D.; LaTorre, A. Toolkit for the Automatic Comparison of Optimizers: Comparing Large-Scale Global Optimizers Made Easy. In Proceedings of the 2018 IEEE Congress on Evolutionary Computation (CEC), Rio de Janeiro, Brazil, 8–13 July 2018; pp. 1–8. [CrossRef]
7. Mahdavi, S.; Shiri, M.E.; Rahnamayan, S. Metaheuristics in large-scale global continues optimization: A survey. *Inf. Sci.* **2015**, *295*, 407–428. [CrossRef]
8. Singh, A.; Dulal, N. A Survey on Metaheuristics for Solving Large Scale Optimization Problems. *Int. J. Comput. Appl.* **2017**, *170*, 1–7. [CrossRef]
9. Del Ser, J.; Osaba, E.; Molina, D.; Yang, X.S.; Salcedo-Sanz, S.; Camacho, D.; Das, S.; Suganthan, P.N.; Coello Coello, C.A.; Herrera, F. Bio-inspired computation: Where we stand and what's next. *Swarm Evol. Comput.* **2019**, *48*, 220–250. [CrossRef]
10. Omidvar, M.N.; Li, X.; Yao, X. A review of population-based metaheuristics for large-scale black-box global optimization: Part A. *IEEE Trans. Evol. Comput.* **2021**, *26*, 1–21. [CrossRef]
11. Omidvar, M.N.; Li, X.; Yao, X. A review of population-based metaheuristics for large-scale black-box global optimization: Part B. *IEEE Trans. Evol. Comput.* **2021**, *26*, 823–843. [CrossRef]

12. Sun, Y.; Li, X.; Ernst, A.; Omidvar, M.N. Decomposition for Large-scale Optimization Problems with Overlapping Components. In Proceedings of the 2019 IEEE Congress on Evolutionary Computation (CEC), Wellington, New Zealand, 10–13 June 2019; pp. 326–333. [CrossRef]
13. Molina, D.; LaTorre, A.; Herrera, F. SHADE with Iterative Local Search for Large-Scale Global Optimization. In Proceedings of the 2018 IEEE Congress on Evolutionary Computation (CEC), Rio de Janeiro, Brazil, 8–13 July 2018; pp. 1–8. [CrossRef]
14. LaTorre, A.; Muelas, S.; Peña, J.M. Multiple Offspring Sampling in Large Scale Global Optimization. In Proceedings of the 2012 IEEE Congress on Evolutionary Computation (CEC), Brisbane, Australia, 10–15 June 2012; pp. 1–8. [CrossRef]
15. Zhao, S.Z.; Liang, J.J.; Suganthan, P.N.; Tasgetiren, M.F. Dynamic multi-swarm particle swarm optimizer with local search for Large Scale Global Optimization. In Proceedings of the 2008 IEEE Congress on Evolutionary Computation (IEEE World Congress on Computational Intelligence), Hong Kong, China, 1–6 June 2008; pp. 3845–3852. [CrossRef]
16. Liang, J.; Suganthan, P. Dynamic multi-swarm particle swarm optimizer. In Proceedings of the 2005 IEEE Swarm Intelligence Symposium, Pasadena, CA, USA, 8–10 June 2005; pp. 124–129. [CrossRef]
17. Marcelino, C.; Almeida, P.; Pedreira, C.; Caroalha, L.; Wanner, E. Applying C-DEEPSO to Solve Large Scale Global Optimization Problems. In Proceedings of the 2018 IEEE Congress on Evolutionary Computation (CEC), Rio de Janeiro, Brazil, 8–13 July 2018; pp. 1–6. [CrossRef]
18. López, E.; Puris, A.; Bello, R. VMODE: A hybrid metaheuristic for the solution of large scale optimization problems. *Investig. Oper.* **2015**, *36*, 232–239.
19. Tseng, L.Y.; Chen, C. Multiple trajectory search for Large Scale Global Optimization. In Proceedings of the 2008 IEEE Congress on Evolutionary Computation (IEEE World Congress on Computational Intelligence), Hong Kong, China, 1–6 June 2008; pp. 3052–3059. [CrossRef]
20. Molina, D.; Herrera, F. Iterative hybridization of DE with local search for the CEC'2015 special session on large scale global optimization. In Proceedings of the 2015 IEEE Congress on Evolutionary Computation (CEC), Sendai, Japan, 25–28 May 2015; pp. 1974–1978. [CrossRef]
21. Qin, A.K.; Huang, V.L.; Suganthan, P.N. Differential Evolution Algorithm With Strategy Adaptation for Global Numerical Optimization. *IEEE Trans. Evol. Comput.* **2009**, *13*, 398–417. [CrossRef]
22. Morales, J.; Nocedal, J. Remark on "Algorithm 778: L-BFGS-B: Fortran Subroutines for Large-Scale Bound Constrained Optimization". *ACM Trans. Math. Softw.* **2011**, *38*, 1–4. [CrossRef]
23. Auger, A.; Hansen, N. A restart CMA evolution strategy with increasing population size. In Proceedings of the 2005 IEEE Congress on Evolutionary Computation (CEC), Edinburgh, UK, 2–5 September 2005; Volume 2, pp. 1769–1776. [CrossRef]
24. Storn, R.; Price, K. Differential Evolution: A Simple and Efficient Adaptive Scheme for Global Optimization Over Continuous Spaces. *J. Glob. Optim.* **1995**, *23*, 1–15.
25. LaTorre, A.; Muelas, S.; Peña, J.M. Large scale global optimization: Experimental results with MOS-based hybrid algorithms. In Proceedings of the 2013 IEEE Congress on Evolutionary Computation (CEC), Cancun, Mexico, 20–23 June 2013; pp. 2742–2749. [CrossRef]
26. Tanabe, R.; Fukunaga, A. Evaluating the performance of SHADE on CEC 2013 benchmark problems. In Proceedings of the 2013 IEEE Congress on Evolutionary Computation (CEC), Cancun, Mexico, 20–23 June 2013; pp. 1952–1959. [CrossRef]
27. Bolufé-Röhler, A.; Fiol-González, S.; Chen, S. A minimum population search hybrid for large scale global optimization. In Proceedings of the 2015 IEEE Congress on Evolutionary Computation (CEC), Sendai, Japan, 25–28 May 2015; pp. 1958–1965. [CrossRef]
28. Hansen, N.; Müller, S.D.; Koumoutsakos, P. Reducing the Time Complexity of the Derandomized Evolution Strategy with Covariance Matrix Adaptation (CMA-ES). *Evol. Comput.* **2003**, *11*, 1–18. [CrossRef]
29. Meunier, L.; Rakotoarison, H.; Wong, P.K.; Roziere, B.; Rapin, J.; Teytaud, O.; Moreau, A.; Doerr, C. Black-Box Optimization Revisited: Improving Algorithm Selection Wizards Through Massive Benchmarking. *IEEE Trans. Evol. Comput.* **2022**, *26*, 490–500. [CrossRef]
30. Potter, M.; De Jong, K. A cooperative coevolutionary approach to function optimisation. In Proceedings of the 3rd Conference on Parallel Probiem Solving Form Nature, Jerusalem, Israel, 9–14 October 1994; pp. 245–257.
31. Liu, Y.; Yao, X.; Zhao, Q.; Higuchi, T. Scaling up fast evolutionary programming with cooperative coevolution. In Proceedings of the 2001 Congress on Evolutionary Computation (IEEE Cat. No.01TH8546), Seoul, Korea, 27–31 May 2001; Volume 2, pp. 1101–1108. [CrossRef]
32. Yao, X.; Liu, Y.; Lin, G. Evolutionary programming made faster. *IEEE Trans. Evol. Comput.* **1999**, *3*, 82–102. [CrossRef]
33. Shi, Y.; Teng, H.f.; Li, Z.q. Cooperative Co-evolutionary Differential Evolution for Function Optimization. *Lect. Notes Comput. Sci.* **2005**, *3611*, 1080–1088. [CrossRef]
34. Bergh, F.; Engelbrecht, A. A Cooperative Approach to Particle Swarm Optimization. *Evol. Comput. IEEE Trans. Neural Netw.* **2004**, *8*, 225–239. [CrossRef]
35. Chen, H.; Zhu, Y.; Hu, K.; He, X.; Niu, B. Cooperative Approaches to Bacterial Foraging Optimization. *Lect. Notes Comput. Sci.* **2008**, *5227*, 541–548. [CrossRef]
36. El-Abd, M. A cooperative approach to The Artificial Bee Colony algorithm. In Proceedings of the 2010 IEEE Congress on Evolutionary Computation (CEC), Barcelona, Spain, 18–23 July 2010; pp. 1–5. [CrossRef]

37. Yang, Z.; Tang, K.; Yao, X. Large scale evolutionary optimization using cooperative coevolution. *Inf. Sci.* **2008**, *178*, 2985–2999. [CrossRef]
38. Yang, Z.; Tang, K.; Yao, X. Self-adaptive Differential Evolution with Neighborhood Search. In Proceedings of the 2008 IEEE Congress on Evolutionary Computation (CEC), Hong Kong, China, 1–6 June 2008; pp. 1110–1116. [CrossRef]
39. Yang, Z.; Tang, K.; Yao, X. Multilevel Cooperative Coevolution for Large Scale Optimization. In Proceedings of the 2008 IEEE Congress on Evolutionary Computation (CEC), Hong Kong, China, 1–6 June 2008; pp. 1663–1670. [CrossRef]
40. Omidvar, M.N.; Li, X.; Yang, Z.; Yao, X. Cooperative Co-evolution for large scale optimization through more frequent random grouping. In Proceedings of the 2010 IEEE Congress on Evolutionary Computation (CEC), Barcelona, Spain, 18–23 July 2010; pp. 1–8. [CrossRef]
41. Li, X.; Yao, X. Tackling high dimensional nonseparable optimization problems by cooperatively coevolving particle swarms. In Proceedings of the 2009 IEEE Congress on Evolutionary Computation (CEC), Trondheim, Norway, 18–21 May 2009; pp. 1546–1553. [CrossRef]
42. Li, X.; Yao, X. Cooperatively Coevolving Particle Swarms for Large Scale Optimization. *IEEE Trans. Evol. Comput.* **2012**, *16*, 210–224. [CrossRef]
43. Ren, Y.; Wu, Y. An efficient algorithm for high-dimensional function optimization. *Soft Comput.* **2013**, *17*, 1–10. [CrossRef]
44. Hadi, A.; Wagdy, A.; Jambi, K. LSHADE-SPA memetic framework for solving large-scale optimization problems. *Complex Intell. Syst.* **2018**, *5*, 25–40. [CrossRef]
45. Tanabe, R.; Fukunaga, A.S. Improving the search performance of SHADE using linear population size reduction. In Proceedings of the 2014 IEEE Congress on Evolutionary Computation (CEC), Beijing, China, 6-11 July 2014; pp. 1658–1665. [CrossRef]
46. Ray, T.; Yao, X. A cooperative coevolutionary algorithm with Correlation based Adaptive Variable Partitioning. In Proceedings of the 2009 IEEE Congress on Evolutionary Computation (CEC), Trondheim, Norway, 18–21 May 2009; pp. 983–989. [CrossRef]
47. Deb, K.; Pratap, A.; Agarwal, S.; Meyarivan, T. A fast and elitist multiobjective genetic algorithm: NSGA-II. *IEEE Trans. Evol. Comput.* **2002**, *6*, 182–197. [CrossRef]
48. Omidvar, M.N.; Li, X.; Yao, X. Smart Use of Computational Resources Based on Contribution for Cooperative Co-evolutionary Algorithms. In Proceedings of the Genetic and Evolutionary Computation Conference, GECCO'11, Dublin, Ireland, 12–16 July 2011; pp. 1115–1122. [CrossRef]
49. Omidvar, M.N.; Li, X.; Yao, X. Cooperative Co-evolution with delta grouping for large scale non-separable function optimization. In Proceedings of the 2010 IEEE Congress on Evolutionary Computation (CEC), Barcelona, Spain, 18–23 July 2010; pp. 1–8. [CrossRef]
50. Chen, W.; Weise, T.; Yang, Z.; Tang, K. Large-Scale Global Optimization Using Cooperative Coevolution with Variable Interaction Learning. In Proceedings of the International Conference on Parallel Problem Solving from Nature, Krakow, Poland, 11–15 September 2010; Ser. Lecture Notes in Computer Science; Volume 6239; pp. 300–309.
51. Zhang, J.; Sanderson, A.C. JADE: Adaptive Differential Evolution With Optional External Archive. *IEEE Trans. Evol. Comput.* **2009**, *13*, 945–958. [CrossRef]
52. Sayed, E.; Essam, D.; Sarker, R. Dependency Identification technique for large scale optimization problems. In Proceedings of the 2012 IEEE Congress on Evolutionary Computation (CEC), Brisbane, Australia, 10–15 June 2012; pp. 1–8. [CrossRef]
53. Molina, D.; Lozano, M.; García-Martínez, C.; Herrera, F. Memetic Algorithms for Continuous Optimisation Based on Local Search Chains. *Evol. Comput.* **2010**, *18*, 27–63. [CrossRef]
54. Omidvar, M.N.; Li, X.; Mei, Y.; Yao, X. Cooperative Co-Evolution With Differential Grouping for Large Scale Optimization. *IEEE Trans. Evol. Comput.* **2014**, *18*, 378–393. [CrossRef]
55. Sun, Y.; Kirley, M.; Halgamuge, S. Extended Differential Grouping for Large Scale Global Optimization with Direct and Indirect Variable Interactions. In Proceedings of the 2015 Annual Conference on Genetic and Evolutionary Computation, Madrid, Spain, 11–15 July 2015; pp. 313–320. [CrossRef]
56. Omidvar, M.N.; Yang, M.; Mei, Y.; Li, X.; Yao, X. DG2: A Faster and More Accurate Differential Grouping for Large-Scale Black-Box Optimization. *IEEE Trans. Evol. Comput.* **2017**, *21*, 929–942. [CrossRef]
57. Mei, Y.; Yao, X.; Li, X.; Omidvar, M.N. A Competitive Divide-and-Conquer Algorithm for Unconstrained Large Scale Black-Box Optimization. *ACM Trans. Math. Softw.* **2015**, *42*, 1–24. [CrossRef]
58. Li, L.; Fang, W.; Wang, Q.; Sun, J. Differential Grouping with Spectral Clustering for Large Scale Global Optimization. In Proceedings of the 2019 IEEE Congress on Evolutionary Computation (CEC), Wellington, New Zealand, 10–13 June 2019; pp. 334–341. [CrossRef]
59. Liu, J.; Tang, K. Scaling Up Covariance Matrix Adaptation Evolution Strategy Using Cooperative Coevolution. In Proceedings of the Intelligent Data Engineering and Automated Learning—IDEAL 2013, Hefei, China, 20–23 October 2013; Lecture Notes in Computer Science; Volume 8206, pp. 350–357. [CrossRef]
60. Mahdavi, S.; Rahnamayan, S.; Shiri, M. Cooperative co-evolution with sensitivity analysis-based budget assignment strategy for large-scale global optimization. *Appl. Intell.* **2017**, *47*, 1–26. [CrossRef]
61. Ge, H.; Zhao, M.; Hou, Y.; Kai, Z.; Sun, L.; Tan, G.; Zhang, Q. Bi-space Interactive Cooperative Coevolutionary algorithm for large scale black-box optimization. *Appl. Soft Comput.* **2020**, *97*, 1–18. [CrossRef]

62. Liu, W.; Zhou, Y.; Li, B.; Tang, K. Cooperative Co-evolution with Soft Grouping for Large Scale Global Optimization. In Proceedings of the 2019 IEEE Congress on Evolutionary Computation (CEC), Wellington, New Zealand, 10–13 June 2019; pp. 318–325. [CrossRef]
63. Sun, Y.; Kirley, M.; Halgamuge, S. A Recursive Decomposition Method for Large Scale Continuous Optimization. *IEEE Trans. Evol. Comput.* **2017**, *22*, 647–661. [CrossRef]
64. Komarnicki, M.M.; Przewozniczek, M.W.; Kwasnicka, H. Incremental Recursive Ranking Grouping for Large Scale Global Optimization. *IEEE Trans. Evol. Comput.* **2022**. [CrossRef]
65. Vakhnin, A.; Sopov, E. Investigation of Improved Cooperative Coevolution for Large-Scale Global Optimization Problems. *Algorithms* **2021**, *14*, 146. [CrossRef]
66. Vakhnin, A.; Sopov, E. Investigation of the iCC Framework Performance for Solving Constrained LSGO Problems. *Algorithms* **2020**, *13*, 108. [CrossRef]
67. Tanabe, R.; Fukunaga, A. Success-history based parameter adaptation for Differential Evolution. In Proceedings of the 2013 IEEE Congress on Evolutionary Computation (CEC), Cancun, Mexico, 20–23 June 2013; pp. 71–78. [CrossRef]
68. Poláková, R.; Bujok, P. Adaptation of Population Size in Differential Evolution Algorithm: An Experimental Comparison. In Proceedings of the 2018 25th International Conference on Systems, Signals and Image Processing (IWSSIP), Maribor, Slovenia, 20–22 June 2018; pp. 1–5. [CrossRef]
69. Hansen, N.; Finck, S.; Ros, R.; Auger, A. *Real-Parameter Black-Box Optimization Benchmarking 2009: Noisy Functions Definitions*; Technical Report RR-6869; INRIA: Paris, France, 2009.
70. TACO: Toolkit for Automatic Comparison of Optimizers. Available online: https://tacolab.org/ (accessed on 31 January 2022).

Article

A Novel Approach to Decision-Making on Diagnosing Oncological Diseases Using Machine Learning Classifiers Based on Datasets Combining Known and/or New Generated Features of a Different Nature

Liliya A. Demidova

Institute of Information Technologies, Federal State Budget Educational Institution of Higher Education, MIREA—Russian Technological University, 78, Vernadsky Avenue, 119454 Moscow, Russia; liliya.demidova@rambler.ru

Abstract: This paper deals with the problem of diagnosing oncological diseases based on blood protein markers. The goal of the study is to develop a novel approach in decision-making on diagnosing oncological diseases based on blood protein markers by generating datasets that include various combinations of features: both known features corresponding to blood protein markers and new features generated with the help of mathematical tools, particularly with the involvement of the non-linear dimensionality reduction algorithm UMAP, formulas for various entropies and fractal dimensions. These datasets were used to develop a group of multiclass kNN and SVM classifiers using oversampling algorithms to solve the problem of class imbalance in the dataset, which is typical for medical diagnostics problems. The results of the experimental studies confirmed the feasibility of using the UMAP algorithm and approximation entropy, as well as Katz and Higuchi fractal dimensions to generate new features based on blood protein markers. Various combinations of these features can be used to expand the set of features from the original dataset in order to improve the quality of the received classification solutions for diagnosing oncological diseases. The best kNN and SVM classifiers were developed based on the original dataset augmented respectively with a feature based on the approximation entropy and features based on the UMAP algorithm and the approximation entropy. At the same time, the average values of the metric $MacroF_1-score$ used to assess the quality of classifiers during cross-validation increased by 16.138% and 4.219%, respectively, compared to the average values of this metric in the case when the original dataset was used in the development of classifiers of the same name.

Keywords: decision-making; oncological disease; kNN classifier; SVM classifier; dataset; features; UMAP algorithm; entropy; fractal dimension

MSC: 68Q32; 68T05

Citation: Demidova, L.A. A Novel Approach to Decision-Making on Diagnosing Oncological Diseases Using Machine Learning Classifiers Based on Datasets Combining Known and/or New Generated Features of a Different Nature. *Mathematics* 2023, 11, 792. https://doi.org/10.3390/math11040792

Academic Editor: Vladimir Balan

Received: 6 January 2023
Revised: 28 January 2023
Accepted: 2 February 2023
Published: 4 February 2023
Corrected: 4 May 2023

Copyright: © 2023 by the author. Licensee MDPI, Basel, Switzerland. This article is an open access article distributed under the terms and conditions of the Creative Commons Attribution (CC BY) license (https://creativecommons.org/licenses/by/4.0/).

1. Introduction

Recently, elements of digital transformation have become increasingly visible and in demand in various areas of human activity, including healthcare.

The digital transformation of healthcare is a continuous process aimed at completely restructuring the mechanisms of work of industry authorities, medical organizations and their interaction with patients. The introduction of advanced digital technologies ensures high standards of medical care and the transition to the "4P medicine" model (preventive, personalized, participatory, predictive medicine) [1].

The introduction of digital technologies in healthcare should ensure a decrease in the level of morbidity and mortality of the population and an increase in life expectancy, including active life expectancy. The use of health monitoring technologies should allow not only for the detection of pathologies at an early stage, but also to prevent the development of diseases.

The development of technologies for analyzing large volumes of medical data, including the use of artificial intelligence, will make it possible to obtain new knowledge in the field of medicine and biology, as well as to develop new methods for diagnosing and treating diseases.

The transformation of healthcare under the influence of digital technologies is taking place everywhere, including such areas as:

- Transition from standardized clinical protocols to a personalized approach to patient care due to the accumulation of a large amount of medical data, as well as the widespread use of individual biomonitoring devices;
- Disease prevention through early diagnosis and regular health monitoring using wearable devices;
- Patient focus and active involvement of the patient in the treatment process.

At the same time, the demand for applied and computational mathematics' tools for digital environments becomes obvious in the case of solving problems of disease prevention through early diagnosis, including cancer [2–5].

Oncological diseases (ODs) are among the most dangerous ones because they can lead to serious consequences for patients, especially in the case of late diagnosis. Such consequences include significant pain and a difficult psychological state. The treatment of oncological diseases is usually lengthy and involves significant financial costs both for the patients and their families and for the state.

An OD is an immune disease that first causes the division and growth of abnormal cells in a single organ of the patient, and then can quickly spread to the entire body.

Obviously, early diagnosis of an OD should allow the oncologist to choose an adequate and effective treatment regimen for the patient in a timely manner. However, the task of early diagnosis of an OD is very difficult: unfortunately, the typical symptoms of ODs appear only in the later stages when the disease is difficult to treat, so the treatment may ultimately turn out to be unsuccessful.

One of the approaches to the early diagnosis of an OD is based on the analysis of test results, in particular, gene tests (GTs) [4,6] and protein tests (PTs) [4,7,8]. GTs reveal hereditary information, they are static, difficult to interpret, and are usually used to detect congenital genetic diseases [4]. Such tests do not detect diseases that occur when there are problems with the immune system and metabolism. In addition, GTs are expensive. PTs, unlike GTs, are dynamic and they allow (if carried out in a timely manner) for identifying the occurrence of an OD and track its development [4]. Additionally, PTs are non-invasive, painless for patients and affordable.

The diagnosis of ODs based on blood protein markers has been increasingly used in the last few years [4,9,10]. Presumably, PT-based diagnostic technologies will allow for predicting the risks of developing oncological diseases 1–3 years in advance, which will make it possible to take advanced preventive measures against the emergence and development of an OD.

There are many different types of protein markers in the blood, and the values of the markers are different for different types of ODs [4]. It is obvious that the use of only one type of marker or some limited group of markers reduces the accuracy of diagnosing ODs, even if this marker (or group of markers) is recognized as the standard for diagnosis. One of the reasons leading to the refusal to use the full range of PTs results is the limited ability of specialists to interpret the data. It is easier to operate with information about the values of 1–2 protein markers than with data on the values of several dozen of the same markers (especially if specialists use a unified table with a priori given limits of the norm and abnormality, followed by a decision based on their knowledge and intuition). It can be reasonably assumed that the use of the full range of PTs results should improve the accuracy of diagnosing various ODs.

It is obvious that the involvement of modern technologies of data mining and machine learning will make it possible to reveal the knowledge about the relationship between the values of blood protein markers in various types of ODs hidden in the PT results.

Currently, data mining and machine learning technologies are actively used to solve various problems of medical diagnostics, including solving the problems of diagnosing ODs [10–19]. In this case, classifiers are developed based on appropriate datasets. The k-Nearest Neighbors (kNN) algorithm [10], SVM (Support Vector Machine) algorithm [11], Decision Tree (DT) algorithm [12], Random Forest (RF) algorithm [15], their hybrids and deep learning algorithms [17–19] are most broadly used in creating such classifiers.

The main problem in the development of tools for solving problems of medical diagnostics is the imbalance of classes in the dataset [10,20]: usually, normal data patterns characterizing cases when the disease is absent constitute the majority class, while data patterns of interest and characterizing cases when certain diseases are present constitute the corresponding minority classes. In this case, for example, instead of developing a binary classifier based on an imbalanced dataset, it becomes necessary to develop a multiclass classifier based on an imbalanced dataset, which is a non-trivial task, since it is necessary to teach the classifier to separate data from different classes that are imbalanced. Obviously, a binary classifier can be obtained even in the case of class imbalance (for example, in a ratio of 10:1), and the accuracy of it will be 90% (which is not bad in the case of balanced classes), but such accuracy should be considered bad if the classifier made errors on all objects from the minority class.

Data scientists have proposed various approaches to solve the problem of class imbalance:

- Approaches using various class balancing algorithms that implement oversampling technologies (for example, SMOTE algorithm (Synthetic Minority Oversampling Technique) [21–23], ADASYN algorithm (Adaptive Synthetic Sampling Approach) [24]), undersampling technologies (for example, Tomek Links algorithm) [23,25] and their combinations;
- Approaches that apply algorithms that account for the sensitivity to the cost of wrong decisions (cost-sensitive algorithms) [10];
- Approaches that implement the transfer of data into a space of a new dimension (with a decrease [26–32] or increase [11,33,34] in dimension), in which data classes will be separated from each other better than in the original space;
- Approaches that implement the so-called one-class classification [34–37].

It should be noted that the transition to the space of a new dimension can be implemented in various ways, for example, using:

- Dimension reduction algorithms (linear [26,27] and non-linear [28–32]) that allow one to move to a space of lower dimension;
- Kernel functions (as it is done in the SVM-algorithm, which allows the transition to a space of higher dimension) [11,33,34,36];
- Algorithms for engineering (generation) of new features for data patterns, which make it possible to move to a space of higher dimension [38].

All of these approaches have their advantages and disadvantages, and there is no universal methodology for choosing the approach that is appropriate to apply to the dataset used in the development of the data classifier.

In each case, it is necessary to perform a comprehensive analysis in order to:

- Avoid loss of information during undersampling or reducing the dimension of the data space;
- Exclude the introduction of false or redundant information during oversampling or increasing the dimension of the data space.

One of the obvious tools that can be used in assessing the quality of the developed classifier is detailed analysis of various classification quality metrics on the test sample, including metrics that allow for accounting for the specifics of the dataset, namely, its imbalance (for example, it is appropriate to use metrics such as *Balanced accuracy* and $F_1-score$).

In addition, it is advisable to use cross-validation, including k-fold cross-validation, which makes it possible to empirically evaluate the generalizing ability of the developed classifier.

A large number of papers have been devoted to the problem of analyzing medical datasets containing information about blood protein markers and making decisions on the diagnosis of ODs. In particular, in the pilot study [4], the task was to identify and surgically localize eight types of resectable ODs (ovary, liver, stomach, pancreas, esophagus, colorectum, lung and breast) based on a multi-analysis blood test using the CancerSEEK test [4,5] based on a machine learning algorithm called the logistic regression algorithm. The dataset used in the study is publicly available and located in the Catalog of Somatic Mutations in Cancer (COSMIC) repository [39] as NIHMS982921-supplement-Tables_S1_to_S11.xlsx, and it is constantly updated with new data. The original dataset is available in the Supplementary Material for the paper as aar3247_cohen_sm_tables-s1-s11.xlsx [4]. The eight types of ODs considered in the dataset were chosen by the authors because they are the most common among the population of Western countries, and also because blood-based tests are not used in clinical practice for their early detection.

The authors of the pilot study [4] proposed to assess the levels of circulating proteins and mutations in cell-free DNA and use the obtained data in the LC (logistic classifier)-based CancerSEEK test. The study used 1005 data patterns received from patients with non-metastatic clinically identified ovarian, liver, stomach, pancreas, esophagus, colon, lung or breast ODs. The CancerSEEK test was based on screening results, such as the levels of protein biomarkers and ctDNA (Circulating tumor DNA). The authors proposed to take into account each person's gender, the levels of eight proteins and the presence of mutations in 1933 different genomic positions, each of which can mutate in several ways.

It was assumed that the presence of a mutation in the analyzed gene or an increase in the level of any of the eight proteins makes it possible to classify the patient's pattern as positive, i.e., a pattern with an identified OD. The authors used logarithmic ratios to evaluate the mutations and included them in a logistic regression algorithm (and, accordingly, in the LC), which took into account both the mutation data and the protein biomarker levels to evaluate the results of the CancerSEEK test. At the same time, the average values of sensitivity and specificity were determined from the results of 10 iterations using 10-fold cross validation.

The results of the experiments in [4] showed that the average value of the *Sensitivity* metric for eight types of ODs is about 70%, the highest value of the sensitivity metric is achieved for the ovary class (98%), slightly less for the liver class (close to 98%), and the lowest value of the sensitivity metric is achieved for the breast class (33%). In general, the values of the *Sensitivity* metric ranged from 69 to 98% in the detection of five types of ODs (esophagus, pancreas, stomach, liver and ovaries, listed in ascending order of values of the *Sensitivity* metric). The value of the metric specificity was above 99%: only 7 of the 812 patterns without known cancers scored positive. At the same time, as the authors write, there is no certainty that several false-positive patterns of patients identified in the normal class do not actually have an undiscovered OD. However, the classification of these patterns as false positives can be considered the most conservative approach to the classification and interpretation of medical data.

The average sensitivity of the CancerSEEK test was 73% for stage II cancer, which is the most common, 78% for stage III cancer, and less than 43% for stage I cancer. The highest and the lowest sensitivity for stage I cancer (the earliest stage) was recorded for liver cancer (100%) and esophageal cancer (20%), respectively.

A liquid biopsy involves deriving mutant DNA templates from dying cancer cells. Later on, these templates serve as specific neoplasia markers. The authors of the pilot study [4] found that the mutation in blood plasma was identical to the mutation found in the primary tumor of the same person in 90% of analyzed cases diagnosed with ODs. This correspondence between the plasma and primary tumor was evident for all eight types of cancer and ranged from 100% for ovarian and pancreatic cancer to 82% for gastric cancer. One disadvantage of liquid biopsies is the inability to determine the type of cancer in patients with positive tests, leading to clinical problems for follow-up.

The authors of the pilot study [4] point out that the vast majority of information about the localization of ODs was obtained from protein markers, since mutations in the driver gene are usually not tissue-specific. They propose the LC that implements the CancerSEEK test for the presence of eight common types of ODs. During the development of the LC, the authors used a training set that combined information about the levels of the gene and protein biomarkers. In doing so, they were able to increase the sensitivity of the CancerSEEK test without a significant decrease in specificity. The authors note that the effectiveness of combining completely different agents with different mechanisms of action is widely recognized in therapy, but not usually used in diagnostics. They also believe that other cancer biomarkers, such as metabolites, mRNA transcripts, microRNAs or methylated DNA sequences, can be similarly combined to increase the sensitivity and localization of a cancer focus.

The followers of the authors of the pilot study continued to offer their own versions of classifiers that implement the diagnosis of ODs based on datasets on values of blood protein markers without taking gene markers into account.

For example, in [10], the authors proposed to use a cost-sensitive kNN algorithm based on a three-class imbalanced dataset containing patterns characterized by 39 blood protein markers and belonging to one of three classes: normal, ovary and liver. In order to include the hidden information in the data analysis and improve the quality of the classification, the authors used two entropy metrics: approximate entropy AE and sample entropy SE. At the time that the study was conducted, the analyzed dataset contained 897 patterns from three classes in the ratio Normal:Ovary:Liver = 799:54:44. The overall accuracy of the classifier was equal to 0.952, and the values of such metrics as *Precision*, *Recall*, *MacroF$_1$-score* and *AUC* were equal to 0.807, 0.833, 0.819 and 0.920, respectively.

It should be noted that the authors of this work abandoned the attempt to develop a classifier for nine classes (eight classes corresponding to patterns of various types of ODs, and one class corresponding to patterns for which no ODs were diagnosed) due to poor separability of the classes.

The goal of this study is to develop the high-precision data classifiers on ODs using modern tools for data mining and machine learning technologies. It is supposed to develop kNN [10,34] and SVM [11,33,34,36] classifiers using oversampling algorithms SMOTE [21], Borderline SMOTE-1 [22], Borderline SMOTE-2 [22] and ADASYN [24], which allow for restoring the balance of classes in the original and extended datasets, formed on the base of the original dataset with the application of various techniques for extracting new features. In particular, it is planned to consider:

- The UMAP (Uniform Manifold Approximation and Projection) algorithm [29–32], which implements non-linear data dimensionality reduction by embedding data into a space of lower dimensionality to generate new features based on pattern features;
- Formulas for calculating entropies [40–45], Hjorth parameters [46,47] and fractal dimensions [48–52] in order to generate new features based on the pattern features.

This study presents the first attempt to generate datasets that involve different tools with the subsequent selection of the best of them to form new features by extracting information hidden in the features of the original dataset. The generation of new features was carried out using the UMAP algorithm, as well as various formulas for calculating entropies, Hjorth parameters and fractal dimensions. Various combinations of new features were selected based on correlation and the perceived ability to distinguish between patterns of different classes were added to the features of the original dataset or combined to form a new dataset. As a result, it becomes possible to work simultaneously with different datasets that describe the subject area. This approach to the generation of datasets is used for the first time in the field of medical diagnostics, including the field of diagnostics of oncological diseases based on blood protein markers. Subsequently, these datasets are balanced using oversampling algorithms and are used in the development of classifiers based on the kNN and SVM algorithms with subsequent selection of the best classifiers based on classification quality metrics.

The rest of the paper is organized as follows. Section 2 briefly describes the aspects of developing the kNN and SVM classifiers. It also discusses the applied quality metrics of multiclass classification, as well as the problem of class imbalance in datasets. In addition, this section provides a summary of the principles of operation of the UMAP algorithm, as well as background information on the investigated nonlinear data extraction tools that are difficult to obtain from traditional statistics, in particular, on entropy characteristics and fractal dimensions. Section 3 presents a description of the novel approach to the formation of the datasets used in the development of the classifiers. Section 4 is devoted to the analysis of the original dataset based on the UMAP algorithm with data visualization, aspects of the generation of new features based on entropy characteristics and fractal dimensions of the data patterns, choosing the best of them. It also discusses all of the steps of the creation of new datasets used for the development of the kNN and SVM classifiers and the results of the development of such classifiers, accompanied by tables and figures. Section 5 presents a discussion of the proposed results. Finally, Section 6 contains conclusions and goals regarding future work.

2. Materials and Methods

2.1. Aspects of Development of Classifiers

The development of classifiers can be performed using various machine learning algorithms, for example, kNN [10,34,53–56], SVM [10,33,34,36,57,58], LR (Logistic Regression) [4,59], DT [12–14], RF [15,60,61] and neural networks [17–19], as well as cascade algorithms and ensembles based on them. We can use the default values of the classifier parameters, or fine-tune them using population optimization algorithms [62,63]. The quality of classification using such classifiers will depend both on the quality of datasets on the basis of which the classifiers are developed, and on the specifics of the mathematical apparatus embedded in the algorithms corresponding to the classifiers. Currently, there is no universal machine learning algorithm that could ensure that a classifier developed on its basis will provide high quality of classification for any arbitrary training dataset. The same can be said about cascade classifiers and ensembles of classifiers. Obviously, it is desirable to minimize the time for developing a classifier that provides high-quality data classification.

Two machine learning algorithms (kNN and SVM) are considered in this study, although all the ideas formulated below can be used in the development of classifiers based on any machine learning algorithm because they affect only the stage of preparation of datasets used in the development of classifiers.

The choice of the kNN algorithm is due to the simplicity of its implementation and, as a result, low time costs for the development of the kNN classifier.

The choice of the SVM algorithm is due to the availability of tools for working with various kernel functions that provide a transition to a higher-dimensional space, and the possibility of generating classification rules in an explicit form by identifying the so-called support vectors located along the class boundary. However, the time spent on the development of the SVM classifier becomes significantly larger compared to the time spent on the development of the kNN classifier.

It is precisely because of the large time costs for the development of the RF classifier that the proposed study does not consider the RF algorithm, although when it is used, it is usually possible to obtain classifiers that provide a very high quality of data classification.

Let $U = \{< x_1, y_1 >, \ldots, < x_s, y_s >\}$ be a dataset used in the development of classifiers, where $x_i \in X; y_i \in Y = \{1, \ldots, M\}; i = \overline{1, s}$; s is the number of patterns in the dataset; M is the number of classes; X is the set of signs of patterns; and Y is the set of pattern class labels [34].

Let classifiers be trained on S patterns and testing be carried out on $s - S$ patterns. The quality of the classifiers is assessed using the k-fold cross-validation procedure.

2.1.1. kNN Classifier Development

The number of nearest neighbors k for the pattern x and the method of voting for k nearest neighbors on the question of the class membership of the pattern x are specified during the development of the binary kNN classifier. The values of the parameters should provide the minimum classification error.

The membership class y of a pattern x is determined by the membership class of most of the patterns from among the k nearest neighbors of the pattern x. Various metrics, such as Euclidean, cosine, Manhattan, etc. can be used to calculate the distance between patterns in the kNN algorithm. Usually, the distance is calculated using the Euclidean distance metric as [34,53,54]:

$$d(x_i, x) = \sqrt{\sum_{h=1}^{q} (x_i^h - x^h)^2},\qquad(1)$$

where q is the number of features of patterns x_i ($i = \overline{1,k}$) and x; x_i^h is the h-th coordinate of i-th pattern x_i; and x^h is the h-th coordinate of pattern x.

Various voting methods can be used to determine the membership class of a pattern during the development of the kNN classifier, for example, simple unweighted voting and weighted voting [34,53,54].

Simple unweighted voting works in such a way that the distance from the pattern x to each of the k nearest neighbors x_i ($i = \overline{1,k}$) does not matter: each of the k nearest neighbors x_i ($i = \overline{1,k}$) of the pattern votes for its assignment to its class, and all k nearest neighbors x_i ($i = \overline{1,k}$) have equal rights in class definition for pattern x. The pattern x will be assigned to the class that receives the most votes:

$$\alpha = \underset{m \in Y}{\operatorname{argmax}} \sum_{i=1}^{k} |y_{x_i,x} = m|,\qquad(2)$$

Weighted voting works in such a way that the distance from the pattern x to each of the k nearest neighbors x_i ($i = \overline{1,k}$) is taken into account: the smaller the distance $d(x_i, x)$, the more significant the contribution to the estimation of the pattern x belonging to a certain class is made by the vote of the nearest neighbor x_i ($i = \overline{1,k}$). The total contribution of the votes of the nearest neighbors x_i ($i = \overline{1,k}$) for the pattern x belonging to the class with the label $m \in Y$ can be calculated as:

$$\alpha_m = \sum_{i=1}^{k} \frac{1}{d^2(x_i, x)} \cdot r_{i,m},\qquad(3)$$

where $r_{i,m} = 0$, if $y_{x_i,x} \neq m$ and $r_{i,m} = 1$, if $y_{x_i,x} = m$.

The class that received the highest value α_m according to Formula (3) is assigned to the pattern x.

The problem of finding the optimal values of the parameters of the kNN classifier, for example, the number of neighbors and the voting method, can be solved using grid search algorithms or evolutionary optimization algorithms, such as the genetic algorithm, differential evolution algorithm, PSO algorithm, bee algorithm, ant colony algorithm, fish school algorithm, etc.

2.1.2. SVM Classifier Development

The SVM algorithm implements binary classification [34,57,58]. In the case of multi-class classification, i.e., for $M \geq 3$, strategies such as OvO (One-vs-One) or OvR (One-vs-Rest) are used, which allow for the use of binary classification solutions to form solutions for multiclass classification [64].

The One-vs-One strategy breaks the multiclass classification into one binary classification problem for each pair of classes. The One-vs-Rest strategy breaks the multiclass classification into one binary classification problem for each class.

In the case of binary classification, the basic SVM algorithm operates on patterns $x_i \in X$ with class labels $y_i \in Y = \{-1; +1\}$.

The development of the SVM classifier can be performed using kernel functions $\kappa(x_i, x_\tau)$ such as linear, polynomial, radial basis and sigmoid kernel functions. Particularly, the linear kernel function has the form $\kappa(x_i, x_\tau) = x_i \cdot x_\tau$, and the radial basic kernel function, which is used in this study, has the form $\kappa(x_i, x_\tau) = exp(-(x_i - x_\tau) \cdot (x_i - x_\tau)/(2 \cdot \sigma^2))$, where $x_i \cdot x_\tau$ is the scalar product for x_i and x_τ and σ ($\sigma > 0$) is the kernel function parameter.

The value of the regularization parameter C ($C > 0$) [57], the type of the kernel function $\kappa(x_i, x_\tau)$ and the values of the parameters of the kernel function (for example, the value of parameter σ for the radial basis kernel function) are determined during the development of the binary SVM classifier. The values of the parameters should provide the minimum classification error.

The development of the binary SVM classifier involves solving the problem of construction of a hyperplane separating the classes. According to the Kuhn–Tucker theorem, this problem can be reduced to a quadratic programming problem containing only dual variables λ_i ($i = \overline{1, S}$) [34,57,58]:

$$\begin{cases} \frac{1}{2} \cdot \sum_{i=1}^{S} \sum_{\tau=1}^{S} \lambda_i \cdot \lambda_\tau \cdot y_i \cdot y_\tau \cdot \kappa(x_i, x_\tau) - \sum_{i=1}^{S} \lambda_i \to \min_{\lambda}, \\ \sum_{i=1}^{S} \lambda_i \cdot y_i = 0, \\ 0 \leq \lambda_i \leq C, i = \overline{1, S}. \end{cases} \quad (4)$$

The support vectors are determined as a result of the training of the binary SVM classifier. These are feature vectors of learning patterns x_i, for which the values of the corresponding dual variables λ_i are not equal to zero ($\lambda_i \neq 0$) [57]. The support vectors carry all the information about class separation since they are located near the hyperplane separating them.

The classification decision rule that assigns a membership class to a pattern with the label "−1" or "+1" is defined as [34,57,58]:

$$F(z) = sign\left(\sum_{i=1}^{S} \lambda_i \cdot y_i \cdot \kappa(x_i, x) + b\right), \quad (5)$$

where $b = w \cdot x_i - y_i$; $w = \sum_{i=1}^{S} \lambda_i \cdot y_i \cdot x_i$.

The problem of finding the optimal values of the SVM classifier parameters, for example, the regularization parameter C ($C > 0$), the type of the kernel function $\kappa(x_i, x_\tau)$ and the values of the parameters of the kernel function, can be solved using grid search algorithms or evolutionary optimization algorithms.

2.2. Quality Metrics of Multiclass Classification

The assessment of the quality of a multiclass classification can be performed using metrics such as *Accuracy*, *MacroPrecision*, *MacroRecall* and *MacroF$_1$−score* [65].

The *accuracy* metric for multiclass classification can be calculated as:

$$Accuracy = \frac{TP + TN}{TP + TN + FP + FN}, \quad (6)$$

where TP is the total number of true positive elements in the multiclass classification problem; TN is the total number of true negative elements in the multiclass classification problem; FP is the total number of false positive elements in the multiclass classification problem; and FN is the total number of false negative elements in the multiclass classification problem.

The *MacroPrecision* metric for multiclass classification can be calculated as:

$$MacroPrecision = \frac{1}{M} \sum_{m=1}^{M} \left(\frac{TP_m}{TP_m + FP_m} \right), \quad (7)$$

where m is the class label index; TP_m is the number of true positive elements for the m-th class label; FP_m is the number of false positive elements for the m-th class label; and M is the total number of classes in the multiclass classification problem.

The *MacroRecall* metric for multiclass classification can be calculated as:

$$MacroRecall = \frac{1}{M} \sum_{m=1}^{M} \left(\frac{TP_m}{TP_m + FN_m} \right), \quad (8)$$

where m is the class label index; TP_m is the number of true positive elements for the m-th class label; FN_m is the number of false negative elements for the m-th class label; and M is the total number of classes in the multiclass classification problem.

The $MacroF_1-score$ metric for multiclass classification can be calculated as:

$$MacroF_1-score = 2 \cdot \left(\frac{MacroPrecision \cdot MacroRecall}{MacroPrecision + MacroRecall} \right), \quad (9)$$

Such metrics as (7)–(9) are useful and effective when developing classifiers using imbalanced datasets.

The $MacroF_1-score$ is used as a maximized classification quality metric. Based on *MacroPrecision* and *MacroRecall*, this metric makes it possible to simultaneously account for information on precision and recall of the solutions generated by the classifiers.

2.3. Solving the Class Imbalance Problem

In most machine learning algorithms, it is assumed that the goal of learning is to maximize the proportion of correct decisions in relation to all decisions made, and both the population and training dataset obey the same distribution. In this case, the datasets used to develop classifiers should be class-balanced, and the cost of a classification error for all patterns should be the same.

However, in many practical problems, one has to work with datasets that are poorly balanced. Learning on imbalanced datasets (imbalance problem) [66,67] can lead to a significant decrease in the quality of the classification solutions obtained using classifiers developed on their basis, since such datasets do not provide the required data distribution characteristics used in training.

For example, in the case of binary classification, the imbalance of the dataset is that more of the patterns in the dataset belong to one class, which is commonly called "majority", and a much smaller set of patterns belongs to another class, which is commonly called "minority".

The cost of misclassifying minority class patterns is often many times more expensive than misclassifying majority class patterns, because minority class objects in real datasets represent rare but most important instances.

For example, in the context of developing classifiers based on a dataset for ODs, the class of normal patterns is the majority, while the classes describing eight types of ODs are minor. Obviously, the correct classification of patterns of minority classes both for the problem under consideration and in general is of significant interest.

There are various approaches to solving the problem of class imbalance based on the application of:

- Class balancing algorithms that implement oversampling, undersampling and their combinations [21–25];
- Algorithms accounting for the sensitivity to the cost of wrong decisions [10];

- Algorithms for transferring data into a space of a new dimension (with a decrease or increase in dimension) in order to improve the separability of data [11,26–34];
- One-class classification algorithms [34–37].

In this study, the imbalance problem is proposed to be solved using such oversampling algorithms as SMOTE [21], Borderline-SMOTE-1 [22], Borderline-SMOTE-2 [22] and ADASYN [24], followed by choosing the best of them in the sense of providing a higher quality of data classification.

The use of oversampling algorithms is due to the fear of losing critical data patterns in the case of using undersampling algorithms in the context of the problem of developing classifiers for diagnosing oncological diseases.

The SMOTE (synthetic minority oversampling technique) algorithm [21] randomly selects a minority class pattern named a and randomly chooses a pattern named b from the k nearest neighbors of pattern a. The synthetic pattern will be located randomly in the line segment between the original pattern a and its neighbor b. The same process will be repeated until the desired number of synthetic patterns is reached.

The Borderline-SMOTE-1 algorithm [22] considers only the minority class patterns that have a number of minority class neighbors in the range $[g/2, g]$, where g is defined by the researcher. These are the borderline patterns and they can be easily misclassified, i.e., they are "in danger". After detecting such original patterns, a basic SMOTE algorithm is applied to create synthetic patterns.

The Borderline-SMOTE-2 algorithm [22] is similar to the Borderline-SMOTE-1 algorithm, but it also considers the neighbors of the majority class.

The ADASYN algorithm [24] is similar to the SMOTE algorithm, since it generates synthetic patterns in the line segments between two minority class original patterns. It uses a weighted distribution for different minority class patterns that takes into account their level of difficulty: the minority class patterns that have fewer minority class neighbors are harder to learn than those which have more neighbors of the same class. The ADASYN algorithm generates more synthetic patterns for the minority class original patterns that are harder to learn and generates less for the minority class original patterns that are easier to learn.

2.4. UMAP Algorithm

The UMAP algorithm performs nonlinear dimensionality reduction preserving both local and global structures of high dimensional data in the best possible way [29,32] compared to other similar algorithms, for example, compared to the t-SNE algorithm [28].

The UMAP algorithm builds a fuzzy weighted undirected graph in the first step and optimizes loss function in the second step [29].

The UMAP algorithm works with a dataset $X = \{\vec{x}_1, \vec{x}_2, \ldots, \vec{x}_s\}$, which contains s objects (patterns). Every object $\vec{x}_i \in X$ is represented by q-dimensional vector: $\forall \vec{x}_i \in \mathbb{R}^q$. The UMAP algorithm embeds objects from the q-dimensional space into the h-dimensional space ($h \leq q$).

In the first step, the UMAP algorithm searches for the k nearest neighbors $Z_i = \{\vec{z}_{i1}, \ldots, \vec{z}_{il}, \ldots, \vec{z}_{ik}\}$ for every object $\vec{x}_i \in X$, where $\forall \vec{z}_{il} \in X$; $i = \overline{1,s}$; $l = \overline{1,k}$, as described in [68]. Then it computes the scalar distance value d_{il} between $\vec{x}_i$ and $\vec{z}_{il} \in Z_i$ using a distance metric. In the case of working with a Euclidean distance metric, the scalar value d_{il} can be calculated as (1), where pattern x_i is replaced by $\vec{x}_i$ and x is replaced by $\vec{z}_{il}$. As a result, for each object $\vec{x}_i \in X$, the UMAP algorithm determines a set $D_i = \{d_{i1}, \ldots, d_{il}, \ldots, d_{ik}\}$, which contains the distances between $\vec{x}_i$ and each of its k nearest neighbors.

After that, a fuzzy simplicial set, represented as a vector $\vec{\mu}_i \in \mathbb{R}^s$, is constructed for each object. First, the UMAP algorithm searches for $\rho_i \in D_i$, such that $\rho_i \leq d_{il}$ for every $d_{il} \in D_i$. After that, a binary search is implemented in order to find σ_i satisfying the following condition:

$$\sum_{l=1}^{k} e^{(\frac{\rho_i - d_{il}}{\sigma_i})} = \log_2 k. \tag{10}$$

Then the j-th component of vector $\vec{\mu}_i$ is represented by a fuzzy value, which shows how similar i-th and j-th objects from the X set are. Therefore, if the two objects, $\vec{x}_i$ and $\vec{x}_j$, are not neighbors, then the j-th component μ_{ij} of vector $\vec{\mu}_i$ is set to 0. If the two objects, $\vec{x}_i$ and $\vec{x}_j$, are neighbors, then the j-th component μ_{ij} of vector $\vec{\mu}_i$ is computed as:

$$\mu_{ij} = e^{(\frac{\rho_i - d_{ij}}{\sigma_i})}. \tag{11}$$

It is necessary to say that $\mu_{ij} \in [0,1]$.

The UMAP algorithm defines a vector $\vec{\mu}_i \in \mathbb{R}^s$ for each object $\vec{x}_i \in X$. This vector encodes fuzzy similarities between the i-th object and every j-th object belonging to the original high dimensional dataset X.

As a result, the UMAP algorithm builds a weighted adjacency matrix $Matr \in \mathbb{R}^{s \times s}$, where each i-th row is represented by fuzzy vector $\vec{\mu}_i$ ($i = \overline{1,s}$).

The weighted adjacency matrix $Matr$ represents a fuzzy weighted oriented graph, which codes pairwise similarities of objects from X. Matrix $Matr$ is not symmetric.

In the second step, the asymmetric matrix $Matr$ is symmetrized using probabilistic t-conorm:

$$\mu_{ij} \leftarrow \mu_{ij} + \mu_{ji} - \mu_{ij}\mu_{ji}, \tag{12}$$

where i and j are the numbers of rows and columns in the $Matr$ matrix, respectively ($\mu_{kk} = 0; k = \overline{1,s}$).

Thus, the transformed matrix $Matr$ will already be symmetric.

The initial low dimensional representations of objects from the set X described by q-dimensional vectors in the space $\mathbb{R}^h$ are calculated using spectral embedding [32] ($h \leq q$). As a result, the matrix $Y \in \mathbb{R}^{s \times h}$ is obtained.

Then the UMAP algorithm starts the optimization process using the weighted fuzzy cross-entropy with reduced repulsion as the loss function [69]:

$$L(Matr, Y) = \sum_{i=1}^{s}\sum_{j=1}^{s}\left(\mu_{ij}\ln\frac{\mu_{ij}}{\nu_{ij}} + \frac{\sum_{k=1}^{s}\mu_{ik}}{2s}\ln\left(\frac{1-\mu_{ij}}{1-\nu_{ij}}\right)\right), \tag{13}$$

where $Matr \in \mathbb{R}^{s \times s}$ is the symmetric adjacency matrix containing fuzzy values encoding pairwise similarities of high dimensional objects from the dataset X; $Y \in \mathbb{R}^{s \times h}$ is the representation of s objects in the low dimensional space $\mathbb{R}^h$; $\mu_{ij} \in [0,1]$ is a scalar value defining the fuzzy similarity of i-th and j-th high dimensional objects from the original dataset X; and $\nu_{ij} \in [0,1]$ is a scalar value defining the fuzzy similarity of i-th and j-th objects in low dimensional space $\mathbb{R}^h$.

The UMAP algorithm determines the pairwise similarity ν_{ij} of the i-th and j-th objects represented by the i-th and j-th rows of the $Y \in \mathbb{R}^{s \times h}$ matrix in the low dimensional space $\mathbb{R}^h$ as:

$$\nu_{ij} = \left(1 + ad_{ij}^{2b}\right)^{-1}, \tag{14}$$

where d_{ij} is the scalar value between the i-th and j-th objects, described by vectors $\vec{y}_i$ and $\vec{y}_j$ corresponding to the rows in the matrix Y.

The scalar value d_{ij} can be computed using a Euclidean distance metric (1), assuming vectors $\vec{x}_i$ and $\vec{z}_{il}$ in (1) are replaced by vectors $\vec{y}_i$ and $\vec{y}_j$, respectively, and q is replaced with h; a and b are the coefficients that are chosen by non-linear least squares fitting of (14) against the curve:

$$\psi_{ij} = \begin{cases} 1, d_{ij} \leq d_{min} \\ e^{(d_{min}-d_{ij})}, d_{ij} > d_{min} \end{cases} \tag{15}$$

where d_{ij} is the distance value between the i-th and j-th objects $\vec{y}_i$ and $\vec{y}_j$ represented by rows in the matrix Y; and d_{min} is the parameter of the UMAP algorithm ($d_{min} \in (0, 1]$), which affects the density of the clusters formed during the loss function (13) optimization process in the low dimensional space $\mathbb{R}^h$.

The UMAP algorithm performs the optimization of the loss function (13) using the stochastic gradient descent (SGD) algorithm [29]. The locations of objects, which are described by rows of the matrix $Y \in \mathbb{R}^{s \times h}$, are specified during each iteration of the SGD algorithm in order to minimize the loss function (13). Other functions given, particularly in [34], can also be used as a loss function.

2.5. Entropies, Hjorth Parameters and Fractal Dimensions

A number of works have shown that the use of nonlinear approaches can help extract some information from the data that is difficult to obtain from traditional statistics. In particular, entropy analysis and fractal analysis are non-linear approaches and provide researchers with new opportunities to extract and explore the knowledge hidden in the data. Entropy and fractal dimension are two diametrically opposed but complementary concepts.

Entropy is a measure of chaos. The value of entropy gives an idea of how far the studied object (pattern) is from an ordered, structured state and how close it is to a completely chaotic, structureless, homogeneous form.

Fractal dimension is a metric for characterizing a fractal pattern (which is often a highly organized structure) by quantifying its complexity as the ratio of change in detail to change in scale.

In this study, we use five entropy characteristics and three fractal dimensions, as well as two Hjorth parameters, such as mobility and complexity, to evaluate the patterns of a dataset on ODs in order to identify such indicators that will allow for improving the separation of data from different classes from each other. The identified best indicators can later claim the role of a tool for generating new features used to expand the original dataset.

The indicators considered in the proposed study are listed below.

Permutation entropy (PE) [40] is a tool that provides a quantification measure of the complexity of the studied object by capturing the order relations between the values and extracting a probability distribution of the ordinal elements.

Spectral entropy (SPE) [41] is a tool that is based on Shannon's entropy. It measures the irregularity or complexity of the studied object in the frequency domain. After performing a Fourier transform, the studied object is transformed into a power spectrum, and its information entropy presents the power spectral entropy of the studied object.

Singular value decomposition entropy (SVDE) [42] is a tool that characterizes information content or regularity of the studied object depending on the number of vectors attributed to the process.

Approximate entropy (AE) [43–45] is a tool used to quantify the amount of regularity and the unpredictability of fluctuations of the studied object.

Sample entropy (SE) [45] is a modification of approximate entropy. It is used for assessing the complexity of the studied object.

Hjorth mobility (HM) [46,47] is a tool that describes the average frequency for the studied object and provides information about its so-called speed.

Hjorth complexity (HC) [46,47] is a tool that describes the variability of the studied object and refers to the similarity of the studied object to a sinusoidal wave.

Petrosian fractal dimension (PFD) [49] is a tool that allows for estimating the fractal dimension of a finite sequence describing the studied object by means of converting the data to a binary sequence before estimating.

Katz fractal dimension (KFD) [50,51] is a tool which makes exponential transformation of fractal dimension values of the studied object with relative insensitivity to noise.

Higuchi fractal dimension (HFD) [52] is a tool which uses an algorithmic approximate value for the box-counting dimension of the graph of a real-valued function for the studied object.

It is necessary to say that HFD yields a more accurate estimation of the fractal dimension values of the studied object than KFD when tested on synthetic data, but it is more sensitive to noise.

The list of indicators similar to those considered above can be expanded.

Typically, these indicators are used to analyze signals, for example, represented by time series. However, there are also works in which these indicators are used to generate new features of objects based on already known features. For example, the work [10] explores the possibility of using entropies AE and SE to generate new features in the problem of diagnosing ODs based on blood protein markers. Obviously, it is possible to use other indicators in order to extract new features of objects based on already known ones using them.

A more detailed description of the indicators chosen during the experiments will be given in Section 4.

3. A Novel Approach to the Generation of Datasets and the Development of Classifiers

The algorithm for developing the best classifier can be described by the following sequence of steps.

Step 1. Scale each feature of the original dataset to the range [0, 1].

Step 2. Check the features of the dataset for correlation and remove features with high correlation (taking into account their correlation with the target feature that determines class labels for patterns).

Step 3. Calculate the values of potential new features based on the not-scaled dataset, from which the correlated features found in Step 1 are excluded, using five formulas for entropy, two formulas for Hjorth parameters and three formulas for fractal dimension, and choose those that are the best at separating patterns of different classes (based on the average values of entropy and fractal dimensions and average standard deviations). Check the potential new features for correlation and remove features with high correlation (taking into account their correlation with the target feature that determines class labels for patterns).

Step 4. Scale each new feature to the range [0, 1].

Step 5. Set the range [2, H], which will be used in the cycle (during the steps 6–10), where each number h from the range [2, H] is the dimension in the low-dimensional space (the number of features); $2 \leq H \leq q - 1$; q is the dimension of the original space (the number of features in the original dataset C1).

Step 6. Implement the UMAP algorithm with the number h from the range [2, H]. Scale each feature to the range [0, 1]

Step 7. Construct 12 datasets (if $h = 2$) or 8 datasets (if $h \geq 3$):

1. C1 is the original dataset (with 39 features) (formed only for $h = 2$).
2. C2 is a dataset based on the UMAP algorithm (from 2 to H features as a result of embedding in a space of lower dimension).
3. C3 is a dataset based on the original dataset and the UMAP algorithm (from 2 to H features).
4. C4 is a dataset based on the UMAP algorithm (from 2 to H features) and one entropy.
5. C5 is a dataset based on the UMAP algorithm (from 2 to H features) and two fractal dimensions.

6. C6 is a dataset based on the UMAP algorithm (from 2 to H features), one entropy and two fractal dimensions.
7. C7 is a dataset based on the original dataset, the UMAP algorithm (from 2 to H features) and one entropy.
8. C8 is a dataset based on the original dataset and one entropy (formed only for $h = 2$).
9. C9 is a dataset based on the original dataset and two fractal dimensions (formed only for $h = 2$).
10. C10 is a dataset based on the original dataset, one entropy and two fractal dimensions (formed only for $h = 2$).
11. C11 is a dataset based on the original dataset, the UMAP algorithm (from 2 to H features) and two fractal dimensions.
12. C12 is a dataset based on the original dataset, the UMAP algorithm (from 2 to H features), one entropy and two fractal dimensions.

Step 8. Rebalance classes for all datasets.

Step 9. Develop classifiers based on the kNN and SVM algorithms. Assess classification quality using cross-validation based on $MacroF_1-score$. Select the best classifiers based on the kNN and SVM algorithms.

Step 10. Increase the number h of dimensions in the low-dimensional space by 1.

Step 11. If $h \leq H$, go back to step 6. If $h > H$, go to step 12.

Step 12. Select the best classifiers based on the results of the algorithm implementation. Complete implementation of the algorithm.

The number of datasets that were used to develop the classifiers was determined as follows.

A total of 12 datasets were used for $h = 2$. Dataset C1 is the same as the original dataset. Dataset C2 contains features based on the UMAP algorithm. Other datasets were acquired by:

- Adding all possible combinations of three groups of features based on the UMAP algorithm, one entropy and two fractal dimensions (as 1 of 3, 2 of 3, 3 of 3) to the features of the original dataset;
- Adding all possible combinations of two feature groups based on one entropy and two fractal dimensions (as 1 of 2, 2 of 2) to the features based on the UMAP algorithm.

Eight datasets were used for $h \geq 3$, because datasets C1, C8, C9 and C10 do not contain features based on the UMAP algorithm. Namely, the number of generated features depends on h whether the UMAP algorithm is used. Thus, it is sufficient to generate the sets C1, C8, C9 and C10 once for $h = 2$ because their composition does not depend on h.

The generation of datasets based on only one entropy and/or two fractal dimensions was not performed due to a significant reduction (convolution) of the initial information in this case.

The choice of the scaling method that implements the transformation of each feature into the range [0, 1] is due to working with the UMAP algorithm, which essentially searches for the coordinates of patterns in a low-dimensional space. In this regard, we decided to scale the values for each coordinate of the patterns in the range [0, 1].

This algorithm uses only one entropy (AE) and only two fractal dimensions (KFD and HFD) because the expediency of using only these out of the 10 indicators specified in Section 2.5 was confirmed experimentally when working with the original dataset based on blood protein markers.

Figure 1 shows a diagram that represents the process of generating the datasets used in the development of classifiers. The upper part of the figure lists the datasets that are generated only once because they are formed without involving the UMAP algorithm.

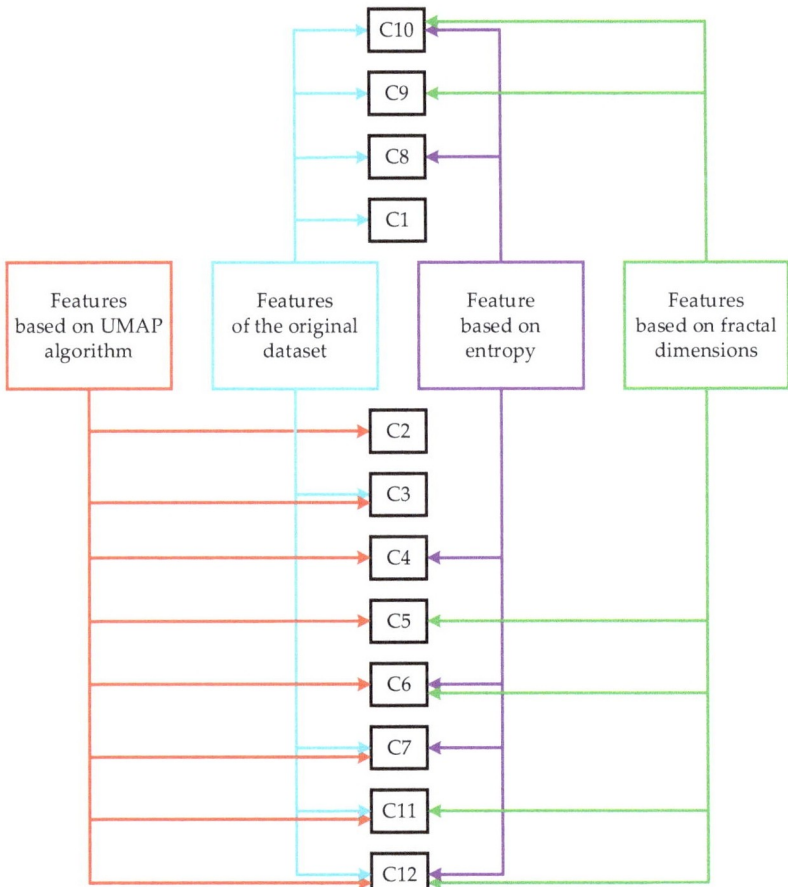

Figure 1. Scheme of generation of the datasets used in the development of classifiers.

Figure 2 shows the enlarged block diagram of the classifier development.

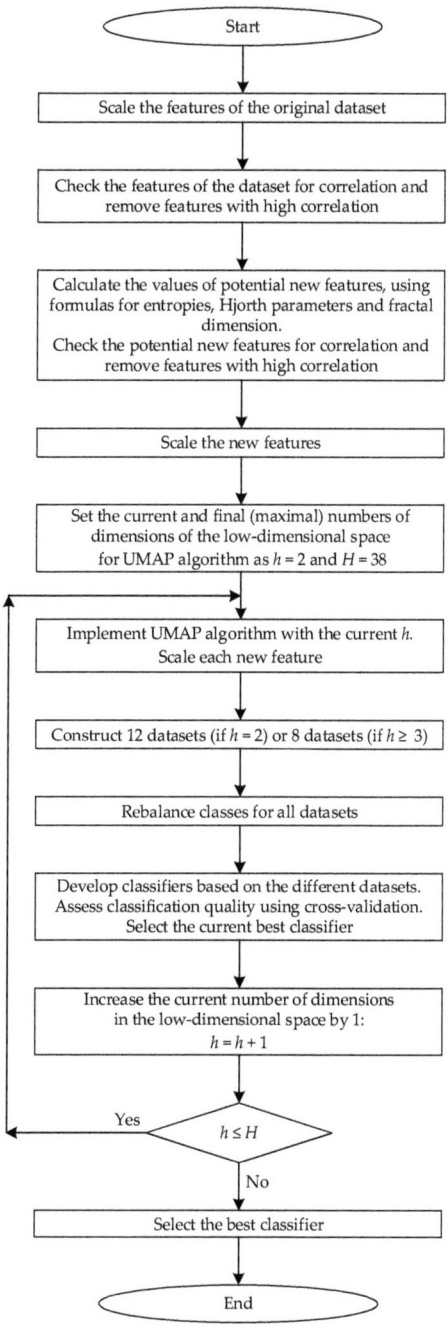

Figure 2. The enlarged block diagram of the classifier development.

4. Experimental Studies

During the experiments, the dataset containing information on 39 serum protein markers for 1817 patterns was used. This dataset includes such classes of ODs as breast, colorectum, esophagus, liver, lung, ovary, pancreas and stomach, as well as the normal class (Norm) corresponding to cases where an OD was not diagnosed. Each protein marker is associated with some feature in the dataset. This dataset is multiclass because it contains information on patterns from nine classes. Accordingly, the classification problem is multiclass and involves the development of a multiclass classifier. This dataset was taken from COSMIC repository [39].

The list of serum protein markers is as follows: AFP (pg/mL), Angiopoietin-2 (pg/mL), AXL (pg/mL), CA-125 (U/mL), CA 15-3 (U/mL), CA19-9 (U/mL), CD44 (ng/mL), CEA (pg/mL), CYFRA 21-1 (pg/mL), DKK1 (ng/mL), Endoglin (pg/mL), FGF2 (pg/mL), Follistatin (pg/mL), Galectin-3 (ng/mL), G-CSF (pg/mL), GDF15 (ng/mL), HE4 (pg/mL), HGF (pg/mL), IL-6 (pg/mL), IL-8 (pg/mL), Kallikrein-6 (pg/mL), Leptin (pg/mL), Mesothelin (ng/mL), Midkine (pg/mL), Myeloperoxidase (ng/mL), NSE (ng/mL), OPG (ng/mL), OPN (pg/mL), PAR (pg/mL), Prolactin (pg/mL), sEGFR (pg/mL), sFas (pg/mL), SHBG (nM), sHER2/sEGFR2/sErbB2 (pg/mL), sPECAM-1 (pg/mL), TGFa (pg/mL), Thrombospondin-2 (pg/mL), TIMP-1 (pg/mL) and TIMP-2 (pg/mL).

All the experiments were conducted using software written in Python 3.10 in the interactive cloud environment Google Colab. The choice of the Python 3.10 programming language can be justified by a large number of various available libraries, including libraries that implement machine learning algorithms.

4.1. Data Analysis Based on the UMAP Algorithm

A preliminary visual analysis of the dataset was performed using the non-linear dimensionality reduction algorithm UMAP. Information on the software implementation of the UMAP algorithm used is available in [70].

With the help of the UMAP algorithm, a 39-dimensional nine-class dataset was embedded into a two-dimensional space (Figure 3). Analysis of the visualization results indicates a complex organization of nine classes in the dataset and their poor separability in general. However, one can try to find such classes in this nine-class dataset that can be well separated from each other.

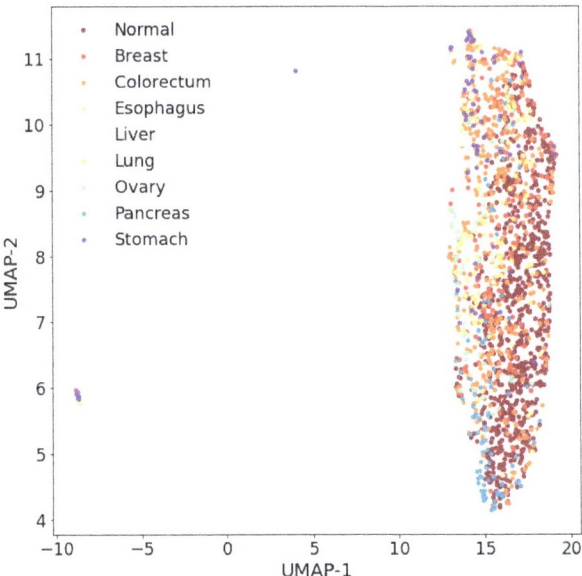

Figure 3. Visualization of nine-class dataset of ODs using the UMAP algorithm. ($n\_neighbors$ = 15, min_dist = 0.1, $random\_state$ = 42, $metric$ = 'euclidean').

For example, if only three classes are left in the dataset, such as normal, liver and ovary, then the results of the visualization of the three-class dataset (Figure 4) allow us to conclude that it is expedient to carry out research on the development of a classifier capable of separating patterns of these three classes with high values of classification quality metrics. It should be noted that a three-class dataset with the same list of classes (normal, liver and ovary) was considered by the authors in [10].

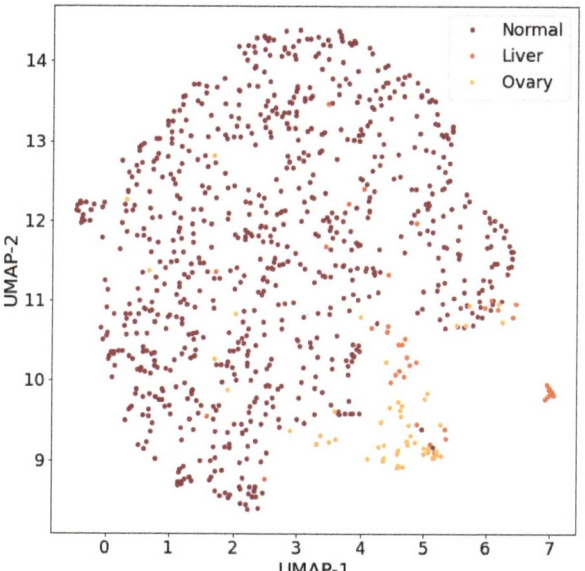

Figure 4. Visualization of three-class dataset of ODs using the UMAP algorithm. ($n\_neighbors$ = 15, min_dist = 0.1, $random\_state$ = 42, $metric$ = 'euclidean').

At the time when this article was written, the ratio of classes in the dataset was Normal:Liver:Ovary = 812:44:54 (which differed slightly from the ratio in the work [10]: Normal:Liver:Ovary = 799:44:54).

It can be assumed that the insufficient separability of patterns of different classes, both in the nine-class dataset and in sets with a smaller number of classes (including in the three-class dataset), is due to the presence of different ODs stages in the patterns presented in the dataset (for example, in the early stages of an OD, separability may be worse). Clearly, further research is needed to answer this question. Insufficiently good separability of patterns of different classes may be due to the insufficiency of the number of features. This problem can be solved by enriching the dataset with new information, either by involving new features in the analysis, for example, based on gene biomarkers, or by generating new features based on existing data, i.e., by extracting knowledge hidden in existing data. In this study, the second approach to enriching the dataset with new information was implemented: an attempt was made to generate new features based on the UMAP algorithm, entropy characteristics and fractal dimensions of the existing data patterns, followed by the selection of new features that satisfy certain a priori selected criteria.

Scaling to the range [0, 1] for each feature was applied to the nine-class and three-class datasets before visualization.

It should be noted that the UMAP algorithm is usually used to embed multidimensional objects in two- or three-dimensional space for visualization, but the results of its application can also be used in the development of data classifiers.

Since the visualization of a reduced three-class dataset on ODs in a two-dimensional space indicates the presence of patterns for which a two-dimensional embedding does not allow for distinguishing some objects in their a priori known classes (Figure 2), then it is advised to study various options for embedding, that is, nesting in spaces, whose dimension is equal to the number h, where $h \in \{2, 3, \ldots, H\}$, H is the maximum dimension of the embedded space. For example, H can be equal to $q - 1$, where q is the dimension of the original feature space (in this example $q = 39$). It is also necessary to develop a data classifier for $q = 39$.

As a result, a group of classifiers will be obtained, developed on the basis of datasets "embedded" in the space of a smaller dimension with the number of features h ($h \in \{2, 3, \ldots, H\}$), as well as a dataset located in the original feature space (i.e., for $q = 39$). It will be possible to choose the best classifier from this group in terms of maximizing the classification quality metric (for example, $MacroF_1-score$ in the case of working with class-imbalanced datasets). Moving to a lower dimensional space may potentially make it possible to improve the separability of classes from each other, even without making any additional effort, such as balancing classes or taking the sensitivity to the cost of wrong decisions into account.

The scaling of each feature to the range [0, 1] was performed twice during the implementation of the UMAP algorithm: before applying the UMAP algorithm and during preparations of the dataset obtained using the UMAP algorithm for developing a classifier. The resulting dataset can be used on its own or to form an augmented dataset. We can add new features obtained using the UMAP algorithm or extracted in some other way (e.g., by computing entropy characteristics and fractal dimensions of the original dataset) to the features of the original 39-feature dataset. The data obtained by reducing the dimensionality of the original dataset can be considered as new features.

4.2. Generation of New Features Based on Entropies, Hjorth Parameters and Fractal Dimensions of Data Patterns

The original three-class dataset was examined for feature correlation before developing classifiers based on variously formed datasets. The examination showed the absence of a strong correlation with the values of the correlation index of at least 0.7 between the features. The maximum value of the correlation index, equal to 0.604, was found only for one pair of traits with numbers 34 and 35 (sHER2/sEGFR2/sErbB2 (pg/mL) and sPECAM-1 (pg/mL)). The values of the correlation index for other pairs of features turned out to be less than 0.6. As a result, the expediency of using all the features in the further analysis and development of classifiers was proved.

In order to improve the quality of data classification, it was decided to generate new features based on metrics such as entropy characteristics and fractal dimensions of data patterns, selecting among them those that do not correlate with each other or the features of a three-class dataset.

Three-class not scaled to range [0, 1] for each feature dataset was used to generate new features based on the entropy characteristics, Hjorth parameters and fractal dimensions of data patterns. Formulas that were used in the generation of new features for each pattern involved 10 metrics. There were five formulas for entropy, such as permutation entropy (PE), spectral entropy (SPE), singular value decomposition entropy (SVDE), approximate entropy (AE) and sample entropy (SE); two formulas for Hjorth parameters, such as Hjorth mobility and complexity (HM and HC); and three formulas for calculating such fractal dimensions as Petrosian fractal dimension (PFD), Katz fractal dimension (KFD) and Higuchi fractal dimension (HFD).

The results of the calculations of the entropy values, Hjorth parameters and fractal dimensions were grouped into three classes. For each of the three classes, the mean value and the mean standard deviation were calculated for each potential new generated feature.

Comparative analysis of the mean values and mean standard deviations of the aforementioned metrics for each of the three classes for each potential new generated feature

(Tables 1 and 2) made it possible to draw the following conclusions. The largest differences between the classes are shown by the entropies AE and SE (Table 1), as well as the fractal dimensions KFD and HFD (Table 1). These metrics were chosen for further consideration. Meanwhile, the mean standard deviations for all the metrics above turned out to be small (and only for the KFD metric they are slightly larger than for other metrics).

Table 1. Mean values for each of the three classes for each potential new generated feature.

Class	Mean Values									
	Entropy					Hjorth Parameters		Fractal Dimension		
	PE	SPE	SVDE	AE [1]	SE	HM	HC	PFD	KFD	HFD
Normal	0.977	0.921	0.943	**0.454**	**0.508**	1.335	1.334	1.068	**1.609**	**2.337**
Liver	0.981	0.913	0.937	**0.257**	**0.425**	1.326	1.336	1.069	**1.548**	**2.271**
Ovary	0.978	0.924	0.975	**0.353**	**0.348**	1.313	1.306	1.065	**1.696**	**2.372**

[1] Bold type indicates the mean values of the metrics that make it possible to distinguish between classes.

Table 2. Mean standard deviations for each of the three classes for each potential new generated feature.

Class	Mean Standard Deviations									
	Entropy					Hjorth Parameters		Fractal Dimension		
	PE	SPE	SVDE	AE [2]	SE	HM	HC	PFD	KFD	HFD
Normal	0.018	0.054	0.043	**0.091**	**0.164**	0.131	0.510	0.005	**0.174**	**0.068**
Liver	0.013	0.085	0.082	**0.105**	**0.105**	0.098	0.021	0.005	**0.266**	**0.138**
Ovary	0.015	0.026	0.021	**0.097**	**0.131**	0.110	0.207	0.004	**0.230**	**0.091**

[2] Bold type indicates the mean standard deviations of the metrics that make it possible to distinguish between classes.

The selected metrics were tested for correlation with each other. The tests showed a correlation between the metrics AE and SE (with the value of the correlation metric equal to 0.931). The metric SE was excluded from further consideration, among other things, because it has a lower correlation with the target feature that determines the labels of pattern classes (the values of the correlation metric for the metrics AE and SE are 0.360 and 0.320, respectively, which corresponds to a moderate direct linear dependence on the Chaddock scale). It should be noted that the experiments confirmed the advantage, albeit insignificant, of the metric AE as a tool for generating the values of a new feature included in the dataset (in terms of ensuring a higher quality of data classification). The correlation between the chosen fractal dimensions KFD and HFD is small: it is only 0.141.

Thus, it is advisable to use one feature based on the approximation entropy AE, as well as two features based on fractal dimensions KFD and HFD.

Below, we briefly describe the algorithms that allow for calculating approximation entropy AE, the Katz fractal dimension KFD and the Higuchi fractal dimension HFD.

The algorithm for determining the approximation entropy AE can be described as follows [45].

Suppose we have a sequence of numbers $u = \{u(1), u(2), \ldots, u(q)\}$ of length q, a non-negative integer ξ ($\xi \leq q$) and a positive real number r.

First, the algorithm defines the blocks $\chi(i) = \{u(i), u(i+1), \ldots, u(i+\xi-1)\}$ and $\chi(j) = \{u(j), u(j+1), \ldots, u(j+\xi-1)\}$, and calculates the distance between $\chi(i)$ and $\chi(j)$ as $d(\chi(i), \chi(j)) = \max_{\kappa=\overline{1,\xi}}(|u(i+\kappa-1) - u(j+\kappa-1)|)$. Then it calculates the value $C_i^\xi(r) = \frac{number(d(\chi(i),\chi(j))\leq r)}{q-\xi+1}$, where $j \leq q - \xi + 1$. The numerator of $C_i^\xi(r)$ defines the number of blocks of consecutive values of length ξ, which are similar to a given block. As a result, the algorithm calculates the value $\phi^\xi(r)$ as

$$\phi^\xi(r) = \frac{1}{q - \xi + 1} \cdot \sum_{i=1}^{q-\xi+1} \log C_i^\xi(r) \tag{16}$$

and approximation entropy $AE(q, \xi, r)(u)$ as

$$AE(q, \xi, r)(u) = \phi^\xi(r) - \phi^{\xi+1}(r), \tag{17}$$

where $\xi \geq 1$; $AE(q, 0, r)(u) = -\phi^1(r)$.

Approximation entropy $AE(q, \xi, r)(u)$ defines the logarithmic frequency with which blocks of length ξ that are close together stay together for the next position.

$AE(q, \xi, r)$ is the statistical assessment of the parameter $AE(\xi, r)$:

$$AE(\xi, r)(u) = \lim_{q \to \infty} \left[\phi^\xi(r) - \phi^{\xi+1}(r) \right]. \tag{18}$$

In the proposed research, we used $\xi = 2$ and $r = 0.25$ (these are values that are usually applied).

In the context of the problem under consideration, we use the description of a certain pattern $x_i \in X$ ($i = \overline{1,s}$; s is the number of patterns in the dataset X) based on blood protein markers corresponding to q features as a certain sequence of numbers u of length q.

The algorithm for determining the Katz fractal dimension KFD can be described as follows [51].

Suppose we have a sequence of points (ζ_j, ϑ_j) of length q.

First, the algorithm defines the length L of the waveform as

$$L = \sum_{j=0}^{q-2} \sqrt{(\vartheta_{j+1} - \vartheta_j)^2 + (\zeta_{j+1} - \zeta_j)^2} \tag{19}$$

and the maximum distance Δ between the initial point (ζ_1, ϑ_1) to the other points as

$$\Delta = \max_{j=\overline{2,q}} \sqrt{(\zeta_j - \zeta_1)^2 - (\vartheta_j - \vartheta_1)^2}. \tag{20}$$

Then the algorithm calculates the Katz fractal dimension KFD as

$$D = \frac{\log(q)}{\log(q) + \log\left(\frac{\Delta}{L}\right)}. \tag{21}$$

In the context of the problem being solved, we consider a sequence of points $\left(j, x_i^j\right)$, where j is the j-th number of the feature in the dataset X ($j = \overline{1,q}$; q is the number of features), as a sequence of points (ζ_j, ϑ_j) of length q; and x_i^j is the value of the j-th feature of the i-th pattern $x_i \in X$ ($i = \overline{1,s}$; s is the number of patterns in the dataset X based on blood protein markers;).

The algorithm for determining the Higuchi fractal dimension HFD can be described as follows [52].

Suppose we have a sequence of numbers $u = \{u(1), u(2), \ldots, u(q)\}$ of length q.

First, the algorithm defines new sequences u_κ^ξ, defined as:

$$u_\kappa^\xi; u(\xi), u(\xi + \kappa), u(\xi + 2\kappa), \ldots, u\left(\xi + \left[\frac{q-\xi}{\kappa}\right]\kappa\right) \quad (\xi = \overline{1,\kappa}), \tag{22}$$

where $[o]$ is the Gauss' notation, which denotes the integer part of o; ξ is the integer defining the initial moment; and κ is the integer defining the interval moment.

As a result, the algorithm defines κ sets of new sequences.

Then the algorithm calculates the length $L_\xi(\kappa)$ of curve u_κ^ξ as

$$L_\xi(\kappa) = \frac{q-1}{\left[\frac{q-\xi}{\kappa}\right] \cdot \kappa^2} \cdot \sum_{i=1}^{\left[\frac{q-\xi}{\kappa}\right]} |u(\xi + i \cdot \kappa) - u(\xi + (i-1) \cdot \kappa)|, \qquad (23)$$

and the length $L(\kappa)$ as

$$L(\kappa) = \frac{1}{\kappa} \cdot \sum_{\xi=1}^{\kappa} L_\xi(\kappa). \qquad (24)$$

Then the algorithm calculates the Higuchi fractal dimension HFD as the slope of the best-fitting linear function through the data points:

$$\left\{ \left(\log \frac{1}{\kappa}, \log(L(\kappa)) \right) \right\}. \qquad (25)$$

In the context of the problem under consideration, we use the description of a certain pattern $x_i \in X$ ($i = \overline{1,s}$; s is the number of patterns in the dataset X) based on blood protein markers, corresponding to q features, as a certain sequence of numbers u of length q.

In the proposed research, we used values for $\kappa \leq 10$ and $m < k$.

4.3. Generation of Datasets Used in the Development of Classifiers

The development of the classifiers was carried out based on the following datasets generated based on new features from Sections 4.1 and 4.2:

1. C1 is the original dataset (it contains 39 features);
2. C2 is a dataset based on the UMAP algorithm (it contains from 2 to H features as a result of embedding in a space of lower dimension);
3. C3 is a dataset based on the original dataset and the UMAP algorithm (it generates from 2 to H features);
4. C4 is a dataset based on the UMAP algorithm (it generates from 2 to H features) and one entropy;
5. C5 is a dataset based on the UMAP algorithm (it generates from 2 to H features) and two fractal dimensions;
6. C6 is a dataset based on the UMAP algorithm (it generates from 2 to H features), one entropy and two fractal dimensions;
7. C7 is a dataset based on the original dataset, the UMAP algorithm (it generates from 2 to H features) and one entropy;
8. C8 is a dataset based on the original dataset and one entropy;
9. C9 is a dataset based on the original dataset and two fractal dimensions;
10. C10 is a dataset based on the original dataset, one entropy and two fractal dimensions;
11. C11 is a dataset based on the original dataset, the UMAP algorithm (it generates from 2 to H features) and two fractal dimensions;
12. C12 is a dataset based on the original dataset, the UMAP algorithm (it generates from 2 to H features), one entropy and two fractal dimensions.

The content of the datasets (namely, the number and selection of features) C1, C8, C9 and C10 does not depend on the dimension h of the space into which the 39-dimensional feature space of the original dataset is embedded when applying the UMAP algorithm. Therefore, classifiers based on these datasets should be developed once. Balancing algorithms, such as SMOTE and its modifications that implement the synthesis of new patterns at the classes' boundary (Borderline SMOTE-1, Borderline SMOTE-2 and ADASYN), are applied once, as well. After this is completed, new classifiers are developed.

The number and selection of features in the remaining datasets C2, C3, C4, C5, C6, C7, C11 and C12 depends on the dimension h of the space into which the UMAP algorithm embeds the 39-dimensional feature space of the original dataset. Therefore, new classifiers should be developed based on the datasets C2, C3, C4, C5, C6, C7, C11 and C12 for each h, both in the case of refusal to use class balancing algorithms, and in the case of their application.

If the dataset is supposed to use a feature based on the entropies, then two variants of the classifier are developed in order to assess the advantages of using the approximation entropy AE and the sample entropy SE in relation to each other, followed by choosing the best entropy for the role of the entropy used for generation of new feature values.

If the UMAP algorithm is not used in the formation of the dataset, i.e., the dataset does not depend on the dimension h of the space into which the 39-dimensional feature space of the original dataset is embedded, then we will identify the names of the classifiers with the names of the datasets corresponding to them. In this case, we will discuss classifiers C1, C8, C9 and C10. If the UMAP algorithm is used when forming a dataset, i.e., the dataset depends on the dimension of the space h into which the 39-dimensional feature space of the original dataset is embedded using the UMAP algorithm, then we will add an indication of the space dimension to the name of the corresponding dataset. For example, we will talk about the C3 classifier (for $h = 5$), if, during its development, a dataset was used that was formed based on the results of applying the UMAP algorithm for $h = 5$.

4.4. Aspects of k-Fold Cross-Validation

The classifiers were developed using the kNN and SVM algorithms, the software implementations of which were taken from the scikit-learn library of the Python language.

It should be noted that it is possible to use other machine learning algorithms, for example, the RF algorithm, but this can lead to significant time costs for the development of classifiers due to the specifics of the algorithm itself.

First of all, we developed classifiers for different values of the dimension h of the space in which the UMAP algorithm embedded the original 39-dimensional space. The classifiers were developed using the kNN and SVM algorithms based on 12 datasets. No balancing algorithms had been applied to the datasets prior to that.

Then we developed classifiers using datasets that were balanced by classes based on four algorithms: SMOTE, Borderline SMOTE-1, Borderline SMOTE-2 and ADASYN. In this case, we used the kNN and SVM algorithms once again.

Before balancing, the ratio of classes in each of the 12 datasets was Normal:Ovary:Liver = 812:54:44.

The classes were balanced with the values of the parameters of the balancing algorithms set by default in the Python program libraries.

After balancing the classes using the SMOTE algorithm, the ratio of classes in each of the 12 datasets became Normal:Ovary:Liver = 812:812:812.

After balancing the classes using the Borderline SMOTE-1 algorithm, the ratio of classes in each of the 12 datasets became Normal:Ovary:Liver = 812:812:812.

After balancing the classes using the Borderline SMOTE-2 algorithm, the ratio of classes in each of the 12 datasets became Normal:Ovary:Liver = 812:812:811.

After balancing the classes using the ADASYN algorithm, the ratio of classes in each of the 12 datasets became Normal:Ovary:Liver = 812:807:806.

In order to assess the quality of each classifier, the k-fold cross-validation procedure, which is an effective approach for estimating the performance of a classifier, was applied.

$MacroF_1-score$ was used as the main metric of classification quality in order to reduce the negative impact on the quality of classification of the existing class imbalance in the original C1 dataset.

A grid search was implemented for the optimal values of the parameters of the kNN and SVM classifiers using the classical approach to the implementation of the k-fold cross-validation procedure. In this case, the k classifiers are trained and evaluated on the k holdout test sets. As a result, the mean performance of the k classifiers is evaluated.

We proposed to perform 10-fold cross-validation (that is $k = 10$) during implementation of the grid search for the optimal values of the parameters of the best classifier. We used a stratified sampling strategy [71,72]. The results of the cross-validation were used to calculate the mean value of $MacroF_1-score$ and the corresponding standard deviation. For the best classifier, similar values were calculated for such metrics as *Accuracy*, *MacroPrecision* and *MacroRecall*. In addition, hyperparameter values were determined for the best classifier.

A grid search was implemented while working with the kNN algorithm. The following parameters were used in the grid search: *n_neighbors*, which corresponds to the number of nearest neighbors, and *weights*, which corresponds to weight coefficients assigned to the neighbors. The value of the number of neighbors *n_neighbors* varied from 5 to 15 with a step of one. The *weights* parameter could take one of two values: *'uniform'* and *'distance'*. In the first case, all neighbors of some object had equal weights. In the second case, the neighbor's weight depended on the distance to the object: the smaller the distance, the greater the weight. As for the rest of the parameters, we used the default values set in the software implementation of the kNN algorithm in the Python scikit-learn library. As a result, 10 * (11 * 2) = 220 model evaluations were obtained with a single pass through the grid.

Working with the SVM algorithm involved the implementation of a grid search, as well. In this case, it was implemented for the values of such parameters as: *gamma*, which is a parameter of the radial basis function of the kernel, and *C*, which is a regularization parameter. The value of the *gamma* parameter varied from 0.4 to 2 with a step of 0.1. The value of parameter *C* also changed from 0.4 to 2 with a step of 0.1.

We used the default values set in the software implementation of the SVM algorithm in the Python scikit-learn library as the values of the rest parameters. As a result, 10 * (17 * 17) = 2890 model evaluations were obtained with a single pass through the grid.

4.5. Development of the Classifiers

We conducted research in order to determine the feasibility of using the approximation entropy or sample entropy when forming the values of new features for each of the kNN and SVM algorithms used in the development of the classifiers. The feasibility assessment was performed for both datasets that were not subjected to class balancing, and for datasets that were subjected to class balancing using four algorithms: SMOTE, Borderline SMOTE-1, Borderline SMOTE-2 and ADASYN.

The preference for one or another entropy was given based on its provision of the maximum mean value of $MacroF_1-score$ at the test sets on a group of the kNN or SVM classifiers developed on the basis of the studied datasets (without class balancing or with balancing using one of the four algorithms). The best class balancing algorithm was chosen for each of the kNN and SVM algorithms used in the development of the classifiers.

The results of our research for the kNN and SVM algorithms used in the development of the classifiers are shown in Tables 3 and 4, respectively. The development of the classifiers was carried out for $h = 2, \ldots, 38$. The maximum mean values of $MacroF_1-score$ in columns AE and SE for each type of classifier are highlighted in bold, and the coinciding values are italicized.

Table 3. Study of the advantages of entropies AE and SE in the development of the kNN classifiers.

Type of Classification Algorithm/ Class Balancing Algorithm	Maximum Mean Value of $MacroF_1$-score	
	AE	SE
kNN/no class balancing	0.842	0.849 [3]
kNN/SMOTE	**0.866**	0.864
kNN/Borderline SMOTE-1	*0.878*	*0.878*
kNN/Borderline SMOTE-2	*0.861*	*0.861*
kNN/ADASYN	*0.842*	*0.842*

[3] The metric value with the largest value in the row is highlighted in bold. Matching metric values in a row are italicized.

Table 4. Study of the advantages of entropies AE and SE in the development of the SVM classifiers.

Type of Classification Algorithm/ Class Balancing Algorithm	Maximum Mean Value of $MacroF_1$-score	
	AE	SE
SVM/no class balancing	0.883	**0.884** [4]
SVM/SMOTE	*0.912*	*0.912*
SVM/Borderline SMOTE-1	*0.911*	*0.911*
SVM/Borderline SMOTE-2	*0.886*	*0.886*
SVM/ADASYN	*0.905*	*0.905*

[4] The metric value with the largest value in the row is highlighted in bold. Matching metric values in a row are italicized.

The experimental results did not reveal a clear advantage of the approximation entropy over the sample entropy. Preference was given to the approximation entropy because of its higher correlation with the target feature. However, it is possible that, in the case of working with the SVM algorithm, preference should be given to the sample entropy SE due to the fact that the time spent on calculating the sample entropy SE is less than calculating the approximate entropy AE.

Based on the results of the analysis of Tables 3 and 4, a class balancing algorithm was also identified, which allowed for obtaining larger maximum mean values of the $MacroF_1-score$. This is the Borderline SMOTE-1 algorithm for the kNN classifier development (Table 3), and the SMOTE algorithm for the SVM classifier development (Table 4). These algorithms will be considered in subsequent detailed studies when developing the corresponding classifiers.

4.6. Development of kNN Classifiers

Euclidean distance metric was used during development of the kNN classifiers. The weights of neighbors for each analyzed object could be equal or dependent on the distance to this object. The Borderline SMOTE-1 algorithm was used to implement class balancing.

4.6.1. Experiment without Class Balancing

Figure 5 presents the results of the experiment in choosing the best kNN classifier in the case of working with the approximation entropy AE when forming some of the datasets used in the development of the classifiers. The balancing of classes in datasets was not performed here.

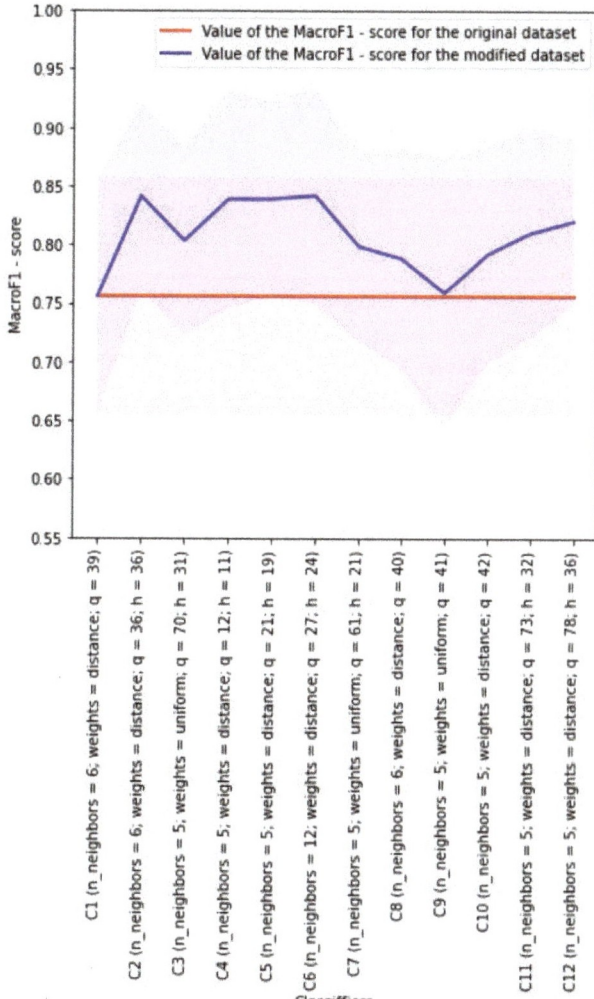

Figure 5. Visualization of the results of the experiment of choosing the best kNN classifier based on 12 datasets without using a class balancing algorithm ($n\_neighbors$ is the number of nearest neighbors; $weights$ is the parameter which assigns weight coefficients to the neighbors; q is the dimension of the space corresponding to the dataset used for development of classifier; h is the dimension of the space into which the UMAP algorithm embeds the 39-dimensional feature space corresponding to the original dataset; the background of each color shows the amount of standard deviation around the mean of the metric $MacroF_1-score$).

The red color indicates the line corresponding to the mean value of the $MacroF_1-score$ obtained for the best C1 classifier developed on the basis of the original dataset, i.e., the dataset with 39 features. The light red shading shows the spread for the $MacroF_1-score$ mean value calculated from its standard deviation. The blue color indicates the line corresponding to the mean values of the $MacroF_1-score$ obtained for the best classifiers developed on the basis of the modified datasets. The light blue shading shows the spread for the $MacroF_1-score$ means calculated from their standard deviation. In addition, the following information is presented in Figure 5 next to the names of the classifiers developed on the basis of datasets: the number of features that depend on the dimension h of the space into which the original 39-dimensional space is embedded, the dimensions h of the space allowing for building the best classifiers, the final dimension q of the space corresponding to the dataset used for development of classifier, and the best values of classifiers parameters are indicated. The same designations are used in Figures 6–8.

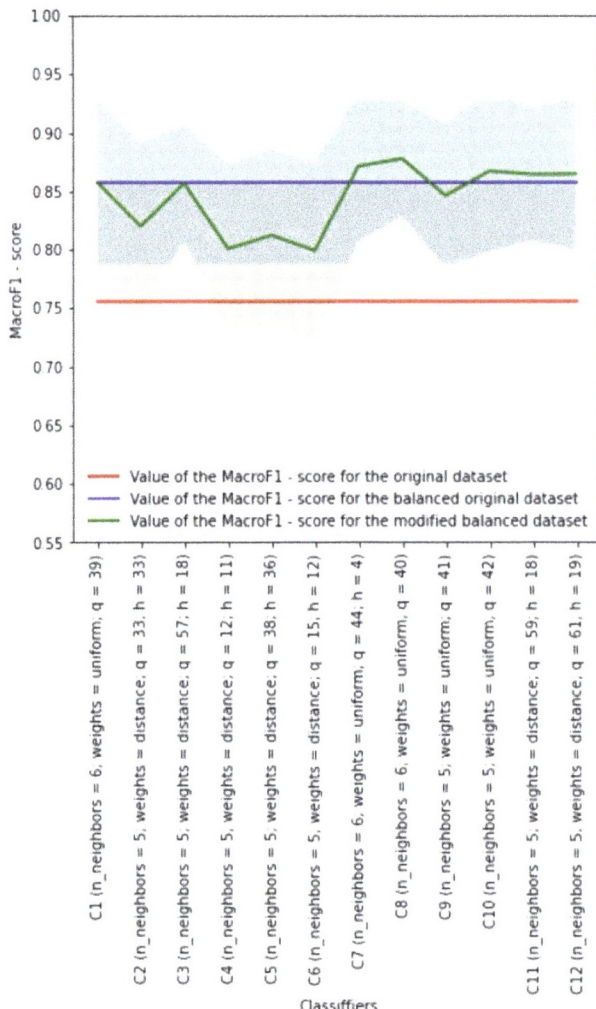

Figure 6. Visualization of the results of the experiment of choosing the best kNN classifier based on 12 datasets using the Borderline SMOTE-1 class balancing algorithm (*n_neighbors* is the number of nearest neighbors; *weights* is the parameter which assigns weight coefficients to the neighbors; q is the dimension of the space corresponding to the dataset used for the development of the classifier; h is the dimension of the space into which the UMAP algorithm embeds the 39-dimensional feature space corresponding to the original dataset; the background of each color shows the amount of standard deviation around the mean of the metric $MacroF_1-score$).

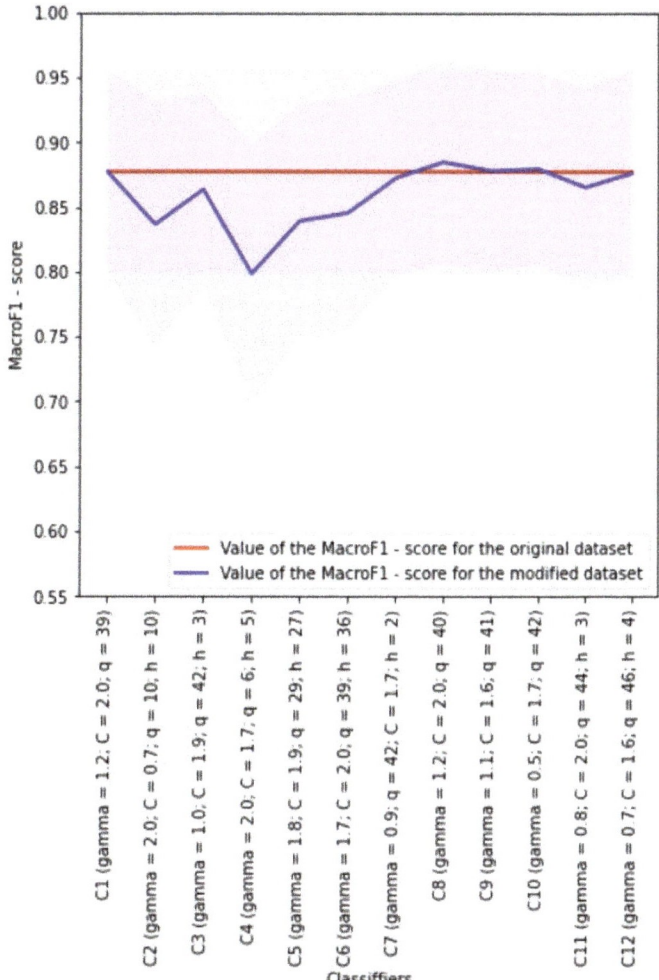

Figure 7. Visualization of the results of the experiment for choosing the best SVM classifier based on 12 datasets without using class balancing algorithms (*gamma* is the parameter of the radial basic kernel function; *C* is the regularization parameter; *q* is the dimension of the space corresponding to the dataset used for development of the classifier; *h* is the dimension of the space into which the UMAP algorithm embeds the 39-dimensional feature space corresponding to the original dataset; the background of each color shows the amount of standard deviation around the mean of the metric $MacroF_1-score$).

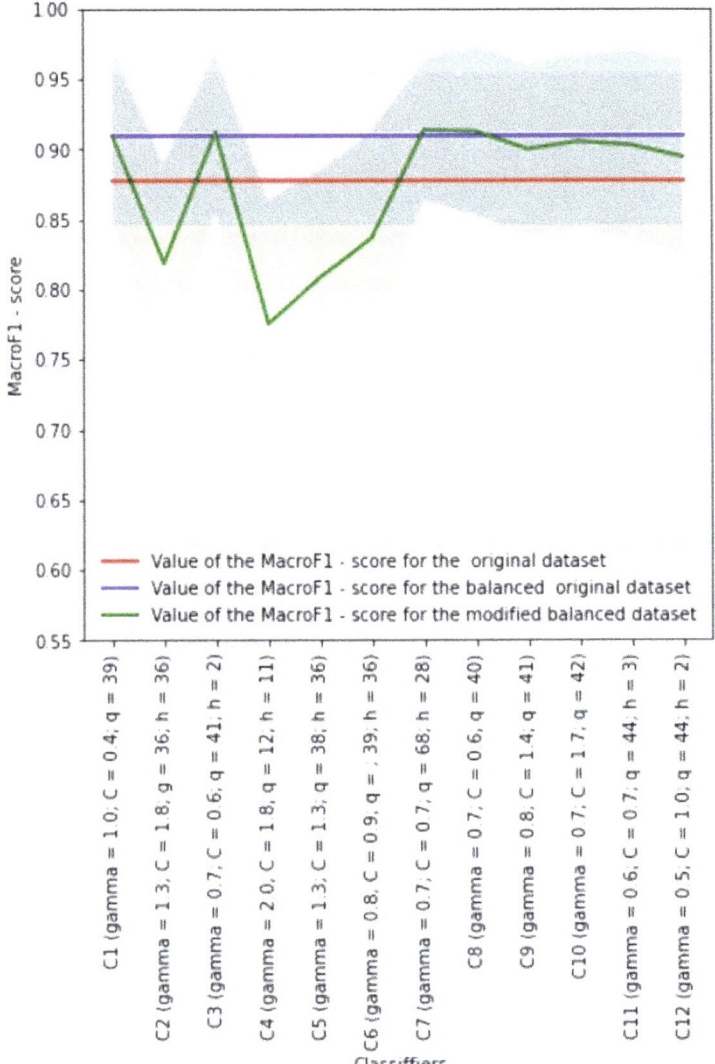

Figure 8. Visualization of the results of the experiment for choosing the best SVM classifier based on 12 datasets using the SMOTE algorithm for class balancing (*gamma* is the parameter of the radial basic kernel function; *C* is the regularization parameter; *q* is the dimension of the space corresponding to the dataset used for the development of the classifier; *h* is the dimension of the space into which the UMAP algorithm embeds the 39-dimensional feature space corresponding to the original dataset; the background of each color shows the amount of standard deviation around the mean of the metric $MacroF_1-score$).

As can be seen from Figure 5, all the classifiers developed on the basis of the modified datasets outperformed C1 classifier developed on the basis of the original dataset in terms of the mean value of the $MacroF_1-score$.

Classifier C6 (with $h = 24$) turned out to be the best: it has a mean value of $MacroF_1-score$ equal to 0.842 (with a standard deviation of 0.080), while classifier C1 has mean value of $MacroF_1-score$ equal to 0.756 (while the standard deviation is 0.101).

The dataset used in the development of classifier C6 (with $h = 24$) was obtained from the original one as a result of applying the UMAP algorithm to it with $h = 24$. This dataset contains 27 features in total, including one feature based on approximation entropy AE and two features based on fractal dimensions KFD and HFD.

Classifiers C2 (with $h = 36$), C4 (with $h = 11$) and C5 (with $h = 19$) also turned out to be relatively good in terms of the mean value of the $MacroF_1-score$.

The worst classifier in this experiment is classifier C9 (independent of h) developed on the basis of the dataset obtained by adding two features based on fractal dimensions KFD and HFD to the original dataset.

Table 5 shows the main characteristics of classifier C1, as well as the best classifier, namely, classifier C6 (with $h = 24$), without class balancing.

Table 5. Characteristics of kNN classifiers C1 and C6 (with $h = 24$) in the experiment without class balancing.

Characteristic	Classifier	
	C1	C6 (with $h = 24$)
Number of features in the dataset	39	27
Number of neighbors (n_neighbors)	6	12
weights	'distance'	'distance'
$MacroF_1-score$ (mean/std)	0.756/0.101	0.842/0.093
Accuracy (mean/std)	0.948/0.017	0.966/0.016
MacroRecall (mean/std)	0.687/0.106	0.803/0.091
MacroPrecision (mean/std)	0.938/0.063	0.919/0.098
Training time (mean/std), s.	0.002/0.001	0.004/0.002
Quality metrics calculation time (mean/std), s.	0.009/0.003	0.009/0.002

In the experiment under consideration, the use of the modified dataset C6 (with $h = 24$) obtained from the original dataset C1 allowed for increasing the value of the $MacroF_1-score$ for classifier C6 (with $h = 24$) by 0.086 compared to classifier C1 (the standard deviation for metric $MacroF_1-score$ of classifier C6 (with $h = 24$) turned out to be less than that of classifier C1). The training time of classifier C6 (with $h = 24$) increased about two times. The quality metrics calculation time during the testing did not change much.

It should be noted that classifier C6 (with $h = 24$), as well as classifiers C2 (with $h = 36$), C4 (with $h = 11$) and C5 (with $h = 19$), outperformed the classifier developed in [10] using the principles of cost-sensitive algorithms based on the mean values of the main quality metrics. At the same time, one can notice slight discrepancies in the number of patterns of the normal class in the proposed study and in [10]: in our dataset there are 13 more such patterns, but this could only negatively affect our results (compared to the results in [10]), which, however, did not happen.

The F_1 of the best classifier in [10] was equal to 0.819, and the values of such metrics as *Accuracy*, *Recall* and *Precision* were equal to 0.952, 0.807 and 0.833, respectively. Unfortunately, the rules for choosing the best classifier in our study and in [10] may be somewhat different (for example, we do not know if standard deviation estimates were calculated in that study), but we assume that our best classifiers (with the best (maximum) values of quality metrics) clearly outperform the best classifier in [10]. To confirm these conclusions, we will provide additional information on classifiers C2 (with $h = 36$), C4 (with $h = 11$) and C5 (with $h = 19$) (because for classifier C6 (with $h = 24$), such information is given in Table 5).

Classifier C2 (with $h = 36$) has a mean value of $MacroF_1-score$ equal to 0.841 (with a standard deviation of 0.093) and mean values of such metrics as *Accuracy*, *Recall* and *Precision* equal to 0.965 (with a standard deviation of 0.015), 0.812 (with a standard deviation of 0.088) and 0.917 (with a standard deviation of 0.065), respectively.

Classifier C4 (with $h = 11$) has a mean value of $MacroF_1-score$ equal to 0.839 (with a standard deviation of 0.094) and mean values of such metrics as *Accuracy*, *Recall* and *Precision* are equal to 0.963 (with a standard deviation of 0.016), 0.818 (with a standard deviation of 0.094) and 0.900 (with a standard deviation of 0.098), respectively.

Classifier C5 (with $h = 19$) has a mean value of $MacroF_1-score$ equal to 0.839 (with a standard deviation of 0.083) and mean values of such metrics as *Accuracy*, *Recall* and *Precision* are equal to 0.964 (with a standard deviation of 0.017), 0.800 (with a standard deviation of 0.095) and 0.930 (with a standard deviation of 0.058), respectively.

Thus, we can conclude that even a simple addition of new features can increase the separability of patterns of one class from patterns of another class.

Analysis of the values of the classification quality metrics (Table 5), in particular, the values of the *MacroRecall* metric, allowed us to conclude that the quality of the classification is not high enough and that it is necessary to take additional actions to improve the quality of the classification. In order to perform such actions, we can use class balancing or cost-sensitive algorithms. In this study, we implemented algorithms for balancing classes in datasets.

4.6.2. Class Balancing Experiment

Figure 6 presents the results of the experiment for choosing the best kNN classifier in the case of working with the approximation entropy AE in the formation of some of the 12 datasets used in the development of the classifiers. In this case, the balancing of classes in datasets was performed using the Borderline SMOTE-1 algorithm.

The red color indicates the line corresponding to the mean value of the $MacroF_1-score$ obtained for the best classifier C1 developed on the basis of the original dataset, i.e., the dataset with 39 features. The light red shading shows the spread for the $MacroF_1-score$ mean value, calculated from its standard deviation. The blue color indicates the line corresponding to the mean values of the $MacroF_1-score$ obtained for the best classifier C1 developed on the basis of the balanced original dataset. The light blue shading shows the spread for the $MacroF_1-score$ means, calculated from their standard deviation. The green color indicates the line corresponding to the mean values of $MacroF_1-score$ obtained for the best classifiers developed on the basis of the modified balanced datasets. The light green shading shows the spread for the $MacroF_1-score$ means, calculated from their standard deviation.

Figure 6 shows that all the classifiers developed on the basis of the balanced datasets provide a higher mean value of the $MacroF_1-score$ than the classifier C1 developed on the basis of the original dataset. At the same time, some classifiers have lower values of the $MacroF_1-score$ than the classifier C1 developed on the basis of the balanced original dataset. In addition, Figure 6 shows a decrease in the standard deviations for the $MacroF_1-score$ for the classifiers developed on the basis of balanced datasets compared to the standard deviations for the $MacroF_1-score$ for the classifiers developed on the basis of imbalanced datasets (Figure 5).

Classifier 8 (independent of h) turned out to be the best: it has a mean value of $MacroF_1-score$ equal to 0.878 (with a standard deviation of 0.050), while classifier C1 has a mean value of $MacroF_1-score$ equal to 0.847 (while the standard deviation is 0.079).

The dataset used in the development of classifier C8 (independent of h) was obtained from the original one by adding one feature based on approximation entropy AE. This dataset contains 40 features in total.

The classifiers C7 (with $h = 4$), C10 (independent of h), C11 (with $h = 18$) and C12 (with $h = 19$) also turned out to be relatively good in terms of the mean value of the $MacroF_1-score$.

The worst classifiers in this experiment were classifier C4 (with $h = 11$) and C6 (with $h = 12$). The first classifier was developed on the basis of a dataset obtained from the original one as a result of applying the UMAP algorithm to it with $h = 11$ by adding one feature based on approximation entropy AE. The second classifier was developed on the basis of a dataset obtained from the original one as a result of applying the UMAP algorithm to it with $h = 12$ by adding one feature based on approximation entropy AE and two features based on fractal dimensions KFD and HFD.

From Figures 5 and 6, one can notice a decrease in the standard deviation of classifiers in the case of using the Borderline SMOTE-1 algorithm to balance classes in datasets.

Table 6 shows the main characteristics of classifier C1, as well as the best classifier, namely classifier C8 (independent of h), with class balancing.

Table 6. Characteristics of kNN classifiers C1 and C8 (independent of h) in the experiment using the Borderline SMOTE-1 class balancing algorithm.

Characteristic	Classifier	
	C1	C8 (*independent of h*)
Number of features in the dataset	39	40
Number of neighbors (n_neighbors)	10	6
weights	'uniform'	'uniform'
$MacroF_1-score$ (mean/std)	0.847/0.079	0.878/0.050
Accuracy (mean/std)	0.957/0.022	0.968/0.013
MacroRecall (mean/std)	0.870/0.079	0.877/0.066
MacroPrecision (mean/std)	0.846/0.085	0.896/0.063
Training time (mean/std), s.	0.012/0.006	0.028/0.002
Quality metrics calculation time (mean/std), s.	0.024/0.009	0.017/0.003

It should be noted that classifier C8 (independent of h), as well as classifiers C7 (with $h = 4$), C10 (independent of h), C11 (with $h = 18$) and C12 (with $h = 19$) outperformed the classifier developed in [10] using the principles of cost-sensitive algorithms based on the mean values of the main quality metrics.

To confirm these conclusions, we will provide additional information on classifiers C7 (with $h = 4$), C10 (independent of h), C11 (with $h = 18$) and C12 (with $h = 19$) (because for classifier C8 (independent of h), such information is given in Table 6).

Classifier C7 (with $h = 4$) has mean value of $MacroF_1-score$ equal to 0.871 (with a standard deviation of 0.065), and mean values of such metrics as *Accuracy*, *Recall* and *Precision* are equal to 0.969 (with a standard deviation of 0.014), 0.864 (with a standard deviation of 0.077) and 0.902 (with a standard deviation of 0.067), respectively.

Classifier C10 (independent of h) has mean value of $MacroF_1-score$ equal to 0.867 (with a standard deviation of 0.070), and mean values of such metrics as *Accuracy*, *Recall* and *Precision* are equal to 0.966 (with a standard deviation of 0.016), 0.870 (with a standard deviation of 0.081) and 0.888 (with a standard deviation of 0.074), respectively.

Classifier C11 (with $h = 18$) has mean value of $MacroF_1-score$ equal to 0.864 (with a standard deviation of 0.057), and mean values of such metrics as *Accuracy*, *Recall* and *Precision* are equal to 0.966 (with a standard deviation of 0.015), 0.866 (with a standard deviation of 0.064) and 0.883 (with a standard deviation of 0.067), respectively.

Classifier C12 (with $h = 19$) has mean value of $MacroF_1-score$ equal to 0.865 (with a standard deviation of 0.066), and mean values of such metrics as *Accuracy*, *Recall* and *Precision* are equal to 0.968 (with a standard deviation of 0.014), 0.864 (with a standard deviation of 0.074) and 0.890 (with a standard deviation of 0.064), respectively.

In the experiment under consideration, using the best classifier C8 (independent of h) made it possible to increase the mean value of $MacroF_1-score$ by 0.031 compared to the C1 classifier (with the standard deviation for $MacroF_1-score$ of classifier C8 (independent of h) being less than that of classifier C1). The training time of classifier C8 increased about 2.3 times. The quality metrics calculation time during the testing even decreased slightly.

Analysis of the values of classification quality metrics (Table 6), particularly the values of the *MacroRecall* metric, allows us to conclude that the classification quality by important metrics has increased. It should be noted that the training time in the case of applying class balancing to the dataset has increased, for example, about two times for classifier C1.

4.7. Development of SVM Classifiers

We used the radial basis kernel function during the development of the SVM classifiers. Experiments with the linear function of the kernel were also carried out, but turned out to be less successful, therefore they are not presented in this study. The SMOTE algorithm was used to implement class balancing.

4.7.1. Experiment without Class Balancing

Figure 7 presents the results of the experiment for choosing the best SVM classifier in the case of working with the approximation entropy AE when forming some of 12 datasets used in the development of the classifiers. The balancing of classes in the datasets was not performed here. Figure 7 uses the same notations as Figure 5.

As can be seen from Figure 7, only classifier C8 (independent of h), classifier C9 (independent of h) and classifier C10 (independent of h) developed on the basis of the modified datasets were able to outperform classifier C1 (which has mean value of $MacroF_1-score$ equal to 0.877 with the standard deviation equal to 0.078), developed on the basis of the original dataset by the mean value of the $MacroF_1-score$. At the same time, classifier C8 (independent of h) outperformed classifier C9 (independent of h) and classifier C10 (independent of h), if we compare them by the mean values of the $MacroF_1-score$: for example, classifier C8 (independent of h) has a mean value of $MacroF_1-score$ equal to 0.885 (with the standard deviation equal to 0.079); classifier C9 (independent of h) has a mean value of $MacroF_1-score$ equal to 0.878 (with the standard deviation of 0.078); and classifier C10 (independent of h) has a mean $MacroF_1-score$ of 0.880 (with a standard deviation of 0.074). The rest of the classifiers turned out to be less successful than classifier C1.

Note that classifier C8 (independent of h), classifier C9 (independent of h) and classifier C10 (independent of h) are developed on the basis of datasets containing 40 (39 + 1), 41 (39 + 2) and 42 (39 + 1 + 2) features, respectively.

It is obvious that preference should be given to the classifier developed using the dataset with fewer features: this is classifier C8 (independent of h). In addition, it has the highest mean value of $MacroF_1-score$.

The dataset used in the development of classifier C8 (independent of h) was obtained from the original one by adding a new feature formed on the basis of the approximation entropy AE.

Table 7 shows the main characteristics of classifier C1, as well as the best classifier, namely classifier C8, without class balancing.

Table 7. Characteristics of SVM classifiers C1 and C8 in the experiment without class balancing.

Characteristic	Classifier	
	C1	C8 (*independent of h*)
Number of features in the dataset	39	40
gamma	1.2	1.2
C	2.0	2.0
$MacroF_1-score$ (mean/std)	0.877/0.078	0.885/0.079
Accuracy (mean/std)	0.973/0.015	0.974/0.016
MacroRecall (mean/std)	0.843/0.088	0.850/0.090
MacroPrecision (mean/std)	0.950/0.053	0.957/0.051
Training time (mean/std), s.	0.123/0.008	0.131/0.007
Quality metrics calculation time (mean/std), s.	0.007/0.001	0.009/0.001

In the experiment under consideration, the use of the best classifier C8 (independent of *h*) made it possible to increase the mean value of the $MacroF_1-score$ by 0.008 compared to the C1 classifier (with approximately the same standard deviations). The training time of classifier C8 increased slightly, which was expected (because the number of features increased by only 1). The same can be said about the quality metrics calculation time during the testing.

Analysis of the values of the classification quality metrics (Table 7), particularly the values of the *MacroRecall* metric, allows us to conclude that the quality of the classification is not high enough and that it is necessary to take additional action to improve the quality of the classification.

4.7.2. Class Balancing Experiment

Figure 8 presents the results of the experiment for choosing the best SVM classifier in the case of working with the approximation entropy AE when forming some of the 12 datasets used in the development of classifiers. In this case, the balancing of classes in datasets was performed using the SMOTE algorithm.

Figure 8 uses the same notations as Figure 6.

As can be seen from Figure 8, only classifier C3 (with *h* = 2), classifier C7 (with *h* = 28) and classifier C8 (independent of *h*) developed on the basis of the modified datasets were able to outperform classifier C1 (which has mean value of $MacroF_1-score$ equal to 0.910 with the standard deviation equal to 0.064) developed on the basis of the original dataset by the mean value of the $MacroF_1-score$. At the same time, classifier C7 (with *h* = 28) outperformed classifier C3 (with *h* = 2) and classifier C8 (independent of *h*), if we compare them by the mean values of $MacroF_1-score$: for example, classifier C7 (with *h* = 28) has a mean value of $MacroF_1-score$ equal to 0.914 (with the standard deviation equal to 0.050); classifier C3 (with *h* = 2) has a mean value of $MacroF_1-score$ equal to 0.912 (while the standard deviation is 0.058); and classifier C8 (independent of *h*) has a mean $MacroF_1-score$ of 0.913 (with a standard deviation of 0.061). It should be noted that classifiers C9 (independent of *h*), C10 (independent of *h*), C11 (with *h* = 3) and C12 (with *h* = 2) outperformed classifier C1 developed on the basis of the original dataset that was not subjected to class balancing (Section 4.7.1) by the mean value of $MacroF_1-score$. The rest of the classifiers turned out to be inefficient compared to classifier C1 developed on the basis of the original dataset that was not subjected to class balancing (Section 4.7.1) and classifier C1 developed on the basis of the original dataset that was subjected to class balancing (Section 4.7.2).

Note that classifier C3 (with $h = 2$), classifier C7 (with $h = 28$) and classifier C8 (independent of h) were developed on the basis of the datasets containing 41 (39 + 2), 68 (39 + 28 + 1) and 40 (39 + 1) features, respectively.

It is obvious that preference should be given to the classifier which has the highest mean value of $MacroF_1-score$: this is classifier C7 (with $h = 28$). However, it was developed using the dataset with the greatest number of features among the three datasets discussed above.

The dataset used in the development of classifier C7 (with $h = 28$) was obtained from the original one (with 39 features) by adding one new feature formed on the basis of the approximation entropy AE and 28 features obtained using the UMAP algorithm.

Alternatively, we can use classifier C3 (with $h = 2$) and classifier C8 (independent of h), which are less accurate by the mean value of $MacroF_1-score$, but developed from datasets with fewer features.

It should be noted that the best classifiers, particularly classifier C3 (with $h = 2$), classifier C7 (with $h = 28$) and classifier C8 (independent of h), outperformed all the best classifiers proposed in Sections 4.6.1, 4.6.2 and 4.7.1 in terms of the main quality metrics.

From Figures 7 and 8, one can notice a decrease in the standard deviation of classifiers in the case of using the SMOTE algorithm to balance classes in datasets.

Table 8 shows the main characteristics of classifier C1, as well as the best classifier, namely, classifier C7 (with $h = 28$) with class balancing.

Table 8. Characteristics of SVM classifiers C1 and C7 (with $h = 28$) in the experiment with class balancing.

Characteristic	Classifier	
	C1	C7 (with $h = 28$)
Number of features in the dataset	39	68
gamma	1	0.7
C	0.4	0.7
$MacroF_1-score$ (mean/std)	0.910/0.064	0.914/0.050
Accuracy (mean/std)	0.977/0.015	0.978/0.012
MacroRecall (mean/std)	0.907/0.081	0.907/0.065
MacroPrecision (mean/std)	0.929/0.058	0.937/0.048
Training time (mean/std), s.	0.886/0.214	0.489/0.021
Quality metrics calculation time (mean/std), s.	0.013/0.004	0.008/0.001

In the experiment under consideration, the use of the best classifier C7 (with $h = 28$) made it possible to increase the mean value of the $MacroF_1-score$ by 0.004 compared to the C1 classifier (with approximately the same standard deviations). It should be noted that the training time and quality metrics calculation time during the testing in the case of applying class balancing to the dataset has decreased approximately 1.8 and 1.6 times, respectively, for classifier C7 (with $h = 28$), despite the increase in the number of features.

Analysis of the values of the classification quality metrics (Table 8), particularly the values of the MacroRecall metric, allows us to conclude that the classification quality in terms of the main metrics has increased.

5. Discussion

The results of the experiments with two machine learning algorithms such as kNN and SVM showed the feasibility of modifying the original dataset by adding new features based on the approximation entropy AE and fractal dimensions KFD and HFD, and also based on the UMAP algorithm, and sometimes by replacing the original dataset with the results of applying the UMAP algorithm to it with the addition of new features based on the approximation entropy AE and fractal dimensions KFD and HFD.

At the same time, due to the high imbalance of classes in the original dataset, it is advisable to use class balancing algorithms and cost-sensitive algorithms. In the proposed study, four class balancing algorithms were implemented (SMOTE, Borderline SMOTE-1, Borderline SMOTE-2 and ADASYN). The Borderline SMOTE-1 algorithm for the kNN classifier and the SMOTE algorithm for the SVM classifier were recognized as the best. However, balancing classes using appropriate algorithms is associated with significant time costs, so the goal of further research is to develop classifiers using cost-sensitive algorithms.

In the context of working with the kNN algorithm using the Borderline SMOTE-1 algorithm for class balancing, classifier C8 (independent of h) turned out to be the best.

The dataset used in the development of classifier C8 (independent of h) was obtained from the original one by adding one feature based on approximation entropy AE. Thus, the development of the kNN classifier was performed in 40-dimensional space (while the original space was 39-dimensional).

In the context of working with the SVM algorithm using the SMOTE algorithm for class balancing, classifier C7 (with $h = 28$) turned out to be the best.

The dataset used in the development of classifier C7 (with $h = 28$) was obtained from the original one by adding new features obtained using the UMAP algorithm to the original dataset with the dimension of the new space $h = 28$ and one feature based on the approximation entropy AE. Thus, the development of the SVM classifier C7 (with $h = 28$) was performed in 68-dimensional space (while the original space was 39-dimensional).

All 12 kNN classifiers developed on the basis of class-balanced datasets using the Borderline SMOTE-1 algorithm outperformed the base classifier C1 developed on the basis of the original dataset, in which features were compared to blood protein markers (Figure 4).

Eight out of 12 SVM classifiers developed on the basis of class-balanced datasets using the SMOTE algorithm outperformed the basic C1 classifier developed on the basis of the original dataset, in which features were compared to blood protein markers. These are classifiers C1, C3 (with $h = 2$), C7 (with $h = 28$), C8, C9, C10, C11 (with $h = 3$) and C12 (with $h = 2$). Four out of 12 SVM classifiers developed on the basis of class-balanced datasets using the SMOTE algorithm turned out to be even worse than the basic C1 classifier developed on the basis of the original dataset. Such classifiers are C2 (with $h = 36$), C4 (with $h = 11$), C5 (with $h = 36$) and C6 (with $h = 36$) (Figure 6).

The classifiers recognized as the best in Sections 4.6.1 and 4.7.1 outperformed the classifier proposed in [10] in terms of the main quality metrics. However, it was decided to use balancing algorithms in order to restore the balance of classes. The classifiers recognized as the best in Sections 4.6.2 and 4.7.2 outperformed the classifier proposed in [10], as well as the classifiers developed in Sections 4.6.1 and 4.7.1, in terms of the main quality metrics. In general, it should be noted that the proposed approach to the formation of datasets by generating new features using different tools with their subsequent combination and use as a new dataset or as an addition to the original dataset turned out to be effective.

The best kNN classifier, C8, was developed based on the original dataset augmented with a feature based on entropy approximation AE. The best SVM classifier, C7, was developed based on the original dataset augmented with features based on the UMAP algorithm and entropy approximation AE. The average values of metric $MacroF_1-score$ used to assess the quality of classifiers during cross-validation increased by 16.138% and 4.219%, respectively, compared to the average values of this metric in the case when an unbalanced original dataset was used in the development of classifiers of the same name. The average values of metric $MacroF_1-score$ increased by 3.660% and 0.440%, respectively, compared to the average values of this metric in the case when a balanced original dataset was used in the development of the classifiers of the same name.

One can assume that applying the population-based optimization algorithms to search for optimal parameter values of the UMAP algorithm and optimal parameter values of classifiers [58,62,63], working with different formulas for calculating the loss function in the UMAP algorithm [32], entropy and fractal dimension, as well as ideas of hybrid classifiers [34] can ultimately improve the quality of data classification.

6. Conclusions

During this research, we proposed a new approach to the development of datasets used in the development of classifiers in the task of classifying ODs based on blood protein markers. It was suggested to use the results from applying the UMAP dimensionality reduction algorithm to the original dataset and the results of calculating the approximation entropy AE and two fractal dimensions KFD and HFD as new features. In some cases, new features can provide an improvement in the quality of classification with different combinations between themselves or with the original dataset.

The goal of further research is to analyze the prospects for the development and application of cost-effective algorithms in the development of classifiers in the problem of classifying ODs based on blood protein markers. In addition, we plan to study the possibilities of improving the quality of classification by using population optimization algorithms for the values of parameters of the UMAP algorithms and classifier parameters, and also to work with various formulas for calculating entropy and the fractal dimension.

Funding: This research received no external funding.

Institutional Review Board Statement: Not applicable.

Informed Consent Statement: Not applicable.

Data Availability Statement: Not applicable.

Conflicts of Interest: The author declares no conflict of interest.

References

1. Global Health Care Outlook. 2021. Available online: https://www2.deloitte.com/cn/en/pages/life-sciences-and-healthcare/articles/2021-global-healthcare-outlook.html (accessed on 3 January 2023).
2. Li, G.; Hu, J.; Hu, G. Biomarker Studies in Early Detection and Prognosis of Breast Cancer. *Adv. Exp. Med. Biol.* **2017**, *1026*, 27–39. [CrossRef] [PubMed]
3. Loke, S.Y.; Lee, A.S.G. The future of blood-based biomarkers for the early detection of breast cancer. *Eur. J. Cancer.* **2018**, *92*, 54–68. [CrossRef] [PubMed]
4. Cohen, J.D.; Li, L.; Wang, Y.; Thoburn, C.; Afsari, B.; Danilova, L.; Douville, C.; Javed, A.A.; Wong, F.; Mattox, A.; et al. Detection and localization of surgically resectable cancers with a multi-analyte blood test. *Science* **2018**, *359*, 926–930. [CrossRef]
5. Killock, D. CancerSEEK and destroy—a blood test for early cancer detection. *Nat. Rev. Clin. Oncol.* **2018**, *15*, 133. [CrossRef]
6. Hao, Y.; Jing, X.Y.; Sun, Q. Joint learning sample similarity and correlation representation for cancer survival prediction. *BMC Bioinform.* **2022**, *23*, 553. [CrossRef] [PubMed]
7. Núñez, C. Blood-based protein biomarkers in breast cancer. *Clin. Chim. Acta.* **2019**, *490*, 113–127. [CrossRef] [PubMed]
8. Du, Z.; Liu, X.; Wei, X.; Luo, H.; Li, P.; Shi, M.; Guo, B.; Cui, Y.; Su, Z.; Zeng, J.; et al. Quantitative proteomics identifes a plasma multi protein model for detection of hepatocellular carcinoma. *Sci. Rep.* **2020**, *10*, 15552. [CrossRef] [PubMed]
9. Kalinich, M.; Haber, D.A. Cancer detection: Seeking signals in blood. *Science* **2018**, *359*, 866–867. [CrossRef]
10. Song, C.; Li, X. Cost-Sensitive KNN Algorithm for Cancer Prediction Based on Entropy Analysis. *Entropy* **2022**, *24*, 253. [CrossRef]
11. Huang, S.; Cai, N.; Pacheco, P.P.; Narrandes, S.; Wang, Y.; Xu, W. Applications of Support Vector Machine (SVM) Learning in Cancer Genomics. *Cancer Genom. Proteom.* **2018**, *15*, 41–51. [CrossRef]
12. Sepehri, M.M.; Khavaninzadeh, M.; Rezapour, M.; Teimourpour, B. A data mining approach to fistula surgery failure analysis in hemodialysis patients. In Proceedings of the 2011 18th Iranian Conference of Biomedical Engineering (ICBME), Tehran, Iran, 14–16 December 2011; pp. 15–20. [CrossRef]
13. Rezapour, M.; Zadeh, M.K.; Sepehri, M.M. Implementation of Predictive Data Mining Techniques for Identifying Risk Factors of Early AVF Failure in Hemodialysis Patients. *Comput. Math. Methods Med.* **2013**, *2013*, 830745. [CrossRef] [PubMed]
14. Rezapour, M.; Zadeh, K.M.; Sepehri, M.M.; Alborzi, M. Less primary fistula failure in hypertensive patients. *J. Hum. Hypertens.* **2018**, *32*, 311–318. [CrossRef] [PubMed]

15. Toth, R.; Schiffmann, H.; Hube-Magg, C.; Büscheck, F.; Höflmayer, D.; Weidemann, S.; Lebok, P.; Fraune, C.; Minner, S.; Schlomm, T.; et al. Random forest-based modelling to detect biomarkers for prostate cancer progression. *Clin. Epigenet.* **2019**, *11*, 148. [CrossRef] [PubMed]
16. Savareh, B.A.; Aghdaie, H.A.; Behmanesh, A.; Bashiri, A.; Sadeghi, A.; Zali, M.; Shams, R. A machine learning approach identified a diagnostic model for pancreatic cancer through using circulating microRNA signatures. *Pancreatology* **2020**, *20*, 1195–1204. [CrossRef]
17. Lv, J.; Wang, J.; Shang, X.; Liu, F.; Guo, S. Survival prediction in patients with colon adenocarcinoma via multi-omics data integration using a deep learning algorithm. *Biosci Rep.* **2020**, *40*, BSR20201482. [CrossRef]
18. Chaudhary, K.; Poirion, O.B.; Lu, L.; Garmire, L.X. Deep learning-based multi-omics integration robustly predicts survival in liver cancer. *Clin. Cancer Res.* **2018**, *24*, 1248–1259. [CrossRef]
19. Lee, T.Y.; Huang, K.Y.; Chuang, C.H.; Lee, C.Y.; Chang, T.H. Incorporating deep learning and multi-omics autoencoding for analysis of lung adenocarcinoma prognostication. *Comput. Biol.* **2020**, *87*, 107277. [CrossRef]
20. Qadri, S.F.; Shen, L.; Ahmad, M.; Qadri, S.; Zareen, S.S.; Akbar, M.A. SVseg: Stacked Sparse Autoencoder-Based Patch Classification Modeling for Vertebrae Segmentation. *Mathematics* **2022**, *10*, 796. [CrossRef]
21. Chawla, N.V.; Bowyer, K.W.; Hall, L.O.; Kegelmeyer, W.P. SMOTE: Synthetic Minority Over-sampling Technique. *J. Artif. Intell. Res.* **2002**, *16*, 321–357. [CrossRef]
22. Han, H.; Wang, W.Y.; Mao, B.H. Borderline-SMOTE: A New Over-Sampling Method in Imbalanced Data Sets Learning. In *Advances in Intelligent Computing*; ICIC 2005. Lecture Notes in Computer Science, Huang, D.S., Zhang, X.P., Huang, G.B., Eds.; Springer: Berlin, Heidelberg, 2005; Volume 3644, pp. 878–887. [CrossRef]
23. Swana, E.F.; Doorsamy, W.; Bokoro, P. Tomek Link and SMOTE Approaches for Machine Fault Classification with an Imbalanced Dataset. *Sensors* **2022**, *22*, 3246. [CrossRef]
24. He, H.; Bay, Y.; Garcia, E.A.; Li, S. ADASYN: Adaptive synthetic sampling approach for imbalanced learning. In Proceedings of the 2008 IEEE International Joint Conference on Neural Networks (IEEE World Congress on Computational Intelligence), Hong Kong, 1–8 June 2008; pp. 1322–1328. [CrossRef]
25. Tomek, I. Two modifications of CNN. *IEEE Trans. Syst. Man Cybern.* **1976**, *6*, 769–772. [CrossRef]
26. Candès, E.J.; Li, X.; Ma, Y.; Wright, J. Robust principal component analysis? *J. ACM* **2011**, *58*, 1–37. [CrossRef]
27. Jolliffe, I.T.; Cadima, J. Principal component analysis: A review and recent developments. *Phil. Trans. R. Soc. A.* **2016**, *374*, 20150202. [CrossRef] [PubMed]
28. van der Maaten, L.; Hinton, G.E. Visualizing Data using t-SNE. *J. Mach. Learn. Res.* **2008**, *9*, 2579–2605.
29. McInnes, L.; Healy, J.; Melville, J. UMAP: Uniform manifold approximation and projection for dimension reduction. *arXiv* **2018**, arXiv:1802.03426.
30. Dorrity, M.W.; Saunders, L.M.; Queitsch, C.; Fields, S.; Trapnell, C. Dimensionality reduction by UMAP to visualize physical and genetic interactions. *Nat. Commun.* **2020**, *11*, 1537. [CrossRef]
31. Becht, E.; McInnes, L.; Healy, J.; Dutertre, C.A.; Kwok, I.W.H.; Ng, L.G.; Ginhoux, F.; Newell, E.W. Dimensionality reduction for visualizing single-cell data using UMAP. *Nat. Biotechnol.* **2019**, *37*, 38–44. [CrossRef]
32. Demidova, L.A.; Gorchakov, A.V. Fuzzy Information Discrimination Measures and Their Application to Low Dimensional Embedding Construction in the UMAP Algorithm. *J. Imaging* **2022**, *8*, 113. [CrossRef]
33. Yu, W.; Liu, T.; Valdez, R.; Gwinn, M.; Khoury, M.J. Application of support vector machine modeling for prediction of common diseases: The case of diabetes and pre-diabetes. *BMC Med. Inform. Decis. Mak.* **2010**, *10*, 16. [CrossRef]
34. Demidova, L.A. Two-stage hybrid data classifiers based on SVM and kNN algorithms. *Symmetry* **2021**, *13*, 615. [CrossRef]
35. Khan, S.S.; Madden, M.G. One-class classification: Taxonomy of study and review of techniques. *Knowl. Eng. Rev.* **2014**, *29*, 345–374. [CrossRef]
36. Scholkopf, B.; Williamson, R.C.; Smola, A.J.; Shawe-Taylor, J.; Platt, J. Estimating the support of a high-dimensional distribution. *Neural Comput.* **2001**, *13*, 1443–1471. [CrossRef] [PubMed]
37. Liu, F.T.; Ting, K.M.; Zhou, Z.-H. Isolation-Based Anomaly Detection. *ACM Trans. Knowl. Discov. Data* **2012**, *6*, 1–39. [CrossRef]
38. Zheng, A.; Casari, A. *Feature Engineering for Machine Learning: Principles and Techniques for Data Scientists*, 1st ed.; O'Reilly Media, Inc.: Sebastopol, CA, USA, 2018; p. 201.
39. COSMIC | Catalogue of Somatic Mutations in Cancer. Available online: https://cancer.sanger.ac.uk/cosmic (accessed on 3 January 2023).
40. Zanin, M.; Zunino, L.; Rosso, O.A.; Papo, D. Permutation Entropy and Its Main Biomedical and Econophysics Applications: A Review. *Entropy* **2012**, *14*, 1553–1577. [CrossRef]
41. Zhang, A.; Yang, B.; Huang, L. Feature Extraction of EEG Signals Using Power Spectral Entropy. In Proceedings of the International Conference on BioMedical Engineering and Informatics, Sanya, China, 27–30 May 2008; Volume 2, pp. 435–439. [CrossRef]
42. Weng, X.; Perry, A.; Maroun, M.; Vuong, L.T. Singular Value Decomposition and Entropy Dimension of Fractals. *arXiv* **2022**, arXiv:2211.12338. [CrossRef]
43. Pincus, S.M. Approximate entropy as a measure of system complexity. *Proc. Natl. Acad. Sci. USA* **1991**, *88*, 2297–2301. [CrossRef]
44. Pincus, S.M.; Gladstone, I.M.; Ehrenkranz, R.A. A regularity statistic for medical data analysis. *J. Clin. Monit. Comput.* **1991**, *7*, 335–345. [CrossRef]

45. Delgado-Bonal, A.; Marshak, A. Approximate Entropy and Sample Entropy: A Comprehensive Tutorial. *Entropy* **2019**, *21*, 541. [CrossRef]
46. Hjorth, B. EEG Analysis Based on Time Domain Properties. *Electroencephalogr. Clin. Neurophysiol.* **1970**, *29*, 306–310. [CrossRef]
47. Galvão, F.; Alarcão, S.M.; Fonseca, M.J. Predicting Exact Valence and Arousal Values from EEG. *Sensors* **2021**, *21*, 3414. [CrossRef]
48. Shi, C.-T. Signal Pattern Recognition Based on Fractal Features and Machine Learning. *Appl. Sci.* **2018**, *8*, 1327. [CrossRef]
49. Petrosian, A. Kolmogorov Complexity of Finite Sequences and Recognition of Different Preictal EEG Patterns. In Proceedings of the Computer-Based Medical Systems, Lubbock, TX, USA, 9–10 June 1995; pp. 212–217. [CrossRef]
50. Katz, M.J. Fractals and the analysis of waveforms. *Comput. Biol. Med.* **1988**, *18*, 145–156. [CrossRef] [PubMed]
51. Gil, A.; Glavan, V.; Wawrzaszek, A.; Modzelewska, R.; Tomasik, L. Katz Fractal Dimension of Geoelectric Field during Severe Geomagnetic Storms. *Entropy* **2021**, *23*, 1531. [CrossRef]
52. Higuchi, T. Approach to an irregular time series on the basis of the fractal theory. *Phys. D Nonlinear Phenom.* **1988**, *31*, 277–283. [CrossRef]
53. Hall, P.; Park, B.U.; Samworth, R.J. Choice of neighbor order in nearest-neighbor classification. *Ann. Stat.* **2008**, *36*, 2135–2152. [CrossRef]
54. Nigsch, F.; Bender, A.; Van Buuren, B.; Tissen, J.; Nigsch, A.E.; Mitchell, J.B. Melting point prediction employing k-nearest neighbor algorithms and genetic parameter optimization. *J. Chem. Inf. Model.* **2006**, *46*, 2412–2422. [CrossRef]
55. Xing, W.; Bei, Y. Medical Health Big Data Classification Based on KNN Classification Algorithm. *IEEE Access* **2020**, *8*, 28808–28819. [CrossRef]
56. Mohanty, S.; Mishra, A.; Saxena, A. Medical Data Analysis Using Machine Learning with KNN. In *International Conference on Innovative Computing and Communications*; Gupta, D., Khanna, A., Bhattacharyya, S., Hassanien, A.E., Anand, S., Jaiswal, A., Eds.; Advances in Intelligent Systems and Computing; Springer: Singapore, 2020; Volume 1166. [CrossRef]
57. Chapelle, O.; Vapnik, V.; Bousquet, O.; Mukherjee, S. Choosing multiple parameters for support vector machines. *Mach. Learn.* **2002**, *46*, 131–159. [CrossRef]
58. Demidova, L.; Nikulchev, E.; Sokolova, Y. Big data classification using the SVM classifiers with the modified particle swarm optimization and the SVM ensembles. *Int. J. Adv. Comput. Sci. Appl.* **2016**, *7*, 294–312. [CrossRef]
59. Schober, P.; Vetter, T.R. Logistic Regression in Medical Research. *Anesth Analg.* **2021**, *132*, 365–366. [CrossRef]
60. Dai, B.; Chen, R.-C.; Zhu, S.-Z.; Zhang, W.-W. Using Random Forest Algorithm for Breast Cancer Diagnosis. In Proceedings of the 2018 International Symposium on Computer, Consumer and Control (IS3C), Taichung, Taiwan, 6–8 December 2018; pp. 449–452. [CrossRef]
61. Acharjee, A.; Larkman, J.; Xu, Y.; Cardoso, V.R.; Gkoutos, G.V. A random forest based biomarker discovery and power analysis framework for diagnostics research. *BMC Med. Genom.* **2020**, *13*, 178. [CrossRef] [PubMed]
62. Cheng, S.; Liu, B.; Ting, T.O.; Qin, Q.; Shi, Y.; Huang, K. Survey on data science with population-based algorithms. *Big Data Anal.* **2016**, *1*, 3. [CrossRef]
63. Demidova, L.A.; Gorchakov, A.V. Application of bioinspired global optimization algorithms to the improvement of the prediction accuracy of compact extreme learning machines. *Russ. Technol. J.* **2022**, *10*, 59–74. [CrossRef]
64. Liu, J.-Y.; Jia, B.-B. Combining One-vs-One Decomposition and Instance-Based Learning for Multi-Class Classification. *IEEE Access* **2020**, *8*, 197499–197507. [CrossRef]
65. Grandini, M.; Bagli, E.; Visani, G. Metrics for Multi-class Classification: An Overview. *arXiv* **2020**, arXiv:2008.05756.
66. Haibo, H.; Yunqian, M. *Imbalanced Learning: Foundations, Algorithms, and Applications*; Wiley-IEEE Press: Hoboken, NJ, USA, 2013; p. 216.
67. Krawczyk, B. Learning from imbalanced data: Open challenges and future directions. *Prog. Artif. Intell.* **2016**, *5*, 221–232. [CrossRef]
68. Dong, W.; Moses, C.; Li, K. Efficient k-nearest neighbor graph construction for generic similarity measures. In Proceedings of the 20th International Conference on World Wide Web, Hyderabad, India, 28 March–1 April 2011; pp. 577–586.
69. Damrich, S.; Hamprecht, F.A. On UMAP's true loss function. *Adv. Neural Inf. Process. Syst.* **2021**, *34*, 12.
70. UMAP: Uniform Manifold Approximation and Projection for Dimension Reduction. Available online: https://umap-learn.readthedocs.io/en/latest/_modules/umap/umap_.html (accessed on 4 January 2023).
71. Prusty, S.; Patnaik, S.; Dash, S. SKCV: Stratified K-fold cross-validation on ML classifiers for predicting cervical cancer. *Front. Nanotechnol.* **2022**, *4*, 972421. [CrossRef]
72. Slamet, W.; Herlambang, B.; Samudi, S. Stratified K-fold cross validation optimization on machine learning for prediction. *Sink. J. Dan Penelit. Tek. Inform.* **2022**, *7*, 2407–2414. [CrossRef]

Disclaimer/Publisher's Note: The statements, opinions and data contained in all publications are solely those of the individual author(s) and contributor(s) and not of MDPI and/or the editor(s). MDPI and/or the editor(s) disclaim responsibility for any injury to people or property resulting from any ideas, methods, instructions or products referred to in the content.